Hoover Institution Publications

FROM PROTEST TO CHALLENGE

Volume 1

Protest and Hope
1882-1934

From Protest to Challenge

A DOCUMENTARY HISTORY OF AFRICAN
POLITICS IN SOUTH AFRICA
1882-1964

Edited by

Thomas Karis and Gwendolen M. Carter

Volume I

Protest and Hope
1882-1934

by Sheridan Johns, III

Hoover Institution Press
Stanford University
Stanford, California

Hoover Press Publication 89

Copyright 1972 by the Board of Trustees of the
Leland Stanford Junior University

First printing, 1972
First paperback printing, 1987
ISBN 0-8179-1892-2 (vol. 1)
ISBN 0-8179-1222-3 (vol. 2)
ISBN 0-8179-6232-8 (vol. 3)
ISBN 0-8179-6612-9 (vol. 4)

Manufactured in the United States of America
91 90   9 8 7 6 5 4

The Library of Congress has catalogued the
first printing of this title as follows:

From protest to challenge; a documentary history of African politics in South Africa, 1882–1964. Edited by Thomas Karis and Gwendolen M. Carter. Stanford, Calif., Hoover Institution Press ₁1972₎-77.

4 v. 24 cm. (Hoover Institution publications, 89, 122–123, 161)

Includes bibliographies.
Contents: v. 1. Protest and hope, 1882–1934, by S. Johns, III.— v. 2. Hope and challenge, 1935–1952, by T. Karis—v. 3. Challenge and violence, 1953–1964, by T. Karis and G. M. Gerhart.—v. 4. Political profiles, 1882–1964, by M. Gerhart and T. Karis.

ISBN 0-8179-1891-4 (v. 1)
ISBN 0-8179-1221-5 (v. 2)
ISBN 0-8179-6231-X (v. 3)
ISBN 0-8179-6611-2 (v. 4)

1. Blacks — South Africa — Politics and government. 2. South Africa — Native races. I. Karis, Thomas, 1919–   ed. II. Carter, Gwendolen Margaret, 1906–   ed. III. Series: Hoover Institution publication; 89, etc.
DT763.F73   323.4'0968   72-152423
                                      MARC

To the African People of South Africa

For the role they have played "during the last 50 years to establish, peacefully, a society in which merit and not race would fix the position of the individual in the life of the nation."

Albert J. Lutuli
Nobel Peace Prize Address
December 10, 1961

PREFACE TO THE 1990 PRINTING

The Hoover Institution has decided to reprint the four volumes of *From Protest to Challenge* in paperback so as to make this source more widely available to scholars and students interested in South Africa. To rescue from obscurity the voices of protest in South Africa was a unique undertaking. Equally important was their publication in the form of documentary histories – a venture pioneered by the Hoover Institution. The background of this project, which took 12 years to complete, therefore is worth noting.

In 1961-1962, following the lead of Hoover curators in other collecting areas, I went to South Africa to establish contacts for receiving materials. Once there, I established a network of collectors and suppliers, most notably Benjamin Pogrund of the *Rand Daily Mail*. Pogrund set about filming the archives, files, and papers of opposition groups and individuals, while I purchased, often clandestinely, political ephemera and long runs of proscribed radical newspapers such as the *Guardian*.

After Pogrund filmed a collection, a copy of the film was given to the group or individual for hiding and a copy was sent to the Hoover Institution. (A few collections never made it to Hoover; for example, the papers of Edward Roux, former executive secretary of the South African Communist Party.) Most of these collections remain at the institution. Others were given to the Center for Research Libraries to facilitate wider use.

With this material and the purchase of the microfilm record of the Treason Trial of 1956-1961, the Hoover Institution had a rare collection of documents. The prosecution in the Treason Trial submitted as evidence some 4,000-5,000 documents, ranging from books and pamphlets to transcripts of meetings, political ephemera, and letters primarily of the period since the defiance campaign of 1952 but also referring to earlier years. In 1962 the Hoover Institution awarded a grant to Dr. Thomas Karis to come to Hoover to prepare a guide to the 25 reels of film (some 19,000 pages). His work was published by the Hoover Institution Press as *The Treason Trial in South Africa: A Guide to the Microfilm Record of the Trial* [Stanford, 1965].

The richness of the material proved such that I suggested to Dr. Karis that he undertake a documentary history of opposition groups in South Africa. He agreed, and asked Dr. Gwendolen M. Carter to join him. The Hoover Institution provided additional honoraria. During extensive field trips to South Africa in 1963 and 1964, funded by the Ford Foundation for research on *South Africa's Transkei: The Politics of Domestic Colonialism* (with Newell M. Stultz, Northwestern University Press), Dr. Karis and Dr. Carter concurrently began to collect and to copy primary historical material and to interview African and other political veterans. The scope of the documentary history was expanded to include politics from 1882 on.

Originally a one-volume work was planned. Subsequently Sheridan Johns III and Gail M. Gerhart joined the effort, and the search for additional source material was extended within South Africa and to British and American private collections, libraries, and archives. The project was enlarged to four volumes and was concluded in 1977, with Johns serving as author of volume one, Karis of volume two, Karis and Gerhart of volume three, and Gerhart and Karis of volume four under the general editorship of Karis and Carter. A companion volume inventorying the primary material that had been microfilmed on 71 reels was published by the Southern African Research Archives Project in Bloomington, Indiana as *South African Political Materials: A Catalogue of the Carter-Karis Collection*.

In addition to the initial stimulus, the Hoover Institution continued to give advice on the project. The press worked closely with the editors of this massive project. Even at a time of rising publication costs, the Hoover Press made no suggestions to abridge the material beyond what the editors themselves thought useful, and the editors were completely free to include or to exclude material and to determine the scope and emphasis of these volumes.

This series reaffirmed Hoover's commitment as a research library to pioneer not only the collecting of material on contemporary history but also the publishing of such projects in order to provide basic building blocks for scholarship.

Peter Duignan
Senior Fellow and Curator,
Africa and Middle East
Collection
Hoover Institution

x

Contents

PART ONE
AFRICAN POLITICS AND THE
PRE-UNION POLITICAL ORDER, 1882-1909

Documents

vii

PART TWO
THE AFRICAN NATIONAL CONGRESS CON
ACCELERATED PROTEST AND APPEALS A

Furth

28. T

Introduction

The Establishment of the South African Native National C

The Land Question

Further Grievances

Appeals Abroad

Documents

29.

30.

31.

32.

33

3

3

3

PART THREE
NEW GROPINGS FOR EFFECTIVE ORGANIZATION AND REPRESENTATION, 1921-1934

Preface

The current situation in South Africa must be evaluated from the perspective that Africans in that country founded and operated nationalist organizations, engaged in political protest, and participated in national political activity earlier than Africans organized such activities in other parts of the African continent. It is, therefore, not only the paucity of current political opportunities for the majority of Africans in South Africa that is so disturbing, but also the fact that, while the political role and influence of most other Africans on the continent expanded, however unevenly, in their preindependence period, the progression in South Africa has been in the opposite direction. Despite patient and continuous efforts by all conceivable means to influence the dominant white electorate to expand their political role, Africans, who in the Cape Colony shared a nonracial franchise with whites, have had even their limited rights taken away. Since 1960, apart from electing a minority of the members of legislative councils in so-called Bantustans, which possess semiautonomous powers over the African rural sections of their areas, Africans have no political representation within South Africa.

The three volumes of documents on African protest and African challenge, of which this is the first, present the drama of more than eighty years of resolutions, requests, anxious arguments, agonizing frustrations, and calls to action by African leaders and organizations. The text provides the background and setting for the documents. The documents underpin the text and enable us to recreate through the words and actions of African leaders the events, tactics, emotions, and personalities of the past.

The collection of documents was the work of many years. Even so, the editors are painfully aware that their holdings do not include many of the records they would like to have. Like others who have studied African politics in South Africa at first hand, particularly in recent years, they were more often met with accounts of police raids, or of the burning of potentially banned material, than with documents to copy or to take. Nonetheless, although there were many stories of material destroyed in the nick of time, or because of fear of involvement, there were also dramatic instances of documents dug up in gardens, uncovered in chimneys, or brought under cover of darkness from hiding places threatened with disclosure. In these latter cases, the material was transferred to the editors with enthusiasm and the hope that it might some day be published.

Much more obvious ways of collecting material yielded a considerable harvest. Trial records, particularly of such long-drawn-out processes as the Treason Trial from 1956 to 1961, the Mandela Trial of 1962, and the Rivonia Trial of 1963-1964, are packed with information for those prepared to spend endless hours patiently putting together the details about persons and movements gleaned from the testimony of different witnesses. Numerous earlier government-sponsored investigations into African conditions and African testimony on pending legislation are often helpful. The records of the government-sponsored conferences of African leaders in the 1920s, of the Natives' Representative Council, 1937-1951, of the annual conferences of the African National Congress (ANC) and of other African organizations (also collected with difficulty and still incomplete) are even better sources of information, however verbose the speakers tended to be.

Newspapers, particularly African papers published in English and in various African languages like *Imvo, Inkundla ya Bantu,* and *Abantu-Batho*, the last-named the official organ of the ANC until the early 1930s, record African meetings and occasionally speeches. *Imvo*, which began publication in 1884, is available at the University of California at Los Angeles (UCLA) on microfilm, but only one copy of *Abantu-Batho* has been found in the United States. *Inkundla ya Bantu*, published in the 1940s as a forum for African opinion, is unavailable in American libraries. After the mid-thirties, African politics can be followed through reflectors of the left: *The Guardian* and its successors, including *New Age*. The English and Afrikaans language newspapers, on the other hand, have usually tended to ignore African organizations unless their activities were regarded as threatening. Nonetheless, in the decades just before and after Union, it was common for the liberally inclined *The Friend* of Bloemfontein to report on the annual meetings held there by African organizations because of its central location, while detailed coverage of Cape ANC meetings in the mid-thirties and of Transkeian developments can be found in the *East London Dispatch*.

In addition to collecting as much documentary material as possible, the editors interviewed at length and on tape as many participants as were available to record their personal accounts of events. The most systematic interviewing was done during 1963 and 1964, mainly in South Africa, but also in Basutoland (now Lesotho), Swaziland, Bechuanaland (now Botswana), Dar es Salaam, Tanzania, and London. All three editors had previously interviewed many African leaders and secondary figures during the course of their earlier researches in South Africa, where Miss Carter worked in 1948-1949, 1952-1953, 1957, 1959 and 1961; Mr. Karis in 1955 and 1957-1959; and Mr. Johns in 1962-1963.

Interviewing Africans in South Africa, particularly those who have been associated with African nationalist organizations and activities, has always been a ticklish business. It has become progressively more difficult, partly because of police surveillance, and partly because extensive bannings, imprisonment and death sharply limit the number of persons available. Nevertheless, a significant number of older leaders and some younger ones were still able to speak privately during 1963 and 1964. The editors would like to pay special tribute to their courage and the patience with which they gave their time unstintingly to help reconstruct the picture of the past. Many African leaders are now outside South Africa and to them, too, goes our appreciation for the long hours they spent answering our detailed questions.

By comparing different stories of events with each other, we were able to answer many questions that arose in our minds as we pored over the documents. Unfortunately, many questions remain unanswered, sometimes because neither participants nor witnesses were available and sometimes because memory was blurred.

Enough material was gathered, however, to fill several large files at the Program of African Studies of Northwestern University. Having collected it, the next and not least difficult task was to bring order to the highly varied documents from many sources and, still more difficult, to select and excerpt those that seemed most suitable for publication. The focus of attention has been on African political activity. Thus, while we have included those African activities that involved cooperative activities with non-Africans, we have left out documents illustrating the independent efforts of Indians and Coloured and of both liberal and left-wing whites. In selecting documents within these limits, we have looked first for those of historic importance and secondly for those particularly illustrative either of major themes or of forms of expression. Only a few personal letters have been included. Despite their bulk, the volumes are only an introduction to the rich materials that should be used in preparing a definitive political history of modern South Africa. They include, however, far more documentary material than has been previously available and thus open up new lines of inquiry and opportunities for gaining a more balanced perspective of South African history.

The field research most directly related to these volumes was done during two intensive periods in South Africa (June-August, 1963, and January-April, 1964) collecting material both for *South Africa's Transkei* and for this documentary collection. The original purpose of the research was to gain perspective toward and to analyze developments in the Transkei as the South African government's first large-scale experiment in territorial separate development. It became quickly apparent, however, that these research periods also afforded major opportunities to secure material on the earlier history of African nationalist organizations and activities and that these opportunities were unlikely to occur again. Without being diverted from our responsibilities for the study of the Transkei (in which we were ably joined by Dr. Newell M. Stultz of Brown University), Mr. Karis, Miss Carter, and Mr. Johns (who was part of our research team from January to April 1964) took advantage of every opportunity to collect documents and to hold interviews relevant to this second, and in many ways more important, purpose.

Without the devoted assistance of our small research staff—Molly Wise, Linda Christianson, and Peter Basquin during our first research trip, and Catherine Eglin, Molly Wise, and Margaret Anderson during the second—it would have been impossible to secure as complete a collection as we did. It was they who spent long hours photostating material we had located, who packed innumerable bundles to ship to the United States, and in countless other ways magnified the effect of what we were able to do. The collection itself and the volumes have benefited from the experience, and efforts of J. Congress Mbata, formerly of the Institute of Race Relations, Johannesburg, then of Northwestern University, and now of Cornell University.

We would also like to express our warm appreciation to the director and staff of the South African Institute of Race Relations, to the librarians of university and public libraries throughout South Africa and of the Parliamentary Library, Cape Town, and to the many others in that country who gave us unstinting aid in our search for material. We have benefited from the rich collection of documents held at the British Museum and Public Records Office, at the African Microfilm Center, directed by the Center for Research Libraries, Chicago, and at the Hoover Institution, Stanford, California. We acknowledge with special satisfaction the initial stimulus to make this collection of documents, and the interest, advice and support extended by Dr. Peter Duignan, director of the African Program of the Hoover Institution, and by Dr. Lewis Gann, also of the Hoover Institution.

Above all, we think with deep appreciation of those Africans who worked so hard, so long and with so little return, to make South Africa the great nonracial country it could have become. Telling evidence of their long, patient and courageous efforts is provided through their own words in this documentary collection.

Thomas Karis
Gwendolen M. Carter

April 1970

Contents

PART ONE
AFRICAN POLITICS AND THE
PRE-UNION POLITICAL ORDER, 1882-1909

Documents

PART TWO
THE AFRICAN NATIONAL CONGRESS COMES INTO BEING:
ACCELERATED PROTEST AND APPEALS ABROAD, 1910-1920

PART THREE
NEW GROPINGS FOR EFFECTIVE ORGANIZATION AND REPRESENTATION, 1921-1934

Preface

The current situation in South Africa must be evaluated from the perspective that Africans in that country founded and operated nationalist organizations, engaged in political protest, and participated in national political activity earlier than Africans organized such activities in other parts of the African continent. It is, therefore, not only the paucity of current political opportunities for the majority of Africans in South Africa that is so disturbing, but also the fact that, while the political role and influence of most other Africans on the continent expanded, however unevenly, in their preindependence period, the progression in South Africa has been in the opposite direction. Despite patient and continuous efforts by all conceivable means to influence the dominant white electorate to expand their political role, Africans, who in the Cape Colony shared a nonracial franchise with whites, have had even their limited rights taken away. Since 1960, apart from electing a minority of the members of legislative councils in so-called Bantustans, which possess semiautonomous powers over the African rural sections of their areas, Africans have no political representation within South Africa.

The three volumes of documents on African protest and African challenge, of which this is the first, present the drama of more than eighty years of resolutions, requests, anxious arguments, agonizing frustrations, and calls to action by African leaders and organizations. The text provides the background and setting for the documents. The documents underpin the text and enable us to recreate through the words and actions of African leaders the events, tactics, emotions, and personalities of the past.

The collection of documents was the work of many years. Even so, the editors are painfully aware that their holdings do not include many of the records they would like to have. Like others who have studied African politics in South Africa at first hand, particularly in recent years, they were more often met with accounts of police raids, or of the burning of potentially banned material, than with documents to copy or to take. Nonetheless, although there were many stories of material destroyed in the nick of time, or because of fear of involvement, there were also dramatic instances of documents dug up in gardens, uncovered in chimneys, or brought under cover of darkness from hiding places threatened with disclosure. In these latter cases, the material was transferred to the editors with enthusiasm and the hope that it might some day be published.

Much more obvious ways of collecting material yielded a considerable harvest. Trial records, particularly of such long-drawn-out processes as the Treason Trial from 1956 to 1961, the Mandela Trial of 1962, and the Rivonia Trial of 1963-1964, are packed with information for those prepared to spend endless hours patiently putting together the details about persons and movements gleaned from the testimony of different witnesses. Numerous earlier government-sponsored investigations into African conditions and African testimony on pending legislation are often helpful. The records of the government-sponsored conferences of African leaders in the 1920s, of the Natives' Representative Council, 1937-1951, of the annual conferences of the African National Congress (ANC) and of other African organizations (also collected with difficulty and still incomplete) are even better sources of information, however verbose the speakers tended to be.

Newspapers, particularly African papers published in English and in various African languages like *Imvo*, *Inkundla ya Bantu*, and *Abantu-Batho*, the last-named the official organ of the ANC until the early 1930s, record African meetings and occasionally speeches. *Imvo*, which began publication in 1884, is available at the University of California at Los Angeles (UCLA) on microfilm, but only one copy of *Abantu-Batho* has been found in the United States. *Inkundla ya Bantu*, published in the 1940s as a forum for African opinion, is unavailable in American libraries. After the mid-thirties, African politics can be followed through reflectors of the left: *The Guardian* and its successors, including *New Age*. The English and Afrikaans language newspapers, on the other hand, have usually tended to ignore African organizations unless their activities were regarded as threatening. Nonetheless, in the decades just before and after Union, it was common for the liberally inclined *The Friend* of Bloemfontein to report on the annual meetings held there by African organizations because of its central location, while detailed coverage of Cape ANC meetings in the mid-thirties and of Transkeian developments can be found in the *East London Dispatch*.

In addition to collecting as much documentary material as possible, the editors interviewed at length and on tape as many participants as were available to record their personal accounts of events. The most systematic interviewing was done during 1963 and 1964, mainly in South Africa, but also in Basutoland (now Lesotho), Swaziland, Bechuanaland (now Botswana), Dar es Salaam, Tanzania, and London. All three editors had previously interviewed many African leaders and secondary figures during the course of their earlier researches in South Africa, where Miss Carter worked in 1948-1949, 1952-1953, 1957, 1959 and 1961; Mr. Karis in 1955 and 1957-1959; and Mr. Johns in 1962-1963.

Interviewing Africans in South Africa, particularly those who have been associated with African nationalist organizations and activities, has always been a ticklish business. It has become progressively more difficult, partly because of police surveillance, and partly because extensive bannings, imprisonment and death sharply limit the number of persons available. Nevertheless, a significant number of older leaders and some younger ones were still able to speak privately during 1963 and 1964. The editors would like to pay special tribute to their courage and the patience with which they gave their time unstintingly to help reconstruct the picture of the past. Many African leaders are now outside South Africa and to them, too, goes our appreciation for the long hours they spent answering our detailed questions.

By comparing different stories of events with each other, we were able to answer many questions that arose in our minds as we pored over the documents. Unfortunately, many questions remain unanswered, sometimes because neither participants nor witnesses were available and sometimes because memory was blurred.

Enough material was gathered, however, to fill several large files at the Program of African Studies of Northwestern University. Having collected it, the next and not least difficult task was to bring order to the highly varied documents from many sources and, still more difficult, to select and excerpt those that seemed most suitable for publication. The focus of attention has been on African political activity. Thus, while we have included those African activities that involved cooperative activities with non-Africans, we have left out documents illustrating the independent efforts of Indians and Coloured and of both liberal and left-wing whites. In selecting documents within these limits, we have looked first for those of historic importance and secondly for those particularly illustrative either of major themes or of forms of expression. Only a few personal letters have been included. Despite their bulk, the volumes are only an introduction to the rich materials that should be used in preparing a definitive political history of modern South Africa. They include, however, far more documentary material than has been previously available and thus open up new lines of inquiry and opportunities for gaining a more balanced perspective of South African history.

The field research most directly related to these volumes was done during two intensive periods in South Africa (June-August, 1963, and January-April, 1964) collecting material both for *South Africa's Transkei* and for this documentary collection. The original purpose of the research was to gain perspective toward and to analyze developments in the Transkei as the South African government's first large-scale experiment in territorial separate development. It became quickly apparent, however, that these research periods also afforded major opportunities to secure material on the earlier history of African nationalist organizations and activities and that these opportunities were unlikely to occur again. Without being diverted from our responsibilities for the study of the Transkei (in which we were ably joined by Dr. Newell M. Stultz of Brown University), Mr. Karis, Miss Carter, and Mr. Johns (who was part of our research team from January to April 1964) took advantage of every opportunity to collect documents and to hold interviews relevant to this second, and in many ways more important, purpose.

Without the devoted assistance of our small research staff—Molly Wise, Linda Christianson, and Peter Basquin during our first research trip, and Catherine Eglin, Molly Wise, and Margaret Anderson during the second—it would have been impossible to secure as complete a collection as

The Authors

Primary responsibility for the selection of documentary material and the accompanying text for Volume I and for Part I of Volume II was undertaken by Dr. Sheridan Johns III, of Duke University. He is particularly well-equipped to handle the material in this period, having written his doctoral dissertation (soon to be published in a revised version) on early left-wing movements in South Africa, and published lengthy articles on the Industrial and Commercial Workers' Union.

Professor Thomas Karis, of City College, City University of New York, undertook comparable responsibility for the remainder of Volume II and for Volume III, covering the periods 1935-1952 and 1953-1964. He is author of the section on South Africa in *Five African States: Responses to Diversity*, Gwendolen M. Carter, ed., (Cornell University Press, 1963), and *The Treason Trial in South Africa: A Guide to the Microfilm Record of the Trial* (Hoover Institution, 1965). He is also coauthor with Gwendolen M. Carter and Newell M. Stultz of *South Africa's Transkei: The Politics of Domestic Colonialism* (Northwestern University Press, 1967).

Professor Gwendolen M. Carter of Northwestern University has aided throughout as collaborator, critic, and editor. She brings to bear her research and writings on South Africa, which include most relevantly *The Politics of Inequality: South Africa since 1948* (Praeger, 1958, rev. 1959), "African Nationalist Movements" in *Southern Africa in Transition*, edited by John A. Davis and James K. Baker (Praeger, 1966), pp. 3-19, *African Concepts of Nationalism in South Africa* (Melville J. Herskovits Memorial Lecture, University of Edinburgh, March, 1965), and her share in preparing *South Africa's Transkei*.

The Documents

In the following documents inconsistencies may occur in punctuation, format, spelling of certain words and proper names, and manner of speech. Because we believe that these variations enhance rather than detract from the value of the papers, we have made no attempt to edit beyond the correction of obvious typographical errors.

PART ONE

African Politics and the Pre-Union Political Order, 1882—1909

Introduction

Under the impact of expanding white power, African society in southern Africa was forcibly and radically reshaped in the course of the nineteenth century and the early years of the twentieth century. White political authorities established hegemony over African tribal groupings and also created political, economic, and social institutions that affected all Africans, rural or urban, illiterate or educated. In the matrix of this imposed system of white-dominated racial coexistence, new patterns of African politics began to emerge which reflected a broad spectrum of viewpoints ranging from rejection of the new system to wholehearted efforts to achieve desired goals through its processes.

In the Cape Colony in the south, the influence of British missionaries and their supporters in Britain and of a few Boers in the Colony spurred the introduction of liberal measures that had far-reaching consequences. In 1828, the Hottentots were assured legal rights equal to those possessed by whites; in 1834, slavery was abolished. In 1852, the grant of representative government, and in 1872, the further move to responsible government opened the possibility of full participation in politics by those Africans and Coloured who could meet nonracial property qualifications and, after 1892, educational tests.

Intermittent warfare with Africans to the east of Cape Colony (the last "Kaffir War" ended in 1878) was succeeded by the gradual extension of mission stations and British control. The Transkei, the largest and most consolidated of contemporary African reserves in South Africa and the first to be granted semiautonomous status as a Bantustan (late 1963), was incorporated into the Cape through a series of annexations stimulated by the settlers' land hunger, desire for frontier security, and trade. These annexations culminated in 1894 with the inclusion of Pondoland.

The strengthening of the mission stations and their growing educational institutions, particularly in the Ciskei and the Transkei, set in motion a powerful process whereby a significant number of Africans were Christianized and given a Western education. They were thus set apart from traditional African society and equipped to take up the promise of common citizenship in the Cape Colony as "civilized British subjects." It was the emergence of this small but visible new social group that brought to the fore new contentious questions about the implementation of the liberal ideal of a nonracial society.

The measures that heartened nonwhites antagonized substantial numbers of whites, especially the Boers, the descendants of the Dutch, Huguenot French, and German settlers who came to the Cape from 1652 onward. By the 1830s, thousands of Boers (later to be called Afrikaners) had begun the Great Trek to the north to escape what they regarded as "oppression" at the hands of the British, particularly British abolition of slavery and alleged failure to protect settlers on the eastern frontier. In the Boers' efforts to establish new states in which their strict white superiority system could be preserved, they came into direct and often bloody contact with African societies that previously had not felt the sustained direct thrust of organized white settlers. Overcoming African opposition and fending off intermittent British efforts at control, the Boer trek communities finally organized themselves into two republics, one in the Transvaal and the other in the Orange Free State. In both states it was clear and explicit that no Africans or other nonwhites could participate in politics. "Liberal" missionaries were not permitted to proselytize in the two republics. In addition, a network of restrictive laws further bound Africans to closely controlled positions of subordination without any of the promises of eventual African emancipation that marked the Cape Colony.

In Natal, the establishment of British control was hastened by fears that the trekking Boers might find an outlet to the sea through Zululand. African society, divided between the consolidated Zulu tribe and those whose unity and spirit had been shattered by the impact of Zulu power, was increasingly influenced by British colonial administration and missionary activity. As Natal, following the Cape, advanced to representative government (in 1856) and then to responsible government (in 1895), it was supposedly in tune with the Cape theory of a nonracial franchise. In practice, however, the Cape ideal was quickly distorted. The whites of Natal were fearful of being overwhelmed by the large African majority in the colony and by the rapidly growing Indian minority that already outnumbered the whites. They used their influence upon and eventual domination of the colonial government to foster edicts and laws that, in effect, barred nonwhites almost completely from any part in the government. Thus, white administrators, by strict insistence that Africans adhere to "Native Law," effectively prevented all but a few Africans from obtaining the vote.

Nonetheless, the intrusion of mission stations, particularly in the parts of Natal outside Zululand (which was not formally annexed until 1887), fostered the growth of a Christian Western-educated group among the Africans. Keenly aware of the greater opportunities open to Africans in the sister British colony of the Cape, this group sharply resented the effects of the restrictive practices of the settler-controlled colonial government of Natal. Thus, in the eyes of its educated Africans, Natal's "Native" policy was aligned to that of the two inland Boer republics of the Transvaal and the Orange Free State.

The discovery of diamonds at Kimberley in 1867 and of gold upon the Witwatersrand in 1886 marked the beginning of modern economic development. These new economic pressures combined with the policies of the white colonial and republican governments and the influence of the missionaries to wrench apart still further the fabric of African life. Simultaneously drawn by the promise of cash earnings and impelled by the necessity to pay new taxes levied by white governments, Africans in areas under white control migrated in increasing numbers out of the crowded African "reserves," the scattered areas left under African communal ownership by the advancing whites. They were joined by a smaller stream of migrants from regions to the north still substantially free from white authority. Some of the newcomers joined the many Africans, particularly in the Transvaal and the Orange Free State, who eked out a subsistence existence as tenants or squatters on white-owned farms. Yet more and more Africans clustered around the new white-dominated urban economic centers, where they became the unskilled core of the emerging South African proletariat or, in the case of a few, the first members of the miniscule and truncated African urban bourgeoisie.

Early African Political Activity

Against this broad backdrop, organized African political activity began to develop in the latter part of the nineteenth century. The new politics centered in the eastern Cape Colony where the well-established activities of various Christian mission churches and schools were furthering the emergence of a class of Africans who were attracted by the hope of full acceptance into a nonracial, Christian, "civilized" society at the same time that they were intimately aware of the hardships and disabilities under which the overwhelming majority of their people lived. Articulate not only in their native Xhosa but also in English, and as property holders or prospective property holders eligible to vote on an

4

equal basis with whites, members of this group began actively to express themselves and to organize for representation of their interests and the interests of their people.

Impressed by white political solidarity, particularly on matters concerning racial issues, and disturbed by divisions along Christian denominational lines, a small group of Africans in the Transkei called on educated Africans in 1882 to form a political organization, *Imbumba Yama Afrika*. Expressly concerned with maintaining African unity so that African interests could be forcefully articulated, the *Imbumba* apparently met in periodic conferences to discuss matters affecting the African people and to plan representations to white authorities (Document 1). In 1884, Africans in the eastern Cape Colony formed two additional organizations, the Native Education Association and the Native Electoral Association. Both groups were concerned with electoral politics and larger issues affecting the African population. From the available evidence, however, it seems that the new organizations like the *Imbumba* led an irregular existence. Nevertheless, their founding marks an important first step in South Africa. Africans had come together in organizations of their own, modeled upon existing white pressure groups, to attempt to work with and through the institutions of the white-dominated colonial political system in order to achieve better representation of African interests.

African political journalism began in 1884 when John Tengo Jabavu, with white financial support, founded *Imvo Zabantsundu* (Native Opinion) in Kingwilliamstown. Its pages chronicled the range of concerns of the new African elite through the latter years of the nineteenth and into the twentieth century. Although Jabavu's editorial comment often reflected personal prejudices and petty concerns, he maintained a consistently high level of analysis which made his newspaper a forum for African interests in the Cape Colony. Already in 1887 Jabavu led the unsuccessful opposition to the Parliamentary Voters Registration Bill. This measure effectively denied tribal Africans the vote by defining qualifications for the franchise so as to exclude land occupied communally or tribally. Jabavu argued insistently that this restriction was contrary to the principles of proper representative government in the British tradition (Document 3). Thus, at the very start of African political journalism, as throughout the history of subsequent African protests, questions of the franchise were central.

That the concerns of Jabavu and his supporters were shared by some tribal leaders in the eastern Cape can be seen from the text of "The Humble Petition of the Native Inhabitants of the Location of Oxkraal in the District of Queenstown, Colony of the Cape of Good Hope" (Document 4). In most respectful terms, the ten signatories of the petition (only one of whom was able to write his own name) endorsed the benefits that they had received under British rule. Then, expressing their fears that the passage of the Parliamentary Voters Registration Bill of 1887 would give added power to the traditionally anti-African Boer population within the Cape Colony, they urged strongly that the British Crown intervene to prevent the final passage of the bill by the Parliament of the Cape Colony. Their pleas went unheeded; nevertheless, they indicated both the commitments of Africans to the provisions of the Cape system and their faith (regularly reiterated by Jabavu) that ultimately the "Imperial factor" would mitigate, if not thwart, anti-African legislation passed by the white minority governments in southern Africa.

In 1889, both Jabavu and the older tribally oriented Africans opposed new proposals to extend pass regulations, in some instances to registered voters. Jabavu promoted a deputation that traveled to Cape Town where it was politely received by the government. The deputation did not succeed in blocking the passage of the Vagrancy Act of 1889, but its performance evoked a favorable response from older Africans who endorsed the efforts of Jabavu and other educated Africans to represent their interests (Document 5).

Through *Imvo*, Jabavu also voiced opposition to many other discriminatory measures that subsequently became regular targets for African agitation. In the second issue of the newspaper, he urged a more lenient application of tax regulations to impoverished Africans on the land (Document 2). Subsequently, articles dealt with such issues as liquor laws pertaining exclusively to Africans, the web of regulations spun around urban Africans, and restrictive legislation aimed at Africans alone. Jabavu did not strongly oppose the Franchise and Ballot Act of 1892, however, which raised property qualifications and introduced educational requirements for the franchise (thereby also affecting rural poor whites). Probably his restraint was in deference to his white allies, J. W. Sauer and James Rose-Innes, who apparently worked from their positions in the cabinet to modify the measure slightly.

In 1894, *Imvo* was in the forefront of opposition to the Glen Grey Act (Document 6), which provided for a labor tax as well as limited individual land tenure and related local district councils. The latter provisions were restricted to the Glen Grey District of the Ciskei and the individual tenure to only a small portion of occupied land. Moreover, the land for which the title was given could not be counted toward the property qualification for the franchise for the Cape legislature. In Jabavu's view, the Glen Grey Act would not only bring hardships upon Africans, but by establishing separate institutions provided a dangerous model for future legislation affecting Africans throughout southern Africa. As a spokesman for African interests in the Cape's pre-Union period, Jabavu was consistent both in his insistence that he and all other qualified Africans possess the same rights as white voters and in his concern for a gradual but, as he hoped, irreversible advance of all Africans to the point where they could share his status as a "civilized British subject."

Jabavu carried his convictions into the sphere of practical politics. As a voter in the Cape Colony and editor of the most prominent African newspaper, at least until *Izwi Labantu (Voice of the People)* was established in 1898, Jabavu used his position and influence both to prod white politicians to be responsive to African demands and to persuade Africans to support those white politicians who gave promise of advancing African interests. It seems probable that as part of the opposition to the Parliamentary Voters Regis-

tration Bill of 1887 he linked up with elements from *Imbumba Yama Afrika* to create an informal organization of the same name that was periodically activated to send petitions and deputations to Cape Town to present the African position. The focus of Jabavu's activities, however, was on electoral politics in the Cape Colony, which he hoped to influence through the establishment of coordinated African support, either for a political party or for selected white parliamentarians who would work to improve the conditions of the African population. Jabavu's efforts brought him into contact not only with African voters, but also directly and indirectly with the leading white politicians of the Cape Colony. In addition, he maintained strong links through *Imvo* with the unenfranchised African majority, the source of new voters and the base of support for any potential African politician.

Jabavu's activities were paralleled by those of other members of the new African elite in the Cape Colony. Disagreements over tactics and policies, and often opposition to Jabavu's maneuverings, spurred the politicization of the small African electorate and the many who aspired to become a part of it. African voters not only developed informal organizations among themselves, but also linked with the unenfranchised African masses in their constituencies to whom they explained the issues of the day and from whom they received reactions in regard to candidates and policies. Africans were often divided in their allegiance to white candidates. Thus, on the periphery of the arena of white electoral politics, a significant group of Africans became involved in the political system of the Cape Colony.

Despite the African opposition led by Jabavu to the Glen Grey Act, its passage in 1894 opened new possibilities for limited political participation outside of Cape electoral politics, at first for the four Glen Grey Districts, and then gradually for all other districts in the Ciskei and the Transkei except the white farming district of Mount Currie. Legislation provided for the establishment of a local council in each magisterial district to which the provisions were extended. This council had limited jurisdiction over certain local matters, such as road building, agricultural improvements and other public works. Four of the six members of each council were elected by local African landowners and taxpayers; the other two members were appointed by the local white magistrate, who also acted as chairman of the council. When extended to Pondoland, the provisions were slightly modified in that only two members of the local district council were elected by landowners and taxpayers, and the other four members were appointed, two by the paramount chief and two by the white district magistrate. In practice, the councils concerned themselves not only with local affairs, but also with measures of interest to all Africans, in particular the franchise and representation. Although the council system provided separate institutions for Africans and was thus suspect to Jabavu, others viewed it as a first step to gradually expanding African participation in government.

Not all Africans, however, were ready to accept even a long-term prospect of gradual evolution into a fully nonracial society, the more so since it was coupled with the short-term prospect of continued white tutelage, if not dominance. Although only isolated armed African resistance challenged white power after the end of the last "Kaffir War" in 1878 and the War of Disarmament with the Basuto in 1881, discontent smoldered in various areas as the whites consolidated their hold over southern Africa.

Among white and African Christians, for example, friction arose early about the role that Africans were to play in the administration and government of various Christian denominations. In 1884, Nehemiah Tile, an African Methodist clergyman in Tembuland, broke away from the Wesleyan Methodist Church to form his own Tembu National Church. Subsequently, other African Christians splintered off from their white-ruled denominations to form independent African churches. Frustrated and incensed by the paternalism of the white ministry, a breakaway group of Wesleyans under the leadership of Mangena Mokone, formed the Ethiopian Church in Pretoria in November 1892. Dissident African Christians focused their activity around the new church, which expanded from Pretoria to link up with separatist groups elsewhere in South Africa. Mokone was joined in 1896 by James M. Dwane, also a former Wesleyan minister. Both cherished visions of a national church that would assume an important role in the Africans' fight for self-determination.

Having heard of the African Methodist Episcopal Church of the United States (formed in 1816 by American Negro Methodists who rejected white control of the church), leaders of the Ethiopian Church of South Africa decided to affiliate with the American organization. In 1896 in Atlanta, Georgia, the African Methodist Episcopal Church accepted the South Africans into membership. In 1898, Bishop H. M. Turner of the African Methodist Episcopal Church in America visited South Africa. The results were spectacular; his reception was enthusiastic; membership doubled. He ordained sixty-five ministers and consecrated Dwane as assistant bishop.

But disappointment with the paucity of financial support from America and frustration over unexpected paternalism by some of the American Negroes soon provoked further fissures among the separatist African Christians. Dwane visited America for a second time to collect money for the church and to seek not only confirmation of his consecration by Bishop Turner, but also elevation to the full bishopric. His mission was a failure. Dissatisfied with the inferior status of his South African church in relation to its counterpart in the United States as implied in the title of assistant bishop, and realizing that the association with American institutions conflicted with the aim of self-determination and the exercise of independent initiative, Dwane decided to leave the African Methodist Episcopal Church and form an autonomous Order of Ethiopia linked to the Anglican (Episcopal) Church. This move provoked further disputes among the Ethiopians. New African-controlled churches broke away from the African Methodist Episcopal Church as well as from the white churches. Violent disagreements over questions of theology, leadership, and organization differentiated the numerous separatist groups from each other, though they were united by a determination to keep control of their organizations in African hands.

Although the Ethiopianism of the separatist African churches was not specifically political, it had broad political implications. Contemporary documents containing specific details of the programs of the various sects are difficult to find, but reports make it clear that the Ethiopians, through the medium of the church, rejected the liberal assumptions of a common nonracial society. Instead, they supported separate but African-controlled organizations, whose ultimate relationships with white society and politics remained ambiguous. Some Ethiopians showed a willingness to accept temporary white predominance, but they were determined to expand the sphere of exclusively African control and administration (Document 8c). Both Africans and whites regarded Ethiopianism as an implicit, if not explicit, challenge to the status quo. Whites attributed Bambata's Rebellion (see below) to Ethiopianism, but its role was peripheral at most. Ethiopians did unquestionably, however, open potentially useful channels of political communication between the Africans of South Africa and the blacks of the new world.

By the close of the nineteenth century, two African approaches to politics were apparent. The dominant approach included both the organizational and agitational activity of the *Imbumba* and similar groups as well as the journalism and lobbying of Jabavu and *Imvo*. Within this approach, Africans organized themselves and worked with sympathetic whites to secure an expanding role in what they believed was an evolving British system that could result eventually in fully nonracial, representative government. For these Africans the slogan "equal rights for every civilized man south of the Zambesi" provided the guide to legitimate political activity. They ignored the fact that the author of the famous slogan, Cecil Rhodes, intended it at first for Afrikaners, then for Coloureds, and only ambiguously for Africans.

Counterposed to the optimistic hopes of those who accepted the implications of Cape liberalism were those of the Ethiopian persuasion. They argued that African self-preservation and advancement could best be realized through exclusively African organiza-

tions, acting without reference to standards of "civilization" as defined by whites in South Africa. Ethiopianism can be seen as a forerunner of subsequent African philosophies and groups whose main thrust was to challenge white power through black unity. In contrast, the other approach placed reliance upon some form of cooperation with sympathetic whites. Neither position was completely exclusive of the other, but they were two distinct poles about each of which much in African politics was to focus.

During this same period, a number of future African leaders were receiving training overseas, some in the homelands of English-speaking Christianity and liberalism whose influences had affected so many Africans in southern Africa. In the Negro community of the United States, South Africans came under the influence of the opposing philosophies of Booker T. Washington and W.E.B. Du Bois. In the writings of two South African students, John L. Dube (who studied at Oberlin College and in Rochester, N.Y.) and Pixley ka I. Seme (who studied at Columbia and Oxford universities), it was possible to see new views evolving in response to overseas experiences. Both Dube and Seme keenly anticipated the emergence of a new spirit of African assertiveness (Documents 19, 20).

Overtones of Ethiopianism were evident in the aspirations of both men, Dube's expressed most explicitly within a Christian framework, and Seme's enunciated in more general cultural terms. Upon his return to South Africa, Dube put to work the education he had received overseas. In Ohlange, Natal, he overcame white skepticism and established the Zulu Christian Industrial School in 1899, the first school founded by a professionally trained African educator.

Hopes and Grievances in the wake of the Anglo-Boer War

The end of the Anglo-Boer War and the defeat of the independent Boer republics in 1902 sharply altered the shape of the political arena for Africans. Africans, most of whom had backed the British, hoped that the extension of British control to the Orange Free

State and the Transvaal would create new possibilities for improvement in their status. In each of the four colonies of South Africa, new African organizations, many explicitly political, began to agitate and pressure British authority for an expanded role in any new all-South African system of government. Largely representing Christian Africans and urban residents, the latter particularly in the north, the new groups seem to have had little formal organization beyond an annual meeting at which the entire spectrum of issues confronting Africans was discussed. Nevertheless, the leaders of various organizations had a keen sense of political relevance and an appreciation of proper procedures.

In the years immediately following the conclusion of peace at Vereeniging in May 1902, Africans expressed their views before official commissions, through petitions to local white authorities, and to the imperial authority in London. These statements indicated the degree to which the new organizations accepted the promises implicit in the teachings of Christianity and the ideals of the British system of government. At the same time they showed a sharp antagonism to any continuation of the political system of the Boer republics as well as an acute awareness of the magnitude of the disabilities under which Africans lived in South Africa.

Africans who were linked to the newspaper, *Izwi Labantu*, and opposed to Jabavu's orientation in white politics, founded the South African Native Congress in 1902 to coordinate African activities in the eastern Cape Colony, particularly with regard to electoral politics. Yet the long statement of the new Congress to the Secretary of the Colonies in London showed that the group was not merely an African vote-gathering committee, but a body intensely concerned that rights due Africans as "loyal British subjects" would be honored fully in all spheres of life in the Cape Colony (Document 7).

From 1903 to 1905 the South African Native Affairs Commission, established to formulate a comprehensive policy for Africans, traveled throughout the four colonies to take evidence from both whites and Africans. The testimony of Martin Lutuli (an uncle of the late Chief Albert Lutuli) spotlighted the desire for full equality under British law of the Christian "detribalized" Africans who made up the membership of the Natal Native Congress[1] (Document 8a). The representatives of the Native Vigilance Association of the Orange River Colony emphasized that they spoke for all "progressive" Africans (by which they meant all Africans in the Colony) in their demands for meaningful local government and compulsory state-subsidized education (Document 8b). Spokesmen from the Transvaal complained especially about the injustice of the pass laws and demanded that Africans be free to sell their labor without restriction (Document 8d). Although the statements reflected in part the distinctive situations of each colony, all the arguments were similarly directed toward expanding the participation of the African in the evolving new society. The emphasis was upon the need for greater economic opportunity and political representation. The key issue for Africans throughout South Africa was the franchise.

In 1906 African attention was suddenly fixed upon disturbances that culminated in armed clashes between Africans and white troops. When the colonial administration in Natal imposed a new poll tax on January 1, 1906, several Zulu groups refused to pay. In scattered incidents several white farmers and magistrates were killed. The Natal authorities reacted with a declaration of martial law and a show of force. Many Zulus were killed, and more were taken into custody. A number were tried and executed for their alleged part in the violence. In the Cape Colony, Africans protested at the harshness of the government action (Document 10).

Meanwhile, Bambata, the chief of a small group near Greytown, received the tacit support of Dinizulu, paramount chief of the Zulus, to organize revolt against the white authorities. With an *impi* of his supporters, Bambata attacked the government troops (which included many "loyal" Africans) and then retreated beyond the Tugela River where

[1] Lutuli's testimony also gives some indication of the nature of this organization. On the formation, leadership and activities of this body and others mentioned below no detailed information has yet been uncovered in the preparation of this volume.

a superior government force defeated him in May 1906, killing Bambata himself and over 500 of his warriors. Several other bloody outbreaks occurred before the Natal government could claim in July that the rebellion had been crushed. Over 4000 Africans had been killed. The unsuccessful armed challenge to white power, which subsequently became known as Bambata's Rebellion, was a recrudescence of the Zulu military tradition established by Shaka. It also marked the last attempt at organized armed resistance against white dominance by the old African order until the Pondoland disturbances of 1960.

Among Christianized Africans there was also discontent with white rule. John L. Dube, who had become the most prominent educated African in the colony with the establishment in 1904, of his Zulu-language newspaper, *Ilanga Lase Natal*, frequently criticized government policy. After the end of Bambata's unsuccessful rebellion he continued his political activity in the Natal Native Congress. A revealing example of the problems faced by Dube and the Congress in their efforts to voice grievances in a colony where they had no effective franchise can be seen in the difficulties encountered in attempting to obtain an official hearing for their views of the pending Native Administration Bills in 1908 (Document 13).

African opinion elsewhere was preoccupied with the proposed grant of responsible government to the whites of the Transvaal and the Orange River Colony. In respectful petitions to the King, the Native United Political Associations of the Transvaal Colony and the Orange River Colony Native Congress (it is unclear whether this organization was the successor to, or a rival of, the Native Vigilance Association of the Orange River Colony) referred to specific discriminatory legislation in force in the northern colonies (Documents 9, 11). Fearful of further injustice at the hands of the white voters in those two colonies, the petitioners pleaded for change in the terms of the Treaty of Vereeniging that postponed consideration of the nonwhite franchise in the two colonies until after the granting of self-government. They requested provisions for African representation or, if this were not granted, retention by the British

authorities in London of the ultimate control over African affairs rather than granting power over Africans to the South African colonial governments.

In resolutions marked by a sharp tone of disappointment, the South African Native Congress in the Cape Colony echoed the concern of the petitioners from the northern colonies that the exercise of the "Imperial factor" on behalf of African interests was being weakened by pressures from local South African whites for British "non-interference" (Document 10). The same resolutions also referred to Ethiopianism and the 1906 disturbances in Natal preceding Bambata's Rebellion. On the former, they argued that Ethiopianism should be viewed as a progressive sign of the advancement of Christianity and in no way a threat to British rule; on the latter, they showed concern about the arbitrary imposition of martial law.

The anxiety of Cape Africans over future developments as well as their assumption that as registered voters they could speak for the interests of all Africans was further shown in the petition submitted to the House of Commons in 1906 by John Tengo Jabavu and thirteen other Africans (Document 12). Not only did they argue against the restrictive terms under which the all-white suffrage was to be preserved in the Transvaal and the Orange River Colony, but they also suggested prophetically that this practice would establish a precedent that might be used subsequently as a wedge to remove Africans from the voters' roll in the Cape Colony.

African Fears at the Prospect of Union

The British government's desire to reduce its responsibilities and to achieve reconciliation with the Boers overrode its solicitude for African interests. Under the terms of responsible government granted in 1907 to the Transvaal and the Orange River Colony, the all-white suffrage was maintained; the Crown did, however, reserve to itself the power to overrule discriminatory legislation against nonwhites. Yet the grant of responsible government to the northern colonies soon ceased to be the burning issue for Africans. Instead, as the postwar situation provided additional impetus for local whites to unite under a single national South African government, Africans found that the fears of Jabavu and his fellow signatories were justified. In October 1908, white representatives of the four colonies met in Durban in the South African National Convention to draft the terms of Union. The overwhelming majority of the delegates clearly intended to limit the role of Africans (and other nonwhites) in any political system devised for a united South Africa.

In this perspective, it is easy to understand the intensity of the renewed demand for franchise rights made by Africans during and after the proceedings of the all-white convention that hammered out the provisions of the Act of Union. In the course of the convention sessions, African inhabitants of the Transvaal petitioned for the inclusion of franchise rights for Africans (Document 14). The Draft Act of Union, however, revealed the intention of the whites not only to maintain the existing system in the northern colonies, but permanently to bar nonwhites from seats in the South African Parliament. Moreover, while the nonwhite franchise in the Cape was given the protection of entrenchment in the proposed constitution, along with equal language rights, the Draft Act provided a method for its amendment or removal by the all-white parliament.

In reaction to the imminent threat to the existing nonracial provisions of the Cape system and the proposed limitations of its implicit promises for an eventual nonracial society, Africans called a counterconvention in Bloemfontein in March 1909. This specially convened South African Native Convention was the most broadly representative African gathering to date. It included such prominent African leaders as John Dube and John Tengo Jabavu and groups and delegates from all the colonies (and Bechuanaland). They represented both the small minority of Cape voters and the overwhelming majority of nonenfranchised Africans and included respected tribal authorities as well as "detribalized" Africans. The South African Native Convention passed a series of resolutions which, while endorsing the principle of Union, declared that the imperial government was obligated to provide equitable rights to all South Africans

regardless of their color (Document 15). Strong protests were also made against those terms of the Draft Act that would arrest the advance of nonracial politics and legalize provisions by which a two-thirds majority of the members of Parliament could disenfranchise any nonwhites on the voters' rolls in the Cape (or Natal).

Africans in the Transkeian Territories General Council also objected to the terms of Union. They forwarded to the governor of the Cape Colony for submission to the King a resolution unequivocally protesting against the color bar in the proposed South Africa Act (Document 16).

When it became clear that the terms of the Draft Act would remain unchanged and would be approved overwhelmingly by the white Parliaments of the Transvaal, the Cape Colony and the Orange River Colony, and by a referendum of white voters in Natal, Africans moved to carry their protests to London. In an unprecedented move, the executive of the South African Native Convention joined with the leaders of the most prominent Coloured pressure group, the African Political [later People's] Organization (formed in 1902), and with sympathetic whites to send a multiracial delegation to London. W. P. Schreiner (former prime minister of the Cape Colony and a long-time white supporter of nonracialism), three Coloured representatives (including Dr. A. Abdurahman), and two Africans (John Tengo Jabavu, the editor of *Imvo*, and Walter Rubusana, an American-educated ordained minister) presented a petition to the British Parliament urging it to remove the discriminatory provisions of the South Africa Act, particularly in view of the loyalty and attachment to British institutions shown by the nonwhite population of South Africa (Document 17).

The appeals went unheeded. The British Parliament passed the South Africa Act unchanged, and the Union of South Africa, a new self-governing state within the British Empire, came into being. In the pages of *Imvo* it was uneasily but unmistakably recognized that a new stage in South African politics was opening (Document 18). In response, *Imvo* called for a new African unity to carry on the struggle for rights within the new political system of the Union of South Africa.

In the three decades preceding Union, African political activity had centered in small bodies led and supported for the most part by Christian Africans in each of the four territories of South Africa. The groups were poorly organized and without an electoral base except in the Cape Colony. As pressure groups operating upon various levels of white authority, the pre-Union African leaders and organizations put forward diverse programs. Yet all displayed sharp concern over the unequal position of Africans in the white-dominated society in which they lived. The statements of African leaders and their organizations focused upon demands for rights which they felt were due them as loyal and educated British subjects, but they also encompassed insistent requests for improvement in the condition of all Africans in South Africa.

With the move toward Union, the leaders and groups in the four colonies were drawn together in their common interest to advance their position within whatever system should develop. They brought with them accumulated experiences of their political activities and unhappy memories of unsuccessful protests. At the same time, Africans were divided on the question of their place in South African society and the strategies to be used to achieve African goals. With the advent of Union, Africans as well as whites were placed in a new arena in which to devise appropriate forms of political action.

DOCUMENTS

Early African Political Activity

DOCUMENT 1. Statement by S.N. Mvambo on the purpose of *Imbumba*, December 1883 [Extract] (Published in An African Bourgeoisie, by Leo Kuper)

Anyone looking at things as they are, could even go so far as to say it was a great mistake to bring so many church denominations to the Black people. For the Black man makes the fatal mistake of thinking that if he is an Anglican, he has nothing to do with anything suggested by a Wesleyan, and the Wesleyan also thinks so, and so does the Presbyterian. *Imbumba* must make sure that all these three are represented at the conference, for we must be united on political matters. In fighting for national rights, we must fight together. Although they look as if they belong to various churches, the White people are solidly united when it comes to matters of this nature. We Blacks think that these churches are hostile to one another, and in that way we lose our political rights.

DOCUMENT 2. Editorial on taxation, in *Imvo Zabantsundu*, November 10, 1884 [Extract]

What the effect of muzzling a race of people, used to settling differences and difficulties after searching inquiry will be, we do not now care to enquire. We are concerned at present with the pointing out of one or two facts which ought not to be ignored by Government. It was to be expected that the people would plead the hardness of the times caused by a succession of dry seasons as a reason for allowing their taxes to fall in arrear. But why the evil day of solemnly calling them to account for seven years neglect should have been put off to this the most straightened of the seven years is, to us, a very difficult problem to solve. We yield to no one in our anxiety to see the Native people standing well with the Government. Indeed, we would do all to assist Government in getting in the money owing. But is it not dealing with the people too harshly to threaten them with summary seizure of stock if there be no visible improvement during the current month? It was pointed out, with truth and force, that

12

cattle were going for comparatively nothing in the market, and still on account of the famine and the taxes they had to sell them. For Government to make a forcible seizure of Natives' cattle on account of taxes not collected for the last seven years would be to deal — well, in a manner that is not kind with their ignorant subjects. The Headman who made the wise request that Government publish notices affecting them in the *Native Opinion*, observed that in many cases most of them did not know exactly the periods when taxes had to be paid. And no doubt this recrimination between Government and taxpayers only serves to involve the issues. Anyhow, be the case involved or not, the fact stands alone that the Natives owe the money, and that it is important it should be paid over to Government without delay. We hold, however, that the present time would be inopportune for the forcible seizure of stock; and for various reasons. While it would create a class of discontented impoverished people the seizure would not adequately pay the Government. This impoverished class would have to live somehow, and, as necessity is a stern master, stock-stealing would lamentably increase. It will be said, as it was said in the meeting, these people must go to work. But it is not easy to get our people to do two things at once. Their excuse just now would be the ploughing season, and we should be the last to cloak them from Government interference did we feel that Government would reap something from such interference. At present these people are destitute, and are at their wits' ends in want of grain for sowing. If a paternal Government could go on without the money for the past seven years, surely they can wait seven months till the people gather in their crops, and may have been to work between weeding and harvest time, ere resorting to the extreme measure of forcibly seizing their drought-stricken beasts.

DOCUMENT 3. "Muzzling the Natives." Editorial in *Imvo Zabantsundu*, March 23, 1887

The Bill which the Sprigg Government has given notice of introducing next Parliamentary Session, with the ostensible object of making 'better provision for the Registration of Persons entitled to the Electoral Franchise' is about the severest blow that has ever been aimed at Native rights since representative institutions were introduced into this country. The Cape Times, a journal which cannot be suspected of negrophilistic tendencies whatever, characterizes it as an attempt "to cloak injustice under the specious pretext of reform."

The "Cape Argus," no blind partisan of the Natives, describes it as a "dishonest measure" which is "miscalled."

Under the first and third clauses of the Bill it is proposed to do away with the present lists compiled four months ago, during the present year. The object of this is of course obvious: The general election coming off next year, the ministry dread an appeal to the country on the present complete lists; and the register must needs be manipulated to suit their designs. Field-cornets are the officers entrusted with the important functions of placing on the roll such persons as they may deem entitled to send a representative to Parliament. Inasmuch, then, as it would be absurd to expect a Field-cornet to have a personal knowledge of any but a few natives in his Ward, it is fair to conclude that Whites alone would be enrolled. Then it is proposed to constitute the Civil Commissioner a final referee to decide upon the claims of those who may have been ignored by the Field-cornet. But what is given with one hand in this proviso, is taken away with the other; for this appeal to the civil commissioner is to involve costs after the fashion of those adjudged in a civil action. Then, as if these stupendous difficulties were not enough to keep our countrymen from their rights as liege subjects of the Queen, the government proceeds to enact in clause 17 that "No person shall be entitled to be registered as a voter by reason of his sharing in any communal or tribal occupation of lands, or place of residence." Such are the provisions of a Bill whereby the aboriginal inhabitants of this portion of her Majesty's dominion are to be deprived of the privileges they have enjoyed in common with their fellow-subjects, the Colonists, since British rule was set up in these parts. This Bill, which seriously affects the rights of the majority of the inhabitants of the country, is to repeal the vital portions of the Constitution Ordinance granted to this country after due deliberation fifteen years ago, for clause 2 reads:—

"So much of every Act, Ordinance, or other statutory enactment having the force of law, which shall be in conflict with the provisions of this Act is hereby repealed." In their endeavor to stifle the feelings of black inhabitants of this country, the Government has gone to the extreme of raking up the Inquisition from the debris of the Middle Ages, for those—black and white—claiming by virture of "salary" or "wage" are to stand cross-examination on "The names of their employers, from whom and the period of employment during which the necessary amount of salary or wage was earned."

Wherefore is all this, is the question which naturally rises to the surface at the contemplation of this coercive legislation. What has the native done to have such treatment meted out to him? That he has in the past exercised the franchise with intelligence and discretion is evidenced by the stamp of gentlemen he has sent to Parliament, and we challenge any one to place his finger upon a single member of the present or previous Parliaments, whose return is due to Natives, who has been a drawback to the House. This is perfectly natural, for it is generally admitted that there is nothing to which the Native of South Africa has, from time immemorial, given more earnest and closer attention than the philosophy of Government. Politics is to him a second nature; and it is to tamper with this that Sir Gordon Sprigg, is introducing his Bill to Muzzle the Natives. It has besides, been over and over again acknowledged that our people have never abused their electoral privileges. To support this statement we can easily and readily cite the opinions of a large number of eminent gentlemen who have taken a leading position in the larger affairs of the country, but, for space exigencies we forbear, and content ourselves with giving the views of two gentlemen at present at the head of the government of the Colony. In a speech which his Excellency the Governor delivered at the Empire Club banquet in 1884, Sir Hercules Robinson observed: "In the Cape and its dependencies the English bear to the Dutch the proportion of about nine to eleven, whilst both together bear to the Natives the proportion of only one to three." By eliminating the Native factor then, Sir Gorden Sprigg establishes the ascendancy of the Dutch in the Colony for ever. We live to see if the English will tacitly allow this to be done. Well, Sir Hercules Robinson went on to say, "Responsible Government, as far as the Cape Colony proper is concerned, has been a complete success, notwithstanding the fact that the Natives within the represented districts exceed the Europeans in the proportion probably of two to one." This testimony of the Governor is very valuable to us. It shows conclusively that, however it may suit certain politicians to trot out what they choose to call the "barbarism of the Natives" as a bogey to frighten the crowd, our people have been on the side of light and progress. But Sir Gordon Sprigg's testimony is even more emphatic. In a truly statesmanlike speech delivered in 1877 by the Prime Minister in East London, Sir Gordon Sprigg argued on grounds both of justice and of expediency that the Franchise should be freely granted to the Natives who possess the necessary legal qualifications. Mr. (not then Sir Gordon) Sprigg said:

"Can it be affirmed that any evil has arisen in the past from our Natives having the same civil rights as ourselves? I am unable to say that it has. In the division of King Williamstown a considerable number of Natives are registered, and many of them at an election record their votes. I may be told of instances when the successful candidate has been put in by the help of the Native vote, and that the defeated candidate had a larger number of Europeans. But the practical question is: Was the successful candidate the inferior man? I do not think that it can be affirmed that he was; and if so the Parliament and the country did not suffer from the Native vote; it might even be said that they gained by it . . . . . I will not now go into the large question of the difference of race and the causes of the superiority of one race to another; but it is my opinion that the black man here distinctly recognizes the superiority of the white man, and that for a very long time to come, perhaps for ever, the recognition will prevail to such an extent as to leave the representation in the hands of men of European descent. It is, in my opinion, extremely dangerous under a representative Government to establish the principle that the larger part of the population shall have no voice in the councils of the country. The true way to remove discontent is to provide a channel for its true utterance. It is the recognition of the soundness of this principle that has been at the bottom of many Reform Bills that have received the assent of the British Legislature. It is the refusal to recognise it that has led to so much disturbance and rebellion on the continent of Europe. Under Parliamentary Government representation is your safety-valve. Tie down your safety-valve and there is an explosion."

DOCUMENT 4. Petition to Queen Victoria, from "the Native Inhabitants of the Location of Oxkraal," July 1887 (Handwritten, 2 pages)

July 1887

The Humble Petition of the Native Inhabitants of the Location of Oxkraal in the District of Queenstown Colony of the Cape of Good Hope

To

Her Most Excellent Majesty Victoria by the grace of God of the United Kingdom of Great Britain and Ireland Queen Defender of the Faith Empress of India—

We your Majesty's most loyal and dutiful subjects the Fingos of the Location of Oxkraal desire humbly to approach your most gracious Majesty. We consider it the highest honour to be under your Majesty's benign sway and the subjects of a Government distinguished for justice mercy and all temporal and spiritual privileges. We are remnants of the once powerful tribes dispersed by Tshaka and prior to the year 1835 were scattered amongst the Amaxosa tribes on the border of this Colony, but when your Majesty's troops led by the then Governor Sir Benjamin D'Urban, Lieutenant Colonel Smith and Colonel Somerset fought against the great and powerful Amaxosa Chiefs Hintza and Hreli we asserted our independence became

allies of the British Government and were finally permitted to enter the Colony and settle down in the District of Peddie and elsewhere. Thirty three years ago Parliamentary Government was conceded to the Colony and a fairly low Franchise was at last agreed upon viz. the occupation of landed property of the yearly value of £25 and for the last thirty three years we have been allowed the great privilege of recording our votes at Parliamentary elections on the same footing as our fellow countrymen of European extraction but during the present Session of the Cape Parliament the House of the Legislative Assembly has already a Bill that will curtail nay in most cases completely take away our privileges under the former just and politic measure. We therefore pray your most Excellent Majesty that in the event of the said measure which is most obnoxious and quite adverse to our best interests as Natives passing both houses of Parliament Your Majesty will exercise Your Royal Prerogative in our favour.

Your Majesty's loyal Subjects deeply lament to learn that the Delegates sent to the late Conference have come back with the intelligence that a distinct understanding if not actual pledges that no further Imperial interference so far as we Natives are concerned shall take place in the future. If this be true Your Majesty's loyal Subjects feel that they are doomed and handed over and sacrificed to their old enemy the Dutch. This intelligence fills us with dismay. We therefore pray your Most Gracious Majesty that the brave and generous English Nation and the British Legislature will not abandon us to the tender mercy of those that are stronger than we are. That Your Majesty and also your Majesty's children and grandchildren may still continue to enjoy the Divine Blessing we will as in duty bound ever pray.

1 The mark X of Zulu Zimuma Chief of the Abambo Tribe

2 The mark X of Hayimpi Kakaza Chief of the Amabele Tribe

3 The mark X of Gontsana Bukani

4 The mark X of William Maqula

5 The mark X of Jafta Msuzwana

6 The mark X of Sikulume Qundeni

7 The mark X of Mtwa Mnyengeza

8 The mark X of Flexis Zinqalwa

9   Thomas Matumbu Dunjana

10   The mark X of Mtshiselwa Kakaza

DOCUMENT 5. Article on the pass law deputation in *Imvo Zabantsundu*, July 25, 1889

Pirie was, on Thursday last, the scene of a large representative and important gathering of Natives of the district of King William's Town to hear the Native Deputation to Cape Town on the Native Pass Bill give an account of their stewardship. Rev. ELIJAH MAKIWANE having, at some length related the incidents of their sojourn in the Metropolis concluded by stating how kindly and courteously they had been received by the Government, and the lively interest shown by the people of the Capital in the success of their mission. The kindness and good will thus shown to them they regarded as intended for their people. That the people listened to the story of the Delegates with deep gratification, goes without saying, and it might interest some if their feelings are given in their own simple and unadorned language. One sentiment seems to run through their utterances. The Natives had given up all hope that Government or Parliament would listen to anything they may ask and, by almost all, the Deputation was looked upon as a sort of wild-goose errand. To such depths of despondency had the Native people succumbed as regards anything good being done for them by the Government. The news, then, that the Deputation had to tell them had the effect of reviving hope, and, doubtless, the relations subsisting between them and the ruling power will improve in a corresponding degree, to the advantage of the country. Thus out of evil good has come. For although the action of Government in this matter savours of "the setting up of a man of straw to knock him down," to achieve the result attained in the exercise is not a bootless one.

Tsewa Bhashe, an old man, who was the first to speak in succession to Rev. E. Makiwane and Mr. Tengo Jabavu, said he was thankful. He does not thank those to whom you had gone. You have been our feet. After this result he felt as if he will shake off some of the bodily afflictions from which he was then suffering. He was suddenly seized by the poetic fire and exclaimed:

> Huku! Ndamtuma nmoto
> Waya wadaka,
> Ndeva nge ngnatguane
> Lindixelela.

Tonyela Mabhengeza, another old man, discerned in this the fruits of educating of their children. It was in grave doubts they sent these children, and they had hearts to venture. It is quite in the hands of these white people to make us slaves. See what education has done.

Tangeni Tabona thanked heaven which gave us the wisdom to give up these young men, and they have succeeded. Although you mention education it had not been sent.

Mbem Njikelana said, the meeting had to do with the expression of thanks, and it might perhaps be advisable to leave it to a committee, but they must have a fitting conclusion for this matter.

Green Sikondla was thankful to the young men before them. They have indicated the only way by which to fight the Government. I have always felt ill at ease about the way we fought Government. Today they have found a capital plan of campaign against the whites — to fight them by means of the law. This is the first Deputation that has been sent to state the feelings of the community. If a similar thing had been done when the guns were taken, war would have been avoided. He related an account of what he gathered from one of the servants on Sir G. Sprigg's farm whom he had accidentally met. He had inquired as to what sort of a master was on his farm, and the servant said he was a very good master and he could not account for the change now he is a ruler. The speaker concluded by saying we had not been acting constitutionally in seeking redress in the past.

After Jacob Dikweni, an old man, and S.H. Mnyanda had spoken

W.K. Ntsikana made observations on the scepticism of many as to the good of sending to Government and dwelt strongly on the importance of education. He concluded by nominating a committee to convey to Government the thanks of the people.

S. Soojica seconded, and after a few more speakers

P. Mali thought they would have commenced by congratulating these young men who had ventured where nobody had ventured and come back again. Thank you. Don't be tired even to-morrow. Thanks are also due to God. I lay not my hand only in thanking him, but go with my feet. He has changed the lion into a man.

Vecashe said these men come from a fight; and it is with feelings of veneration we now look upon them. They have taught us a very great lesson of which we had been previously ignorant. Whenever we felt aggrieved at what Government did to us we hurled the assegai, the result being orphans, but today a victory has been won although there are no orphans. At such a meeting all the Kafirs, the Tembus, and other Native races should have been present for what has been done has been done for all. We feel now we old people can depart in peace.

After J. Pamla and S. Sitela had spoken in a similar strain

Craig, a son of Gaika, thanked Government at what has taken place, and expressed his feeling that the Kafir nation would never have been dispersed if the course that had been pursued in this matter had been resorted to.

DOCUMENT 6. "The Future of the Bill." Editorial in *Imvo Zabantsundu*, August 15, 1894

The next stage that the Native Bill has to pass is the Governor's. On Sir William Cameron, who is now administering the Government, rests a heavy responsibility in regard to such a Bill. The Governor has the power to assent to Bills as the Queen's representative; and, usually, he exercises that power on the advice of his Ministers. The way the Native Bill has been passed through the legislature may not be sufficient reason for the Queen's representative to refuse assent to a measure; but it should be borne in mind that under Letters Patent constituting the Office of Governor and Commander-in-Chief of the Colony, there are Bills that the Governor is enjoined to reserve for Her Majesty's pleasure. The Native Bill just passed is clearly one of these, and must first go to England before it becomes law in the Colony. Mr. Jas. Molteno,

the other day, found on enquiry that the Bill providing for the Annexation of Pondoland had been sent to the mother country for her Majesty's assent. The same course has to be followed in regard to the Bill dealing with the lands of the Natives. The Governor is expressly instructed not to assent to Bills "inconsistent with treaty obligations," and it is a notorious fact that the Natives' lands — with which Mr. Rhodes would deal as he likes, and against the wishes of the people — under the Native Bill, are all secured to them by Treaties and Proclamations. In view of this fact, therefore, the following Petition, to be followed, no doubt, by others, has been forwarded from the Natives here to his Excellency the General for transmission to her Majesty the Queen in Council: — The Petition of the undersigned, loyal subjects of Her Majesty, and Natives of South Africa, residing at _____ , Cape Colony.

HUMBLY SHEWETH:

1. That a Bill has been passed by the Cape Parliament, entitled a "Bill to provide for the disposal of lands, and for the administration of local affairs within the District of Glen Grey and other Proclaimed Districts."

2. That the said Bill was introduced to Parliament by the Prime Minister who stated that if the measure was read a second time it should stand over for a year to allow of discussion.

3. That subsequently, and by a forced all night sitting the measure was carried, and is now about to become an Act and submitted for Your Majesty's approval.

4. That in the opinion of your petitioners this measure prejudices the rights and property of Your Majesty's subjects; and is inconsistent with Your Majesty's treaty obligations with large numbers of Natives who are now forced to surrender their rights to lands occupied by their fathers and themselves, under Your Majesty's Treaties and Proclamations, and to pay a labour tax such as is at best a qualified slavery.

Wherefore your petitioners humbly pray that Your Majesty will refuse your assent to this Bill, or grant such relief as may seem just to Your Majesty.

And your petitioners will ever pray.

Hopes and Grievances in the Wake of the Anglo-Boer War

DOCUMENT 7. "Questions Affecting the Natives and Coloured People Resident in British South Africa." Statement by the Executive of the South African Native Congress, 1903 [?] (Printed, 11 pages)

To the Right Hon.
Joseph Chamberlain, P.C., M.P.,
His Majesty's Secretary of State
for the Colonies.

HONOURED SIR,

We are glad of the opportunity afforded us of approaching you and through you the British Government in the manner prescribed by the constitutional forms of the country for the expression of public opinion and feeling.

The loyalty of the Native people of South Africa is satisfactorily testified to by the reports of the official heads of Native Departments in their recent Blue-Books. We fully confirm them now. Much as our people have suffered through the late war, their confidence in the justice of that war made them all the more willing to bear the hardships imposed upon them in common with the Mother Country. We would not lose this opportunity of testifying their indebtedness to His Excellency Viscount MILNER and his able administrators in the great work of repatriating the Native refugees, and for all that has been done in protecting, housing, and feeding them in the Concentration Camps. The cause of the sufferers can be confidently left in the generous hands of the Imperial Government in its anxiety to do the best for all classes.

The Church

The question of loyalty raises the larger question of the indebtedness of the Native races to the Government and people of Great Britain. How much is implied in the thought that out of the self-sacrificing faith of the Christian nations, foremost among whom are the people of the British Isles, the Gospel of Salvation, has been brought to the people that sit in darkness and the shadow of death, cannot be adequately expressed. No mere words can describe the spiritual blessings brought by the Messengers of Peace and good-will from the Church Catholic in fulfilment of the Divine commission.

The strides which education and Christianity are making are giving rise to fresh impulses, and creating a demand for reforms in the religious and educative methods of the past, but the old conservatism looks askance at the movements generated by these impulses both in Church and Mission field. Some of the clergy have failed in great part to catch the spirit of the times, and charges involving the loyalty of the people have been made, and being taken up by the anti-Native Press have been freely used to create suspicion and alarm. Doubtless much blame is attachable to the conduct of untrained men taking upon themselves responsibilities for which many of them are eminently unfitted by character and culture, and entering the mission field as preachers and teachers when their own knowledge is circumscribed. Thus complaints are rife of interference with vested interests, of the invasion of ecclesiastical rights, of trespassing within Ministerial preserves, of setting up opposition churches and mission schools, of proselytising parishioners, and in other ways creating schism and division amongst the churches. These church secessions are responsible for much bitterness, but as they have been interpreted as aiming at the eventual overthrow of the established authority of the Government and the white clergy, it would perhaps be well for us to emphasise the fact as already explained to the Prime Minister of the Cape Colony, that these movements are purely a matter concerning those churches affected, and have no anti-racial significance. The black races are too conscious of their dependence upon the white missionaries, and of their obligations towards the British race, and the benefits to be derived by their presence in the general control and guidance of the civil and religious affairs of the country to harbour foolish notions of political ascendency. The idea is too palpably absurd to carry weight with well-informed minds, and tends to obscure the real issues and to injure the people as a class. The Common law of the country is amply sufficient to protect the rights of the individual or the Church.

Education

The parlous condition of education in South Africa may be judged by the anomalous attitude of former Ministries under Responsible Government towards Native Education. Through the retrograde influence of the Africander and British anti-Native party the education of the native and coloured people has been hampered and the instructions of the Government of the day to the Education Commissions of 1891, and the findings of the Commissions of 1896 and 1900, as recorded in the reports of the Education Department will amply bear out this serious assertion.

At the present time, under the improved management of the Supt.-General of Education the disparity between the grants allowed per pupil to white and black, as shown by the Education Report, will be seen from the following table: —

First Class Public School (White)	£3	17	4½
First Class Public School (Black)		12	2¾
Third Class Public Schools (White)	£2	1	3¼
Third Class Public Schools (Black)		13	3½

The salaries paid to teachers are scandalously illiberal, forcing many to adopt other means to obtain a livelihood. The spirit that animates this attitude was expressed thirty years ago by Sir Langham Dale, the distinguished predecessor of the present Superintendent-General of Education, when he remarked (we quote from the Education Report for 1900):

"I do not consider it my business to enforce education on all the aborigines, it would ruin South Africa. If I could produce 60,000 educated Tembus or Fingoes tomorrow, what could you do with them? Their education must be gradual."

The President of the Education Commission (Sir J.D. Barry) reported *(inter alia)* as follows in 1900:—

"The schools for aborigines have practically all been promoted, and are maintained and managed by Church associations. The teachers, who are for the most part natives, are also indebted to these Church associations for any special training they have had for their work. The school age children of the aborigines cannot number less than 200,000, but the whole of the schools frequented by the children have never had a tenth of that number on their collective rolls at any one time. It cannot, therefore be said that so far as facilities for schooling are concerned there has been any tendency to make the education otherwise than 'gradual.' But while, speaking generally, school destitution is very noticeable, there are complaints that school areas in some cases 'overlap,' that is to say, schools promoted by competing agencies are needlessly numerous in parts.

"It is part of the Colonial system of public education that trade-classes are to be allowed for native day schools. But it is to be doubted whether any single native day schools have such an adjunct. Probably in none of the 269 schools has any serious effort been put forth to provide 'manual training' for the boys. In their case the whole of the four hours daily attendance required by the bye-laws of the Department is devoted to 'literary' work. Time-tables compiled on this plan are in some disfavour, for nearly every witness who had anything on the question of 'native' education to say to the Commission—and its witnesses included some missionary superintendents of native schools urged that manual training ought to form an essential part of the native course.

"We cannot but think, said the Commissioners, that Sir Langham Dales' dread of the ruin to South Africa lurking in some thousands of 'educated Tembus or Fingoes' a dread in the entertaining of which Sir Langham Dale by no means stands alone amongst colonists—owes its origin and justification to the character of the education supplied to the children of these people.

"Meanwhile, said the Commissioners, we perceive first that in matters pertaining to their education the aborigines are not supposed to have any opinions that are worthy of notice; secondly, that the methods sanctioned for the education of this class are either on

19

their trial or are already widely condemned; and thirdly, that the State, while assuming only a minimum of responsibility for the character of the education, year after year votes money for carrying it on."

The Natives have much to learn and unlearn, and the power of resistance to the will of the ruling caste having been effectually broken down, they are now applying themselves to the newer conditions imposed upon them by Christianity and civilisation with a common faith in the necessity of British rule, as the best and most liberal system for the Government of the various tribes and the settlement of their conflicting interests. There is, therefore, no longer a Native problem, but the Problem of the Ruling Caste, how to govern and educate on those broad and impartial lines which, while insisting on a policy of judicious firmness without prejudice, of sympathy without weakness, and justice with moderation will, at the same time, ensure the protection of the weak and law-abiding, and be a terror to evildoers.

The Judicial Aspect

Of the administration of justice by the High Courts, there is no complaint. Occasionally grave charges are made against the Natives, such as those of rape on white females, and ill-behaviour and rudeness in the public streets and thoroughfares. Of the more heinous and revolting crime of rape, it may be said that it has no sanction by tribal systems, and we therefore view with regret the attempts that are being made in the North to bring the law under subserviency to mobocracy. The comparative absence of such crimes is a testimony of the abhorrence in which they are held by the Natives generally, and they would support the enforcement of the severest punishments conformable to justice, irrespective of class. On the other hand the frequent cold-blooded murders of Natives, so uncommon even among the most barbarous races, and the difficulty of securing convictions under the Jury System, is having a marked effect in lowering the high prestige of the Bench, and the seasonable remarks of the Judge President of the High Court of Kimberley will be welcomed by the friends of law and order. We are glad to pay our respectful tribute to the high character of the Colonial Bench by quoting briefly from the learned Judge's charge to the Jury in a recent murder trial: —

His Lordship reminded the Jury that inflexible justice must be administered, not only between the European race in this country but between men of European races and those who were not. The basis upon which the Empire was built up was not material force or numerical strength and accumulated wealth. These things singly or collectively would not hold the Empire together. It was the fact that equal justice was meted out to all, irrespective of race or creed. The question of the administration of inflexible justice, irrespective of colour, was one in connection with which every citizen of the Empire, when called upon, must do his duty.

We think that no fair-minded man will deny that the Jury System of South Africa has too often degenerated into a mockery from its frequent abuse in cases between White and Black. It was pointed out by the late Professor ANDREW SMITH of Lovedale, "That a certain ignorant class, despising perjury as jurymen and actuated by race-hatred are resolved to allow none of their party to suffer for murdering a Native. Such shameful crimes as the murder of helpless prisoners in the Langeberg Campaign and the brutal massacre of friendly Natives by Geluk Burghers, in which no verdict from the jury could be obtained, creates a profound impression on the Native population and encourages the establishment of a bitter and lasting hatred such as exists between White and Black in the United States of America. It has been thought that it would be better for the Natives if the Jury Trial were abolished altogether, but to destroy the Palladium of Liberty — the gift of the Anglo-Saxon race — to mankind is not popular." The learned Professor suggested that a remedy might be found in a High Court of Justice, after the manner of *Court of Cassation* in France, which has the power to review the verdict of juries, to-quash sentences and to deal with all cases, where there is a violation of justice. The business of this tribunal would be to deal with cases where the verdict of juries to acquit or condemn were in gross violation of the evidence, or where the sentence was not in accordance with justice. And cases could be brought before such a Court by the Judges in the Circuit Courts, by the Public Prosecutor, by the advocates for the accused, or by others. We commend this question to the serious consideration of the British Government.

Civil Appointments

It was the wish of Sir Bartle Frere that the natives should be encouraged to fill responsible positions in the Civil Service, and to aid in the administration of the country. There is a tendency to narrow down their position to one of preferential treatment on colour lines. While we can cordially appreciate the necessity of preserving the race ascendancy of the whites in a country inhabited by a preponderating coloured race, such as the Bantu, the employment of men of thorough training, character, and abilities to positions of trust and responsibility should at least find more favour in the future than it has in the past. The opinion of President Roosevelt in the recent agitation over this question in America will perhaps be interesting, in its appositeness to these remarks.

It seems to me that it is a good thing from every standpoint to let the coloured man know that if he shows in marked degree the qualities of good citizenship – the qualities which in a white man we feel are entitled to reward – that he will not be cut off from all hope of similar reward.

Colonists can lose nothing by taking a more liberal if careful view of the issues involved in questions of this nature.

Administration

The natives of South Africa are naturally Imperialistic in their sympathies, having come through the experiences of early Colonial history, and the frequent wars and tragedies that have been enacted in this country in which they were by no means the least sufferers. Throughout the severe trials which our race has undergone in the past nothing impressed us more than the high sense of fairness, justice, and humanity displayed by Governors of British birth in their administrative capacities. There are, for example, the names of Lord Glenelg, Sir Andries Stockenstrom, Sir George Grey, Sir Bartle Frere, and others who, in the midst of difficulties,

opposition and the strongest prejudices, contrived to maintain the traditional prestige of the Imperial power in the fulfilment of its obligations to the native races of this country, while at the same time conserving the highest interests of the white races and the Empire. How much also the natives owe to the untiring zeal and humanitarian sentiment of the much-abused Exeter Hall party and the Aborigines' Protection Society, and similar associations, which it is now the fashion to condemn indiscriminately, it would be hard to realise. With all their defects, whatever they are, we cannot cease to cherish the memories of those courageous men.

It is interesting to enquire if the British ideal is being maintained. To our mind Colonial prestige has suffered a decline through the deteriorating influences of a low standard of Government in the neighbouring Dutch States, previous to the late war, and which has been unfavourably reflected in the administration of Native affairs in this and the sister Colonies of Rhodesia and Natal. To adduce examples of this decline in the Cape Colony we need not revert to matters so remote as the disarmament of the Basutos, which resulted in the failure of the peaceful mission of that great Imperial patriot, the late General Gordon, or the deliberate infringement of the Habeas Corpus Act, by the arbitrary arrest and detention in gaol of the Pondo chief, Sigcau, whose anomalous position at the present time is worthy of the special attention of the British Government.

The principle involved in the Langberg campaign, whereby the doubtful precedent of confiscating native lands and selling them to Boer farmers, and apprenticing the prisoners, male and female, to the Western Province farmers was established, although confiscation of the lands of the Dutch rebels was held to be illegal.

The case of Fleur and his Griqua accomplices in a seditious agitation in or about 1896, does not contrast reasonably in their sentence of fourteen years' imprisonment which they are now expiating on the breakwater, with the Cape Treason Bills, and the amnesty of Boer rebels and the disfranchisement of others, who had no votes, for a period of five years, as a punishment for the serious crime of rebelling against the established authority.

Or the provisions of the labour clause in the Glen Grey Act, which can only be interpreted as a concession to the forced labour party, when applied generally, but if applied to a particular class of youthful idlers, loafers, and vagrants who by their increase may become a menace to the country, revenues derived from any taxation which may be placed on such, ought to be expended on local improvements and should not go into the General Treasury. The completion of the survey of Native lands under the Glen Grey Act should discover this class of Natives, who cannot otherwise be properly distinguished under tribal tenure. In this form a "gentle stimulus" cannot be reasonably opposed looking to the existing conditions.

Recent Events

Coming to more recent events it cannot have escaped the notice of attentive students of Colonial policy how public feeling is being influenced against the native, and the formidable attacks by press and platform which aim at the destruction of the liberties granted to them by the benign rule of the British Government.

Much as the natives can respect all reasonable legislation which will safeguard the power of the ruling caste in the social and political affairs of the country, and which will conduce to the preservation of order and the general improvement of the Native people as labouring factors in the country, they cannot view without misgivings the persistent attempts of prominent public men, backed by a powerful section of press, both here and in Great Britain, to bring about a subversion of their constitutional rights.

The Franchise

In a communication which we sent to you, Honoured Sir, in May last, through His Excellency the Governor of the Cape Colony, the principle of the "open door" under the formula of "equal rights to all civilised men" which was favoured by the sagacious statesman, the late Right Hon. CECIL JOHN RHODES, was advanced in relation to the Franchise as the only sound construction to our mind of the Constitution, and we took up the ground that as the power of the British Government was potential, it was bound to protect the rights of all classes in the reconstruction and admission of the newly-formed States into the Union.

We must record a firm but respectful dissent to the interpretation of Great Britain's duties at this crisis by any one section, however powerful, against the fundamental interests of any other section, however weak. That responsibility lies entirely in the hands of the British Cabinet, in the same manner as it has borne it in the crisis which ended in the Boer War. If, as the Boer leaders say, the Natives must be taught that there is to be no alteration in the political relation of the whites to the blacks, it might be remarked that there is no colour distinction in the realm of morality and justice. We pointed out that under the proposed Federation the terms of Section VIII of the Articles of Peace appeared to justify the belief that the Imperial Government desires to vest in the Federal States the right to decide the vital question of the Enfranchisement of His Majesty's Native and Coloured subjects in South Africa. The question also occurs of the status of those qualified voters of the Cape Colony who enter those States, and the application of the principle of taxation and representation of these and also those Native residents of the States who may be fully qualified by education, property, and domicile, to vote as free citizens. Your advice, Honoured Sir, to the citizens of Maritzburg that it was necessary for unity on common objects, and to beware of speaking with a divided voice upon such matters as Customs, Railways, and Native Administration in case their influence would be weakened in the Councils of South Africa, suggests the thought whether in view of the expressed utterances of the Premier of Natal on this subject which agrees with that of the Boer Leaders, viz., that there must be no political equality granted to the Natives, these views are to be the criterion for the guidance of public opinion to the rest of the South African States and the British people in arriving at the ideal of unity upon which you so eloquently touched.

We are of course aware that while no good ground exists which might be construed as an abuse of the Franchise by the Natives, but on the contrary their choice of representatives in Parliament has been generally creditable and wise a powerful agitation has been proceeding to deny these rights to the Natives, and the recent agitation for the suspension of the Constitution of the Cape Colony has been interpreted as aiming at that object among others. The extreme advocates of this policy are prepared to put it to the test under the new Federation. Herein lies the germ of much future trouble.

The idea is thus expressed by the Secretary for Native Affairs of Natal, and it is supported by the utterances of most of the candidates for Parliamentary honours in the elections of 1901.

They should manage their own affairs, he said, and regenerate a desolated country, and let Dutch and English tender their advice to England to let them manage their own affairs, and especially the Native Question. If they were to be dominated by outsiders, and to have the constant interference they had in the past he felt that there would be still further trouble between the Dutch and England, and between England, the Dutch and Natives.

The *Times of Natal*, in endorsing these sentiments, also remarked: —

But these things once accomplished the new order once firmly established on a lasting basis, there will be no room for the direct Imperial factor in South Africa. The official legend of Downing Street will pass away like a tale that is told.

The voice of Mr. MOOR is merely the first articulate echo of public opinion, and that opinion will become more pronounced as time goes on. Those who read the signs of the times will acknowledge the truth of what we say. Up to the present the wave of Imperial patriotism has carried us over all obstacles, but we cannot always remain on the crest of the wave.

That there is some reason to suspect a collusion of sentiment and premeditated design between the extreme British anti-Native Party in South Africa and the Bond or Dutch Party, which aims at the elimination of the Imperial Factor to the ruin of the subject races of His Gracious Majesty, will be seen from the following comments by *Ons Land*, Mr. HOFMEYR'S organ:—

The new Colonies are directly governed from Downing Street, and Mr. CHAMBERLAIN is directly responsible for their administration. If his visit has the object of as speedily as possible putting an end to the present condition of affairs and giving self-government to the inhabitants of those colonies, then we cannot do otherwise than rejoice at the visit. If, however, the object is to strengthen the domination of Downing Street over the internal affairs of South Africa, then we anticipate little good as the result. This latter course, unfortunately, appears to be the impression of many in England, for latterly much has been heard of the new Imperialism, and they seem to be departing from the principles upon which the great over-sea colonies have had the management of their affairs.

It is a singular commentary upon the wisdom that would call upon the Natives at this period of the world's history to defend the use of rights which are firmly established upon the impregnable basis of human liberty and justice. It is plain, therefore, from the statements quoted that an *imperium in imperio* may be created *sui generis* within the realm of British operation and policy, by the advocates of deprivation, on the one hand, and of a moderate Franchise on the other, which may materially affect the future relations of the people of this country.

The Labour Question

In regard to the Native Labour question it is commonly asserted that there are sufficient and more than sufficient, able-bodied men in the country to do all the work needed, but living in absolute idleness, and not helping in the slightest degree to advance the progress of the country. It is also apparent that more labour is absolutely essential to the development of the natural industries of South Africa. There is just sufficient truth in the former statement to mislead the unwary, for it raises the inference that the native will not work. To say the native will not work is to argue against the visible progress of the country which has in great part been built up with the aid of native labour whatever its deficiencies may be. On the contrary, the natives are willing to work. They have been accustomed to obedience under their own chiefs, and the changing conditions from barbarism to civilization with its increasing necessities are forcing them out to work in greater numbers every year, although it must be recognized with regret that the evil of adding to their hereditary defects the vices of

European civilization is a deteriorating factor in the economy of the land. The labourer or servant should be made to strictly observe his contracts, but he should also be protected in them, and contracts should be made with individuals, not the Chiefs, and properly drawn up before responsible officials in order to safeguard the rights of all parties and to prevent fraud.

Roughly, there are two classes of labourers, the husbandman who tills his own land, and the hired labourer or servant. Both these are as yet unskilled and their greatest misfortune is that they have not yet become accustomed to the strenuous life, the practical, consistent, and constant exercise of their best faculties of body and mind. To develop these to the best advantage it is necessary that there should be administrative co-operation, but when we look around to see what has been done we find that, apart from the attempt made by that distinguished statesman, the late Cecil John Rhodes, who established a Labour Bureau which met with poor support at the hands of the officials, and which he had not time to properly develop before he died, when it was abolished, no serious attempt has been made to encourage or regulate the supply of labour on right lines by any of our statesmen. The whole question has been left with the mines and the farming community, and the terrible results of the absence of administrative control, in the scandalous irregularities under the old regime at the Rand made such a deep impression on the native mind, that there can be no surprise at the scarcity of labour. The sudden depression of wages before the effects of the war, or the impressions formed of the evil conditions of the old regime had had time to subside, was a master-stroke of bad diplomacy, by whomsoever invented. It also reveals the attitude of the mine-owners—a cold, hard, unsympathetic, calculating, determination to reduce wages at any cost. Only the other day a question was asked in the Cape Parliament as to several cases of alleged ill-treatment of labourers under the new regime at the Rand, which drew from the Premier a promise to investigate the matter in the interests of this Colony, which profits largely by money brought down by the labourers who go there.

The idea which also has found favour with many that the natives are demoralised by high wages received from the military during the war is as false as the assertion that they live by stock stolen from the farmers. Such views may mislead the ignorant, or suit the sinister designs of the forced labour party, but they add nothing to a satisfactory solution of the difficulty, and in view of the increasing poverty which sees extensive districts threatened with starvation through the failure of crops, are positively injurious. In this relation, Sir, we have noted with satisfaction your statement in the British House of Commons, "that no policy of actual physical compulsion brought to bear on the black to work, would have the slightest support of the Government." These attempts to precipitate the British Government to a policy of force have been watched with keen anxiety by the natives and their friends, and we deprecate the attempts inspired from interested sources to denounce the natives as a class in the sweeping manner so fashionable with the prejudiced press. The natives are willing to be led. They are accustomed to obedience. They cannot throw off the lethargy of ages in a day. However much we may deplore their unreadiness to meet the changed conditions brought about by the influx of an increasing white population, with its higher and more expensive standards of living into a country accustomed to the simple habits of a pastoral life, and the demands which the former make on the latter for a cheap labour supply in order to support their more expensive habits, nothing constructive or useful to our purpose can be got from mutual recriminations. The capitalist demands cheap labour. The labouring man has not, in this or any other country, had a satisfactory interpretation of the term.

For South Africa, labour troubles are just commencing, and the statesman who will deal successfully with them must first sweep his mind clear of the prejudices that have been heaped around it. It is not a race question, although radical differences in life and language, and such questions as general treatment, rates of wages, accommodation, food, etc., etc., give rise to more bad feeling on this, and the Master and Servant question, than any other subject, for it touches the country on its tenderest spot—the economic—and the attempts to reconcile low wages with high living, we may readily believe from the example of other countries will continue to agitate the country long after the present generation has departed.

Again the Department of Native Affairs in the Cape Colony, unlike Natal, has no available statistics of a complete and reliable kind to guide us in framing a correct estimate as to the number of able-bodied men available for work, the number engaged in remunerative occupations of their own and who, therefore, do not require to take service, the number of idlers and vagrants, the amount of taxes directly paid to the Government by the Native people, their contribution to the Commonwealth by indirect means as producers and consumers, and as customers on our railways, telegraphs, postal and other sources by which the Government coffers are advantaged. These and other statistics should be the common text-book and guide to the formation of sound and authoritative opinions. The Secretary for Native Affairs of Natal, speaking on Native taxation in 1898, said: —

It was said that Natives do not contribute enough to the revenue, but there was something to be said on the other side from the point of view of themselves. The sum of £1,000 had been received in passes from Natives leaving the Colony and coming into it, and from the figures at his disposal he made bold to say that of the Natives of a working age in Natal there were not 10 per cent, who did not put in work somewhere during the course of twelve months. By indirect taxation the Natives had contributed nearly £110,000 as compared with £5,000 contributed by Europeans with indirect taxation. Apart from what they contributed in the purchase of clothing, agricultural implements, &c., the Natives contributed £140,000 to the revenue. The Natives also contributed largely to the revenue of the railway. During the last eight months of the last year they had travelled on the Natal line to the number of 170,000, bringing in a revenue of £30,000. There was very nearly half of the Native population of the Colony on their railways as passengers within eight months. He was sorry they had forced labour in Natal, because he did not believe in it, regarding it as a slight upon industry. Until they shook themselves free from this incubus he feared they would not hold their own with those countries that had free labour.

Possibly later statistics would show still better results, and we are of opinion that the Cape Colony natives proportionally would improve upon these.

We can assure you, Sir, that the intelligent native mind is impressed with the extreme importance of the great issues lying at the root of the labour supply, involving as it does the vital interests of the industrial, commercial, and economic life of the country as well as the highest interests of the natives themselves, as the principal labouring factor.

But one thing we should like specially to remark, is the desire, often expressed, that conferences on the labour question should not be left entirely in the hands of the mining fraternity. We advocate co-operation. No practical schemes which leave the natives out of consideration in matters affecting them can be satisfactorily dealt with in that manner. We suggest an Imperial Commission, which would include the labour question in a larger investigation of the condition of Native Affairs in South Africa, with a view to securing some measure of uniformity between the laws of the different states, and the systems of civil and municipal administration and management of the native subjects of His Gracious Majesty, and to find, if possible, a grand solution of the whole question, in view of approaching Federation.

One remarkable feature is that while merchants are not loud in complaining of the scarcity of native labour, the mine owners and farmers are loudest in their outcries. This is explained by the difference in wages, the former paying more, while the latter are not paying a living wage (vide Report of the Cape Commissioners Messrs. Halse and Visser, on the treatment of farm hands in Australia, as compared to native treatment in Cape Colony). After all is said and done the question whether this country can supply all the labour required for present use and future developments would be best answered by satisfactory statistics controlling the labour supply at the different centres in order to deal practically with surplusage. These, we have already said, are not available, but we would again urge the necessity of a Commission on which the natives should be represented.

We believe that there is room for co-operation between the different administrations and the mine managers to develop on proper lines the labour supply south of the Zambesi, and we are glad to observe from your speech to the mining magnates that you also impressed this view upon them, although from the attitude of mine managers it is to be feared that their impatience would contribute materially to the difficulty of a proper solution of the question on broad and rational lines. Their haste inclines to prejudice the rights of the labouring classes. We also think that in dealing with this question satisfactorily, the cooperation of the educated leading natives should be sought, and they should also be allowed to take part in the deliberations of such conference.

Polygamy

On the effect of Polygamy on the labour market, we attach little importance, for numerically Polygamists are not a large class, and as an independent class they are generally capable of maintaining themselves without going out to work in the same manner as the aristocracy in England. We attach more importance to the results of the custom in degrading the womenfolk and by the force of example on the young manhood destroying all legitimate desire for self-improvement, and the cultivation of the higher arts of civilisation and the moral and religious elevation of the people. The only remedy for this is education and Christianity; but here again we are faced by defects of administration, which were called attention to by amongst others, the late Bishop BRANSBY KEY of revered memory, who pointed out to the Commission on "Native Laws and Customs" in 1881, "that the Government and administration of the Native tribes lacked "executive force," besides other notable authorities who impressed upon the Commission the necessity of the gradual abolition of poligamous marriages. Although the Commission made it an instruction that evil customs should be gradually abolished, there are evidences of administrative failure to carry out this wish. The effect of this neglect is now being felt on the labour question and other matters.

Locations

The location system of the country does not encourage the Natives to migrate with their families to the labouring centres, as the Natives are taxed in the locations without security of tenure which kills all ambition to improve their surroundings or to aspire to a higher state of life. In many cases it is to be feared that such taxes are applied to other purposes than the improvement of the sanitary condition of the locations and the efficient regulations of the municipal needs of the inhabitants, the result being generally seen, in the lamentable spread of diseases, the high death-rate, and the depraved moral status of the people who occupy these locations. In place of pure and healthy townships we have a condition of squalor which is already a byeword in many cases.

The Liquor Question

Closely associated with the Master and Servants' question, and labour generally, is that of liquor. The connection between liquor and crime is shown by the fact that one-half of the serious crimes with which the Circuit Courts have to deal are the result of drink, even in the Transkeian Territories, where restrictive measures short of total prohibition are in force. Its effects on the morale of the Native people in lowering their respect for authority, and their manners and behaviour, and its demoralising consequences generally, are such as no sane country would tolerate without incurring serious loss and injury. The debasing effects of drink on the mass are testified to by Ministers, Magistrates, and others in authority, and there is an almost unanimous opinion on the part of the public, that the traffic must be restricted in its operations. The efforts of the Temperance Societies and the Missionary bodies show encouraging signs of success, and the work of these devoted people has been greatly aided by the measure known as the Innes Liquor Bill which falls short of total prohibition. But the question is aggravated by the conduct of Licensing Boards, and legislation which gives the power of "local option" to the Divisional Councils upon which the Native taxpayers are not represented. Total prohibition of the sale of liquor is strongly advocated by many, but on this subject there is a division of opinion, some fear being expressed that the objection-

26

able feature of class-legislation would thus be introduced as an injurious precedent. Much satisfaction is expressed at the stringent regulations enforced by the new regime at the Rand for protecting the Natives, and the industries, against wholesale demoralisation. It is felt, however, that something more is needed in the Cape Colony to deal effectively with liquor and Kaffir-beer in the best interests of the country.

Native Government

The beneficial results of Magisterial authority are most strikingly apparent in the cessation of tribal wars, and their presence is a corrective to sedition, insubordination, and lawlessness among the more turbulent tribes. At the same time it is noticeable that in the Native Territories, the administration, to quote a well-known authority, "lacks executive force."

The personal influence of the Magistrates in the encouragement of that progress which is indispensible to the "material wellbeing, increase in knowledge, and improvement in conduct," is, with a few exceptions, wanting. The premature concession of Responsible Government has doubtless resulted, as in other things, in a lack of sustained effort such as that recommended by the Native Laws and Customs Commission of 1881 to be observed, and the Government has not been able in the multitude of its responsibilities to give effect to those reforms which are so necessary to the proper administration of Native affairs in regard to the improvement of the laws and the social condition of the people.

On a general survey of Native policy in South Africa, the necessity of endeavouring to arrive at some connected system between the States in order to give more uniformity of administration is made more apparent by the condition of Native affairs in the otherwise progressive Colony of Natal.

Amongst intelligent Natives the conditions there are a bye-word, and may not incorrectly be described, we think, as one of "nursing barbarism in the lap of civilisation." The system of Native government in the Sister Colony affords cause for grave anxiety, and appears to call for more extended inquiry.

The land laws both there and in the Cape Colony and the other States, in so far as they apply to the Natives, require careful revision with a view to the protection of the people in their tenure and individual rights which at present is on an unsatisfactory footing.

It appears that in Natal the Government is alienating large tracts of land from the Natives, who are to remain in future as squatters on land formerly held by them, giving their services without payment to the farmers for the right of occupation. This system appears to be in direct conflict with solemn treaties entered into by the British Government to protect them in their possession. A double profit is thus secured to the farmer in the labour and the product besides the advantage of owning the land and practically enslaving the people. The disabilities placed in the representation of the intelligent Natives on the Franchise are also a subject of remark.

Unity

Speaking of Unity it is painfully apparent that this sentiment conveys nothing more to some of the leaders of public thought in this country, as well as a large class of the European public than of uniting Briton and Boer so as to present what is called a "solid front" to an alleged "black menace."

The cardinal principle of reconciliation between the whites is said by the leaders of Dutch thought to lie in the concession of complete self-government being accorded to the people of this country.

These two schools of thought, although differing on the question of race predominance, meet on the common ground of antagonism to the Natives, and this feeling has been fostered by the actions in legislation and utterances on the public platform and Press of leading public men. On the simple question of admitting the Native subjects of the King to participate in some degree in the defence of the Empire we have the recommendation of our Premiers of the Cape and Natal to the conference of Premiers in London, which is suggestive of the political ostracism of His Majesty's Native Subjects. Added to this is the recommendation to raise the strength of the defensive forces of the Cape Colony ostensibly for the protection of one class—the whites, against the other class—the blacks.

Just as we believe that the Unity of the Natives for the purpose of attempting to overturn the established authority of the white man is the "chimera" of ill-informed minds, and an idea which is belied by traditional tribal disunity, so also do we believe that the conception of uniting the white races in a league against the Native as a class is bound to failure.

We were of opinion that conditons had undergone a change, and that the Natives were no longer to be looked upon as a class for special and exclusive treatment, or to be governed by a policy of continued suspicion. We thought that they were now to be received with confidence within the political family circle as true citizens of the Empire, and that the doors of the Temple of Peace would be thrown widely open that they also might enter freely in with their white brethren to share in the coming prosperity which has been so eloquently described by the great advocates of the Commonwealth.

To say that the Natives feel perfectly secure in the protection of their liberties, would, in face of the examples already advanced, be misleading and contrary to fact. In the honesty and integrity of British feeling towards them, and the Christain conscience behind it. Yes! In the loyal execution of the dictates of that feeling by those Colonial Statesmen at present charged with the duty of giving expression to it under the systems of Responsible Government at present in vogue in the Cape and Natal, we say No! In them that sense of security has been greatly shaken, and the confidence which the Natives are accustomed to give to those in authority has been sadly abused in the desire to pander to a mistaken sentiment of suspicion and enmity against them for party purposes and other selfish aims.

How the British Government is going to reconcile such sentiments and aspirations which are powerfully supported in this country with its solemn pledges of protection to the weaker races is the cardinal question for us. How those who have been traditionally opposed to the Natives in their conduct and government in the past, such as the Dutch anti-Native class, and the other class of British anti-Natives who support them, are to be granted absolute control of the Natives under the new Federation before they have furnished satisfactory evidence of a change in their attitude and feelings, is a question that will interest others besides the Natives themselves, and it should engage the serious attention and jealous regard of all true lovers of constitutional liberty.

It is not sufficient for the Boer leaders to say that the Natives must be treated with justice and fairness. Our experience in the past leads us to know how little we can expect from such professions on their part, and we have the experience of other countries before us, and especially of the Southern States of America where, on the authority of such men amongst others as ex-Governor PINCHBACK in a review of the political status of the Afro-American people, he says:—

It is noticeable that wherever coloured men have been deprived of the ballot, unjust class-legislation has speedily followed, race antagonism has been intensified, and lawlessness and outrage against the race increased.

The time does not appear to us to be ripe for Great Britain to entirely divest herself of her obligations of Empire, or for the British people to seek to be relieved of their trust. However desirable the unity of the white races may be, and we are conscious of its necessity in the best interests of the ruling caste any conception of Unity which is founded on the political extinction of the Native element towards which a section of public feeling appears to be drifting in South Africa would, to our mind, be unwise and in the highest degree unstatesmanlike. Our own conception of our duties as loyal subjects is sadly deficient in the ignorance of the mass of the people which will call for strict management in which the support of the intelligent Natives will be cordially pledged to the British Crown in maintaining law and order, and that Ideal of Policy which has been so well expounded by a contemporary, English writer, and by the great American Statesman, WILLIAM J. BRYAN :—

A Britain worthy of the name of great—great as the mother of free communities beyond the sea—great in her loyalty to her old traditions as the land of religious liberty, the home of constitutional freedom—great as the protector of the weak against the strong, the champion of the oppressed against the oppressor—great, not by reason of the extension of her military frontier but in the strength of her moral position; Britain, great for CHRIST and for humanity.

It must be by beneficent laws, it must be by a just government which a free people can love and upon which they can rely that the nation is to be preserved. We cannot put our safety in a great navy; we cannot put our safety in expensive fortifications along a sea-coast thousands of miles in extent, nor can we put our safety in a great standing army that would absorb in idleness the toil of the men it protects. A free government must find its safety in happy and contented citizens, who, protected in their rights and free from unnecessary burdens, will be willing to die that the blessings which they enjoy may be transmitted to their posterity.

His Majesty's black and coloured subjects must be made to feel in a way they have never felt before, that the question of social equality and other impediments which are drawn across the trail are not made the lever for the subversion of the highest civic and political rights which, conformable to constitutional limitations, and the predominance of the ruling caste, are freely and impartially extended to all classes under the benign rule of His Gracious Majesty EDWARD VII.

DOCUMENTS 8a-8d. Minutes of Evidence, South African Native Affairs Commission, 1903-1905

DOCUMENT 8a. Testimony of Martin Lutuli of the Natal Native Congress, before the South African Native Affairs Commission, May 28, 1904 [Extracts] (Published in *Minutes of Evidence. South African Native Affairs Commission, 1903-1905*)

32,069. You have got an institution in Natal called the Natal Native Congress?—Yes.

32,070. Who is that composed of? Tell us what it is?—So far as I know, the Natal Native congress is the voice of the Natives; they come together and talk about things, and if we find anything wrong, we can go to the Government about it, and present it to the Government,

tell the Government what we think and what we see during that meeting.

32,071. How many of your people belong to that Congress?—I cannot say how many. Of course, they come from all parts of the country.

32,072. You know whether it is a hundred or a thousand; which is it nearest to?—When the meeting is called, sometimes there will be about 50, sometimes about 70, sometimes about 100; it never was more than 100 in the meeting called.

32,073. May everybody go to the meeting?—They are free to go.

32,074. Are you the chairman?—I was the chairman for three years.

32,075. How often do you hold meetings? Do you hold them many times in the year?—Once a year.

32,076. Is that all the meetings you have? Have you a committee, for instance. Have you a committee or a council?—We have the Missionary meetings and church meetings.

32,077. You have not a committee which meets often?—The Natal Native Congress meets once a year.

32,078. Have you got, besides the Congress, a committee or council that meets at other times?—Yes, we do appoint a committee if there is anything necessary to call a committee together for; it is called when we find there is anything for it to do.

32,079. You say the Congress is the voice of the people?—Yes.

32,080. What are really the objects of the Congress firstly; then, secondly, what is it that the Congress aims at?—The object is, so far as I know, this. If we want to talk to the Government, one man cannot talk alone, we must come together and decide things, and hear the opinion of others on a certain thing. Then if it is necessary for it to go to the Government, we appoint some delegates from that meeting to talk with the Government on that subject.

32,081. What are your aims?—The welfare of the Native population under the Government.

32,082. What are the things that you discuss in your Congress?—Sometimes we discuss about how we should approach the Government to let the Native have the franchise, so that the Native can have a voice in the Parliament; because here in Natal we have no voice in Parliament whatever. That is another thing we talk about, but we have not brought that before the Government yet, to ask for it. Some say it is now the time to do it, and others say it is not the time, so we have not brought it before the Government yet, although we do talk about it. We also want to approach the Government to let the Natives be free in everything, let them buy lands if they like, if they are able to, and let them trade in the towns or out of the towns, and so on. Those are the things we talk about. We also talk about education; we say we have not got enough education. We do not think the Government is educating the Natives as far as it ought. That is what we talk about.

32,083. Are these the principal things?— Those are the principal things.

32,084. You spoke about the franchise. You said that the Natives have no voice in Parliament?—Yes.

32,085. I will ask you some questions about this afterwards. The next question I want to ask you is, in this Congress of yours are you suffering from any grievance at the present time?—I cannot say we are suffering from any grievance.

32,086. Do you not feel that the Magistrate, the Secretary for Native Affairs, the Under Secretary for Native Affairs, and the Governor, represent the Natives?—Yes, they do represent the Natives. We take the Secretary for Native Affairs in this way; he is there as Secretary for Native Affairs, but he is representing other parties. He is sent to the Parliament by other parties. He is not sent by the Natives to the Parliament. Those who send him to Parliament will be against the Native and will not like it if he does not do as they tell him to do. He is all right enough, we recognise him well enough, and we deal through him, and we like him, but there is that point.

32,087. Then there is the Under Secretary, who is a permanent officer?—The Under Secretary for Native Affairs is a permanent officer, but he will talk of the matters through the Secretary for Native Affairs. They will go through the Secretary for Native Affairs. He is all right enough at his office, and we like him

very much. We are pleased he is there at his office. We will be very sorry if he loses the office, but all matters which go through him go through the Secretary for Native Affairs, and the Secretary for Native Affairs is sent by other parties.

32,088. You evidently do not think that at the present time you are fairly represented?—Although we have discussed many things, we have not brought them all before the Government; some say it is time to bring it to the Government now, and some say it is not.

32,089. I am asking you what you think?—I think myself that it is time we had a voice in the Parliament.

32,090. How do you think that voice can best make itself heard—in what way?—There should be some members who are there to represent the Native sent there by the Natives, and they will know they are to represent the Natives, to do Natives' work only, to look after the interests of the Natives.

32,091. How should these men be appointed; should they be nominated, or should they be elected?—They should be elected.

32,092. Elected by the Natives themselves?—In whatever way the Government thinks fit to elect these men.

32,093. I mean, should the election be by white people and by Natives, or by Natives only?—Elected by white people and the Natives.

32,094. They should represent only Native affairs?—They should represent Native affairs. The member should know he is there to represent Native interests.

32,095. Should he sit in Parliament, and have a voice and vote in Parliament, too?—Yes.

32,096. You would like to see representatives of the Natives appointed specially for that purpose, sitting in Parliament?—Yes.

32,097. Will you carry your views a little further? Do you think these representatives ought to be white men?—Yes, they ought to be white men.

32,098. Not Natives?—Not Natives.

32,099. You have said that one of your grievances was that you were not free in every way, that you could not purchase land as you wished to. Do many Natives want to purchase land?—Now they do; they have seen that they must have land of their own. Everybody wants to have land of his own.

32,100. They wish to purchase land?—Yes.

32,101. Then you went on to say you wished to be able to purchase land in the town and out of the town?—Anywhere we can.

32,102. Are you prohibited from purchasing land?—No, we are not prohibited from purchasing land, but there are some places where Natives are not allowed, say, for instance, at Eshowe; there they have passed a law to say that the Native has no right to have land.

32,103. In Zululand?—In Zululand. The Natives look at it in this way. Zululand was our own land, and although now it is under the Government, we ought to be the first. We ought not to be prohibited.

32,104. You wish to be able to buy land in the towns?—Yes.

32,105. Are you allowed to do that?—Yes, we are allowed to do it.

32,106. You wish to have the right to trade in towns?—Yes.

32,107. Are you allowed to do that?—Yes, we are allowed to do that.

32,108. And outside also?—And outside also.

32,109. What is it you complain of?—I bring this before the Commission because there are some places where you cannot go free; and I bring this before the Commission because I have heard it spoken of at meetings many times, so I must bring it before the Commission as they ask me.

32,110. You went on to say that the Government does not do enough for education. How would you have the Government do more?—We have no Government school for Natives in Natal.

32,111. Nevertheless, does not the Government subscribe a good deal of money towards Native education?—Yes, Government pays the money to have education in Mission schools to teach the children.

32,112. What changes would you like to see?—I would prefer that the Government should build a Government school to teach everything—to teach the knowledge in head and hands and everything, to know how to work at trades such as blacksmiths, carpentering, mason work, and all those things.

32,113. Would you like to have industrial schools supported by the Government?—Yes, when we meet together, we talk about it; I like it too.

32,114. Do you think the pupils of these schools ought to pay for that education?—The children pay even now, if we send them to colleges. There are colleges under the Missionaries, and if we send them there they do pay; though it is little, they do pay something.

32,115. What I ask you is, supposing the Government were to put up a lot of money to build such schools as you indicate, do you think the pupils who go to these schools ought to pay sufficient to keep these schools going?—Yes; they must pay for their education. Those who send their children there must pay something.

32,116. Do I understand you rightly when I infer that what you want is the opportunity for your children to be educated?—Yes.

32,117. It is not that you are asking for money, but you are asking for opportunity?—Yes, opportunity.

32,118. Is that quite clear?—Yes, that is quite clear.

32,119. Have you ever lived much in the locations in Natal?—No.

32,120. You do not know much about location life and the tribal system, and so on?—I have not lived on a location. I have been always in a Mission station—all my life.

32,121. The matters in which you are interested are those relating to representation, education, and such like?—Yes.

32,122. I suppose you know something about the land question. Do you like the present location system, under which the Natives hold the land in communal right under the Chiefs?—Yes.

32,123. You like that?—As at the present time?

32,124. Yes?—Yes; but it will not always be as it is. We are afraid that it will not always be like it is. For myself I would suggest that everyone should have a little piece, and know where he is, because in future there will be many troubles, and we are afraid that in time to come the Government might sell it, and the European might buy it all, and buy the

Native's also, and he will not have anywhere to stay.

32,125. That is what is known as individual tenure?—Individual tenure.

32,126. That is what you would like—that each Native should be able to own a plot of ground of his own?—If he can.

32,127. Should it be his own in freehold?—In any way the Government think best, to secure it for him and his generation.

32,128. Would you let him sell it?—I would not like him to sell it.

32,129. The Government should prevent him from selling it?—Yes.

32,130. Even to Natives?—Even to other Natives. Let them secure it for that individual for him and his generation.

32,131. Should it go from father to son?—From father to sons.

32,132. And if any man misbehave himself, would you take it away?—The Government can make a law that, if he does not behave himself they would do this and that to him.

32,133. Do you think the Natives of Natal would like such a change as that?—Now they would like such a change. They all see what is going on.

32,134. Would that not break up Chieftainship?—It would not break up Chieftainship. A man may have land of his own, but he will recognise his Chief still.

32,135. In what way?—In every way.

32,136. If the land belongs to the man, what is the good of the Chief coming along and giving him orders? The man might say, "No, I will not obey your orders"?—I take it this way: At the present time those who have their own land, under their own Chiefs, do recognise their Chief, if they have their own lands. I know, too, that the Natives are people to recognise those who are superior over them.

32,137. What I mean is that the Chief has a power over the common man, that is to say, he may turn that man out, he may make it unpleasant for him; but if the common man be the owner of his ground, the Chief could not disturb him?—Even now the Chief, unless the man is going against the law, cannot do as he likes with him.

32,138. Do you think Chieftainship is a

good thing? Do you think it can go hand in hand with individual land tenure?—Chieftainship helps the Government very much in many ways.

32,139. Do you think the Chiefs also would like this change of land system?—Some of them do; some do not. They would like to have the land to themselves, and we call that greediness.

32,140. What opportunity have you had of learning what the views of the great mass of the Natives in Natal are on this subject?—I go to the meetings, and meet the people, and we talk about many things. We talk about what is going on, and what is coming on, and what has passed. We talk about all these things. I see and meet the people, and talk with them about many things.

32,141. Do you think the Natives of Natal as a whole would like such a change as that?—I think, if that way is opened to them, they will welcome it.

32,142. Do you think the Natives of Natal are backward?—They are not backward; they are advancing.

32,143. They are advancing now?—They are.

32,144. Are they advancing fast enough?—Not fast enough.

32,145. In what way would you hurry them?—I would put it in this way—they are not advancing as fast as they should. The Government does not assist them to advance fast enough. If the Government were to throw education open to them, they would advance more.

32,146. Do you think that education alone is all that is required to advance them?—I do not mean just education alone, but industrial training, and trades, and so on.

· ·

32,170. Is there anything you have got in your mind that you would like to express your opinion on?—Such as what?

32,171. Anything that I have not asked you about?—There is a thing I would like to say a few words upon to the Commission, about which I hear most from the Natives, that is "isibahlo," the compulsory labour. The Natives cry about that everywhere.

32,172. Why do they cry?—Because they are turned out to go and work on the road parties.

32,173. That is the law?—That is the law, and they do it, but they are not pleased with it.

32,174. Why are they not pleased with it?—Because they go and work and it is not their own wish, and they get paid just what they are offered. The Government says, "We will give you so much." I hear many people talking and crying about that.

32,175. They prefer to seek labour where they wish to?—Yes, they prefer to go and work where they wish.

32,176. And would they be prepared to give something to the Government in exchange for this right that the Government has of calling them out for public works?—I do not know whether they would turn round and say, "We pay our taxes."

32,177. Is that a grievance?—Compulsory work?

32,178. Yes?—To the Natives it is.

32,179. But only a very few out of the population are affected by it?—It is not a very few; it affects mostly every Chief, especially those in the locations.

. . . .

32,217. You say that the Natives would like representation in Parliament, and you say that their representatives should be chosen by the white men and the Natives together, and that they should only look after the black man and only vote on Native questions. What about the white men who helped to send those representatives to Parliament? Could not the white men turn round and say, "You are only looking after the Natives; what about our share?" Do you not think it would be better for the Governor to say, "I am going to choose you four men who will go to Parliament (or two men), and they must look after the Native interests only, and must not vote upon any white question. They must be the eyes and ears of the black men. These men are good white men, and they will go and sit in Parliament, and look after your interests." Would that not be better?—That would be just the same as it is to-day.

32,218. No, to-day they are voted for?—It would be just the same as it is to-day if the Natives did not elect their representatives but the Governor just took the men he thought fit to take and said, "Here you are."

32,219. How would it suit you if all the Natives came together and ten men were put before them, and the Governor said, "You must pick out four men from these ten; you must settle amongst yourselves which two or three or four men out of the ten shall represent you in Parliament." Would that not be a better plan?—That the Natives should elect those men themselves?

32,220. Yes, would that be better than the Governor saying, "You four must go to Parliament," without any talking to the Natives?—Yes.

32,221. You would prefer the Natives to pick out four men from the ten?—Yes.

. . . .

32,241. *Mr. Samuelson.*] You are not Chairman of the Natal Native Congress now, are you?—Not this year.

32,242. Who is Chairman this year?—Skweleti Nyongwana; I am only the Vice-Chairman.

32,243. How long were you Chairman?—I think for about three years.

32,244. Did you not take for your cue or for your example the formation of the Farmers' Conference of the Colony in the formation of the Native Congress?—I would not say that.

32,245. There are communities all over the old part of this Province, that is of Natal proper, who send representatives to the Natal Native Congress?—Yes.

32,246. These communities who send delegates have committees for the local management of the affairs of the Congress?—Yes.

32,247. The Congress has a secretary?—Yes.

32,248. And the office of that secretary is at Verulam?—Yes.

32,249. How many Natives in this Colony are represented at the Congress?—I think I have already said.

32,250. I do not mean the persons representing the Natives, I mean the communities themselves, such as Driefontein, Innyanyadu, Edendale, and so on—the communities represented?—There are representatives from the Mission stations and some from Zululand, and there are delegates from Innyanyadu, Driefontein, Ladysmith, and other places.

32,251. You could not give us the number?—I have not got the number.

32,252. There are various districts in the Colony represented?—Yes.

32,253. None of those districts which send representatives to the Congress are of heathen tribes, that is to say, tribes under heathen Chiefs?—No.

32,254. It is only the Christian and civilised Natives who are represented on the Natal Native Congress?—Yes.

32,255. Many of them have been exempted from Native law, and many of them are still under Native law?—Yes.

32,256. You cannot say that the Natal Native Congress, which is really formed from the Christian and civilised Native community, in any way represents the great bulk of the population which is under Chiefs and in heathenism?—I cannot say that, but the object of it is to represent the whole.

32,257. Native Chiefs and Headmen of Native tribes have not participated in the Native Congress so far?—No, they do not send their representatives.

32,258. They have been invited, have they not, to send delegates to the conference?—Yes.

32,259. And they have not done so?—They have not done so.

32,260. Why?—I cannot say why.

DOCUMENT 8b. Testimony of the Rev. E.T. Mpela, the Rev. B. Kumalo, J. Twayi, A. Jordaan, J. Mocher, J. Lavers, and Peter Thaslane, of the Native Vigilance Association of the Orange River Colony, before the South African Native Affairs Commission, September 23, 1904 [Extracts] (Published in *Minutes of Evidence, South African Native Affairs Commission, 1903-1905*)

39,127. *Chairman.*] I have got a letter here signed by Mpela, saying that the Native Vigilance Association of the Orange River Colony would like to give their evidence before this Commission; did you write this letter?—*Mpela:* Yes.

39,128. We should like to know who the members of this deputation are?—*Lavers:* I am in business here, and I formerly belonged to the Cape Colony.

39,129. *Mr. Stanford.*] What tribe do you belong to?—I am a Tembu.

39,130. *Chairman.*] What business are you following?—I am making bricks and am a cartage contractor.

39,131. And the next one?—*Mocher:* I am a mason.

39,132. From what country are you?—From the Transvaal.

39,133. What tribe?—Matlonka.

39,134. And the next?—*Jordaan:* I am a Cape boy.

39,135. And you?—*Twayi:* I am a Fingo.

39,136. What are you doing?—I am a dray cart driver.

39,137. And you, Kumalo?—*Kumalo:* I am a Zulu.

39,138. You are a minister?—Yes, I am a minister of the African Methodist Episcopal Church.

39,139. And the next?—*Mpela:* I am a Basuto, and I am also a minister.

39,140. From where do you come?—From Basutoland.

39,141. *Mr. Stanford.*] What Church do you belong to?—To the African Methodist Episcopal Church.

39,142. *Chairman.*] And you, Thaslane?—*Thaslane:* I am from the Transvaal, and am a cartage contractor.

39,143. Are you all members of the African Methodist Episcopal Church?—No.

39,144. How many are members of that Church?—*Kumalo:* Two; Mpela and myself.

39,145. Who is to be the spokesman of this deputation?—*Twayi:* The Rev. Kumalo has been appointed spokesman.

39,146. Now, Kumalo, what is it that you are appointed and desire to state to this Commission?—*Kumalo:* We considered that we were going to answer the questions put us according to the items as they appear on the list of subjects—on each subject.

39,147. Have you answered those questions already in writing?—No, we have not answered them yet; we have only had a discussion about them.

39,148. Are there not some particular subjects upon which you wish to speak which are on this list?—Yes, there is the subject of land.

39,149. What do you want to say about land?—It is only that, as you are aware, we have no right to buy land in this country. It has been our desire all along to have the right to buy land, as the black people have in the old Colony and in Natal. Their having the right to buy land in the other Colonies has made all the people here, who have not that right, desire also to be able to do so. They consider it to be slavery not to be allowed to buy land, especially as they have to live on those town lands known as locations where, especially at some places, the police have the right to enter when they wish. We consider, further, it is enlightenment and progressiveness, and those who wish to speculate must have the freedom to do so that other people have in speculating and buying land. We say that it is the desire of all our Natives to have a piece of land, either on a farm or in a town, and that they should not be prohibited from buying land wherever they think fit if they are in a position to do so, and that they should have in their possession their title deeds.

39,150. You are aware that the great number of Natives in South Africa are living under what is called the communal tenure system? — Yes.

39,151. Do you see any objection to that system?—As I said before, we consider it slavery. Every man has the right to go on his land, and even the Town Council makes laws to affect even our wives, simply because we live on that ground.

39,152. Would you like a new law made which would enable you to buy land at pleasure?—Yes.

39,153. And that would bring you more or less under the European law?—Yes.

39,154. And would you like to be brought under the European law in all ways?—Yes; that is our desire, too, to be brought under European law.

39,155. Then, I suppose, under these circumstances it would be necessary to cancel all the old laws; such laws indeed as protect all the Natives in South Africa in the reserves which they now occupy?—We here will not represent that class of people who are still far in heathenism and in darkness, but for those who have already advanced it is so much the better that they should be cancelled, and let

those people be governed by the one law governing all British subjects.

39,156. How many people do you represent?—We represent what we call the enlightened people; we do not represent those people who are still under Native law in the true sense of the word. We are more or less governed by the Church laws, although, in the eye of the law, we are considered to be under Native law; and the Church laws are those which are governing civilised people.

39,157. Then you recognise that Government must have two kinds of laws, one for the unenlightened and one for the enlightened?—Yes; because we feel that it would not be fair to press those people who are still in heathenism to come up to those who are already enlightened. Still, we think that they should be encouraged to be brought to enlightenment.

39,158. And the whole point of your view is that those who have advanced and who desire to progress should be afforded facilities for their progressiveness?—Yes.

39,159. That is the gist of everything?—Yes.

39,160. But with regard to the great mass you have nothing to say; they and their lands should be let alone?—May I ask one question: Do you refer to the Orange River Colony?

39,161. I refer to South Africa?—I confined my mind to the Orange River Colony, the Colony we represent; I do not allude to other places.

39,162. Well, answer for the Orange River Colony?—We consider that the most of the people here in the Orange River Colony are civilised.

39,163. Most of the people?—Yes.

39,164. What is your population?—I could not exactly say.

39,165. How many Christians have you?—At the different Churches?

39,166. Yes?—I do not consider that Christianity forms what we call civilisation only.

39,167. Well, how many can read and write?—Even that I do not consider as civilisation.

39,168. What is civilisation?—Civilisation is the state of living and of progressiveness, even whether you write or cannot write; if you live in a state of progressiveness, that is civilisation.

39,169. Is that in the dictionary?—I did not look at the dictionary; but I consider, in my explanation of the thing, that that is the position. Of course, the knowledge of writing and reading must come in sometimes to cause civilisation, but that is not the most essential factor.

39,170. Do you mean that the first footsteps that a Native may take towards civilisation at once make him a civilised man?—No; it is the mode of his living. If he shows in his living, in his deeds, and in his works, that he is progressive, that causes civilisation. I can say this by way of illustration: Here is old Father Lavers; he can neither write nor read, and yet his mode of living in his home is that of a civilised person. I would therefore call him a civilised man.

39,171. You have expressed yourself on this point, and have covered what you might call the subject of land tenure?—Yes.

39,172. Is there any other point upon which you would like to speak?—The franchise.

39,173. What have you to say about the franchise?—That is another desire we have. We wish also to enjoy the privilege of the franchise.

39,174. That is, if you acquire the qualification laid down by the law, you should be allowed to exercise the right of voting?—Yes.

39,175. Do you say that in view of what you have just said with regard to the progressiveness of the Natives?—Yes; I would not force those Natives who are still in darkness; I only refer to those who are progressive in their minds and civilised in their modes of living.

39,176. Then your arguments are practically the same as those you used in regard to the acquisition of land?—Yes.

. . . .

39,194. What is the next subject?—Administration of local affairs; I would like a little explanation of this.

39,195. In a word it is this: In some parts of South Africa there are what are called District Councils of Natives, formed of Headmen and other appointed representative Natives, presided over by the Magistrate. In those Councils they discuss matters relating to

the Natives in the respective districts where they exist, such matters as schools, roads, and other things, and the people pay a special tax of 10s. a year towards the upkeep of the schools?—That is done under the Glen Grey Act?

39,196. Yes; they have a certain share in the management of their own affairs?—In this Colony we have locations belonging to the Town Council. We have not, as they have in the Cape Colony under the Glen Grey Act, District Councils; we have Town Councils.

39,197. And so they have in all large towns, such as Cape Town and Port Elizabeth?—Yes. If that is included in this heading, "Administration of Local Affairs," I would recommend that the Natives should look after their own work in the location. They should appoint men to discuss matters; and even monies that are collected from the location should be used to improve the location.

39,198. Is that not done?—No, it is not done.

39,199. It is done in some parts of South Africa, where they have a Council of the leaders of the location, who are consulted on matters affecting that location?—I do not remember any.

39,200. At any rate, that is what you think might well be done?—Yes, to manage their own local affairs in the location. We especially consider it a great grievance in regard to these policemen. The Town Council here says our wives must have tickets, and of course, sometimes they forget those tickets; then for a man to catch hold of another man's wife and say, "Give me your ticket," is a thing we do not like—because these policemen handle the matter in any way. I know we have a remedy in Court, but the thing has happened as I have described it, and we consider it to be a great grievance about these Municipal tickets.

39,201. Tickets for the women?—Yes, tickets for the women. People who are living in a good mode. And for men also, I may say.

39,202. You recognise, I suppose, that it is necessary for any Municipality to keep a proper control over the people living within the Municipal limits?—Control can be kept without that.

39,203. Have you not got a very large number of what we may call loose and irresponsible men and women living in this location?—I will not say that we have not; we have such people at different places.

39,204. Is it not, perhaps, with the object of creating a better moral atmosphere that the Municipality has taken this measure?—No, it is not on account of that; it is merely to increase their monies.

39,205. Supposing it was for some moral reason—would you approve of it on that ground?—Yes; although we must bear in mind that when people come together, it must always occur that the morals become affected in some way. With every civilised people that must occur; and it must occur in all countries, with all classes and colours of people.

39,206. The view you want to express is, that such a regulation as you have described can be administered too harshly?—Yes. I think, if the Natives themselves were managing their own affairs, they would work it better, and the morals of the people could be better looked after. The Town Council makes laws for these people, but they do not take much interest in their progress. If we have to have such locations, I would recommend that they be on landed property that is bought by the people themselves, because if the people buy the land they will improve it, and Natives will have no right to go and cluster there, because the owners will be held responsible for their advent. I should say that it is the fault of the Municipality that this immorality is going on.

39,207. In all these things, you mean to say, you think the Native should be consulted?—Yes; and furthermore, when they do consult the Natives, they do not consult those people who will give them enlightenment, but they always go to those people who will not give them enlightenment on things affecting the Natives. Even if they do go sometimes to an enlightened person, I think that we, who are the leaders of our people, are the persons who should be consulted on anything affecting the interests of the Natives in the country. We are the people who should be consulted, but what do they do? Even the Government will sometimes go to those raw Natives, and want the Natives to give them ideas as regards us who have left that state of heathenism and darkness. The desire may be to uplift the

Natives, but by going to enquire of those people who are still in darkness, is to press those who are already enlightened down.

39,208. I want you to deal with the general principle, and not to be particular as to what is happening in the town of Bloemfontein. It is not a part of the scope of our enquiry as to what is being done by Bloemfontein particularly, or by any particular Government; but we are enquiring into principles. Well, we have heard your views upon that. Is there any other subject?—Education.

39,209. What have you to say upon the subject of education?—The best form of education is compulsory education; compulsory education for us would be a very good thing. And when we have education, I think it would be better that we should have it for a certain object. If a person wants to be a teacher, he must study for that purpose, and if he wants to be anything else, he should study with that end in view. We are accused of having a little education, which is spoiling us, and yet in view of that accusation which is brought against us, even the Government has set a standard where the Native must end his education—a standard which does not enable the Native to reach that point in education which will not spoil him. And in regard to industrial education, it is only training to go and plough the ground and sow seed. The Natives all do that. Every Native knows how to plough ground, and to sow seed, and how to do all that kind of thing. That is not what is wanted. They must be taught to study the soil, and they must be enabled to study everything, so that they can improve. With the industrial education given at present, even in becoming a mason, they are only taught to take a brick and some clay, and to put it down in its place. That is not industrial education enough. When they know those things, they must learn how to make contracts, and they must know all the other branches of work which will make them skilled workmen.

39,210. What is it that you are now aiming at? Is it the opportunity to learn those trades?—What we have now, is merely to have a young man sent to school and apprenticed, and he has to take two pieces of wood, and knock them together with a nail; and when he comes out of school he does not understand a trade at all.

39,211. Why do you say that? What is your experience? Have you been through it yourself?—I have been studying the Natives as I have been looking at them.

39,212. Have you been to the industrial schools where those things are being taught?—No, I have not been there; but I have studied the result of the industrial schools.

39,213. Where have you studied it?—Amongst the Natives who have come from those places.

39,214. Do you think that all they learn is to knock two bits of wood together with a nail?—Yes, or to make a box, or a table, and such little things. But they know nothing about a trade. They do not become skilled workmen.

39,215. And what is it now that you wish?—If Natives are taken to be taught industrial work, they must be taught to understand all about it. If, for instance, a Native is to become a carpenter, he must be a skilled man. Of course, I know that they cannot all become skilled men, but that is not the point. If they are taught to do anything, such as ploughing or carpentry work, as I have mentioned, they must be taught thoroughly those things, so that their mind will always be desirous of doing the thing properly. Sometimes, when they have not got enough education in the doing of those things their mind becomes benumbed, and they get tired, and cannot go on to reach those places which would improve them, and make their earnings better. They get discouraged, because they have not got the right thing. Therefore, I say, if this compulsory education comes about, it must be that kind of education which will improve them.

39,216. Do you want compulsory education?—I think it would be a good thing.

39,217. Do you think the State ought to pay for it?—I think it ought to be taken from the taxes paid by the Natives towards the revenue of the state.

39,218. With regard to the high form of industrial education which you have indicated, do you think that the Natives themselves ought to pay for that?—Yes; but the Government must help them.

39,219. In what way?—The Government can help them by erecting those institutions, and receive from each of the pupils a small fee on entering for that work.

. . . .

39,223. It is difficult for Natives to find work?—[Mpela] Yes.

39,224. What you would like is that when once a man is educated he should always be able to secure work?—Yes; he should be able to secure work from the Government.

39,225. Many educated Natives have not got work: Is that it?—Yes.

39,226. Does not that rather open your eyes to the fact that there is a danger in over-educating the masses, because there will be no work for them to do?—That is just the thing. If the Native could be given a proper and thorough education it would not be like educating the masses. You would get the proper men in the proper place; but now you view all Natives alike, and that is where the trouble comes in.

39,227. What work would you find for them if they were educated in the way you allude to?—If you could get thoroughly-educated Natives, and if you could put them anywhere, to be Magistrates' clerks, or anything like that, that would be good for them, and it would also be good for other Natives, because they are looking after those children when they send them to school. Boys, when they come back from school, must take a prominent place in the country.

39,228. That is your aim: that your children should be well educated, and made able to occupy the offices of the State?—Yes. I would also speak about the indirect taxation. We think that there is too much of it at present upon the shoulders of the Natives, especially in the way of these travelling passes, Municipal passes, and other things like that.

39,229. You call that indirect taxation do you?—Yes, if a man has to pay for a pass when he gets it, then it is indirect taxation.

39,230. Do you mean that when the Native has to get passes they ought to be free and not paid for?—Yes; because it is for the protection of good people. The Native is made to pay for that pass, and by that he is made to contribute to the State too much, because when the monies are aggregated at the end of the year, you will find that the Native has paid more than he expects, and has benefitted very little.

. . . .

39,235. *Mr. Stanford.*] You seem to advise that a very distinct line should be drawn between the Native who still practises the old heathenish customs and the Native who has emerged therefrom and adopted a certain measure of civilisation?— *Kumalo:* Yes.

39,236. Would there not be a difficulty in placing individuals in respect of such a line? How is the Government to gauge the measure of civilisation which has been arrived at here and there by any individual Native?—As I have said, in this Orange River Colony, our people are already reaching this stage of civilisation, and are reaching it daily, whilst in such places as Basutoland and others, the people are not civilised.

39,237. Are you really justified in saying that the majority of the Natives in the Orange River Colony are more advanced than the Natives in Basutoland?—Yes, I am justified in saying so. I think they are even more advanced than the people in the old Colony, because in the old Colony they have education, but they are not progressing in their mode of living in their homes. Educationally, the old Colony is far superior to this country, but in the mode of living, these people are far more civilised than those in the Colony.

39,238. Is it not a fact that a great many of these people living on the farms hardly use any European clothing at all, and are living very much in the old Baralong style?—No; the majority would be those that are living in the European style of clothing.

39,239. On the farms?—Yes.

39,240. Where they are at service amongst the European farmers?—Yes.

39,241. Then your contention is, that the majority in this Colony are now fit to exercise the rights of franchise, and to be freeholders in respect of landed property?—Not those who are still at the back, but for all those who are showing their progressiveness in their mode of living and otherwise, I say yes.

39,242. *Mr. Thompson.*] I would like you to give me your opinion on this scheme: If the Government of the Orange River Colony were to-day to move you all—you and the unenlightened—to a spot a couple or three miles out of Bloemfontein, there cut up plots of half-acres, sell you those plots, and keep you in there, right out of town, away from the white people, would that meet your idea?—Not fully, because that would not give the black man the right to buy land in town. He ought to have the right to buy land in the town even, and to speculate if he wishes to.

39,243. But answer this first: Would you not like to see, in the first place, all the Natives moved from these slums and all about, and put a couple of miles out of the town, with a proper railway system to bring them out in the morning, and take them back at night, ring the curfew bell at night, at nine o'clock, and keep them in their town. Do you not think that would be in the interests of the Natives as a whole round Bloemfontein?—Yes, it would be a good plan; you mean also that they should manage their affairs there?

39,244. Yes, they can have their own Council to manage their own affairs. You would not consider it a hardship if the Native was told, "You cannot live here, but you must go out to your own township"?—Yes, that would be a proper thing; it would teach them to recognise and to know each other. That would be the best, I think; but not to interfere with their business things.

39,245. They could come in and carry on their business, but there they must go for their homes?—Yes, I think that would be the best.

DOCUMENT 8c. Testimony of the Rev. Samuel Jacobus Brander, the Rev. Joshua Mphothleng Mphela, and Stephen Nguato of the Ethiopian Catholic Church in Zion, before the South African Native Affairs Commission October 4, 1904 [Extracts] (Published in *Minutes of Evidence, South African Native Affairs Commission, 1903-1905*)

40,782. *Chairman.*] Who do you represent?—*Brander:* I represent the Ethiopian Catholic Church in Zion.

40,783. What is that?—It is an organisation which we have commenced lately since we resigned from the A.M.E. Church.

40,784. Where is it situated?—In Pretoria.

40,785. Is this the first centre of it?—Yes.

40,786. Are you the head of it?—Yes.

40,787. What were you belonging to before?—To the A.M.E. Church.

40,788. And before that?—We belonged to the Church of England before we joined the A.M.E. Church.

40,789. Why did you leave that Church and start one of your own?—When we found that we could not get ahead, Makone and myself came together to raise the Church of Ethiopia, and later on we joined the A.M.E. Church of America, because we found at that time that it would go better if we joined the American Church, as they had education and other things better than we had. We considered that it would be better for us to join them, so that they could help us, being coloured people themselves.

40,790. What nation are you?—My father is Mokhatla of this country, but I was born in the Cape Colony.

40,791. And Mphela?—He is of the Bapedi, Transvaal.

40,792. And the other man?—That is Nguato, from British Bechuanaland.

40,793. What are your aims and objects in this new Church of yours?—Our aims and objects are to teach our people the Gospel, and later on, when we are strong enough to erect schools as industrial colleges, to educate our people in the Transvaal.

40,794. Have you many people who follow you?—I have got a lot of branches; I have got over 600 people who are following me; that is, since May.

40,795. Were you ordained in the English Church?—I was ordained as deacon in the English Church.

40,796. Did they withdraw that office from you?—No.

40,797. In coming here to-day, I suppose there is something particular that you wish to say?—There is something that I would like to say. That is about education and our schools. We are very weak, and we have not got the money, and our people are still in darkness, and we want aid from the Government to help us with the schools. That is our great disappointment which we wish to speak about. I made an application last year while I was in the A.M.E. Church for a grant in aid for the Ethiopian school, which was refused to me by one who said that the Ethiopian Church was not recognised as yet by the present Government. So we have to wait until such a time comes, when we can bring up all our complaints and what we want from the Government. That is all we can say: we want the Government to help us.

40,798. Were those 600 children, or people of whom you spoke, not afforded the opportunity to get education under other missions before you gathered them to yourself?—They were all in the A.M.E. Church with me; those people have all followed me from that Church.

40,799. Have you done much damage to the Ethiopian Church in taking them with you?—I cannot tell; I have not heard of any.

40,800. Is that the only thing you wished to say?—That is the only thing I wished to say.

40,801. *Mr. Sloley.*] What is the object of your people in desiring this education?—It is because our people cannot come up to a proper standard, or come up to the white people, and do what they want; and education is the only thing we find that will bring us up to a standard like that.

40,802. Can you explain it more fully; do you mean it will improve their chances of getting wages and property, or what?—The first thing is that they would be allowed to buy farms outside for themselves, and to erect schools on them, whereon they could be taught industrial work. I think that would help them a great deal. That is the only thing that can make our people not lay in the kraals; and, while they lay there, there is nothing to make them work. The Chiefs sit with them there, and only make Kafir beer, and now and again send their people out to work to get money for the taxes. When they can be taught how to work in the industrial schools, and are brought up to a higher standard, that will be a good thing. Then, with regard to the wages, the wages are only for the town Natives. For those who are living in the locations the wages are very small. And we have a lot of taxes to pay, after which we find our people cannot afford to pay for schools, or anything. That is an application that has been made already by the people here to the Municipality, and I do not think that I can bring up anything of that.

40,803. Where were you yourself educated?—I was educated in the Colony, in the mission schools, and then, later on, I was with Archdeacon Gaul, who is now Bishop of Mashonaland.

40,804. You were educated at Zonnebloem?—No, at Lovedale.

40,805. *Mr. Krogh.*] Why did you leave the English Church?—We came together in a meeting that we called, and said, "Let us go and teach our own people by ourselves." That was all.

40,806. How far do you want to educate your people?—We think, if the Government will help us, we would bring them up to matriculation, if we can.

40,807. The object, I take it, would be to bring them on an equality with the white man?—Not at present, but for the future.

40,808. *Mr. De la Harpe.*] Have you many churches in the Transvaal belonging to your persuasion?—I have them on a paper, but I cannot tell them out of my head.

40,809. You do not know how many members you have belonging to your Church?—I have over 560, from here to Basutoland and British Bechuanaland.

40,810. Over 500 members?—Yes, those who have joined me since I started the organisation; it is only five months since I opened the Church here.

40,811. Is that only men, or men and women put together?—That is men and women.

40,812. Are they increasing very fast?— They are increasing.

40,813. How long is it since you actually commenced, since you were the head of the Church?—Since May this year.

40,814. *Captain Dickson.*] What was your object in leaving the A.M.E. Church and starting a Church of your own?—We left on account of the promises they gave us when we joined them not being kept. They promised that they would give us a school from America at their own expense, with teachers and all, and this they did not do. It is now six years since we were united with them, and all those promises they failed to keep. We had to support our schools and everything here ourselves, and at the same time collect our yearly income, and also take collections for Easter Day, contingent moneys, and all that money had to be forwarded to America. When we asked for help when we were in debt, or anything, they refused to help us. I did that three times, when the Church was in danger of debt; three times I sent an application to America for them to help us, and they said they could not help us, at the same time saying we had to forward all our moneys to them. So I said it was no good for us, they would not help us from America, and it would be better for me to stay in Africa and help my people. That is my reason.

40,815. During the six years you were a minister of the American Church, did you receive any grants from America at all?—Not one.

40,816. Was there any political teaching in the Church during the six years you were a member of it?—Not to my knowledge.

40,817. Have you in the Church that you have just lately started no white supervision whatever?—No.

40,818. What is your object in starting a Church independent of the white man and of white control; seeing that your first attempt at that was a failure, what is the reason that you made a second attempt?—We have not seen that we have become a failure as yet.

40,819. Did you not say you made a mistake by joining the A.M.E. Church?—In joining the American Church we thought that, as they were our own colour, they would help us up, but we found they helped us down, and they took all the best positions without telling us a word, sending men from America, and putting them into those positions, and taking us away, without giving us any notice.

. . . .

40,850. What was the original object of the African Methodist Episcopal Church in coming out from America?—We called them out here.

40,851. You called them out?—We called them out. Makone, who was with me, was a man who had a young lady from here. She went to America with a choir and when she was there she met the church and sent a letter to him. After she had sent the letter to him he brought that letter to the meeting, and the meeting found it good to ask those people if we could unite with them, and if they could give us help, and the answer came, "Yes, with the greatest pleasure."

40,852. Your motto and the motto of the A.M.E. Church is "Africa for the Africans"?—Yes, "Africa for all nations."

40,853. Like the motto for the Afrikander was "Africa for the Afrikanders"?—Yes.

40,854. And you are working on those lines; that is to say "Africa for the Africans"?—Yes, on the lines "Africa for the Africans," besides the others. I will give you a little explanation of what I mean. We were united to the Americans because we thought they would help us, but we were cheated by them. They told us, "Look here; we will show you and teach you and bring you equal in education with the whites, so they will recognise you through the education which we will give you." And they did not give it to us.

40,855. Do you think it would be a good thing for you Native races to run side by side with the white races in everything, just like the two rails of a railway line?—Not at present, but in the future I think so.

40,856. When?—In years to come; it may be after 50 years.

40,857. Do you not think it will be better for you to keep always separate like the two rails on a railway line, so that you will not come into conflict, and perhaps into ill-feeling with one another, and so get into trouble with each other in some way?—No; I think when we are educated we can be united and we can be one with the white all over, and I think we will have peace later on.

40,858. You think at the same time you should all have the same right to the franchise, the same political rights and the same social rights?—Yes, when our people are educated to such a standard.

40,859. And you would also like in time by constitutional methods, that is by lawful measures, to get yourselves into the control and management of public affairs in the Government as you have done in the church?—Yes, I should think so.

40,860. Mr. Thompson.] And where would you end; would you like the races to amalgamate?—Yes.

40,861. Would you like the white man to marry the Native woman?—I should think so.

40,862. And the Native man to marry the white woman?—I should think so.

40,863. Mr. Stanford.] Did you quite understand that question about getting ultimate political control into your hands; do you mean that you want to govern the white people of this country?—No, it is not so. While we live together?

40,864. That is what you said?—While we live together it would not be for us to govern the white people, but to be with them. We are under the whites, and I do not think we would ever come up to a standard like them to govern the white people.

40,865. You recognise that the white man must always govern in this country?—I recognise it in that way.

40,866. What is it then you desire: religious freedom?—Yes, religious freedom.

40,867. Do you in your church preach loyalty to the Government and obedience to the white man?—Yes.

40,868. Captain Dickson.] Do you not look forward to the day when you will be capable of governing yourselves, both whites and blacks?—No, I do not think so; when I look into that I do not think so at all. I think we can be pleased if we are educated so far that the Government can recognise us so that we can become members of Municipalities or anything like that. I think that would do for us. The white people would be with us and have a supervision over us, and when we are in the meetings we could advise for our people and speak for them. I think that would do for us.

40,869. Chairman.] That is all you wish to say?—Yes.

DOCUMENT 8d. Testimony of James B. Mama and John Makue, Transvaal, before the South African Native Affairs Commission, October 7, 1904 [Extract] (Published in Minutes of Evidence, South African Native Affairs Commission, 1903-1905)

42,055. Chairman.] I understand that there is something that you wish to say to the Commission, and that the first thing you wish to speak about is the franchise?—*Mama:* I wish that the Natives of this Colony should have the franchise.

42,056. Why?—Because that is a thing which will make a people of us. We have no place to which we can go, or to which we can get out of the way of Colonies like this, and the only safety for us is to have the right of voting.

42,057. *Mr. Samuelson.*] When you have reached what stage of civilisation do you think you ought to have the franchise?—I think that when Natives have got to that degree of knowledge that they understand what the meaning of franchise is, and of voting, they ought to have it.

42,058. *Chairman.*] Not before?—Not before.

42,059. The next point that you have marked on this list to speak about is labour. What have you to say about that?—Work here in the Transvaal is carried out under pressure and is a hardship. You are given four days in which to obtain employment, and to get a master who will pay you that amount of money which will satisfy you, and if you are unable within the four days to get an employer who will pay you the wage you want for your services, you are compelled, in order to save yourself, to take employment from a man who will pay you only £1 a month. There is also another matter. That is with regard to passes. If you happen to be in the country without a pass, or happen to have stepped into a place where you should have a pass and have not one, then you are subject to arrest at once. The only object of compelling Natives to have a pass in a town like this, is really to force them into obtaining employment within four days, at rates unfavourable to themselves. There cannot be any other reason for it, because if people want us to work here they should not require us to take out passes when we go to seek work. That matter causes a great deal of hardship to us Natives. Again, we get no special rewards or bonuses for our services in this country; all we get is the wages; and we are forced by this system to go into places where only lower rates of wages are obtainable than we could get if we had more time.

42,060. Do you know anybody in this town of your own age, who is a grown man, who is getting £1 a month as wages?—There are men working about here in the town sweeping the streets who are getting £1, £1 10s., up to £2, who have come into it that way. If reference is made to the Pass Office it can be definitely ascertained what wages are paid to Natives who have come in under passes.

42,061. How many days do you want to look for a master, for work?—Why should there be any restriction or limitation at all? When we come here to seek work, we should be free. And there is another thing. You cannot leave your master to whom you have contracted your services until you have completed that time which is fixed in the pass. That is where the danger to us Natives who come to work is. It is in the pass.

. . . .

42,073. Then you wished to speak on the subject of taxation?—The tax here is heavy. It is £2 per head of the manhood. We living in towns have, in addition, to pay a rent, which amounts to 18s. Here in town we have also to pay 10s. dog tax; we have to pay 2s. 6d. for the removal of rubbish; we have to pay 7s. 6d. for w.c.; and we have to pay 7s. 6d for a stand.

42,074. Are you obliged by law to keep a dog?—A dog is a man's property, and when he becomes possessed of one, then he has to pay a tax for it.

42,075. Do you pay unless you have a dog?—No, I do not pay, because I have not got one. These taxes in the municipality here, I say, are heavy; these only, without reference to the poll tax. In addition to these municipal taxes, the Government has placed upon us the poll tax of £2 a head. We are men, we are not slaves. We are only servants to our employers. We are not in the same position as Natives out of the country, because while they pay tax they have ground to cultivate. We think the Government ought to see into this for us. The tax which is paid outside the town, the poll tax itself of £2, is heavy; and the rates and payments we have to make here to the municipality in themselves are heavy without any additional taxation. Then, at the same time, the wages here are very low. The time has not come when men receive wages such as would enable them to meet comfortably these taxes.

42,076. What work are you doing?—I am working in a lawyer's office.

42,077. What are your wages?—£4 a month.

42,078. *Mr. Sloley.*] Are these municipal rates you speak of monthly?—They are monthly with the exception, of course, of the dog tax.

42,079. *Chairman.*] Is the 7s. 6d. for sanitary rates the same as paid by the Europeans?—We cannot be compared with the white man and the white man's servants. Here, in this municipality, they do not do what is done for us in other towns of South Africa, where water closets are erected for the use of the Natives. Here that is not the case. If the residents of the location were not forced to set up these w.c.'s, it would be all right, because then the poor man could go to the general w.c.'s which the municipalities should put up.

42,080. *Mr. Sloley.*] What means have you of approaching the Government and stating anything you want to state?—We have no other means of reaching the Government except through the Native Affairs Office.

42,081. *Captain Dickson.*] What religious denomination do you belong to?—I am a Wesleyan. *Makue:* I belong to the Congregational Church.

42,082. You complained about the passes and said that four days was not long enough to get employment in a town like Pretoria. How long has that been the case, that four days was not long enough to get any employment whatever in the town of Pretoria?—*Mama:* That difficulty has existed ever since I came to Pretoria.

42,083. Is not four days quite long enough to get some kind of employment in the town of Pretoria?—Sometimes one day is quite sufficient for you to find an employer who will pay you the wages you want, but in other cases it takes longer; sometimes it takes more than four days.

42,084. If employment is to be got in the town of Pretoria, surely four days is long enough to find that employment if it is to be got?—Yes, if one can find work within those four days, then the time is sufficient, but we do not see why there should be any restrictions of this sort. Why should there be pass regulations?

42,085. Is it a hardship, or is it only a matter of sentiment?—It is a trying thing, and it makes work a troublesome matter.

(Mr. Sloley took the Chair.)

42,086. *Acting Chairman.*] Have you anything that you wish to say, Makue?—*Makue:* As regards voting, I think it would be much better that we should get the franchise and be able to vote. I do not mean that the raw Native should, who does not understand what it is. I think we would trust one another better if the Native were to get the vote. The case is like when there are two children in the house, and one will have bread and butter, and the other only soup. That creates a feeling that he does not believe in his father, because the father does not treat him well. One has soup and the other has bread and butter. As regards the work of the black man, to force him to work is not good. It is not good under any circumstances to be forced to work. Our earning power is very small. I think when we are forced to work there ought to be big pay. There is no decent black man that can manage to exist on £8 a month, pay all the taxes, and the upkeep of his house in the proper manner—I mean a civilised Native. I do not mean the raw man who comes from the kraals. As regards the liquor law, I think it is better to throw it open, not to prohibit liquor to the Native. There are so many that drink, and so many that do not drink, and they are both good. There are some that do not drink who are bad. According to the eye of the white people, who look after us, they cannot draw a line between a good and a bad black man. If liquor were thrown open to the Native it would be found that there are as good black men as there are white. Then they could be classified. Now we are all blacks and are measured with the same measure. I might be a good man, but I am looked upon, perhaps, in the same light as a bad one. I know the black man is not as good as the white, as far as civilisation goes. I am sorry that I have had to condense my remarks as I have done. I am

44

afraid I may not be understood.

42,087. Do you realise that this liquor law was originally imposed because the Government wished to take care of the coloured people and prevent them destroying themselves?—It is so, but now I am measured with the same measure as the man who cannot look after himself, and who is not in the same position as I am. The white man does not know that there are some Natives who are decent; they are all put into one pot, as it were.

42,088. What do you mean by being forced to work? I do not see that you are forced to work in any other way than we are all forced to work. All the men you see in this room have been forced to work all their lives?—Should the Native not be able to obtain work within the four days he is punished. A decent man, who has a house and family, cannot procure a master in four days who will pay him handsomely.

42,089. The regulation as to the four days is a municipal regulation, I presume, to prevent a lot of idle and disorderly people coming into the town without having any lawful reason for being here?—Yes; although it is a municipal law, we are punished all the same.

42,090. *Mr. Samuelson.*] In Durban and Maritzburg, in Natal, the same law is in force, but the man who is not able to get work in four days can go again to the police office and get his pass extended, if he can show good reason that he has not been able to get work in those four days. Is that not the same case here?—It can be done, but there is a lot of trouble. No good man can get work in four days, sometimes not within the month.

DOCUMENT 9. Petition to King Edward VII, from the Native United Political Associations of the Transvaal Colony, April 25, 1905 (Typewritten, 3 pages)

TO HIS MOST EXCELLENT MAJESTY EDWARD THE SEVENTH, by the Grace of God, of the United Kingdom of Great Britain and Ireland, and of the British Dominions beyond the Seas, King, Defender of the Faith, Emperor of India.

— — — — — — — — — — —

THE PETITION of the Members of the Native United Political Associations of the Transvaal Colony, and of the Natives of that Colony humbly sheweth:

1. That your petitioners are loyal subjects of Your Most Excellent Majesty, residing in the Transvaal Colony.

2. That your petitioners have noticed with apprehension during the past two years the tendency towards class legislation in the Transvaal Colony to the detriment of the status and position of the Natives of the Transvaal.

3. That your petitioners humbly beg leave to refer to the following instances of such legislation:

(a) The Morality Law, inasmuch as it does not protect Native women.

(b) The infliction of the lash in all cases of Assault by Natives on Whites.

(c) The infliction of the Death Penalty in all cases of Outrage or Attempted Outrage by Natives on White women, while comparatively brief terms of imprisonment are provided for similar offences by White men on Native women.

(d) The prohibition of Natives from walking on the Footpaths of any street, except in the case of respectable and well conducted Coloured persons, not being Aboriginal Natives.

(e) The exclusion of respectable Natives from First and Second Class Compartments on the Central South African Railways.

(f) The prohibition of Natives from purchasing Landed Property in the Transvaal Colony.

(g) The prohibition of Natives from holding Public Meetings in the Transvaal Colony.

4. That your petitioners are informed and verily believe that in terms of the Vereeniging Peace Conditions, the Constitution of a Representative Government for the Transvaal Colony is now engaging the attention of Your Majesty's Imperial Government.

5. That under Article 8 of the said Conditions the question of granting the Franchise to Natives of the Transvaal Colony will not be decided until after the introduction of Self-

Government, the effect whereof is that Natives are not allowed to vote at Municipal Elections and their interests in Municipal matters are at present unrepresented.

6. That for the reasons above mentioned Your Petitioners fear that when Representative Government is granted by Your Majesty's Imperial Government to the Transvaal Colony it will be the object of the majority of Your Majesty's white subjects in that Colony to exclude Natives from enjoying the liberty, freedom and equality to which as British subjects they claim to be entitled.

7. That in proof thereof Your Petitioners would refer to the anti-Native utterances on the part of the Rand Pioneers at Johannesburg in their many attempts to legislate against colour and especially to the recent discussions in the Johannesburg Municipal Council on the subject of Native Cyclists, showing that it is the intention of the speakers to base their arguments entirely on the question of colour.

8. That your petitioners for the above reasons fear that unless the interests of the Natives in the Transvaal Colony are in some way protected by Your Majesty's Imperial Government in framing the Transvaal Constitution, the position of Natives in that Colony, under Representative Government, will be a degrading and humiliating one, and one on which your petitioners look with considerable alarm.

WHEREFORE your petitioners humbly pray that it may please Your Most Excellency Majesty, taking the above facts into consideration, to safeguard, when framing the Constitution for the Transvaal Colony, the interests of the Natives of that Colony, either by reserving to Your Majesty's Imperial Government through Your Majesty's High Commissioner the entire control of Natives and of legislative enactments regarding Natives in the Transvaal Colony, or by reserving to Your Majesty's Imperial Government a vetoing power as regards such legislative enactments, until such time as it shall be deemed expedient to accord to the Natives of the Transvaal Colony a franchise similar to that enjoyed by Your Majesty's Native subjects in the Cape Colony and Rhodesia or in such other way as to Your Majesty and to Your Majesty's Imperial Government may seem fit and proper.

AND YOUR PETITIONERS as in duty bound will ever pray.

DOCUMENT 10. Resolutions of the South African Native Congress, April 10, 1906 [Extracts] (Published in *The Aborigines' Friend*)

The Native Congress feels called upon to record its deep regret at the apparent decline of British views in the treatment of the native question from those high standards which were once the pride and the crown and the glory of British statesmanship. Without going into all the causes which contributed to this condition, Congress feels that the attitude of the late Imperial Government in relaxing those bonds which bind the native and coloured races to the Imperial Government has contributed materially towards the regrettable conditions in which native affairs are placed at the present time in the several South African colonies, and especially in Natal and the Transvaal. The tendency in the colonies has latterly been in the direction of eliminating the prerogative of veto which is a repository of the Crown, and which has an important bearing in the relations of the native races to the British Government. As this Imperial factor is the only moderating influence between the races, so sharply divided as they are in South Africa by different causes, they view with extreme gravity any relaxation on the part of the British Government of this all-vital principle.

Congress desires to impress upon the Home Government, and especially upon the present Ministry, the obligation of surrendering nothing of vital importance to the natives to the prevalent cry of 'no interference' on the part of the capitalistic Press which dominates the situation in South Africa and claims to voice public opinion. Congress also feels called upon to express the opinion, with much regret, that responsible government has been prematurely granted to the colonies, considering the very low moral tone of the average colonist in regard to native treatment and their feeling and demeanour towards the native races. It is also regrettable to observe that the moral influence of the Church appears to have declined in its power to counteract these degrading tendencies or to raise the standard of thought and feeling towards the aborigines.

Much has been made of the outcry of Ethiopianism, and all sorts of charges have been laid at the door of this new feature, interjected into the relations of the people of the country by designing minds and an alarmist Press, which works upon the superstitious feelings of the community and adversely agitates the public mind, to the detriment of sober judgment in the governments of the colonies in dealing with large masses of natives in South Africa. The whole outcry is intangible, and no satisfactory evidence has been produced by those who make these charges upon which a verdict could be based, which would justify the conclusion that the natives, or any section of them, are disloyal or meditating mischief against the supreme authority.

Much has also been made of the numerical preponderance of the natives of this country, with the sinister object of agitating the public mind and keeping it in a condition of perpetual ferment, and Congress observes with regret that several colonial politicians, ministers of religion, and public speakers, have sought, at various times, to impress upon British statesmen and the Imperial authorities the need of unity among the white races in order to present a solid front against the imaginary bogey of a colossal native combination to oust the whites from South Africa. Congress feels that the effect of the spread of such views is to intensify suspicion, and unsettle the public mind, and to widen the relations between the races. Its effects are apparent to some extent in the regrettable Natal crisis where the "Ixopo farmers" have appeared to be most vindictive in demanding that mercy should not be shown to the unfortunate victims of this deplorable state of public feeling.

Congress states emphatically its opinion that if there is any disloyalty in the country it should be placed at the door of those who agitate the public mind in this manner.

Congress believes that Ethiopianism is a symptom of progress, brought about by the contact of the natives of Africa with European civilisation making itself felt in all departments of the social, religious, and economic structure. The natives of the South African colonies are loyal to the Imperial factor and the Crown, and this is verified by the official statements of Blue books and reports of Departments of Native Affairs.

With reference to the recent crisis in Natal, Congress desires to place on record its opinion that the imposition of taxation without representation is a crime; that to that cause must be traced the origin of the disturbances which led up to the unfortunate death of Inspector Hunt and Trooper Armstrong in Natal and the natives who were subsequently executed.

With regard to the execution of the natives under martial law, Congress desires to ascertain from the Secretary of State for the Colonies: (a) Whether the execution of the twelve natives sentenced to death under martial law in Natal, having been postponed beyond the date fixed originally, is legal; (b) whether martial law can be proclaimed where a state of war does not exist without a previous ultimatum and declaration of hostilities.

If martial law can be proclaimed, arbitrarily, to any portion of the country, the unsettlement of the native mind must be increased, and all sense of security and confidence in the government of the native races destroyed. The general feeling of the native races is that the proclamation of martial law in Natal was arbitrary and unnecessary, as Natal has a police force which was sufficient to deal with the slight disturbance at Richmond in its initial stages. The execution of these men before their relatives and friends, Congress considers, was a tactical mistake, which has left a bad impression on the native mind generally. The employment of undisciplined native forces to quell native disturbances is regarded as reprehensible on the part of a professedly civilised and Christian government.

Congress considers that, if the government of the natives and coloured races in the colonies is to continue on the pernicious and retrogressive lines advocated by Natal and the Transvaal as well as by extremists in the other colonies, it would be preferable for the natives to be taken over by the Crown and be governed from Downing Street through a Department of Native Affairs in the Home Government.

DOCUMENT 11. Petition to King Edward VII, from the Orange River Colony Native Congress, June 1906 (Printed, 1 page)

TO THE KING'S
MOST EXCELLENT MAJESTY.

The humble Petition of the loyal Native Subjects of His Majesty Edward VII, King of all Britain, her Colonies and Dependencies, sheweth:—

(1) "That those of His Majesty's loyal Native Subjects residing in the Orange River Colony are much gratified that His Majesty has been pleased to attach to himself as his servants the Leaders of the Liberal party, whose discharge of the trust committed to them will, they believe, conduce to brighter and more prosperous days for all races and colours of British subjects.

(2) "That your petitioners are humbly confident that the condition and welfare of His Majesty's Native subjects in this Colony will not be forgotten or occupy the background when the interests of other races of British subjects are being consulted:

(3) "That your petitioners respectfully desire to bring before your Majesty the importance of the problem of Native Representation when Self-Government is conceded to this Colony:

"That your petitioners earnestly deprecate the clause in the Vereeniging Peace Terms which compromised the claim of the Natives to what they feel is a legitimate franchise. Indeed, it seemed to them deplorable that before bloodshed ceased the avowed cause of Justice, Freedom, and Equal Rights, for which the war had been undertaken, should have been so easily abandoned.

"That your petitioners believe that without some measure of representation in the legislatures of this Colony their interests will ever remain in jeopardy, and that however they may conform to the rules of civilized life they can never hope to enjoy those of its privileges as, for instance, liberty to trade and to own land, which are at present withheld from them.

(4) "That your petitioners, therefore, humbly pray that the Imperial Government, when preparing a Constitution for the Self-Government of this Colony, would insert some clause which will either grant some representation to its Native subjects or retain the Administration of Native Affairs under its direct control until their enfranchisement is accomplished.

(5) "That your petitioners desire also to bring before your Majesty their position under Municipal Governments in this Colony:

(i). In the large Municipal locations there are thousands of civilized and tolerably educated Natives who have entirely discarded the customs and practices of such Natives as are still living in tribal fashion. Despite the fact that they live in conformity to the rules and requirements of civilization, they are debarred from any form of civil rights. In Municipal Councils, which possess enormous powers for making laws and regulations for the management of locations and of natives in locations, they have no voice and no means of making their grievances and needs known to the Councils; their deputations are more often refused than granted a hearing.

(ii). To show the position of Municipal Councils, your petitioners respectfully tender, inter alia, the following information:-

In Bloemfontein recently blasting operations were undertaken in a stone-quarry in Waai Hook location. These operations subjected the property and lives of house-owners to great danger. But in spite of remonstrances from the occupants in that locality they were not discontinued until recourse was had to legal measures, and the High Court ordered their immediate cessation.

(iii). Next followed the valuation of houses in the land expropriated for the extension of the same quarry. Considerable losses were incurred by the house-owners, who were forced to accept compensation without arbitration, and ordered to remove at once. A deputation sent by the house-owners was refused an interview with the Mayor.

(iv). At the present moment new laws under the title "Zogt Regulations for Bloemfontein Municipality" are awaiting the sanction of the Lieut.-Governor. These are in principle identical with the methods in vogue in countries where slavery is still countenanced, and in practice will be nothing short of enforced labour.

(v). One of the most painful things to your petitioners is the carriage of street and residential passes by Native women, who, under pretext of this requirement are examined (sometimes indecently) by the police in the streets.

(vi). Your humble petitioners hold the opinion that it is only just and constitutional that where sufficiently large numbers of civilized Natives are congregated who contribute towards Municipal revenues, they should be granted some means of making their voice felt and recognized by the Municipality in matters affecting themselves.

(vii). In Bloemfontein and Kroonstad, for instance, their contributions towards Municipal revenues take the form of Water and Sanitary Rates, monthly rent for house stands, and the monthly street and residential passes required of male and female persons over 16 years of age. Hence the conviction of your humble petitioners that their qualifications and contributions towards Municipal finances fully entitle them to some rights of Municipal representation, if not of separate Municipal self-government."

And your petitioners will ever pray.

DOCUMENT 12. Petition to the House of Commons, from J. Tengo Jabavu and thirteen other signatories, July 13, 1906 (Published in *The Aborigines' Friend*)

"The petition of the undersigned British subjects, natives of South Africa resident in the Cape Colony, humbly showeth:—

"1. Your humble petitioners, native residents in the Cape Colony, are loyal British subjects who, under the equitable franchise established by the grant of a constitution to the said colony, have long enjoyed the right for which they are fully qualified to vote at popular elections, and have admittedly exercised that right to the advantage of its great

native population and of the whole people of that colony.

"2. Your humble petitioners fear that in the constitution proposed to be granted to the Transvaal and Orange River Colonies South African natives, though in justice they are entitled to special consideration, may, as some desire, be singled out for exclusion from all popular elections merely on the ground of their colour, however well qualified they may be to exercise the franchise.

"3. Your petitioners strongly sympathise with natives in the said colonies, and may in the exercise of their lawful avocations desire to emigrate to those colonies, as they have every right as British subjects to do, and they consider that any exclusion from the franchise on account of colour alone would be an unmerited degradation of all natives, an injustice to them, and a deep injury not only to them but to the whole of the inhabitants of South Africa, a departure from the constitutional principles of the British Colonial Empire, and the taking away of an indefeasible right conferred upon the new colonies by the acts which annexed them to the Empire.

"4. Your humble petitioners fear also lest the grant of constitutions to the new colonies, by which a portion of their inhabitants should be excluded from the electoral franchise on the ground of colour alone, would establish a new departure in South African British colonies, and give a fulcrum and an attempt to deprive coloured men not only of a privilege due to them in the Federal Union which is much sought after, but of those which they hold in the Cape Colony itself.

"5. Your humble petitioners hope, for the above-stated reasons, that the natives of the new colonies now resident therein or who may emigrate thither may not be handed over to Governments to be created by a Constitution now to be granted without such reservations as may secure to them a progressive measure of representation through the franchise.

"The humble prayer of your petitioners, therefore, is that your Honourable House may devise such measures for their relief as to your Honourable House may seem wise and fitting.

"And your humble petitioners, as in duty

bound, will ever pray.

"J. Tengo-Jabavu, Editor *Imvo*."
And thirteen other signatories.

DOCUMENT 13. Petition to the Secretary of State for the Colonies, from the Natal Native Congress, October 1908 (Typewritten, 13 pages)

TO THE RIGHT HONOURABLE THE SECRETARY OF STATE FOR THE COLONIES.

THE PETITION OF THE UNDERSIGNED NATIVES OF THE COLONY OF NATAL,

HUMBLY SHEWETH:—

THAT on the 30th of April 1908 there was held at Pietermaritzburg a meeting of Natives from different parts of the Colony of Natal to consider the following three Bills which the Government had notified its intention to introduce into Parliament.

"To increase the number of Members of the Legislative Council".

"To provide for the better administration of Native Affairs".

"For the creation and Administration of Native Lands Settlements".

THAT a representative Committee of this gathering had an interview with the Honourable the Minister for Native Affairs when he suggested that the Natives should take further time to consider these three Bills and meet him on a future occasion.

THEREAFTER many Chiefs and Headmen of Natives in this Colony held meetings in their districts and over two hundred delegates were appointed to consider these three Bills.

THESE delegates met at Pietermaritzburg on the 9th day of June 1908 and having spent the whole of that day and the greater part of the 10th June in deliberation unanimously adopted the following resolutions:-

(1):- The Native Delegates from different parts of Natal, while highly appreciating the Government's desire and intention to give the Native people of the Colony of Natal Parliamentary representation by the nomination of four members to represent them in the Legislative Council, would most respectfully point out that such members cannot be truly said to be their representatives but Nominees of the Governor in Council; and would, therefore most humbly beg to ask for the extension of the Franchise to the Native Races of this Colony.

(2):- With regard to Bill No 2 the Delegates wish to humbly express their inability to endorse it, inasmuch as it contains in its provisions several points which, in their opinion, may prove detrimental to the interests of the Native people.

(3):- The delegates further consider No. 3 unnecessary, and humbly request that it be not introduced to Parliament. They would, therefore, beg to strongly urge that Title Deeds be given in Freehold to those residing on Mission Reserves according to the terms of the original grants. With regard to Native Locations the Delegates would most respectfully request that they be left alone; but that Act No 37 of 1896 be repealed, as it is considered not conducive to the welfare of the Native people.

THE Delegates met the Honourable the Minister for Native Affairs the same day and presented to him the foregoing resolutions.

The said meeting of Delegates, (known as the Native Congress of Natal) appointed a Committee of fifteen of its members to watch the progress of the said Bills and to take such action as might be considered necessary to oppose the passing of these Bills into Law.

Your Petitioners are members of the said Committee.

[The petitioners then recount the following: their petitioning the Legislative Assembly with "no result"; the futile efforts of Congress's white solicitor to arrange for a deputation to meet the Governor; warnings from the Minister for Native Affairs and from his officials that intervention by an intermediary in "purely administrative" matters could not be permitted, that Natives must deal with the Minister, and that chiefs as "Government Servants" must secure approval from magistrates before leaving their districts; and petitioning of the Colony's Legislative Council.]

THAT notwithstanding the said Petition the Bill,

"To provide for the better administration of Native Affairs"

has been passed by both Houses of Parliament, but has, your Petitioners believe, been reserved for the signification of the pleasure of His Majesty the King.

THAT your Petitioners now respectfully pray that Your Lordship may be pleased to advise His Majesty not to assent to the said Bill, on the following amongst other grounds.

(a) It would confer the authority and powers now held by His Excellency the Supreme Chief alone, under the 39th and 40th section of the Code of Native Law, also known as the Schedule to Law 19 of 1891, on an indefinite number of officials who would not be answerable for their acts in any of the Courts of Law of the Colony. In support of which statement Petitioners respectfully refer Your Lordship to the sections of the Native Code above referred to and Part 3 of the Bill.

THE section of the Native Code reads as follows:-

(39) "The Supreme Chief in the exercise "of the political powers which attach to his "office has authority to punish by fine or "imprisonment or by both, for disobedience "of his orders or for disregard of his author-"ity.

(40) "The Supreme Chief is not subject "to the Supreme Court, or to any other Court "of Law in the Colony of Natal, for, or by "reason of, any order or proclamation, or of "any other act or matter whatsoever, com-"mitted, ordered, permitted, or done either "personally or in Council".

PETITIONERS view with alarm the extension of the powers conferred by these sections, more particularly since, as is shown by the correspondence with His Excellency the Governor, the Secretary for Native Affairs, and the speech delivered by the Honourable the Minister for Native Affairs on the 3rd September, it will be practically impossible for the Natives to approach His Excellency the Governor and Supreme Chief, or the Secretary for Native Affairs, save through the Magistrates who, under the 13th section of the Bill, are to be deemed officers of the Native Affairs Department when exercising adminstrative functions in Native Affairs.

PETITIONERS are informed and believe that the powers given under the above sections of the Code are exercised not infrequently, and they respectfully submit that these powers are likely to be exercised still more frequently under the Bill just passed, while by the decision given by His Excellency the Governor in the letter of the 28th August, above quoted, natives are practically debarred from laying their grievances before His Excellency as the representative of His Majesty save through the Minister for Native Affairs.

(b). That such provisions are opposed to the spirit of good and just Government and constitute an infringement of the rights and liberties of your Petitioners and the whole Native population of this Colony.

(c). That the proclamation of the Bill (which is now well understood by a large number of the Natives) as Law, will cause widespread alarm and discontent and create unrest amongst the Natives.

(d). That the 39th and 40th sections of the Code, even as they now stand, are opposed to the spirit and letter of the Law of the British Empire, and are repugnant to the spirit and principles of just Government, and any extension of such powers will render the condition of Petitioners and the Natives generally worse than it has been at any time since such powers were conferred.

(e). That the said sections as they now stand are not in accordance with the principles of our Native Law; no such powers as they confer were vested in any Supreme Chief before the Colonization of Natal by Europeans.

(f). That the passing of the said Bill into Law would tend to create artificial offences and subject Petitioners and other Natives to punishments without the right of appeal to the Courts of Law.

(g). That the provision in the said Bill as to the Council for Native Affairs, are inadequate and more likely to retard than advance the interests and condition of the Natives.

(h). That the Bill will create a number of officers who are not required in the interests of the Colony and the appointment of these Officers entail a considerable annual expenditure of money which could be used to much better advantage in the interests of all sections of the inhabitants of Natal.

(i). The powers conferred by the Bill on such officers amount to an interference with the Courts of Law and the administration of justice.

PETITIONERS earnestly submit that any legislation affecting the Petitioners and Natives generally should be framed so as to gradually elevate and improve the condition of the Natives and to afford them the fullest protection of the Law.

LEGISLATION of such a character would create a feeling of security and contentment on the part of the Natives and tend to the peace and welfare of the whole Colony.

THAT one of the first steps to that end would be to give the Natives the same rights in the Courts of Law as other sections of the inhabitants. This would afford Petitioners and the Natives generally a full assurance of the protection of the Law.

ANOTHER step would be to give the Natives the fullest opportunity of laying their grievances before HIS EXCELLENCY the Supreme Chief, the Government and Parliament.

IN support of the objections of Petitioners they annex hereto marked "C" a copy of the Petition recently presented on behalf of the Native Affairs Committee (consisting of representatives of all sections of the community) to the Honourable the Legislative Assembly.

PETITIONERS also beg leave to quote the following passage from a speech delivered by the late Right Honourable Harry Escombe then, and for many years after, one of the leading public men of Natal, and also at one time, since the establishment of Responsible Government in the Colony, Prime Minister.

"We know quite well, notwithstanding "the complete fairness and honesty with "which the Natives have always been treated "in the past, that the great danger in party "government in this colony (Natal) is with "respect to native Government, and that "danger will become nearer our doors in case "the natives are left without representatives to "speak for them in the popular Assembly, "which is the taxing house. For if it is right to "tax people, it is right to give them represen- "tatives to say whether the taxes should be "lessened or made as light as possible.

PETITIONERS would respectfully urge Your Lordship to adopt such a course as Your Lordship may deem advisable to obtain for the Natives of Natal the same freedom of access and rights in the Courts of Law as are enjoyed by all other sections of the inhabitants of this Colony, (a step which the Petitioners regard as a vital necessity for the protection of the Natives), and the adoption by the Government of Natal of a policy that will tend to improve the lot of the Native population, restore confidence in the Government of the Colony, and bring about contentment and peace.

AND YOUR PETITIONERS AS IN DUTY BOUND WILL EVER PRAY.

Natal, October, 1908.

As Witness to all the signatures of Petitioners.

> STEPHEN MINI
> M.S. RADEBE
> A. MTIMKULU
> THEO NTOMBELA
> DYER NXABA
> POSSELT GUMEDE
> C. LUTAYI
> M. SIVETYE

As Witnesses:

> J. Warwick Tainton of Pietermaritzburg,
> Solicitor
> A.C. Parsons of Pietermaritzburg,
> Solicitor's Clerk.

African Fears at the Prospect of Union

DOCUMENT 14. Petition to the South African National Convention from "aboriginal natives of South Africa, resident in the Transvaal," October 22, 1908 (Published in *The Aborigines' Friend*)

We, the undersigned, being aboriginal natives of South Africa, resident in the Transvaal, beg to bring before your honourable convention our just claim to be granted representation in the Parliament of a United South Africa.

We desire to remind you that the natives in this colony have hitherto been totally unrepresented in the local Parliament, notwithstanding the fact that they contribute largely in direct taxation to the treasury, in addition to bearing a full share of the indirect taxation through pass-fees, the railways, and the Customs tariff.

We attribute the advancement in prosperity, contentment, and loyalty, which is such a marked characteristic of the natives of Cape Colony, to the generous policy which has permitted them to qualify themselves as citizens, and to enjoy the privileges of citizenship. And we submit that the same happy result may be expected to follow the extension of the Cape franchise to our people throughout South Africa.

We therefore submit to the favourable consideration of your honourable convention our claim to be permitted to qualify for the full political privileges such as may be granted to the European population in the constitution you are preparing for submission to His Majesty the King, while praying that the interests of those of our people who may be unable to qualify for this franchise may be protected by a measure of separate representation following in part the method suggested in the report of the South African Native Affairs Commission.

[Published in *The Aborigines' Friend* of January 1909, which notes that the petition was "very extensively signed."]

DOCUMENT 15. Resolutions of the South African Native Convention, March 24-26, 1909 (Published in *Izwi Labantu* [Voice of the People])

The South African Native Convention composed of delegates from the Cape Colony, Natal, Transvaal, Orange River Colony, and Bechuanaland, assembled at Bloemfontein on the 24th, 25th, and 26th March, 1909 to discuss those clauses of the Draft Act of the South African National Convention relating to Natives and Coloured people, and the reports of delegates submitted by their various congresses and associations, has after careful consideration of Act, arrived at the following decisions, to wit:

1. This Convention recognises the principle of Union amongst all His Majesty's subjects in the South African colonies to be essential, necessary, and inevitable, the ultimate object of which seeks to promote the future progress and welfare of all.

2. The Imperial Government, of which we are now all loyal citizens interested in, and sharing alike its responsibilities, is bound by both fundamental and specific obligations towards the natives and coloured races of South Africa to extend to them the same measure of equitable justice and consideration as is extended to those of European descent under the law. It has been well said that the King and the Empire owe good and just government to every class of their subjects, but no such good or just government is possible, where one class is left at the mercy of another class by being absolutely deprived of the right of equal representation, which is a fundamental obligation.

3. This Convention places on record its strong and emphatic protest against the admission of a "colour bar" in the Union Constitution as being a real vital basic wrong and injustice, and respectfully pleads that a clause be inserted in the "Charter" providing that all persons within the Union shall be entitled to full and equal rights and privileges subject only to the conditions and limitations established by law and applicable alike to all citizens without distinction of class, colour or creed. The franchise has been enjoyed for more than 50 years by the native and coloured races of the Cape Colony, but is not extended to the native and coloured races of Orange River Colony, the Transvaal and the Colony of Natal, and this Convention seriously deprecates the absence, in the said Draft Act, of the principle of equal rights for all the races in the South African Colonies; a principle which was sustained by the leading statesmen of the Country and which was also the constant motto of the late Cecil John Rhodes (to whom an united South Africa was also an ideal), viz:—"Equal rights for all civilized men from the Cape to the Zambesi."

. . . .

6. With regard to clauses 25 and 44 and their sub-sections (d) and (c) the Convention

desires the deletion of the words "of European descent."

7. That with regard to clause 35, sub-section (1), this Convention desires the amendment of the clause by the omission of all the words following after the words—"race or colour only," leaving sub-section (2) as it stands. The clause would therefore read as follows, viz:—"Parliament may by law prescribe the qualifications which shall be necessary to entitle persons to vote at election of members of the House of Assembly, but no such law shall disqualify any person in the province of the Cape of Good Hope, who under the laws existing in the Colony of the Cape of Good Hope at the establishment of the Union, is or may become capable of being registered as a voter, from being so registered by reason of his race or colour only."

8. With regard to clause 33 the Convention desires that after the word "European male adults"—wherever those words occur in the clause and sub-sections—the words "and native and coloured voters" should be added, making the sentence "European male adults" read "European male adults and native and coloured voters."

9. With regard to clause 153 the Convention desires that the words "thirty-five and" in line 7 of the clause should be deleted and substitute the word "section" for "sections" in the same line, and add after the words "of both Houses" in line 11 of the same clause the following words:—"Provided still further that clause 35 remains unalterable."

DOCUMENT 16. Petition to the Governor of the Colony of the Cape of Good Hope, from the Transkeian Territories General Council, June 21, 1909 (Typewritten, 4 pages)

To His Excellency the Honourable Sir Walter Hely-Hutchinson, Knight Grand Cross of the Most Distinguished Order of Saint Michael and Saint George, Governor and Commander-in-Chief of His Majesty's Colony of the Cape of Good Hope and of the Territories and dependencies thereof, etc., etc.

The Petition of the undersigned humbly sheweth:

1. That your petitioners are members of the Transkeian Territories General Council and as such representatives of nearly all the Native tribes resident in the Native Territories of His Majesty's Colony of the Cape of Good Hope.

2. That your petitioners beg humbly and sincerely to express to Your Excellency the devotion and loyalty of themselves and the people whom they represent in this Council to the throne and person of His Most Gracious Majesty the King.

3. That some of your petitioners, and many of the people whom they represent in this Council, have under the benign and fostering rule of the British Government acquired rights and privileges as subjects of the British Crown which to them are of inestimable value and that foremost amongst these are that equality in the eye of the law conferred upon all British subjects, and the possession of the franchise.

4. That your petitioners and the people whom they represent in this Council have for many years exercised the rights which they enjoy under the peace and security afforded them by the protecting folds of the British flag.

5. That it has ever been the desire of your petitioners and of the people whom they represent in this Council to be the loyal and law-abiding subjects of His Most Gracious Majesty the King.

6. That in no instance has it ever been shown that your petitioners, or the people whom they represent in this Council, have ever, as a people, misused the privileges of the franchise so freely and ungrudgingly conferred upon us and them by the British Crown.

7. That your petitioners and the people whom they represent in this Council have followed with great interest and concern the deliberations of the inter-Colonial Convention appointed to consider and to formulate a scheme for the Union of His Majesty's several Colonies in South Africa.

8. That your petitioners and the people whom they represent in this Council view with great apprehension the Act of Union known as the South Africa Act which has been passed by the several Parliaments of His Majesty's South African Colonies, and which introduces a principle hitherto entirely absent from and foreign to the law of His Majesty's

Colony of the Cape of Good Hope, that principle being the colour line running through the various sections of the Act, descriptive of the qualifications necessary for members of the two Houses of the Union Parliament.

9. That by this colour line your petitioners and the people whom they represent in this Council are for ever excluded from entrance into the Parliament of United South Africa.

10. That as an instance of the operation of the colour line in the South Africa Act, your petitioners beg to point to Section 32 of the Act which fixes the number of members assigned by the Act to each of His Majesty's South African Colonies, and to clause 1 of section 33 of the Act which defines the principles upon which the number of members so assigned is based: and that in their opinion His Majesty's Colony of the Cape of Good Hope has already been deprived by the colour line of a great part of the preponderance of members in the House of Assembly in the Union Parliament which it would have otherwise enjoyed.

11. That even though none of your petitioners or the people whom they represent in this Council have ever desired to or attempted to enter the Legislative Houses of His Majesty's Colony of the Cape of Good Hope, yet they enjoyed the right of doing so had they so desired and it is now felt that the explicit introduction of a colour line into the franchise and the consequent exclusion of British subjects of African descent are not only a grievance to the Natives of His Majesty's Colony of the Cape of Good Hope, but are a withdrawal of the rights which they have enjoyed and which they have in no instance abused.

12. That your petitioners therefore, humbly and with the respect due to the exalted position which Your Excellency occupies, beg that Your Excellency may be pleased to submit for the consideration of His Most Gracious Majesty the King the prayer of his devoted and loyal native subjects, your petitioners, that the colour line in the South Africa Act may be expunged.

13. And as in duty bound your petitioners will ever pray.

SIGNED: DALINDYEBO.
VELDMAN BIKITSHA
  his X mark.
SIMON P. GASA.
ENOCH MAMBA.
GEORGE JAMANGILE.
BUCHANAN MOSHESH.
AARON NJIKELANA.
S. MILTON NTLOKO.
MBIZWENI JOJO
  his X mark.
PAUL NKALA.
FALO MGUDLWA
  his X mark.
HENRY SHOSHA.

DOCUMENT 17. Petition to the House of Commons, from W.P. Schreiner, A. Abdurahman, J. Tengo Jabavu, et al, July 1909 (Published in *Hansard*)

1322. The Petition of the undersigned representatives of the coloured and native British subjects resident in the British Dominions in South Africa.

Humbly sheweth,

Your humble Petitioners are by resolutions of five coloured and native congresses, and by resolutions passed at public meetings held at very many different centres in South Africa, empowered and authorised to approach the Imperial Parliament by Petition or otherwise.

Those whom your Petitioners represent are, according to the testimony of all leading statesmen, loyal and dutiful subjects of His Majesty.

In the colony of the Cape of Good Hope political rights have been granted to all without discrimination of race or colour by the Constitution granted to that colony by Great Britain.

Nowhere has it been suggested that those rights have ever been abused; on the contrary, the judicious manner in which they have been exercised on the whole has received the unstinted approbation of many colonial statesmen.

By the original Constitution granted to Natal, and also in Rhodesia, no discrimination in obtaining or exercising political rights has been sanctioned, though in Natal subsequent local legislation has introduced such discrimination on the grounds of race or colour.

Your humble Petitioners respectfully submit that the only practical and efficient means whereby fair and just administration and legislation can be attained, peace, harmony, and contentment secured, is by granting equal political rights to qualified men irrespective of race, colour, or creed.

Your Petitioners fully approve of union of the self-governing Colonies of British South Africa.

The Bill now before the Parliament of Great Britain and Ireland for the purpose of enacting a Constitution to unite the self-governing British Colonies of South Africa into a legislative union under the Crown would for the first time in the history of the legislation of that Parliament by virtue of the phrase "of European descent" in Clauses 26 and 44 create a political discrimination against non-European subjects of His Majesty, and thus introduce for the first time since the establishment of representative institutions in the year 1852 into the Colony of the Cape of Good Hope a colour line in respect of political rights and privileges.

Your Petitioners are deeply disappointed at the non-extension of political and civil rights and privileges to the coloured people and the natives in the Transvaal and Orange River Colony.

Your Petitioners feel aggrieved that solely on account of differences in race or colour it is contemplated by the proposed Constitution to deprive the coloured and native inhabitants of the colony of the Cape of Good Hope of their existing political rights and privileges.

Your Petitioners fear that the franchise rights of the coloured people and natives of the Cape Colony are not adequately protected under the provisions of the proposed Constitution, but are indeed threatened by the provisions of Clause 35.

Your Petitioners apprehend that by the racial discrimination proposed in the aforesaid Bill as regards the qualification of members of the Union Parliament, the prejudice already existing in the Transvaal, Orange River Colony, and Natal, will be accentuated and increased; that the status of the coloured people and natives will be lowered, and that an injustice will be done to those who are the

majority of the people in British South Africa, who have in the past shown their unswerving loyalty to the Crown, their attachment to British institutions, their submission to the laws of the land, and their capacity for exercising full civil and political rights.

Wherefore your Petitioners humbly beseech your Honourable House so to amend the aforesaid Bill as to protect the existing political rights of His Majesty's coloured and native subjects and to ensure permanently to them the continuance thereof.

Your Petitioners further respectfully and earnestly pray that your Honourable House would hear them either through the Hon. W. P. Schreiner or through one other of your Petitioners at the Bar of your Honourable House, or for such other relief as to your Honourable House might seem fit.

Your Petitioners, as in duty bound, will ever pray.

W. P. SCHREINER.
A. ABDURAHMAN.
J. TENGO JABAVU
&c. &c. &c.

DOCUMENT 18. "Latest Developments." Editorial in *Imvo Zabantsundu*, August 31, 1909

THE blow has fallen, and the British Government and House of Commons have passed the Union Constitution Act without the amendments we had hoped for. In another column will be found the cable account of what has been said and done in this matter, which our readers may study for themselves.

There are, however, a few points to which we wish to give prominence. The first is that we should be truly grateful that Mr. SCHREINER and the Native and Coloured delegates did appeal to the people and Parliament of England, though the time was too short and the conspiracy of silence too great to allow of their really arousing the British conscience. But for their action we should never have had such weighty utterances of British statesmen against the colour blots—utterances which will tend to make some of our South African rulers more willing than they otherwise would be to remove these blots from the Constitution; and we say, hesitatingly, that if ever the South African Union Government does the right thing and remove the colour disabilities it will be largely due to the action taken at the present time by the civilized Natives and Coloured people and their delegates and friends.

Secondly, we wish to say that we are entirely one with Mr. SCHREINER in the position he takes up in his letter to the *Morning Post* that the reservation for signification of the King's pleasure of any legislation of the Union Parliament which is entirely in accord with the provisions of clause 35, is of no value whatsoever, for the King will most certainly not veto action taken in [consonance] with a clause which the Imperial Parliament has now approved of, and those who are trying to make the Natives to believe otherwise are encouraging them to live in a fool's paradise.

We desire also to express our deep regret, from the Native point of view, that the idea that the first Union Ministry should be a Coalition seems to be abandoned. A Coalition Ministry of 6 South African Party and 4 Progressives would have been the surest safeguard of such rights and privileges as are left to the Natives by the Constitution, and would have meant the real healing of the racial divisions between Boer and Briton, which will now continue to hinder the progress of South Africa and damage its prosperity.

We cannot credit the correctness of the rumor as to Mr. WINSTON CHURCHILL'S being in the running for the Governor-Generalship of British South Africa. Such an appointment would be, we think, resented by the whole of South Africa. We want a man of fixed and steady principles not a political mountebank however clever.

We know nothing of Lord PENTLAND and his character or capabilities, but we can conceive of no reasons profound or cogent enough to justify the appointment of anyone but Lord SELBORNE as the first Governor-General; and as to the Premiership the superior claims of Mr. MERRIMAN cannot well be overlooked, whoever may be Governor-General.

The Native and Coloured people must now realize that an entirely new chapter in South African history is opening, in which they will have to depend on themselves and their South African European friends for the securing and maintenance of their civil and political rights. They must become united politically and refusing to cling to any of the present political parties must work for the creation of a new political party in the State which will unite the religious and moral forces—European and Natives—of South Africa upon lines of righteous legislation, justice and fairplay irrespective of race or colour.

The Natives—men, women and children must bend their energies to the advancement of themselves in all that civilization and true Christianity means, so that their claim to equality of treatment for all civilized British subjects may be irresistible. Let us have faith in the GOD who rules over all, and in the justice of our cause, and let us be patient in the well doing, and be willing like the Syro-Phoenician women to accept thankfully even the crumbs of justice which fell to our lot from the Constitution, while mentally and constitutionally claiming our full heritage.

PART TWO

The African National Congress Comes into Being: Accelerated Protest and Appeals Abroad, 1910-1920

Introduction

The continuity of South Africa's racial policy was evident during the first decade of the Union, when the new white government confirmed some of the worst fears held by African leaders. Freed from the threat of the "Imperial factor" (the retention of which had been a key demand of African petitions in the pre-Union period), the government under General Louis Botha moved to consolidate white hegemony within the system established by the South Africa Act. For most whites, but not for the nonwhites, the question of the franchise was settled, the Act of Union having retained the exclusively white franchise of the former Boer republics and entrenched (that is, put beyond the power of a simple parliamentary majority to change) the qualified nonracial franchise of the Cape. Immediately following Union, the vital issue of land relationships between black and white became the focus of attention. Around this question the government spelled out its philosophy of unequal racial coexistence in all spheres of life. Debate over this policy and over the franchise was to be a chronic preoccupation of African politics.

The Establishment of the South African Native National Congress

The first spur to restructuring African political life came from Pixley ka I. Seme, who had returned from overseas to open a law practice in Johannesburg. In an effort to translate his earlier ideas about the "regeneration of Africa" into organizational forms, Seme in 1911 took the initiative in calling another national meeting of African leaders. In the face of the fact of Union, however, Seme considered it necessary to organize not merely another gathering of leaders such as had come together in the South African Native Convention in 1909, but a new African political organization encompassing all four provinces and the three adjacent British territories of Basutoland, Bechuanaland, and Swaziland. Seme argued that regional and tribal differences among Africans had to be overcome by promoting a spirit of African nationalism. The organization he envisaged would provide a forum for all African viewpoints, forcefully present African grievances to the new government and to white public opinion, and serve as a new rallying point for political pressure on behalf of Africans throughout South Africa (see Document 21).

In response to Seme's call, representatives from provincial associations, leaders of local vigilance groups, chiefs, and other prominent Africans from throughout South Africa and the neighboring British territories assembled in Bloemfontein in January 1912. At a conference which was not reported in any white South African newspaper (nor in the pages of *Imvo*, whose editor, John Tengo Jabavu, opposed Seme's move lest it further separate African leaders from sympathetic whites), hundreds of African delegates endorsed Seme's proposal and established the South African Native National Congress (changed in name in 1923 to the African National Congress or ANC) as a permanent national federation of African organizations. John L. Dube was elected president-general of the Congress; Pixley ka I. Seme was named treasurer; and Solomon Plaatje, an erudite, self-taught African clerk who had never left South Africa, was chosen secretary-general.

It was almost six years before the draft of a permanent constitution of the Congress was completed by a committee headed by Richard Msimang, a young lawyer trained in

England. The long rambling document finally approved in 1919 indicated that the leaders of the organization saw its mission as a consolidated pressure group continuing and expanding the scope and tactics of the numerous African organizations that had preceded it (see Document 23). Elaborating upon Seme's original conception, the constitution outlined an organization which was to formulate uniform policy upon African affairs for presentation to the Union government, while at the same time both educating white public opinion to African concerns and Africans to their rights and obligations. From an unequivocal platform of opposition to the color bar, the organization was to agitate and pressure government bodies for measures it judged favorable to African interests.

The constitution explicitly stated that the Congress would seek its goals through constitutional means, including petitions, deputations, and propaganda campaigns. It looked forward to the time when the Congress would back its own candidates for legislative office, although carefully refraining from identification with white political parties (in contrast to the earlier tactics of John Tengo Jabavu in the Cape Colony). More significantly, in what was perhaps a reflection of the impact Gandhi's passive resistance campaigns among the South African Indians had made upon African opinion, the constitution specifically endorsed "passive action" as a means to be used. The orientation of the Congress as it appeared in the clauses of its first permanent constitution stamped it as the most ambitious African political organization that had yet appeared in South Africa.

John Tengo Jabavu opposed the forming of the Congress. Still deeply convinced of the nonracial potential of the Cape system, Jabavu felt hostile to an organization that did not center its activities upon working with sympathetic whites to exert pressure within the established parliamentary system. (He was possibly also wary of an organization in which he was not the central figure.) The editor of *Imvo* therefore called together his supporters in the Cape Province to form their own Unionwide organization called the South African Races Congress. In his inaugural address, Jabavu invoked his past efforts on behalf of the African cause (see Document 22). His statements suggest that he did not oppose the broad goals which the rival Congress had enunciated. Yet the tenor of Jabavu's remarks suggested that he conceived his organization, which was claimed to be the direct successor to *Imbumba*, as a means of continuing the electorally oriented pressure group politics he had practiced since the 1880s. It is probable that Jabavu also saw the organization as a section of the Universal Races Congress whose inaugural meeting he had attended in London in 1911.

The Land Question

Almost immediately after their foundation, the two new Congresses were tested in the hard crucible of white determination to fix the terms upon which both white and black could occupy the land of South Africa. The South African Native Affairs Commission of 1903-1905 had urged the reservation of a set amount of land for exclusively African occupation. The commission's recommendation that land delimitation be done "with a view to finality" implied that the principle of territorial segregation should become the basis of "Native" policy in South Africa. Shortly after the formation of Union, a Select Committee of Parliament considered the question of African land settlement with particular reference to the problem of "squatting." Its proposals for legislation included limitations upon collective land ownership by Africans outside the reserves and sharp limits on the number of Africans allowed to squat upon white-owned farms as sharecroppers.

The reaction of African public opinion to the threat of this "Squatters' Bill" can be seen in the indignant speeches of the African participants in the meeting of the Cape Peninsula Native Association held in March, 1912 (see Document 24). It was the unanimous conclusion of all the speakers that the bill would benefit only the white mine owners and white farmers, for it would force Africans off the land into white hands on terms that would be equivalent to slavery.

That particular "Squatters' Bill" was not enacted, but upon sudden notice in late April 1913, the new minister of native affairs, J. W.

Sauer, introduced a measure of far broader scope. Building on proposals outlined by his predecessor, General J. B. M. Hertzog (who had resigned from General Botha's cabinet in a dispute over English-Afrikaner relations), Sauer proposed the Natives Land Act of 1913.[1]

In less than two months, Sauer piloted the bill through Parliament. In June 1913, it became the law of the land and the main hallmark of the African policy of the Union government.

The kernel of the new legislation was the principle of territorial separation under which Africans and whites were to occupy and acquire land in separate, designated areas. A commission was to be appointed to determine the exact designation of all land within the Union. In the interim, Africans were to be barred from purchasing land except from other Africans or in existing tribal reserves.

The clear impact of the legislation was to restrict African land ownership to the so-called "scheduled areas," some 10.5 million morgen (a morgen is 2½ acres). This represented only about 7.3 percent of the total land area of South Africa, the bulk of which was the tribal reserves, the areas from which the Africans could not be pushed by the advancing white settlers in the nineteenth century. The measure also envisaged the release of additional land, whose boundaries should be determined by an expert commission, but nothing was done in this regard until the 1930's when the Hertzog land legislation of 1936 increased the potential maximum African area to 12.3 percent.

The 1913 bill also put an end to leasing arrangements by Africans in the Orange Free State and forbade the practice of tenant farming. Africans living on white-owned farms were left with the alternatives of accepting labor service with white farmers for a minimum of three months, seeking a share of communal land in the already overcrowded reserves, or migrating to the burgeoning African locations on the outskirts of South African cities where freehold rights were scarce and only low-paid unskilled or semi-skilled work was available.

In the light of Sauer's long record as supporter of nonracialism in Cape politics, Jabavu felt that he could not desert his previously steadfast white ally. Summoning a meeting of the South African Races Congress, Jabavu obtained a resolution in favor of the new legislation. He argued further that the land law would confirm land for African ownership and would immediately make more land available to landless squatters. He affirmed his belief that Sauer would not possibly let the Africans down. But Jabavu's stand met opposition even in his own stronghold of the eastern Cape Province. When in 1914 he ran for the Cape Provincial Council against the incumbent African member, Dr. Walter Rubusana, and a white challenger, the split of African votes was sufficient to give the white politician the seat. By opposing Rubusana and contributing to the defeat of the only African ever to be a member of a provincial council, Jabavu lost the political prestige that he had so long enjoyed in the Cape. At the same time his personal political organization, the South African Races Congress, was thoroughly discredited.

The South African Native National Congress, neither enmeshed in links to white politics nor the instrument of one person, reacted with shock to the Natives Land Act of 1913. In a series of meetings during the brief parliamentary debate, the Congress repeatedly declared its opposition to the legislation. In the months after its passage, the Congress drew attention to the great hardships the law was causing thousands of Africans. At a meeting early in 1914, it decided to organize a deputation to protest the legislation within South Africa and if necessary to proceed to England. The domestic campaign concentrated upon resolutions, a deputation headed by Dube and a petition to the prime minister, General Botha (see Document 25). In that petition, Dube declared that Africans made "no protest against the principle of separation so far as it can be fairly and practically carried out". But he strenuously objected to the

[1]It was ironical that the bill should be introduced by Sauer, long regarded by the Africans as a friend. Professor D. D. T. Jabavu suggests in his paper, "Native Unrest, Its Cause & Cure," that Sauer had to perform "an odious task under the political whip hand of a refractory negrophobist section of the then government." See Document 34.

Natives Land Act of 1913 as primarily a measure to compel Africans to accept service with whites upon disadvantageous terms that would result not in separation but further inequitable integration. His arguments reflected the views of those Africans who were willing to consider the possibility of "equitable" separation (at least in the short run), but rejected any system drawn exclusively to white specifications. Even with its suggestion of possible compromise, however, Dube's appeal fell upon deaf ears. The Congress' leadership then decided to send another delegation, headed by Dube, to Great Britain to present their grievances to the King, Parliament, and British public opinion. But this approach had no more effect than those they had tried in South Africa.

With the outbreak of World War I, Africans spontaneously declared their loyalty to the British cause and resolved to suspend the agitation against their disabilities for the duration of the war. Yet the voice of protest was only muted. When the Beaumont Commission, appointed under the terms of the Natives Land Act of 1913, made public in mid-1916 its recommendations for land delimitation, the Congress reacted sharply. The commission's recommendations reflected the pressures of the entrenched white farmers and voters. The areas it suggested for African occupation only slightly expanded the small amount scheduled for African ownership; furthermore, most of the recommended areas were recognizably inhospitable to human habitation or agriculture. In a meeting in Pietermaritzburg in October 1916, the Congress asserted that not even in terms of the principle of territorial separation had the commission given the slightest basis for a fair and equitable settlement (see Document 26). The resolution of the Congress charged that, on the contrary, the report of the Beaumont Commission indicated the determination of the Union government and the white population to relegate the Africans permanently to second-class citizenship in every aspect of their existence.

Further signs of the depth and extent of African feeling over the distribution of land were given in testimony before various local committees, which took evidence for the government in 1916-1918 (see Documents 27a, 27b, 27c). While occasional African spokesmen suggested support for the measure, the overwhelming majority of those Africans who testified (many of them members of the local committees of the Congress) expressed opposition to the segregation provisions of the Natives Land Act of 1913. Frequently, they stigmatized the land laws as a travesty of British rights and a return to the old system of the Boer republics.

Further Grievances

Nonetheless, in a conscious effort further to circumscribe the place of the African in South Africa, the Botha government introduced the Native Administration Bill of 1917. The first section of the proposed measure confirmed the principle of territorial segregation, while the second section formulated a scheme for African administration. This plan placed administration in the designated African areas under a permanent commission of whites chaired by the minister of Native affairs. The governor-general was to be given authority to legislate for these areas by proclamation, a provision which, in effect, would have given almost unlimited powers to the Union government. As a first step toward African involvement in this white-directed process, the measure proposed the gradual introduction of local Native councils (roughly corresponding to those already in existence in the Transkei) through which Africans could voice opinions. A third section of the bill dealt with the place of Africans in non-African areas and specified that only limited categories should be given permission to reside outside the designated African lands.

African reactions to the proposed legislation were highly antagonistic. In testimony before a Select Committee of Parliament, representatives of the Natal Native Congress (since 1912 a branch of the South African Native National Congress) echoed many of the complaints that had already been made repeatedly in connection with the Natives Land Act of 1913 (see Document 28). Yet, since the legislation was primarily concerned with African administration, the hearings also provided an opportunity for Africans to stress their desire for political representation. They unequivocally objected to the proposal to give the governor-general the power to legislate by proclamation. Instead, they wanted the franchise extended so that Africans outside Cape Province would also be able to participate in parliamentary elections. If there were to be a Native commission, the representatives of the Natal Native Congress wanted Africans to have some role in the selection of its white members, instead of having them appointed by the government.

The most original proposal from the representatives of the Natal Native Congress, however, was one that was to be reiterated and amplified in coming years. They suggested calling a national convention of representatives of both races to determine the future of the country (particularly if the principle of territorial separation was to be seriously entertained). By their appearance before the Select Committee of Parliament, the Natal representatives showed that they were willing to use the narrow constitutional avenues for limited representation left them by the Act of Union. Although they continued to oppose the principle of territorial segregation, they asserted their desire for some voice in its application if the white minority was to insist upon it. Simultaneously, their testimony affirmed the fact that they had not abandoned the ideal of a greatly expanded role for Africans within an all-Union political system.

When World War I came to an end, the government made no move to reward the wartime loyalty of the Africans by even the slightest concessions. It merely suspended consideration of the Native Administration Bill (and a more limited Native Urban Areas Bill regulating African residence in the towns) pending agreement among white parliamentarians upon uniform terms by which segregation could be introduced for both land and politics in light of the distinctive position of Africans in Cape Province.

In the economic sphere Africans also fared poorly. Sharp postwar dislocations fell particularly hard upon African workers, many of whom had been drawn into the work force for the first time with the unexpected wartime economic expansion, particularly in secondary industries. The well-organized skilled and semi-skilled white workers were able to exert pressures, including strikes, to further their economic demands which often included additional entrenchment of their privileged position. In contrast, the low-paid African workers, many of whom were housed in isolated compounds under strict controls, were hamstrung by the terms of the pass laws and by their labor contracts which provided no legal means of exerting pressure on their employers.

In the face of white South Africa's unconcern for African grievances, and despite the hazards involved, a wave of protests spread through the African community. Although left-wing white socialists in Johannesburg had encouraged the formation in 1917 of an African trade union, the Industrial Workers of Africa, the organization did not take root. Yet in 1918 sanitation workers in Johannesburg attempted to strike. Early in 1919, African workers in Bloemfontein demonstrated in the location (see Document 30) and in October, the locally based Industrial and Commercial Union of Cape Town, organized earlier in the year, led a strike of African and Coloured dock workers. In 1918, and again on a much larger scale in 1920, African mine workers on the Witwatersrand refused to work. In each instance the demonstrations were broken by white authorities.

In the political sphere, the Transvaal section of the Congress began to despair at the ineffectiveness of the representations through petitions and deputations. In the Orange Free State in 1913, African women already had gone beyond petitions and deputations by refusing to carry passes; they backed their action with peaceful demonstrations before local white authorities. Mrs. Charlotte Maxeke, who in 1905 had earned a bachelor of science degree at Wilberforce University in Ohio, founded a women's section of Congress that demonstrated widely and occasionally successfully against passes for women.

Following the example of the women (and perhaps also that of the Indians led by Gandhi), the Transvaal section of the Congress called its first passive resistance campaign in March-April 1919. Upon the Witwatersrand, several thousand Africans defied the pass laws by turning in their required documents.

Though citing the denial to Africans of both civil and human rights, Congress leaders promised that the demonstrations would be orderly (see Document 31). The demonstrations were peaceful, but they were broken by the brutal action of police and white vigilantes. Some demonstrators were killed; others were jailed. The pass laws remained intact on the statute books of the Transvaal as well as elsewhere in South Africa.

Although the African strikers and the passive resisters had not achieved their goals, new tactics had been used to express African protest. Furthermore, Africans from outside the small middle class circles that dominated the leadership of the existing organizations had become involved in political action.

Profound disillusionment and anguish, strangely mixed with continued hope, marked the comments of African leaders in the immediate postwar period. In the Cape Province, Meshach Pelem, a teacher who had acted as an agent for a prominent white politician, John X. Merriman, in the pre-Union days, attempted to fill the organizational vacuum left by the collapse of the South African Races Congress and the apparent failure of the South African Native National Congress to establish itself strongly in the eastern Cape Province. Out of a series of meetings in late 1918 and early 1919 came the Bantu Union, a new political pressure group under Pelem's presidency. In his inaugural address, Pelem showed how deep was the impact on African leaders of the announced democratic aims of the wartime Allies, in particular the Fourteen Points of President Wilson (see Document 29). He was emphatic that he did not want Afrikaner generals and political leaders Botha and Smuts to be the spokesmen for South Africa when the implementation of these ideals was discussed in the postwar peace conferences. Equally striking was his ambiguous attitude to the British: on the one hand, a sense of betrayal at the way Africans had been handed over to the Afrikaners, and on the other, a passionate faith that the "true" British ideal would ultimately be realized for Africans in South Africa.

Pelem's rival for the leadership of African political organizations was Samuel Mapogo Makgatho, a long-time resident of Pretoria, who had been active in African politics in the Transvaal in the pre-Union period. Makgatho had been elected in 1917 to succeed Dube as president of the South African Native National Congress in the wake of a dispute within the Congress over whether or not the principle of territorial separation might be accepted in theory. He represented the dominant wing in the Congress that was unprepared to compromise with the ideal of an ultimately nonracial society. In his address to the annual meeting of the Congress in 1919, Makgatho voiced his anguish and indignation about deterioration in the situation of Africans (see Document 32). He focused upon a specific list of grievances that had captured African attention in the postwar months, yet he was also anxious to bring out the nationwide character of African problems. Thus, he gently chided Africans in the Cape Province for their failure to identify fully with their brethren in the three other provinces. In Makgatho's eyes there could be no special approach in the Cape Province merely because it was there that Africans had franchise rights.

It remained for an African college teacher, unconnected with either the Congress or the Bantu Union, to provide the most complete catalog of the grievances stimulating unrest among Africans. In *The Black Problem: Papers and Addresses on Various Native Problems*, published in Lovedale in Cape Province in 1920, Davidson Don Tengo Jabavu, the eldest son of John Tengo Jabavu and the first African to become a professor, surveyed the condition of the African in South Africa (see Document 34). His extensive statement was not oriented toward political action (except that he specifically attacked socialism as anti-Christian), but to pinpointing the many areas of African discontent. He recommended training "well-educated Native leaders" to deal responsibly with African problems and the government. It reflected the orientation of the educated African elite, who suffered most directly from the failure of the system to fulfill the liberal promise of the 19th century nonracial franchise in the Cape and who stood to gain the most in any movement toward an expanding nonracial society.

Important tactical differences, however, existed within this elite. These differences showed vividly in African reactions to the Native Affairs Act of 1920. In preparing this measure, Prime Minister Botha's successor, General Jan Christiaan Smuts, had rejected the idea that "Native policy" as a whole could be handled within a single bill. Thus, in his administration's Native Affairs Act, he sidestepped the contentious question of the Cape franchise by underlining the fact that it had been entrenched in the Act of Union. Yet, in effect, he took the same path as had the proposals of 1917 by calling for the establishment of a Native Affairs Commission of whites and an associated system of limited local councils for Africans. In addition, he proposed machinery through which Union-wide conferences of African leaders would be called by the government for purposes of consultation.

Africans were offered an opportunity to express their views on this act before a Select Committee of Parliament. John Tengo Jabavu, in one of his last public appearances before his death in 1921, did not directly question the principle of the legislation (see Document 33a). He urged that Africans be made members of the proposed Native Affairs Commission; yet he was also anxious to involve white traders in the eastern Cape Province in any new local councils that might be established under the terms of the legislation. He thus remained true to his ideal that no South African institution should be restricted exclusively to one racial group. Meshach Pelem also apparently accepted the principle of the legislation but wished to modify its terms through a complicated scheme that would have converted the Native Affairs Commission into a partially representative body for Africans (see Document 33b).

In sharp contrast, the Rev. Z. R. Mahabane, president of the Cape Congress, who was to be a stalwart spokesman for Africans for more than four decades, forthrightly condemned the principle of political segregation upon which the act rested (see Document 33c). He did agree, however, that in the short term he would be willing to accept certain temporary measures of segregation, in particular a series of special constituencies from which Africans could elect members of their own race to the all-white South African Parliament.

Each of the spokesmen urged that opportunities for African political representation be expanded beyond the modest schemes contained in the Native Affairs Act, yet only Mahabane went outside the government's proposals to challenge the segregated nature of South Africa's highest legislative body. In so doing, the Congress spokesman forcefully reaffirmed the African commitment to the attainment of equal political rights.

Appeals Abroad

Throughout the first decade of Union, Africans had striven for a hearing in South Africa by all peaceful means at their disposal: petitions, deputations, appearances before government bodies, pamphleteering, and ultimately, civil disobedience. At the same time, Africans were also continuing and expanding the range of their activities overseas in an effort to bring outside pressure to bear upon the South African government. Testifying to the strength of African faith in British institutions, the Congress twice within the decade sent its own delegations to Great Britain to plead the African cause. In their lengthy formalistic petition to the King, carried to London by the 1914 deputation, the Congress protested against the Natives Land Act of 1913 and dwelt closely upon the moral and legal obligation of the Crown to uphold nonracial principles (see Document 35). They urged the King to annul the measure that had been passed without consultation with Africans, that deprived them of their rights as British citizens, segregated them in the land of their birth, and forced them off the land of their ancestors. The subsequent appeal by the delegation to members of Parliament and the British public detailed the Congress' unsuccessful efforts to obtain redress in South Africa and the consequences suffered by Africans after the passage of the act (see Document 36).

When the Congress campaign was suspended with the outbreak of war, Solomon Plaatje remained in Great Britain as a publicist for the Congress. With his *Native Life in South Africa* (see bibliography) he vividly chronicled the devastating impact of the

Natives Land Act of 1913 upon African squatters. In powerful language he dramatized for the British public the difficulties under which Africans labored in any effort to combat white domination (see Document 37).

In different terms his pleas were taken up in 1918 by the Congress as a whole in another petition to the King (see Document 38). After an almost embarrassingly long list of instances of African loyalty in the war, the Congress respectfully requested the intervention of the King throughout southern Africa to overturn the policy of the Union government. Looking beyond South Africa to the interests of Africans elsewhere on the continent, the petition specifically requested that South-West Africa should not be placed under Union government control and that the Congo should be removed from Belgian rule.

The international and Pan-African aspirations of the Congress were further demonstrated when the Congress delegation that carried the petition to England traveled on to Versailles to present the African position to an unhearing Peace Conference. Subsequently, John L. Dube attended the Second Pan-African Congress in 1921 on behalf of the South African Native National Congress. Thus a tactic of overseas appeals that had begun in the late nineteenth century was greatly extended and amplified, although with no more effect than before.

By 1920, the situation of the Africans of South Africa seemed measurably worse than it had been in 1910. Yet new stirrings were apparent in African politics. While the methods of the Cape African liberals had not been discredited, their limitations had been borne in on many African leaders. Organized African political activity, such as existed, was increasingly centered in the South African Native National Congress, whose approach combined the narrower concerns of those who could play electoral politics in the Cape Province with a more inclusive strategy that accepted any peaceful means as legitimate for the presentation of African grievances. Instead of the earlier separate colonial or provincial organizations, the goal was now a coordinated national federation — although fluctuation of membership, irregularity of meetings, inadequacy of finance, and intraorganizational disputes testified that the reality was still far from the ideal. Yet the range of political action had been broadened, and groups outside of the small middle class had been somewhat involved. Although white South Africa had proved unreceptive to the pleadings of the Congress (and its rivals), there was still hope (tempered by disillusion) that progress could be made toward a larger role in South African society.

DOCUMENTS

The Establishment of the South African Native National Congress

DOCUMENT 19. "A Talk Upon My Native Land." Pamphlet by the Rev. John L. Dube, 1892 [Extract]

I appeal to all Christians who may chance to read these pages, to aid in some way in this great work. "Truly the harvest is great, but the reapers are few." Millions of those for whom Christ died, are sitting in the darkness of sin and superstition, and almost crushed beneath the iron heel of heathen oppression. They are longing for something to satisy the hunger of their famishing souls, but fail to find satisfaction in idols. No one points them to the only living and true God. Why an all wise Providence has allowed all these years to elapse before opening the way for the gospel in Africa, we may never know. God in His wisdom seems to have appointed this time and this generation for the accomplishment of this work. God has in the past raised up a few heroes, such as were Dr. Livingstone, Robert Moffat and Bishop Hannington and others, who have gone forth into the dark continent and told to a people who are victims of heathenism, the story which was first told to the shepherds of Bethlehem Judah "Glory to God in the highest and on earth, peace, good will toward men." Wherever this story of Jesus and his love has been told, the curtain of darkness is lifting. May the soldiers of the Lord arise and press forward until all the kingdoms of this earth shall become the kingdoms of God and of this Christ. Every true Christian must sympathize with the cause of missions, and with the conversion of the heathen. It is not the business of Christians to speculate as to whether or not the heathen can be saved without the gospel, but it does concern every Christian to ask himself if he can reasonably expect to be saved himself if he refuses to obey Christ's last injunction and send the gospel to them. As one has quaintly said, the time has come when the demand of Christian missions is to every Christian, the imperative demand of the highwayman, "Your money or your life."

Oh! how I long for that day, when the darkness and gloom shall have passed away, because the "Sun of Righteousness has risen with healing in His hand." This shall be the dawning of a brighter day for the people of Africa. Christianity will usher in a new civilization, and the "Dark Continent" will be transformed into a land of commerce and Christian institutions. Then shall Africa take her place as a nation among the nations: then shall her sons and daughters sing aloud: "Let us arise and shine, for our light has come. The glory of the Lord has risen upon us." May the day speedily come when "Ethiopia shall stretch out her hands unto God."

> "Hail, O Africa, thy ransom!
> Raise to heaven thy grateful song!
> Last in rank among the nations,
> Thou shalt lead the choral throng, —
> Land of promise!
> Thy Redeemer's praise prolong!"

DOCUMENT 20. "The Regeneration of Africa." Article by Pixley ka Isaka Seme, in *The African Abroad*, April 5, 1906

I have chosen to speak to you on this occasion upon "The Regeneration of Africa." I am an African, and I set my pride in my race over against a hostile public opinion. Men have tried to compare races on the basis of some equality. In all the works of nature, equality, if by it we mean identity, is an impossible dream! Search the universe! You will find no two units alike. The scientists tell us there are no two cells, no two atoms, identical. Nature has bestowed upon each a peculiar individuality, an exclusive patent— from the great giants of the forest to the tenderest blade. Catch in your hand, if you please, the gentle flakes of snow. Each is a perfect gem, a new creation; it shines in its own glory—a work of art different from all of its aërial companions. Man, the crowning achievement of nature, defies analysis. He is a mystery through all ages and for all time. The races of mankind are composed of free and unique individuals. An attempt to compare them on the basis of equality can never be finally satisfactory. Each is self. My thesis stands on this truth; time has proved it. In all races, genius is like a spark, which, concealed in the bosom of a flint, bursts forth at the summoning stroke. It may arise anywhere and in any race.

I would ask you not to compare Africa to Europe or to any other continent. I make this request not from any fear that such comparison might bring humiliation upon Africa. The reason I have stated,—a common standard is impossible! Come with me to the ancient capital of Egypt, Thebes, the city of one hundred gates. The grandeur of its venerable ruins and the gigantic proportions of its architecture reduce to insignificance the boasted monuments of other nations. The pyramids of Egypt are structures to which the world presents nothing comparable. The mighty monuments seem to look with disdain on every other work of human art and to vie with nature herself. All the glory of Egypt belongs to Africa and her people. These monuments are the indestructible memorials of their great and original genius. It is not through Egypt alone that Africa claims such unrivalled historic achievements. I could have spoken of the pyramids of Ethiopia, which, though inferior in size to those of Egypt, far surpass them in architectural beauty; their sepulchres which evince the highest purity of taste, and of many prehistoric ruins in other parts of Africa. In such ruins Africa is like the golden sun, that, having sunk beneath the western horizon, still plays upon the world which he sustained and enlightened in his career.

Justly the world now demands—

"Whither is fled the visionary gleam,
Where is it now, the glory and the dream?"

Oh, for that historian who, with the open pen of truth, will bring to Africa's claim the strength of written proof. He will tell of a race whose onward tide was often swelled with tears, but in whose heart bondage has not quenched the fire of former years. He will write that in these later days when Earth's noble ones are named, she has a roll of honor too, of whom she is not ashamed. The giant is awakening! From the four corners of the earth Africa's sons, who have been proved through fire and sword, are marching to the future's golden door bearing the records of deeds of valor done.

Mr. Calhoun, I believe, was the most philosophical of all the slaveholders. He said once that if he could find a black man who could understand the Greek syntax, he would then consider their race human, and his attitude toward enslaving them would therefore change. What might have been the sensation kindled by the Greek syntax in the mind of the famous Southerner, I have so far been unable to discover; but oh, I envy the moment that was lost! And woe to the tongues that refused to tell the truth! If any such were among the now living, I could show him among black men of pure African blood those who could repeat the Koran from memory, skilled in Latin, Greek and Hebrew,—Arabic and Chaldaic—men great in wisdom and profound knowledge—one professor of philosophy in a celebrated German university; one corresponding member of the French Academy of Sciences, who regularly transmitted to that society meteorological observations, and hydrographical journals and papers on botany and geology; another whom many ages call "The Wise," whose authority Mahomet himself frequently appealed to in the Koran in support of his own opinion—men of wealth and active benevolence, those whose distinguished talents and reputation have made them famous in the cabinet and in the field, officers of artillery in the great armies of Europe, generals and lieutenant generals in the armies of Peter the Great in Russia and Napoleon in France, presidents of free republics, kings of independent nations which have burst their way to liberty by their own vigor. There are many other Africans who have shown marks of genius and high character sufficient to redeem their race from the charges which I am now considering.

Ladies and gentlemen, the day of great exploring expeditions in Africa is over! Man knows his home now in a sense never known before. Many great and holy men have evinced a passion for the day you are now witnessing— their prophetic vision shot through many unborn centuries to this very hour. "Men shall run to and fro," said Daniel, "and knowledge shall increase upon the earth." Oh, how true! See the triumph of human genius to-day! Science has searched out the deep things of nature, surprised the secrets of the most distant stars, disentombed the memorials of everlasting hills, taught the lightning to speak, the vapors to toil and the winds to worship— spanned the sweeping rivers, tunneled the longest mountain range—made the world a vast whispering gallery, and has brought foreign nations into one civilized family. This all-powerful contact says even to the most backward race, you cannot remain where you are, you cannot fall back, you must advance! A great century has come upon us. No race possessing the inherent capacity to survive can resist and remain unaffected by this influence of contact and intercourse, the backward with the advanced. This influence constitutes the very essence of efficient progress and of civilization.

From these heights of the twentieth century I again ask you to cast your eyes south of the Desert of Sahara. If you could go with me to the oppressed Congos and ask, What does it mean, that now, for liberty, they fight like men and die like martyrs; if you would go with me to Bechuanaland, face their council of headmen and ask what motives caused them recently to decree so emphatically that alcoholic drinks shall not enter their country— visit their king, Khama, ask for what cause he leaves the gold and ivory palace of his ancestors, its mountain strongholds and all its august ceremony, to wander daily from village to village through all his kingdom, without a guard or any decoration of his rank—a preacher of industry and education, and an apostle of the new order of things; if you would ask Menelik what means this that Abyssinia is now looking across the ocean—oh, if you could read the letters that come to us from Zululand—you too would be convinced that the elevation of the African race is evidently a part of the new order of things that belong to this new and powerful period.

The African already recognizes his anomalous position and desires a change. The brighter day is rising upon Africa. Already I seem to see her chains dissolved, her desert plains red with harvest, her Abyssinia and her Zululand the seats of science and religion, reflecting the glory of the rising sun from the spires of their churches and universities. Her Congo and her Gambia whitened with commerce, her crowded cities sending forth the hum of business, and all her sons employed in advancing the victories of peace—greater and more abiding than the spoils of war.

Yes, the regeneration of Africa belongs to this new and powerful period! By this term regeneration I wish to be understood to mean the entrance into a new life, embracing the diverse phases of a higher, complex existence. The basic factor which assures their regeneration resides in the awakened race-consciousness. This gives them a clear perception of their elemental needs and of their undeveloped powers. It therefore must lead them to the attainment of that higher and advanced standard of life.

The African people, although not a strictly homogeneous race, possess a common fundamental sentiment which is everywhere manifest, crystallizing itself into one common controlling idea. Conflicts and strife are rapidly disappearing before the fusing force of this enlightened perception of the true intertribal relation, which relation should subsist among a people with a common destiny. Agencies of a social, economic and religious advance tell of a new spirit which, acting as a leavening ferment, shall raise the anxious and aspiring mass to the level of their ancient glory. The ancestral greatness, the unimpaired genius, and the recuperative power of the race, its irrepressibility, which assures its permanence, constitute the African's greatest source of inspiration. He has refused to camp forever on the borders of the industrial world; having learned that knowledge is power, he is educating his children. You find them in Edinburgh, in Cambridge, and in the great schools of Germany. These return to their country like arrows, to drive darkness from the land. I hold that his industrial and educational initiative, and his untiring devotion to these activities, must be regarded as positive evidences of this process of his regeneration.

The regeneration of Africa means that a new and unique civilization is soon to be added to the world. The African is not a proletarian in the world of science and art. He has precious creations of his own, of ivory, of copper and of gold, fine, plated willow-ware and weapons of superior workmanship. Civilization resembles an organic being in its development—it is born, it perishes, and it can propagate itself. More particularly, it resembles a plant, it takes root in the teeming earth, and when the seeds fall in other soils new varieties sprout up. The most essential departure of this new civilization is that it shall be thoroughly spiritual and humanistic—indeed a regeneration moral and eternal!

O Africa!
Like some great century plant that shall bloom
In ages hence, we watch thee; in our dream
See in thy swamps the Prospero of our stream;
Thy doors unlocked, where knowledge in her tomb
Hath lain innumerable years in gloom.
Then shalt thou, walking with that morning gleam,
Shine as thy sister lands with equal beam.

DOCUMENT 21. "Native Union." Article by Pixley ka Isaka Seme, in *Imvo Zabantsundu*, October 24, 1911

I have been requested by several Natives, Leaders and Chiefs, to write a full and concise statement on the subject of the South African Native Congress, so called. I feel, however, that I shall better meet their desire as well as more properly treat this subject if I disregard the pretentious title and write on the simple subject of Native Union, for after all, this is what the Congress shall be.

There is to-day among all races and men a general desire for progress, and for co-operation, because co-operation will facilitate and secure that progress. This spirit is due no doubt to the great triumph of Christianity which teaches men everywhere that in this world they have a common duty to perform both towards God and towards one another. It is natural, therefore, that there should arise even within and among us this striving, this self-conscious movement, and sighing for Union. We are the last among all the nations of the earth to discover the priceless jewels of co-operation, and for this reason the great gifts of civilisation are least known among us today. I repeat, co-operation is the key and the watchword which opens the door, the everlasting door which leads into progress and all national success. The greatest success shall come when man shall have learned to co-operate, not only with his own kith and kin but with all peoples and with all life.

The South African Native Congress is the voice in the wilderness bidding all the dark races of this sub-continent to come together once or twice a year in order to review the past and reject therein all those things which have retarded our progress, the things which poison the springs of our national life and virtue; to label and distinguish the sins of civilisation, and as members of one house-hold to talk and think loudly on our home problems and the solution of them.

Such national Conferences of the people are bound to give a wide publication of the Natives' own views on the questions which primarily concern him to-morrow and to-day. Through this Congress the Native Senators in the Union House of Parliament will be able to live in close touch with the Natives of the whole country whose interest each Senator is supposed to represent. The Government also will find a direct and independent channel of informing itself as to the things uppermost in Natives' mind from time to time, and this will make it easier for the Union Government to deal with the Natives of the whole of South Africa. If we wish to convince the Government that it is possible to have a uniform Native policy for the whole of South Africa then let us form this Congress. Again, it is conclusively urgent that this Congress should meet this year, because a matter which is so vitally important to our progress and welfare should not be unnecessarily postponed by reason of personal differences and selfishness of our leaders. The demon of racialism, the aberrations of the Xosa-Fingo feud, the animosity that exists between the Zulus and the Tongaas, between the Basutos and every other Native must be buried and forgotten; it has shed among us sufficient blood! We are one people. These divisions, these jealousies, are the cause of all our woes and of all our backwardness and ignorance to-day. A great Paramount Chief accepting that his name be included in the honourable list of Native princes who endorse and support this movement, writes that "He however wishes to point out that whilst the objects and the aims of a Congress appear to be good and reasonable, much of the success depends upon the attitude of the members. There should be among other things a firm resolve on the part of every member to eliminate factors which have in the past proved fatal to the continued existence of such Societies. They should set their faces strongly against the jargon of racial feeling, the ebullition of the Xosa-Fingo element, and the excessive display of political partisanship."

In conclusion, I do not feel that it is at all necessary that I should preach Union even in this article. The Natives everywhere now and to-day know that a South African Native Congress such as is proposed in these columns, will give them the only effective means whereby they will be able to make their grievances properly known and considered both by the Government and by the people of South Africa at large. Through this Congress the Natives will have the opportunity and means with which to influence the public opinion of this country and to greatly assist the South African Statesmen who are working for the peace, prosperity, and the development of this land.

The Executive Committee, which is simply a Committee elected by a part of the people, is busy performing the thankless task of organising this movement. As one of the

Committee, I am pleased to say that we have been greatly encouraged by the support which we have received from all the great sections of our country. Today this movement is known, and in a great measure is openly supported by nearly all the leaders and the greater Chiefs of at least three Provinces and all the Protectorates. The Committee, therefore, intends to summon the first sitting of the Congress in the early part of December. This will certainly be an important day in the annals of our Native history; we shall have come together to bury forever the greatest block to our security, happiness, progress and prosperity as a people. We shall have come together truly, as we are, the children of one household to discuss our home problems and the solution of them.

This is a general announcement sent to all the Native leaders, Societies and Editors asking them to explain this important news to the people at large, and to advise them to arrange for the sending of delegates so that every section of the people shall be represented in that Conference of the races.

The chief business for their important deliberation will, for convenience, be divided into two sections.

First Section

1. To formally establish the South African Native Congress as a National Society or Union for all the Natives of South Africa.

2. Consider, amend, and adapt, the Constitution and Rules for the Society, Union or Congress.

3. To elect Officers for the ensuing year.

Second Section

1. The installation of Officers.

2. To take a Vote of Confidence on —

(1) General the Right Honourable Louis Botha, P.C.

(2) The Honourable the Minister for Native Affairs.

(3) The Honourable the Native Senators.

3. General discussions —

(1) Native customs and union.

(2) Native Marriages and Divorce.

(3) Native beer, is it a national beverage?

(4) Native Schools and Churches.

(5) The Black Peril and White Peril.

(6) Native Lands and Reserves.

(7) Native Courts — civil and criminal.

(8) Native labour.

4. General Concert and farewell Reception for the Delegates, Members and friends.

DOCUMENT 22. "The South African Races Congress." Inaugural Address by J. Tengo Jabavu, President, South African Races Congress, April 2, 1912 (Published in *Imvo Zabantsundu*)

S.A. Races Congress

At the South African Races Congress held at Toleni the inaugural address, of which the following is the substance, was delivered by

The PRESIDENT (J. TENGO JABAVU) who cordially welcomed the Chiefs, delegates and people, some of whom had travelled long distances to be present. Anthropologists classified people in an ascending scale — as Individuals, Families, Clans, Tribes, Nations, with Humanity at the top — according to the ties of Friendship, Sympathy and Love. Unfortunately Natives are still in the meshes of the Fourth Group, and are only able to act as Tribes, with the jealousies and feuds inseparable from that crude state of development. At the stage reached the controlling and governing power is the Chiefs. But in their earlier history the power of the Chief was modified by its delegation to the Counsellors, and thus, even in our rude and crude state we, as a people had realised the important principle which in more civilised countries is comprehended in the saying that "The King can do no wrong." It means that in practice counsellors are responsible for any mistakes that occur in the government of the people, and not the chief. It is earnestly to be hoped that in the development of their people the chiefs will ever bear this in mind and not think that they, as Counsellors are, or can be their rivals, but that they would regard them as what they really are — their servants and protectors. (Cheers.)

Their Congress, he might state is

As some may recollect it was called into being by Sir Gordon Sprigg's Native Disfranchisement Bill some 25 years ago. The aim and effect of that measure was to declare all land occupied by Natives as of no value in computing the qualifications of a registered voter for the Parliamentary Franchise. That was the first attack on Native rights and liberties as British subjects levied at them. They then found that they were unable to resist the invader hampered by tribal antipathies and jealousies; although the Bill itself aimed at all the Native races without distinction of tribe. It was then that they felt that some organisation, over and above and beyond their tribal arrangements should be formed to cope with this uncalled for assault on their privileges as the subjects of the Queen. An informal Congress of representatives of their tribes, was summoned by himself and met in King Wm's Town in 1887. Delegates came not only from all the Native tribes in what was then the Cape Colony, but also from the Coloured people of Stockenstrom. The tribes then stood as one man and decided on an appeal to the Imperial Government and empowered him to summon the Congress when occasion required. It was under that authority that they were represented on the Color Bar Deputation despatched to England in 1909. The Executive Committee has now decided to make provision for the regular conduct of the work of the Congress by drafting a simple and effective Constitution which will be submitted to them for approval during this sitting.

The Constitution

is made as broad and comprehensive as possible. The name South African Races Congress is selected to indicate the view of the promoters that they wish to live in absolute peace and harmony with every race in this country be it black or be it white, green or yellow. They are perfectly convinced that race and color hatred are the curse and blight of any country, and are determined to fight them to the utmost. They would order themselves under Providence to co-operate with all who work for the best interests of this land to promote the happiness and prosperity of every member of the community. Having said that much as to their aims he would glance at some of the

Questions of the day,

noting how they would apply their long and broad aims to them. First and foremost at all Native gatherings is the gratuitous insult which the founders of the Union of South Africa, for some unaccountable reason, thought fit to cast on a great and deserving section of the people of this country and their posterity by the insertion of the Color Bar in the Constitution. They are proud of the color they wear, because Providence designed it for them, and woe betide him who would reproach them on it. Unfortunately their leaders were so badly advised that they used this rotten stuff as one of the foundations of the future of this country. As they were aware, they protested earnestly against this miserable and shortsighted policy, and carried their protest to the Imperial Government and Parliament where its justice was acknowledged by all parties in the State. The Imperial Government made no secret that they would have removed the regrettable blot, but for the fear that it would have retarded Union; and the British Premier publicly and earnestly announced that the Imperial Government had urged it upon the delegates of the Uniting States to remove the blot themselves and he expressed a hope, amounting to a conviction, that this would be done by the South Africans themselves, and that sooner than later. (Cheers.) Until this is done, it must ever be the cardinal policy of every Native gathering to call attention to this deplorable blunder in their constitution "lest they forget, and lest they forget." (Hear, hear.)

Clause 147

Those interested in the privileges conferred by Clause 137 of the Constitution are moving heaven and earth to have effect given to it. Now as Natives, certain valuable rights were conferred on them by Clause 147 of the same instrument whereby all Native Affairs were taken out of Municipal, Divisional and Provincial Councils, which are minor bodies, and reserved to be dealt with by the pick of the Statesmen of the Union. But what do they find? They still find Natives harried and harassed by town and divisional bodies with the most exasperating regulations ever devised to vex and worry a people. It is high time they claimed their rights under the clause indicated, and had these things brought under review by the Union Minister responsible for their wellbeing and happiness as a people. Under the same clause they might consider matters affecting

Their Education,

which at present seems to be nobody's because it is everybody's affair, for while they are expressly removed in every respect from the local Councils, by another section of the Act of Union elementary education is reserved to the Provincial Council. The question is where, as Natives, they came in? As Mr. Malan once put it, the question of Native education is inseparable from the Native question; and he believed he was right. As no Minister of Native Affairs could deal satisfactorily with the Native problem with the factor of Native education excluded. Hence it is to the Department of Native Affairs they must go with their educational troubles, and by clause 147 of the Act of Union it cannot legally divest itself of responsibility, and pass its burdens on to a subordinate Provincial Council Department such as the Department of Education at the Cape. (Hear, hear.) Again, in view of the great failure of Native students at their Missionary Institutions they think that the remedy is in introducing into the management boards of these Institutions a dash of Native representation. The children now being taught at them are sons and daughters of those who were themselves educated in them, and it is very curious that the standard reached by the children is inferior to that attained by the parents. That there is something wrong in the state of Denmark everybody feels convinced and the remedy they suggest seems to be the only one if they are to exert control on the appointment of those who are to teach, direct

and mould the future of the coming Native generation. Then as to Mission schools, such is the rivalry of sects that schools are placed with an utter disregard to efficiency. This procedure has outgrown their requirements, and the next step would probably be to combine missionary managers with intelligent Natives in Missionary District School Boards, so that schools might be planted where they are required by the people not where a sect wishes them in its zeal for No. 1. (Cheers.)

On Labor,

Among the reforms that are being carried out, for various reasons they attach great importance to Government seeing that small allotments are given to Natives with families in towns and labor centres so that they can live with their families and lead decent lives. (Hear, hear.) Dealing with

The Squatters' Bill

he condemned the principle underlying it of rooting Natives out of farms and old established locations under the specious title of Crownlands, the tendency being to establish whites rather than Natives on the land. The policy is futile since the Native is naturally a peasant while experience has shown that the poor whites cannot compete with him on small allotments. He earnestly begged Government to desist from such a policy and rather follow General Hertzog's of endeavouring to raise the standard of comfort of the Natives until they are on competing terms with the poor whites. The question was a pure economic one, and should not be dealt with on color lines.

Liquor Restrictions.

Lastly they felt that it is impossible to restrict the sale of fire water too much from their people, if they are to thrive and prosper. They hoped the effort to run their Congress on approved lines would tend to the services of the Natives as well as that of the other sections of the South African people. (Cheers during which the speaker resumed his seat.)

DOCUMENT 23. Constitution of the South African Native National Congress, September 1919 [Extracts] (Typewritten, 29 pages)

1. WHEREAS there existed in the Provinces of the Union of South Africa several small and Independent Associations, Organisations or Vigilant Committees each one established for the purpose of advancing, observing and considering interests within its own tribal or local limits;

2. AND WHEREAS the subjects and problems with which the said free spontaneous and independent Associations, Organisations or Vigilant Committees had to consider and deal, were essentially of general interest to and affected the whole Bantu people in South Africa;

3. AND WHEREAS the good work of the aforementioned bodies was being rendered futile by the apparent indifference, ignorance and want of cooperation between one another;

4. AND WHEREAS there also existed in some of the Protectorates and Territories in South Africa certain bodies or Councils each constituted to consider and deal with the subjects and problems within its own tribal and local limits and no further;

5. AND WHEREAS there met at Bloemfontein O.F.S. on the 8th day of January 1912, certain Chiefs, delegates and other leading men in all representing the said Territories, Protectorates, the Provinces and also the aforesaid bodies throughout South Africa; AND the said meeting, there and then, resolved that it was expedient and desirable that a well-digested and accepted native opinion should be ascertainable by the Government and other constituted Authorities with respect to the Native problem in all its various phases and ramifications. And it was then further resolved to invite all aforementioned Associations, Organisations or Vigilant Committees and Councils to unite together and form as affiliated bodies, a Federation of one Pan-African Association the name thereof to be "THE SOUTH AFRICAN NATIONAL CONGRESS" (hereinafter in these recitals called the "National Congress") and to be composed and consist of two sections or Houses — to wit, one section then to be known as the Upper House and the other the Lower House;

6. AND WHEREAS an Extraordinary Meeting of the Executive Committee of the National Congress was held at Bloemfontein on the 1st day of August 1914 wherein (inter alia) the draft Constitution of both the said Houses was considered, amended, read and confirmed and was declared henceforth to be the Constitution of the National Congress its Rules, Regulations and Bye-laws in the manner and all respects as therein contained and provided;

7. AND WHEREAS by a Resolution passed and agreed upon in the fourth annual meeting of the National Congress held at Kroonstad, O.F.S., on the 3rd day of August 1915 convened (inter alia) to consider the amendment of the Constitution of the National Congress. After declaring that the said meeting was not satisfied with the then existing Constitution of the National Congress in that it did not contain adequate or uniform provisions necessary to safeguard the material interests of a National Organisation and more particularly in the respects therein mentioned. It was thereby resolved, inter alia, that the amendment of the Constitution be referred back and a Select Committee of ten members be appointed to consider the proposed amendments and either to prepare further or other amendments, or to revise same or draft a fresh constitution. And the Select Committee to present its report thereon to the Executive Committee of the National Congress.

8. AND WHEREAS the Executive Committee of the National Congress met on the 2nd day of August 1918 at Bloemfontein to receive the report of the Select Committee embodying the revised constitution of the National Congress when in the said meeting the Constitution was read [and] discussed clause by clause, when certain alterations and amendments were made and the same as altered and amended was adopted and agreed upon;

9. AND WHEREAS it is intended and it is hereby declared that the National Congress be made a corporate body to exist as such in perpetuity by the Registration of the Constitution hereof and in pursuance thereto the President and the General Secretary being the executive officers of the National Congress

shall sign and execute the constitution hereof on behalf of the National Congress and that no other authority for the execution thereof shall be required and these presents to be called "THE CONSTITUTION OF THE SOUTH AFRICAN NATIVE NATIONAL CONGRESS."

Chapter II

Interpretation of Terms

10. Throughout this constitution, if not consistent with the context: −

"Association" shall mean the incorporated body known as the "South African National Congress."

"National Congress" shall mean the Annual Meeting of and including the South African Native National Congress as an Association.

"Convention" shall include any ordinary special extraordinary or annual meeting of the National or Provincial Congress and Branch and any Committee Meeting.

"President" shall mean the president of the National Congress and no other with full discretionary and executive powers as such under this constitution.

"Chairman" shall mean the Speaker, Deputy Speaker, President of the Provincial Congress, Vice Chairman and other person holding or presiding in a meeting or in a Committee held under these presents.

"Officer" shall mean any person holding an office or a member of the Committee as well as the Committee as a body under these presents.

"Chief" shall not include a Headman or Induna, but shall mean one ruling over a tribe or tribes.

Chapter III

Objects

11. The Provincial Office of the Association shall be situated within the Union of South Africa.

12. The objects for which the Association is established are: −

(1) To form a National Vigilant Association and a deliberative Assembly or Council, without legislative pretentions;

(2) To unite, absorb, consolidate and preserve under its aegis existing political and educational Associations, Vigilance Committees and other public and private bodies whose aims are the promotion and safeguarding of the interests of the aboriginal races.

(3) To be the medium of expression of representative opinion and to formulate a standard policy on Native Affairs for the benefit and guidance of the Union Government and Parliament;

(4) To educate Parliament and Provincial Councils, Municipalities other bodies and the public generally regarding the requirements and aspirations of the Native people; and to enlist the sympathy and support of such European Societies, Leagues or Unions as might be willing to espouse the cause of right and fair treatment of coloured races.

(5) To educate Bantu people on their rights, duties and obligations to the state and to themselves individually and collectively; and to promote mutual help, feeling of fellowship and a spirit of brotherhood among them.

(6) To encourage mutual understanding and to bring together into common action as one political people all tribes and clans of various tribes or races and by means of combined effort and united political organisation to defend their freedom, rights and privileges;

(7) To discourage and contend against racialism and tribal feuds or to secure the elimination of racialism and tribal feuds; jealousy and petty quarrels by economic combination, education, goodwill and by other means;

(8) To recommend, propose and lay before the Government for consideration and adoption laws for the benefit and protection of the Native races. And also to watch Bills introduced in Parliament for proposed legislation as well as in other bodies for legislation affecting Natives and to draft and present amendments thereto.

(9) To agitate and advocate by just means for the removal of the "Colour Bar" in political education and industrial fields and for equitable representation of Natives in Parliament or in those public bodies that are vested with legislative powers or in those charged with the duty of administering matters affecting the Coloured races;

(10) To promote and advocate the establishment in Parliament and other public bodies of representatives to be under the control of and for the purpose of the Association.

(11) To record all grievances and wants of native people and to seek by constitutional means the redress thereof, and to obtain legal advice and assistance for members of the Association and its branches and to render financial [aid] where necessary with the objects hereof;

(12) To encourage and promote union of Churches free from all sectarian and denominational anomalies;

(13) To establish or to assist the establishment of National Colleges or Public Institutions free from denominationalism or State control;

(14) To originate and expound the right system of education in all schools and colleges and to advocate for its adoption by State and Churches and by all other independent bodies in respect thereto;

(15) To encourage inculcation and practice of habits of industry, thrift and cleanliness among the people and propagate the gospel of the dignity of labour;

(16) To acquire land by purchase, lease exchange, gift or otherwise for erection of halls and other public buildings for the use and purposes of the Association;

(17) To sell, dispose, manage, develop, let and deal in any way with all or any part of the property of the Association;

(18) To borrow or raise money by mortgage or charge of all or any part of the property of the Association; and also to grant loans on security of mortgages in the manner hereinafter provided;

(19) To establish a National Fund for the purposes of the Association either by means of voluntary contributions, periodical subscriptions, levies, contributions charges or other payments; and to hold and manage all funds raised for the objects of the Association;

(20) To all and everything directly or indirectly to maintain and uplift the standard of the race morally and spiritually, mentally and materially; socially and politically.

(21) AND GENERALLY, to do all such things as are incidental or conductive to the attainment of the above objects or any of them;

PROVIDED ALWAYS:

(a) That the Association shall not support with its funds or endeavour to impose on, or procure to be observed by its members or others any regulation, restriction or condition which, if an object of the Association, would make it a commercial or proprietary concern;

(b) The income and property of the Association whensoever derived shall be applied solely towards the promotion of the above objects, and no portion thereof shall be paid or be transferred directly or indirectly by way of interest bonus or profit to the members of the Association.

(c) Provided nevertheless that nothing herein contained shall prevent the endowment by the Association of any public useful object or the payment in good faith of reasonable and proper remuneration to any officer or servant of the Association or any of its members or other person in return for services actually rendered to the Association; nor be deemed to prevent the making of a gratuity of honorarium to its officer, servant or member or any other person for special services rendered to the Association voluntarily or otherwise.

Chapter IV

Methods or Modus Operandi

13. The work of the Association shall be affected and advanced (a) by means of resolutions, protests and a constitutional and peaceful propaganda; by deputations and other forms of representations; by holding enquiries and the investigation of grievances and other matters; and by passive action or continued movement; (b) by means of education, lectures, and distribution of literature on the objects of the Association; (c) by means of united action and when time is ripe for this method to secure the election to all legislative

and administrative bodies of candidates, who shall form a group of members and shall primarily stand and promote the interests of the Association so far as it is practicable and expedient, without identifying themselves with any political party or section. Such candidates to be under the control of the Association.

[No paragraph is numbered 14.]

Chapter V

Constitution and Government of the Association

15. The Association shall consist of and be constituted as follows:-

(a) The Provincial Congresses;

(b) District and Local Branches;

(c) Agricultural and Educational Societies;

(d) Industrial and Economical Unions; and

(e) any other bodies formed for such specific purposes as are closely allied with the objects of the Association, may with the approval of the Executive Committee attach themselves to the Association, and be represented in its annual mortjoin [sic] the Association under and subject to the provisions of these presents.

16. The Territories and Protectorates shall be within the pale of the Association and shall be represented at its annual meetings by the Chiefs or their nominees and with such representation and no other they shall be deemed to be incorporated with the Association.

17. The existing Provincial Congresses and the District and Local Branches and all other organisations hitherto forming part of or under the pale of the Association shall each and every one of them hereafter be deemed to be the branches of the Association and shall herein after be governed by and be subject to the provisions of these presents and no other.

National Congress

18. The Government and management of all and singular the affairs of the Association shall vest in a governing body called the "Annual Meeting of the South African Native National Congress (hereinafter referred to throughout in this constitution as the National Congress subject to and under the provisions of these presents.

19. The National Congress shall be composed of

(a) The hereditary Kings, Princes and Chiefs;

(b) The Elected Representatives of the Territories and the Protectorates.

(c) The Executive Committee;

(d) Official Delegates of the Provincial Congresses;

(e) Delegates representing certain bodies allied with and under the aegis of the Association.

20. The National Congress shall meet each and every year during the Easter Holidays at such place or places as the Executive Committee shall appoint.

21. A SPECIAL MEETING of the Association may be held whenever the Executive Committee shall think it fit. AN EXTRA-ORDINARY MEETING of the Association shall be called by the Executive Committee whenever a requisition in writing and in the form of a resolution is made by not less than two Provincial Congresses and passed by a two-thirds majority of those present at each meeting; such requisition to be signed by the Chairman and Secretaries of the said Congresses and lodged with the Secretary of the National Congress stating fully the objects of the meeting. Each Provincial Congress so making the requisition shall on lodging same deposit with the Treasurer of the National Congress the sum of £20 for the purpose of the requisition.

22. The National Congress shall meet as aforesaid to receive the Report of the Executive Committee, the Treasurer's accounts and to transact any other business which under these presents may be transacted by the National Congress. And the business of the National Congress may be adjourned to any day that may be appointed by the meeting or from day to day.

23. All business transacted at the Special and Extraordinary Meetings of the Association shall be deemed "Special or Extra-

ordinary" as the case may be. And all that is transacted at an annual meeting of the Association shall also be deemed "Special" with the exception of the report of the Executive Committee, Statement of Account and election of Officers.

24. No meeting of the National Congress (including a special as well as extraordinary) shall be held or considered constitutional under these presents unless at least 24 ordinary delegates shall have answered the roll. And no decision resolution or matter whatsoever of such meeting shall be valid and binding in any manner howsoever unless at least 20 ordinary delegates shall have been present and voted in such meeting.

25. The National Congress shall be the supreme authority of the Association and the final tribunal of all appeals matters and things submitted for its decision under this constitution. And in the meetings of the Association and in all matters in question, the act of the majority in number assembled as aforesaid shall be had, taken and be accepted as the act of the whole meeting and be binding on the Association and its constituents and all and singular its members to all intents and purposes and construction whatsoever.

26. All the decisions, resolutions, orders and work of the National Congress shall be administered by and through the Executive Committee who are by these presents appointed general agents of the Association and invested with all the necessary powers as such for direction and control, subject always to the approval and confirmation of the National Congress as hereinafter provided.

Chiefs

27. All Kings, Princes, Paramount Chiefs and Chiefs by heritage and other persons of Royal blood in the direct line of succession among the various tribes of the Bantu races in South Africa (hereinafter all referred to as Chiefs) shall have the right to attend the meetings of the Association either in person or by representation.

28. They shall be allowed the distinction of Honorary Vice Presidentship of the National Congress and those present shall be deemed to represent their districts and places under their rule or control respectively.

29. In any of the meetings of the Association, Chiefs shall be assigned a separate place of honour and respect. They shall also have precedence in reference to all rights audience.

30. Whenever in the meeting there shall arise a matter which in its purport affects the interests of all or any one or more of the Chiefs or their places, the matter in question shall be referred to the Chiefs themselves and they shall be allowed a separate session for consideration thereof and whose decision shall be final on any such matter.

31. No motion, resolution or decision of any of the branches of the Association, either in the Provinces or in the Territories, which in the opinion of the President for time being is hostile to the interests of the Chiefs and people or in direct conflict with the expressed desire of the majority of the Chiefs shall be considered valid and operative.

32. Every Chief in the Territory affected thereby as in the preceding clause mentioned may appeal through the elected Representatives (hereinafter referred to) direct to the President of the National Congress to contravene thereon as herein before provided.

33. If any such motion or decision arise within provinces the Chief therein affected as aforesaid, shall have the right to appeal to the Chairman of the Provincial Congress for intervention there on, subject to the confirmation of the President.

34. All disputes between Chiefs, upon being reported to the President, shall be referred to arbitrators in that Province or Territory nominated by the President through and by the advice of the Chairman of the Province or elected Representatives of the Territory (as the case might be). The said arbitration shall in all and in every case be conducted under the direction of the Chairman or elected representative the sum of ten pounds or to give adequate security thereof for the purpose of the arbitration. And the Party who on the day of Arbitration has failed to deposit the said sum or to give security thereof, shall not be heard in the enquiry; for all purposes thereof he shall be treated as a person in default.

35. Any party dissatisfied with the award may request the Chairman of the Provincial Congress to refer the matter for review in the ensuing meeting of the National Congress by a Council of Chiefs in which review at least ten Chiefs shall be present. The party so appealing shall deposit with the Chairman thereof a further sum of £20 for the said purpose. The decision of the said Council shall at the absolute discretion of the Executive Committee be final. Any dispute between the Chief and any of his people, upon being referred to the National Congress for Arbitration the Chairman of the Provincial Congress shall appoint a board of the Arbitrators consisting of three men. And for all purposes of this provision, clauses 43, 44, and 45, hereof shall apply in all respects.

36. Whenever there is a separate session of Chiefs as herein before provided, the president or his deputy shall preside. All the members of the Executive Committee and including the elected Representatives of the Territories shall have a right to sit and therein except that all matters of dispute between the Chief and Chief they shall have no right to vote.

37. In each Territory there shall be appointed by the President at the nomination and approval of the Head Chief a Representative of the National Congress in the Territory. His duties shall be to receive all notices and edicts and matters of the National Congress and communicate same to that Territory through the recognised channels. And shall also receive collect and transmit all matters and things therein to the President. He shall hold his position under the direction and control of the President and shall be the official representative in all meetings of the Association.

38. Each Territory through its Chief Ruler shall contribute to the funds of the Association a fixed sum. And every district of the Chief within the Province shall contribute through its ruler, a sum not exceeding £50 per annum according to the size and proportion of the district. A special session of the Chiefs during the sitting of the National Congress shall determine the amount to be contributed by each district thereof within the extent aforesaid with the advice of the Executive Committee.

39. All monies of whatever nature or purpose intended for the Association from and contributed by the Territories shall be paid to the Senior Treasurer of the National Congress. Also all monies of similar description from and contributed by districts of Chiefs within the Provinces shall be paid to the Treasurer of the Provincial Congress who shall pay over to the General Treasurer one-third thereof.

40. All Chiefs shall be ex-officio members of the Association with the right to attend and speak in all its meetings whenever and whensoever.

41. Chiefs within the Provinces shall be Honorary Vice-Chairmen in all districts and local branches and be delegates for their districts in the meetings of the Provincial Congress with a separate place of honour and a right of preference to audience. Each shall pay an honorary membership fee to the Association of one guinea.

42. In every district of a Chief within the Province with the approval of himself there shall be appointed an official representing the interests of the Association under the control and direction of the Chairman of the Provincial Congress and through whom all the affairs of the Association shall be made known to the Chief and his district. He shall attend all the meetings of the Provincial Congress and be ex-officio member of its Executive Committee. All reports grievances, notices, etc., to and from and affecting the district shall be made through him and the Chairman of the Provincial Congress. He shall be designated the "District Agent" of the Association.

43. The District Agent shall attend the meetings held by the Chief in his district and read all notices, etc., from the Chairman of the Provincial Congress and generally report the result thereof. He shall attend the meetings and Committees of the Provincial Congress at the expense of his district.

44. For the purpose of these presents, the undermentioned places, are hereby declared to be the Territories for the time being, viz.:- (1) Basutoland, (2) Swaziland, (3) British Bechuanaland and (4) Bechualand.

45. The National Congress (through the Executive Committee) shall define, declare, demarcate and subdivide the Territories, Prov-

inces, Divisions, Districts and Branches and shall also from time to time create new ones with demarcations or subdivisions and form Associations therein and appoint officers or representatives thereon, under control of the Association. The Transkeian Territories with the existing boundaries are hereby declared a Province and to have a Congress constituted in all respect and with powers and functions of a Provincial Congress within the meaning of Chapter VII of these presents.

The Land Question

DOCUMENT 24. "The Squatters' Bill." Article in *Imvo Zabantsundu*, March 19, 1912

The Cape Peninsula Native Association inaugurated its campaign against the proposed Squatters' Bill of the Union Government the other day at a meeting called by it in the Ashley Hall, Cape Town. There was a full attendance, with the Rev. Nyombolo in the chair.

The Rev. Chairman said he was very glad to attend anything which marked a spirit of real progress and enlightenment among their people and he heartily thanked them on forming such an Association as that which had called them together that evening. He sincerely desired to see it go and prosper if it continued to watch over the rights, privileges and social and political welfare of their people. (Hear, Hear.) These were very worthy objects and he must again congratulate them. He would ask one of the Executive officers of the Association to explain fully the purport of their gathering.

Mr. T. Zini (President of the P.N.A.) said he would not detain them for any great length of time but it was necessary to explain their attitude to the Squatters' Bill, and their reasons for adopting that attitude. Turning to the more immediate subject they were met to discuss - the Squatters Bill which it was proposed to introduce into the coming session of Parliament - he would ask them to bear in mind that they were commencing a campaign which would be a strenuous one. The harder the struggle the better they should fight.

(Hear, hear.) It was simply and solely in the interests of the farmers and miners and of no other section of the community. He had been at some pains to make himself acquainted with the provisions of the Bill, and he could assure them that all he could find it to contain was indifference to the interests of the bulk of the community, and the oppression of the Natives. It was a most iniquitous measure, and they should oppose it to the very last. If, unhappily, they were not successful in preventing its becoming law, they would at least have it on record that from first to last they had entered an emphatic protest against it. He was certain all Natives would combine in that. (Loud applause.) The whole measure was one gigantic invasion of their liberties. It would most adversely affect hundreds of thousands of Native families which had, up till then, lived on landed estates and farms, paid rents to the owners, and tilled the soil for a subsistence, happy and contented in their way of life. Why, in the Zoutpansburg district of the Transvaal alone there were 168,000 families thus living. Think what it would be to them and to all so living, if that mischievous proposition became law. They would be driven into locations with the sole object of forcing them to work in the mines or on the farms. If the former, they could hardly fail to prove victims of that terrible scourge, miners phthisis, while if they went on farms they would be subject to the treatment for which the great majority of the farmers were notorious in their dealings with the Natives. (Indignation.) The Bill took the cruellest harshest form of assailing the sacred right of every man to choose for himself in what manner he should earn his daily bread, and use the mental and physical attributes God has endowed him with. And yet the Ministry in power was never tired of proclaiming that it was the real friend of the Native and would see to it that he had justice. Yes! Miners phthisis "justice" or the "justice" of the farmers, the greatest sweaters of labour in South Africa. Such was what was proposed to be done by the men who made £ 2,000 a year each - very largely from the Natives, by the way. That most unjust and iniquitous measure would form one of the subjects for discussion at the Native Congress at Johannesburg on the

8th January. Many other important matters affecting the Natives would also be thought out, and he appealed to them to see that the P.N.A. was represented there by a delegate. (Hear, hear.)

Mr. B. Abrahams reminded his hearers of the very important feature of the proposed legislation, that it shamelessly sought to benefit the large gold mining companies and the big land owners at the price of the ruin of the health of the Natives, and with an utter disregard of all other sections of the people. The Government really played into the hands of the capitalists in Europe who held gold mining shares or owned vast tracts of undeveloped country - men who had never even seen South Africa, in many cases, but whose already bloated money bags the Government wished to swell to a still greater extent. (Indignation.) In no other country in the world did the Government seek to condemn men to contract a fell disease, saying (for that was what it meant) if they did not do that they must work for the farmers, at the expense of their future happiness and with no prospect of advancement. He (the Speaker) knew of nothing more unjust or tyrannical, a greater pandering to the capitalistic few at the expense of the many. (Applause.)

Mr. Umlamlelli asked them to remember General Botha's professions. The General had said time and again that he was going to assist the Natives to rise in the social scale, to be happy and contented. And what was the result of it all? He now sought to rush through Parliament a measure which would destroy their health and be detrimental to the State. Was that the Act of a sincere well-wisher of the Natives or of a wise far-seeing statesman? (No! No!) A more obnoxious manner of interfering with the freedom of the subject as to the disposal of his labour he could not conceive. Worse still: it made them court death at the instance of the mining community with the alternative of being hewers of wood and drawers of water all their lives at 10s. or 6s. a month. In one hand death; in the other slavery. (Indignation.)

Mr. T.H. Mobutha characterised the proposed legislation as cruel and diabolical. He trusted they would let their protest against be a most emphatic one, ringing from end to end

of the land. (Applause.) It was a callous and shameful playing with their lives, happiness, and all their future welfare. ("It is.") It was bad enough, nothing could be worse, to so affect those who worked in the mines or on the farms, but the Natives were mistaken if they thought those would be the only people it would affect. It concerned them all. The returning men from the mines would bring the seed of disease with them, to spread it far and wide among their people. (Fierce indignation.) Where was the vaunted superiority of the white man, if the Government thought it necessary to so unjustly and cruelly bolster him up against the competition of the Native? (Hear, hear.) Their people were to be pushed into the gutter for the only reason that they happened to have the unfortunate colour - black. The farmers complained of shortage of labour, but it was they themselves who were to blame. They drove labour away. Men were to work for them each day and every day, from sunrise to sunset on poor food and a miserable pittance, too often filched from them on one pretext or another. And when their hard labour had made them physical wrecks, old before their time, they were to be turned adrift to starve. (Renewed indignation.) The Native was not lazy; he was a willing worker, if fairly treated. Look at the Diamond-fields! Was De Beer's ever short of labour? No! Was German West Africa ever short of labour? And why? Because at both places the men were treated fairly. The Natives asked for nothing but fair treatment. The farmers were harming themselves by their oppression and injustice, for they humbug the Native once, but never again - he was built that way. (Laughter and applause.)

A speaker, whose reason for wishing his name withheld from print was accepted by the Chairman as valid, thought that, consciously or unconsciously, the Government was playing into the hands of the capitalists. In his opinion it was not the backveld farmer who wished for an Act of this description of the Squatters' Bill. At the present time there were thousands of Natives on their farms, Natives paying rent in money or kind, and it was not they who desired to drive them into locations. Some hundreds of thousands of Natives had done nothing else but farm all their lives; it was their work, and they were perfectly willing to rent suitable land from the white landowners, and so live there free, contented and peaceful lives. But now came this Bill to drive them into the locations where it would be impossible for them to live the lives for which alone they were suited, and to which alone they had been accustomed from their earliest years. The idea was that with the impossibility of existence in the locations, they would be forced into the mines. They would earn good wages there, no doubt, but at what a terrible risk? - a risk not only to themselves, but as had been pointed out by a previous speaker, to their whole people when they should return to the Native territories broken down in health and disseminators of the disease which had seized hold of them. (Hear, hear.) The alternative to the mines was to go on the farms to be treated like dogs, to work hard for a miserable pittance. (Cries of "true, true".) One could not understand some of our legislators. They were like so many acrobats, continually turning bewildering somersaults. (Laughter.) The speaker was indebted for the phrase "legislative acrobats" to perhaps the greatest of all in that line, the Right Hon. J.X. Merriman. (Renewed laughter.) You never knew where to have these people or what side of them they would show next. There was, too, the ex-Premier of Natal, Sir Frederick Moor. In England Sir Frederick had been their very good friend, he would do this, that and the other for the Natives; he would see to it that justice was done to them. Well, as he had said, that was in England. In Natal a few days ago he had openly expressed himself in favour of driving them into locations, and had laid it down as his policy that the Native should never be anything else than the servant of the white man. What did he really mean? Were it not so serious, it would be too funny for anything. (Loud laughter.) And when they turned to the members of the Cabinet, they saw the same sort of gymnastics even more wonderfully done.

The Chairman, in bringing the meeting to a close, had only one regret that the lateness of the hour made it impossible to do otherwise. He must again congratulate the Association. Its members showed an energy

altogether to be praised, and conducted their meetings in a reasonable manner. They did not ask for impossibilities and for anything out of the way. All they urged was that the Natives should be treated fairly and justly. That was as it should be, and he hoped the Association would gain in strength and always watch over, safeguard and advance the interests of the Natives. (Applause.) When the speaker first heard that a Squatters' Bill was to be introduced into Parliament he had high hopes that it would prove an entirely satisfactory way of dealing with one phase of the Native problem. He could not help but regret saying that he was thoroughly disillusioned. To him it appeared that the Bill simply means pauperising thousands of Natives, and consigning them to untold misery. In his journeyings in South Africa he had met many Natives who had worked 30 or 40 years on particular farms but were then being turned adrift for the only reason that their physical powers were on the wane. No provision was made for their old age; no consideration shown them whatever. They had been content to remain on the land, well assured what labour they were still capable of would provide for their simple wants. They were willing, perfectly willing, to pay, and asked only that they should be left in peace to continue to the end the work they had served apprenticeship to. But no! The Government said they must go into locations and, of course, where they went the younger generation would have to go also, with the unhealthy work at the mines, or rigorous labour on the farms as their only prospect. (Indignation.) They must firmly protest against such treatment, by all lawful methods.

DOCUMENT 25. Petition to the Prime Minister, from the Rev. John L. Dube, President, South African Native National Congress, February 14, 1914. (Published in *The Cape Argus*)

Humbly showeth:—

1. That your petitioner is the Principal of the Zulu Christian Industrial School as

above, and president of the South African Native National Congress, which represents practically all the native tribes of South Africa, and it is on their behalf, and by their commission, that he now makes this petition. [A reply to the petition, signed by the Secretary for Native Affairs and published in *The Cape Times* of February 26, 1914, observed, "Your statement that, as President of the South African Native National Congress, you are making this petition on behalf of practically all the Native tribes of South Africa is scarcely correct, as the Government is well aware that there are large and important tribes and various sections of the Natives of the Union which your Congress cannot truly claim to represent in this matter."]

2. You, Sir, are no doubt aware that money is now being raised to send a deputation to England to make an appeal to the King against the injustice of the Native Lands Act, which became law on 19th June of this year, a step which you deprecate, as appears from your speeches. You are reported to have said that a political question of this kind would be better settled here, with which we entirely agree. But it has been pointed out to you, Sir, that we have already done all that we found possible to do with the Government here, before the Bill was passed; but scarcely any notice was taken of our representations.

3. Now, however, lest it be said that we have not exhausted every possible means to get redress of our grievances from the local authorities before sending our deputation to England, we are making this appeal to you, Sir, and propose making a final one to Parliament if not successful.

4. Your petitioner avers that practically all the well-informed natives of South Africa feel that never under the British flag have they suffered an act of greater injustice and one which is more likely to embitter the hearts of the most loyal native subjects against the Union Government.

5. We make no protest against the principle of separation so far as it can be fairly and practically carried out. But we do not see how it is possible for this law to effect any greater separation between the races than obtains now. It is evident that the aim of this law is to compel service by taking away the means of independence and self-improvement. This compulsory service at reduced wages and high rents will not be separation, but an intermingling of the most injurious character of both races.

6. It has been stated that the law is of advantage to us; but there is no assurance in the law that it will protect us from rapacious land-agents. Any European holding land in a native area is not prohibited to sell, and, furthermore, we have not been protected from landlords, to whom we pay rent, who take advantage under the law to charge high rents, knowing we cannot move away with our stock or find admittance to any other farm as rentpaying tenants. We are more at their mercy than ever we were before, as competition is shut out.

7. But even supposing a little protection were there, the wrongs which might be suffered in that line are as one to a hundred in comparison with what we must now endure from the rapacious farmer who seizes the opportunity to raise our rent and reduce our wages.

8. It may be said that we misunderstood the law, and that when it has been properly explained, we shall find that it is not so grievous as we supposed. It is true there seems to be a great deal of misunderstanding about it, even by those highest in authority. But we heard it explained both to natives and Europeans and we cannot help noticing a difference in the explanation which is given to Europeans from that which is given to natives. As it has sometimes been explained to natives it does not seem to be so objectionable, and some natives have expressed themselves in favour of it. But we have seen that explanation utterly refuted by statesmen when before European audiences. Whatever may be the explanation, we can now speak from what we have seen of the effects even in the beginning, and which must inevitably grow worse and worse. We have seen our people driven from the places dear to them as the inheritance of generations, to become wanderers on the face of the earth. We have seen rents raised to the point of desperation. We have seen many of our people who by their frugality have laid by a little money in the hope of buying a small piece of land where they might make a home

for their families and leave something for their children now told that their hopes are in vain; that no European is now permitted to sell or lease land to a native. We do not need any plainer explanation than what we have already seen.

9. For the above reasons your petitioner humbly protests against the summary prohibition of the sale of land to natives, and prays that you, Sir, may exercise your power as Minister of Native Affairs to bring about an amendment to the effect that there may be no prohibition of the sale of land to natives till after the report of the Commission has been accepted by Parliament and the natives adequately provided with land.

10. We also ask that the law regarding the leasing and ploughing of land on share be left as it was before this Act came into operation. This prohibition is causing much hardship without benefiting anyone.

In conclusion, we pray that one native be appointed by the Governor-General to the Commission now sitting from among three to be nominated by the South African Native National Congress; or alternatively, one from two European gentlemen to be nominated by the same body.

As in duty bound, etc.

DOCUMENT 26. "Resolution against the Natives Land Act 1913 and the Report of the Natives Land Commission," by the South African Native National Congress, October 2, 1916 (Typewritten, 3 pages)

Having heard the main features of the Report of the Natives Land Commission on the Natives Land Act of 1913, and having learnt its principal recommendations, this meeting of the South African Native National Congress held at Pietermaritzburg, Natal, this 2nd. day of October 1916, resolves: —

1.

THAT looking to the interests and welfare of the Bantu people within the Union, the Report of the Natives Land Commission as presented to Parliament is disappointing and unsatisfactory, and fails to carry out the alleged principle of territorial separation of the races on an equitable basis for the following reasons:-

THAT it confirms all our previous apprehensions prior to the passing of the Act: That it offers no alternative for the restriction of the free right to acquire land or interest in land: It recommends no practical or equitable remedy for the removal of the manifold objectionable disabilities imposed on the Natives by the Natives Land Act.

THAT it has failed to fulfill the official promises made to the Natives and also to satisfy their anticipations that the Report of the Commission would provide more land sufficient for occupation for themselves and their stock.

WHEREAS the land now demarcated or recommended by the Commission is inadequate for permanent settlement or occupation in proportion to the needs of the present and future Native population: And Whereas the said land is, in most parts, unsuitable for human habitation as also for agricultural or pastoral requirements, seeing that it has been studiously selected on the barren, marshy and malarial districts more especially in the Provinces of the Transvaal and the Orange Free State:

AND WHEREAS according to the evidence given before the Commission there is conflict of opinion amongst the whites as to the approval or disapproval of the principle of the Natives Land Act - the majority of the whites in the Northern Provinces are opposed to the Natives having the right to purchase land or acquire any interest in land in their own names: Nor are they in favour of any large tracts of land being granted to Natives for occupation or settlement except in the unsuitable districts as aforesaid.

BY REASON of these facts the Report of the Commission as presented for consideration by Parliament cannot be acceptable as a basis for the alleged intended territorial separation of the races or as a fair application of the alleged principles of the Act, on just and equitable lines.

ON THE OTHER HAND, while the ostensible aim of the Natives Land Act is that of territorial separation of the races, the evidence in the Report of the Commission shows that the ulterior object of the Government as well as the real desire of the white population of the country, is:-

To deprive the Natives as a people of their freedom to acquire more land in their own right: To restrict or limit their right to bargain mutually on even terms for the occupation of or settlement on land: To reduce by gradual process and by artificial means the Bantu people as a race to a status of permanent labourers or subordinates for all purposes and for all times with little or no freedom to sell their labour by bargaining on even terms with employers in the open markets of labour either in the agricultural or industrial centres. To limit all opportunities for their economic improvement and independence: To lessen their chances as a people of competing freely and fairly in all commercial enterprises.

THEREFORE this Congress, representing all the tribes of the Bantu Races within the Union, earnestly prays that Parliament unhesitantly reject the Report of the Natives Land Commission and instantly withdraw the Natives Land Act 1913 from operation as a statute.

11.

With regard to ZULULAND it can only be pointed out as an acknowledged historical fact that the parcelling out of this territory into private farms for whites by the successive Colonial Governments was a breach of the Royal proclamation especially making this territory of Zululand a permanent reserve for the original owners. Having regard to the breaches of the aforesaid Royal proclamations and apart from the Natives Land Act 1913, this Congress urges Parliament to take the bold step of restoring the status quo in Zululand by proclaiming it a territory and a permanent place for the original owners thus securing an act of justice where it is due.

111.

FINALLY, this Congress begs to point out that the great bulk of the Native population in South Africa has no protection or any privilege under the Constitution of the Union, no legal safeguard of their interest and vested rights as subjects of the British Empire, no channel for any other intervention on their behalf in the redress of their just grievances,

no recognised means whereby they can effectively make their legitimate objections felt on any proposed legislation in the Union Parliament; and that as things stand the Executive for the time being in its own initiative and their interest and that of their supporters may (without any previous consultation with the Natives and their Chiefs) impose any law on the Native people without let or hinderance and regardless of the principles of that law and its effects on the people concerned. Guided by these facts and by the light of political experiences in the past we cannot accept the projected solution of the land question. We regard the Natives Land Act as one-sided and as inconsistent with the ideals of fair Government by reason of the disabilities it imposes on the Native people of the Union, while the Report of the Lands Commission is based on the objections of the European people only. Consequently, instead of establishing good relationship it is creating friction and racial antipathies between the blacks and the whites.

That the welfare of this country depends upon its economic development while this Act is calculated to retard the law of supply and demand. The Act as designed is wrong in principle as violating the laws of nature that every man is a free agent and has a right to live where he chooses according to his circumstances and his inclinations. Any system therefore of settlement on land to be lasting and beneficial without the least injury to any section of the community can only be on natural lines, and not by means of artificial legislation. Further that partial territorial separation of the races already obtains in every sphere of life in the urban and rural places: and therefore this cannot effectively be met by retaining the Natives Land Act on the statute Book. We submit there should be no interference with the existing conditions and vested rights of the Natives, and there should be no removal or ejectment of them from their ancestral lands or from lands they have occupied for generations past: but they should have unrestricted liberty in every Province to acquire land wherever and whenever opportunity permits.

For these and diverse reasons this Congress consisting of delegates representing the various Native tribes of South Africa in declaring its unshakable opposition to the Natives Land Act 1913 reiterated all its former resolutions with respect thereto and hereby further resolves to employ all means within its power to secure the repeal of this mischievous Act and the non-enforcement of the Commission's Report.

In spite of our previous promises to desist from agitation in connection with the Natives Land Act 1913, and recognising the Act is still in operation with detrimental effects to our people, the Executive Committee is instructed to immediately inaugurate a campaign for the collection of funds for the purposes of this resolution and to educate the Bantu people by directing their attention towards this iniquitous law.

That this resolution be sent to the Governor-General, the Missionary Societies and other interested bodies, and to the Anti-Slavery and Aborigines Protection Society. That the Chief Executive appoint a deputation of three to place this resolution before the Union Government at the earliest opportunity and also to lay same before the Union Parliament next session.

DOCUMENTS 27a-27c. Minutes of Evidence, Eastern Transvaal Natives Land Committee, October 1917 — January 1918

DOCUMENT 27a. Testimony of Saul Msane, Sprinkhaan, and Jonas Mapope before the Eastern Transvaal Natives Land Committee, October 23, 1917 [Extracts] (Published in *Minutes of Evidence, Eastern Transvaal Natives Land Committee*)

SAUL MSANE:

I live at 9, Kruis Street, Johannesburg. I am a Zulu.

I am pleased to be before you. You spoke in your address (referring to the opening remarks of the Chairman, in which he explained the intent and purpose of the Bill), of the great principle established by Act 27 1913. I wish to remind you, Sir, that when that act was passed we fought against it. I was one of the delegates sent to Cape Town to represent the case of the natives. We pointed out to Mr. Sauer, the then Minister for Native Affairs, that the Act pressed severely upon us and we asked that before the Act was passed a Commission should be sent round the country to ascertain the views of the natives. We asked the Government not to legislate in the dark, but the Government would not listen to what we said, and the Act was passed. The Government carried that law knowing well that it took away rights that we formerly possessed. We were astonished that such a thing should happen under the British flag. After this, certain men were chosen to go to England and make representations on our behalf. I am one of these delegates. Then the war spoiled everything. We did not care to press our case whilst our King was troubled by war. We suspended our agitation, but we have not dropped it. We mean to take it up again so soon as the war is over.

The principle established by the Act of 1913 is really a travesty of Queen Victoria's Proclamation of 12th May, 1843. It robs us of the rights we enjoyed under that Proclamation. We are surprised that rights given us by the English should now be taken away again. The war has proved that we are submissive. If we resist, it is because our great right was taken away from us.

You have come here to-day, Sir, to speak to these people of the land which will be given to them in various parts. These natives think this area will be given to them. But the Bill does not say that. It says they will be given the right to buy. But how are these natives here who have lost all their property to buy? I say that the authorities do not wish us to have a place where we can settle down quietly. Look at the matter of the registration of contracts before the Magistrate. Only those who have money with which to buy will go into the native area. The others will have to stay in the white area. Those who stay will find that the conditions under which they must reside are not the conditions to which we Bantu are accustomed. These conditions savour of slavery.

Again, take Section 16, Sub-section 17. You will see that the native is deprived of his wife and children. (The Chairman pointed out that the effect of the section was exactly the contrary.) I am glad to hear you say that it is not so. I say it is not right to come to natives like these here to-day who do not understand what is being done, and to expect them to give an opinion on so complicated a matter. The Committees are meeting this class of people everywhere—the most primitive.

Under Section 147 of the Act of Union the Governor-General-in-Council is the supreme chief of the natives. What we ask is that the Governor-General-in-Council should meet all the natives and discuss this Act with them and tell them exactly what is being done. When I ask that we people should be able to settle down quietly I want also that we should live in harmony and help one another.

I refer again to Act 27 of 1913. Out of a total of 143,000,000 morgen within the whole Union, Act 27 of 1913 provides only about 10½ millions for the natives. The Beaumont Commission has added, I think, another 8 1/3 millions, bringing it up roughly to 20 million morgen. That is for 4½ millions of natives. The white people who are 1¼ million, will have the rest. Can you rightly say that there is justice in that? It makes us think that you don't wish to help us, you want to destroy us. To put all these people and their increase in one small kraal! I have grown up under the British flag. I know how the British live and act. This is not the way they act. You are not doing justice to Great Britain.

You will see, Sir, that the Act provides for a South African Native Commission which will be over us, in other words, we shall be deprived of the protection of Parliament. Parliament will no longer be over us. You are taking away a right from us. Section 60 of the Act of Union provides that after a Bill has passed both houses the Governor-General may assent to it or reject it, or reserve it for the Imperial Parliament. Section 65 gives the King the right to alter a Bill after it has been assented to by the Governor-General. We went to England under that clause. Now it is proposed to rob us of that right. The law is unjust to us, it destroys us.

Then, again, we are to have a court of our own and not go to the judges of the Supreme Court. The court will consist probably of two magistrates or two commissioners, or sub-native commissioners. Here too, we are de-

prived of the protection given us by the Act of Union which provides that the Appellate Division of the Supreme Court of South Africa shall be the highest court within the Union. There is no provision enabling us to appeal to that court. Do not then be surprised that we do not approve of the Bill. We cannot approve of it. Our prayer is that this Act 27 of 1913 be repealed and the Administration Bill be not proceeded with until after the war. Then when everything is settled a convention can be summoned of all the chiefs and leaders of the natives to meet the Governor-General-in-Council and evolve what you call a native policy. (The *Chairman* at this stage pointed out that the speaker was wrong in regard to the right of appeal.)

We are very much afraid of this Bill. In the Free State now they are making women carry passes. We urge that the Government take no further action to have this Bill made law until our people have returned to this country from Europe and have had an opportunity of discussing the bill. We simply want the thing to drop until the war is over.

The *Chairman* at this stage dealt with the various points raised by the speaker and pointed out to the meeting the necessity for indicating the area they wanted.

SPRINKHAAN: Examined by Chairman.

I thank you very much, Sir, to-day. We are cattle and have come to the kraal. When I left Sekukuniland I came away from the big kraal. At that time there was no water there. Even now you hear that natives are leaving Seku-kuniland because there is famine.

We discussed this matter with our people and they said to us: "When you go from here tell them we have no eyes, we are blind." The only eyes we have are the eyes of our Commissioner. He is the one to hear our grievances.

To-day our children are in England for the Government, and while they are away you come here and say you want to decide the matter of the ground that is to be given to us. I ask if this Bill is to become law while our children are still in England.

We are very sad when you say we must go away and look for other places in which to live. There are no other places to go to. Please assist us and let us remain where we are to-day.

Diamond was my chief, and when he died I buried him there where we live to-day. If I go away, the white people will come and plough up his grave. Diamond's last words to me when he died were: "Remain here where I shall be buried and look after my son."

I cannot say where the boundary ought to go. I wish the Commissioner to speak for me.

JONAS MAPOPE: Examined by Chairman.

I speak to endorse the words of Saul. We heard a little time back that there was another Commission which went round the country. When they went back to Parliament we heard what they said there. We saw that their recommendations were a great mistake. I think that is what Saul means. We stand here to-day and say again that those recommendations were a mistake, and I say the authorities make a mistake too in pressing this legislation. Now we hear there is another Commission that has come with good. I heard of this at my home in Spelonken.

All that Saul has said we think is right. I say that you should listen to what Saul has said. We don't say that the Government must not give us an area. But what we say is that we don't want the area at the back of beyond. We are not afraid of what is to-day, but of what is to come. You tell us that we will be well looked after by our Commissioners. If they were all like Colonel Damant here we should be satisfied. We support him in the matter of the areas. What we refuse is a small area.

DOCUMENT 27b. Testimony of the Delegation of the South African Native National Congress, Ermelo, before the Eastern Transvaal Natives Land Committee, January 8, 1918 (Published in *Minutes of Evidence, Eastern Transvaal Natives Land Committee*)

After the magistrate and the Chairman had addressed the gathering [about 200 Africans] the following representative natives were heard:

Solomon Tutu.] I am a representative of the South African Native National Congress. Our Congress has fully considered this new Law. The sore point with us is this proposed segregation between black and white. We ask that this matter be postponed until twelve months after the war. Then upon the matter being brought up again it could be dealt with by meetings of our people and the thing decided one way or the other. Another point to which we wish to draw the attention of the committee is that there has been no land set apart for natives on the high veld.

Joseph Hlubi.] I am a Swazi and representative of the South African Native National Congress.

The Chairman has explained to us very fully the circumstances under which we are to live in future. It is repugnant to us that we should be made to live apart from the white people. We want to live among them. Before you white people came, there was a great deal of bloodshed and trouble among us. Then when you came, we lived among you and we became men. We rose in the scale of civilisation, and instead of fighting among ourselves we became well ordered under the rule of the white man. The white man showed us the light. Now you wish to remove us from the light and make us stay apart by ourselves. I say chief, that when the English were subject to the Romans and if the Romans had segregated them, they would not be what they are to-day. You wish to separate us from you so that we may not have the same opportunities of advancement as you have had. That is why this proposed legislation is not acceptable to us. You want to keep us underfoot. That is why we say this Bill must remain in abeyance because it is killing us.

There is another point in connection with the control of our people who remain in non-native areas. The provisions relating thereto are very unpleasant. What we object to is that a native and his family living on a white man's farm should have to be registered. That man is no longer free. He would never be able to rid himself of the shackles of the white man. There are many little things like that to which I could refer. The white people should protect us and help us, because we need them. We need to live among you to get the light that you have had.

John Msimang.] Our request is that the Government should give us the right to possess land in the Ermelo district. I have ground on Spitzkop. My request is that the Government should allow us to buy ground in the whole of the district among the white people. The native wants to live among the white people. We ask the committee to receive our request to-day that we be allowed to live among the white people. When a father has given his child cattle he does not go behind his back and take them away again. Our father gave us the right to purchase land, now our father turns round and asks us to give up that right. His children say "No."

Rooikop Sheba.] I am an Induna of the Ermelo district, and live on the farm Mooiplaats.

[To the natives:—I am surprised that you have elected men to represent your views who have not my knowledge or the knowledge of many of us. I hear that Tutu claims to speak for us. I deny that.]

We have come to represent our views to the committee, but I wish first of all to put certain questions to the committee. I appear before you but I did not know where the areas were. I had never gone into this question of ground. I grew up among the white people for whom I worked, and even now I work for them.

What I want to say is that I am surprised that our daughters and our wives are allowed to board trains at will and leave their kraals without the authority of their fathers and guardians. Secondly there is the question of Lobola. We wish the Lobola system to continue the same as before.

I am not prepared to make any representations with regard to native areas because it is a matter that I have not previously gone into. I should like to be given the opportunity of meeting my people and discussing the matter with them. I do not want to make a separate representation as an individual.

John Tabeti.] I am a Swazi and live at Carolina. I was elected by the headmen to appear before the committee.

I am surprised that we natives are not in agreement before you. It appears that there is no union among us. There are many important people in Ermelo. It is surprising to me that they did not know before what the provisions of this Bill are. I thought that this had been made known among the natives and that they had agreed to have their representatives. The induna who has just spoken has no right to voice our views. He is not a chief.

We do not accept the areas recommended by the first commission, because the ground is low-lying, infertile and unhealthy. We wish to have the ground upon which we were born. We do not wish to leave it. All of us say that. The Government being in authority has power to give us ground to suit our purposes.

Mashosha.] I am a Swazi and live at Steynsdorp.

I notice that there is no union among the natives of the Ermelo district. I think there ought to be a meeting of the natives now that the Chairman has explained the position and that they should come forward later and express their views. Some of us know about this matter, and others do not. We should all retire and come to some understanding.

Simon Siluma.] I am a member of the committee of the South African Native National Congress. I agree with what has been said by our representatives.

Bonifacius.] I am a Basuto. I was born in the Free State and have been here three years.

There are a few of us here who own land. Where I am at New Ermelo there are about fifty of us. Before we had finished buying, the law came and prevented us from buying. We want these stands to be thrown open. It is now three years that this has been going on. The difficult thing about these meetings is that we go back just as stupid as we came.

In this question of parting the ground between black and white there is only one thing which presses hardly upon us. We do not object to the principle of the thing, but what we do find hard is that we should have to go to country in which we are unable to live because it is unhealthy. We want the Government to give us ground on the high veld where it is possible for us to live. Things will not come right if we have to go into the low veld and into Swaziland. We should be glad if the Government gave us ground on the high veld. That is the whole thing. We do not want to go into the unhealthy parts of the country.

The meeting adjourned at this stage to give the natives an opportunity of consulting further. On the resumption the following persons were heard:

Rooikop Sheba.] I am not in favour of having the ground cut up. We should like to remain as we have been in the past. I speak for those of my people who agreed to the resolution just taken.

Joseph Hlubi spoke to the same effect, and the meeting closed.

DOCUMENT 27c. Letter to the Sub-Native Commissioner, Pietersburg, from Filipus Bopape, November 23, 1917 (Published in *Minutes of Evidence, Eastern Transvaal Natives Land Committee*)

c/o Private Bag, Leshoane Mission,
via Pietersburg,
23rd November, 1917.

The Sub-Native Commissioner,
Pietersburg.

Honourable Sir,

We humbly beg you by this letter, that you may please carry our complaints and our requests before the Government, concerning to the "Native Land Act" we already agreed upon year 1913 together with the Chiefs of the Zoutpansberg District, we asked the Government that each chief had to remain in big place together with his own people. Should Government be willing to take care of us, may kindly give us pieces of land where we are found.

In this year we are still asking as we already have asked in the year 1913, as well as in reign of Queen Victoria. The English Government had pleased us by ordering the Republic Government that natives must be given Locations, that every chief and his people must be given a piece of land their birth place. Locations were granted to the people, at which we were thankful, they insufficient for the people to live in [*sic*]. The different Denominations were founded in these Locations, to worship God in them, we were pleased that even we natives were allowed to purchase portions of farms through our own names. A thing which was (prented) prevented in the time of Republic was that a native had

no right to purchase same through his own name. Therefore we commenced to purchase farms through the Government permission, and we paid due prices for doing same and we were given their Titles in which our names were entered. And we did not go far away from our Locations to buy these pieces of Farms, we bought only the neighbouring to our chiefs. Churches were erected in these farms and schools which are under the care of Government. We had much hope that a thing is confirmed by Government would not be changed. Now we are threatened by hearing that our lands are fallen in the European side. Though the European's pieces of farms in this land are few among we natives who are counted by thousands. If Locations and native farms should fall into the European's side, then the Union Government will have broken the commands of the late reigners who slept in peace upon whom we still make recommendations while dead. Continually, the Union should be careful of the Churches and Schools which are in the Locations and Native farms. If, after the natives are sent or removed to the mentioned states towards the East, and their Churches and schools remaining used stalls of the white people Domestical herds, as for horses, cattle, pigs and sheep, whether to be used like bedrooms or dining or bar houses. These rooms are founded for worshipping God of every nation. Subsequently from the year 1913 to 1917 the Union Government have bound the black races with an old law of time of the (Repl) Republic for a native is again bracked to buy his own farm. This law is carried against the natives, of course any white man can buy a farm whenever he is in need, he will buy it without any hindrance, several natives have kept their money in their purses, they wish to buy their own farms, but the Union Government prevented them to buy. Even these farms of Europeans which are amongst our chiefs Locations. If the owners wish to sell these to some of our native races, the Union prevents them.

These are awful extremities which meet the natives in Union. Consequently we beg that the Government should not only keep care under Locations, but also remember to other natives living outside the Locations by cutting or gratifying to them pieces of lands approximately to the chiefs' Locations. Because if the Government only wants to crowd all the natives in Locations without allowing them to buy their own pieces as they want, of course that will mean the inhumanity of the Government, because native populations are already densed in the Locations; there are no meadows for their herds, there are no ploughing places for their lives. Starvation ranges awkwardly amongst the locations that the people can with greatest difficulty obtain money for the Government revenue income.

There is another awful branch of this bad law that: A native is not allowed to hire a white's farm by money, except by working for nothing "Boroko". We are really ignorant of the place where the Government wishes to be living for to the heaven we are unable to go in order to avoid the cruelty of these laws. The Government knows, then if he, a native, has no farm for himself to live, where will he live if he does not hire a white's farm with money for his life, because the Europeans have occupied the whole country, and natives are living through the help of white people and the white's also through natives. To hire a farm by money is far better than to work for nothing like a slave who is caught from the battle. Queen Victoria made peace to the natives from their slavery lives, that every one might live in the way he likes. The Union Government also decreased the law (Boroko) working for nothing, in the last years. By ordering the owners of the farms that natives have to work (Boroko) for three months in a year, and that for the remaining nine months work for their houses and also for the Government Tax Receipts. The law said, if any of the farmers overgoes this law, and make natives work "Boroko" for the time exceeding three months, he will be liable to be fined £50 sterling, or to be thrusted gaol [sic] for a period of six months. Still a lot of white farmers overgo that law, by making natives to work twice every week in a year. A native has to work with his wife and children that are over twelve or thirteen years of age without giving them food. If a man has six children, they are all set to work for one man along with their parents without food. We even do not know what amount of money did these white farmers buy their portions of farms. Schools which are in the white people's farms are even closed for good, because native children are on the work for "Boroko".

Although the Union Government knows very well that these schools were under his care, still these schools are shut without compensation to the Government. The Government does not even attempt to blame or punish the Transgressor of his laws, because heavy laws are set for black races only. Another law which inunderstoodable [sic]! For living to buy the Permit or Licence in our farms which we bought through the Government allowance or permission, be damaged as if we have stolen these farms. These show plainly how that although the Government would compel us by force without our own free-will, he will within few years of our living there come and remove us again toward the East, until we are finally thrown in the Seas, and there as for instant [sic] is where the Union Government would be quite contented for the natives live, and that place, even the wisest or cleverest people of the world cannot live in it. As about the East continues, the place where the Government wants to through or send the Natives by saying that it is a good living country prepared for natives. That in reality puts the natives in grieves, their hearts are gloomy, and are leading a lamentation live for the rumour that natives are going to be thrown towards the East. If the Union Governor is going to decide by force and remove all Zoutpansberg chiefs with their tribes to the said country, then Union Government will be like a butcher who drives his herds to a butchery house to be all slaughtered at a time. Because the country is liable for people to live in, but for wild beasts and people who were born in it. The country is as hot as fire. That how it possesses diseases of different kinds and deaths.

The said country must belong to the Government, he will go and kill elephants and other wild animals, whenever he goes for hunt. We beg that the Government should grant us another country which is very near or close to our birth place, instead of the East country which will belong to the Government for ever, because all countries are belonging to him. He is the Government of Locations farms.

These are our complaints and our requests from the Government.

(Writer: Sgd.) FILIPUS BOPAPE.

Further Grievances

DOCUMENT 28. Testimony of Chief Stephen Mini, J.T. Gumede, and the Rev. Abner Mtimkulu of the Natal Native Congress, before the Select Committee on Native Affairs, June 15 and 18, 1917 [Extracts] (Published in *Minutes of Evidence, Select Committee on Native Affairs*)

Chief Stephen Mini, Josiah Tshangana Gumede and Rev. Abner Mtimkulu, examined.

4392. *Acting Chairman.*] You are President of the Natal Native Congress, Mini?— (*Chief Mini.*) Yes.

4393. And you are the Secretary, Gumede?—(*Gumede.*) Yes.

4394. And you are a Wesleyan Minister at Pietermaritzburg, Mtimkulu? — (*Rev. Mtimkulu.*) Yes.

4395. And you are all appearing before this Committee as delegates from the Congress recently held at Pietermaritzburg?—Yes.

4396. What part of Natal do you come from, Mini?—(*Chief Mini.*) From near Maritzburg.

4397. Was this Congress representative of the Natives of Natal proper or also of Zululand?—Both Natal and Zululand.

4398. What tribe do you belong to?—The Christian people at Edendale.

4399. What race are you all?—(*Omnes.*) Zulus.

4400. Did the Congress discuss the *Native Affairs Administration Bill?*—(*Chief Mini.*) It was discussed several times.

4401. Will you give us the Congress' views with regard to the Bill?—The view of the Congress is that nothing good will arise from the Bill. The Bill takes away the rights of the people which they have enjoyed for seventy years, especially the right to acquire land where they please and the hiring of land. They

feel that the rights they have been accustomed to for such a long time are being taken away from them. The Proclamation of 1843 laid down that there should not be any discrimination and it also forbids slavery in any form. The Congress is of opinion that this Bill discriminates from the very start—it discriminates according to colour—and takes away the rights which all enlightened nations have enjoyed according to law. The Bill is quite against the spirit of the Proclamation of 1843 because there is equality for all under the Proclamation. The Congress considers that the people cannot find out where this law is driving them to. The Native people only recognize what their superiors and Chiefs tell them. When that Proclamation was issued there was peace and order in the country which has lasted for seventy years. The people regard the Proclamation as having come from the King and they trust and cling to it always. In Natal we have gone on for all these years on that principle. In 1848 another Proclamation was issued and those who were in authority in Natal at the time pointed out that the Natives were not so civilized as other nations in the British Empire. They said that what they had to do was to educate the people so that they could also be enlightened so as to follow the laws of civilization intelligently.

4402. Do you know that under this Bill the white people are treated in exactly the same way as the Natives?—There are some differences in regard to Native and European areas.

4403. Do you know that the Bill provides that there shall be certain Native areas and certain white areas and that the restrictions which apply to the purchase and hire of land in a Native area apply to the white men in a Native area?—I recognize that, but at the same time I also recognize there is a difference.

4404. The Proclamation of 1843 states "that there shall not be in the eye of the law any distinction or qualification whatever, founded on mere distinction of colour, origin or language or creed; but that the protection of the law, in letter and in substance, shall be extended impartially to all." I would like to know in what way you think that this Bill is an infringement of the Proclamation of

1843?—They have been going on for seventy years in Natal under that Proclamation and nothing wrong has happened all the time.

4405. But that is not my question?—For the last seventy years we have been under that Proclamation and nothing went wrong and we had nothing to complain of. The new Bill is contrary to the spirit of the Proclamation of 1843.

4406. I would point out to you that the restrictions which are applied to the Natives in certain areas are also applied to the white people in their areas?—There is something in the new Bill contrary to the old law.

4407. What is that "something"?—This Proclamation of 1843 came from the British Government and it allows us to do exactly as we please. It is a law of freedom. The new Bill directs that the people can only buy and hire land in certain places. One place is for Europeans and another place for Natives.

4408. But the white man is also restricted. He cannot buy land in a Native area?—You must also remember that as things are the Natives have not enough land as it is, and this law is restricting them from extending.

4409. Do you know that in this Bill certain areas are given to the Natives, and they are protected in those areas, whereas under the present law, unless they are protected, the white man can come and take even the land they already hold?—In 1864 the land in Natal was surveyed into locations and reserves for the Native people, it being recognised that the Natives must have land set apart for them. Those locations and reserves were given to them, and after that they still had the right to purchase and acquire land, and farms were sold to them by European farmers without restriction. The Natives do not complain if that door is still open to them to purchase land; they do not want to go through any other door but the door which has been opened to them for all time. They would not complain if that were still the case and if the locations could be extended—the locations given in 1864.

4410. Under the Letters Patent of the 27th April, 1864, Natives were exclusively confined to their own locations and were not allowed to go outside?—What I say is that for the last seventy years a Native has had the right to hire land from any outside location.

4411. Would you be prepared to agree that the white man should come and purchase and hire land in your locations?—That would be all right, because the European has been restricted for the last seventy years from buying land in Native locations.

4412. But is not that against the Proclamation of 1843, which laid down that the white man and the Native should have the same right. If the white man cannot go into the location that is not treating him fairly?—I do not think it would be unfair to the European, because it has been there all the time, and he has not the same claim as we have—over 70 years. There are places set aside in Natal where Natives cannot buy land, and there is no complaint about that.

4413. The Proclamation of 1843 laid down the same law for both. There are restrictions now with regard to certain areas for the Natives. What wrong can it do the Natives to give what one might say white locations? You have Native locations, so why not white locations?—We have enjoyed certain rights for the last seventy years, which the Europeans have not, and we wish to retain that right.

4414. Is there any other point you wish to bring to the notice of the Committee?—I have a lot to say in regard to Chapter I. of the Bill, but at this stage I would prefer that the Secretary to the Congress should give his evidence. (Gumede.) The first Clause of this Bill restricts transactions relating to Natives and prevents other than Natives to purchase or hire land, a thing which is unknown to us. As Chief Mini has stated, I have only to refer you to the Proclamations of 1843 and 1848, which created one law for white and black in Natal, and that was the case until Natal went into the Union.

4415. How can you say that when there are areas in which the white man cannot buy?—There never were areas where white men could buy. In her wisdom the late Queen Victoria set apart land for the people who were found in the country who were the aborigines of the country. That is British rule all over.

4416. You say that the Native must be able to buy land everywhere and the white man restricted. That is not equality?—I do not say that. The Queen in her wisdom, finding the Natives in their own country, set apart certain pieces of land for them, where they were to live with civilised people, who would come there with different ideas amongst them, so that they could do something to protect the people.

4417. Suppose Parliament now says, "We want further to protect the Natives," and lays down that in these additional areas where the Natives live they shall live there alone, and the white people cannot go there?—Under the provisions of the Bill I fail to see that, as I shall point out later on.

4418. There is no inequality. What is done for the white man is done for the Native too?—In this Bill?

4419. Yes?—That is not so.

4420. In what way?—The freedom and liberty of the Native, which he has enjoyed ever since Natal became a British Colony, is to-day being restricted. It is laid down that the Native must buy here and not buy there, and the same with the white man. It is all so confused to us. The white man makes that law, and the Native is not consulted. The white man is represented in Parliament, and his Parliament can restrict him, but Parliament is also restricting me without consulting me, and taking away my freedom and liberty—restricting me against my will. The law under the Proclamations have bound together the European and Native to live under peaceful conditions all these years.

4421. I have no objection to your stating your claim on the grounds that you have not been consulted, or that you are not represented in Parliament, but you cannot complain that we are infringing the law of 1843, because that law says, what you do to the Native you do to the white man, and we do not interefere with that law. I want you to clearly understand that we are not breaking the law of 1843?—I do say that the Proclamations of 1843 and 1848, as far as the Natives in Natal are concerned, are being infringed as I will prove later on. I would refer you to Law No. 28 of 1865 (Natal). In speaking to Chief Mini you stated that the Natives were not restricted, and that there were equal rights under the Bill before the Committee. There are European land settlements in Natal that were created for people who could not buy back their farms, and in these settlements Natives were not allowed to buy or hire land.

. . . .

We fail to see what this Bill is going to give us. A right is being taken away from us and nothing is being put in its place. As I have pointed out before much of the land proposed to be reserved is very unsuitable. Secondly, the Government or Parliament having passed this law has not provided for Natives who would refuse to accept the conditions laid down in this Bill for their occupation of farms.

4441. *Mr. Clayton.*] What Natives are you referring to?—The Natives on the farms.

4442. Those at present on private farms?—Yes.

4443. *Mr. King.*] Do you mean the squatters?—Yes. When these conditions came before them they wished to leave the farms and go to these places, but these were found unsuitable for occupation.

4444. *Sir Bisset Berry.*] Will there be many of that class?—Yes, a great number.

4445. How many?—Thousands who are living on the farms.

4446. Will you tell me why you think that the Natives would leave the farms if this Bill is passed?—Because of the conditions under this Bill, the provisions of which will compel the Natives to leave the farms.

4447. Do you mean the Bill will bring about conditions that the Natives are not accustomed to?—Before the Natives Land Act a Native could work on a farm, and he could put his children to work for the owner of the farm. A man who did not want to work could rent a hut at the rate of from £3 to £5 a year.

4448. And then he could live there with his wife and family?—Yes, and that has been the custom for years.

4449. Are there grown-up sons living with the family also?—Yes.

4450. The farmer who owned the land did not object to that?—No. Some of the farmers had grown up with the Natives and some had got old with the Natives. The Natives lived on the farms under very peaceful conditions.

4451. Did they make written agreements?—No, the agreements were verbal, and never has any breach of agreement occurred, to my memory.

4452. The Natives were allowed to live on the farms for giving their labour?—Yes.

4453. What labour did that mean?—Some of them herded cattle, and others worked on the lands, and so on.

4454. Do they work all the year round?—No, for six months at a time. If a man has three sons, one goes for six months, then the other and then the third, and the girls work for the farmers as well.

4455. What did the men do after they had completed their six months' labour?—Some of them went to Johannesburg to work.

4456. When they came back were they taken on again?—Yes.

4457. There were no restrictions?—No. They were all allowed to live together; those who wanted to work did so, and others paid rent.

4458. The Commission which went up to Zululand—the Dartnell and Saunders Commission—did they set aside a piece of land for sugar planting?—Yes.

4459. And that was to be taken from the Natives' portion of Zululand?—That was done.

4460. Who are on it now?—The sugar planters.

4461. Did they buy it?—I think they bought it from the Government under the Crown Lands system.

4462. Are there any Natives living on it?—There are some Natives living there—some of them are working.

4463. Not all of them?—No, only some, and they seem to be quite content. I never heard of any harshness being exercised by the farmers there.

4464. I understand that your principal objection to this Clause is that until this Bill came forward and before the 1913 Act was passed, you were not restricted in any way in your rights to buy land outside of your locations?—Yes.

4465. This Bill proposes to limit your rights in that respect?—Yes.

4466. And to limit you to certain areas which are stated in the Schedule?—Yes.

4467. And you think your rights should go further—that you should have an unre-

stricted right to purchase land where you desire?—Yes, that is so.

4468. You hold that the same thing does not apply to the white man who wants to go into the locations, because the Queen set aside those locations for you?—Yes, in her wisdom.

4469. Then you mean that your people have grown in numbers to such an extent that you cannot part with any of that land to the white man?—Yes, most of the locations are very much congested.

4470. And, therefore, in order to provide for your increasing numbers you want to go outside and hire or purchase land?—Yes.

4471. The substance of your complaint is that in this Bill you are restricted in that respect?—Yes.

. . . .

Chief Stephen Mini, Josiah Tshangana Gumede and Rev. Abner Mtimkulu, further examined.

4629. *Mr. Stuart.*] Have you any notes in connection with Chapter II. of the Bill?—*(Rev. Mtimkulu.)* Yes.

4630. What is your first note?—My first note is in regard to Clause Four in connection with the appointment of a Native Affairs Commission. We consider that the Native people should have a voice in the appointment of the Commissioners. The Clause says that a permanent Commission shall be constituted, consisting of the Minister, "and not less than three or more than five." This Commission being the only outlet by which the Native people can keep in touch with the Administration, and seeing that most of the Native people at the present time are not directly represented in Parliament, we consider that if the Commission were to be appointed by them, it would serve as some kind of relief. The men they appoint would be their mouthpieces, and would be able to redress any grievances. The members would be accessible to them, whereas if the Commission were appointed by the Government, it would be looked upon as all other officials and departments of the Government, when, unless one is directly prepared to prove what he has to say he would have no access at all. If the Commissioners were appointed by the people themselves, their confidence would be obtained, and their grievances would be better known by the Government.

4631. *Mr. Clayton.*] What is your idea as to what that Commission should be?—I consider that the Commission should consist of one man from each of the Provinces.

4632. *Mr. Stuart.*] Have you any comments to make on sub-section (2) of the Clause?—I consider that the appointment of permanent officials who could not be removed unless within a statutory time would immediately lead to dissatisfaction.

4633. That is inadvisable?—Yes. The position of the Commissioners should be regarded as permanent, but they should also be removable.

4634. *Chairman.*] Would you object to the permanent appointment if the appointment was not made by the Government, but in some other way?—Yes, we would object in any case if it was permanent.

4635. *Mr. Stuart.*] What are your comments on sub-sections (3) and (4)?—The questions involved there are very broad indeed, and seeing that they touch the whole of the Native people, we feel it would be unwise to suggest anything. I think the people as a whole should be consulted, through their Chiefs and other principal Natives, and then some common meeting ground would be arrived at.

4636. Supposing that in places where you have direct councils, such as in the Transkei, the Councillors were consulted generally, and that in particular areas, such as in Natal and Bechuanaland (where there are no district councils), advisory councils were appointed by the Government, which would be consulted by the Commission, do you not think that would be a possible solution?—As representing the feelings of the people the position is that this question is a very broad one. Even if they had district councils it would be better to have a general meeting of the Natives, and in that way they could be consulted.

4637. You open up the broad question of representation, but you are not discussing any particular form?—No.

4638. Under the circumstances, have you any suggestion to make as to how this Commission should be appointed?—My opinion is that the Commissioners in all the districts should be in touch with the Native

Chiefs and the principal people, so that the Government should consult all the Natives of the Province with a view to ways and means being adopted for a common meeting ground.

4639. You feel that with regard to Chapter II.—administration and legislation in Native areas—the Government must get into touch with the people?—Yes. *(Gumede.)* Our feeling is that this question is a very broad one. It is proposed, for the first time in the history of South Africa or of any other British Dominion, to separate the races, this having been agreed upon by Europeans through their representatives. We have not been consulted on a matter which touches us deeply. Therefore, in our minds, after considering the matter, we feel that if this separation must be done a Convention of the two races concerned is necessary to consider the question; two races that have lived together under different conditions for all these years. We beg to urge for this Convention of the two races to go into the whole question. Again, it is proposed to give the Commission powers and functions which are quite beyond the layman.

4640. Why?—Powers are given and work is assigned them which is more suitable to men who hold legal attainments.

4641. You think the nature of the work of the Commission would lead to the appointment of lawyers?—Judges or experts—people who have qualification in law. Again the period of appointment is another objection. The number of members is also very small to consider business that concerns about 5½ millions of people, and if the Protectorates come in as part of the Union, as was indicated in General Smuts' speech in London, I do not think that three or six men would represent 7 millions of people.

4642. The number would be considerably increased, from 3 to 5 millions, if the Protectorates were handed over to the Union?—Apart from that, the number of Commissioners is too small to represent 5½ millions of people. In view of the greatness and deepness of this matter as affecting the Native population we urge for a Convention of the two races.

. . . .

4645. *Chairman.*] How would you call this Convention together?—We would leave it in the hands of Parliament, who propose this measure.

4646. The suggestion in regard to this Convention has come from you, and I would like to know how you would propose to call the Convention together?—The Government would call it together.

4647. Would the Government have to invite the educated class or the Chiefs?—All the classes concerned.

4648. I would like you to explain the position, because there exists a difference of opinion on this point. For instance, you have your Chiefs in Natal whom you pass over and you call the educated people your masters. Would you invite a number of the Chiefs as well?—No. The members from each Province would be elected by the people to go to that Convention. If it is necessary that Chiefs should also attend, and they were elected, it would be so much the better. It could be done. Each Province should select its own representatives.

4649. *Mr. Stuart.*] You think that a reasonable basis of agreement could be arrived at?—Yes.

4650. Do you agree sufficiently with the appointment of the proposed Commission to make it worth while to give evidence in regard to sub-sections (5), (6) and (7)?—No.

4651. *Chairman.*] Do you wish to give evidence on any other point?—I would like again to refer to sub-section (3) of Clause Four, which provides that "no appointed member shall be removed from office except upon addresses from both Houses of Parliament passed in the same session and praying for his removal." Our objection is that it is made difficult to remove a member once he has been appointed. He might have been wrong in something and the Government may have found him to be wrong, yet the Government would be impotent to remove him. Parliament is represented by parties and it may happen that a certain Commissioner may belong to a particular party, and on his case coming before Parliament that party would hold he should not be removed.

4652. The Commissioners are appointed for at least five years. That is provided in sub-section (2)?—I object to that length of period.

4653. *Mr. Stuart.*] You realise that it is difficult to make appointments of this nature unless there is some guarantee of tenure?—I admit that it is difficult.

4654. *Chairman.*] You object to the appointment for a term of five years?—Yes.

4655. What period would you lay down? —There should be no time limit. As long as he behaves himself he can carry on for twenty years.

4656. You do not want Parliament to decide; you want the Government to decide? —Yes.

4657. *Mr. Collins.*] Who must decide when a Commissioner must go?—The Government— the Native Affairs Department.

4658. *Mr. Stuart.*] Have you any views to express on sub-sections (5), (6) and (7)?— Before coming to those sub-sections I would like to refer to sub-section (4), which lays down that no appointed member shall be, or be qualified to become, a member of either House of Parliament, or of a Provincial Council.

4659. Do you think it unwise?—We think that a man who takes up a position as Commissioner should be a man of great responsibilities and have the necessary qualifications for Parliamentary representation.

4660. Have you anything to say in regard to Clause Eight of the Bill?—We feel that government by proclamation as provided for in this Bill will be a great hardship to the native people, especially the native people of Natal.

4661. Why?—Because we have always been accustomed to rely on the Government and the Magistrates to interpret the law for us, and not to have an official to only proclaim those laws. Government by proclamation would tend to diminish the confidence that we hold. It is a hardship inasmuch as government by proclamation is being specially made for the native people, and it would be liable to misinterpretation. It would not be such a great hardship if we knew it came from responsible people who have studied the ins and outs of the land, and the things that should be done and things that should not be done. Again, some laws would remain with the Commissioners for some time and when they come out there would not be sufficient advertisement of the laws. They will simply take people by surprise and it would not prepare the people for what is coming. When a law comes in at the present time we have a chance of discussing it and, as in the present case, make our representations before a Select Committee, and in that way it is some source of satisfaction. Government by proclamation divides us altogether—it puts us aside from the Government; it creates a government within a government, and in that way we are not able to reach headquarters. It is suggested that we shall be a separate nation in the same Empire in that we shall have our laws laid down by proclamation.

4662. You agree that it is laid down in the Act that every proclamation, except in cases of urgency, should be published for some period so that the people should be made aware of the fact and be in a position to make any protests. Do you not think that would meet the case to a considerable extent?—At the present time there is no knowing. If an urgent need should arise we are simply told that such and such a thing would be done on such and such a day. In the past that has been done without any hardship. If we are set aside, our connection with authority is cut away altogether—we have no means of bringing our grievances to notice. We are separate from the Government.

4663. *The Minister of Education.*] The Commission which it is proposed to appoint will be directed under the Government. What you have in mind is that it separates you from Parliament?—Yes, we feel we are separated from Parliament, and we would like still to have some connection. We view with concern the coming generation of native people—the cutting away of the only connection we have.

4664. *Mr. Stuart.*] Legislation by Holland for you?—It should not be cut away; it should continue.

4665. *The Minister of Education.*] Do you not think that a Commission, which would consult the Natives direct and be in touch with them, will know the wants of the Natives better than Holland, in which the Natives are not represented?—I do not think so. As a rule Native people do not give their minds to Magistrates and officials. They would accept a certain thing and say: "It is alright," whereas, in fact, they mean quite just the opposite. You must remember that the Natives will always be in South Africa, and you now propose to cut away our only connection with Parliament.

4666. *Chairman.*] Surely this body consisting of five men, whose sole object will be to look after Native affairs, would bring you more into touch with the Government than anything you have had before. Is not that so?—According to this Bill it would not be so because the members of the Commission are not to be elected by the Native people. It is very hard on the Natives to go and see a Commissioner or a Magistrate who knows nothing of their grievances. We consider that the Natives would have no access to the Commission.

4667. *Mr. Clayton.*] Supposing you had advisory boards elected by the Natives themselves who would be in touch with the Commission, would not that bring you closer to the Government?—No, not if the door is to be closed for all time to the Native people in regard to access to Parliament, as this Bill suggests. We consider that an agreement could be arrived at by a responsible party of people attending such a Convention such as we have urged.

4668. *Chairman.*] In regard to your statement that "The door is to be closed for all time," I would call your attention to subsection (7) of Clause Eight, which reads "Nothing in this section contained shall be construed as limiting the power of Parliament to make laws in respect of any part of the Union which is within a Native Area." All proper nations are brought under review by Parliament?—It comes to what the Rev. Mtimkulu has said. Government by proclamation is unknown in the whole world. In the Transkei the people are represented in Parliament; other Native people are not represented in Parliament. In regard to people who are represented in Parliament, if there is any proclamation which is contrary to their wishes they have their safeguard and remedy to get it removed. In our case there is no such safeguard. Government by proclamation under British rule was condemned long years ago. In view of that we cannot accept it. It simply amounts to this: that the door is being removed for all time against the black man being represented in Parliament. That being the case and it being proposed to separate the two races, why not have a Convention of these two races to consider the question of separation and come to an agreement in regard thereto. We cannot be expected to be competent enough to make suggestions in this connection, but suggestions from the people could be considered.

DOCUMENT 29. "To the Native Conference at Queenstown." Address by Meshach Pelem, President, Bantu Union, February 26, 1919 [Extracts] (Printed, 8 pages)

The Basis of the Meeting

Now, to come to the subject that has brought us together, it is necessary that I should put you in the way of understanding the basis upon which our meeting is founded. You will remember that four years ago the whole world was placed under a fearful and ominous shadow by the outbreak of a terribly devastating war, the like of which has never been experienced before. And when the warring nations felt that they should come to a settlement of their differences after much bloodshed, they proclaimed an armistice in order to the discussion of definite peace terms. The Government then informed our chiefs, headmen and people, that the war was ending, and of the hope that peace would be resumed. This great and welcome news came upon us unexpectedly, like a thief in the night, as we in South Africa were quite unprepared for the announcement. We had the misfortune to be surprised by this war while we were unprepared for such an emergency. Both our representative Associations, the S.A. Native Congress and the Mbumba, existed only in name, being practically lifeless, but in the good providence of God another effort taking its rise in the Transkei came into being. I am glad to say that the Native Convention of the Transkei, having heard the news of peace, without delay proceeded to convene at Toleni, under the Chairmanship of the Rev. Jonathan Mazwi, on the 16th December, 1918, and the issue of their dis-

cussions there are the present meetings at Queenstown.

The first meeting was held here last month (22nd January, 1919) and the result of that Convention was the formation of the present Bantu Unie.

The Bantu Unie

The poet was right in saying "God moves in a mysterious way His wonders to perform." Who could have foretold at the beginning of this great war what the issue would be to mankind and the world. Those who take a keen interest in the solution of world problems, will have a vivid recollection of the incidents which led up to this terrible struggle. Among the old-standing animosities that precipitated the war between France and Germany in 1871, the German Empire started a song of victory, and all the other great Powers joined in the refrain, which was the "Survival of the Fittest." All the little nations and big danced to the tune and desperately armed themselves for the coming orgie. Wicked eyes peeped out from behind bristling bayonets, the whole civilised world was converted into one huge arsenal, and children were trained to play with fireworks and explosives. All the diplomatic skill of men like Edward the Peace-Maker, the late Czar of Russia, W. T. Stead, and a host of other humanitarians, failed to effect a reduction of armaments, and international pourparlers leading up to the famous Peace Conferences at the Hague ended in complete fiasco. I am sorry to say, gentlemen, that amid the turmoils and upheavals which unsettled the times, British statesmanship, which had always stood for the protection of native rights on principle as a long settled policy of the British people, lost its balance, suffered an eclipse, and surrendered their obligations and our rights accordingly to the Afrikander Party represented by Generals Botha and Smuts. By this ignominious surrender they imposed a terrific strain upon our loyalty, they have shaken the confidence of a people who have learned to look to the British Sovereign for impartial justice, have aimed a mortal blow at British institutions which have stood the test of centuries, and have taught the people of this country the new doctrine unparalleled in English Constitutionalism that "white" is supremacy and "black" is slavery. It would be impossible to promulgate a more monstrous doctrine than that which has as its war cry, "Africa a White Man's Country." with the eventual deprivation of its black inhabitants of every shred of citizen rights, land rights, and other liberties and privileges.

The Survival of the Fittest

When things reached this climax it is evident that God withdrew, and said to the sons and daughters of men—sing your war songs, sharpen your swords, on with the dance, but suddenly you shall sing another song. Who will deny the truth of this? To-day we are singing another song, and the demons of Racialism find that the sword, or in other words, brute force, offers no true solution of the problem of the social and international relationships of the nations of the world. The doctrine of the survival of the fittest (an infidel doctrine, which has no faith in the over-lordship of a Sovereign Ruler of the universe), will find fewer advocates to-day than it did yesterday. The great song to-day is the Peace song at Paris, in which all the kindred nations are rejoicing—"Peace and goodwill toward men." Armaments must be limited, arsenals demolished, and armies reduced. We must beat our swords into ploughshares, and our spears into pruning-hooks. All the Great Powers must come together to lay broad and deep foundations for a lasting peace, and the idea so fondly cherished by these fully armed race-survivalists, that the millions of the weaker races, and only weak perhaps because they have no arsenals, should be left exposed to the tender mercies of the few swashbucklers like our statesman soldier, Smuts, for example, to play with, is utterly condemned except in the imaginings of our Union men of affairs, as an evil dream of the past. We should all be grateful to God that in His merciful Providence, He should have set it in the hearts of nations to realise, that the time has come when all the races of the earth must be freed from the tyranny of the few, and be granted equal rights and liberties in all things without distinction of race, colour, or previous condition. To-day the nations are all provisionally agreed that equal justice must be done to all men without distinction, in order to remove the causes of war, and it is on these grounds that you and I are assembled here to-day.

Causes of Race Division

We wish to take counsel together upon those matters which are embittering our relations, our position in the land of our forefathers, and to find out how far these provisional agreements made in Europe are likely to affect our destiny for better for worse in South Africa. The presence of our chiefs, ministers and delegates, from all parts of the Union, is a sign of the general feeling that has so profoundly disturbed your minds. As your fellow-countryman, I am in perfect sympathy with your motives, aspirations, and desires, as well as your grievances, and tribulations, because your pains, sorrows, tears and anxieties, are parts of my own experiences, and moreover the heroic endurances and sacrifices of this war must have taught you that there is nothing more honourable than that a man or woman should lose even life itself for the love of country, the honour of their people, and the graves where the ashes of their forefathers rest. If the celebrations of peace, and all the rejoicings connected therewith, cannot stir up your hearts, and fire your blood to rise up and strive for our rights, and interests, which is our lawful and legitimate duty; if we neglect or trample underfoot the grand opportunity presented by this war, after all the meritorious services you have performed, and which were acknowledged and appreciated by the British people in the hour of their extremity; if we cannot accept the utterances of statesmen, and national leaders, who speak for England, her allies and America, who said that their reasons for entering the war was to fight for the liberties of the weaker peoples like ourselves; then you will deserve to carry no weight in the counsels of the civilised world, and to go down to your graves for ever disgraced, "unwept, unhonoured and unsung." The American Republic, by the mouth of its great President, frankly declared, that it fought for the regeneration of the world, and its reconstruction upon an entirely new basis, after the principles which all faithful Christians realise are enunciated by the Lord Jesus Christ.

The Mind of the People

You have been summoned, chiefs and fellow-countrymen, to discuss and ascertain the mind of the people, in relation to those supreme interests, which are agitating men's minds at the present time. Even as we speak, a memorial setting forth the grievances of the coloured people by the African Political Organisation is now crossing the ocean on its way to Lord Milner, the Secretary of State for the Colonies. Another memorial from the Native National Congress of the Transvaal has been accepted by His Excellency the Governor-General for transmission to His Majesty the King. The Nationalist Republicans among the whites who are agitating for the dissolution of the Union, a Union which was aimed against the black man, are also proceeding across the water to lay their complaints before the Peace Conference. We also feel that the time is propitious for us to move in unison, and proceed to relate our cause to our sympathetic sovereign, King George V. I know, and doubtless you also are aware, that there are some among us who are opposed to this step. They contend that we have Messrs. Botha and Smuts as our representatives, and I should like to ask such, if they really understand that Botha and Smuts represent a Union from which we are excluded. If therefore they are our representatives, by whom is the Union represented? Have they had a revelation of the inner secrets and purposes governing the motives of these men, and are they aware that those motives impelled them to protest at the peace conference at Vereeniging that they would under no circumstances accept the British sovereignty unless it was clearly demonstrated that there would be no equal rights extended to black men in the surrendered republics? Were they present at the conferences at Bloemfontein and Durban, which settled the question of Union, when their friends Botha and Smuts, with ruthless violence of speech and utterance, opposed the very thought of granting civil rights to natives,

until the atmosphere of the Convention building was surcharged with vituperative invective hurled against us as a people, insomuch that the Cape members were stunned, or hypnotised, into insensibility of their first duty, which was at all costs to maintain the principles of the British Constitution unblemished and undefiled in spite of the hurricane of scurrilous abuse which sought to pervert and unbalance their reason. . . . .

. . . .

Chiefs, fellow countrymen and fellow-delegates, I think that I have to the best of my abilities endeavoured to demonstrate to you, that from the day the terms of peace between Great Britain and the South African Republics were signed at Pretoria, and the subsequent inauguration of the Union of South Africa, the British policy and principles of Government, which have always commanded the respect of the world, are, so far as the Bantu are concerned, being gradually eliminated, replaced, and superseded, by the introduction and resuscitation of the old, crude, savage ideas and methods of the defunct Republics of the Transvaal and Free State. Again, you will observe that Great Britain which once stood as liberator of the oppressed peoples; Great Britain which always threw her influence and often her sword into the scale of those who struggle for freedom; Great Britain who has always encouraged and subsidised small and weak nations during periods of despondency and destitution; and has therefore been known throughout the civilised world as the bulwark, guardian and protector of human rights everywhere on the broad universe, has been compelled by a new school of political advisers in this country, and in England, to uphold a wicked policy of selfish exclusiveness and greed, which aims at the exploitation of the natives of Africa for profit. With stoical indifference and cynical disregard of the sacred rights of millions of His Majesty's subjects, the safeguards set up for their security by constitutional mandates of the past, and in direct violation and contravention of the solemn treaties, obligations, agreements, and assurances, which have been made from time to time with our chiefs and people, British Ministers have been found or forced to become traitors to the ancient constitution of England, and have sold the Bantu under a fraudulent Union. We are not without hope that these conditions will be changed, for if British Ministers who are charged with the duty of advising His Majesty on questions affecting our welfare, can be allowed so lightly to bargain and trade with the sacred rights of millions, then it would seem that a question of paramount and constitutional importance, to the Empire is raised, which can only be dealt with satisfactorily by the Imperial Government.

This new school of advisers, seem to think that the power, wealth, and glory, of the British nation has been founded like their own crude, primitive, and barbarous systems, upon the rapacity and plunder of the weaker, and more ignorant races of this Continent; whereas the British power is founded upon industry, commerce, and just dealing with the subject races, as a principle of policy and humanity. The inspiration that caused us as natives to follow the flag to France, is finely set forth in the words of Albert J. Beveridge in a speech which I am sure you will endorse, delivered at a banquet of the Union League Club at Philadelphia on 15th February, 1899, because it means to us larger liberty, nobler opportunity, and greater happiness, besides all other blessings to which we are inheritors under the British Empire.

"What is England's glory? England's immortal glory is not Agincourt or Waterloo. It is not her merchandise or commerce. It is Australia, New Zealand, and Africa reclaimed. It is India redeemed. It is Egypt, mummy of nations, touched into modern life. England's imperishable renown is in English science, throttling the plague in Calcutta, English law administering order in Bombay, English energy planting an industrial civilisation from Cairo to the Cape, and English discipline creating soldiers, men, and finally citizens, perhaps, even out of the fellaheen of the dead land of the Pharaohs."

In conclusion, although I am not a prophet, I will venture to say that as long as the foundations of Union are based upon oppression and injustice, they shall never unify, but on the contrary, evil and division shall reign, because it does not rest upon that righteousness which exalteth nations. In spite of all our difficulties the time is not far distant, when the poetic vision shall be realised which is set forth in these lines:—

"O Thou on Whom the islands wait,
　And nations far away,
Who midst the Gentiles shall be great,
　Whom all men must obey.

"Behold the lands where Satan reigns
　Upon his cruel throne,
That sit in darkness and in chains,
　And bow to wood and stone.

"Thine ancient heritage behold,
　Thy faithful Abraham's seed,
And lead them to the holy fold
　Wherein the ransomed feed.

Far from the West bid hatred flee,
　And unbelief and pride,
How long shall those that love not Thee
　Thy seamless robe divide?

"How long shalt Thou forget the East,
　Where first Thy truth was spread,
Where Bishops first Thy Name confessed,
　And holy martyrs bled?

"Lead sinners from the paths of sin,
　Let scorners hear Thy voice;
And let all heretics come in,
　And make Thy Church rejoice.

To God, the Mighty and the Just,
　All praise and glory be;
To Him in Whom the isles shall trust,
　And Holy Ghost, to Thee Amen."

DOCUMENT 30. Address on disturbances in Bloemfontein location, by I.J. Nthatisi, March 4, 1919 (Published in *The Friend*)

At the request of the leaders of the location, the Resident Magistrate, Mr. J. A. Ashburnham, and the Mayor of Bloemfontein, Mr. D. A. Thomson, motored out to Waalhoek Location yesterday afternoon to address the natives of the location on the recent disturbances. About 1,000 natives gathered near Fichardt Siding where a trolley formed the impromptu platform, from which the addresses were delivered. I. J. Nthatisi read an address to the Resident Magistrate and the Mayor, which, after expressing their loyalty and thanks for the visit of the recipients, proceeded as follows:—

"It is not pleasant to recall the circumstances which have necessitated your visit to us this day, inasmuch as they eclipse the good reputation which the residents of this place have always borne. However, we are confident, sirs, that your presence amongst our people will result in restoring peace and harmony, which have been suddenly and temporarily disturbed.

"As it is of absolute importance, sirs, that peace and order should be restored and be made permanent, we beg to point out in a most respectful manner and with all due submissiveness, that such permanence can only be maintained when the internal grievances of the people have been fully disclosed to you in your capacity—one as a representative of the Government in the Native Affairs Department, and the other as Mayor of the town—positions which place you under a common obligation to protect the interests of the native people within the limits of your jurisdiction. These grievances must not only be ventilated by the people on the one hand, but they must also be redressed by the governing authorities on the other hand.

"We would, therefore, humbly request that an opportunity be granted to lay before you all matters which disturb the peace of the locations, with a view to adopting a much more satisfactory mode of governing the people.

"With regard to the burning question of the increase of wages, we beg to thank you from the bottom of your hearts, your Worship the Resident Magistrate, for the kind words you addressed to our people from the bench on Monday, the 3rd instant. It was a relief to us to learn that there is no law to prevent agitation for increase of wages, provided it is done in a lawful manner. This assurance has given us strength against intimidation, and we therefore wish to avail ourselves of the opportunity we have to lay before you and before his Worship the Mayor that this agitation for an increase of wages is not a matter that has

been thought of on the spur of the moment, or brought into the minds of the people by outside influence. It is a movement which is spontaneous among the people, only it has been lying dormant in their minds on account of their obedience to the order of General Botha that people should refrain from making any agitations during hostilities; and by their obedience to this order they have materially helped to accelerate the termination of the war; and now that the war is over they feel it is time that they should raise the question.

The Minimum Wage Demand

"People are sincere in their demand for a minimum wage of 4s. 6d. a day, and to say it is absurdly high is to show glaring ignorance of the conditions under which our poor people live ever since the coming into force of the Native Lands Act which has recently been declared by Mr. Neser, M.L.A., that its results have been cruel. On top of these cruel results there has come the high cost of living occasioned by the war; and the people who feel the pinch came to the conclusion to ask the masters to raise them from the miserable position by granting them this minimum wage of 4s. 6d. a day. We therefore humbly beg to request you, sir, in your capacity as Mayor of Bloemfontein, to use all your influence over the Town Council and the other bodies employing native labour in town to reconsider your decision with regard to this matter, and kindly allow yourselves, as good and sympathetic masters, to come to the rescue of your poor but honest and humble servants. The cry of the people is, 'We are perishing, masters; please make the rope a little longer so as to be within our reach and then pull us up.'

"We equally apply to you, sir, in your capacity as Resident Magistrate, to communicate this request to the Government on behalf of the men employed on the railway and other Government institutions, using all your influence over them to secure relief for these poor people. While we are on this point it is only fair to express our gratitude to those firms in town which have acceded to the request of their servants and are already paying them the 4s. 6d. a day. We can assure them they will never be poorer for that; by their kind act they have made themselves the friends of the needy.

The Friday Disturbance

"We feel it our duty to express the most profound regret that, owing to the attitude of the authorities in handling the incident of Friday, a very unusual disturbance took place in the locations. Whatever happened that day was due wholly and principally to the most unfortunate oversight on the part of the police, which made them take the role of alarmists in making the whole town believe that a most depressing cloud was hanging over Bloemfontein, which fact rendered the irresponsible and unruly class of our people practically unmanageable. We would urge that in future immediately after the arrest of one of the leaders the police should see their way to get into contact with the leaders to warn them of what has taken place, in order to save a calamity; and that before any drastic steps are taken the opinion of the natives should be consulted.

"However, in spite of this unfortunate oversight, sirs, we cannot allow this opportunity to pass without expressing our appreciation of the able manner in which the police handled a most delicate situation, which passed off without loss of life. We particularly wish to mention the name of Lieut. Raftery, who, by a rare combination of patience, tact and presence of mind, averted a catastrophe on Sunday afternoon. The work he did at that critical moment deserves recognition."

DOCUMENT 31. "Pass Law Resisters, Native Case Stated." Report on interview with I. Bud Mbelle, J.W. Dunjwa, and P.J. Motsoakae of the South African Native National Congress, April 1, 1919 (Published in *The Star*)

Three natives, who, to a great extent must be regarded as responsible for the present local movement among their compatriots in town and on the Reef called at "The Star" this forenoon with the object of submitting their case to the public. They were Horatio L. Bud Mbelle, a Fingo, who had been educated at Lovedale, and who came to the Transvaal in 1912; J. W. Dunjwa, a schoolmaster, with nine years' residence in Johannesburg, and P. J. Motsoakae, a Baralong, from the Free State. They stated that their object in initiating passive resistance was not to challenge the Government in any way. There was no disloyalty on their part, and they owed absolute allegiance to the King and the British Constitution.

Asked why they had resolved on passive resistance, Mbelle said they had tried to get redress through making representations from time to time for the alleviation of the grievous difficulties under which the natives in the Transvaal laboured, but all their efforts had been without avail. Asked what their principal grievances were, the deputation stated that apart from many minor difficulties connected with the administration of the pass law in the Transvaal, their grievances could be grouped under two heads:

1.–The denial of the rights of citizenship.

2.–The denial, through the operation of the colour bar, of the rights of ordinary human beings.

In the course of general discussion, the natives said that, for instance, a native in the Transkei led an honourable life, he respected his Magistrate, and in turn was respected by him and by every white citizen with whom he came in contact. Although born in South Africa, the same native on entering the Transvaal had to report to the Pass Office, had in the generality of cases to wait hours upon hours in the glaring sun before he was received by an official, and when he had gained admission to the office, was not received with anything approaching courtesy.

Asked what their programme was, they said they would insist on order being maintained by their people. They had formed a group of special constables to collect sticks, and every weapon which any of the natives may be possessed of, and from every platform the natives would be told that there were to be no shouts or threats or anything that would incite public feeling. In case of arrest, the natives were told that they must submit quietly, and must go to gaol. No picketting had been authorised, and the natives had simply been invited to stop work.

Yesterday a sack full of passes and exemption papers which were collected as the result of the meeting on Sunday afternoon were taken to the Pass Office, and in handing them over the officials were told that the natives had resolved to resist the Pass Law. "We hold", said Mbelle, "that the Pass Law is nothing more or less than a system of slavery." He had, he said, always been taught in his boyhood days that the British Government was the most liberal and most freedom-loving of all Governments, and he had seen it in the days of Queen Victoria and King Edward, but those days seemed to have finished and the fathers of Joseph are dead. Last night a native at Jeppes, Mbelle added, was set upon by three Europeans and very seriously injured. The natives would do nothing to molest any white person, and they asked in return that the white people would not interfere with them.

Questioned as to the extent to which they propose to carry the movement, the deputation said they simply invited all natives, whether working in stores or in houses to stop work, and invitations were also being sent to the natives working on the mines.

DOCUMENT 32. "Presidential Address" by S.M. Makgatho, South African Native National Congress, May 6, 1919 (Printed, 9 pages)

CHIEFS, LADIES AND GENTLEMEN,

I am glad to welcome you to this first Annual Conference of our Congress ever held in the dear old Cape Colony. As Mr. Pelem will remember, this is not the very first occasion on which our Congress was held on Cape soil, for, in 1914, I met him at the Kimberley Congress in Griqualand West; but this is really the first time that the South African Native National Congress ever assembled in what is known as the Colony proper; and we are looking forward to that far-famed hospitality for which the Komani River is noted.

Chiefs, ladies and gentlemen, many changes have taken place since we last met at Bethlehem. The Native Lands Act still operates as mercilessly in different parts of the Union, and as a result many native families are still working for white farmers only for their food. It will be remembered that, after the representations of this Congress and the pleadings of our Missionary and other friends, the Government has consented to postpone for a year enacting the Native Affairs Administration Bill, which was nothing but the confirmation and perpetuation of the harsh provisions of the Native Lands Act and all its sorrows. Another Bill has likewise been postponed: that is

The Native Urban Areas Bill

That it had any good points was a matter of opinion. For instance, it says: No white man, under pain of £100 fine or six months' imprisonment, shall rent or sell a house to a Native in any town or village in the Union, unless that Native be a registered voter. This means that only a few Natives will retain the right to acquire town property in the Cape Province; and none at all in the other three provinces. How such a provision can be acceptable to us, only the Government knows. It adds that men and women should not get work unless they carry passes, and pay 1/- a month for them. Such a provision will introduce, into the Cape, new difficulties hitherto unknown outside the Free State, and it is a proposition our people can NEVER accept. When the Bill came out, I was assured in the Transvaal that our people there would forestall it by organising a movement against the present male pass laws before their extension to our women. The passive resistance against male passes, which began in Johannesburg on March 30th, and which I shall refer to presently, is now history in the Transvaal. There have been serious strikes and

Labour Troubles Among Europeans

in South Africa. In every instance where well paid white men, getting as much as £1 a day or more, struck for higher pay, they got it; but our first strike for 6d. a day over 2/- and 2/6 was met on the part of the Government by violence, arrests, heavy fines and imprisonment.

In response to a long telegram from our Secretary and other representations to the Prime Minister and to the Minister of Justice, some of the sentences were vetoed by the Government.

We asked for a reason of

This Striking Difference
Of Treatment

between white and black strikers; we were told that colour had nothing to do with it; that the only difference is this: while the Native holds a service pass, contracting him to his employer for several months, his strike amounts to a criminal offence. The white man, on the other hand, can strike at any time because he has no pass, but a Native worker going on strike commits a breach of contract—his service pass.

Thereupon, at Bloemfontein, last July, the Johannesburg branch of the Transvaal Native Congress brought to the Executive Committee a resolution demanding

The Abolition of the Pass Law,

so that Natives must work unshackled by contract passes. The resolution was duly sent to the Government, and the matter was discussed at various interviews between the Transvaal Congress leaders and the Government officers, and also with the Prime Minister and other Ministers at different times; the reply in each instance being that the matter will be attended to. Eventually, in March of this year, the Johannesburg Branch, followed by the Benoni and other Witwatersrand Branches, decided to throw away their passes and secure the Government's attention to our grievances by courting arrest. Thousands of men and women have been arrested and sentenced to fines and various terms of imprisonment with hard labour, and, refusing to pay fines, they nearly all elected to go to gaol. They were driven like cattle, trampled by mounted policemen under their horses' hoofs, shot at by white volunteers, and some men and women are in their graves as a result of their refusal to buy any more passes.

The principle involved has wide ramifications from both points of view. The authorities insist that they cannot abolish the passes, which are

A Great Help to the Natives,

as they serve to identify dead ones, and stop living ones from committing crimes. But, Chiefs, ladies and gentlemen, you will understand how illogical is this allegation when I say there were no passes in Johannesburg before 1893, and there was less crime proportionately in those days; but since the multiplication of passes Johannesburg has been known as the University of Crime. Again, like the Cape Natives, who carry no passes, white men also die in Johannesburg, and it has never been suggested that they, too, should carry identification passes.

What is so difficult for us Natives to understand is that a form of help should be forced upon us against our wish, that we should be fined, imprisoned, and ridden to death by mounted policemen, with our women also under the horses' hoofs, and shot at simply because we say we are not in need of the help that is offered. What kind of protection is so compulsory? While our people were shot at and clubbed by civilian whites, and our women-folk ridden down by the mounted police of Johannesburg, there was, at the same time, a strike of well paid white men in the same city, agitating for

More Pay and Less Work.

Not content with doing that, they forcibly seized the local Government property, and practically ejected the constituted authority. Nobody shot at them. Their wives were not ridden down or beaten with sticks. The real reason for this insistent enforcement of the pass law is kept in the background. No mention is made of the amount of revenue raised by the Government from our people by means of this badge of slavery. The Government retains a share of the spoil. The Transvaal Provincial Council alone gets £340,000 annually, from the scant earnings of our poorly-paid people, to build and maintain schools for white children while our educational needs remain unattended. Thousands of Natives are suffering imprisonment at the present time, and, in spite of the law, many thousands since last month are courting arrest by working without any passes. And it is for you to call on the Government to

Abolish the Transvaal and Free State Passes,

and let us live peacefully as our kinsmen in the Cape Province and elsewhere. That will dispose of the Native Affairs and Urban Bills postponed till 12 months after peace.

Now, ladies and gentlemen, I am told that there is a difference of opinion as to the wisdom of sending

A Deputation to England.

I cannot understand how anyone could call it a crime to send a delegation to the headquarters of the Empire. What sort of a King have we that we should never go to see him. Have we got the Republic already that we should not go to the seat of the Empire? Our Vice-President, Mr. Sol Plaatje, returned from England two years ago with an illuminated framed address presented to him by certain Englishmen. One of the Englishmen who signed this address was Sir Richard Winfrey, Secretary for Agriculture in Mr. Lloyd George's Ministry, and it contained the following passage:

"At the close of the war we shall do all in our power to help you to regain that justice and freedom to which, as loyal British subjects, your people are justly entitled."

Only commonsense should guide us to send him back, now that the war is over, to ask these gentlemen to redeem their promise. Since the cessation of the Great War our Vice-President has received letters and one cable urging him to come, and it seems to me a pity we did not arrange a little earlier for this deputation. At the December Special Congress he was elected with myself and seven others to carry our grievances to the British public. Two of the delegates have already left, and as funds are forthcoming others will follow shortly; and I ask everyone, on returning home, to urge his friends to contribute

liberally towards the deputation fund so that their families may not starve.

To-day we are informed that we are represented at the Peace Conference by

Generals Smuts and Botha.

Did any of the two Generals ever inform any Native that they were going to represent him? I read that General Botha on leaving Capetown in a Japanese ship told some Europeans that he was going to represent the two great races. So, where do we come in?

President Wilson before leaving America for the Peace Conference duly consulted the American Negroes. He took with him a Negro adviser, and the Negroes also sent their own representatives. The Indian Government came over with their Indian advisers; and what do our two Generals know about the abomination of the Pass Laws or the atrocities of the Native Lands Act, enacted by them? What do they know about our starving widows and dependants whose bread-winners fell during the Great War in German West and East Africa, on the Ocean, in France, and other battle fronts?

Chiefs, ladies and gentlemen, if we send no representatives to the seat of the Empire now our families will only have ourselves to thank; so let us do our best at this moment, so that when the hard time comes and the threatened class laws are enacted, posterity may not charge us with inattention.

Our people in the Free State have also had their chapter of misfortunes. Like us in the Transvaal, their troubles are two-fold—the need for a living wage and the infernal "pass." All this on top of the mischief of the Natives Land Act, which, in the Free State, allows the buying of land from Natives by Europeans, while it strictly prohibits any purchase or lease of land by a Native. Even sales between Native and Native are strictly forbidden.

I must apologize to the Free State delegates for my inability to visit them during this time of trouble. I hope they will understand when I say that in recent months these manifold troubles have increased my work in Pretoria. I have been in constant attendance at Union Buildings and other offices, where I have had numerous conferences with Heads of

Departments, and at various times with General Botha, before he left, and with other Ministers, such as Mr. Malan, Mr. De Wet and Mr. Burton on various questions more or less serious.

Chiefs, ladies and gentlemen, when we met

At Bethlehem Last Year

the Free State Natives were very restless because of the easy manner in which Natives were shot by farmers, without any protection from the Courts, as the juries could always be relied upon to discharge every white man who shot one Native or a Native couple.

When the Bethlehem Congress rose, four fresh shooting outrages were again reported in rapid succession. It was difficult for me to return to the Free State at the time, but I sent Mr. Sol Plaatje, and, with the able help of Mr. Fenyang, our good President of the O.F.S. Native Congress, he managed to get at the Boers in his own way each time the Courts failed us. The result is that there is apparently a stoppage of these outrages in the Free State—no shooting has been reported in the Free State since eight months ago, when he settled with the last Boer.

It is to be regretted that there is at this moment

A Split in The Natal Congress,

where the heads don't seem to pull together. Perhaps you can advise them on how to heal their harmful differences. At a time like this, when we are face to face with some of the worst upheavals that ever overtook our people, it is imperative that we should stand together.

It would seem that the easy life under the the more sympathetic administration of the Cape has had the effect of sending some of our Colonial people to sleep. It seems to me that, moving about as they do, like white men, without any passes, they fail to appreciate the difficulties under which the Natives are groaning in the Transvaal, in Orange Free State and in Natal, so that we have received more help from Europeans than from the Natives of the Cape who enjoy the franchise. This is not as it should be, and

The Cape Natives

ought to understand that the dictates of humanity should impel them to show a bit of fellow feeling for their own kith and kin. We are their flesh and blood, and if they show no concern for our suffering their day of reckoning will follow as a matter of course. We ask for no special favours from the Government. This is the land of our fathers, and, in it, we wish to be treated at least as well as foreigners and with the same consideration extended to foreigners, including foreigners of enemy origin.

It is my pleasant duty to express the thanks of our people to the small band of Englishmen in and out of Parliament, together with our friends and sympathisers of the Missionary Associations who have stood by us throughout the dark days under the pitiless yoke of the

Natives Land Act,

and also during the present "no-pass" agitation. It is for us to see that their confidence in us is not misplaced.

Ladies and gentlemen, I bid you welcome to this Eighth Annual Conference of the South African Native National Congress, and I hope that the session will be a useful one.

DOCUMENTS 33a-33c. Minutes of Evidence, Select Committee on Native Affairs, June 1920

DOCUMENT 33a. Testimony of J. Tengo Jabavu, before the Select Committee on Native Affairs, June 15, 1920 (Published in *Minutes of Evidence, Select Committee on Native Affairs*)

77. *Chairman.*] Have you read the *Native Affairs Bill* which is now before Parliament?— Yes.

78. What remarks have you to offer in connection with the provisions of the Bill?—I would first like to refer to the Commission. I have been translating your speech in the House top to bottom and I can quite follow what your views are for the establishment of confidence between the natives and whites of

this country. To begin with, I think that confidence should be established in connection with the Commission, and that depends upon its personnel, if it is to be of any help both to the Government and the natives. Of course, you must have Europeans on the Commission, but there should also be a member or two of the native races in order to ensure that the whole thing, from top to bottom, is a native affair and a native arrangement to meet the views and wishes of the natives. I find in connection with church matters, which I am interested in, where the church keeps natives out of positions and committees and so on, we have trouble where we least expect it and I find that this is always due to the fact that the native side of the question has probably not been studied by those from outside and members of that sort would be a help to the Commission to see the natives from the inside and would give satisfaction. Those are my remarks on the Commission itself. Its appointment with me is a simple matter—leave it to the Prime Minister and his colleagues, because he knows what is best to carry out his ideas and even in that respect I would not interfere with the appointment by making any recommendation as to how the members should be elected. Start it going until we have had some experience.

79. So you think that natives should be members of the Commission?—Two would be better than one. Two would be necessary to correct each other's ideas. One member alone would have to bear a good deal of responsibility for any mistakes and two members could better share the responsibility.

80. You are not afraid that the appointment of one or two natives on the Commission would have the effect of rousing jealousy among the various native tribes of South Africa?—I do not know that in practice it would mean much—it is only sentiment.

81. Would a Zulu member of a Commission carry any weight with natives of the Transkei?—Yes, if he was a generally recognised man, if the people knew who he was, that he was capable, suitable in regard to character and also in regard to ability. I suppose that is the rule followed in regard to

other matters with the Government in the Union.

82. We have a South Africa still divided by very distinct racial differences in various native races and do not you think that the selection of one or two of these races for representation on the committee will tend to weaken the Commission rather than strengthen it, as other sections of the native population will consider that they are not represented. If white men who know them and sympathise with them and who are impartial are on the Commission, they would not mind that but if natives belonging to their particular races were not appointed they would have no confidence at all in the committee. Is there not a danger of that?—We always find that as long as there is a native on any committee they are satisfied and where such is not the case you will find trouble.

83. So you have not this fear?—Not the slightest. I think it will strengthen your Commission. Whereas otherwise the agitator will point out and say, "Where is your mandate," and that weakens the whole idea.

84. Are you in favour of these local councils?—Absolutely, because they will help to improve the conditions of the natives, because they will be managing their own affairs. I am not quite certain as to what size you are going to make the districts.

85. We will have to deal with each case on its merits, and I think it will mean in many cases a good deal of education among the natives themselves before they will accept this local council government?—I am afraid there you are going to make the matter a dead letter because they are very conservative and even the existing councils had to be forced upon them.

86. You think these local councils must be imposed in some places?—Yes, it was done in regard to Glen Grey district, it had to be forced upon them. If you leave it to them it will be a dead letter.

87. As the natives themselves will not do it?—They are divided and the backward element will be strengthened.

88. The conservative element amongst the natives I take it is that which will be influenced by the chiefs?—Yes, they think they are

going to lose power, and I know that they have that fear. It was always the fear from the beginning that certain powers would be taken away from them.

89. We have taken some evidence as to whether the councils should be nominated by the Government, after consultation with the area concerned, or elected by the area concerned?—I would like to know how big the councils would be. I come from King William's Town, which is a very largely populated district. If you are going to have only one council of nine members for the entire district the effect will not be felt. You have 100,000 natives in one division.

90. The idea is to have workable areas where a council can supervise matters and carry out local government properly. The view has been put to me that in these very large areas the councils are not so useful. It must be a smaller and more workable area?—Yes, and I may say that in this connection my views are represented in the report of the Commision appointed by the Cape Government in 1910.

91. What were your views?—I advocated smaller districts. In King William's Town they carved out three areas. I expressed the view in favour of the smaller areas and they argued the matter very closely, and were convinced with my arguments. I would suggest that a district area should be formed from these smaller councils.

92. You would group them and have a council representing the local ones?—Yes, we would have a King William's Town council elected from the smaller local councils, and this will represent King William's Town fully. It will be in charge of the smaller ones and from the district council communications could pass between it and the Commission. We are also in favour of something being done in favour of a general council to make general arrangements for the district councils—a sort of Transkeian General Council.

93. You say that your views are in that report?—Yes, they are there represented. There should be two councils in the Cape—the Transkeian and the Ciskeian—I think it would work very well as a general council.

94. Do you think the Conference would be a useful institution?—Very useful, but

before coming to the Conference there is a remark I wanted to make. I think the Europeans in the native council area ought to work with the natives in that area, and I do not see how else it could be worked. Take the traders in a native district, how can they work apart from the Council?

95. It would never do to put white people in such a district as King William's Town under a native council?—They would be in the council themselves and it would be very helpful.

96. Would the natives be satisfied with that. Once you give whites a chance on these councils there is a serious danger of the whole matter falling into their hands?—But there are so few of them in the native areas—you may have three or four traders and they would be a sort of "goats which lead sheep" in working the councils. Even in the Transkei there was a difficulty in that respect but the Europeans enjoyed the fruits of the local councils without taking responsibility.

97. The matter of the relations between the Provincial Council system on the one hand and the local council system which we propose to establish is one that will have to be worked out and seeing that there is a clause in the Bill under which the Government may settle the relations between them and be guided by experience, we will be able to see how to arrange these councils?—I would leave it to regulation and experience. It is a matter worth considering because the natives are at sea with these new institutions. The whites need not have a preponderating influence. In the Transkei the natives are guided by their own Magistrates in the council. I would like the position of the European in a native area carefully considered by the Committee, but I agree it is a matter which should be considered by experience and on the advice of the Commission. The conferences should also dovetail and these local councils and provincial territorial councils might elect a certain number of representatives to the general conference.

98. The idea of the conference is to have a means of meeting the natives and discussing the question?—If you have members elected by the general council you will have men experienced in the areas.

99. *Mr. P. W. le R. van Niekerk.*] If you adopt that system solely you must have an outstanding native who belongs to these councils, but he might not be representative. The idea here is to get representative natives from different parts of the Union to discuss native questions?—I think the representative native should come from a smaller council.

100. He might represent his own locality but there are some natives who are more advanced and regard the question from a general policy point of view?—If he could be asked with representatives of the lower council that would be good.

101. But the conference would deal with questions affecting the Union?—But they are initiated in the smaller councils and the representatives will be quite familiar with the questions in the lower council and would be able to discuss matters with a certain amount of intelligence, but when new men come in without experience they may prove the snare of the conference.

102. *Chairman.*] The idea was more to have occasional meetings when natives of large areas could be met through their representatives and talk matters over?—The idea with us is the same only there is a little difference in detail.

103. *Mr. Gow.*] Do you represent any section of the natives?—We have an organisation which we call the Native Races Congress and I am President of it.

104. Did they give you any particular views to express here?—We discussed matters with those members near by as to what was proper to be done.

105. You have no formal mandate from the Congress?—There was no time.

106. Would it spoil the spirit and intention of the Bill if the Commission was composed entirely of Europeans?—It would, a great deal. You must have somebody on it who understands the native people. Take a case like the Lovedale trouble. If they had a native on that Committee I feel no trouble would have taken place. You have white missionaries without natives amongst them, and they discuss the native from their own point of view. The question might crop up whether you would not have the native side fully expressed on the Commission; local councils are outside the Commission, and my fear is that the European would look upon this from the European point of view. The natives would be satisfied if they had two natives appointed to the Commission.

107. In regard to the local council system, you may have one area adjoining another where there may be very few natives. Would you go by the number of people in an area or according to the size of the area?—The size I would say.

108. You might have one area purely agricultural and another one an industrial area. Do you suggest that it should be according to areas with community of interests?—Yes, I should say so.

109. Are the people satisfied with the council system in the Transkei?—Yes, they would not part with it.

110. Should the natives on local councils be elected by the votes of the natives or be appointed?—By a hybrid arrangement.

111. Do you think all areas will understand the method of election and realise their sense of responsibility?—I can only speak of the Cape, and in the Cape they would understand the elective element and also understand the reason for the nomination.

112. You say that traders in native areas should be on these councils in order to guide the natives. Why should we consider Europeans at all, seeing that the proposal in the Bill is to establish councils for natives?—These Europeans are one and the same with the natives, and would they not do just as well because they are familiar with the natives at the bottom.

DOCUMENT 33b. Testimony of Meshach Pelem, President, Bantu Union, before the Select Committee on Native Affairs, June 11, 1920 [Extract] (Published in *Minutes of Evidence, Select Committee on Native Affairs*)

1. *Chairman.*] The House of Assembly has appointed this Select Committee to take evidence on the Native Affairs Bill which is before the House. I do not know whether you have read the Bill?—I have read the Bill.

2. The Committee is very anxious to know whether you have any views, any

opinions, which you would like to express to the Committee on the provisions of this Bill. Have you any remarks to make or any criticisms which might help us to frame a good Bill?—Yes, I have prepared a memo of my views on the Bill, which I will read. It is as follows:—With regard to the name "Native Affairs Commission," we would suggest the adoption of the name "The Supreme Council of Native Affairs."

Membership and composition of Councils under section 1.—We would suggest that if there are five members two shall be qualified educated natives, who shall be freely elected by the native people themselves through their recognised organisation for the approval of the Prime Minister.

Functions and duties under section 2.—We would suggest that the Government consider seriously the creation of a separate portfolio of Native Affairs to take charge of:—

(a) Native industries and the promotion of handicrafts; (b) agriculture in all its general phases; (c) education; (d) social problems with supervision of local and general councils, including the Glen Grey Council as applied at present to the Native Territories, and all administrative matters related to Municipalities, Village Management Boards and native urban areas. The native question is a growing one, and is becoming too unwieldy to be dealt with by the Prime Minister's Department alone, of which it is merely an annexe. This is not meant to affect the Prime Minister's control over the civil administration of Native Affairs. The Supreme Council would be the connecting link between the Prime Minister's Department and the new Minister suggested, coordinating the work of both Departments. What about the question of direct representation of natives in Parliament, as those local Council Bills do not dispose of that question?

My further suggestions are:—

(1) Establishment of a Native Affairs Board or Commission for the Union; (2) Local Councils in Native areas; (3) convening of native conferences; (4) Bill evidently modelled on the schedule of the South Africa Act, the Glen Grey Act, and the Moffat Commission (report); (4a) composition of Board to consist of Prime Minister and not less than three and not more than five other members; (5) duties

of the Board, to consider all matters relating to Native administration or legislation specifically affecting the native, and to make recommendations thereon, with an appeal (a) to the Governor-General-in-Council (b) to Parliament in event of diversity of views; (6) period of office and salaries not yet fixed, to be dealt with by regulation, the body to be elastic as possible. It will, however, be a permanent Advisory Board on Native matters generally; (7) powers of local or district Councils to provide for all Divisional Council matters:—(a) sanitation; (b) establishment of hospitals; (c) improvement of farming methods and educational facilities, etc., they can also make bye-laws and prescribe fines for contravention of the Act not exceeding £2. They can also levy a rate not exceeding £1 on each adult native male. The revenue accruing from these will constitute the revenues of the Councils; (8) election of members of District Councils, appointment of officers, salaries and method of rate collection are left to be dealt with by regulation; (9) Native conferences to be composed of chiefs, members of District Councils, prominent natives and native delegates from associations purporting to represent any native political or economic interest, the idea being to remove the complaint that legislation is passed over the heads of the natives. Districts for conferences in the Cape Province might be grouped as follows:—(a) Upper Tembuland or the districts of Umtata and Engobo; (b) Willowvale, Kentani, Butterworth, Idutywa, Nqamakwe and Tsomo; (c) Lower Tembuland, including the following districts:—Queenstown, Glen Grey, Cofimvaba and Cala (d) King Williamstown, Victoria East and Peddie.

The principle of the Bill has been accepted and is not in any danger. From this point then we would move along with less speed. I would suggest if it was possible that after the Bill had been thrashed out in Committee of the whole House, that the Government should proceed to elect the Supreme Council, and that these officers get to work to frame the constitution and details of Departments of administration and call conferences after which, if a special session of Parliament would be too much trouble, perhaps the Prime Minister might suggest some other way, all this could be done within six months. My object being to save circumlocution and needless correspondence. (10) *Education.*—There was an influential Commission appointed on Native Education recently, but their report is still awaited. We have long felt that a radical reform of native education is necessary in various directions. A Director of native education in each province is, I think, necessary, who should work with a council of education composed of nominees of the various churches, District Councils, Ratepayers and the Government. This council should sit periodically and would form a link between the Provincial Administrators Department which governs education, and local educational boards or committees which should be created to control education in the districts under the Director and Council of Education for the Province. According to my previous memo, I suggested that a new Portfolio should be created under a new Minister and if this plan is adopted, native education might be turned over to his department *in toto.* The great complaint is that mission schools have no responsible authority to control education and to enforce regulations and proper attendance.

(II.) *Constitution of Native Conferences.* In order to facilitate representation it might be advisable to group areas as I have already shown, and allocate to each area a number of delegates proportioned by the population of rate-payers or taxpayers. These delegates should be freely elected by the people and not nominated. The Government reserving its right to nominate its own representatives. A clause providing for election of representative delegates should be embodied in the Act itself and not left to regulation.

DOCUMENT 33c. Testimony of the Rev. Z.R. Mahabane, President, Cape Province Native Congress, before the Select Committee on Native Affairs, June 15, 1920 (Published in *Minutes of Evidence, Select Committee on Native Affairs*)

113. *Chairman.*] You are the President of the Cape Province Native Congress?—Yes.

114. You have read the *Native Affairs Bill* which has been referred to this Committee?— Yes, and I have come before you to give the views of the Association which I represent. When we met at Queenstown last we had not seen the text of the Bill, but we knew what was going to be in the Bill.

115. How did you know if you had not seen the Bill?—From the Governor-General's speech at the opening of Parliament. I have seen the Bill since the Congress closed, and at the Congress we passed a tentative resolution, although we had not seen the Bill and had not sufficient information about it, to the effect that we could not accept the Bill and since reading the Bill I feel compelled to endorse the resolution. In the first place I consider that the Bill involves and perpetuates the objectionable principle of the political segregation or separation of the Bantu races and their exclusion from the political rights of the country. That is the first objection to this Bill. To my mind it amounts to a denial of the black man's rights of direct representation by members of his own race in the legislature of the country and carries into effect the principle of the colour bar in the South Africa Act, which lays it down that only persons of European descent can become Members of Parliament. If I am right in that view, that would be in conflict with what we consider to be our legitimate aspirations—the right to be represented in Parliament which is charged with the duty of making laws for the peace, welfare and orderly government of the country and also for disbursing the public funds of the country. There is an important House which is responsible for shaping the destiny of the land and determining its fate and we feel in a House like that we should be directly represented and we feel that the time has arrived when the question of our representation therein should be seriously considered and that nothing short of this can satisfy the wants of our people. In connection with this Bill, our Congress passed a resolution authorising the executive committee to petition Parliament with a view to amending the Act of Union by deleting the phrase which constitutes what is now commonly called "the colour bar." An objection has generally been raised in connection with this matter of doing away with the colour bar that the native vote would swamp the European vote, and, in order to avoid that possibility, I would suggest

(this is my own view, not that of Congress, and I do not know whether they would concur in that view) creating native constituencies. My personal opinion is that separate native constituencies should return native members to Parliament. I would not press for equal representation in Parliament at present with the Europeans, but I would say some modicum of representation. These constituencies might be: three in the Cape Province, two in the Transvaal, one in the Free State and one in Natal, each returning two native Members of Parliament. If that were done, it might also apply in the case of Provincial Councils. Then with regard to the local councils which are proposed to be established under the Bill, I consider they cannot give general satisfaction because they are local, divisional or of a parochial character and they would only deal with matters of a local nature, matters affecting the native in areas which might be called native areas or districts, and the natives in other parts of the country would not come under the scope of these local councils and therefore they would not have a share in the management of the affairs of the country. Those who are in native territories or districts would have a privilege in the management of their own affairs but others would be left out—those outside those territories. Local councils are to possess I think advisory powers and no powers of legislation, whereas I consider legislation of the utmost importance—more important than advisory power.

116. Local committees are not merely advisory, but, to a large extent, deal with their own affairs, and they also advise the Commission on general questions of policy. In that respect they are advisory, but in their local affairs they deal with them?—I see. Moreover, these local councils will be adopted in various parts of the country and, to my mind, that would not conduce to their unifying the people, but would tend to divide the interests of the native people according to districts and localities.

117. You think that the establishment of local councils would be to accentuate divisions?—That is my view. There is a doubt in my mind if the Commission would be in the position to link the interests of all the natives throughout the Union. The creation of a Native Affairs Commission itself to my mind seems to be a superfluous arrangement. It is what I call the segregation of native affairs, and I am against that. If the Bill passes through Parliament I would respectfully suggest that the Commission be composed of 5 members, of which 3 should be native.

118. You are really against the Commission, but if it is appointed the native representation should be in the majority?—It will not be a majority because the Minister of Native Affairs will be a member of the Commission and another official of the Government will be a member in addition.

119. Apart from the attitude which you are adopting that there should be no political separation, no colour bar, that the political institutions of the country should be the same, do you not think, seeing that the native races are far behind the whites in this country in civilisation and development, that it would be a good thing to have local institutions established for the natives by themselves as in the Transkei? Would not that help them forward in development and education and also looking after their own affairs?—I think that would be a satisfactory arrangement. If care is taken in the selection of the members of the local councils and if the local councils are given ample powers in regard to local affairs. I see from the Bill that they have charge of agricultural, irrigation, hospitals and educational matters, and so on. If they get self-government in these matters they must be raised and educated up to a higher political standard.

120. Would it not be a good thing for the Government and Europeans in this country to try and get a closer understanding with the native because for years past we have been drifting apart. One of the proposed methods is to call big conferences of important natives at which questions of policy can be discussed. The present position is that white people pass a law affecting the native, and if we want to have peaceful development of this country, which contains both black and white, we must hold conferences with important, leading natives, and discuss things with them?—That would be a good thing, and I have always held that such conferences would be very useful.

121. You do not look upon your ideal of political fusion between the whites and natives of this country as practicable, as something which can be carried out?—I believe that if the statesmen of the country really mean to do business it is a thing that can be brought within practical politics, because I feel that this political division is not in the interests of peace in this country. It tends to divide the white people and the native people and that, to my mind, is very dangerous—more dangerous than political fusion. I am against social equality with the white man, because I know we are not equal, but as far as politics are concerned, I see no danger in equal rights. I would give the same franchise to the white and the native; I would not make any distinction. I am against the idea of making a distinction whether on the lines of colour or the state of civilisation. If there is manhood suffrage for whites it should be for blacks; but in view of the present condition of things, I would advocate the creation of separate native constituencies for the present.

122. At the same time you face the ultimate ideal and result that in the end if there is perfect equality, the whites, forming a minority in the country, will also be in a minority in the political life of the country?—I admit that it will be very hard for the white people of this country to agree to that fusion, and that is why I suggest the other alternative.

123. I take your attitude to be this: Apart from your political ideal, which you have very clearly and ably expressed, if you set it aside and look at the Bill on its merits, you are not opposed to its provisions. You think it is a step in the right direction?—Yes, I agree that it is a step in the right direction, and if I am against the Bill it is because I fear it is drifting farther away from the ideal of the Native Congress. As an instrument of government for the natives, it is undoubtedly a step in the right direction.

124. *Mr. Keyter.*] Supposing you had a district with 12,000 whites and 12,000 natives, do you wish two members to be appointed to Parliament for that district—one for the blacks and one for the whites?—Yes, that is my idea, when I spoke of native constituencies I suggested there might be three of them in the Cape Province. I would select a limited number of native constituencies electing natives to Parliament. We are petitioning to alter the South Africa Act so that the qualification for members of Parliament might not be the colour or origin of the man, but that any British subject may become a member of Parliament. For the present I would not press for equal representation of natives in Parliament with the white representation. I feel the state of dissatisfaction in the native mind is more dangerous than the native outnumbering the white people in Parliament, because even if they outnumber the white people in Parliament, the native would never be able to outclass the white man intellectually, even if there were a hundred natives in Parliament against 30 or 50 white members the word of the white man would always carry the day.

125. *Chairman.*] You think that the native mentality is in such a state, it would be better to give them direct representation to Parliament and face any opposition of the whites to such a policy?—Yes.

126. *Mr. P. W. le R. van Niekerk.*] To what extent does your Congress represent the natives? Have you branches all over the country?—Our Congress represents natives throughout the Union of South Africa. In the Cape Province—we only started a provincial branch in October last year—we have at present three district branches, one at Queenstown, one in the Cape Peninsula and one in Port Elizabeth. The one in the Cape Peninsula has 4 sub-branches, one at N'dabeni, one at Cape Town, one at West London and one at Huguenot. The one in Port Elizabeth has sub-branches at Richmond Hill, Korsten, New Brighton, Uitenhage and Humansdorp, and the one at Queenstown has sub-branches at Queenstown, Lesseyton and Kamastone. New branches are now being organised at Barkly West, De Aar, Naauwpoort, Herschel, Aliwal North, Tembuland, Maclear, Engcobo, Pondoland, Matatiele and Cala. At the last annual convention we had representatives from these places I have mentioned. In regard to the membership, I only know as far as the branches already in existence are concerned and the total number is about 1,200, and already we are able to influence native

opinion of those who are for the present outside the Congress. Their sympathies are entirely with the Congress. In the Transvaal the Congress is stronger than in any other part of the country. I may say that I am not averse to the local councils if the Bill goes through, provided they are given ample powers to deal with local affairs, because at present—I am not speaking from direct knowledge but from what I hear—the council in the Transkei has not much power. They discuss matters, pass resolutions and after passing them the magistrates have separate meetings of their own and sift and modify resolutions before they are forwarded to the Government. That is the objection I have always held against the councils. I lived in the Herschel district for six years before I came here and they were strongly against the council system, because they felt they were not in a position to carry out their resolutions—no effect could be given them. I think that the larger mass of uneducated thought and opinion clamours for direct representation in Parliament and what makes me think so is because when we hold meetings with them or speak with them that is what they say. The native believes in Parliament because they had their own parliaments (called "courts") and every adult male was a member of the court and if he was not a member of the court he was not regarded as a man. The native court was not elected because every adult was a member of it. There were persons who were recognised as permanent members of the court, but everybody could attend and take part.

127. *Rev. Mr. Mullineux.*] Do you think it would be in the interests of the country as a whole that the franchise should be granted to the native people?—Yes.

128. Do you not think that would be going a little faster than the native people could keep pace with?—The uneducated native knows very little about franchise and he wants some representation in Parliament by members of his own race. He does not mind how it is effected, whether by popular vote as in the case of the white people or by native people being given the right to elect a certain number of native representatives—that would satisfy him.

129. Do you not think that the development of the native people might be more sure, if slower, under the Bill. It would be more sound along the lines suggested by the Bill?—My objection is that the councils are of a local character and confined to certain districts only.

130. *Mr. Keyter.*] You have stated that the majority of the natives are against segregation. In 1917 they were not against it, so since then have they changed their minds?—I do not know who gave evidence in 1917, but in 1913 when the Land Act was passed, we objected to it because it contained that principle of segregation and we also objected to the 1917 Bill on the same grounds mainly.

131. You are personally against segregation, but not the majority of the natives?—I represent the Native Congress and the members of that Congress are opposed to the policy of segregation. I represent the Free State natives who belong to the Congress.

132. If a native from the Free State came before this Committee and said they would be satisfied with this policy, would that be a story?—The natives of the Free State were bitter opponents of the Land Act, but I could not say they would be telling a story if they said they were satisfied.

DOCUMENT 34. "Native Unrest." Paper by Professor D.D.T. Jabavu read before the Natal Missionary Conference, July 1920 (Printed, 17 pages)

The Bantu people throughout the Union of South Africa are in a state of positive discontent. One need not be regarded as an alarmist for making such a statement. These people are, as it were, beginning to wake up out of their age-long slumber and to stretch themselves out and speak through their press and platform-demagogues in municipal areas like Johannesburg, Cape Town and Bloemfontein, their voice waxing louder and louder; while even in the rural districts of Natal, Pietersburg, the Transkeian reserves and among Free State squatters there is a growing feeling of distrust in the white man's lordship, loss of faith in his protestations of just intentions, and loss of confidence in the old-time kindly protection of the British

Constitution. These feelings are largely not expressed, for the Native is not given to confiding the secrets of his inmost feelings to Europeans, as in many cases he dare not; but nevertheless the feelings are there, and are seething like molten volcanic lava in the breasts of these inarticulate people.

It is only the bolder spirits who have ventured to give the world this secret by means of their scathing criticism in their press (the *Abantu-Batho* of Johannesburg being the most outspoken organ), and through their deputations to Great Britain.

And unless something is done at once to mitigate the causes of present dissatisfaction it will not be very long before the whole white community must deal with a situation overwhelmingly beyond their control.

1. The most immediate cause of unrest, although there are two or three more equally serious, and others less serious though individually and collectively serving to create an atmosphere of suspicion, the most immediate cause of unrest is the present economic pinch.

The Natives have been far harder hit by the prevailing high prices of the strictest necessities of life, than has been the white man. This needs no proving for the daily press reports unusual prosperity and extravagant spending of money by those who have made fortunes out of the high prices of merchandise. Government estimates display greatly increased salaries and wages; white employees and clerks everywhere are being paid in accordance with the times, either as a consequence of strikes, threatened strikes, or other persuasion. This is all due to the fact that the European, being well educated, knows how to speak out his sufferings, plead his case intelligently in the press, organise to the point of perfection, enlist public opinion in his cause, and finally force the hands of Government.

What about the black man? Behind him he has no European public opinion, the thing that counts in this country; for his power to influence it is negligible because three fourths of his fellowmen in the Union being without the franchise he has no political pull on Government. Hence he is expected to be satisfied with pre-war wages plus a rise of only five per cent. where the cost of living has advanced by from fifty up to a hundred per cent. The prices of rice and sugar are fixed; but maize, the staple food of millions of black people, is left to the mercy of speculators. A native labourer in East London recently asked in the "Dispatch" how he could be expected to be honest on a pound a week when his food, rent and light alone cost him far more than that a week. The fact is that in most cases to-day the wages earned by a black man cannot buy his food and the barest needs of life. It should be remembered too that the labourers in the Rand and elsewhere are there to raise money not only for their personal needs but for the support of their people at home. Fireside discussions of these things are more rife than they have ever been before. The cure for this is the sympathetic revision of the scales of wages by employers everywhere, the alternative being that the blacks will be obliged to learn the methods of white trade-unionists and be gradually drawn into socialistic organisations to compel the employers to pay at their dictation, just as the American Negro has done who to-day receives 15s. a day for the same type of unskilled labour for which the Bantu get two shillings.

2. Successive droughts with failures of crops have rendered agriculture, on the lines of the ante-diluvian African cultivation, unprofitable, neglected and unpopular. Wonderful opportunities in this connection are being lost by the Union as a whole, for the Natives are capable of being made important factors in the development of production. On this point the Native Farmers' Association of Middledrift, C.P., last year prepared a memorandum for the Native Affairs Department where, however, it received no attention, a memorandum recommending the purchase of a farm by Government in which Natives would be taught how to make a living out of an "isikonkwane" (six-acre plot) by means of a one-horse or one-ox American plough on the lines of Southern State negroes, to be taught by an American negro familiar with the system. Incidentally, dipping has produced much ill-feeling, for Natives do not understand its aim, and they ignorantly imagine it to be a white man's dodge to kill off their cattle, as witness the Matatiele disturbances in 1914; and Natives value cattle above all their other worldly possessions. This is therefore a

sore point with them. The cure here lies firstly in the educational training of headmen and chiefs who will encourage the pursuits of agriculture; secondly in the multiplication of native farm demonstrators on the American style to teach dry-farming methods; and thirdly in the establishment of agricultural schools for Natives; for it does not escape the knowledge of the more intelligent Native, that while Government spends £100,000 yearly on agricultural schools for whites, plus overseas scholarships and experimental stations, it provides next to nothing for black people who pay much of the taxes and stand in sorest need for this training.

3. In politics the black people are in the predicament of the American colonists of the eighteenth century who were taxed without representation. Whatever else has held good heretofore the time has gone past when the Bantu of this Union could be treated as children, however uneven be their development in the mass. They have vivid recollections of how their political rights were bargained away in the pacification of Vereeniging (1902). They reckon that the Union Act of 1910 unites only the white races and that as against the blacks; for the colour bar clause struck the death-knell of Native confidence in what used to be called British fair play. "That cow of Great Britain has now gone dry," they said, and they must look to themselves for salvation. All their deputations were referred back to the adjudication of the very government they appealed against and which had now by some dexterous manoeuvre made itself its own final Court of Appeal! Then immediately after the achievement of Union the Dutch Reformed Church in her capacity as a Christian Church piloted through parliament in the teeth of glaring heterodoxy an act calculated to stamp herself indelibly as an anti-Native Church. Behold the contradiction in terms!

Out of this seed-bed of racial antipathy and out of a sense of self-preservation there sprang up several native and coloured political organisations, chief of which was the "South African Native National Congress," which to-day represents the strongest single volume of Native feeling in the Union, although its methods and spokesmen are open to criticism by certain sections of natives. The next thing which has probably done more than any other political event to rouse and antagonise Native feeling against whites is the passing of the 1913 Native Land Act. The irony of it is that the Act was engineered by a man long acknowledged as a great friend of natives, a friend who had to perform an odious task under the political whip hand of a refractory negrophobist section of the then government. Had Mr. Sauer lived to administer the Act he would in all probability have mitigated its hardships. As it was, he died immediately, and its rigour in the Orange Free State was and still is Procrustean, whatever may be said for it in other provinces; for in this province its effect was to dispossess and reduce the native to a veritable bondman. A lurid picture of its torments is to be found in "Native Life in South Africa" by S. Plaacje. Mr. Selby Msimang, the editor of a Bloemfontein Native paper, has collected a number of verifiable cases of its recent victims; while an eloquent sketch of the political position of Natives at that time may be seen in the "Dream of Alnaschar" speech by Dr. Abdurahman, a coloured political leader of Cape Town. Other political events that are factors in the present state of native unrest are (i) The 1914 Native deputation to the Imperial Parliament to appeal against the Lands Act. True, it returned fruitless, but its pertinacious labours have gone a long way in educating the British public on the political disabilities of the aborigines in this country. (ii) The 1918 Urban Areas Bill which sought to bestow unprecedented legislative powers upon town councils, including the power to create municipal beer canteens, the effect of which would have been to demoralise town natives. (iii) The Native Administration Bill of 1917, whose impracticability caused it to break in the hands of its own forgers. (iv) The 1918 Rand strike of Native Sanitary labourers with the summary and notorious treatment they received at the hands of the local magistrate. This incident has served to unite Native miners because they have ever since been confirmed in the idea that Government favours white strikers but represses the black. As the late Mr. J. B. Moffat pointed out in his report this idea is a delusion so far as the law goes; nevertheless it remains in the Native mind and it is for the powers that be to eradicate it. (v) If ever one race in the world did ever seek the most signal way to repress and humiliate another, human invention could not have done it more effectually than the system of Pass Laws now obtaining in the Northern provinces. For decades, from the days of the Dutch Republics, has this system enslaved the Native, and the Union, instead of palliating its incidence, has not only continued it, accentuated it, but has actually threatened to make it universal or "uniform," to put it in the cunning language of the law-maker. This thing, as one man expressed it on the Reef, is simply perpetuated martial law in peace time.

The revulsion of Native feeling came to a head in a general Passive Resistance movement in Bloemfontein, Kroonstad, the Witwatersrand, and elsewhere in 1918, when people mutually agreed to throw away these passes and undergo voluntary imprisonment. Particularly painful and distressing were these laws on women in the Free State and Natal.

(vi) Certain utterances by Europeans of eminence appearing from time to time in the press have further alienated many Native minds. Such are the words of the Johannesburg magistrate to the sanitary strikers. The famous Savoy speech by General Smuts in London in 1917 has remained an enigma to Natives of this land.

Remarks like those made by a Mr. Van Hees lately in parliament on justice being only for whites and not for blacks do a great deal of damage. Also, what does the expression "to make this a white man's country" mean? Whoever is responsible for coining it must have meant the repression and destruction of black races. (vii) The 1920 Native Affairs Bill is moving Natives who have studied it for two reasons: (a) No attempt has been made to consult them generally before it was framed or discussed in parliament, in view of the permanent character of the machinery it seeks to put up; (b) It has been feverishly rushed through parliament, just as was the Lands Act of 1913, which itself is now proclaimed as the first instalment of the Union Government policy. This feverish hurry has of itself engendered suspicion.

Its powers are so elastic that everything is going to depend upon the personnel of the commissioners; and it seems only fair that Natives should be consulted upon the choice of such plenipotentiaries. (See also the "Grievances Memorial" pamphlet recently prepared by Messrs. Pelem and Soga, Queenstown, C.P.—perhaps the most comprehensive document, written by Natives of the Cape Province in exposition of the Native Question from the political point of view; the present writer did not see it until this paper had been completed.)

4. In the Department of Justice the Native has gradually lost faith. i. In a country like South Africa, the jury system can never be a success inasmuch as it bolsters up the distortion of justice nurtured by racial hatred, and cloaks it over with an appearance of legal rectitude. Even a tyro can tell that a black man in a country such as this can hardly expect fairplay from a white jury, when he is pitted against a white man. ii. The sentences of magistrates are a puzzle, and in their severity are distinctly anti-native. For the crime of failing to dip, a magistrate in Kafraria recently fined a Native £20, a fine indubitably disproportionate both to the offence, and the circumstances of the defendant, as compared with the same magistrate's fine against a European who had committed a similar offence. iii. Suspended sentences, as was remarked lately, in the House of Assembly by Mr. Langenhoven, seem to have been invented for the sole benefit of the European and to bear little or no reference to Natives. iv. Natives do not fail to notice that Europeans get off lightly and quietly in crimes against Natives, such as murder and rape, while Natives are unmistakably punished with the utmost rigour of the law amidst press trumpetings and fanfare. v. A high court Judge was not long ago reported in the "Daily Dispatch" as practising and upholding the differentiation of punishment as between whites and blacks for similar offences. Under these circumstances can one wonder that Natives should lose confidence in British Justice?

5. In social life the "School Native" cannot move anywhere without being made to know that his black skin is his life-long damnation. He is practically not recognised as

a citizen entitled to a place under the sun, (particularly is this the case in Northern provinces). For instance in Pretoria I had three simple Post Office transactions to negotiate. I entered the main post office to buy stamps, for I saw several natives entering and being served. Peremptorily I was told in a discourteous and gruff manner, that Natives could not buy stamps there but had to go some two hundred yards round the block of buildings to the next street, where after much search, I eventually discovered a back-kitchen sort of arrangement with Indian salesmen behind the counter, and got my stamps. To despatch my parcel to East London, I was told to go back to the General P.O. On getting there it was duly registered; and I desired to purchase a postal order, but was then told to travel back to the Native P.O. for that! My feelings are best left undescribed. Again when in Pretoria, I moved between friends at the East end of the town and others near the Indian bazaar, a distance of about two or three miles across town, covered directly by a 6d. tram ride. Being a black man I was not allowed to use the trams, and was compelled either to foot it daily all the way along the very tram route or pay half-a-crown each time for a private cab.

Socially speaking, the black man in all public places is either "jim-crowed" or altogether ostracized. In stores he has to wait until all whites are served; in public offices, he is bullied by officials; in markets his stock and produce are by tacit agreement earmarked for low prices; his sugar cane is not accepted at the Zululand mills; evening curfew bells restrict his freedom of movement among his friends and he is cut and snarled at throughout his life.

6. In railways he is at the very start of his journey buffeted by booking clerks; in the goods sheds he is unnecessarily anathematised in language that cannot bear repeating. His waiting rooms are made to accommodate the rawest blanketed heathen; and the more decent Native has either to use them and annex vermin or to do without shelter in biting wintry weather. His accommodation in trains is frequently not equal to the money he pays in fares.

To travel 3rd class is often a test of physical endurance specially on some lines where there are more people than the half coach or single coach can contain. Travelling first class from Alice to Durban recently my first class compartment was in many cases only an old second redubbed "First" and, as it was, I was recklessly dumped with second class passengers—the very privacy for which I had paid being denied. Reserved bookings by Natives are frequently ignored. Several times have I had to claim refunds from railway divisional superintendents when after fulfilling all legal requirements for reserving a seat, I had to go third or not go at all. A number of Native teachers last winter wrote to Umtata a fortnight ahead of time to have second class seats reserved for them. When they came to join the train not only was there no accommodation made for them but no second class tickets would be issued to them and they had either to abandon travelling or go third class. When I joined the same train at Butterworth I was offered pretty much the same treatment, but I stood my ground, threatening to take legal proceedings against the delinquents when after half an hour's palaver an extra coach was attached, to the relief and joy of many black passengers who included a native doctor qualified in Edinburgh University. Such incidents often render railway travelling a perfect misery, as the decent Native has constantly to engage in ugly altercations with supercilious officials in claiming his privileges. Much heart-burning has come from the system of replacing blacks by poor whites in railway sheds and workshops. Refreshment stalls like those at Amabele, Komgha and Sihota are doing incalculable harm, converting otherwise peaceful natives into bitter malcontents by their disgusting contempt for native passengers in peculiarly native districts. In fact Transkeian Europeans by their policy of pin-pricks against natives are gradually accentuating racialism. For example rank prejudice is shown in the very Council Hall at Umtata where Natives may use only a certain door to enter or leave the hall in the Bunga sessions, this peculiar piece of snobbery even necessitating crossing the hall in front of the magisterial benches—all this in a Native reserve.

The cure here lies in the appointment of officials with tested sympathy towards

Natives, in all departments of Government.

The above six points constitute, in my view, the most important factors in the general ferment of unrest, which need urgent solution. Now I wish to take eight other points which contribute not a little to the charged atmosphere that has been electrified by racial distrust.

7. Native Housing: This question deserves the attention of all interested in the welfare of Natives. In most municipalities these people live in squalid surroundings, shockingly over-crowded, these quarters being favourable breeding beds for disease and epidemics. From their nature they are cesspools of drunkenness and demoralisation. Conveniences are distant, sometimes nonexistent; water is hard to get; light is little; sanitation bad; while there are no common laundry buildings, no gardens, no amusement halls or clubs. Some are located near sanitary dumps, e.g. Klipspruit and Springs in the Rand. The favourite solution of the problem is to threaten to remove them further away from the towns without promising improvement of conditions.

The cure for this is to be found in the suggestions made in the newly-published Government Commission Report on Housing. Many constructive proposals may be gained also from the speech of Mr. P. D. Cluver, Mayor of Stellenbosch, given at Grahamstown in the 1920 Municipal Congress and from the "Municipal Control of Location," a paper by Dr. F. A. Saunders, F.R.C.S., of Grahamstown (now published in pamphlet form) delivered before the same Congress.

8. Insecurity of land tenure: Like the owning of cattle the possession of land, to Natives, is a natural ambition. But the possibility to buy land or hire it has been seriously circumscribed everywhere by the Land Act of 1913. The worst case is that of the Orange Free State which has rendered confusion for the black man worse confounded. Before 1913 the Native could hire land or plough on the half-share system for a white master and could not purchase land under any conditions. To-day he is not allowed under this law to hire land or to contract to plough on half-shares. He is a literal serf, landless, unable to hire land, and must only be a paid servant of the Dutchman.

Also in many urban locations there are no facilities for Natives to buy property, hence there is no inducement for them to beautify, and improve with gardens even if they did feel so inclined, the property that is rented from a town council and liable at any time to be moved away by a resolution of the town council.

9. Missions. Missionaries will for ever be remembered with gratitude by Natives as the people who befriended them in times of trouble and danger at the risk of their own lives. They faced opprobrium for the sake of black people, founded countless mission stations and bequeathed unto them the present foundations of the entire educational structure that is to-day theirs. Today however there is a danger that the type of earnest missionaries associated with the founders of prominent mission stations and Native Training Institutions is being steadily replaced by ministers and other staff members of a more and more secular spirit, who not only fail to understand the Native, much less to love him, but adopt a socially distant attitude of master to servant. Success in Christian work without Christian love is an impossibility. Now many a missionary of to-day has no hand-shake for a black brother and he feels distinctly embarassed when he is among other whites and meets him in town.

His position is lordly, his discipline military. These doubtless form a small fraction of the whole but as in all things in the world, the many are apt to be judged by the few erratic cases. On one occasion I was invited by a Principal of a Native Training Institution to lecture to his students. He, as my host, took no steps to let me even see the inside of his house—perhaps with all my ten years of English University life I was not good enough for him—but boarded me among the boys in their dining hall where he only came to say prayers and to depart. There was high feeling among the boys and Native Teachers over this treatment of me but I asked them earnestly to say nothing about it for the day of Nemesis was bound to come, since this attitude was characteristic of certain missionaries.

One mentions this incident as a warning to a Conference of this kind for this is where racial sectarianism takes its source, for even in synods, presbyteries and conferences the spirit of racial discrimination is so powerful that the black delegates have again and again to be sorted out from the rest like goats from the sheep. Therefore do not rest on your laurels for Natives are watching you at every step. Their docility does not spell stupidity.

10. Education. The present condition of Native education in the Union is one of chaos, for while at the Cape and Natal there are signs of organisation to improve things, there is nothing of the sort being done in Transvaal and the Free State. Natives here have a just grievance. They see Government spending lavishly in putting up majestic educational edifices for European primary, secondary and University education staffed by highly paid teachers, while they have to be satisfied with having their children taught in mission rooms with walls dilapidated and furniture rough and scanty, teachers receiving miserable pittances, so miserable that a raw and illiterate Zulu policeman in Durban to-day gets better pay than the best paid Zulu school teacher. Provincial grants to Native education are very tiny by comparison with those for white schools and infinitesimal as compared with the enormous revenue derived from Native taxation. There is no pension for a Native teacher in Natal.

The inspectoral system there however is a model one and a contrast to that of the Cape, where its terrorism over teacher and pupil is such that at a certain school near King William's Town the inspector not long ago actually failed an entire school of seventy, passing only four. Such a system needs overhauling. Cape Native teachers would be considerably benefitted in their work by an instructive and sympathetic, even humorous paper like the Natal Native Teachers' Journal published by the Education Department instead of the lifeless dry-bones of the Cape "Education Gazette."

The report of the Native Education Commission 1919 is a capital document worth studying as it contains valuable proposals, which would change a great deal of what is antiquated, if acted upon.

Useful for Cape Teachers would be Winter School courses such as those yearly organised in Natal by Dr. C. T. Loram, M.A., author of "The Education of the South African Native."

11. The Civil Service is greatly injuring Native sentiment with its policy of weeding out competent Natives where they can serve their people better than can other people. Even in a Native reserve like the Transkei Territories, Native youths with good qualifications are put on a special Native scale of salaries lower than that of whites with inferior credentials. Why not give the Native a fair chance in his own reserve? Why must he after due training have to work under an inferior "black scale" of remuneration in a Native district? Where is *our* civil service? Why not give us a chance to rise according to our ability and professional qualifications? Such questions are being asked by people who wield no small influence among the less enlightened.

12. Bolshevism and its nihilistic doctrines are enlisting many Natives up-country. Socialism of the worst calibre is claiming our people. The main alarming features are (a) That Christianity must be opposed and rooted out, for it is a white man's religion which the white man himself does not act upon. "Let us fabricate a religion of our own, an original, independent African religion suited to our needs," say they. (b) "Let us unite to compass our freedom, opposing the white man tooth and nail as he has taken our country and made us economic slaves." The cure here is that we should have in this country counteracting forces. There should be more social workers such as Dr. D. Bridgman and Rev. Ray Philips in Johannesburg who are organising for Natives a sort of Y.M.C.A. sheme to provide recreation, a large club with reading, writing and restaurant rooms plus playing fields, debating and musical societies. This is needed in every location, rural and urban, to heighten the tone of Native life.

13. Agitators. There has sprung into life a large number of Natives from the better educated class who have seized the opportunity of the general state of dissatisfaction to stir up the populace to desperate acts. A sensational report of something of this kind appeared in the vernacular in a recent issue of "Imvo" by a Rand correspondent. Personally I do not blame these men for the conditions that have called them into being are positively

heartrending and exasperating in all conscience. They poignantly feel the sting of the everlasting stigma of having to carry passes in time of peace in the land of their birth. They are landless, voteless, helots; pariahs, social outcasts in their fatherland with no future in any path of life. Of all the blessings of this world they see that the white man has everything, they nothing.

Like Catiline and his conspirators of Roman history, they believe that any general commotion, subversion of government and revolution are likely, out of the consequent ruins and ashes, to produce personal gain and general benefit to Natives and sure release out of the present state of bondage. They harp upon the cryptic and dangerous phrase "to make this a white man's country," which as we all know has become Parliamentary platitude. Armed with rallying catch phrases and a copious Socialistic vocabulary they play as easily as on a piano upon the hearts of the illiterate minelabourers. It must be remembered too that the Socialism they acquire is not the harmless commonsense system advocated by Phillip Snowden and Ramsay Macdonald in their books; but the atheistic and revolutionist doctrines of Count Henri Saint Simon of the early 19th century introduced into England by Robert Blatchford, Charles Bradlaugh and J. M. Robertson in latter days, and now somehow imported into South Africa.

The cure here lies in our being able to produce well educated Native leaders trained in a favourable atmosphere, who will be endowed with commonsense, cool heads, with a sense of responsibility, endurance and correct perspective in all things. The Native College at Fort Hare has this as one of its aims and if sufficiently supported it ought to be a real help to the country and the government.

14. Finally the Native Labour Contingent that did work in France during the Great War has imported into this country a new sense of racial unity and amity quite unknown heretofore among our Bantu races. Common hardships in a common camp have brought them into close relation. They had a glimpse at Europe and even from the closed compounds they got to discover that the white man overseas still loves the black man as his own child, while on the contrary some of their white officers, including two chaplains, forsooth, made themselves notorious by their harsh treatment and slanderous repression of them when French people befriended them. All this was carefully noted and published among their fellowmen in this country when they returned. The result is that there is among the diversified Bantu tribes of this land a tendency towards complete mutual respect and love founded upon the unhealthy basis of an anti-white sentiment. They thus provide plastic material for all sorts of leaders and agitators who may use it for good or ill.

It is the duty then of every loyal citizen of the Union to be familiar with these causes of unrest and discontent, with a view to each one taking his share in providing a solution that will save the country from what will, if not arrested in time, surely come up sooner or later as an anarchist disruption of this land.

Appeals Abroad

DOCUMENT 35. Petition to King George V, from the South African Native National Congress, July 20, 1914 (Published in *The Cape Argus*)

The "Argus" to-day is in a position to publish the full text of the petition protesting against the Native Lands Act, which a deputation representative of the various South African native sections now in London, have handed to Mr. Harcourt (Secretary for the Colonies) for presentation to the King.

The petition runs as follows:—

To His Most Excellent Majesty, George V., by the Grace of God, of the United Kingdom of Great Britain and Ireland, and of the British Dominions beyond the Seas. King, Defender of the Faith, Emperor of India:

May it please Your Majesty:

The humble petition of the undersigned most humbly and respectfully showeth:

That petitioners are Your Majesty's most loyal and humble subjects, who have always been loyal to Your Majesty's throne and person, and still desire to continue being loyal to Your Majesty's throne and person.

That petitioners, in their capacity as representatives of the South African National Native Congress, which is again the representative body of natives of the Union of South Africa, most humbly approach Your Majesty as their King, their father and protector, and say:

(1.)

That petitioners are descendants of a race that for many years have had a respect and love for the British people, and a most loyal and respectful disposition for Your Majesty's throne and person, whose beneficent rule the petitioners and their forefathers have experienced, more especially when this the land of their birth was under Crown rule.

(2.)

That petitioners represent a vast number of Your Majesty's subjects, the denizens of this land, the former owners of this land, whose all in all is in this land, and who have no other country to go to, as all others of Your Majesty's subjects have, and who love this their land with a most intense love.

(3.)

That petitioners are descendants of a race which, when their forebears were conquered by Your Majesty's might, and their land taken from them, their laws and customs mangled and their military and other institutions brought to nought, loyally and cheerfully submitted to Your Majesty's sway in the full belief that they would be allowed to possess their land as British subjects, and would be given the full benefits of British rule like all other British subjects.

(4.)

That on the 12th day of May, 1843 [sic] the British Government in the reign of that most gracious and most Christian of the world's sovereigns, Queen Victoria, whose memory will never die with us, and whose most beautiful influence bound us to the British throne and people, and will ever remain in our hearts as a memento of what such influence can effect among a subject race, issued a proclamation to the first emigrants, both English and Dutch and others, who were the first to come to this land of our birth, whose special terms were as follows, with regard to the denizens of this land:

"That Her Majesty's said Commissioner is instructed distinctly to declare that the three next mentioned conditions—all of them so manifestly righteous and expedient as to secure, it is to be hoped, their cheerful recognition by the inhabitants of Natal—are to be considered as absolutely indispensable to the permission which it is proposed to give the emigrants, to occupy the territory in question, and to enjoy therein a settled Government under British possession.

"1st. That there shall not be, in the eye of the law, any distinction or qualification whatever, founded on mere distinction of colour, origin, or language, or creed; but that the protection of the law, in letter and in substance, shall be extended impartially to all alike.

"2nd. That no aggression shall be sanctioned upon the natives residing beyond the limits of the Colony, under any plea whatever, by private person or any body of men, unless acting under the immediate authority and orders of the Government.

"3rd. That slavery, in any shape, or under any modification, is absolutely unlawful as in every other portion of Her Majesty's Dominions."

(5.)

That petitioners claim that proclamation, in letter and in spirit, as their gift and Charter from the British Government, and as a contract by the British Government, as guardian and protectors of the native races with all the white races that have settled in this land, and they most humbly pray that Your Majesty may see that that contract is implemented.

(6.)

That petitioners say that there was an attempt to carry out the spirit and letter of that proclamation while this land was under Crown rule, but that since Crown rule was withdrawn that proclamation has been quite ignored, and the treatment of the natives and all that concerns them has gradually drifted, and is still drifting, from the sweet influence of that memorable rule of Queen Victoria, our mother and Queen, to a state of things, the issue of which we shudder to contemplate unless a return from that course is made very soon.

(7.)

That petitioners say that when their forebears submitted themselves to the rule of the British Government, and paid homage to them, they fully accepted the Sovereignty of Great Britain and no other, but fully believed that their land would be reserved for them, and that they would have the full right of British subjects, more especially with regard to the possession of land and all the right incident thereto.

(8.)

That petitioners wish to be allowed most humbly and respectfully to refer to the proclamation of Sir Garnet Wolseley, made in June 1880, after the Zulu War, with regard to the future of Zululand, which was a clear pronouncement from him, as the representative of the Crown, to the effect that so long as the sun ran its course the Zulus would not be deprived of their land, but that the best parts of Zululand have since, by Colonial legislation, been surveyed into [acres?] and sold to any but the natives.

(9.)

That petitioners have never begrudged members of the white race, who are British subjects, getting a share of the land, but protest most strongly and solemnly against being gradually squeezed out of rights to and in land, and claim that the natives should be put into possession of land in proportion to their numbers, and on the same terms and conditions as the white race.

(10.)

That petitioners say that the only portion of the South Africa Act aforesaid, which has reference to the natives is Section 147, which reads as follows:—

"The control and administration of native affairs throughout the Union shall vest in the Governor-General-in-Council, who shall exercise all special powers in regard to native administration hitherto vested in the Governors of the Colonies or exercised by them as supreme chiefs."

(11.)

That the petitioners say that they consider themselves and the native races to be still under the direct rule and control of Crown through the Governor-General-in-Council, and therefore appeal to the Crown.

(12.)

That the petitioners say that they have never accepted the Union Government in place of the Crown, but have only accepted the Union Government as advisers of the Governor-General, through their Ministers, for and on behalf of the Crown.

(13.)

That petitioners say that they and the native races have been friendly and still desire to be friendly, to the Union Government and all Your Majesty's subjects, but in all matters affecting them adversely look to Your Majesty for the security of their rights and protection of themselves and such rights as Your Majesty's subjects.

(14.)

That petitioners most humbly say that the Native Lands Act No. 27 of 1913, passed by the Union Government, is an Act that has shown to the natives that the Union Government have overlooked the Queen's Government Proclamation, as quoted in paragraph 4 of this petition, and have started to pursue a policy towards the natives of entirely eliminating them from the interests of this country, and of ignoring their rights as British subjects, and are taking a course that must inevitably lead to disaster.

(15.)

That petitioners say this Native Lands Act has caused the greatest disappointment to, suspicions among, and the deepest opposition from, the native races.

(16.)

That petitioners say that they recognise that it is necessary to initiate without delay a policy dealing with the land question, and other questions affecting the Europeans and natives in this land, but most humbly and respectfully submit that the Union Government failed to do what was right with regard to the said Land Act.

(17.)

That the petitioners object to the said Land Act as being generally an act of class legislation, and one that would never have been dreamt of had only Europeans been in this land, and see in it the beginning of that policy towards the natives which will end in making them slaves.

(18.)

That petitioners beg permission to draw attention to the fact that it was the European who came to this land and settled in it alongside the native, and the native could not help it, and that they (the natives) most keenly feel and resent the spirit exhibited by the Europeans towards the native races by that Land Act.

(19.)

That the petitioners and the native races, while admitting the wisdom of initiating a policy to deal with the land question, and other cognate questions in this land without delay, most earnestly protest against the following with regard to the Native Lands Act of 1913 passed by the Union Government of South Africa, viz.:

(a) It was conceived, framed and bought [sic] into the Union House of Parliament without any previous notice to the natives, and without consultation with the natives and without the taking of the natives into confidence as should have been done, seeing that the question at issue affects the natives more than any other subjects of Your Majesty.

(b) It was dealt with in both Houses of Parliament in a most reprehensible hurry, and without consideration, and passed into law with such haste, as could never have been the case if the European subjects of Your Majesty were to be alone affected by the provisions thereof.

(c) Its conception, its framing, and the manner of its being passed into law, is a precedent for future legislation in the Union Parliament with regard to questions affecting the natives, who are entirely unrepresented, though they pay a large sum in taxes, and are the majority of labourers and inhabitants of the Union of South Africa.

(d) It was passed in such a crude and ambiguous shape that it is difficult to understand its true import, even after many explanations by those who think they can explain its meaning.

(e) It has not been yet explained to most of the natives whom it affects as it should have been, and a vast number of natives have no explanation of it at all, but have commenced to feel its cruel effects.

(f) It is an Act which instead of being based on the principles observed in the Cape Colony with regard to the natives and the land there, has been based on principles subversive of all that is right, just and likely to conserve the peace, prosperity and happiness of the various races of the Union of South Africa.

(g) It is an Act whose provisions, if they are carried out as they stand, will mean the deprivation of the natives of their most sacred rights as British subjects, will turn them into slaves, and will create such a strained and bitter feeling between the white races and the native races as will always in the future mean opposition between the two races and continual conflicts.

(h) It is an Act that ignores the natives and his [sic] feelings, and leads them to believe that the Union Government consider them nonentities in this the land of their birth, and they may only expect worse things in the future.

(i) Its provisions are entirely opposed to the principles of British policy and justice, and are laden with dynamite tendencies which mean agitations, schemings, upheavals, and conflicts in this land we love so much, and the scandalising of the British name and prestige.

(20.)

The petitioners say, that they and the native races object most strenuously and earnestly against all the provisions of the Native Lands Act, passed by the Union Government in 1913, which have for their object, viz.:—

The segregating and separating of the natives and the Europeans, as if they were so many animals, because:

(a) The natives are the original denizens of this land, and the white races came and located themselves alongside the native in their own land, and it was not the native who went to the white man's country and located himself alongside the white man.

(b) The native does not recognise any wrong he has committed to deserve this segregation and separation.

(c) The natives are as fully British subjects as are all the other members of the various races constituting the Union of South Africa, and claim for themselves equal consideration and treatment.

(d) The effect of segregating and separating the natives will be to at once satisfy the natives that the white people intend evil to them, and they (the natives) will deeply resent the treatment and combine against the white people, and the white people will combine against the native, and that inevitable and continual conflict between the two races will be initiated, which the natives do not desire, as they wish to live as friends of the white race, in peace with the white race, in co-operation with the white race, and in loyalty to the British Crown and Throne, from which they have received so many blessings.

(e) The natives most solemnly protest against any policy which will drive them into conflict with the white races, for it would be to the serious disadvantage of both, and they submit that a policy of segregation and separation will immediately lead to such conflict.

(f) The natives have had all their institutions broken up by the white race conquering them, and have been driven by circumstances and choice to the light of civilisation, and they do not want segregation and separation, which will have the effect of throwing them backward.

(21.)

The petitioners and the native races most strenuously and earnestly object to the provisions of the Union's Native Lands Act, where they differentiate against the natives.

(a) In that they limit the right of the native to the free purchase of and dealing in land on the same terms as the white subjects of Your Majesty.

(b) In that with regard to natives on the farms of the white people, they interfere with the vested rights of the natives exercised for generations, on land once theirs, and on which lie buried their ancestors, by altering the right they have as British subjects to bargaining in any way they please with the owners of these farms, for a place for their homes and a means of existence, which is not done to any other of Your Majesty's subjects, and which exposes them to a condition that will enable and even force the farmers to eject them from their farms, leaving them to wander about or submit to living on the farms, on the sole terms of giving three months' service, which at once turns them (the natives) into slaves.

(c) In that they have for their object the forcing of the native to labour by making it the only condition of his living on a white man's farm; that they are to bargain with the owner of the farm on the sole condition of supplying three months' labour.

(d) In that they have for their object the expropriation of lands already held in freehold by the natives, where the native is found to live on land in an area which it is intended to convert into a white man's area.

(e) In that they have for their object, in the Orange Free State, the deprivation of the natives of all rights of purchase of land, and any right to or in any land.

(f) In that they have for their object the most unjustifiable interference with the rights of races the common subjects of the King, and the common inheritors with the white race of lands of the Union of South Africa.

(g) In that they even place the other natives of the Union of South Africa in a less favourable position than their brethren and cousins in the Cape Province, whose rights are secured to them, while the mighty and most beneficial influences of Victorian rule existed, were safeguarded in the South Africa Act of Union, to the eternal credit of those who took part, on behalf of the Cape Colony, in drawing up that Act of Union.

(22.)

The petitioners, therefore, ask for themselves and the native races they represent, that Your Majesty may be graciously pleased to protect them, and stave off from them the calamities impending over them by reason of the passing of the Union's Native Lands Act of 1913, by refusing to confirm it, and by remitting it to the Union Government of South Africa for the deletion therefrom of all the obnoxious provisions we have complained of, and by the insertions of such provisions as we have suggested, and more especially by such provisions as would have been in the said Act, nad it been drawn by Your Majesty's Home Ministers in matters appertaining to Your Majesty's subjects at Home.

(23.)

The petitioners further ask for themselves and the native races that Your Majesty may be graciously pleased to advise the Union Government of South Africa to secure to them in addition to the locations and native reserves already existing, substantially large additional areas of land, within the Union, commensurate with the proportion in num-

bers of the natives and the white races, so that there may be land whither the natives leaving farms or evicted from farms may go to and live.

(24.)

The petitioners, for themselves and the native races, most humbly respectfully, and loyally assure Your Majesty of their continued homage and loyalty to Your Majesty's throne and person, and their friendliness to General Botha and his Government, and to all Your Majesty's subjects.

We are, Your Majesty,
Your Majesty's most humble subjects
and servants.

DOCUMENT 36. "An Appeal to the Members of the Imperial Parliament and Public of Great Britain." Petition from the South African Native National Congress, 1914 (Printed, 7 pages)

The signatories of this Appeal have been sent to this country by The South African Native National Congress, an organization for focussing native opinion, and consisting of paramount chiefs, headmen, councillors, educated native leaders, and representatives of the various native tribes and races within the Union of South Africa.

This Congress, gravely disturbed at the menace to native rights under the Natives' Land Act, passed a strong resolution against the Bill. Furthermore the following Religious Conferences of South Africa have passed resolutions against the passing of the Bill:— Anglican, Wesleyan, Congregational, Baptist and Presbyterians. But in spite of these resolutions the Bill was hurriedly passed through Parliament.

A deputation waited upon the Government asking that the Bill should be delayed until the natives could study its provisions. These efforts failed, and the Bill which had been introduced only in May became law on June 16th, (1913). The natives, already suspicious of the measure, were now greatly alarmed at the haste with which it was forced through Parliament. Accordingly, the Native Congress,

July 19th, 1913, resolved to send a deputation to His Majesty the King, praying that the Act might be disallowed. The President of the Congress in July, 1913, sent a deputation to the Hon. F. S. Malan, Acting Minister of Native Affairs, requesting that the Act, on account of the hardships it was inflicting upon the natives, although it was only six weeks old, might be suspended.

All these endeavours having failed, the Native Congress meeting at Kimberley, February, 1914, re-affirmed its resolution to send a deputation to England. But, once more, it petitioned the Union Parliament and the King's representative. The petition, however, was not presented, as its presentation was discouraged by the Prime Minister, who also is now Minister of Native Affairs.

Between the resolutions passed by the Native Congress and the deputation it sent to Government, to the Minister, and the Acting Minister for Native Affairs, its executive was also in frequent correspondence with the Prime Minister, first to secure the withdrawal of the Bill, then to effect a change in its most drastic clauses; but General Botha did not so much as promise the possibility of a change in the Bill. Instead of a promise he said to the deputation, in the interview with him in 1914, given on the eve of its departure for England: "If I went to Parliament with a proposal to modify the Act, Parliament would think I am mad." Similarly the executive of the Native Congress applied at three different times to the Governor-General, Lord Gladstone, for an interview; in the first instance, in 1913, to stay his assent to the Bill; in the second instance, also 1913, to point out the mischief the Bill was doing to the natives. On each of these occasions the Governor-General declined to receive a deputation, for the alleged reason that it was not within his constitutional function to meet them. He vouchsafed an interview in May, 1914, but beyond merely urging the deputation to abandon their mission to England, he held out no hope that his good offices would be used to modify the more obnoxious clauses of the Act.

After exhausting all these constitutional means in South Africa, for the redress of our grievances in connection with the Natives' Land Act of 1913, it was decided by the South African Native National Congress that we should proceed to England, as their delegates, to lay our cause before the Imperial Government and the people of Great Britain.

What was uppermost in the collective mind of the Native Congress was this—they wished to save the Union from the disintegration which must inevitably follow the enforcement of the Natives' Land Act.

The Act

The Land Act which the Governor-General of the Union of South Africa signed on June 16th, 1913, declares in its first clause:—

"Except with the approval of the Governor-General—

"(a) A Native shall not enter into any agreement or transaction for the purchase, hire, or other acquisition from a person other than a native, of any such land, or of any right thereto, interest therein, or servitude thereover, and

"(b) A person other than a native shall not enter into any agreement or transaction for the purchase, hire, or other acquisition from a native of any such land, or of any right thereto, interest therein, or servitude thereover."

It may be said that according to this Sub-Section, Europeans are restricted as well as Natives. But this is a restriction on paper only, as the Natives have no land to sell; besides, no European would think of settling in the scheduled native areas, already crowded, except for trading purposes. Consequently, the provisions of the Act really operate only against the Natives.

The Effect

The effect of the enforcement of these provisions is that when a native leaves a farm on the expiry of his tenancy or otherwise, he is at once rendered homeless because the Act does not allow him to purchase, hire, or lease land anywhere for farming purposes. He can live on a farm only as a servant to the farmer.

Thus Section 5 reads:—

"Any person who is a party to any attempted purchase, sale, hire or lease, or to any agreement or transaction which is in contravention of this Act or any regulation made thereunder shall be guilty of an offence and liable on conviction to a fine not exceeding One Hundred Pounds or, in default of payment, to imprisonment with or without hard labour for a period not exceeding six months; and if the act constituting the offence be a continuing one, the offender shall be liable to a further fine not exceeding five pounds for every day during which that act continues."

The operation of the Act has produced six classes of sufferers, viz.: —

"(a) Persons under notice to quit.

"(b) Persons actually evicted from farms.

"(c) Migrants to territories outside the Union.

"(d) Homeless wanderers with families and stock in search of new homes.

"(e) Persons who had to leave their crops unreaped, or who had not ploughed this season; and;

"(f) Persons who yield unrequited labour."

The above classes of sufferers are the result of Parliament legislating natives off the farms without making provision for their settlement.

The first section of the Act provides that the permission of the Governor-General should be obtained before any purchase, hire or lease of land can be effected, but applications for the permission of the Governor-General have been almost invariably refused by the authorities.

Out of thousands of cases which might be cited we give a few, indicative of the severe hardships inflicted by the Act.

For example:—In the Cape Colony, where we are repeatedly told that the Act is not in force, the Magistrates of East London, King Williams Town and Alice prohibited native tenants from re-ploughing their old hired lands last October, and also ordered them to remove their stock from grazing farms.

About 9 months ago, application was made on behalf of 400 natives by Mr. Wilcox, of the Weenen Division, in Natal, to purchase a farm between two native holdings. The Governor-General's permission was not granted, and the farm has now passed into the hands of a white man, who forthwith demanded annually from the old occupiers of the farm six months' unpaid labour.

At a meeting held at Thaba Nchu, on Sept. 12th, 1913, attended by some thousand natives amongst whom were several evicted tenants seeking such permission of the Governor-General, through Mr. Dower, Secretary for Native Affairs, who addressed them— Mr. Dower said, *inter alia:* "The Act does not allow for any special cases in the Free State being submitted to the Governor-General under the First Section of the Act, so my best advice to you is to sell your stock and go into service."

Only last mail (June 23rd) we received news of great unrest amongst the Natives in these Districts. In the Districts of Peters, Waschbank, Colworth and Weenen (Natal), 522 families are under notice to leave at the end of this month (June).

These are but typical of the evictions that have been taking place, almost weekly, in the four provinces of the Union, namely, Transvaal, Orange Free State, Natal and the Cape since the Act came into force last June.

We would like to point out that one of the reasons which led to the coming of the present deputation to England, was, if possible, to avert the danger of our people being forced to commit acts of violence.

Objections to the Act

The Native races most strenuously and earnestly object to the provisions of the Act, where they differentiate against them, because—

(a) They exclude the Native from the free purchase of and dealing in land, a right never challenged hitherto.

(b) With regard to Natives on the farms of the White people, they interfere with rights the Natives have exercised for generations. In particular they interfere with the right the Natives have as British Subjects of bargaining with the owners of these farms. In effect this produces a condition of slavery. This is due to a provision which encourages the farmer to exact unpaid service from the native tenants. In the event of eviction the tenant is unable to settle upon any other farm, except as a farm servant, and therefore is forced to accept almost any conditions the farmer likes to impose upon him. This we claim is slavery.

(*c*) In point of fact the avowed object of the new law is that of forcing the Native to labour, by making it the only condition of his living on a White man's farm.

(*d*) Under the new Law also no native may occupy or own any land in the Orange Free State.

The natives of South Africa are loyal subjects of His Majesty the King, but they have no voice in the Legislative Councils of the country in which they live (except to a limited degree in the Cape Province), and their appeal was first made through us to His Majesty's Representatives in South Africa. This having failed to secure redress we then approached the adviser of His Majesty the King in this Country on Colonial affairs (The Rt. Hon. Lewis Harcourt), but without avail. Among the natives of South Africa His Majesty is looked upon as their natural protector, and it is their faith in His Majesty's sense of justice that has impelled them to send us here.

We append herewith our memorandum to the Rt. Hon. Lewis Harcourt and a letter from the Anti-Slavery and Aborigines Protection Society, and we are confident that these documents, together with the foregoing statement, establish the reasonableness of our appeal, and the urgent necessity of some public action on the part of the Parliament and people of the United Kingdom.

DOCUMENT 37. *Native Life in South Africa,* by Solomon Plaatje, 1916 [Extracts] (Printed, 382 pages)

General Hertzog's Scheme

It may interest the reader to know that General Hertzog is the father of the segregation controversy. The writer and other Natives interviewed him before Christmas, 1912, at the Palace of Justice, Pretoria, when he was still in the ministry. We had a two hours' discussion, in the course of which the General gave us a forecast of what he then regarded as possible native areas, and drew rings on a large wall-map of the Union to indicate their locality. Included in these rings were several Magistracies which he said would solve a knotty problem. He told us that white people objected to black men in Government offices and magistrates in those areas would have no difficulty in employing them.

General Hertzog was dismissed shortly after, and it has been said that in order to placate his angry admirers the Ministry passed the Natives' Land Act of which this Report is the outcome. Judging by the vigour with which the Union administration has been weeding Natives out of the public service and replacing them with Boers without waiting for the Commission's Report, it is clear that they did not share General Hertzog's intention as regards these magistracies. I cannot recall all the magistracies which General Hertzog mentioned as likely to fall in native areas; but I distinctly remember that Pietersburg and Thaba Nchu were among them; while Alice and Peddie (and possibly a neighbouring district) were to be included in a southern reserve into which the Natives round East London and Grahamstown would have to move, the land vacated by them to be gradually occupied by the white settlers now scattered over the would-be native block. He went on to forecast a vast dependency of the Union in which the energies and aspirations of black professional men would find their outlet with no danger of competition with Europeans; where a new educational and representative system could be evolved for Natives to live their own lives, and work out their salvation in a separate sphere. But the lands Commission's Report places this plausible scheme beyond the region of possibility, for no native area, recommended by this Commission, includes any of the magistracies mentioned.

General Hertzog's plan at least offered a fair ground for discussion, but the Commission's Report is a travesty of his scheme. It intensifies every native difficulty and goes much further than the wild demands of the "Free" State extremists. Thus even if it be thrown out, as it deserves to be, future exploiters will always cite it as an excuse for measures subversive of native well-being. In fact, that such legislation should be mooted is nothing short of a national calamity.

How They "Doubled"
A Native Area

Near the northern boundaries of Transvaal there lies a stretch of malarial country in which nothing can live unless born there. Men and beasts from other parts visit it only in winter and leave it again before the rains begin, when the atmosphere becomes almost too poisonous to inhale. Even the unfailing tax-gatherers of the Native Affairs Department go there only in the winter every year and hurry back again with the money bags before the malarial period sets in. A Boer general describes how when harassed by the Imperial forces during the South African war, he was once compelled to march through it; and how his men and horses—many of them natives of the Transvaal—contracted enough malaria during the march to cause the illness of many and the death of several Burghers and animals. Of the native inhabitants of this delectable area the Dutch General says: "Their diminutive, deformed stature was another proof of the miserable climate obtaining there."[1]

When the Land Commissioners contemplated this "salubrious" region, their hearts must have melted with generosity, for whereas in our own healthy part of South Africa they have indicated possible native areas by little dots of microscopical rings (as in Thaba Nchu for instance), here, in this malarial area, they marked off a reserve almost as wide as that described by General Hertzog himself at our Pretoria interview. It is possibly in this way, and in such impossible places, that the Commission is alleged to have "doubled" the native areas. In the rest of the country they ask Parliament to confiscate our birthright to the soil of our ancestry in favour of 600,000 Boers and aliens whose languages can show no synonym for Home—the English equivalent of our IKAYA and LEGAE!

The Britishers' vocabulary includes that sacred word: and that, perhaps, is the reason why their colonizing schemes have always allowed some tracts of country for native family life, with reasonable opportunities for

their future existence and progress, in the vast South African expanses which God in His providence had created for His Children of the Sun. The Englishman, moreover, found us speaking the word *Legae,* and taught us how to write it. In 1910, much against our will, the British Government surrendered its immediate sovereignty over our land to Colonials and cosmopolitan aliens who know little about a Home, because their dictionaries contain no such loving term; and the recommendations of this Commission would seem to express their limited conception of the word and its beautiful significance.

Natives Have No Information
About the Coming Servitude

All too little (if anything at all) is known of the services rendered to the common weal by the native leaders in South Africa. In every crisis of the past four years-and the one-sided policy of the Union has produced many of these—the native leaders have taken upon themselves the thankless and expensive task of restraining the Natives from resorting to violence. The seeming lack of appreciation with which the Government has met their success in that direction has been the cause of some comment among Natives. On more than one occasion they have asked whether the authorities were disappointed because, by their successful avoidance of bloodshed, the native leaders had forestalled the machine guns. But, be the reason what it may, this apparent ingratitude has not cooled their ardour in the cause of peace.

To-day the Native Affairs Department has handed over £7,000 from native taxes to defray the cost of the Land Commission, consisting of five white Commissioners, their white clerks and secretaries—the printing alone swallowed up nearly £1,000 with further payments to white translators for a Dutch edition of the Report. But not a penny could be spared for the enlightenment of the Natives at whose expense the inquiry has been carried through. They have been officially told and had every reason to believe that the Commission was going about to mark out reservations for them to occupy and live emancipated from the prejudicial conditions

[1]*My Reminiscences of the Anglo-Boer War* (General Ben Viljoen), p. 222.

that would spring from contiguity with the white race. For any information as to the real character of the contents of the Dutch and English Report of this Commission, they would have to depend on what they could gather from the unsalaried efforts of the native leaders, who, owing to the vastness of the sub-continent, the lack of travelling facilities and their own limited resources, can only reach a few localities and groups.

It may be said with some reason that English leaders of thought in South Africa have had a task of like difficulty: that they worked just as hard to get the English colonists to co-operate loyally with a vanquished foe in whose hands the Union constitution has placed the destiny of South Africa. It could also be said with equal justice that the Boer leaders' task has been not less difficult, that it required their greatest tact to get the Boer majority—now in power—to deal justly with the English who had been responsible for the elimination of the two Boer flags from among the emblems of the family of nations. But the difficulties of their task is not comparable to that of the native leaders. English and Dutch Colonial leaders are members of Parliament, each in receipt of £400 a year, with a free first class ticket over all systems of the South African Railways. They enjoy, besides, the co-operation of an army of well-paid white civil servants, without whom they could scarcely have managed their own people. The native leader, on the other hand, in addition to other impediments, has to contend with the difficulty of financing his own tours in a country whose settled policy is to see that Natives do not make any money. His position in his own country approximates to that of an Englishman, grappling single-handed with complicated problems, on foreign soil, without the aid of a British consul.

Bullyragging The Natives

For upwards of three years the Government of the Union of South Africa has harassed and maltreated the rural native taxpayers as no heathen monarch, since the time of the Zulu King Chaka, ever illused a tributary people. For the greater part of our period of suffering the Empire was engaged in a titanic struggle, which, for ghastliness is without precedent. I can think of no people in the Eastern Hemisphere who are absolutely unaffected by it; but the members of the Empire can find consolation in the fact that almost all creation is in sympathy with them. Constant disturbance has brought a realization to the entire universe that nature, like the times, is out of joint. The birds of the air and the fishes, like other denizens of the deep, are frequently drawn into the whirlpool of misery; and a mutual suffering has identified them as it were with some of the vicissitudes of an Empire at war. And they too have in their peculiar way felt impelled to offer their condolence to the dependants of those who have fallen in the combat on land, in the air, on sea, and under the sea. And while all creation stands aghast beside the gaping graves, by rivers of blood, mourning with us the loss of some of the greatest Englishmen that ever lived, South Africa, having constituted herself the only vandal State, possesses sufficient incompassion to celebrate the protection conferred on her by the British Fleet and devote her God-given security to an orgy of tyranny over those hapless coloured subjects of the King, whom the Union constitution has placed in the hollow of her hands.

Is there nobody left on earth who is just enough to call on South Africa to put an end to this cowardly abuse of power?

We appeal to the Colonists of Natal, who have declared themselves against the persecution of their Natives; and would draw their attention to the fact that in spite of their disapproval, expressed to the Lands Commission, the Union Government, at the behest of a prisoner, is still tyrannizing over the Zulus.

We appeal to the Churches. We would remind them that in the past the Christian voice has been our only shield against legislative excesses of the kind now in full swing in the Union. But in the new ascendency of self and pelf over justice and tolerance, that voice will be altogether ignored, unless strongly reinforced by the Christian world at large. We appeal for deliverance from the operation of a cunningly conceived and a most draconian law whose administration has been marked by the closing down of native Churches and Chapels in rural South Africa.

We appeal to the Jews, God's chosen people, who know what suffering means. We would remind them that if after 1913 there was no repetition of a Russian pogrom it was largely because the native leaders (including the author) have spared neither pains nor pence in visiting the scattered tribes and exhorting them to obey all the demands of the South African Government under the Grobler law pending a peaceful intercession from the outside world. But for this self-imposed duty on the part of the native leaders, I am satisfied that numbers of the native peasantry would have been mown down early in 1914, and humanity would have been told that they were justly punished for disobedience to constituted authority.

We appeal to the leaders of the Empire—that Empire for which my own relatives have sacrificed life and property in order to aid its extension along the Cape to Cairo route, entirely out of love for her late Majesty Queen Victoria and with no expectation of material reward. We ask these leaders to honour the plighted word of their noble predecessors who collectively and severally assured us a future of peace and happiness as our membership privilege in the Empire for which we bled. They were among the noblest Englishmen that ever left their native shores to create a prestige for their nation abroad. They included heroes and empire-builders too many to mention, who all told us that they spoke in the name of Queen Victoria and on behalf of her heirs and successors. What has suddenly become of the Briton's word—his bond—that solemn obligations of such Imperialists should cease to count? And if it is decided that the Victorian Englishman and the Twentieth Century Englishman are creatures of different clay (and that with the latter honour is binding only when both parties to the undertaking are white), surely this could hardly be the moment to inaugurate a change the reaction of which cannot fail to desecrate the memories of your just and upright forebears.

We would draw the attention of the British people to the fact that the most painful part of the present ordeal to the loyal black millions, who are now doing all they can, or are allowed to do, to help the Empire to win the war, is that they suffer this consummate oppression at the bidding of a gentleman now serving his term for participating in a rebellion during this war. We feel that it must be a source of intense satisfaction to Mr. Piet Grobler in his cell, that the most loyal section of the King's South African subjects are suffering persecution under his law—a fact which, looked at from whatever standpoint, is equal to an official justification of the ideals for which he rose in rebellion. And if there is to be a return to the contented South Africa of other days, both the Natives' Land Act—his law—and the Report of the Lands Commission—its climax—should be torn up.

Courting Retribution

For three years and more the South African Government have persecuted my kinsmen and kinswomen for no other crime than that they have meekly paid their taxes. I had come to the conclusion, after meeting Colonials from all quarters of the globe and weighing the information obtained from them, that in no Colony are the native inhabitants treated with greater injustice than in South Africa.[1] Yet in spite of all I had seen and heard, I must say that, until this Report reached me, I never would have believed my white fellow-countrymen capable of conceiving the all but diabolical schemes propounded between the covers of Volume I of the Report of the South African Lands Commission, 1916, and clothing them in such plausible form as to mislead even sincere and well-informed friends of the Natives. There are pages upon pages of columns of figures

[1]Some white South Africans in recent years have migrated to the Katanga region in the Belgian Congo. I have read in the South African daily papers, correspondence from some of them complaining of their inability to make money. They attributed this difficulty to the fact that the Belgian officials will not permit them to exploit the labour of the Congolese as freely as white men are accustomed to make use of the Natives in British South Africa.

running into four, five or six noughts. They will dazzle the eye until the reader imagines himself witnessing the redistribution of the whole sub-continent and its transfer to the native tribes. But two things he will never find in that mass of figures; these are (a) the grand total of the land so "awarded" to Natives; and (b) how much is left for other people. To arrive at these he has to do his own additions and subtractions, and call in the aid of statistics such as the Census figures, the annual blue books, etc., before the truth begins to dawn on him. They talk of having "doubled" the native areas. They found us in occupation of 143,000,000 morgen and propose to squeeze us into 18 million. If this means doubling it, then our teachers must have taught us the wrong arithmetic. Is it any wonder that it is becoming increasingly difficult for us to continue to love and respect the great white race as we truly loved it at the beginning of this century?

We would submit a few problems in this Report for the British People and their Parliamentary Representatives to solve:—

First: Who are to become the occupants of the lands from which the Commission recommends the removal of the native proletariat?

Secondly: In view of certain upheavals which we have seen not very long ago, and others which might take place in the future, it is pertinent to ask, concerning the "very small minority of the inhabitants"—the Whites—alluded to by Mr. Schreiner at the head of this chapter, (a) what proportion is in full sympathy with the ideals of the British Empire; (b) what proportion remains indifferent; and (c) what proportion may be termed hostile?

Thirdly: Does the autonomy granted to this "small minority" amount to complete independence, or does it not?

Fourthly: Would it not be advisable also to inquire: Of "the vast majority of the inhabitants" the King's Black subjects, doomed by this Report to forfeit their homes and all they value in their own country, (a) how many of these are loyal, and (b) how many are not?

Finally and solemnly we would put it to all concerned for the honour and perpetuity of British dominion in South Africa, can the Empire afford to tamper with and alienate their affections?

As stated already, this "very vast majority of the inhabitants" of South Africa has been strafed by the "very small minority" for over three years. And when the burden loaded on our bent backs becomes absolutely unbearable we are at times inclined to blame ourselves; for, when some of us fought hard—and often against British diplomacy—to extend the sphere of British influence, it never occurred to us that the spread of British dominion in South Africa would culminate in consigning us to our present intolerable position, namely, a helotage under a Boer oligarchy. But when an official Commission asks Parliament to herd us into concentration camps, with the additional recommendation that besides breeding slaves for our masters, we should be made to pay for the upkeep of the camps: in other words, that we should turn the Colonials into slave raiders and slave-drivers (but save them the expense of buying the slaves), the only thing that stands between us and despair is the thought that Heaven has never yet failed us. We remember how African women have at times shed tears under similar injustices; and how when they have been made to leave their fields with their hoes on their shoulders, their tears on evaporation have drawn fire and brimstone from the skies. But such blind retribution has a way of punishing the innocent alike with the guilty, and it is in the interests of both that we plead for some outside intervention to assist South Africa in recovering her lost senses.

The ready sympathy expressed by those British people among whom I have lived and laboured during the past two years inspires the confidence that a consensus of British opinion will, in the Union's interest, stay the hand of the South African Government, veto this iniquity and avert the Nemesis that would surely follow its perpetration.

DOCUMENT 38. Petition to King George V, from the South African Native National Congress, December 16, 1918 (Typewritten, 11 pages)

Memorial

To His Most Gracious Majesty King George V of Great Britain and Ireland including the

Dominions and Colonies, and Emperor of India.

May It Please Your Majesty—

1. We, the Chiefs and delegates assembled at Johannesburg, this 16th day of December, 1918, in the Special Session of the South African Native National Congress, a political body representing the various tribes of the Bantu people in South Africa, record the expression of our satisfaction and thankfulness in the triumph of righteousness in this great war by the victory of the forces of Great Britain, her noble Allies, and the United States of America.

2. We beg to convey to Your Majesty our affectionate loyalty and devotion to Your Majesty's person and Throne and the sincerity of our desire that Divine Blessing and prosperity may attend Your Majesty and all Your Majesty's Dominions in the dawn of a better age.

3. We further express the hope and wish that during Your Majesty's Reign all races and Nations will be treated fairly and with justice, and that there will be no discrimination on account of colour or creed; and will enjoy the right of citizenship, freedom and liberty under your flag.

4. It would scarcely be necessary to recite the active part played by ourselves—Your Majesty's subjects—in the prosecution of the Great War, but the occasion and the purposes of this Memorial justify such a recital:—

(a) It will be remembered that up till August 1914 the National Congress had a Deputation of its men in London to petition Your Majesty to exercise the right of veto against the Natives Land Act 1913, and at the outbreak of hostilities in Europe, Congress prompted by a sense of loyalty to Your Majesty's Throne and the British Empire made representations to the Governor-General of the Union of South Africa informing His Excellency that the Bantu people were prepared to render every assistance in the defence of Your Majesty's Throne and Empire, which pledge was greatly appreciated by His Excellency, the Governor-General and High Commissioner of South Africa.

(b) We offered 5,000 strong men to go and fight the Germans in South-West Africa, but we regret to say that the offer was refused by His Excellency the Governor—General's Ministers of the Union of South Africa on the ground that this war was waged between white people only, whereas we were as vitally affected by the results of the war as any white subjects of Your Majesty.

(c) Thousands of our men went to German South West Africa as drivers and to assist in the Railway construction into that Territory for military purposes.

(d) It will be significant to every one that during the trying and provocative times of the Rebellion in this country, we remained perfectly quiet and passive, without causing the slightest embarrassment to the Union Government, when difficult circumstances offered dangerous and ill-advised temptations to an oppressed people.

(e) 17,000 of our men took part in the campaign in German East Africa under the Right Honourable Lieutenant-General J. C. Smuts, Minister of Defence of the Union, and there participated in fighting and transport capacities—many of whom died with malaria fever and suffered severe hardships and privations.

(f) We heartily responded to the call of your Majesty's Imperial Government and the Army Council, for 25,000 men to do manual work in the French docks, and behind the trenches in Flanders. Our men braved the oceans and endured the hardships of European cold weather, all under new and rough war conditions; 615 of our men sank in the S. S. Mendi while in the service of Your Majesty and the Empire. Owing to circumstances beyond our control, but we believe them to be due to the Union Government's political prejudices, the South African Native Labour Overseas Contingent was demobilised against our wish and much to our despairing regret, while we were still prepared to send more men to assist in the World-wide war of Justice, Freedom and Liberty.

(g) For a period of four years and since the commencement of hostilities our countrymen steadfastly maintained the supply of labour in the Gold Mines on the Rand, thus affording a continued output of gold and the availability of cyanide for purposes of war: coal Mines and Harbours and all other industries necessary for the prosecution of the war were adequately supplied with the labour of our people, which was indispensable.

(h) While our men were engaged in the various theatres of war, in non-combatant capacities as already shown, those of us remaining at home gave contributions in money and kind according to our means, towards the support of the various War Funds. Chiefs gave cattle, mealies and curios—all of which have been gratefully acknowledged by Your Majesty's representatives in this country.

(i) Your Majesty will no doubt recognise that all the assistance given by us in this great war was entirely voluntary and made without any coercion or inducements. There was no promise of pension or bonus to our men and no provision made for their dependents out of the Governor-General's Fund or any other War Funds.

Compensation for those injured or killed in war during employment was extremely inadequate, and yet the Chiefs and our Leaders continued to hold meetings throughout the country, exhorting people to remain quiet and loyal during the war, and also encouraging the recruiting of our men for labour, and expressing the insistent desire to be allowed to bear arms and fight as soldiers of Your Majesty.

All these acts were performed and rendered by Your Majesty's subjects who—except in the Cape Province—have no voice in the disposition of the affairs of the country of which they are the aboriginal inhabitants, and your subjects who are admittedly loyal and law-abiding, are without any recognition or safeguard under the constitution of the Union of South Africa.

5. In the appreciation of the service and loyalty of Your Majesty's subjects recited in the preceding paragraph 4, we are reminded by Your Majesty's message to our Chiefs and people delivered to the representatives of the South African Native Labour Contingent at Abberville in France on the 10th July 1917, saying:—

"This work of yours (meaning ourselves) is second only in importance to that performed by the Sailors and Soldiers who are bearing the brunt of the battle. But you also form part of my great Armies which are fighting for the liberty and freedom of my subjects of all races and creeds throughout my Empire. Without Munition of War my Armies cannot fight: without food they cannot live. You are helping to send these things to them each day, and in doing so you are hurling your spears at the enemy, and hastening the destruction that awaits him.

"A large Corps such as yours requires drafts and reinforcements. I am sure your Chiefs will take upon themselves this duty of supporting your Battalions by ever increasing numbers. I wish them and their people to share with all my loyal subjects that great and final victory which will bring peace throughout the world.

"I desire you to make these words of mine known to your people here, and to convey them to your Chiefs in South Africa."

And also the message of His Excellency Lord Buxton, the Governor-General of the Union, before a Mass Meeting of the Bantu people representing many of our tribes assembled at Johannesburg on the 8th Dec. 1918, on the occasion of the Peace Thanksgiving Service, as follows:—" . . . .My second duty which gives me much pleasure, is to thank you, on behalf of His Majesty the King, for the assistance and loyalty which you and the natives you represent throughout South Africa, have shown to him and to the Empire, during these four years of strain and stress. To thank you also for the help that you have in various ways given to him against his enemies. I was especially glad to be received today by the Members of the Native Labour Contingent, who have done such good work in Europe . . . . But in spite of all these difficulties and temptations, the natives have remained steadfastly loyal. The war has proved to you that your loyalty was well placed; and I can assure you it will not be forgotten."

Again we are encouraged to mention the appreciation expressed in the Parliament of the Union of South Africa on the occasion of the Mendi disaster when the Right Honourable General Louis Botha, Prime Minister of the Union said:—

"If we ever lived in times when native people of South Africa have shown great and true loyalty, it is in time like the present. Ever since the War broke out the Natives have done everything possible to help where such was possible, in the struggle, without ever doing that which was in conflict to their loyalty to the flag and the King. Nearly all my life long I have had to deal with Native questions, but I have never experienced a time when the Natives have displayed greater tact and greater loyalty than they have done in the difficult and the dark days through which we are now going. It has never happened in the history of South Africa that in one moment by one fell swoop such a lot of people have perished, and I think that where people have died as they have done, it is our duty to remember that they have come forward on their own accord, of their free will, and that they have said—'If we can help, we'll do so, even if we have to show our loyalty with our hands.' They insisted on going, and I think, they deserve every credit for the good work they have done. These people said, 'this war is waging and we want to help'. In doing so they have shown their loyalty to their King, their Flag, and their Country, and what they have done will redound to their everlasting credit."

Lastly we cannot refrain from mentioning the expression of appreciation by Field Marshall Sir Douglas Haig, Commander of the British Forces in France, of the splendid services rendered by the members of the South African Native Labour Contingent on the occasion of their return from France through the message to Lt. Col. Sir S. M. Pritchard, the officer commanding the Native Labour Contingent in France.

6. We are mindful of the great main fact that Great Britain and her Allies as well as the United States of America went into war (inter alia) for the protection of small and weak nations: for the enforcement of international treaties and agreements; to liberate oppressed nations; to grant every nation, great or small, the right to determine its sovereign destiny and the free choice of its own government and flag; and to allow subject races to express their voice in the final control and disposal of their territories and to choose the flag under which they desire to be protected; to make the world fit and safe for every man to live in with freedom to choose his own destiny.

7. The Bantu people of South Africa have ever been impressed with the high ideals permeating the British Constitution, and in this connection have always held the memory of the late Queen Victoria, The Good, with reverence and devotion. It was in her illustrious reign that the black people were emancipated from slavery in 1834.

In Her late Majesty's Proclamation of Natal in 1843, any discrimination in the eyes of the law on account of race, colour, or creed, as well as slavery in any shape or form, were distinctly repudiated. Even under the two Conventions in the Transvaal in 1881 and 1884, the late Queen Victoria discountenanced slavery in any shape or form. All these Proclamations and Conventions contain principles which are still regarded by Your Majesty's subjects as their Magna Charter [sic].

It is with painful regret that we remind Your Majesty that these Victorian principles with which our people associate with the high ideals of the British Constitution have been departed from and in the main dishonoured and ignored by Your Majesty's representative Governments in South Africa.

We humbly submit to Your Most Gracious Majesty that the black inhabitants of this land who are Your Majesty's subjects, on account of their race, colour, language and creed, live under a veiled form of slavery. The subject's inherent right of freedom and the right to move at liberty is unwarrantably restricted, and the individual cannot bargain, under existing laws with his labour as he chooses. Equal opportunities for trading are denied and the avenues of civilized advancement are limited.

8. We wish to inform your Majesty that the policy proposed by the successive Governments in South Africa have from time to time been detrimental to the original rights of your subjects in land ownership and occupation followed by calculated encroachments on their inherent rights to acquire land, as also the projected administrator of Native Affairs, —all of which have confirmed previous apprehensions and misgivings and have created serious alarm and mistrust accordingly.

(a) Your Majesty's humble subjects pray that the Territory of Zululand should remain integral for the use and occupation of the original inhabitants in terms of Her Late Majesty's Annexation Proclamation in 1897, and that in any event no delimitation or other encroachment on the remaining portion of the land delimited in 1902 should be allowed and that such attempt is considered by Your Majesty's subjects as a breach then given to the people of Zululand that the delimitation then made would be final. The Union Government's projected land Legislation threatens a further encroachment as against that undertaking.

(b) Your Majesty's subjects further pray for a review of Her Late Majesty's Proclamation of 1848 in conjunction with the Convention of 1854 relative to certain lands in the Orange Free State belonging to and claimed by the Batlokoa and the Bagolokoe tribes. These claims afford a just case for review and readjustment in the Orange Free State because the undertakings then given under the said Proclamation and Convention have been departed from without any compensation or other relief being granted to the original owners of the land. The recognition of the Orange Free State Independence as a Republic was never intended to violate or sacrifice any inherent rights of the inhabitants therein nor did Her Late Majesty concede to forego Great Britain's responsibility in connection therewith.

(c) Your Majesty's subjects further pray for a review of the Conventions of 1881 and 1884 relating to the Transvaal, wherein under Article 19, Freedom to acquire land and the setting aside of tribal land or locations were, amongst other things, assured to the Native inhabitants. These assurances have scarcely ever been carried out and today Your Majesty's subjects in the Northern Transvaal find themselves dispossessed of land and their original holdings encroached upon.

(d) Your Majesty's subjects pray for a review of the Proclamations affecting what is now termed the Transkeian Territories in the Cape Province; as also an exhaustive review of the landed rights of the peoples of Mashonaland. Each and every one of these claims are justly and reasonably subject for reconsideration having regard to the projected land Legislation of Your Majesty's Representatives in South Africa, of which Your Majesty's subjects are seriously apprehensive and alarmed; and a feeling of discontent and mistrust would considerably be allayed by means of a Royal Judicial Commission to enquire into and to make a permanent adjustment of the several land claims and to right past wrongs and injustices.

9. In pursuance of Great Britain's war aims and her love for free institutions for all peoples under her flag and these aims being adapted and conconant with those of Her Allies and the United States of America, the only solution therefore is to have those principles applied to South Africa so that we may have a voice in the affairs of the country, and have full protection so as to check reactionary legislation and unpopular one-sided laws. To put these principles into effect it may please Your Majesty to cause a revision of the South African Constitution in such manner as to grant enfranchisement of natives throughout the Union; and further so as to make provision for the protection of the aboriginal national institutions being respected and developed, and further so as to give effect to the principle contained in the Royal Letters Patent of 1865 in Natal in regard to the franchise.

10. Great Britain has committed wrong in the past by omitting to consult the wishes of the people concerned. We desire to appraise Your Majesty of the fact that when the Protectorates called Basutoland, Swaziland and Bechuanaland sought protection of Her Majesty Queen Victoria, they never surrendered their tribal land and their sovereign rights. They remain this day integral dependent Nations. Particularly the independence of Swaziland as recognized under the London Convention of 1884 in the Transvaal.

They were never conquered and they never at any time waived or surrendered their sovereign rights. They have faithfully adhered to the original terms of protection in reverend memory of Queen Victoria, under whom they sought protection. They have remained loyal. It is their wish and of ourselves that not one of these Protectorates should be transferred to the Union without the consent of the peoples concerned being first obtained.

Further, it will ever be borne in mind that

these Protectorates have played a part in the prosecution of the Great War in men and money.

11. Neither Great Britain, nor the Allies and United States of America fought a war for territorial acquisition, therefore the conquered territories in Africa should not be disposed of or their future destiny determined without the wishes of the inhabitants being first ascertained.

That both German South West and German South East should never be handed to the Union Government of South Africa unless its system of rule be radically altered so as to dispel colour prejudice; but that these territories and the Congo States be placed under the control of the United States of America (subject to the wishes of the peoples concerned), in trust for and to be developed in the interests of African inhabitants until they become sufficiently advanced for their own civilized government.

That the question of the control in the Congo States be re-opened so as to divest Belgium of any right thereto, since her atrocious crimes and misdeeds have caused de-population, proving that she is unable to control African Colonies.

12. Having regard to the prevailing desire for independence amongst white races in South Africa under the form of Republicanism, it is recorded that we shall never consent or tolerate such independence without the consent of the Native inhabitants who are quite content to remain under British Rule.

In conclusion, we, Your Majesty's most loyal and humble subjects, lay this Memorial before Your Majesty on this supreme and unique occasion of the cessation of hostilities with thankfulness and satisfaction that Your Majesty's Memorialists have taken an active part in bringing about victory and peace, and in full confidence that the position of Your Majesty's subjects under the sun will be improved and be readjusted in terms of this Memorial.

We are, &c.,
By order of

South African Native National Congress in its Special Session at Johannesburg on the 16th day of December in the year of Our Lord One thousand Nine hundred and Eighteen.

(sgd)   S. A. Makgatho,
PRESIDENT.

(sgd)   I. Bud-M'Belle
GENERAL SECRETARY.

PART THREE

New Gropings for Effective Organization and Representation , 1921-1934

Introduction

The postwar era opened inauspiciously for Africans in South Africa. The unrest which had been evident in the immediate postwar months continued into the early 1920s and culminated in a series of direct confrontations with white authorities. In October 1920, demonstrations by Africans in Port Elizabeth in support of an arrested African trade union leader sparked a reaction from white vigilantes and policemen in which twenty-three Africans and one white were killed. In May 1921, frustrated white authorities finally resorted to the use of force after the Israelites, a millenarian separatist sect, had repeatedly refused to move from ground outside of Bulhoek in Cape Province, where they had squatted for over a year. When a reinforced police unit was sent to eject them, the Israelites resisted with primitive weapons. In a one-sided struggle, 163 Africans were killed and 129 were wounded. In 1922, Bondelswarts tribesmen in South-West Africa challenged the imposition of new taxes by the South African administration of the former German colony; in a series of raids against the rebels, the government reestablished its authority at a cost of numerous African dead. These incidents underlined the determination of the white government to suppress ruthlessly what it regarded as serious challenges to its authority.

Yet it was not direct black-white confrontations that shaped the overall viewpoint of the government on the "Native question" during the 1920s and 1930s, but rather a series of developments within the white community itself. The key mining industry of the Witwatersrand had long attracted both white and nonwhite workers. Tradition, entrenched by legislation, allotted a monop-oly of the skilled, highly paid positions at the top of the labor pyramid to the white minority, most of whom were English immigrants familiar with militant trade unionism; the nonwhite majority, overwhelmingly new African immigrants to the urban areas, was restricted to the unskilled, poorly paid positions. Faced with rising costs and declining profits, the mine owners began to hint that the color bar should be breached so that Africans and other nonwhites could advance into skilled positions—albeit at wages well below the rates for whites. White labor, already suspicious of the mine magnates on ideological grounds, reacted with determined opposition to the threat to their privileged position.

The issue was further complicated by the intrusion of another factor: the steady influx of poor white Afrikaners into the urban areas. Squeezed off their farms by persistent drought and the growing infertility of land, displaced Afrikaner *bywoners* flooded to the racially segmented labor markets of the cities. *Bywoners* were rural Afrikaners who squatted on the farms of the white landowners. Since the early twentieth century, tension had been growing between *bywoners* and landowners as a result of land becomming progressively less available, repeated droughts, and increasing concern for profits in agriculture. Although the Afrikaners, like the Africans, were initially untrained for skilled work, particularly in a new environment dominated by English, which to them was a "foreign" language, they demanded inclusion among the ranks of highly paid white labor on the basis of their skin color. Their presence sharpened the already tense relations between white capital and organized white labor.

During World War I, confrontation

between capital and labor had been postponed. In a spirit of patriotism, the English-led trade unions and the Chamber of Mines had agreed to maintain the status quo for the duration of the war; both sides, in fact, benefited from the war-induced expansion, which drew substantial numbers of whites and Africans into the labor-hungry South African economy.

With the coming of peace and the spread of postwar economic difficulties, the issues of the color bar and of white wages came to the fore. Labor disputes multiplied throughout the Witwatersrand. A crisis was reached in 1922 when a dispute between a section of the white workers and the Chamber of Mines escalated into a general strike. The key issue for the white workers was the retention of their privileged position through the maintenance of the color bar. When a section of the strikers, including both English-speaking left-wing socialists and Afrikaner militants, used armed action to support their demands, the Smuts government invoked martial law, broke the strike by force, and restored public order. In the eyes of the defeated white strikers the Smuts government had aligned itself with the Chamber of Mines.

The crushing of the "Red Revolt" set the stage for a radical realignment in South African white politics. Previously, the rurally based Nationalist Party, dedicated to Afrikaner republicanism and racial segregation, had been wary of the socialism of the English-speaking white workers. From its side, the professedly socialist South African Labor Party, anchored among the English-speaking white workers and committed to the maintenance of their privileged position, was hostile to the republicanism of the Nationalists. In the wake of the 1922 strike, however, the determination of both groups to oust their common political adversary, General Smuts, provided a new and compelling incentive to compromise in the interests of a common political platform. After a series of delicate negotiations, the Nationalists and the South African Labor Party agreed early in 1923 to an electoral pact under General Hertzog in opposition to the South African Party of General Smuts. In return for Nationalist agreement to postpone republican demands, the

South African Labor Party agreed to postpone its socialist goal. Both parties were united in their conviction that additional segregation was imperative for the welfare of white South Africa.

The Africans had remained aloof during the 1922 disturbances, except when they reacted to unprovoked attacks by white strikers. A resolution passed by the Industrial and Commercial Workers' Union (see below) at a meeting in Cape Town indicated their feelings about the situation. The resolution condemned the attacks on non-Europeans and called on the government to protect the people; at the same time it blamed the color bar for the trouble on the Rand, and demanded its abolition. In response, however, to a "Republican Resolution" passed by certain elements among the white strikers at a meeting in Johannesburg, and to their open urging of armed revolt, the ICU called on nonwhites to be loyal to government, King, and country. On its side, the government assured the country that the Africans had done nothing to cause trouble; yet it pushed forward with its restrictive program.

In the following year, the Smuts administration passed the Natives (Urban Areas) Act of 1923, which provided for a standardized system within which white municipalities could limit and regulate the burgeoning African settlements within their boundaries. Municipalities were empowered to establish new "locations" for Africans outside or on the edge of white residential areas. These locations were under the control of white superintendents, but provision was made for setting up "Native Advisory Boards" to act as channels for the expression of opinion by their African residents. Municipalities could also define the categories of Africans who were permitted to live in urban areas. The legislation thus authorized influx control; yet there were no complementary measures to provide more land in rural areas for those Africans excluded from the cities.

With the victory of the Nationalist-South African Labor Party coalition in the general elections of 1924, a further impetus was given to segregationist policies. The Nationalists, increasingly concerned about the rapidly growing poor white population (almost 60 percent of the Afrikaner population at the height of their distress), and the Labourites, determined to preserve the protected position of the privileged white workers, moved quickly to satisfy the demands of their supporters. In its first two years in office, the Pact government unveiled a far-reaching program to entrench the position of white labor.

Under the guidance of Col. F.H.P. Creswell, the leader of the parliamentary wing of the Labour Party, who was appointed to the newly created post of minister of labour, a series of measures was passed that reinforced the privileged position of white workers and further differentiated their status from that of African labor. The Industrial Conciliation Act of 1924 had established machinery for the negotiation of labor disputes but specifically excluded "pass-carrying natives" (i.e., African males, the vast majority of the African labor force) from its provisions. Building upon this legacy of the Smuts administration, the Pact government passed the Wages Act of 1925 for the governmental determination of wage rates within specific industries. Agricultural and domestic workers (the largest categories of the lowest paid African workers) were specifically excluded from coverage under the legislation. The Mines and Works Amendment Act, 1926, overrode a court ruling of 1923 and once again made the color bar legal in the mining industry. The Pact government also pursued a much-publicized "civilized labor policy" under which poor white Afrikaners increasingly replaced Africans and other nonwhites at inflated wage rates in a wide range of relatively unskilled jobs in government-operated enterprises such as the railways.

The most comprehensive statement of the segregation policy of the Pact government was made by Nationalist Prime Minister Hertzog in a carefully reported speech made on November 13, 1925, in the small Orange Free State town of Smithfield. The program for his "solution" to the "Native" question was an elaboration of views that he had broadly outlined much earlier, prior to the introduction of the Natives Land Act of 1913. It consisted of four points:

1) Removal of all African voters from the common roll where they voted for the same candidates as did whites in the Cape Province.

2) A final delimitation of land within the framework of the Natives Land Act of 1913.

3) The establishment of electoral machinery by which African voters could indirectly elect a small number of white members to the South African Parliament, and

4) The establishment of partly nominated, partly elected local "Native councils" in the areas designated as African with further provision for an all-Union "Native council" to advise on African questions.

In a parallel proposal directed at the Coloureds, General Hertzog offered guarantees to fix their legal and political status at an intermediate point between those of the Africans and the whites. Early in 1926, he presented his proposals to the Parliament in what came to be known as the "Native Bills." Simultaneously, his proposals regarding the Coloureds were introduced as the Coloured Persons Rights Bill.

Up to 1935, Hertzog's Native Bills hung as an ever-present threat over the African population of South Africa. In keeping with his grand scheme, Hertzog insisted the bills be passed in toto and not separately. But in accordance with the "entrenched" clause of the Act of Union, the crucial provision to remove Africans from the common roll in Cape Province, where they had long voted for the same candidates as did whites, required a two-thirds vote of a joint sitting of both houses of Parliament. While most of the white opposition agreed with part of Hertzog's scheme, he was not able to win the necessary extraordinary majority during the period the Pact government or its successor Nationalist Party government was in power.

The failure of the Pact government to gain passage of the Native Bills did not mean that it desisted from efforts further to regulate African affairs. In 1927, supported by the opposition and opposed by only three dissident members of the Labour Party, the Pact government passed a Native Administration Bill. The measure enacted into law many of the provisions of the Native Administration Bill that had been proposed by the Botha government in 1917. The governor-general was given power to legislate by proclamation on African affairs, a power in effect exercised by the white-controlled government of the day. Most dramatically, the new bill included a "hostility clause" under which anyone inciting hostility between the races was liable to prosecution and punishment.

In 1929, General Hertzog went to the white electorate under the banner of the "Black Manifesto" in which the *swart gevaar* (black danger) was made the central issue, and the Nationalist Party heralded as the most effective protector of white supremacy. Elected to office upon a rising tide of votes sufficient to give the Nationalist Party an absolute majority in Parliament, General Hertzog was able to form a Nationalist Party government without the aid of the English-speaking South African Labour Party, although two of its leaders were included in the new cabinet. For the first time since Union, the South African government was controlled by an all-Afrikaner party.

The new government moved swiftly against a rising wave of African discontent that centered in Natal. Backed by the prime minister, the new Minister of Justice Oswald Pirow led a show of force in November, 1929, against Africans in Durban who had been boycotting municipal beer halls. In this same spirit, he piloted the Riotous Assemblies (Amendment) Bill through Parliament in 1930. This measure provided power to exile within South Africa persons deemed to create hostility between the races, thus giving new means to control radical political movements.

By other means, the government moved to assure its electoral base, and that of any future white government. White women were given the vote, as had been done in the United Kingdom in 1928, and at about the same time the property and educational requirements were removed for the white electorate, though not for the nonwhite voters of Cape Province. Temporarily thwarted in its objective of removing African voters from the common roll, Hertzog's Nationalist Party government compensated for this situation by substantially enlarging the white electorate.

The government's priorities were further revealed by its efforts to combat the impact upon South Africa of the worldwide depression. New welfare schemes for poor whites were devised, but not for Africans and other nonwhites, already at the bottom of the labor pyramid. Moreover, in 1932, the Native Service Contracts Act increased penalties for breach of contract and tightened restrictions on the movement by African labor outside the reserves. Although Africans were more involved than ever in the industrializing South African economy, the white-determined rules for their participation were being progressively strengthened to prevent any possible challenge to white superiority in any field.

Africans "Respectfully Submit"

It was against this unpromising backdrop that African protest continued to express itself from 1920 to 1935. Painfully aware of their growing disadvantages within the system, African leaders were still hopeful that the post-Union trend could be diverted into channels that were more promising for African advance.

At the conferences of African leaders which the governor-general called in accordance with the Native Affairs Act of 1920, Africans attempted to utilize the officially established advisory institutions. In terms of the act a group of Africans, selected each year by the government from among chiefs and other prominent persons, were invited to Pretoria for a three to six day meeting with the all-white Native Affairs Commission and a small number of white officials of the Native Affairs Department. Government thinking on key issues of importance to the African population was presented directly by responsible white ministers, including General Hertzog himself in 1925. In response, many of the invited Africans regularly challenged the paternalistic prescriptions of the white government, and constantly attempted to extend the platform from which they could discuss governmental policies.

The "civilized labor policy" of the Pact government soon came under fire. At the conference session in 1924 Africans also voiced concern that a differential standard of justice was being administered in the South African courts (see Document 39b). Yet it was the issue of African participation in the political process that most concerned the invited African delegates at these conferences.

They argued consistently that the government was failing to consult African opinion before it introduced measures affecting African affairs. Referring specifically to the institution of the conference itself, they proposed that its structure be altered to make it more representative, that Africans elect some of the delegates, and that it be given statutory powers guaranteeing consultation. In these arguments, always couched in respectful parliamentary language, African representatives showed themselves prepared to accept, at least temporarily, a restricted franchise coupled with a gradual extension of their political participation. Yet their speeches constantly reflected their commitment to an eventual full share in the South African political system (see Documents 39a, 39c, 39d).

In several instances there had been open differences between the African representatives of the three northern provinces and those of Cape Province. This was particularly the case in the discussions of the Registration and Protection Bill put forward by the Smuts administration in 1923 (see Document 39a). The bill proposed a standard system of African registration to replace the multitude of special local passes carried perforce by all African male residents of the northern provinces (and some in the Cape Province). Opposition to the pass system was universal and widespread, but the northerners, not surprisingly, were more willing than those from the Cape Province to accept a simplified and standardized system for all African males outside the reserves, including those in the Cape Province who had previously been exempt. The bill was not passed, but its discussion showed that some northerners might be willing to compromise the "privileges" of the Africans of the Cape Province in order to obtain some improvement of their own situation.

Despite their differences, Africans were unanimous in their reaction to General Hertzog's proposed Native Bills. Barely a month after his 1925 Smithfield speech, General Hertzog made his first (and only) appearance before the conference with a condensed version of his grand scheme for the "solution" of the "Native problem." He was received respectfully, even to the point where delegates expressed their appreciation for his willingness to tackle the complex "Native problem," but almost immediately voices were raised to attack the very concept of segregation upon which Hertzog's formula was based (see Document 39c). When the conference met in 1926 (after the publication of the Native Bills) it was nearly unanimous in its opposition both to the basic idea of segregation and to the specific proposals contained in the Native Bills (see Document 39d). Although the protests of the delegates brought no change in the government's intent, they testified again to the African elite's steadfast commitment to the ideal of a nonracial South Africa, to the depth of its opposition to any strengthening of the inequalities within the South African system, and to its awareness of the crucial significance of the common voters' roll in Cape Province.

Africans further elaborated on their attitudes to the Native Bills before the Select Committee of Parliament that considered the legislation (see Documents 40a, 40b). African witnesses testified to the necessity of maintaining the Cape franchise and its inherent nonracial promise — although, despite vigorous dissent from his fellow Africans, one witness (Meshach Pelem of the Bantu Union) indicated that he would be willing to accept separate representation. Professor Jabavu, deeply involved in Cape Province politics as president of the Cape Native Voters' Convention, specifically rejected arguments often made against the common voters' roll and defended its retention as an important sign of African progress within a common Western civilization. The representatives of the Transkeian Territories General Council argued from a strong mandate against the main provisions of the bills. Aware of the circumscribed limits within which their own representative institution operated, they warned that Africans in the proposed Native councils would tend merely to be "government men" and not representative of African opinion. While the Africans were willing to accept separate African provincial councils as forums to deal with specific regional problems, they were not prepared to abandon the Cape system of national African representation.

Africans and Whites in Dialogue

The government-sponsored conferences and committee hearings were institutions linked to the government's policy of expanding the machinery of segregation. In contrast, a small but growing number of whites, largely associated with Christian organizations, attempted to extend informal African-white contacts in an atmosphere where there could be sympathetic discussion of other possibilities for meeting South Africa's racial problems.

As the migration of Africans to the urban centers steadily increased, welfare societies among the whites undertook to investigate African living conditions and to extend charitable work into African townships. Following the 1921 visit of the Gold Coast educator, J. E. G. Aggrey, on a Carnegie endowment mission to study African education, concerned whites and members of the African middle class came together to form Joint Councils of Europeans and Bantu in the major South African cities. In 1929 the leaders of the Joint Council movement led in the creation of the South African Institute of Race Relations, a nonpartisan body oriented to research and conciliation to ameliorate racial tensions. The welfare societies, churches, the Joint Councils, and the Institute helped to focus attention on the social and economic conditions of the nonwhites. Moreover, in the multiracial meetings organized by these groups Africans found new opportunities to express their views.

African opinion varied in its estimate of the value of the meetings. In 1922, R. V. Selope Thema, a journalist who had been closely associated with Congress since its foundation and had been a member of its 1919 deputation to Europe, endorsed biracial meetings as a useful device to provide information (see Document 41a). He urged that the inextricably integrated nature of South African society should be recognized by a commitment to equal rights for all. If such a commitment was not forthcoming, however, Selope Thema felt that serious consideration should be given to an equitable separation of the races.

The Rev. Abner Mtimkulu (a member of an African delegation that had testified in 1917 before a Select Committee of Parliament against the proposed Native Administration Bill) supported the concept of joint meetings between white and black, with particular reference to the Cape Native Welfare Society (see Document 41c). In Mtimkulu's view, such conferences were especially useful in helping Africans who were caught in a new and strange urban environment.

But James Thaele of Cape Town, a self-styled "professor," presented a dissenting view with specific reference to the first Conference on Native Affairs held under the sponsorship of the Dutch Reformed Church in 1923 (see Document 41B). Recently returned from the United States where he had become a supporter of Garveyism, Thaele articulated the skepticism of those who were dubious about any solution of the "Native problem" posed strictly within the framework of Christianity. Thaele argued, instead, that explicitly political and trade union actions were the only means by which the African could achieve his ends. Although later in his political career Thaele became antiradical, he represented in 1923 the tradition of African politics that placed primary reliance upon independent African action. In contrast, both Selope Thema and Mtimkulu, the latter perhaps more than the former, were anxious to work with sympathetic whites in order to improve the African's position.

Dr. A. B. Xuma, a future president of the ANC during 1940-1949, made a still more detailed survey of the possibilities for interracial cooperation in a speech to the Conference of European and Bantu Christian Student Associations in 1930 (see Document 41d). From the perspective of more than a decade of medical training in the United States and Europe, he criticized South African race relations in the post-Union period in comparison with those in the United States. Yet he saw hope in the activities of the Joint Councils, in the integrity of the South African courts, and in the neutral attitudes of certain white newspapers. Leaning to the position of Selope Thema and Mtimkulu, yet incorporating Thaele's concern for self-reliance within the African community, Xuma urged expansion of opportunities for Africans and that

African views be seriously considered. Like Professor Jabavu a decade earlier, Xuma explicitly argued that the educated African was both the hope and the bridge linking black and white South Africa.

Both the potentialities and the limitations of unofficial joint conferences are reflected in the reports of conferences organized by the Dutch Reformed Churches and by the Joint Council movement. In conjunction with the official government-sponsored conference for African leaders in 1923, the Dutch Reformed Churches called a conference of their own in Johannesburg (the one of which Thaele had spoken); a second conference of this type was held in 1927 in Cape Town (see Documents 42a, 42b). The participants at both conferences — whites concerned with "Native affairs," most of them connected with religious groups, and African leaders from a wide variety of groups, including political organizations and trade unions — devoted considerable attention to discussing welfare measures. Yet African speakers also focused upon the main grievances agitating the African community, including unequal land distribution, the restrictions on Africans in urban areas, and lack of African political representation. Resolutions urged further joint conferences to discuss many issues. In 1927, however, the crucial issue of the Cape African franchise split the conference, many of whose white members were drawn from the ranks of the predominantly Afrikaner Dutch Reformed Churches.

Many of these same persons participated in the National European-Bantu Conferences, called yearly from 1929 on by a committee representing the Joint Councils of Europeans and Bantu. The National European-Bantu Conferences that were subsequently incorporated into the framework of the newly formed South African Institute of Race Relations, touched on most questions of concern to the African community (see Documents 43a, 43b). Although the discussions and resolutions of the conferences were never undertaken in a specifically political context, they tended to support those who were arguing for a sharp reversal of government policy away from the accelerating trend to segregation.

While the debates and statements of these conferences perhaps carried weight with those committed to the ideal of growing cooperation between African and white as partners or potential equals, they had relatively little effect on the overwhelming majority of white South Africans who saw Africans at best within a paternalistic framework. The conferences can be seen as a new form of common enterprise in the spirit of the "liberal" tradition implanted in the Cape Colony; yet the hopes they inspired were restricted to a small minority of white South Africans.

Non-Europeans Meet Together

Work with sympathetic whites for the advancement of the African cause was paralleled by the first coordinated efforts to bring together all groups of South African nonwhites in a united front to present their grievances to white South Africa. For the first time since the joint delegation of 1909, which had traveled to London in a vain effort to block passage of the Act of Union, Africans and other nonwhites attempted to devise a common strategy. On the initiative of Dr. Abdullah Abdurahman, president of the African People's Organization (and the leading Coloured representative in the 1909 delegation), a Non-European Conference was convened in 1927; three more were subsequently held in 1930, 1931, and 1934. The procedures of the Non-European Conferences with their emphasis upon discussion of nonwhite grievances and the passage of numerous resolutions recording opposition to government policy were much the same as those of the joint white-African conferences. Yet as gatherings restricted to nonwhites they represented an important extension of the range of African political activity.

The proceedings of these conferences indicated, however, the difficulties of achieving any common nonwhite front. Representatives of Indian organizations (in attendance for the first time at a meeting with South African Coloured and African organizations) sought to preserve their distinctive status in relation to the British Indian representative appointed to negotiate with the South African government on behalf of the

Indian community; accordingly, in 1927, they requested and obtained conference agreement that they could maintain a certain aloofness from any active political involvement (see Document 44). Divergent political approaches among the delegates were particularly evident in 1930 when a small group of delegates, who favored a more radical strategy of direct confrontation through passive resistance and demonstration (supported at the time by the Communist Party of South Africa), unsuccessfully challenged the majority, who favored continuation of the more traditional methods of respectful resolutions and deputations (see Document 45). Even efforts to establish a more permanent organization for coordination of nonwhite political activity foundered on the fears and unwillingness of many existing organizations to yield their separate independence (see Document 46).

Despite disagreements and the inability to advance beyond discussion and resolutions, the conferences did highlight the extent to which different nonwhite groups held common positions of opposition to government policies, in particular to the Native Bills and to the legislation of the first years of the second Hertzog government. As was often emphasized, the delegates felt that their meetings were not a substitute for, but a supplement to, joint cooperation with sympathetic South African whites. It was in an extension of this spirit that the Non-European Conference of 1931 decided (over opposition in its own ranks) to send a delegation to Great Britain to counter General Hertzog's efforts to obtain a voice for South Africa in the determination of policy throughout the British Empire in Africa. Although the delegation was subsequently reduced to one man, Professor Jabavu, it gave an opportunity for the conference through him to provide the overseas public with an exhaustive list of grievances that was an expanded and strengthened reformulation of the points he had presented in 1920 (see Document 47). In addition to this action, the Non-European Conferences established patterns of consultation between Africans and other nonwhite groups although consultation did not go beyond sporadic meetings. Nor was there any attempt to establish a mass-based political organization.

Africans Acting Alone

The focus of African political activity remained within African organizations. The Bantu Union, founded by Meshach Pelem in 1919, stayed a small organization in the eastern Cape Province, rivaling and sometimes cooperating with the Cape Native Voters' Convention. Yet it was the latter organization which became the focal point for African involvement in the electoral process. Continuing his father's practice of organizing registered African voters, Professor Jabavu led the convention in efforts to exert some influence upon government policies through participation in electoral politics. The convention's 1928 petition to Prime Minister Hertzog graphically revealed the deep anxieties of the group most immediately threatened by the Native Bills (see Document 50a). Discussion at the December, 1928, meeting of the convention showed that the membership proposed to throw its support to white politicians solely upon the basis of their stand on the Cape African franchise (see Document 50b).

Yet participation in electoral politics in Cape Province was at the periphery of African concern. The South African Native National Congress, renamed the African National Congress (ANC) in 1923, kept its position at the center of African politics throughout most of this period, although it was for a while eclipsed by the Industrial and Commercial Workers' Union which at the height of its power became political rather than strictly industrial in character. Nonetheless, the ANC, drawing adherents from the African middle class throughout South Africa, continued to bring together Africans from each of the four provinces in periodic meetings to discuss grievances and to try to organize means to present the African viewpoint to white authorities. Still hampered by poor organization and limited finances, the ANC focused its activities around its annual conferences in Bloemfontein, although it also made sporadic representations to the government, particularly in response to specific measures proposed by the Hertzog administration.

In the Rev. Z. R. Mahabane's 1921 presidential address to the Cape branch of the South African Native National Congress, and in the significantly named Bill of Rights formulated in 1923, the ANC leadership had reiterated its identification with the standards of British practice and justice at the same time that it attempted further to legitimize its demands by placing them in the context of inalienable democratic and human rights due the Africans of South Africa (see Documents 48a, 48b). It was from these premises that the ANC launched its protests against specific government legislation throughout the 1920s and into the 1930s.

Resolutions of the ANC regularly repeated Mahabane's arguments against the segregationist intent of government legislation. The Natives (Urban Areas) Act of 1923 was opposed because it did not give Africans full freehold rights in urban areas (see Document 48b). Later, the ANC newspaper *Abantu-Batho*, strongly criticized proposed amendments to the Natives (Urban Areas) Act on the grounds that it would perpetuate and strengthen segregation (see Document 48g).

Moreover, the government-sponsored conferences of African leaders, authorized under the Native Affairs Act of 1920, were attacked on the ground that their members were not elected and therefore not representative of African opinion (see Document 48c). Respectful demands were also made that the Union government undertake to provide compulsory education for African children (Document 48c).

With the publication of Hertzog's Native Bills in the wake of his Smithfield speech, ANC protests centered on the threat to the limited political rights still held by Africans, in particular to the nonracial franchise in Cape Province. The reports of the 1926 meeting of the ANC indicate differences of attitude toward Hertzog's proposals to "solve the Native problem," but its resolutions, and those of the House of Chiefs assembled by the ANC in 1927 in accord with its constitutional procedures, displayed the depth of African feeling against the Native Bills (see Documents 48d, 48e).

In its efforts to register its protests and achieve its integrationist ends, the ANC until the mid-1920s kept well within the constitutional means Mahabane had supported in his 1921 address. The ANC made no attempts to

organize any protest campaigns like the passive resistance movement of 1919. Resolutions taken at the annual conferences were regularly presented by ANC deputations to white authorities. In 1924, it urged cooperation with other nonwhite groups, and accordingly its leaders subsequently participated in the Non–European Conferences (see Document 48c). For the most part, the ANC seemed content to act as a national African forum and informal political pressure group, concentrating its efforts at the time of its annual conference.

By the late 1920s, disagreements over strategy and principle produced new controversies within the ANC. After the publication of the Native Bills in 1926, an ANC conference agreed to embark upon a nationwide campaign of demonstrations in alliance with the ICU (see below); but the leaders subsequently backed away from this endorsement, and the campaign remained stillborn. Younger members of the organization chafed under the ineffective methods of the past and became receptive to radical slogans and cooperation with the Communist Party of South Africa. A representative of this more activist group, James Gumede, of Natal, a founding member of the ANC and a member of the 1919 ANC delegation to Great Britain, was elected ANC president in 1927. In his inaugural message, he made a specific appeal to the left and right wings to join in a united front on behalf of the African people (see Document 48f).

Shortly thereafter, Gumede, who had attended a Communist-sponsored Congress of Oppressed Nationalities in Brussels and then traveled to the Soviet Union, indicated his readiness to cooperate with the Communists in joint efforts to influence the government, including mass demonstrations. Since association with liberal white sympathizers and respectful protests had done nothing to halt the expansion of government restrictions on Africans, Gumede was ready to make a tactical alliance with Communists to further the goals of the ANC. But his policy provoked dissension within the ANC's already fragile structure, particularly after 1928, when the Communist Party in response to directives from Moscow endorsed the goal of an "Independent Native Republic as a stage toward a workers' and peasants' republic." A vivid indication of the degree of the ANC's disorganization was embodied in the report of the secretary-general in 1930 (see Document 48h). The controversy that Gumede's approach aroused came to a head at the annual conference that year, where he was challenged by Dr. Pixley Seme, the ANC's founding father. Running on a sharply anti-Communist platform, Seme captured the presidency of the organization, but it was a Pyrrhic victory for the cohesion of the ANC was shattered (see Document 48i).

For the first five years of the 1930s, the ANC was unsuccessful in reconstituting its unity even to the extent of meeting regularly to pass resolutions and to organize the deputations that had been the focus of its activities in the 1920s. Thus no serious consideration was given the imaginative proposal made in 1930 by Mweli Skota, a journalist and ANC secretary-general, for the convocation of a continent-wide Pan-African Congress to coordinate opposition to General Hertzog's efforts to influence British African policy (see Document 48h). In 1931, a call at an ANC meeting in the Transvaal for a passive resistance campaign against the pass laws in the tradition of the 1919 demonstrations was similarly unheeded (see Document 48j).

President Seme had his own definite ideas for reconstructing the ANC. These first centered around a new constitution which would have given greater powers to the generally more conservative chiefs. Later, in 1934, they involved African Congress Clubs, economic self-help groups that would seek to give the ANC a sound economic base (see Documents 48l, 48m). His opponents shared his concern for achieving African unity, particularly when economic dislocations and new measures of the Hertzog government spotlighted the disabilities of the African people (see Document 48k). Yet Seme and his opponents were unable to resolve their differences. The ANC disintegrated further into competing cliques. Nevertheless, the unaccepted proposals of both Seme and his opponents, including the abortive plans advanced by the latter in 1931 for a passive resistance campaign, all highlighted African grievances and gave rise to new suggestions for means to express them forcefully. Inability to organize did not mean the abandonment of the goals that had animated the ANC since its foundation.

The other focal points for the articulation of African grievances were nonwhite trade unions. In the postwar labor unrest that erupted in most major South African cities, small trade unions mushroomed as Africans and Coloureds attempted to organize themselves for the effective expression of their grievances as workers. In 1920, a conference of local nonwhite trade unions organized by Selby Msimang, a founding member of the ANC, and Clements Kadalie, the Nyasa founder of the Cape Town ICU, agreed upon the formation of a federation of nonwhite trade unions called the Industrial and Commercial Workers' Union of South Africa. Under the presidency of Msimang, the new organization placed its greatest emphasis upon the need for African workers to organize carefully so that advances could be obtained through peaceful negotiation with white employers. Msimang's speech, delivered before the second conference of the federation in Cape Town in 1921, listed the major grievances of African workers. They ranged from strong dissatisfaction with restrictive governmental machinery to antagonism to the industrial color bar that prevented the employment of nonwhites in skilled positions (see Document 49a-1).

A more limited organization, the Transvaal Native Mine Clerks' Association, was founded by A. W. G. Champion in 1920 to bring together the generally literate Africans who occupied the small number of low-level clerical and supervisory positions open to Africans on the mines. Although the program of the organization was oriented to the interests of the "educated Native," whose role in the supervision of the mass of illiterate mine workers was explicitly noted, it also attempted to speak for all African workers in demanding that they be given a voice in the industrial system of which they had become a part. Its 1922 memorandum to the Mining Industry Board was couched in respectful, almost obsequious terms, yet through the accommodating language protruded an unmistakable questioning of the basic principles of a system that held the African worker at the unskilled, low-paid bottom rungs of the economic ladder (see Document 49a-2). In a similar vein, the organization welcomed the Prince of Wales to South Africa in 1925, while explicitly warning him not to be deceived as to the true conditions of African workers on the basis of his carefully guided tour of the mining compounds (see Document 49a-3).

Yet neither Champion nor Msimang provided sufficiently dynamic leadership to establish their organizations upon a national basis. It was Clements Kadalie, the leader of the local ICU in Cape Town, who made nonwhite trade unionism a significant force in African politics in the 1920s. Denied the position of secretary-general in Msimang's organization, Kadalie had retired to his home base in Cape Town. In 1922 he convened a conference of Msimang's trade union federation (of which he technically remained a member) and apparently succeeded in taking over the machinery of the organization from Msimang, who retired gracefully to avoid disruption of the union. From his new position Kadalie embarked upon a campaign to convert the slightly renamed organization, the Industrial and Commercial Workers' Union of Africa (ICU), into a nationwide mass-based organization which could claim to speak for all the nonwhite workers of Africa.

The obstacles to success were great. The African proletariat of South Africa, an ethnically diverse group of largely unskilled workers, many of whom were still migrants closely linked to African reserves, did not readily lend itself to regular and cohesive organization. Furthermore, white management, which especially in the key mining industry isolated African workers through the compound system, hampered and harassed ICU efforts. In addition, the government frequently invoked weapons from its arsenal of restrictive legislation to limit any African trade union activity.

Despite the difficulties before it, the revitalized body, known simply as the ICU, caught hold in the mid-1920s. Although poorly organized and unevenly led, it expanded into the major urban centers and even into the countryside, particularly in Natal and the Orange Free State. Its trade union concerns had clear political overtones; indeed, by the mid-1920s Kadalie's ICU was implicitly challenging the preeminence of the ANC in African politics.

The thrust of Kadalie's appeal was visible in an editorial in the ICU newspaper *The Workers' Herald* in December 1923, on the eve of the annual conference that launched the first national organizing campaign (see Document 49b-1). In its revised constitution of 1925, the ICU's goals were set forth, both with regard to trade union concerns and to welfare interests (see Document 49b-2). The preamble of the constitution, retained from the constitution of the original Cape Town ICU, explicitly dedicated the trade union to a socialist goal. The specific grievances of the ICU and its animosity to segregationist white trade unions reflected the particular disabilities of nonwhite workers in South Africa. Yet at the same time, the ICU identified itself with all workers, regardless of race. It held out the ultimate goal of a color-blind socialist society. Like the ANC in its more explicitly political sphere, the ICU as the spokesman for labor argued for the full inclusion of the African within a nonracial integrated system.

Although the ICU constitution specifically eschewed political involvement, the nature of its concerns and the situation in which it operated extended it beyond this commitment. In 1924, Clements Kadalie was active on behalf of the anti-Smuts coalition of the Nationalists and the South African Labour Party, probably being persuaded that the ouster of a government closely associated with the Chamber of Mines might be to the benefit of African labor. As the segregationist intent of the Pact government became clearer, the ICU became progressively disenchanted with the government whose election it had encouraged. With the Smithfield speech and the publication of the Native Bills the break was complete. The resolutions of the ICU against the Native Bills show great similarity to the arguments and demands made by the ANC in the same period (see Document 49b-3). Like the ANC, the ICU called for an end to the pass laws, the abolition of the color bar, limited legislative power for Africans through a shift in the format of the government-sponsored conferences for African leaders, and retention of the direct vote for Africans in the Cape Province. But although at one time the ICU considered joining the ANC in a nationwide campaign of demonstrations against the Native Bills, it failed to act upon the proposal.

Like the ANC, the ICU in the mid-1920s became partly preoccupied with internal struggles complicated by debate on the nature of the relationship it established after 1924 with the sympathetic Communist Party. When the Communists moved to challenge the leadership of Kadalie and Champion (who had joined the ICU from the Transvaal Native Mine Clerks' Association in 1925), Kadalie was able to rally support within the executive to oust Communist officers, and subsequently in March, 1927, to forbid any member of the ICU to hold membership simultaneously in the Communist Party. Subsequently, the ICU claimed to continue its expansion throughout South Africa, making exaggerated estimates of a membership of 100,000 in early 1928.

Cut away from the option of a left-wing alliance with the then white-run Communist Party, Kadalie placed new reliance upon the traditional approach of deputations to government authorities, which he buttressed by efforts to obtain significant overseas support from British and European socialists and trade unionists. The "soft" side of this tack could be seen in Champion's respectful letter written (while Kadalie was on tour in 1927 in Britain and Europe) to Prime Minister Hertzog, requesting a meeting to discuss the grievances of the ICU in an atmosphere free from polemics (see Document 49b-4). Its "hard" dimension was visible in the appeal by Kadalie to the white workers of Britain for support against the segregationist practices of white South Africa (see Document 49b-5). Kadalie was particularly anxious to mobilize British public opinion against passage of the Native Administration Act of 1927 under which those convicted of inciting "hostility" between the races in South Africa were to be liable to imprisonment or fines.

Upon his return from Britain in late 1927, Kadalie attempted to reorganize the ICU along the lines of a properly established British trade union. Yet it was clear that he had no intention of abandoning agitation by the ICU against those government policies it considered inimical to the interests of African workers. The *Economic and Political Program for 1928*, for which Kadalie obtained the approval of the ICU at its conference in April 1928, represented one of the most comprehensive and forthright statements of ICU concerns (see Document 49b-6). The program focused upon economic demands, but it explicitly argued that the ICU must also be concerned with politics. In this spirit it not only favored a petition opposing the withdrawal of the Cape African franchise, but also efforts by the ICU to find its own candidates for the Cape Provincial Council (still legally open to nonwhites). On the key question of passes, the program urged that the government be petitioned to make a test withdrawal of pass law enforcement for a six-month period. In the event that the government proved unreceptive to this request, the program argued for a campaign of pass-burning and civil disobedience. With these proposals Kadalie tried to place the ICU within the political tradition for which the ANC stood.

But the program was only a stillborn testament to the political aspirations of Kadalie and the ICU. At the very moment it was being passed by the annual conference, the ICU was in the process of irreversible disintegration. Organizationally overstrained by a too-rapid expansion, criticized by an impatient rank and file, and challenged on all sides by white South Africa, ICU leaders began to squabble over alleged corruption, local autonomy and political tactics. When Champion was suspended pending an investigation of the financial affairs of the Durban and Natal sections of the ICU which he headed, the ICU lost its strongest branches. Shortly thereafter, Champion became president of a separatist ICU *yase Natal* based on a platform of provincial autonomy.

In mid-1928, William Ballinger arrived from Britain as adviser to the ICU. His efforts to reorder the organization sparked new dissension. Amidst recriminations about financial irregularities and irresponsibility, Kadalie finally withdrew in early 1929 and made an effort to form an independent ICU out of the dissidents, who by that time were united in their opposition to Ballinger. But neither he nor Ballinger was successful in recreating a strong viable African trade union organization. Neither could attract national support, and their local efforts were hindered by organizational weaknesses, continued factionalism, and (in the case of Kadalie) government harassment in the wake of an attempted general strike by African workers in East London early in 1930.

In Natal, and more particularly in Durban, however, Champion showed signs of mustering support for an action-oriented group ready to challenge government policy. The constitution of the ICU *yase Natal* spelled out the wide scope of activities which the provincial trade union organization reserved for itself (see Document 49c-1). In 1929, Champion attempted to channel discontent among African workers against a provincial regulation that gave a monopoly on the brewing and sale of *utshwala* (African beer) to white municipal authorities. In disturbances between Africans and whites in June 1929, partially centered around the Durban headquarters of Champion's organization, six Africans and two whites were killed. In Champion's discussions of the disturbances and their aftermath, resentment against the regulation of African affairs by white "experts" was sharply expressed in the context of a demand for African participation in deliberations about African policy and combined with an appeal to the Nationalist government to intervene against locally based English-speaking administrators of Native policy (see Document 49c-2).

Champion's latter appeal was acted upon by the Nationalist government — but with disastrous results for the ICU *yase Natal*. In response to the June demonstrations (and in order to counter expected Communist-sponsored demonstrations scheduled for late 1929), Oswald Pirow, the new minister of justice in the Nationalist government, directed reinforced police units in mass raids upon Africans in Durban in November 1929. Then in 1930, Pirow piloted the Riotous Assemblies (Amendment) Act through the South African Parliament. Under this legislation, Champion became the first African to be banished from his place of regular political activity, being exiled from Durban for a three-year period from 1930 to 1933. In his absence, the ICU *yase Natal* dwindled into a small sect of the sort that Kadalie and Ballinger led in East London and Johannesburg, respectively. The ICU as a national nonwhite trade union primarily for Africans was dead.

The significance of the ICU for African politics, however, had been considerable. In its meteoric rise and fall can be seen the gropings of the new South African proletariat for an effective means to articulate their demands as workers and increasingly to link themselves with broader African efforts to participate politically in South Africa on an equal and nonracial basis. Africans had taken up the promises of advancement implied both in the capitalist ideology of the mine owners and industrialists and in the socialist ideology imported by white workers to South Africa. That white society rejected this interpretation of its ideologies is not surprising, yet its rejection did not prevent the reformulation of this variant of the African claim for equality in subsequent years, particularly in relation to the workers of the key mining industry. The activities of the ICU opened a new dimension of African political activity, dramatically forcing attention to the problems of a significant group of Africans who had become irrevocably enmeshed in the "integrated" economy of South Africa.

In a less spectacular fashion, the concerns of Africans as urban residents were also increasingly articulated, in part in response to the provisions made for limited African representation under the 1923 Natives (Urban Areas) Act. Although African leaders, and the ANC in particular, had not overlooked urban problems, they had not focused their attention upon them. In 1930, the voice of a long-time activist, Mrs. Charlotte Maxeke, who had achieved political prominence in 1919 as a leader of women demonstrators against proposals to extend the pass system to women, was heard in a plea for joint conferences of Africans and whites to analyze the situation of urban African women (see Document 51c).

African concern for the problems of urban areas found organizational expression in the Location Advisory Boards' Congress of South Africa, founded in 1929 by representatives from the advisory boards selected in African urban locations under the terms of the 1923 Natives (Urban Areas) Act. R.H. Godlo's presidential address in 1929 and the memorandum the Congress submitted to the minister of Native affairs in 1930 reflected preoccupation with the particular problems of the urban areas (see Documents 51a, 51b). Yet it is evident that these problems were seen as an integral part of the situation faced by all Africans in South Africa, and that in this sphere, as in others, Africans were demanding that they be consulted about their fate, even if temporarily within a restricted framework. Thus, the first "elected" representatives of urban Africans tried to explore new avenues for political expression.

In the early 1930s, white South Africa was temporarily diverted from its preoccupation with the "Native problem." To cope with the rigors of economic depression, the two major white political parties, the Nationalist Party under General Hertzog and the South African Party under General Smuts, came together in 1933 to form a coalition government. In 1934, they fused into a single party, the United Party, under the leadership of Hertzog with Smuts as his first deputy. Only a small group of dissident Nationalists refused to follow Hertzog's lead; under Dr. Daniel Malan, the latter regrouped their small forces in the Purified Nationalist Party to continue the fight for their ideal of an Afrikaner-dominated republican South Africa. Yet the overwhelming parliamentary majority of the new United Party government overshadowed the break-away Nationalist opposition. The new administration began to tackle the country's pressing economic problems and, more ominously, to coordinate white efforts further to shape multiracial South Africa in line with white segregationist feelings.

To the outside observer, the existing disarray of African politics might have indicated unbridgeable disagreements. There had been divisions over the proper organizational forms for African politics and the type of strategies most relevant to African needs. All African protests had proved ineffectual in the face of governmental determination to limit African opportunity and mobility. Both the ICU and the ANC were fragmented into squabbling factions that were unable to rally their own former memberships, let alone challenge the white government.

Yet Africans were basically united in their conviction that the accelerating trend toward political segregation in South Africa must be reversed. The variety of new modes of expression that had developed in the 1920s and 1930s showed determination to continue to seek channels through which the African cause might be advanced more forcefully. In the short run, prospects for effective African organization or amelioration of African grievances seemed highly unpromising, but the foundations of a greatly expanded African political consciousness had been laid. Immediately after this period, an outside catalyst, the revised Native Bills of the United Party government, brought Africans together for a new surge of political activity.

DOCUMENTS

Africans *"Respectfully Submit"*

DOCUMENTS 39a — 39d. The Governor-General's Native Conferences

DOCUMENT 39a. Proceedings and Resolutions of the Governor-General's Native Conference, 1923 [Extracts] (Published in *Native Affairs Commission [Union] Report for 1923*)

Pass Laws.

The *Chairman* stated that the first subject with which the Conference would deal was the Bill relating to the Pass Laws and called upon Colonel Godley to address the Conference.

Col. Godley: The question of the pass laws was a burning one. It was essential that something should be done at once both from the point of view of the Europeans and the Natives. Government had long realised that the Natives in the Northern Provinces are suffering from too many restrictions and must be afforded some relief. On the other hand

Europeans throughout the Union were pressing Government to tighten up the pass laws. That pressure come not only from the Northern Provinces but also from the Southern portion of the Union.

It was very important that the Conference should devise some measure which, while meeting the reasonable requests of the Europeans will afford relief for the Northern Natives. If the Conference was unable to do this there was little doubt that the position would become worse.

The Government instructions to the Department and the Native Affairs Commission were to bring up a measure based on the Bill now before the Conference (A.B. 24/23) which would apply to those areas where pass laws are in force.

He had been the Chairman of the Pass Committee which had travelled throughout the Union and had taken much evidence from Natives. The Committee submitted a report upon which the Bill was based.

The Bill was designed to secure the protection of a Native by a life-long document which will enable him to travel freely in rural areas and secure perfect identification when he entered industrial areas.

The necessity of identification would be appreciated by the Conference when he stated that there were hundreds of unclaimed estates, through faulty identification records. For the same reason the Department was unable to deliver messages from Natives at home to their relatives in industrial areas.

Conference must bear in mind that the Bill was an earnest and honest attempt to secure the minimum of control and the maximum measure of protection to the Natives.

It only remained to discuss the Bill clause by clause and he would only be too glad to furnish any explanation which might be desired.

The Bill would have to be recast on account of clauses 9 and 14 having been incorporated in the Natives Urban Areas Act.

Clause 1 considered.

Mr. S. Msimang considered that the age of registration should be 21. If a boy of 18 were registered it would weaken parental control.

Mr. Lehana agreed with Mr. Msimang and thought the Registering Officer should make special investigation before issuing certificates.

Mr. Makgatho enquired how would a Registering Officer know the age. He had seen cases at the Pass Office where boys of sixteen were put down as 21 and *vice versa.*

Col. Godley said there was seldom difficulty in fixing approximate age by reference to some historical event or the year of circumcision.

Mr. Mahabane supported Mr. Msimang's view. At 18 Native boys required strict parental control.

Mr. Mapikela inquired whether it was in order to discuss this clause before they agreed to the principle.

The Chairman replied in the affirmative. The position was that there were too many passes in the Transvaal. Different systems in Natal and Orange Free States. Object of Bill is to get uniformity. A man would get an identification certificate at 18 for whole life.

Take the case of a young man of 19, who wants work—he could not go without certificate—if not, would require temporary document. He quite saw the point of parental control until 21. It was for the delegates to suggest how this could be attained.

Mr. Ndhlovu thought the boys should be given temporary documents until they reached 21. To prevent boys from going out to work, would be great hardship on some families.

Mr. Fenyang suggested that registration should only take place with consent of parents.

Mr. Zibi understood that that Bill was for protection of Natives who left their homes, but, it made every one register.

Col. Godley pointed out that a man might wish to leave home and then he need not go to a Pass Officer or Official for permission.

Mr. S. Msimang said he was not opposed to the registration of boys, except that registration would take them out of parents' control.

He suggested that parents should keep registration certificate until boy went to work, any boy working without one, to be treated as a deserter from home.

Mr. Bikitsha said that any boy getting a

certificate, could hand it to his parents, or they could demand it.

The Chairman said if you handed the certificate to a boy, and he left the district for work, the parent might lose control. If Conference wanted parents to have control, a boy might be given a temporary certificate up to 21.

Mr. Fenyang objected to registering a boy twice. The age should be 21.

Mr. Jabavu said he understood the Bill would only operate where pass laws were in force—this would leave the Cape untouched. But he would like to have his impression confirmed in black and white. He had strong resolutions from the Cape against any system of pass law. There were certain mild pass laws existing in a portion of the Cape, and these the people did not mind.

They were afraid the Government was taking away privileges.

Uniformity was a good word, but they were not prepared to give up anything.

After Union they had thought that the Cape spirit would permeate north—not *vice versa.*

The Cape Natives welcomed the relief from the pass laws to the Northern Natives, but would give up no privileges.

Mrs. Maxeke pointed out that three-fourths of the earnings of the Cape Natives were got from their employment in the Transvaal. Not six Transvaal Natives go to the Cape. The Cape Natives should remember this.

Mr. Langa said the Natives were very satisfied with the existing conditions. It was quite easy for them to come out to work. Government should leave things as they were.

Dr. Molema pointed out that the use of the word "pass" had been avoided. But registration and exemption were the same thing. His views were very much like Mr. Jabavu's, namely that the pass laws of the Transvaal and Orange Free State were being introduced into the Cape.

Freedom in the Cape would be sacrificed for uniformity. Cape Natives felt strongly on this point. They welcomed the simplification of the pass laws in the Northern Provinces until Government could apply the Cape spirit to the North.

He accordingly *moved*:—

"That the Bill should only apply to the three Northern Provinces and the Cape Province should continue to enjoy the freedom from the pass law hitherto enjoyed."

Mr. Jabavu seconded.

Mr. Makgatho understood one of the reasons put forward was that money was lost by Natives. If this applies to Transvaal then he said they did not want the pass. The time would come when the pass system must be removed. It caused bad feeling between Natives and Europeans. The actual carrying of a pass was not objected to but the irritating interference of the police.

The Chairman pointed out that some system of identification was necessary when people went from District to District or from Province to Province. This was in the interest of the Native. If this were accepted then what was the position as regards the Cape. If the Cape was excluded no Native could come to the Transvaal unless he got a certificate, *not* from the Cape but from the Transvaal.

The proposal in the Bill was to divide the Cape into three parts, (1) the Transkeian Territories, (2) British Bechuanaland and (3) the remainder of the Cape. A man wishing to go from one part to another would require a certificate.

If Cape Province were taken as a whole, would it be advisable to give a man a certificate who wants to leave the Province.

Mr. Zibi enquired whether a man must be registered who did not leave his home.

Col. Godley replied that nearly every one left his home at some time or other —possession of a certificate would enable him to avoid going to an official sometimes 50 miles away for a pass.

The Conference adjourned at 12.45 p.m. and resumed at 2 p.m.

Col. Godley in the chair.

The Chairman stated that he would allow discussion on the general principles of the Bill—each delegate might speak once.

Mr. S. Msimang gathered that the Bill was to grant relief and contained one important principle, namely, that all Natives should be registered *once*, but if the Cape were excluded some Natives would be treated as aliens. At present pass laws in the Transvaal do affect the Cape to a large extent because a Cape

Voter loses all his rights as soon as he crosses the Orange River, his position being lower than that of the exempted Native. People who were used to freedom were right to feel sore at being subjected to such a law in another Province. The Native working class from the Cape would be found in all parts of the Transvaal—the mines depended on it. Such people got a pass from their Magistrate to take them to the Transvaal, and as soon as they arrived they were treated exactly as Transvaal Natives.

If the Bill were not to apply to the Cape then Natives coming to the Transvaal from that Province would be in a very much worse position.

He could not see why the Cape Natives were making such a noise. To secure privileges let them agree to the registration.

Many Cape Natives domiciled in the Transvaal complained about the pass laws.

Chief Bokleni said he agreed with the principle of registration. Lots of Natives lost touch with their people. He understood that a man would use the registration certificate when he wanted to travel. Such a document would act as a protection. Even the Transkeian Territories Natives were worried with passes when they wanted to go to the Transvaal. Sometimes it took a Native three days to obtain a pass. With registration there would be no need to go to the Magistrate.

Further, registration would protect their young people.

He supported the principle of registration.

Mr. Thema asked the Conference not to discuss the matter from the provincial point of view, but with an open mind.

He appreciated the Government's efforts to grant relief to the Northern people, but at the same time he must point out that those people wanted the entire abolition of the pass laws.

He appreciated the Government's difficulty on account of the European view. In effect the Government said in response to the Native agitation for the abolition of the pass laws "I will introduce a system of registration." The Transvaal Natives in reply said "That will be a better system than the present one."

Now, he asked, should the registration system apply to the Cape? He thought that if the Government had power to abolish the pass law it would do so. Cape Natives should remember that the agitation for the abolition of the pass law would not cease even when this Bill passed. The application of the Bill to the Cape would be taking away rights from the Transvaal Natives and the Cape Natives.

The Conference should not take up the attitude: "If the law is to apply to us let it also apply to the Cape."

He did not think it would be difficult to meet cases of Natives coming to the Transvaal.

He drew the attention of the Conference to Mr. Welsh's views in Pass Committee Report, page 21 [U.G. 41–22.].

Mr. Mapikela said he had listened carefully to previous speakers, and especially Mr. Jabavu, but some seemed to have forgotten that the Cape Native would not be able to enter the Northern Provinces without a pass.

Delegates had come to the Conference to give and take and not to be selfish.

A pass system *did* exist in the Cape, whose Natives should remember that half a loaf is better than no bread. They should help their poor brothers in the Northern Provinces. They said: "Our forefathers used to carry passes but we are free to-day." But the Free State Natives were not.

Later on a time would come when all might say: "Let the pass system be abolished." But in the meantime let all accept the registration system proposed. If the Cape Natives went to the Orange Free State they would agree to it fast enough.

Mr. Pelem asked the Conference not to forget that the Cape was the oldest Province. As far as pass law was concerned the Natives had already been through the mill. This very registration proposed in the Bill had existed in the shape of a certificate of citizenship.

Some of the speakers wanted the Cape Natives to take a backward step instead of the Transvaal Natives climbing up to them.

As a representative of the Cape he stated that the Natives there were *not* prepared to take a retrograde step.

Mr. Ndblovu said, after listening to previous speakers, the point seemed to be what was the Cape going to do with the masses of labourers who came to the Transvaal. He understood that they would be under disabilities. Were Cape Natives going to lessen these. He wished the Cape delegates to understand that he would like the Northern Natives to come up to the same standard as the Cape Natives; but could they at present? He did not think so.

He asked the Cape delegates whether what they had said would be for the benefit of those who come to labour centres in the Transvaal.

Mr. Matoti said he sympathised with the Northern people.

He could not see what harm would be done if the registration system were extended to the Cape.

The existing stock theft law did not prevent stealing, for a man could change his name. A person would be registered for his own area, need not travel 60 miles to get a pass.

The Conference should not forget the interests of stock owners: everyone should have an identification.

By accepting the principle of registration stock thefts would be lessened, no bogus names would be possible and a certificate of registration would not be bulky.

He agreed with the principle of registration.

Dr. Loram said that the Acting Prime Minister had indicated:—

(1) That there were only three days to get through the business if delegates wished to attend the Johannesburg meeting;

(2) that delegates would speak not for themselves but for all Natives, and, therefore Provincialism should be dropped;

(3) that the Native Affairs Commission existed to advise.

These three things impelled him to speak.

One of the grievances in the Transkei was that Magistrates did not speak in the Bunga, but only at the subsequent Magisterial Conference, but he thought that the most helpful Magistrates spoke more in the Bunga than in the Conference.

Conferences such as the present one had made a good start at Bloemfontein—one reason was that at the Conference facts had been recognised and advice tendered accordingly.

The present Conference should recognize one or two facts regarding the pass law, namely:—

(1) It was only a temporary measure and in the course of time would disappear;

(2) a pass system would have to be continued in the Orange Free State, the Transvaal and Natal;

(3) the Government had decided that the pass law need not apply to the *Cape proper*, but that a pass system would continue in the Transkeian Territories, British Bechuanaland and Northern Provinces.

He felt that the spread of education would make the pass law unnecessary.

Those who had the pass law in force should not complain just because the Cape did not have it: they should not ask the Cape to carry their burden, but rejoice that the Cape was free from it.

What was necessary was to find out how a Cape Native entering the Transvaal should get a certificate.

He could not see why a Native living in the free and glorious Cape should apply for registration before he went to the Transvaal. So the Cape Native would be free until he went to the Transvaal.

He suggested that the Conference should direct its attention to finding this out.

Mrs. Maxeke said she was sorry to see the spirit of division in the Conference.

It would not serve the Natives' cause if the Cape were to be treated differently to the Northern Provinces. The policy of the Europeans was to divide the Natives and rule.

If the Cape accepted the registration system the Natives would be enabled to fight their grievances together.

She hoped the pass law would include the Cape so that the Natives could get together quickly.

Mr. Makgatho said it was a case of half a loaf and that was better than nothing.

On the other hand, the Natives said: "One King, one law." The question was: "Is there any help in the registration certificate; if so, why does the Cape object?"

If the Cape Natives said they were to be free then there was no necessity for the Transvaal Natives to have the law. The Cape delegates seemed to be in the Conference simply to tell it all the bad laws from which they were free.

If there is any help in the proposed law the Natives had better accept it—but let it apply throughout the Union.

He proposed that the principle of registration be accepted.

Mr. S. Zibi said he understood that Cape Natives would be required to be registered when they entered the Transvaal, and he agreed to this. But he failed to understand why his Northern friends wanted to place the Cape people in the same position as they would be on entering the Transvaal.

Mr. Sikiti said it appeared that Natives would have to register when they left their homes for work and he thought the Conference should agree to the principle of registration.

Dr. Roberts said that for 40 years his views on the pass laws system had never changed—they were well known—and during the few years remaining to him they would not change.

He asked whether in order to enable one body of people to move forward it was necessary for another body to go backward.

One great speaker had advised mankind to guard with their souls the privileges they had gained.

He hoped the Natives would never relinquish the freedom won by them in the Cape as the results of the efforts of men like Merriman, Sauer and others.

From some of the statements made one might think that the whole of the Cape Native population—nearly two millions—came to the Transvaal! And for a few thousands—50,000—some of the delegates wanted to put a burden on 1,640,000.

He thought it quite possible to have a change for the better in the Northern Provinces and yet leave the Cape alone.

He did not think the Conference so stupid as not to be able to find a way out.

Mr. Mabhabane moved:

"That in view of the fact that the pass laws system operative in the Province of the Cape of Good Hope appears to be more calculated to produce more harmonious relations between the white and the black races of this land and to promote a more peaceful govern-

ment of the Bantu population of this country this Conference recommends that the system existing in that Province be extended to the other Provinces."

Speaking to the motion *Mr. Mabhabane* said he failed to see the necessity for the registration of all the people. They were already registered through the payments of poll tax and hut tax. If registration was required in order to provide identification he failed to see why the tax receipt could not serve as such.

If one exemption were the 5th Standard why not others. There were too many divisions of the people: it was also proposed to leave out the Cape. Now, travelling passes were taken in the Cape setting forth the name, residence, etc., if the law made the holder keep his travelling pass it would identify him.

There being no seconder, the motion dropped.

General Lemmer said it was clear from the debate what an important matter this was. The Transvaal and Natal had too many passes and some alteration was necessary.

He thought that any new law should apply to all the Provinces.

He did not want to interfere with the rights and privileges that some Natives enjoyed, but he thought the principles in the Bill were reasonable. Under the Bill Cape Natives would not be touched until they travelled. If the Bill included the Cape it would make things more easy for the Natives.

In matters such as this there are two classes of interest to be considered—white and black. It was impossible to think that all pass laws could be abolished at that time.

He hoped that Natives would recognize that the provisions in the Bill were in their interests. It was better for a Native to have such a document than to have to run to a Magistrate or an official for a pass.

He could not see how the Cape System could possibly work in the Northern Provinces.

If one or more Provinces was to be left out of the Bill uniformity could never be attained.

He would be glad if Natives had reached the position when a pass was unnecessary, but they knew that until the Natives reached a certain standard restrictions were needed for their own protection.

Mr. S. Msimang moved, seconded by *Mr. Matoti:*

"That the principle of the Bill be accepted."

Mr. Thema moved, seconded by *Dr. Molema:*

"That this Conference appreciates the efforts made by the Government, and is ready to consider the methods to alleviate the disabilities imposed by the Pass Laws upon the Bantu communities in the Transvaal, Natal and the Orange Free State, but is strongly opposed to the Registration and Protection Bill being applied to the Bantu people of the Cape Province."

The Chairman said he wished to make it clear once more that the Government's instructions were that the Bill was only to apply in areas in which a pass law was in operation, that is in the Orange Free State, the Transvaal, Natal, the Transkeian Territories and British Bechuanaland.

From the debate it seemed to him that the feeling of the Conference was in favour of the principle of registration, as the Government proposed to apply it, and he suggested that Messrs. Msimang and Thema might withdraw their motions and a motion brought forward giving expression to this feeling.

Messrs. Msimang and Thema, with the leave of their seconders, withdrew their motions.

Mr. S. Msimang, seconded by *Mr. Thema,* moved:

"That this Conference adopts the principle of registration as explained by the Chairman, namely, that it shall only be extended to those areas in which a pass law is in operation."

Agreed to unanimously.

. . . .

Constitution of Conference.

The Chairman intimated that as the Acting Prime Minister had specially asked the delegates to assist by their advice in evolving some scheme for the constitution of future Native Conferences he wished to invite full discussion on the subject.

Mr. Majozi said that if the delegates discussed the matter for the whole day they would find no solution. There was no machin-

ery in existence. If the Natives were asked to elect delegates it would cause great trouble. The Prime Minister had mentioned how hard it was for the people to appoint their own councils. The Conference was in its infancy.

He suggested that the selection of delegates be left in the hands of the Government—which has the advice of the body representing all Natives in the Union, namely, the Native Affairs Commission. This should continue for two or three years.

The Government should endeavour to see that all portions of the Union should be represented.

If the people elected delegates the latter would only be recognised by certain sections.

Mr. Bikitsha said he agreed with Mr. Majozi, that the matter should be left in the Government's hands. The Conference was in an experimental stage and delegates should go slowly.

The desire to select delegates was due to a wish to send firebrands to the Conference.

Mr. Sikiti admitted that the election of delegates was difficult, but in the Cape they had the machinery, for in that Province there were Native parliamentary voters. In the other Provinces there were no voters. He did not think that every man in those Provinces should be entitled to vote.

He thought that the Government should continue to nominate delegates.

Mr. Mahabane moved, seconded by *Mr. Zibi:*—

"Whereas in the opinion of this the second Conference of Native Chiefs and other representative Natives with members of the Native Affairs Commission held in Pretoria this 24th day of September, 1923, the interests of the more satisfactory administration of Native Affairs would be better served if the Conferences contemplated by section 16 of the Native Affairs Act No. 23 of 1920 were partially selective, partially nominative and partially elective.

"The Conference therefore respectfully yet strongly recommends the Government to consider the advisability of introducing machinery whereby one-third of the members of the Conference would be selected by the Government, one-third nominated by Native Chiefs domiciled in the several Provinces or Native

Territories of the Union, and one-third elected by the various Bantu political or industrial associations in the country."

He considered that these Conferences were good. They should inspire confidence at the outset, but selected Conferences did not do so, as they raised opposition. This had been recognized by the Acting Prime Minister.

The difficulty of election could be met by giving the right of election to existing Bantu Associations, which represented the organized sections of the people. The unorganized sections would be met by the Chiefs' nominations. In the Urban Areas delegates could be elected from existing organisations.

The time would come when the Native people should be governed with their consent. He appreciated the Government's action.

Mr. Jabavu supported Mr. Mahabane's views. Some people saw only wrangling for the choice to be present at a Conference and this might happen if badly done. But he would draw attention to the Transkei where election and nomination were both recognized in the Councils.

The single aim should be to get the confidence of the Natives in the Conference.

He thought the principle of one-third nominated by the Government and one-third nominated by the Chiefs good.

But he differed from Mr. Mahabane in regard to the Bantu political organizations— not on account of any suspicion but because it would leave out the representation of some people.

He suggested that all Natives owning property valued at £75 or earning £50 p.a. be given the right to vote for delegates. This would facilitate machinery, for those qualifications were what were fixed for parliamentary voters and he was looking forward.

The Conference adjourned at 12.45 p.m. and resumed at 2 p.m.

Mr. S. Msimang said he was in sympathy with Mr. Mahabane's motion but he felt that any election by Bantu associations would *not* succeed. Before accepting the proposal they would have to know the standing and strength of the Associations as well as the qualifications of the members.

He knew of course that associations were contemplated under the Native Affairs Act,

1920, but was the Conference prepared to accept *any* Association. If so there would be a multitude of Associations.

Furthermore there was no system by which Chiefs could come together to select representatives.

He was sorry it had not been possible for the Government to establish Native Councils in Native Areas—but they would come and in the meantime something else had to be put forward.

He suggested that for the next Conference the Government should nominate one-half of the delegates and the remainder should be chosen as follows:—

(a) In the Cape by the election of candidates for whom registered voters would vote;

(b) in the Transvaal, Natal and Orange Free State, exempted Natives should furnish lists of names from which delegates could be selected.

Mr. Pelem agreed with Mr. Msimang. He said he represented Glen Grey—a district with a Native population of 55,000—where the Glen Grey Act was in force. Location Boards were elected every year and his experience was that the people did not understand the responsibility attached to the election of members.

Mr. S. Msimang's idea of one-half the number of delegates being nominated by the Government was good.

Mr. W. Msimang advised the delegates to hasten slowly. They should place full confidence in the Government. The Conference had just been born and was not even creeping. If the delegates returned home and told the people they must vote it would only create a disturbance. Where election was concerned he found that the people voted against an intellectual man. The people were backward especially the chiefs and councillors. How could such people elect proper representatives.

He thought the matter should be left in the hands of the Government.

He suggested that the Government should nominate delegates not for one year, but for a period of years.

Mr. Zibi said he was under the impression that Chiefs were specially mentioned in the Native Affairs Act.

He did not fear Native Organizations which

were working for the benefit of Natives, and he thought the election of delegates should be in their hands.

Mr. Makgatho emphasized the fact that suspicion would be created.

Dr. Roberts addressed the Conference.

Mr. Thema said it appeared to him that the Conference was not quite ready to consider the question of election.

He pointed out that the number of delegates should be increased as there were many important districts in the Transvaal which were not represented.

He moved:—

"That the question of the Constitution of the Conference be held over till next year."

Mr. Ndhlovu seconded the motion.

Mr. Mahabane pointed out that the days of government by nominated persons were when autocracy ruled, but democracy now ruled.

He had no objection to the postponement of the consideration of the Constitution.

Mr. Mahabane, with leave, withdrew his motion.

Mr. S. Msimang suggested the appointment of a Committee to deal with the question.

The Chairman said he could not accept the suggestion.

The Chairman put Mr. Thema's motion, namely:—

"That the question of the constitution of the Conference be held over till next year".

The following voted:—

For the motion:
1. Bokleni, W.
2. Fenyang, Z. W.
3. Kuzwayo, M.
4. Langa, J.
5. Lehana, S.
6. Majozi, S.
7. Matoti, S.
8. Maxeke, Mrs.
9. Moiloa.
10. Molema, S. M.
11. Mopeli.
12. Msimang, H. S.
13. Msimang, W.
14. Mphahlele, P.
15. Ndhlovu, W. W.
16. Pelem, M.

17. Takalani.
18. Thema, R. V. S.
19. Zibi, S.

Against the motion:
1. Jabavu, D. D. T.
2. Mahabane, Z. R.
3. Makgatho, S. M.
4. Mapikela, T. M.

Motion carried.

DOCUMENT 39b. Proceedings and Resolutions of the Governor-General's Native Conference, 1924 [Extracts] (Published in *Native Affairs Commission [Union] Report for 1925*)

Chairman's Address.

Mr. Roos, in addressing the meeting, said:—

"I have pleasure in welcoming the delegates to the third Conference under the Native Administration Act of 1920.

"The Prime Minister's intention was always to open this Conference in person, but unfortunately his duties have called him away, and on his behalf and at his request I am welcoming you here.

"The principal matter before you for discussion is the proposed Bill to secure uniformity of taxation.

"As you will discuss that Bill very fully, I will content myself by saying that the Bill provides for a general tax payable by every male Native in the Union of 18 years and upwards of £1 per annum, and in addition a local tax payable by such Natives resident in Native locations of 10s. per annum.

"The way in which the proceeds from this taxation will be utilised is set forth in the Bill, and discussion will show the extent to which it is applied to the benefit of the Natives of the Union.

"I may refer in passing to the segregation policy generally associated with the name of the Prime Minister.

"That policy is largely in the interests of the Native population, and the Prime Minister's intention is by its use to secure the development of that population along lines natural to itself.

"It would be inadvisable for me to make any further statement on this subject, as the Prime Minister proposes at the next Session of Parliament to lay his views before that body.

"It may perhaps not be out of place for me to make some remarks on the recent campaign pursued in the Press and elsewhere regarding maltreatment of Natives.

"The point of the attack was the diversity of treatment meted out to Europeans for offences against Natives and to Natives for offences against Europeans.

"As far as the higher Courts of Justice are concerned, a Native accused may of course call for trial by a judge alone. He is therefore always able to escape trial by jury if he distrusts a body of that nature.

"The European has the same option, and the complaint is that a jury in the case of crimes against Natives is prone to acquit or convict of a smaller offence than that actually perpetrated. In so far as this is a complaint which is rightly founded, it seems to me that it is only by the proper moulding of the character of the community that a reform can be obtained.

"It must be borne in mind that the punishment inflicted is not confined to the verdict or the sentence. To that must be added the arrest, the long drawn out legal process, and the expense involved.

"In addition, the aggrieved party has his remedy in a civil action for damages, and it would be well if this were made generally known, because under Native law and custom many offences which are under European law punishable as crimes only give rise to compensation for the damage sustained. In South Africa criminal steps are taken generally speaking for the wrong against the majesty of the State, against the infraction of law and order in the State and to prevent at the instance of the State any interference with the safety and security of its inhabitants.

"The aggrieved party himself has his civil action for damages, which is not cut down or removed by the criminal steps which the State has taken to vindicate its own dignity.

"I personally believe that there is more cause of complaint in the lack of courtesy obtaining in Magistrates' Courts and the way in which Natives are treated there considered quite apart from the merits of the complaints brought against them and the justice of the judgments and sentences imposed upon them.

"I am enquiring closely into this matter with a view to ameliorating present conditions.

"In your position as leaders of the Native people it must be apparent that in many respects their conduct is worse than it was in the past, and it is a matter of regret that Native women, many of whom are still children, roam uncontrolled about the towns at any hour of the night whereby immorality and criminality amongst the Natives are greatly increased.

"Many of the wiser Chiefs in the country view this evil very anxiously indeed, and desire that by proper control it should be lessened and finally stamped out.

"In conclusion I need scarcely say that the value of your deliberations remain as great as in the past, and that the conclusions at which you arrive will receive the earnest and serious consideration of the Government, which desires to give its assistance to the important portion of your population which you represent and thereby enable that population to develop itself in the interests of the whole community of which it forms a part.

"I declare this your third Conference formally opened."

Mr. Dube, in moving a vote of thanks to the Minister, stated that he appreciated Mr. Roos' address, and was voicing the feelings of the delegates in expressing that appreciation.

As regards the question of taxation this was a very difficult proposition, but they appreciated the fact that the Government was giving them an opportunity and plenty of time to discuss it.

In regard to segregation, the principle would be acceptable if the Government were benevolent, but the Natives did not see how they could be segregated and yet be given sufficient land for development. They were greatly disappointed to see Crown land being cut up for poor white settlement when the whites had already so much land at their disposal. He spoke for the Zulus who saw large tracts of Crown land hitherto regarded as their own now being cut up for Europeans. Large tribes were being moved away from those territories. Where, he asked, were the lands to be given to them as indicated by the Natives Land Act? A large proportion of the Natives squatted on European land. Yet the Natives were continually told that they were to have their lands where they could develop.

Anyone knowing the land question was aware that only in Pondoland and Transkei did Natives have sufficient land to develop.

Natives were being driven from towns, discharged from jobs in which thousands had sacrificed their lives in the interests of the white people. He prayed the Government to be generous and to bear in mind the interests of the Natives as well as those of the whites.

In regard to the treatment of Natives in Courts, the white people seemed to have it in their minds that the lives of Natives were of no account. Natives had been recently murdered by Europeans and the punishment inflicted had been very small. They were glad to have the Minister present to express their feelings in connection with this serious grievance.

The case of a girl who was tied to a cart and beaten made their blood boil. They were here as Natives of this country, and God had placed the whites here to administer justice and see fair play.

Natives were not hard-hearted, and responded to justice, but when outrages of this kind were so lightly punished it did not help the Natives to become more loyal to the powers that be.

The white people wished to segregate the Natives but they would have a difficult job to do so. God had ordained that they should live together, to work together and that the Natives should benefit by the thousand years of European civilization.

If the Europeans threw the Natives far away and told them to develop on their own lines the former would be evading and shirking their responsibilities.

In the ill-treatment of Natives—blame attached to both white and black. Native policemen "bashed" prisoners and this encouraged young men in Court to ill-treat blacks. It was horrible to see the punishment of Natives without trial in Johannesburg Courts on Monday mornings.

A Native is asked "U ne cala na?" (are you guilty) and he replies "Yes" meaning "Yes, I have a case against me" but not intending to plead guilty to the charge, and he is immediately sentenced.

The faulty interpretation was a real grievance.

The majority of Natives did not know of the privilege of being tried by a Judge alone.

The European rulers were largely responsible for the looseness of Native women. Nowadays the Chiefs were figureheads with no authority and the parents had still less authority over their children. For small offences which could be tried by the Chief or his council, Natives were dragged to Court.

The only way to enable parents to control their children was by adjusting the relations between the people and their Chiefs.

Mr. Jabavu, in seconding, stated that Mr. Dube had spoken what they really felt. They felt highly honoured to see a Minister among them in the flesh and they appreciated the personal contact as it did more than correspondence or press reports. He was glad to hear the Minister's intentions. The only hope of happiness was for both sides to approach a question with sympathy.

The Natives realized their helplessness and for that reason Europeans should therefore be more sympathetic and remember the motto *"noblesse oblige"*.

He asked the Minister not to take too much notice of violent language from Natives which appeared in the press. That was merely a psychological development of the Native from childhood to boyhood. It was precocious but harmless.

Mr. Thema endorsed the remarks of the previous speakers.

The Natives felt very keenly the attempt to replace their labour by European labour for they had played a great part in the development of the country and its industries.

At one time the idleness of the Natives was considered a curse by the Europeans and pressure was brought to bear on the former. The poll tax was imposed to drive the Native from the kraal to the mine compounds. Europeans had also encroached on land occupied by Natives and now the latter were without land and compelled to work.

The Natives had helped to build up civilization and industries when the whites were only a handful but now they were regarded as dangerous.

They felt ill-treatment keenly and thought that if such were suffered by Europeans they would certainly take up arms.

Lawlessness on the part of the Europeans would lead to lawlessness on the part of the Natives. He pleaded for justice and a spirit of co-operation and referred to Dr. Malan's encouraging address at Fort Hart in which it was said that the country was the common heritage of both white and black.

Mr. Makgatho said he would like an explanation from Mr. Roos with regard to an alleged statement that a Native should not be treated as lightly as a European and also that Father Rand's remarks were nonsense. The Standerton case was a travesty of justice. They heard a lot about justice but he did not know of a single European who had been hanged for the murder of a Native.

The Minister of Justice thanked the delegates for the vote of thanks.

He stated that Mr. Makgatho had misread in the press what he (Mr. Roos) had stated. What he had stated was that the Standerton case was exceptional and that it was nonsense for Father Rand to say that in the Northern Transvaal Natives scurry away from white people. Father Rand had, he believed, contradicted this.

Further, in reply to Mr. Makgatho he pointed out that in 1922 Europeans had been hanged for the murder of Natives.

He (Mr. Roos) had said that the Judge in fixing punishment had to consider its burden, the expense involved in the trial, and the effect of its infliction. A certain differentiation in punishment was necessary if the Judge or the Magistrate was doing his duty properly.

He could not tell Judges or Magistrates what punishment to impose—that was their duty. But, after the imposition of a sentence, any accused who thought it too severe had the right to put the matter before the Minister directly by letter or petition. If he (Mr. Roos) thought the punishment too hard he recommended the Governor General to reduce it. Since he had been in office he had made recommendations in a large number of cases—both European and Native.

The question of interpretation in the Courts was already under his consideration and he would try to remedy matters.

The Minister added that Mr. Dube had tried to inveigle him into a discussion on the Prime Minister's policy of segregation. In doing so he had made two assumptions, firstly, that the Natives were to be pushed aside from the whites in certain areas, and, secondly, that those areas would be too small. The delegates would find, however, that when the Prime Minister made his statement to Parliament next session, General Hertzog would avoid the difficulties mentioned by Mr. Dube. The Natives would receive assistance in their areas from enlightened white men and he hoped that this would only be initial assistance and that Natives would eventually work out their own salvation under segregation.

In conclusion, he wished the Conference success in their deliberations, and thanked them for their vote of thanks.

. . . .

At this stage Col. F. H. P. Creswell, Minister of Labour, entered the Conference Hall and addressed the delegates on the following lines:

"You have asked me to come down to explain to you what is the Government policy with regard to labour, and particularly what is known as the civilized labour policy. Well, it is simple. It is the desire of the Government to open up every avenue of employment in which a man can earn a wage that a European and a man who desires to live like a European can live on. And this, so far from being directed against the interests of the Native peoples, is entirely in the best interests of Native peoples.

"We have been drifting along into a condition which anybody with intelligence can see is not to the interest of the European or of the Native peoples. Just let us understand the position and what are the causes that have brought us to the present state of affairs. What has brought masses of Natives out of their natural surroundings and into the white man's big industries and white man's towns?

"Go back a long time—when diamonds were first discovered. The man used to dig them for himself at first. Then the Natives came along and they were employed because they worked for a very low wage. Then the white man went to the Native territories and brought Natives from there to the mines, and thus gradually the recruiting system began. Enormous sums of money had been spent on recruiting Natives in large masses for the gold, coal and other mines and industries.

"At a very early date there were not enough Natives content to work at this very low wage among our own Natives and so Natives were brought in from Mozambique, and then you will remember, more than 20 years ago it was said that there were not enough Natives in the Country, and so they sent to China and got Chinese to come out to work for the same low wage. When the Chinese went away the Government helped in trying to get Natives to come from the Cape Colony at the same low wage. Now this has not been good either for the Native people or for the European workers.

"For the Natives one effect has been that their territories have been looked upon principally as a place from which to get cheap Native labour instead of looking upon them as territories in which Natives should be helped to discharge their responsibilities and make their territories happy, and where they could develop along their own lines. The present system works out badly for the European workers because all the avenues are crowded with Natives working under contract on a wage on which a European cannot exist. Now the question the Government and the country is faced with is this: Are we to go on drifting like a log in a stream, or are we going to study what is best both for the European and the Native and try so to arrange things that each can develop his own nature with the least possible interference one with the other? When you have a thing of many years' standing and it is all tangled up as this is, you cannot suddenly take it and tear it apart without hurting people. You have got to go very carefully, disentangling one string at a time lest you break one and injure people. I want to progress now when there is a great deal of unemployment among Europeans—I should like to do—a great deal more than I have done—but the Government has to realize the difficulties of the situation. Here is a European and there is a Native. When I want

to go so far my friends here (the Minister indicated the members of the Native Affairs Commission and the officials of the Department) say 'No, we must make arrangements for the Natives.

"Now this native taxation measure which you have been discussing for the last two days, and particularly with regard to the large sums of money for agricultural education and instructors is just part of the machinery to help the Natives. While provision is being made on the European side the native side is also receiving attention."

Proceeding Colonel Creswell said: "that more and more Europeans should take part in every phase of activity. Now all that was not a thing which could be done suddenly. They would have to go very carefully because the habits of the Europeans and the Natives could not be changed by 'just saying so'.

"The Government fully realize their responsibilities towards the Native peoples of this country. The Government fully realize two things: First of all that those Natives who wish to advance in civilization should have the opportunity of doing so; and they realize that in order that there shall be the least possible clash between the Europeans and the Natives that they should direct and focus their help mainly towards Natives in their own territories so that these may be a centre of their own advancement. And while we recognize that, we also recognize the necessity for maintaining the European civilization in this country as a vigorous and strong one. You know that the Native peoples in this country own their present security and much else to the civilization which the European people have brought to Africa. You also owe some evil things which are due to the Native being taken out of his more natural conditions. Well, we want to try to preserve the good and diminish the evil as much as we can. What I have sketched to you in speaking of the present conditions of affairs is merely an indication on broad lines.

The Minister continuing, said with regard to particular measures the question would have to be considered whether the time had arrived for a particular action, and various circumstances would have to be taken into account in order that justice might be done to both Natives and Europeans. Not only from the European side would they be warned if they went too far. From the Native side, from the Native Affairs Commission and the Department, it would be said to them, "You must think about the Natives in this case."

"So you need be under no anxiety, under no alarm, that the measures which we may feel bound to take in the interest of the Native peoples will not be brought to our attention by the Native Affairs Department and the Native Affairs Commission."

Mr. Thema, in moving a vote of thanks to the Minister, said when the Natives were first recruited for labour they would have been content to remain in their kraals. The Europeans, however, had not been content to remain in Europe, and they caused the great changes in this country. It is most unfair for the Europeans, therefore, not to consider the interests of the Natives at the present time.

If the Government wished to do something for the Natives they would have to consider the question of land. He was not referring to segregation, but he thought that Natives were entitled to more lands on which to develop. The Natives Land Act was introduced to provide farmers with cheap labour, but the effect was to drive the Natives into urban areas. There was no danger to white civilization to-day, because it was established in the midst of the barbarism of the people. How could anyone expect the Natives to go back from a civilization to which they were awakening? He realised the gravity of the problem, but he thought it would lead to greater understanding if the blacks and whites conferred more frequently. In the past, measures for Natives were brought forward without consulting the Natives. In conclusion he appealed to the Minister to make ample provision for Native settlement on the lands if an adjustment of the labour problem was to be attempted, and he drew attention to the fact that Europeans had turned their eyes to North Zululand, essentially a Native territory.

Mr. Jabavu seconded the motion, and said that Sir George Grey had employed cajolery to get the Natives off the land to work for Europeans. The great Cecil Rhodes had employed similar means. In the Cape out of 260,000 square miles only 3,000 square miles were in possession of Natives, and over a million Natives populated that small area.

If the Natives were being taken off the land where would they go? With regard to urban areas, the opposite was the case, because Natives who were born in towns could not go back to the land. He hoped the Minister would consider sympathetically all the points raised.

Mr. Mahabane associated himself with the previous speakers, and eulogised the work of the Native Affairs Commission in their endeavours to persuade the Government not to act too quickly in the replacement of Natives by whites.

He appealed for greater race co-operation, and mentioned the work which Dr. Jesse Jones and Dr. Loram had done in this respect. There could only be race co-operation if all sections of the population were consulted on vital questions, otherwise wrong impressions might easily be created. The great congestion of the Native people should also be considered, and by replacing Natives by whites this congestion was being increased. It was regrettable that the Government had set the example, especially on the railway, of this replacement of the Natives.

He hoped in conclusion that the Government would not bring forward any more oppressive and repressive measures. The Natives were by nature socialists and communists, and they knew what oppressive measures had produced in Russia—Bolshevism. By introducing oppressive measures the Government were creating a fertile field for Bolshevism, Ghandiism and other evils.

Colonel Creswell, in reply, said that about two years ago he had read an article written by one of them, Mr. R. V. S. Thema, Johannesburg. It was entitled "Race Problems." Mr. Thema was the first among the Native race he (the Minister) came across who recognized that what was called the "Native problem" was a problem which was on the one side the white problem, and on the other the Native problem.

But it seems to me, proceeded the Minister, that Mr. Thema this morning was looking upon the whole matter from the Native point of view.

"Might I ask Mr. Mahabane," Col. Creswell

said here, "is it wrong for the European people in their industries to employ Europeans?"

(*Mr. Mahabane*: No, sir.)

"You say the Native has nowhere else to go," the Minister went on. "And the European? Is he to starve outside?"

"Mr. Mahabane had spoken of the country being divided—one-half European and the other half Native. Do the Europeans, asked the Minister, teach the Natives nothing in regard to the methods of agriculture, and so on? Do the Natives own nothing?

"Some of the delegates to-day have spoken as if the Government intended to take all the Natives wholesale out of the towns and fling them on to the veld. There is no ground for any such apprehension.

"May I say I have seen in the Press many remarks which might give Natives that impression. I am afraid behind that feeling are many, many Europeans who principally look upon the Natives as convenient people to exploit in the industries.

"I thought I had said the Government, in pursuing their policy, are going to be even-handed. And we realize—as one of the speakers stated—that we have got land. There are two things about land. There are two ways of increasing land, you know.

"One is by taking more acres; the other is by successful agriculture, to be able to produce more on the same land. What we have already begun—what we have continued in this Native Taxation Bill—will be the setting aside of considerable sums of money merely to instruct and educate the Natives in agriculture.

"Don't you approve of that? Is not that a good thing to do. Should not that money be expended?

"I want to get out of your mind what may have been suggested—from other quarters—that it is the intention of the Government to take all the Natives out, like you take a lot of apples in a basket, take all the Natives out of the towns and throw them away like that.

"There is no such intention. But we have also a responsibility to the European, and the European youths in this country, so that they have a fair and good entry into the activities of this country.

"Mr. Thema said there was no danger to European civilization from men like himself, and many others. Of course there is not—not a particle! But there is danger to the European civilization of this country if by the arrangement we have drifted along into, increasing numbers of Europeans cannot earn a living in the country.

"There are many other elements in the situation which produced the present condition of affairs. He (the Minister) would be very pleased to discuss the whole matter with any deputation.

"I want to finish up on the note that Mr. Thema himself struck in the article," Col. Creswell concluded.

"This problem is not the Native problem. It is the Native and white problem; it is the race problem. And if you are to make progress with it you must not do what Mr. Mahabane suggested we are doing—using material entirely from the exploiting idea.

"No; you have got to regard it with a long view to the future. We believe we are doing so in the way we are tackling it—in trying to get towards a position where there will be less tendency to race antipathies, and more real co-operation instead of pretended co-operation.

"Don't imagine, on the one hand, that the policy of the Government is to throw the Natives away like you would a kitten.

"On the other hand, don't presume to think that in this country the European has not got the right to get employment in every possible occupation. I am sure there is no such assumption on the part of the Native population."

Colonel Creswell then retired.

DOCUMENT 39c. Proceedings and Resolutions of the Governor-General's Native Conference, 1925 [Extracts] (Published in *Native Affairs Commission [Union] Report for 1927*)

Prime Minister's Address.

General Hertzog addressed the meeting on the following lines:—

"Unfortunately I shall not be present at this Conference for any length of time and I wish to say a few words to you. Possibly there may be questions put to me for enlightenment, and if I have time this morning I shall answer them with pleasure. Unfortunately I have to be elsewhere at 11.30. Consequently if I am not in a position to give the necessary explanation, I hope to have the chance at a later opportunity.

"This Conference is meant to ascertain the feelings of the Natives in connection with Native administration, concerning which it is possible that proposals will be placed before Parliament at the next Session. The matters which are being brought to attention will be of great importance and in certain respects far reaching.

"Before I speak about them, I shall say a few words about the constitution of this meeting.

"This Conference consists of twice as many members as its predecessors. In addition other methods have been followed in choosing the delegates. It is not necessary for me to state the principles in accordance with which the Government has acted in this matter. But I may say, shortly, that the desire was to reach every portion of the Native people and above all where possible to place the Natives in a position to send their own delegates.

"As I mentioned at Smithfield I hope that in a short time this Conference will by law become the Union Native Council with most of its delegates chosen by the people. Its duties will be weighty and important.

"This Conference is therefore the forerunner of the future Union Council which I have no doubt will be of great use and power. But the extent of its utility will depend on how the delegates show their ability: If they play to the gallery or don't look to the benefit of the people the Council will fail. The Native population is looking for leaders; and, these should be progressive not retrogressive. In the choice of leaders will depend how much the true interests of the Natives will be served.

"With my parliamentary experience, I have found that long and beautiful speeches are not always fruitful.

"The Native is in general a good orator and, in addition, he has a natural talent for debate. It is necessary for you therefore to know in the first place how to consult with each other, how to give advice, but at the same time how to take advice. If you do this there will be no necessity to look for eloquence. This will come of itself without your seeking for it, and when it comes it will beautify the fruit of your work.

"Be assured that the whole country has its eyes fixed on what may be done here; and let me assure you that the eye of the white man is on this meeting, not because of any ill feeling, towards you, but because he desires that you will attain the blessing and the happiness of the Native people.

"I feel certain that you have placed great importance on the views I voiced in my address at Smithfield.

"Now I wish to say at once that the reception of those views by the press as well as by other portions of the people—whites and blacks—has given me great pleasure.

"This gives me proof of how the whole of South Africa are in agreement that this problem must be solved, and also that the whole population is ready to think over it long and earnestly before taking action. This is as it should be.

"The Native problem is the most difficult one with which South Africa has to deal. Every earnest suggestion for its solution deserves consideration. And I feel convinced that South Africa is ready to give consideration to what I have proposed, and, at the same time come to some definite decision in the matter.

"I wish to repeat here what I said at Smithfield: I feel convinced that it is best both for the Native and for the European that so far as the occupation of land is concerned the Native should be separated from the European. This is the plan followed in the Transkei where one finds the most favourable conditions in so far as Natives are concerned.

"That is also the view put forward by Government Commissions and by nearly all writers on Native matters. And I feel convinced that this is also the opinion of the great majority of the Natives. But if there is to be territorial segregation then provision must be made for the necessary land. How that will be obtained I will not now go into. But I will say that according to the administration begun by the former Government there is no reason why the necessary ground cannot be obtained for the Native, whether by purchase or lease. What the necessary additional land will be has already been fixed in general by two Commissions and I have full confidence that I shall be in a position to place proposals before Parliament which will extend the Act of 1913.

"I have mentioned 'purchase' and 'lease,' because the Native must clearly understand that no land is to be given by the State. But that the opportunity will be given to him by means of purchase or lease to enable him to acquire a reasonable extent of land in addition to what has been reserved for him.

"I wish here to emphasize that it is clear to me that there is a misapprehension about this matter. There are Natives as well as Europeans who seem to think that the Act of 1913 intended to make a free gift to the Natives of the land described by the Beaumont Commission. That was never the intention, nor is it the present intention.

"The Native must endeavour, just as the European does, to obtain land by means of purchase or hire. Where he has not the means the State will lend him the assistance in so far as he deserves it and the State is able to do it.

"I want you to know that the policy is the same as has been the case in the past. Where the Natives need land and wish to buy the Government has stepped in. I may inform you that for this year an amount of £50,000 has been placed on the Estimates for the purchase of farms in the Glen Grey District. For these, Natives will pay rent in the usual way.

"Further the Native must be assured that he will have the right to extend by purchase or hire the land already reserved for him.

"That is an implied right under the Act of 1913 and he must therefore be placed in that position, in other words, the Native must up to a certain point extend his territory, but this he must do by acquisition in the usual way possibly with the Government's help.

"I hope he will be placed in that position by legislation which I intend to lay before Parliament.

"Local Councils will be constituted on different lines within the Native Areas according to circumstances, development, national character and habits. While therefore in certain cases a Council will be constituted of Native Chiefs, there will be others consisting of Chiefs and representatives of the people. An eye will have to be kept continually on the progress and development of the Natives in such areas.

"So far as the duties of these Councils are concerned, these will naturally depend in each specific case on the capacity of the Council to deal with matters. As a guide all such matters will be entrusted to the Council as they have the power to deal with satisfactorily.

"I wish to add that these Native Areas will never become the independent or semi-independent states of which some Natives sometimes speak. The Native Areas will be under the leadership of the Government, more or less on the lines of municipalities or divisional councils amongst Europeans with defined rights and responsibilities.

"Then there will be further a Union Native Council which will in the course of time be charged with very responsible duties in regard to the affairs of Natives, what may be described as the Natives' Parliament.

"Some Natives doubt whether these different councils will ever be created. They point out that although five years have elapsed since the Native Affairs Act was passed by which provision is made for Native councils no such councils exist as yet. This is due to the fact that, according to the opinion of the late Government not sufficient provision was made in the Act for the proper control by Government of the finances of these councils. As this omission has since been remedied by the Native Taxation Act there can no longer be any reason why these councils should not be established. That the Government takes these councils seriously is proved by your presence here to-day. There was no obligation on the Government to increase the number of delegates of this meeting, or to bring about improvements in the method of selecting them. This has been done solely to give the Natives a larger number of delegates in the consultations on these questions.

"I wish to assure you that the creation of Native Councils is an essential part of the Native policy of the Government.

"Therefore nothing surprises me more than when I see that according to some Natives it would be the policy of the Government to divide the Natives among themselves and to throw them back into the ordinary tribal system.

"Now I come to the question of the field of labour for Natives within Native Areas.

"Within a Native Area a Native ought to feel at home. So far as he is concerned, therefore, there should be no limitations within his area except those which exist in a well-managed community. As I have already said, it is my object that, so far as the Native is capable to do so, he will himself lay down the rules according to the demands of civilization, which will suit him. I not only desire that he shall be his own legislator within his own house, but he must also control his own administration by means of Native effort. Within these areas there will be opportunity for the Native statesman as well as for the Native civil servant. The employment of the European must be the exception, and as a general rule no white person shall be employed for work for which a Native can be found.

"In European areas conditions will naturally be the opposite to a certain extent. Where the European is almost wholly excluded from doing work in Native Areas it would not be right to place the European in his own area in a position of unrestricted competition on the part of the Native. Both have the right to protection; and the question to me is to give this protection in such a manner that justice shall be done to both.

"To obtain this end the basis for the employment of Europeans within white areas must be extended in favour of the European, so that, within his own areas, he will always have the assurance of obtaining employment — as will be the case with Natives in the Native areas generally. It is for this reason that I will continue to support the Colour Bar Bill. It does not appear to me to be anything more than reasonable to restrict the activities of the Native in regard to certain matters.

"I come now to the question of the Native vote. As regards the arguments for and against the position in the Cape, I must refer you to history. It is clear that the arrangement which was come to in 1909 was only a compromise. Now we must accept it as a fact that the European portion of our population is against the enfranchisement of the Natives on the same basis as themselves. The European feels, quite rightly, that the right to vote is the fruit of centuries of civilized government and that he is the result and the heir of a civilization in which the Native does not share. The European is, however, prepared to agree that the Native should determine the method and personnel of the Native Council but, in the matter of Parliament, the European insists that this is a matter in which he alone shall have the say.

Meanwhile it must be admitted that there are certain Native interests indissolubly bound to those of the European and because Parliament is entrusted with the management of these interests it is felt that, in so far as the Native is concerned, there should be representatives in Parliament to speak and act on his behalf.

"My proposal is that there should be seven Europeans in Parliament entrusted with the care of Native interests. These will be elected directly by the Natives independently of the white vote. These seven members will represent the whole Native population and will be able to speak and vote on all subjects except those affecting the principles of parliamentary representation.

"I have been told that the retention of the Cape coloured vote and its extension to the coloured people of the Northern Provinces is the least satisfactory of my proposals so far as the Native is concerned. It seems to me that this is a point of greater interest to the coloured man and to the European than to the Native. In the Cape there exists a large number of coloured people already in possession of the vote. They owe their origin to the white man. They speak the language of the European. They live among Europeans and share their outlook and philosophy in a measure totally different from what we can expect from the Native. Like the European they possess no tribal Chiefs and no tribal laws. It is therefore impossible to deal with them in the same way as the Native, or to give them separate councils or separate areas. They can best justify their existence where they are to-day and all I propose is that the rights possessed by them in the Cape will not be confined to the Cape.

"It is incorrect to say that the Native will be worse treated by this proposal. There is a difference in the treatment but that is a difference which is calculated on the needs and interests of two different classes of the population. I hope you will agree with me that there is no injustice done when different grazing is given to sheep than that given to the cattle.

"I am anxious that the views of the Natives be heard on these weighty problems. I have decided therefore that next year after the various Bills have been laid on the table of the House, this Conference will again be summoned to discuss the Native problems raised by them in an effort to reach a solution whereby the interests of both Natives and Europeans will be safeguarded.

"My wish is that this will happen eventually to the general satisfaction of all.

"It has been said, I understand, that the search to-day for a solution is the result of fear. That may be so. But then I must also say that this fear has its origin in reason and prudence not in cowardice."

The Prime Minister then withdrew from the Conference, and it adjourned until 11.45 a.m.

. . . .

At this stage the Prime Minister accompanied by the Minister of Finance entered the Conference.

Mr. Jabavu moved:—

"That this Conference thanks the Prime Minister most sincerely for his courtesy in opening the proceedings of the Conference, for his lucid explanation of his policy, this being the first occasion for a Prime Minister to address us, for his visit to the Native Territories, and for granting us this additional visit."

Speaking to the motion *Mr. Jabavu* said that General Hertzog was the first Prime Minister to take the trouble to travel extensively among his (the speaker's) people in their own homes. He thanked the Prime Minister cordially for all his trouble and his usual courtesy in listening to their representations.

Amongst the items on the agenda were some having direct reference to the Natives Land Act of 1913 and which involved the principles of segregation. With regard to the matter of segregation the Natives had never been consulted about it directly. Possibly there was no need because the Natives are the ruled. But in their humility they would like to offer a suggestion: if the academic theory of segregation is desirable, the logical thing is to begin with territorial segregation as the industrial and political aspects are dependent on it.

If the Natives were taken away from industries, they should have territories to which they could go.

If political segregation were contemplated, the Natives should have their own Magistrates and the machinery of self-government. As a voter in the Cape he had always exercised his vote to further the protection of his own interests which were involved with those of the European.

The Natives had been told to develop on their own lines, but when the Europeans came they found us developing on our own lines which they then judged to be a danger to civilization. The Natives were therefore removed to industries to learn the dignity of labour and to assimilate themselves to European civilization.

Now the Natives had to go back to their own civilization and develop along their own lines. That was logical, if territorial segregation were applied, for the land question overshadowed all other questions.

The Natives also wanted an opportunity to confer annually. At the present moment their time was too short.

They would also like to see the resolutions passed in the Annual Conference tabled in the House of Assembly for then the members would at least be familiar with Native views. Thus there would be direct communication between them and Parliament.

Mr. Plaatje in seconding the resolution thanked the Prime Minister for allowing the people of Griqualand West to have a representative at the Conference. He praised the administration of the Prime Minister. Although some of the Natives desired a separate Minister of Native Affairs they had no sympathy with this proposal in Griqualand

West, for the sympathy of the Prime Minister was necessary in Native Affairs.

He thought that General Hertzog must have used much "lampoil and electricity" in the study of Native Affairs, and if the Native now got a "brand new white fellow (splinternuwe Duusman)" it would be a long time before the latter would learn the "A.B.C. of Native Affairs," and in the meantime their clock would stop.

He was of opinion that seven members were too few to represent the Natives.

General Hertzog, in reply, said he was very pleased to be present at the Conference that morning and to be able to reply to any grievances and to thank them for his reception.

He was attending not for the purpose of exercising his authority but as a representative of the Government and to see that as far as possible the desires of the Native population are granted.

He acknowledged that many of their grievances were justified, but even the Europeans had grievances.

As regards the presence of the Prime Minister at the annual Conference he could not be present the whole time but he would attend each Conference for a reasonable time as long as he was Minister.

He agreed that the Conference should be held annually.

He favoured the idea that the Conference Resolutions might be laid before Parliament, but unfortunately no Government could allow all classes of documents to be laid on the Table by every body or society as this would mean too many papers would have to be considered.

The period usually allowed for the meeting of the Conference would be increased, but the length of time must always depend on the business to be discussed.

He thought that the Natives agreed with him that they should be represented in Parliament only by members elected by themselves.

The land question had been raised and it had been said that if segregation is to become an accomplished fact the Natives must have the requisite extent of land and security in respect of that land. This ought to be the case. As to the size of the land it depends on the meaning attached to the term segregation. They knew that some people were of opinion that segregation means separate land for Europeans and separate land for Natives, and that the European must keep to his own territory, in which the Natives would not be allowed and *vice versa.* The people who support this, desire that there should be two kraals — one for the sheep and the other for the goats. This would not happen unless it was in the interest of either the Europeans or the Natives. If that had been his intention he would have been accused of depriving the Native of every opportunity of advancement.

His proposals were largely identical with the Natives Land Act, 1913. By that Act the Native could work in towns and in the country for wages, and, this was also his own suggestion.

He wanted to make increased provision for the Native who worked on the farm not for wages but for the right of staying on the farm, but he wanted to prevent abuse of such provision.

The Act of 1913 had already limited the right of the Native to obtain land, and he would not allow the Native to be deprived of the land set aside for him by that Act. It was felt at the time of the Act that not enough land had been so set aside for the Native and a Commission was appointed to determine how much more land could be earmarked for him as a compensation for his right of settling in any area of which he had been deprived.

Unfortunately, although two Commissions have been appointed both Natives and whites offered such strenuous opposition that the Government decided to leave matters alone.

He felt that the Act of 1913 contemplated that the Native should have undisputed rights to land within certain areas and it was time that this should be given effect to.

In regard to the size of the Native Areas and their position in the Union it was no more than right that the recommendations of the Commission should be considered.

He considered that the new areas should be adjoining or as close as possible to the land already reserved for Natives. The size must, however, be considered in relation to the segregation scheme.

He was busy considering methods of securing more ground. He had nearly completed his task, and he would explain the scheme to the people during the next parliamentary session.

With reference to councils the law of 1920 makes provision for them and they will come into existence in five or six months' time whether his scheme was accepted or not.

The extension of Native territories was contemplated under the Act of 1913 and it seemed to him to be necessary, for it was one of the first duties of the Government to see that the interests of the Natives should be considered as far as possible. There were many Natives in the towns but they formed a small proportion of the Native population. He felt that the Natives throughout the Union were fully justified in demanding the assistance of the more educated and developed Native of the towns.

Under the Bill brought before Parliament and rejected by the Senate, there was no curtailment of the Native's industrial activities, but their activities would be dependent on subsequent proclamations by the Governor-General, who might decide on the industries in which the Natives were to be allowed to participate, but certain industries would be reserved for whites and certain for Natives.

Referring to Mr. Plaatje's remarks he doubted whether one race could take over the civilization of another, each had to develop its own. They might approach each other, and he hoped the time would come when the Natives would assimilate European civilization.

Criticism had been offered that seven members were too few to represent the Natives in Parliament but on the other hand some Europeans thought the number too many. He thought seven sufficient and asked them to remember that there would be an Annual Conference and the seven members would be compelled to bring forward its Resolutions in Parliament. He did not think the Northern Provinces would agree to more than seven representatives.

Mr. Mahabane asked for an assurance that land set aside for Natives should not be taken away for white settlement. This had happened in the cotton areas in Zululand.

He asked if arrangements could not be made for Natives to obtain loans from the Land Bank.

The Prime Minister replied that the Land Bank could lend money to Natives or Europeans, but unfortunately the Bank wanted security which the Natives were unable to give.

If the Natives could not buy land they could hire it from the Government.

The land reserved by the Act of 1913 could not be taken away from the Natives except by a special Act passed by Parliament.

Mr. Dube pointed out that land at Amanzimtoti had been taken away from the Natives without their knowledge for the purpose of white settlement.

The Prime Minister replied that only a small portion of land at Amanzimtoti had been expropriated by Parliament itself for certain necessary development. For that land £ 30,000 had been paid to the Natal Native Trust and the money was to be used to purchase other land for Native occupation.

The Conference adjourned from 1 p.m. to 2.15 p.m.

. . . .

The Chairman invited the submission of motions.

Mr. Jabavu moved, seconded by Mr. Sikiti:
"That the period of the Conference be extended from three days to six days."

Agreed to.

Mr. Jabavu moved, seconded by Mr. Sikiti:
"That the Minister arrange to send the agenda to the members at least 30 days before the meeting of Conference."

Agreed to.

Mr. Jabavu moved, seconded by Mr. Sikiti:
"That the Minister should place the resolutions of this Conference on the Table of Parliament previous to the introduction of legislation on any Native question."

Agreed to.

Mr. Thema moved, seconded by Mr. Zibi:
"The Government having recognised the fact that it is in the interests of South Africa that Natives should be provided with facilities for higher education in this country, and having translated this recognition into action by financially supporting the Native College at Fort Hare, it is the opinion of this Conference that the Government should be urged to seriously consider the matter of raising the standard of education in the Transvaal and

Orange Free State so as to enable the existing Training Schools to prepare students to enter the Native College without having to go to Institutions in the Cape and Natal.

Alternatively that the scheme suggested by Dr. C. T. Loram in his book 'The Education of the South African Native' should be put into operation, namely, that Provincial High Schools should be established in each of the Provinces of the Union for the purposes of feeding the Native College with students."

Agreed to.

Mr. Zibi moved, seconded by *Mr. Morosi:*—

"That legislation by which it is proposed to place the Native question on a more stable basis should be made conditional on a clear statement of the Government's policy in regard to land for Natives throughout the Union."

Agreed to.

Mr. Fenyang moved, seconded by *Mr. Singqandu:*—

"That in order to relieve the congestion of the Seliba Reserve Government be requested to buy the farm "New York" and adjoining farms belonging to Europeans, and bounded on all sides but one by the Native Reserve, as an additional Native Area where Natives may buy or lease land."

Agreed to.

Mr. Mahabane moved, seconded by *Mr. Plaatje:*—

"That in the interests of the moral and tribal integrity of the Bantu races of the Union of South Africa this Conference respectfully recommends that Native Chiefs or Headmen be appointed in terms of section *one* (5) of the Native Administration Bill in such Non-Native Areas of the Union where a desire for such appointment exists."

Agreed to.

Mr. Fenyang moved, seconded by *Mr. Plaatje:*—

"That the heads of families residing in Thaba 'Nchu Native Reserve holding temporary and other similar certificates be allowed to fence their residential sites."

Agreed to.

Chief Sioka moved, seconded by *Mr. Kumalo:*—

"That the Conference strongly appeals to the Government that when sending out the

Native Affairs Commission to enquire into any matters affecting Natives same should consult leading Natives' opinions as well as Europeans'."

Agreed to.

Chief Senthumulo moved, seconded by *Mr. Thema:*—

"That the education of Native children, especially the sons of chiefs, should be made compulsory in the Transvaal."

Agreed to.

In closing the Conference *Major Herbst* wished the delegates a pleasant journey home. The session had been short, but much work had been done.

The Bill which they had discussed was most important and far reaching — and, as the Conference consisted not only of educated Natives but also of the backward representatives, progress was necessarily slow. He hoped their homes would be blessed with good rains.

Dr. Roberts said they would pardon him if he stated that he regarded the Conference as the child of the Native Affairs Commission. He was pleased with it and when he looked back on the small beginning four years ago and saw its size to-day he was very gratified.

He congratulated them on the manner in which debates had been carried on.

One of the delegates had thought that the members were at fault in not speaking at the Conference. As far as he was concerned he intended no disrespect but he had realized that the time allotted for the Conference was short and there were quite enough able men among the delegates to keep the discussion going. Further he wished the considerations and conclusions arrived at to go forth as those of the Natives themselves.

General Lemmer said he was pleased to say a few words now the Conference had finished its labour. He agreed with Dr. Roberts as to the members of the Commission taking part in the discussion. Their decisions should be arrived at without the influence of the Commission which found it necessary sometimes to disagree with the views of the Conference. He was content with the work which had been done by the Conference. It was not complete, but it could be completed.

The Act of 1920 contemplated consultation of Natives regarding legislation which affected them and every one taking part in the Conference knew that that body would slowly and gradually increase.

Everyone wanted to see a solution of the Native problem and when both Europeans and Natives come together and reasonably discuss difficulties a solution will be nearer.

He hoped that when the Government put its legislative proposals before the Natives they would not blindly throw them aside but give them the most reasonable consideration.

Dr. Loram said that the first impression which the Conference had left on him was how necessary education was for the Native people. Anyone who tried to prevent their obtaining it was no friend of the Natives.

The second impression was that in a gathering like this how quickly people improved with practice. There were the old stagers from the Transkei who showed their skill at once.

The third impression was how quickly people got together in a meeting like this.

Mr. Mahabane moved a vote of thanks to Major Herbst for the able and impartial manner in which he had presided over the Conference.

He admired the progress which had been made since the inception of the annual conferences. This year's Conference was a good augury for the future.

In the past it had been believed that white men could not sit in conference with black people, but this Conference proved the contrary. He was hopeful of the future and his hope was that black and white should work together to bring about a great South African country with no divisions of race and colour.

Mr. Singqandu seconded the motion.

Major Herbst expressed his thanks.

The Conference closed.

DOCUMENT 39d. Proceedings and Resolutions of the Governor-General's Native Conference, 1926 [Extracts] (Published in *Native Affairs Commission [Union] Report for 1927)*

Mr. Herbst welcomed the delegates on behalf of the Native Affairs Commission and the Department of Native Affairs. The date of the Conference had been fixed as late as possible, inasmuch as after the Bills had been discussed by the Conference the Government would reconsider them again. There would be much work to be done before the Bills could be submitted to Parliament.

He drew attention to the various maps in the Conference Hall which would show the various areas dealt with in the Bill.

On the suggestion of the Chairman the Conference decided to discuss the "Representation of Natives in Parliament Bill."

Dr. Roberts explained the provisions of the Bill.

Mr. Thema said that the Conference was asked to consider a very grave matter. The Acting Prime Minister had asked them to speak frankly and freely and they would do so. Year after year Natives were invited to the Conference to take away rights from their people in the Cape. The purpose of the Bill was *not* to give the Native people franchise rights throughout the Union but really to take them away: and the reasons for that step were clearly stated by the Prime Minister in his speech at Smithfield. He read the following quotation:—

"On closer examination we are struck by the fact that, unless the Cape state of affairs is changed it will be impossible for us to avoid that the Natives in the Northern Provinces will, within a relatively short period, obtain the franchise in any case.

"I say this in all seriousness. I say this not in order to intimidate, but in order to inform the people, so that the necessary steps may be taken in good time to avert the threatening evil. To-day I wish to explain to you what I intend proposing to that end. The danger is one threatening the ruin of both Natives and whites, but let me tell you first why, in existing circumstances, the northern provinces cannot possibly in the long run withhold the franchise from the Natives. I say in present circumstances, that is to say, as we are drifting now. The reason for this is directly connected with the right the Cape Native has to vote together with the white man for a member of Parliament. Unless this franchise is taken away from the Cape Native or at least fundamentally altered, the northern provinces, I repeat, cannot possibly continue to close the door against the Native franchise within their boundaries, too.

"According to expert judgment it will not be long, say 50 years or so, before the number of enfranchised Natives in the Cape exceeds the number of white voters. This contention may appear exciting to more than one of you, but there is not a single ground for contesting it. Everything points to this being a correct deduction from facts and figures. However, long before the expiry of those 50 years the Native voter in the Cape will be of much greater significance for and exercise a much greater influence on the Native franchise question in the three northern provinces than it does to-day. I am not exaggerating when I say that, as things are going now, within the next 40 years there will be but few among the 50 and more Cape M.L.A.'s who will dare publicly to oppose the extension of the Cape Native franchise to the rest of the Union."

The danger, continued *Mr. Thema*, is in about 50 years' time! Natives in Natal and in the Transvaal *may* then obtain the vote! So, in order to prevent that the Prime Minister says the vote must be taken away! The Conference was asked to agree to the Cape vote being abolished. The Prime Minister had said he would substitute something — not because he wanted to give the Native something, but because he wanted to take away the Cape vote. If it were true that the Natives in the Transvaal would get the Native vote in 50 years then the Natives in the North were prepared to wait that length of time. They could not in justice agree that the right given to the Cape should be taken away — even if they got two white men with no status to represent them. Those two men would not be regarded as "white men." No decent European would go to Parliament on the conditions laid down in the Bill, even if the Natives really elected them, but the Bill said they must be elected by nominees of the Government. Progressive Natives were not recognized in the Bill. The whole idea was to drive Natives back to tribal conditions.

The Conference was asked to help the Government to violate the constitution of the country. When Union was formed certain safeguards were fixed in regard to the Native people of the Cape, and they had hoped the promises then made would be kept and that the Cape policy would be followed. But year after year proposals were made infringing on Cape rights.

In this particular case they were *not* going to concur. If the Government were honest and wanted to give the franchise in some form in the North they should not interfere with the Cape franchise.

The North would then welcome the proposals in the Bill as a step in the right direction.

Under the Bill all hope of getting full citizenship rights was closed.

In regard to the principle of separate representation the idea seemed to be that the people of South Africa — white and black — were not one nation. Apparently the Government thought that certain matters only affected Natives or whites. He knew of no such matters. For example, the farmer would like free Native labour, enforcement of the Pass Laws, etc. These effect Natives as well as farmers. If they must have separate representation then political segregation was necessary, that is, firstly territorial separation and then political separation so as not to be under the control of the white Parliament.

It was impossible to evolve a Nation within a Nation. They could not have a separate Bantu Nation and a separate European Nation in South Africa so long as the two races live side by side.

The three Bills showed that segregation has failed.

The only conclusion they could come to was that Natives must be represented in the Councils of the State on equal terms with whites.

Chief Sioka supported the last speaker. He had discussed the Bills thoroughly. It was unfortunate that the three Bills were tied together. If they had been treated separately one or two might have been discussed, but as far as the present Bill was concerned they did not want to discuss it.

He had been strictly requested by those whom he represented not to discuss such a serious proposal as the abolition of the Cape franchise.

It was impossible for a white man to represent Natives truly. Not because he did wish to do so, but because when matters arise where action should be taken in the interests of Natives as against the interests of Europeans it was only natural he would fail.

Chief Tombela said the Government had a good thing to offer them, but seemed to want to close and bar the door to Native progress seeing that Europeans were to represent them. Why could they not have Native representatives.

He could understand why it was proposed to take away the Cape Native vote. The Natives looked upon the Cape as the most enlightened Province. It was the hope of Natal and the Natives there did not want the franchise taken away from the Cape.

The seven members would be useless, they would be knee-haltered, dummies and mummies.

The Cape franchise should remain and the vote extended to Natal, the Transvaal and the Orange Free State.

Mr. Fenyang supported the last speaker. The Orange Free State Natives had always looked forward to the time when they would get the same vote as the Cape, and they were not prepared to agree to anything which would result in the Cape franchise being abolished.

He accepted the Prime Minister's explanation as to the object of this Bill, namely, the danger of the European vote being swamped, but Mr. Roos' explanation was quite otherwise.

The Government was always proposing to take away rights and to give nothing in return, and it was the Government's fault that there were so many agitators.

The Cape Natives had never abused the franchise.

Chief Zibi said that Mr. Thema had voiced the views of the Transvaal Natives by saying they would wait 50 years.

They rejected the Bill — for they were asked to take a retrograde step.

It is not the detribalised Natives who always progress but the tribal — it is the detribalised man, cut away from tribe, parents and children who joins the amalaita.

It would be a pity if an educated man were to be asked to vote in the way suggested by the Bill.

The Natives said "No" in regard to this Bill.

Rev. Mtimkulu said they were asked to advise the Government to amend the South Africa Act and they were afraid. The Prime Minister said the reason for the Bill was "self-preservation." So in order to preserve his own people the Natives must suffer. That could not be fair. The vote was the only weapon left to the Natives after they had thrown down the assegai. If they gave "this" up what was the return? Seven dummies!

They were not prepared to suggest the removal of the vote from the Cape, nor were they prepared to advise the Minister to interfere with its entrenchment.

Mr. Bokleni said every time they came to Pretoria some of the Native rights were taken away. He suggested the extension of franchise rights to the Transvaal. Why deprive the Cape Natives for the benefit of those in the North?

He had been instructed to oppose the Bill.

Mr. Tladi agreed with previous speakers. The Native Affairs Commission had been appointed to voice Natives' views. It had greater powers than the seven proposed representatives. He was prepared to wait 50 years for the vote unless it was shown that the Commission had failed.

The Conference adjourned from 12.45 p.m. to 2.15 p.m.

Mr. Sakwe moved:—

"That this Conference of Native representatives convened to discuss and to give the Native views on the proposed Union Native Policy as outlined in the Prime Minister's four Native Bills assures the Prime Minister of its willingness to co-operate with him in the adjustment of the racial relationship between the Black and White races, in the occupation and acquisition of land, and political matters within the Union, but that the task of doing so is rendered very difficult, if not impossible, owing to the Bills in question having been made interdependent.

"The Conference takes cognizance of the fact that just as it is not in the interests of the country to leave conditions created by the political Colour Bar in the South Africa Act and the Natives Land Act to continue, it is equally unwise and not in the best interests of the country to force the Bills — interdependent as they are — upon the country.

"The Conference therefore respectfully requests the Prime Minister to kindly remove the difficulty confronting the Conference by consenting to the deletion of the words from "Provided" to "Acts" in the Short Title section of each of the four Bills; and to consent to each Bill standing, and to be dealt with, on its own merits.

"The Conference further urges that its findings on any one or other of these Bills must not, in any way, be regarded as an acceptance of the Bills being introduced in Parliament in their present form."

Speaking to the motion, *Mr. Sakwe* said that if they accepted one Bill it meant accepting the others. If they rejected one Bill they rejected the others. The delegates had come prepared not only to advise but to offer constructive proposals.

He could not understand what the Europeans meant by talking of the Native problem which seemed only to lead to such laws as the Natives Land Act, the Natives Urban Area Act, the Colour Bar Act and the proposed Native Administration Bill.

The Government was acting well in consulting the Natives before passing laws and they thought the Government really needed their assistance.

Hence he could only ask that the Prime Minister be requested to delete the last clause of each Bill.

He was a delegate from the Transkeian Territories General Council, which had passed a resolution on the Bill, and this gave the feeling of the people.

As a man from the Cape he was glad that the delegates from the other Provinces had expressed themselves against taking away the Cape franchise.

It would take too long to recapitulate the privileges due to the franchise. Their progress was largely due to this. They told their children to learn, to build better houses and to be thrifty, all with the object of getting the vote so as to escape the curfew regulations, be able to walk on pavements, and gain the respect of others.

The Bill would kill all these incentives to progress.

Mr. Jabavu seconded the motion, and said that the indivisible character of the Bills made it most difficult to deal with them. It meant that if one was rejected all were rejected. There were some things in the Bills which they would like to discuss frankly.

They could not compromise on the Cape Franchise.

The Government has wrongly assumed that the policy of uniformity is the right thing. He was there to say that uniformity in every phase was neither possible nor desirable. Even Europeans after 15 years of Union were not unified—they still had four provincial systems.

The Cape Natives feel a sense of injury from the Prime Minister's proposals. The obvious application is that he does not wish the Natives of a lower status to rise to the higher status of the Cape but to bring the latter down to the lower.

The policy is to bring down the best to the level of the worst.

In a recent speech General Hertzog said he regarded the Orange River as a purely artificial boundary for Natives. That is not so. It is the boundary of two different policies: the one a liberal policy of allowing the black man to advance as high as he can, the other an illiberal policy based upon fear. It was indeed luck that the Cape Natives had the liberal policy on their side of the river.

The Cape Natives had to defend that heritage for it was held by them, not for themselves alone but for their children and for the future development of the other Provinces.

He remembered the speeches at Westminster on the Union Act which insisted that the heritage of the Cape Natives must be maintained at all costs.

They valued this heritage which was the slight thread connecting the Natives with England.

They believed that it was entrenched designedly to preserve their privileges.

It was a fallacy to say that the uplift of the black man meant the downfall of the white. His belief was that however highly civilised the black man became he could never stand up against the white. The latter had had too long a start — the engines of war were at his disposal.

If the Natives were driven to believe that injustice was being meted out to them then they might be a real danger to the whites, and the grandsons of all those present might have to face that position.

The safest policy was to prove and convince the Natives of the justice of every proposal and to give them liberty to develop to the best of their ability.

The stopping of the franchise would be purely transient — it could not last. Their future generations would be in a position to insist upon getting fair play.

If injustice were committed to-day it would result in a legacy of discomfort, suspicion and ill will.

In the West Indies white and black live happily together — there is no fear of the black man there. In America negroes are living amicably with the whites with full opportunity to develop.

If the Government wished white dominance to endure the best way was to give fair play to the black man.

Delegates came to the Conference with full realization of their responsibilities: but the resolutions passed were never referred to Parliament. If those resolutions were not to be noticed it might be as well if the delegates remained at home.

He asked that Mr. Sakwe's resolution be submitted to the Acting Prime Minister in order to ascertain whether the Bills could be taken separately.

If the Bills were taken on their individual merits they might be able to help the Government, but if the Bills were indissoluble they might as well go home.

Rev. Kuzwayo could not understand why Government treated the Natives differently.

He did not want the Cape Natives to be deprived of their franchise which they regarded as a ladder for the Natives' success.

Mr. Mabonga wanted to know whether the King was aware of the proposal to take away the franchise.

He had been instructed to object to the Cape vote being taken away.

Mr. Gonyane intimated that the Northern Natives had hoped for the extension of the Cape franchise. The principle of the Bill was bad.

The Cape franchise should remain and franchise in some shape extended to the North.

No Native outside a lunatic asylum would agree to the Cape vote being taken away.

Mr. Mlandu requested that the views of the Acting Prime Minister be obtained.

The Chairman said he could see no difficulty in the Bills being discussed on their own merits.

The Prime Minister had informed him some time ago that the four Bills must all become law or none at all.

Mr. Plaatje agreed with Mr. Jabavu regarding the fallacy of black supremacy.

He moved that the Conference should reject the Bill.

Mr. Fenyang seconded.

Mr. Thema agreed that the Bill should be rejected but in such a way that there might be no mistake or twisting in the future.

The Natives tried to swamp the whites at Fish River — unsuccessfully. History shows that Natives had helped the whites against other Natives: not only in wars but in exploiting and opening up the country.

As a race the Natives were good natured, but if they were told every day they were a danger then they *would* become a danger.

The Natives recognized that the whites had come to stay and had brought the good things of Western civilization and it would not be to the advantage of the black man to drive them out.

The whites had resources in European immigration, or, let them give white women the vote.

He moved:

"In view of the strong and unanimous feeling expressed by the Transvaal, Free State and Natal representatives against the abolition of the Cape Native franchise as proposed under the Representation of Natives in Parliament Bill, and in view also of the fact that the proposed Native legislation affecting franchise emanates not from a desire to grant franchise to Natives in the Northern Provinces but rather from the mistaken fear on the part of the European public that white civilisation and white supremacy will be endangered; this Conference finds itself unable to consent to this measure which is directed against the future political rights of the people of the Union. It rejects the Representation of Natives in Parliament Bill.

"Further the Conference suggests that the Government should enfranchise all European women as a safeguard against any possible swamping of Europeans by Natives, and then extend the Cape Native franchise to Natives of the Northern Provinces as this is the only policy which will ensure goodwill and harmony between the races, and peace and prosperity for the country.

"Or, alternatively, we ask the Government to initiate a small beginning of a grant of franchise rights to the Northern Province Natives but leaving the Cape Native franchise untouched."

The Conference adjourned until the following day.

Second Day.

Wednesday, 3rd November, 1926.
Mr. Herbst in the Chair.

Mr. Jabavu said that in regard to Mr. Sakwe's motion he had listened to the Chairman's views. But the point was that the Bills were a reconstruction of Native policy. The delegates had to carry out their duty to their people. They had to put the views of the Native people no matter how impracticable they appeared to European officials.

He asked that Mr. Sakwe's motion be transmitted to the Minister.

Mr. Sakwe's motion was read and put to the Conference.

Motion unanimously adopted.

The Chairman enquired whether it was the wish of the Conference to postpone further discussion until the Acting Prime Minister met the Conference at 4 o'clock on Thursday.

Mr. Jabavu said that they had come to an impasse. They wanted an assurance that their action would not be misconstrued. They would be in a false position if they accepted one Bill. He thought the Acting Prime Minister should attend the Conference the whole time so as to decide on questions which arose. The Conference was more valuable than others where Ministers were present all the time.

Mr. van Niekerk thought it would be advisable to get the Acting Prime Minister's

opinion, but in the meantime if a motion were tabled that the principle of the indivisibility of the Bills was not accepted the Conference could go on with the business.

Mr. Gonyane thought the Bills were like the ten Commandments — if one broken, all broken.

They were afraid that if they agreed to one they might be held to agree to all.

The Chairman suggested that the Bills could be considered separately if the last clause were deleted.

Mr. Fenyang stated that they had acted on the lines of the Chairman's suggestion at previous Conferences, but at no time had their proposals been mentioned in Parliament.

The Resolutions of the Conference should be mentioned in Parliament.

The Chairman reminded Mr. Fenyang that the Prime Minister had explained at the last Conference why the resolutions could not be formally tabled.

He would adjourn the Conference and put the resolution before the Acting Prime Minister.

The Conference adjourned and resumed at 10 a.m.

The Chairman stated that he had seen the Acting Prime Minister who had furnished the following written reply: —

"As far as I know Gen. Hertzog's policy is to make the three Acts interdependent.

"In some respects the Natives may feel that they lose something, a position which I do not admit, but taking them as a whole the Native population is certainly benefitting greatly.

"If I were in charge of these measures I should certainly not permit one measure to be passed and the others to be rejected.

"I am therefore strongly in favour of the maintenance of the position that they are interdependent.

3.11.26."
      T. J. ROOS.

Mr. Jabavu wished to make it clear that the position of deadlock due to this reply was not the fault of the Natives. They were unable to accept the principle of interdependence. That fact committed the Conference if they discussed the Bills to-day.

The strength of a chain of Bills depends on its weakest link. He realized the position taken up by the Government: it was "buy this by giving that." He would be doing a great injustice to his people in accepting one or two points in the Bills while they are unalterably against the principle of interdependence.

They must wait until the Prime Minister returned and then thrash out the principle with him or allow him to carry out his full will in the knowledge that they were against the principle.

They were labouring under a full sense of their responsibility to their people and if they compromised they would betray their people.

The Bills were drafted on a wrong principle and could not be accepted.

He did not mean that all the Bills were entirely bad, but the price they were asked to pay for the advantages offered was too dear.

Mr. Thema associated himself with Mr. Jabavu's remarks. The Bills, he pointed out, would have to be passed by a joint sitting and the experience of such a sitting did not make them want another.

The Government seemed to want to steamroller the Bills. The Government wanted them to say that if one Bill was good then the others were also good.

Everything revolved on the fact that the Government wished to take away the Cape vote.

There could be no compromise on the Cape vote.

They felt they could not do anything but to decline to discuss the Bills until the Prime Minister separated them.

They were only an advisory body, but they did not like that the Government should be able to say it had consulted the Natives when the Conference resolutions were not put before Parliament.

They were in a difficult position and knowing that the interests of their race were at stake they were content if they could not get the concession to let the white people legislate as in the past.

They were not unwilling to assist the Government but it has placed us in the position which should be made known to the country. The fault was the Government's.

Mr. van Niekerk explained the parliamentary procedure in regard to objecting to the principle of the Bill and then trying to make its details as good as possible.

He suggested that having made their protest they should tackle the details of the Bills.

The Chairman said that the matter should not be disposed of so lightly. The position was serious as their attitude to-day might affect the whole question of consultation with the Natives. Delegates had stated that the Conference was an advisory body called together to advise the Government. Were they acting as such? or were they adopting the function of a parliament?

The Government had asked them to consider the policy enunciated by the Prime Minister, and owing to the rules of parliamentary procedure that policy had to be dealt with in four Bills, each to be considered in accordance with such rules,

As far as he understood the proposals of the Government the Conference was not tied down by the clauses making the Bills interdependent. All they were asked to do was to consider the Bills on their merits. The clauses in question were meant to bind Parliament, but Parliament might reject them or the Government at the last moment might delete them.

By merely asserting the fact they could not throw the responsibility on the Government.

Chief Zibi moved that the Conference adjourn for an hour.

Dr. Roberts said he spoke under some difficulty. He had always been proud of the Conference and he had never hesitated to speak of it as an example of the patience and wisdom of the Native people.

When he had pressed for a Council Bill he knew it would give forth the wisdom of such a conference.

He asked them not to do anything which would bring down the honourable past lying behind the Conference and which would cause them to be misjudged by the people of the country.

On some of the matters he felt as strongly as any man in that hall and when the opportunity was given to him in Parliament he would take it. But he was not such a coward as to say "I won't have anything to do with this." He would discuss it.

Where they had objections and protests let them make them as strong as possible. That was the road for sensible men to pursue.

They had already protested against taking away the Cape franchise! Why had they not taken up the position at the start? They *had* already discussed one Bill! They had gone one-third of the journey — were they going to return?

If in the middle of the proceedings they said they would not go any further they would give a most unfavourable impression to the country.

He hoped they would go on and indicate their dislikes.

He hoped the meeting would not be abortive.

Rev. Mtimkulu seconded Chief Zibi's motion.

Motion put and carried.

The Conference adjourned until 11.30 a.m.

Chief Zibi said that as their protests had already been registered the delegates were prepared to go with the discussion of the Bills.

Mr. Thema's motion was read.

Mr. Fenyang seconded the motion.

Mr. Qamata moved that all reference to women in the motion be deleted.

Chief Sioka seconded the amendment and said that women's franchise depended on the abolition of the Cape Native franchise. Both parties in Parliament had agreed to give the vote to women if it could be confined to white women.

Mr. Jabavu said Mr. Thema's motion expressed what they wanted, but he did not wish to express an opinion on the question of votes for women. It was only in the motion as a constructive proposal and he did not think it wise that the Conference should formulate a resolution on the matter. He supported the amendment.

Mr. Thema said he could not accept the amendment. It was said that women would get the vote when the Native franchise went. There was therefore more reason for them to get it now as this might abate the fear of the white man.

Mr. Qamata's amendment was put and carried (only three voting against it).

Mr. Thema's motion, as amended, was read:—

"In view of the strong and unanimous feeling expressed by the Transvaal, Free State and Natal representatives against the abolition of the Cape Native franchise as proposed under the Representation of Natives in Parliament Bill; and

"In view also of the fact that the proposed Native legislation affecting franchise emanates not from a desire to grant franchise to Natives in the Northern Provinces but rather from the mistaken fear on the part of the European public that white civilization and white supremacy will be endangered.

"This Conference finds itself unable to consent to this measure which is directed against the future political rights of the people of the Union.

'It rejects the Representation of Natives in Parliament Bill.

"Alternatively it asks the Government to initiate a small beginning of a grant of franchise rights to the Northern Provinces' Natives, but leave the Cape Native franchise untouched."

Motion put and carried (3 against).

Mr. Plaatje said he did not understand where they were. They had fully discussed the Bill and did not want to go into details.

The Chairman pointed out that the Conference had objected to the principle of the Bill, but that did not mean they need not discuss each clause.

Instead of rejecting the Bill the Conference should have advised against it.

The Government may send the Bill in its present form to Parliament and the Conference should advise on each clause, *e.g.*, in regard to method of voting, number of members, etc.

However, he left it to the Conference to decide.

Mr. Jabavu said the delegates really meant what the resolution said.

The Conference would reject each clause. There was not one clause they liked. He suggested that the Conference should pass on to the next Bill.

This was agreed to.

The Chairman said that the Natives Land Act Amendment Bill was a most intricate one and no doubt after the delegates had read it the first time their heads were in a whirl.

Anyone who had read the Natives Land Act, 1913, would realize that territorial segregation of land was now a dead question. That principle was decided and accepted in 1913 and the whole administration of the Act was on that principle.

The 1913 Act contemplated that until definite areas were set aside where Natives could enjoy the right to purchase and lease the position of 1913 was to be maintained. That is to say, no Native could acquire land except in the Scheduled Native areas.

Mr. Sauer promised to assign by Act of Parliament as soon as possible areas where Natives could buy.

The Beaumont Commission was appointed and reported in 1916.

In 1917 the Government brought in a Bill which contained a schedule of areas where Natives could buy land. That Bill passed its second reading and was referred to a Select Committee.

Then the trouble began. The Select Committee reported that owing to the mass of evidence challenging the Beaumont Commission's recommendations, it was unable to make any recommendations in the short time it had.

It suggested the appointment of Committees to revise the Beaumont recommendations and submit proposals.

The Government, in view of the agitation and of the fact that Natives were assisting in war areas, accepted that suggestion and postponed the matter.

Local Committees made investigations and submitted proposals.

Nothing further was done, and the result was that no Native can buy land outside a Scheduled Native Area — except by the grace of the Government.

That was not the position, however, in the Cape owing to the franchise qualifications. There a Native could buy where he liked subject to the Cape Squatters Laws.

From 1913 it had been necessary to deal with the needs of the Natives by administrative means, otherwise great hardship might have occurred, and for this purpose the Government laid down conditions under which Natives could purchase.

Various stages had been passed through since 1913.

At first until the issue of the Beaumont Report Government had strictly followed the Act of 1913 and no Natives were allowed to buy land in European areas.

When Parliament turned down the Beaumont Report another stage arose and the Government acted then as if that Report would in general be accepted by Parliament later on, and gave Natives permission to buy in specific cases.

After the issue of the Committee's Reports the third and existing stage was reached and the Government allows Natives to purchase and lease land in the Committee areas.

Thus there was little difficulty in getting permission to purchase in the areas called "released areas" in the Bill and marked "red" on the maps in the Hall.

They must realise that the Natives had acquired no *right* to buy in the "red" areas. It was only the policy of the Government to allow them to do so.

The policy had not been legalized by Parliament.

The difference between the Beaumont recommendations of 1917 and the Committees' proposals affected Natives mostly in regard to Crown land. He had not heard Native opinion on that point and he would like to know whether their opposition to the proposed areas in 1917 was not a mistake. For he believed that it was largely because of the Native opposition assisted by certain Europeans friendly to the Natives that the Bill of 1917 did not become law.

Now in 1927 it was impossible to get the land they could have got in 1917. This was due to many causes, which it was unnecessary to state. But speaking from inside knowledge he knew it was impossible and he thought that every friend of the Native regretted that the Bill of 1917 did not pass.

Take the Crown land — there was still some in the Transvaal — nothing in the Cape — very little in Natal — none in the Orange Free State — while in 1917 there were thousands of morgen available. They had disappeared and Europeans were in occupation.

The Act of 1913 would stand and the Bill was to be read as one with that Act.

If necessary an explanation of each section would be given.

He wished, however, to refer to the drastic

squatting provisions in the Bill, but they must remember that squatting laws existed in all the Provinces, and strange to say the strictest law was in the Cape.

If a landowner allowed one Native to live on his farm without service he broke the law.

Now, although the Cape law allowed 100 Natives to buy a farm only one of them had the absolute right to live on it. If the other 99 wanted to enjoy rights of residence they had to make application to the Divisional Council and if that Council agreed the Magistrate would then issue licences to the 99 and each would have to pay £2 p.a. for the licence.

This would perhaps be news to the Transvaal delegates.

Chief Tombela hated the mention of the Natives Land Act which he compared to lysol.

The Bill would make them pay licences, while all the Natives wanted was to be allowed to reside on farms if the farmers were agreeable.

The Bill looked to the farmer to pay licence fees and if *he* paid them he would regard the Natives as slaves.

He failed to understand why the released areas in Natal were so small when the Native population was so great.

The Natives should have broad lands as small plots meant quarrels and fights.

The Bill made no mention of wages for farm labour; this should be fixed.

Adjournment from 12.30 *p.m. to* 2.30 *p.m.*

Chief Sioka asked that Mr. van Niekerk should explain Chapter II.

In the Bill the Government gave a good thing with one hand and a bad thing with the other.

Mr. Plaatje said that the previous day they had had a full discussion on the rights of the subject but that day they had to discuss the most vital right — the right to live on the soil of South Africa.

He had compared the maps with the Schedule of the Bill and that of the principal Act and he did not place much reliance on the maps.

The Bill reminded him of a jackal trap — a nice piece of meat with poison inside. If the Native accepted the Bill they would be more stupid than a jackal.

The Natives had as much right in the Union as those people who had the right to buy in the white areas.

His title to live in the Union was not based on birth alone, or as a member of a tribe seeing that his forefathers fought side by side with the voortrekkers.

Land legislation on the lines of the 1913 Act was the most cruel ever devised.

Mr. Fenyang pointed out that leave had been given in all the provinces to Natives to buy land since 1913 except in the Orange Free State on account of Chapter 34 of the Law Book.

The people in the Orange Free State did suffer through the 1913 Act. Families trekked from Thaba' Nchu and unscrupulous people took advantage of them in Rhodesia where thousands perished in fever areas of that country. Officials — with the knowledge of the Union Government — came and touted, although the Government knew the nature of the country.

The Beaumont Commission recommended all the Native owned farms as "Native Areas" and those farms were included as "additional Native areas" in the Bill of 1917. The Natives of the Orange Free State did not oppose that Bill.

The Committee only recommended some of those farms as "released areas" — 9 valuable Native owned farms are left out.

Further the Committee ignored the Beaumont recommendations in regard to the Districts of Fauresmith, Edenburg and Hoopstad.

The Chairman stated that the Government was acting on the Committees' reports — it did not support or defend them.

Mr. Thema considered the Bill to be a most important one. They looked at the maps and saw red "spots" and the green "spots" — reserved for 5,000,000 Natives — while the 1½ million whites were to have the immense remainder.

The protest to the Act of 1913 was based on the proposition that the land should be found before the law was made. Natives were buying land in the Transvaal and the whites saw that the best land was going hence they passed a law to stop that; thus the 1913 Act was rushed while the Natives were told it was only temporary.

The Beaumont areas were opposed by the Natives on the ground that they were insufficient and unhealthy and by the whites because they were too much.

The Natives were told that the idea of the Act was to find land and set it aside for Natives only to buy. The Smithfield speech gives the same idea. But now the Government seems to find that the farmers are unwilling to give up land, so that the released areas are to be thrown open for both Europeans and Natives to buy.

This shows that segregation has failed?

If Natives are to compete with the Europeans in the released areas why are they to be debarred from competing in the white areas.

The Natives have no chance in the "red" areas where platinum exists and cotton planted. How could Natives compete with wealthy Europeans? Besides where would the money come from?

The Conference might consider the Bill if the "released areas" were made "Native areas."

As a matter of fact most of the released areas are already owned by Natives as is the case in the Rustenburg District.

There was no reason why Natives should not have an opportunity of buying land in the high veld.

The Bill would inevitably drive the progressive Natives back to tribalism. If he wanted to buy a farm the Government would have to know his father and grand-father and if he said they came from Pietersburg a "red area" would be pointed out; and then if his tribe had already bought its quota of land he would be debarred from buying any more.

In fact the Bill said "You were divided into tribes in the past and you must remain tribes for the future."

Some Natives had worked since Union to break down tribalism because they did not like the conditions and wanted to think for themselves. So they had bought townships like Lady Selborne, Alexandra and others. They wanted to buy land where they liked.

It was hateful to be divided into tribes for land purchase.

Rev. Kuzwayo urged that the farms Redikerswel, Vergelegen, Goodgeloof, Wilderness, Tradouw and Spes Bona in the Emtonjaneni District should be constituted a released area.

Chief Kumalo thought the areas in the Orange Free State too small.

He suggested the repeal of the 1913 Act.

He came from Ladysmith and the tiny "red" spot on the map indicated Native owned farms one of which his grandfather had bought. He could not understand how these farms could be "released areas."

Rev. Mtimkulu said that after he had read the four Bills he understood the definition of the phrase "developing on our own lines" and this was "send the Natives back to tribalism."

There was to be free competition between whites and blacks in the released areas but their respective resources were not equal. The Native had no money and his earning capacity was being kept down by the Colour Bar Act.

The Bill prevented Natives from living where they liked. What farmer was going to take the trouble to register black men to work for him. A burden was being placed on the farmer who would have to pay licence fees.

Could not the Government follow the example of America, New Zealand and Australia?

There were the various Masters and Servants Acts in existence and now this Bill proposed further burdens for the Natives.

He suggested that everything in section *one* referring to tribes be deleted.

He pressed for the deletion of all sections dealing with squatters and labour tenants.

In conclusion, he said, the land was not sufficient.

R. Mona asked the Government to pay special attention to the conditions in which the Natives lived in the Cape and give them additional areas. Their Reserves were too small. The released areas were very small — only two little farms in the Queenstown District.

It seemed that they would only be able to buy communally or tribally. The Natives were of different tribes and scattered about for work, and they were not living under tribal conditions.

They wished to be able to buy anywhere.

He suggested that the released areas be made additional Native areas to accommodate landless Natives.

Mr. Jabavu pointed out that the Cape was going to suffer most under the Bill. Firstly by the loss of privileges. The proposals in the Bill were most unsettling. Congestion was worst in the Cape. The density of the population in the Cape was 90 to 100 per square mile as against 40 in other parts.

The Bill prevented the Natives from buying where they liked and this was a serious matter.

Section *one* dealing with tribalism is most unsettling for the Cape. Take the District of Herschel — there the tribes were intermixed. This would give rise to claims to chieftainship which had been turned down. The Government was assuming the power to say who were a tribe. They wished to inform the Government that it did not know much about the matter.

Headmen were appointed by the Government which did not recognize hereditary claims.

He was anxious that the door be left open for individual tenure. Communal occupation was all right for the masses.

The Natives did not want the released areas to be limited for specific tribes. A Native should be able to buy anywhere in a released area. On this point he spoke for all black men.

The sources from which the Land Purchasing Fund would get its moneys would not give substantial sums. He suggested that it be laid down that money *must* be voted each year by Parliament.

The existing difficulties were due to the 1913 Act which had been invented by the Europeans with whom he sympathised in having to carry out the moral duty of a fair distribution of the land. Such a duty required christianity which the Natives had not seen as yet.

The white spaces were 80 per cent. of the Union and from them the Natives were to be debarred for ever and ever. Amen.

Chief Msinyane complained that Zululand had only two delegates. He deplored the changes which had occurred since the days of Queen Victoria.

The Conference adjourned until the following day.

Third Day.

Thursday, 4th November, 1926.
Mr. Herbst in the Chair.
Certain questions addressed to the Acting Prime Minister and notices of motion were handed in.

The discussion on the Land Act Amendment Bill was resumed.

Chief Sekukuni said he was glad that the Government had given the Natives an opportunity of expressing their views on the proposed legislation. Consultation was appreciated by them. He hoped the Bills would be altered to meet their representations.

Chief G. Makapan pointed out that the Natives were poor and unable to buy land.

Mr. Ramuba said the released areas were too small. He would like things to be as they were in the old times. The Natives had helped the Europeans with their lives but got no benefits. They were given scorpions for bread.

Mr. Sakwe considered that too little land was being released.

Tribal rule had been abolished in the Transkeian Territories where they had Government Headmen. The tribal position as laid down in the Bill prohibited Natives of one Province from getting land in another; this was not the case where Europeans were concerned and they could get land even in a released area.

The Europeans should be generous if they wished for industrial and land segregation. The land possessed by Natives was really Crown land. In a sense the Natives were squatters paying a perpetual quitrent.

It was alleged that the Natives did not make proper use of their land. Well, whose fault was it? Did the Government allow the Natives the same facilities as European farmers in the way of agricultural education and the Land Bank?

Chief Zibi said he wished to thank the officials of the Department of Native Affairs for the assistance they had given him in connection with his settlement in Rustenburg.

He asked that conditions in the Reserves should be made such that educated Natives would stay in them. It was a pity that all the educated Natives left for the towns and none left to uplift the masses. A people was not judged by the few but by the masses. The Cape had recognized this hence individual tenure had been introduced. He suggested that in tribal purchases the land should be surveyed and only the grazing be communal. Chiefs must grow with their people. The Bill assumed that the tribal people were not growing. In the Transvaal they really had Paramount Chiefs because they really owned the land; in the Cape the Natives might be described as paramount squatters.

Just as Natives respected the ownership of cattle they must learn to respect the ownership of land.

Chief Tombela enquired whether he could purchase land in the Orange Free State.

He enquired why the Government could not repeal the 1913 Act which was like a poison to the Natives.

Mr. Njokweni pointed out that the Peddie Natives were suffering on account of the insufficiency of land.

Mr. Langa was surprised to hear that the Natives in the Cape were paramount squatters. He pointed out that in Pondoland the land was reserved by Treaty rights.

Chief Sioka mentioned that he was a Basuto and under the Bill he would be unable to buy land in Natal.

He thought the Government should call a round table conference with all the leading Natal men.

Natal could not accept the Bill on account of the squatters provisions.

He asked that land be given to Chiefs who were landless.

There was no released area in Maritzburg District except a little farm "Weltevreden" already owned by Natives.

Mr. Morosi pointed out that Europeans could buy in released areas. This was in conflict with the legislation foreshadowed by the 1913 Act.

The released areas were said to be 7,000,000 morgen but much of this was already owned by Natives and if that were deducted little was really available for Natives.

Native farms in European areas would have to be sold to whites.

He objected to the differentiation in the tribal opportunity to buy land.

He suggested:—

(1) That all Native-owned farms be taken out of the released areas and added to the Scheduled Native areas;

(2) that Europeans in the released areas be allowed to sell only to Natives or to the Government;

(3) that Natives be allowed to buy land within released areas wherever situated irrespective of their tribes.

The Chairman pointed out that the Government had granted permission to Natives to buy in the released areas during the last ten years.

Rev. Mtimkulu said the Bill was something new in the history of South Africa. It proposed to give a man a licence to live upon the earth. It savoured of slavery. It said nothing about the coloured man, the coolie and any foreigner who came to the country. The Natives must suffer all the hardships. They must not progress. The underlying principle was to keep the black man down. They were second to none in their loyalty but they were not getting a square deal.

Referring to the Orange Free State he would point out that in his own home the Prime Minister had no room for the Native.

He moved:

"This Conference expresses its deep disappointment that the Prime Minister's Land Bill contains no message of hope for the landless Native of the Union and would respectfully appeal to the Union Parliament to defer legislation on land matters pending the introduction of a more liberal measure."

Mr. Plaatje seconded the motion.

He invited attention to the Cape map showing the small released areas and considered that the fairest segregation proposal would be to divide the Cape by a line following the railway line from Port Elizabeth to Bloemfontein.

In the Cape he could buy where he pleased and if the Government wanted him to give up this right they must make the released areas attractive.

Nothing was offered to the Natives in return for giving up their most cherished rights.

Chief Kumalo considered that the Act of 1913 was a failure and no amendment could make it good.

The Natives wanted liberty.

The 1913 Act should be repealed.

Mr. Qamata thought that provision should be made for the surplus population of the Cape where they were like ants.

He wanted the right to buy land anywhere in the Union.

Mr. Nkamane said they would be lunatics to accept the Bill. If the Government had no hole to bury them it should send them to heaven.

Mr. Thema said the Government was abandoning the principle of the 1913 Act and only releasing certain areas. Thus it admitted the injustice of the Land Act and that the separation of the races was a failure.

The 1913 Act did not apply in the Cape, and as the Representation Bill was rejected on account of the Cape, the Conference should reject the Land Bill in respect of the Cape.

He moved:—

"1. That in view of the rejection of the abolition of the Cape Native Franchise by this Conference, the Conference finds that the Cape is faced with the similar danger in this Bill, and therefore strongly opposes its application to the Cape Province.

"2. This Conference, realising that the Government have abandoned the policy of segregation, recommends that the whole country be released from the operation of the Natives Land Act, 1913.

Or alternatively, "(a) the Government should adopt the Beaumont and Committee Areas in the Northern Provinces as minimum areas in which Natives only could buy.

"(b) That the allocation of areas according to tribes as prescribed in the Bill is strongly opposed as such will retard progress and civilisation among the Bantu people.

"(c) That the restrictions on Associations of Natives to purchase land be removed.

"(d) That Land Boards as suggested by the Beaumont Commission should be established for further adjustment of the land question.

"(e) That a Native Land Bank be established on the basis of the European Land Bank.

"3. That farms bought by Natives and scheduled areas situated in European areas be added to Native areas.

"4. That the whole of Chapter II be deleted as the ultimate effect of its application will bring about an economic enslavement of Natives. The Conference recommends that this Chapter be substituted by one dealing with Native development in agriculture and industry.

Mr. Jabavu seconded.

The delegates wanted to offer constructive criticism by this motion.

Their position was simply that they wanted to hold what they had and get more.

They did not want to prejudice the position in the Cape.

The 1913 Act had broken in the hand that forged it. The Europeans had been obsessed with the abstract idea of segregation without having considered the practicability of putting it into effect. They had been in a feverish hurry to put the idea on the statute book.

The first thing any reasonable man would have done was to find the land and then pass the Act. But the white people would not listen to the Natives.

He hoped the authorities would realise that the suggestions to repeal the Act were not made in a flippant spirit.

Rev. Kuzwayo hoped the Government would realise from the speeches that there was something wrong with the Native people on account of the 1913 Act. They were sick and the sickness was due to lack of land.

Chief Senthumulo said that the Bill should provide for the creation of new released areas when those set aside were full.

Chief Marcus Masibi pointed out that farms in the released area near his Location were of value owing to discovery of platinum. Europeans had already bought some and erected buildings valued at £5,000.

Europeans should not be allowed to buy in the released areas.

Mr. Gonyane hoped the Conference would support the motion.

At this stage the Hon. T. J. de V. Roos. Acting Prime Minister, entered the Conference Hall.

Mr. Roos stated that he had only come to answer the questions which had been placed in his hands.

He had received the list of cases from Mr. Plaatje. The names were not mentioned but he would enquire into every case and a reply sent to him and published in the press.

He proceeded to reply to the various matters namely:

1. *Question by Mr. Jabavu*: Could not the Prime Minister make his visit to this Conference one of a round-table character in which we may put questions to his answers?

Reply: He promised to lay this before the Prime Minister on his return.

2. *Suggestions by Rev. Mtimkulu*: "That the best interests of the Bantu will be served by the appointment of Native Postmasters in purely Native localities, and the appointment of Native Clerks in central Post Offices like Johannesburg, Pretoria and Durban to the Native work."

Reply: He promised to get this question gone into by the Minister of Posts and an answer given at a later stage. No answer could be given then as the suggestion meant a change of policy.

3. *Question by Mr. Qamata*: "In view of the fact that nothing has been granted to the Cape in regard to land acquisition in fresh areas by Natives what steps does the Government propose to take to allow Natives to buy land outside their Provinces?"

Reply: This was a question on which discussion and advice had been asked, and he had no doubt the Conference would set out its view for the Prime Minister's consideration. If they were not against Natives buying land in other Provinces they should say so.

The Bill was not yet law and would have to go to a Select Committee. It was not stereotyped. A resolution on the point would be valuable.

4. *Interpretation: Mr. Plaatje and Chief Tombela*: (a) Much of the hardships suffered by litigants in our Courts is due to the employment of interpreters who are incompetent in the knowledge of Native languages. A further grievance is that able Native interpreters who have served the Government for twenty or thirty years are always confined in the Department of Justice to the junior scale of pay. Could not the Minister effect a change in his Department so as to put his Native interpreters in line with those of the Native Affairs Department? (Plaatje.)

(b) That Natives in Natal suffer a grievance through lack of Native interpreters in certain country offices such as Municipal and Government. There being competent Native linguists in Natal, there seems no reason why Indians only should serve Natives. (Tombela.)

Reply: As far as Municipal offices were concerned he could do nothing. In Government offices Indians were not used as interpreters. There were some Indians employed for other purposes but he personally wanted to reduce them as far as possible. He hoped to do so except as far as they were actually required for the needs of the Indian population.

It was right that good interpreters should be available. What they should do was to report wherever they found an Indian interpreting.

He was not prepared to introduce two scales of pay in the Department of Justice, as he did not wish to add to the great increase in the cost of administration.

5. *Representations by Mr. Fenyang*: The definition of the phrase *"bona fide Barolong"* in the Moroka Ward Relief Act, 1924, is likely to create hardships for members of other tribes — landowners and non-landowners — who having lived among the Barolong since the early 'thirties have acquired vested interests in the District and are regarded by Natives as members of the Barolong tribe. This definition appears to limit landownership to purely Barolong people. Representations have already been made to the Native Affairs Department for an early removal of this anomaly since our apprehension is that possible difficulties may arise in the event of succession of children to landownership.

Reply: His own opinion was that the definition was unlikely to cause hardship. From his experience in Native cases he knew that a man could become a member of a tribe by subjecting himself to the authority of that tribe. But if this view were wrong hardship might be caused. Men regarded as Barolong since 1830 should be so treated.

He would obtain a legal ruling.

6. *Proposed motion by Mr. Koza*:"This Conference strongly opposes the provisions of the proposed Liquor Bill whereby it is intended (a) to extend the 'tot' system in vogue in the Western districts of the Cape to

the Northern provinces and (b) to give the Government the right to open canteens in Urban Areas for Natives, the right to brew and sell Kaffir Beer in Native Reserves."

Reply: It was not his intention to introduce the Cape system to the Transvaal but to extend the Orange Free State system to the Transvaal rural areas. Under that system the farmer had the right to give his servant one drink per day.

As regards the brewing and selling of beer in Reserves all he knew about it was from the Natal members of Parliament who claimed to know all about Natives.

They knew what the position was in Johannesburg and the Reef towns where there was an immense amount of illicit drinking of skokian. They would be horrified at the amount of yeast used for that purpose. He thought his proposal would help to combat drunkenness.

The Bill was still under consideration and he did not intend to do anything to increase drunkenness.

7. *Suggestion by Chief Senthimulo and Chief Moiloa*: (a) "That white people be not allowed to dig corundum in Native Locations but Natives only and if whites are allowed that should be with the approval of Chief and Tribe.

"(b) That locations granted to Native Tribes by the old Republican Government be treated as tribal property. That the tribal Chiefs continue to exercise the right of control and allocation of lands and the admission of traders and prospectors into the Reserves. That the proceeds of such trading licences be treated as tribal property."

Reply: The Locations do not belong to the tribe but are set aside for their occupation. The mineral rights belong to the Government which had no intention of giving those rights to the tribe.

As regards traders the general rule is that Chiefs are first consulted but the final decision must rest with the Department.

Under the Land Bill trading rents are assigned to the Land Purchasing Fund.

8. *Request by Chief Sioka*: "That the Government be urged to withdraw the word 'kafir' from all Government documents when referring to Natives as the use of the word 'kafir' is an insult to the Native race."

Reply: The tendency was to use the word "Native" exclusively. Here and there "Kafir" was used but then it was wrongly used as a synonym for "Native." He would see that the legal draftsmen made a note of this.

9. *Request by Mr. Plaatje*: That, having regard to their scant earnings, the Native people as a class are too highly taxed already. This Conference therefore requests the Government to take the earliest steps to exempt all Natives from the additional burden of paying to the provincial authorities entertainment licences and amusement tax which are proving so troublesome in missionary endeavours, since even sacred concerts in aid of church funds cannot be held without the written consent of the authorities, to be applied for direct from the administration of each provincial capital.

Reply: This was a provincial matter which he would have sent to the various Administrators.

10. *Suggestion by Mr. Plaatje*: In view of the frequency of the complete breakdown in the administration of justice in serious cases involving a clash between black and white in our Courts the Minister of Justice be requested to amend the Criminal Procedure Act, so that all such cases in future be tried by judges and assessors instead of judge and jury.

Reply: Personally he believed in the jury system. There might be an occasional but not frequent breakdowns. A Native as well as a European could claim trial by a Judge.

He would not hesitate to take action if he were convinced that his view was wrong.

11. *Proposal by Mr. Plaatje*: "That this Conference makes an urgent appeal to the Union Government to take immediate steps to relieve the Provincial Councils of the burden of administering Native Education and place it entirely under the control of the Union Government."

Reply: He thought the Provincial Administrations would agree to this on account of their being relieved from the financial burden. But if the Government took away education from the Councils there would be little left for them to do.

12. *Suggestion by Mr. Plaatje*: "That the

allowance for delegates attending the Conference be increased to 40 shillings per day."

Reply: He was afraid that the delegates would have to fight this out with Major Herbst, the Head of the Department. Heads said, "Ministers come and go but we go on for ever."

After furnishing the foregoing replies the *Minister* said he thought that the delegates were dealing with the matters before them in the right spirit. They should debate fully and give their views which would not always be right. Much depended on the point of view. If they got fullest information on differing views the road would be easier to improve things.

They were there not to get ideal conditions but to get some improvement and to hold on to that. He never threw away half a loaf while looking for the whole.

He was pleased to be with the gathering again and hoped their stay would be fruitful.

Mr. Jabavu tendered their sincerest thanks for the Minister's presence and for his geniality. They were sometimes too serious in their discussions.

It was the first time a Minister had answered their questions and this constituted a record.

However much they might disagree it might be that some desired to give the Natives fair play.

Rev. Mtimkulu joined in Mr. Jabavu's thanks.

The Minister thanked the Conference and withdrew.

DOCUMENTS 40a — 40b. Minutes of Evidence, Select Committee on Subject of Native Bills, May 1927

DOCUMENT 40a. Testimony of Charles Sakwe, Elijah Qamata, and William Mlandu of the Transkeian Native General Council, before the Select Committee on Subject of Native Bills, May 6, 1927 [Extracts] (Published in *Minutes of Evidence, Select Committee on Subject of Native Bills*)

67. By the Chairman. (Mr. Charles Sakwe.) We are here for the purpose of giving evidence upon the Native Bills now before the House. We are all members of the Bunga and

are giving evidence in that capacity. We have been delegated by the Bunga to do so. We have a report of a Select Committee of the Bunga on the three bills. We all served on that Committee and the report is signed by us as well as by the other members. The views expressed therein are the unanimous conclusions of the Committee. The following is the report:

Your Committee met on the 22nd, 23rd and 25th instant and considered the following Bills:—

1. The Union Native Council Bill.
2. The Natives' Land Act 1913 Amendment Bill.
3. The Representation of Natives in Parliament Bill.

Your Committee has appreciated the grave responsibility placed upon it and has conducted its deliberations with the earnest desire to find a via media which will not only be acceptable to the Government but will also give satisfaction to the people whom the Committee represents.

Your Committee realises that the proposed legislation discloses an honest effort to cope with certain aspects of the much debated "Native Question" and feels that the adoption by Parliament of the measures under consideration will, according to the form in which they may be passed, have very far reaching effects upon the future peace and welfare of the Union of South Africa and will according to their final character earn the approval or condemnation of the whole civilised world.

Certain members of your Committee were present in an accredited capacity at the recent Native Conference at Pretoria and at the European-Bantu Conference in Cape Town in January last so that they have a knowledge of public opinion as there expressed.

It is in the spirit and with the knowledge indicated above that your Committee has carried on its duties.

Your Committee is unanimous in the following statements and conclusions:—

General.

Though the three Bills under consideration may be corelated in substance each should be dealt with in Parliament as a separate independent measure.

The Natives' Land Act 1913 Amendment Bill.

Your Committee has found the greatest difficulty in arriving at detailed conclusions on this measure. It appears that the professed intention of the Bill is to palliate the harshness of the operation of the Natives' Land Act of 1913, to grant further facilities to Natives to acquire land and to provide in general for greater fixity and security in land tenure, but the advantages to be obtained are so circumscribed with conditions and restrictions as to place the suggested privileges beyond the Natives' reach. For example, section 1, subsections (3) and (4) limit the right to acquire land in released areas to members of a recognized tribe thus restricting co-operative effort towards acquiring land.

In the competitive quest for land between European and Native; the latter on account of his less advantageous economic position is only too sure to be ousted.

In the opinion of your Committee sections 2 and 10 which make fencing a condition to the acquisition by a Native of land in a released area or the holding of land in a scheduled or released area places an almost insurmountable obstacle in the way of his acquiring or holding land. The provision is moreover a physical, heartless and unnecessary colour discrimination.

In the opinion of your Committee the effect of the operation of Chapter II of the Bill will be to create a new landless, homeless class of Natives many of whom will inevitably drift to urban centres, not only to their own disadvantage but to that of the European community.

Your Committee respectfully suggests that the whole tenor of the Bill appears to be a tendency to give with one hand and take away with the other. As a single reason for stating this view your Committee draws attention to section 20 under which permission may be given to aged, infirm and destitute persons to reside upon land, which permission may be withdrawn at any moment.

Your Committee in the limited time permitted to it has made some brief enquiry into the history of Native land tenure in South Africa and has found that from earliest times landlessness has led to lawlessness. This fact was realised in the Cape Colony so far back as 1828 when an Ordinance was passed giving Natives right to acquire land and giving them security of tenure.

Coming to modern times we find that in the earlier part of the late great war farmers for purposes of economy found it necessary to dispense with the services of a large proportion of their Native and Coloured farm servants. These banded themselves together in groups committing in their desperate case thefts and robberies and creating a condition of general lawlessness.

Your Committee has reason to urge that as the operation of the Bill is likely to have the effect of driving large numbers of people from the land they at present occupy, this contingency should be anticipated by making suitable provision for such persons.

Your Committee in brief feels that such merit as the Bill may contain is nullified by the disabilities it imposes.

Union Native Council Bill.

In stating its views upon this Bill your Committee wishes to make it plain that it in no way commits itself to an acceptance of the principles of the Bill on the understanding that such acceptance suggests a surrendering of the Franchise. Your Committee believes itself to be justified in stating that the Natives of the Cape Province would be prepared to forego all the legislative and other privileges included in the Bill provided they are permitted to retain the Franchise.

Your Committee suggests that the name "Pretoria" be deleted from section 2 (1) of the Bill and the words "some suitable place" be inserted in place thereof. Your Committee does not consider Pretoria to be a central or suitable place for the meetings of the Council.

Your Committee suggests that the Council itself and not the President should have the power to alter its rules, and that section 2 sub-section (2) should be altered accordingly.

Your Committee considers the mode of election provided to be cumbrous, involved and generally unsatisfactory. If the proposed method of election is to operate, elected members of Council will almost all be Government employees (Chiefs and Headman) the other members being Government nominees, so that practically the whole weight of voting power will be that of persons who are in a sense committed to a Government point of view. Your Committee strongly recommends the preparation of a roll of male persons to be entitled to a straight and final vote for the election of members of Council, the right to vote depending upon the person concerned being a tax payer or upon some other similar suitable qualification.

Your Committee recommends that the words in section 3, sub-section (4) from "Provided" to "prescribed" be deleted so that members of Council hold office for three years and do not retire by rotation.

Your Committee considers that the Council should have the right to legislate of its own volition, such legislation to be subject to the veto of the Governor-General, and recommends that section 4, sub-section (3) be amended accordingly.

The Representation Of Natives
In Parliament Bill

Your Committee holds that the right of the Natives of the Cape Province to vote for full members of the Union House of Assembly as confirmed by the terms of the South Africa Act was in intent entrenched for all time.

Your Committee is absolutely and entirely opposed to the terms of this Bill in so far as it entails the withdrawal of the franchise from the Natives of the Cape Province, and it cannot conceive of any present set of circumstances warranting such withdrawal. Your Committee knows of no precedent in history for the deprivation by the Government of a state of the full citizen rights possessed by a section of its law abiding subjects, and holds that it has never been shown that the exercise of the franchise has been abused by those Natives of the Cape Province who have enjoyed it.

Your Committee acknowledges with deep appreciation the proposal to grant a measure of representation to the Natives of the Transvaal, Natal and Orange Free State, but it is in a position definitely to state that whatever merit the proposed legislation now under consideration may contain such merit

in the eyes of the Natives of the whole Union will be entirely nullified by the withdrawal of the franchise from the Natives of the Cape Province which would engender in the Native mind a deep and everlasting sense of injury and injustice. On the other hand your Committee has good grounds for stating that if the Native franchise in the Cape is guaranteed, the Natives throughout the Union will incline to the support of the principles in the three Bills now under consideration.

Your Committee wishes to stress the point that their claim to the retention of the franchise are in no way coupled with claims to social equality.

In conclusion your Committee wishes to state that it has endeavoured to express itself with all modesty, moderation and reserve and it trusts that if this end has been achieved this Council and the Select Committee of Parliament before which it is desired this report shall be placed, will believe that your Committee has placed upon itself such restraint in dealing with the vital matters laid before it as will indicate the deepest earnestness of purpose.

We still hold the views expressed by us in that report, and those are the views which we wish to lay before this Committee. We have nothing to add except in reply to questions you may wish to ask us. We admit in the report that there is an honest effort made in these bills to cope with certain aspects of the native question. We think it will be better if these bills are dealt with as separate and independent measures, and not have them connected as at present. When considering the *Natives Land (Amendment) Bill* we had before us the bill that was discussed by the official Congress at Pretoria last, which is the only copy we had. We interpret sub-section (3) of Clause one to mean that only tribal land can be bought by natives within the released areas. We want the natives not only as a tribe but by co-operative means to have the right of buying land as an association or company, and even the individual should be allowed to buy. It is not clear to us that by this Bill individuals as well as tribes are allowed to buy land. If that is made clear in the bill we will be satisfied as far as that point is concerned. We are agreeable that companies or associations which are purely native should be able to buy land. (*Mr. Qamata.*) The point is this: At present individual natives are unable to buy land by reason of their economic position unless they club together as an association. In the meantime while tribes are still unable to buy land for themselves, native companies or associations should be allowed to acquire land in the areas set apart for natives. (*Mr. Sakwe.*) You draw attention to cases where an association of about 100 natives have bought a farm and when one dies the farm has to be subdivided, or where the farm has to be subdivided where any one of the 100 desires it, which results in great cost to the other natives, but that aspect has never occurred to us. (*Mr. Qamata.*) Will it not be possible when land is bought by an association to insert a condition in regard to subdivision which will not run them into expense? We express the fear in our report that in the competitive quest for land in the released areas between the European and the native, the European will in every case have the better of the native. You say, however, that the experience of the department is that when a released area is created the inclination is for the European to get out of it and not to buy land there, and we accept your word. Our experience is derived from Scheduled Areas themselves. The Europeans living in these areas very seldom part with their land on account of the quality of the land. I am speaking about land about the Transkei. (*Mr. Sakwe.*) I think it is quite the natural thing as stated by you that the Government finds it easier to get money to buy land for native purposes in a released area than it would be to get money to buy land in amongst Europeans, and I think that that supports our contention when we tell you that it is difficult even to get Europeans to part with their land in scheduled areas. (*Mr. Qamata.*) We would like it to be distinctly laid down that Europeans have no right to buy land in the released areas set aside for natives. (*Mr. Sakwe.*) We do realise that we are more likely to be efficiently assisted by the Government in the matter of improving our agricultural conditions within the released areas than if we were spread all over the country, and we would be better off if that can be done. We next take exception to the conditions in regard to fencing. We consider they are far too harsh. (*Mr. Qamata.*) We must consider that from the economic position of the native. He will exhaust all his means in buying the land and will have no money for the purpose of erecting the fence. We had clause twelve (2) in mind when we drew up our report, but it still does not do away with the difficulty. The man will have to borrow the money, it will be advanced to him on loan and will be a debt due by him to the State.

We say in our report that Chapter II will create a landless, homeless class of natives that will drift to urban centres. We think that will be the effect of the licence fees and other things in the Chapter which will force the natives to leave the farms, and they will have no homes to go to. The bill does provide that the licence fee shall be paid by the farmer, but by experience we have had we know the farmer will get it out of the squatter, and that is going to drive him from the farm owing to changed conditions. It is a fact that to-day under the Cape law squatters are not allowed on farms in the Cape Province unless a licence is granted by the Divisional Council for which the farmer has to pay £2. It does not matter to us whether the licence is £2 or £3 our point is that the farmer, notwithstanding any provision in the Bill, will pass that burden on to the squatter. If the squatter refuses to pay the amount the farmer is at liberty to tell him to leave the farm. That is a hardship we foresee. We quite appreciate your view that this is not a hardship now created by this Bill. (*Mr. Mlandu.*) You must bear in mind that when the Cape law was framed the natives were not consulted, but now we have been taken into consultation and we say that provision should be made to overcome this hardship so that the natives on account of what I have stated will not be forced to leave the farms. We have taken into consideration the fact that under this Bill the money derived from licences will go to a fund for assisting the natives in fencing and buying land. In the Cape this law has never had any bad effect upon the natives, but in the other provinces it is just the opposite, and we fear that with the progress of time we may have the same conditions here in the Cape. The natives have been driven out and scattered about on account of the operation of such law in other provinces. I am alluding to the operation of the Native Land Act in the other provinces. It is a well known fact that when that Act was put into force many natives who were living on the farms had to go, and trekked from one farm to another and lost their stock on the way, and even some of the people died on the road. Some of them never got a place to go to. This information was in the newspapers at the time. (*Mr. Sakwe.*) With regard to the Union Council Bill, we say that instead of Pretoria being made the seat of the Council the Bill should simply say "some suitable place." We also say that the Council itself and not the President should have the power to alter the rules of the Council. The Bunga has not that power, we simply make recommendations to the Governor-General. In regard to electoral qualification we say that all native tax payers, irrespective of educational qualification, should have the power to vote. We do not like the idea of the elected members being merely Government nominees. That is why we are opposed to the provisions as they stand in the Bill. We wish every man to have the right of choosing his own representative. The electoral practice in the Transkei is this: A Government official will go round to a certain location where a general meeting has been called, and he will take the votes of the people. Voting will not always necessarily be by ballot. It may also be by a · show of hands. The Government officials could go to all the location centres and take the votes of the people in this way instead of having one day set apart for a general election which will draw all the natives away from their work to go to the ballot box. The method suggested by me will differ very much from that provided for in the Bill. The difference is that according to our practice every man has the right of saying who will be his representative. The natives on the farms can vote by a centre being arranged for them there rather than that they should leave the farms. (*Mr. Qamata.*) It is so that the natives on the farms will have to go to the ballot box or to some place equivalent to the ballot box on a certain day. You ask whether we have considered the effect that this system will have on the economic position of the country. To-day in the Cape, even with the ordinary general election, it has never as far as the natives are concerned, especially in respect of those on the farms, dislocated the work of the European at all. The main consideration is that most of the natives on the farms have not yet reached the standard of exercising the right to vote or else they do not care to exercise it. We wish the present practice not to be disturbed. It has never interfered with the work of the country and has never caused trouble during general elections. (*Mr. Sakwe.*) The people scattered on the farms are also in a minority. We are speaking about the mass of the people in the locations. (*Mr. Qamata.*) With regard to the costs that will be involved there will be nothing beyond the expense of the official who will go round from one meeting to the other taking the votes. (*Mr. Sakwe.*) A mass meeting on one day will include all the locations round about and no expense will be incurred. We also ask that retirement of members by rotation should be done away with, and that the Council have the right to legislate of its own volition upon any subject, subject however to the veto of the Governor-General. With regard to the *Representation of Natives in Parliament Bill* we are entirely opposed to the withdrawal of the franchise from natives in the Cape Province. We are aware that the Bill provides for the substitution of another native franchise. We do not accept the principle of having native representation apart from that of the Europeans, because we are living together with the Europeans and our interests are interwoven with theirs and we see no necessity for having them separated. Your scheme would work well if we natives were living in our own territory all by ourselves where there are no Europeans, and where nothing is in common between the native and Europeans. Our reply is a general reply covering the provinces as a whole. We are not confining ourselves to one particular district or locality. We are in principle against the separation of representation between Europeans and natives in Parliament. (*Mr. Qamata.*) You ask whether we are prepared to make any suggestion better than what is provided for in the Bill on the basis of separate representation by natives in the Cape.

That question suggests something which is outside the scope of the report of the Native Select Committee, and we do not desire to deal with any matter that was not dealt with by that Committee. That suggestion would really require a new Bill and would have to be put before the people again for consideration.

68. *By Gen. Smuts.*] (*Mr. Sakwe.*) This report is the report of a Select Committee appointed by the Bunga to consider the Native Bills. The Bunga has discussed this report and approved of it, and has sent us here to give evidence. The report represents the views of the Bunga. Our position is that we are afraid that the Cape natives will lose under the Bills. At present we can buy land freely as we like, and under his *Land Bill* we will be restricted to buy only in the released areas. Our land rights are therefore going to be curtailed. We also stand to lose our present franchise for Parliament. We think that the sacrifice asked from us in the Cape is too great although the natives in the other provinces will be the gainers by being given rights under these Bills. The Bunga is not prepared to make these sacrifices. We wish natives only to have the right to buy in the released areas. If the Government takes the *Land Bill* entirely by itself independent of the other Bills and our franchise rights are not going to be effected we will be prepared, for the sake of the natives in the other provinces who are not free to buy land as we are, to accept this Bill if the right to buy in the released areas is restricted to natives only. We wish this to be clear that we only agree to the condition that natives only be allowed to buy, and that we do not accept the whole of the Bill as it stands. We object to Chapter II of the Bill. (*Mr. Qamata.*) We think the effect of the licence will be to drive the natives from the farms, and there is not enough other land for them to go to. We do not like Chapter II of the Bill, and we do not like the fencing clause of the Bill. If the fencing clause and the licences are made right or taken away we are prepared to accept the *Land Bill* if it is confined to natives. (*Mr. Sakwe.*) That will not yet satisfy us with the whole Bill. Even suppose the released areas are solely for natives there is not enough land for the natives as far as the Cape is concerned. There is too much congestion. We think the

released areas for the Cape should be larger. We have not enough land in the Transkei even if cultivated properly. It is not only individual tenure that is making it difficult for us in the Transkei. The people there still go in for both individual and communal tenure. Some prefer one form and some the other. Those who go in for individual tenure like it, and those who go in for communal tenure have no definite opinion. We say there is not enough released area given in the Cape and that the congestion is too great.

In regard to the *Native Council Bill*, there is a great difference between the natives in the various provinces. (*Mr. Mlandu.*) Personally as far as we are concerned the suggestion to have native provincial councils for the provinces instead of one big council for the whole of the Union would be a good arrangement for the Cape. Experience has shown us when we meet at these conferences that some of the natives from the other provinces have not kept pace with the Cape in development, and differ in their psychology and their policy differs from ours because we came into contact with the white man before they did. We find at these conferences our views are in advance of theirs and we may accordingly be retarded in our progress. A provincial council at the Cape for the natives will suit our interests better (*Mr. Qamata.*) With regard to the franchise question our report deals only with the mode of election but does not deal with the qualification of electors. We leave that open and it still can be arranged to deal with the qualification. What we like to see is that the native males vote for themselves and not the chiefs and headmen to vote for them. If the Government says that not every male must vote and that there must be some qualification for civilised natives we will accept it, but we would add that the natives who are living under the tribal system in the Transkei have accommodated themselves to the present system existing there and are fully satisfied therewith. For those who prefer the other mode of election the Government can lay down a qualification. The tribal system in the Transkei is different from the tribal system in other parts. Under the Bunga system they have learned to exercise their vote and if they are to come under the system proposed in the Bill they will not

201

accept it and carry on as they are doing at present.

With regard to the *Representation of Natives in Parliament Bill*, we are opposed to taking away the votes of the Cape natives under any circumstances. (*Mr. Sakwe.*) You ask us whether we would be prepared to consider a compromise that the natives who are on the roll at present remain there but that no further natives be put on. We have discussed this matter very fully and the people have come to this one conclusion that they will accept no compromise on this question. They simply stand on their existing rights. (*Mr. Qamata.*) That includes voting in the white constituencies with the whites. We want the Cape to be left as it is and rights given to the other provinces as the Government may desire. We do not want to make any sacrifice on the franchise question. (*Mr. Sakwe.*) We are prepared to make a sacrifice on the land question to some extent.

DOCUMENT 40b. Testimony of Professor D.D.T. Jabavu, Walter Rubusana, and the Rev. Abner Mtimkulu of the Cape Native Voters' Convention and Meshach Pelem of the Bantu Union, before the Select Committee on Subject of Native Bills, May 30, 1927 [Extracts] (Published in *Minutes of Evidence, Select Committee on Subject of Native Bills*)

253. *By the Acting Chairman.*] (*Professor Jabavu.*) Besides the Cape Native Voters' Convention I represent the following bodies:—

The Wesleyan Methodist Conference of South Africa.

The European-Bantu Conference.

The Cape Native Voters' Convention.

The Cis-Kei Native Convention.

The Government Native Conference (Act 23 of 1920).

The S.A. Native Farmers' Congress.

The S.A. Native Teachers' Federation.

The S.A. Native and Coloured Health Society.

I wish to speak of the Representation of Natives in Parliament Bill. I have embodied my views in a pamphlet which has been submitted to the members of this Committee and which I wish to be taken up in my evidence. It is as follows:—

The franchise was first granted to the Natives of Cape Colony in 1854, without distinction as to white and black. Before this privilege was conferred upon the Natives, the evidence of both oral tradition and Cape historical records of the years 1848-1854 enables us to judge that the motives inspiring the officials of the then British Parliament were born of the essential Christian ethic, namely: "Do unto others as you would have them do unto you." They were founded on a system of unimpeachable equity to all human beings regardless of colour, race or creed.

Translated into practical politics by Sir George Grey and his contemporaries, who meticulously eschewed all discrimination based on the colour of a man's skin, they were finally crystallized by Cecil Rhodes in his formula of "Equal rights to all civilised men south of the Zambesi." This Rhodesian dictum imposed the criterion of civilisation on everybody alike, excluding both white and black uncivilised men. It was an equitable standard, because it threw the door open for all to qualify for true citizenship and a voice in the counsels of a State in which civilized men were bound for the same destiny.

Under such a scheme it was no disadvantage to wear a black skin, because all men who could prove their civilisation by a recognized educational and property test were eligible for the franchise and Parliamentary membership. Judged from the religious standpoint this was perfectly Christian and at the same time sound economics. The Ministers of Queen Victoria thus made Britons of all civilized black men under the Union Jack on a uniform equality of citizenship with all other British subjects elsewhere in the Empire on which the sun never sets. The old Cape Colony adhered to this policy for nearly half a century, producing a progressive, contented and sane Bantu population.

At the conclusion of the Boer War and pacification of 1902 a compromise was made by which the Britishers yielded to the tradition of the Northern ex-Republics on the principle that a man's black colour should prohibit him from the right to the franchise.

A worse compromise was pressed from the same quarter in 1909 when under the Union Act, the right of membership to Parliament was taken away from the Cape Native and Coloured voters. We know that in the deliberations of the 1908 Convention it was the Northern members who pressed for the exclusion of non-Europeans from Parliament; and that it was only under inexorable pressure that the Cape delegates were brought to give way to the notorious Colour Bar Clause No. 26 of the Constitution, and to Clause No. 35, which made it a possibility to dispossess the Cape Natives of their franchise, and which constitutionally placed it under the jeopardy of election vicissitudes whereby all non-Europeans could some day be disqualified by a two-thirds majority in a Joint Sitting.

The spirit that produced this clause was without doubt illiberal, un-Christian and subversive of all that is best in British tradition, resulting in palpable unrest among the people thus stigmatised, as well as considerable mystification and perplexity in the Imperial Parliament when the Draft Union Act was taken thither for ratification. Memorable speeches were made in the House of Commons by the Prime Minister, Mr. H. H. Asquith, and in the House of Lords by Lord Crewe, all urging the South African delegation to abandon the un-British and shortsighted Colour Bar in the Constitution; but to no purpose. In view of this adamant position on the part of the South African delegation King Edward VII took the extraordinary step of preserving the right of the Cape Native franchise against future dispossession in his "Letters of Instruction" to all future Governors-General. Again, the Imperial Commoners in their despair, after endeavouring to influence the Convention delegates to a more humane attitude, exhorted the delegates to modify their policy on their return so as to seek a way to withdraw the Colour Bar and extend the Cape Native franchise northwards.

It was not a question of uninformed English negrophiles unduly intermeddling in the local affairs of South Africa; but a case of independent external examiners criticising the patent failure on the part of South African politicians to observe the universal laws common to all humanity. Locally, it was the historical conflict between the ideals of the liberal Cape and the inflexible Northern Provinces habituated to governing their subject races on the principles of so-called "firmness." The Imperial Parliament and the King of the British Empire, in their capacity of unbiased judges, could not forbear to censure the Convention delegates for the glaring injustice committed against the inarticulate Bantu races.

Less than two months ago a prominent Cape politician gave expression in a public speech to the following apposite remarks:

"A new spirit had come into Native policy in recent years as far as the Union was concerned — a policy of repression, a policy of injustice, and a policy that went back entirely on the policy of the old Cape Colony. He would go as far as to say that had they at the Convention, or had the leaders of the old Cape Colony in those days, known the position as it was to-day, there would have been no Union. That was absolutely certain. If they could have foreseen the Bills which were now before Parliament for discussion next session, they would never have dreamt of going into Union. They thought at that time that, with the experience which the Union Government would get, the policy of the old Cape Colony would gradually extend and be supported by the whole of the people of the Union. The policy now was to go back on the policy of the old Cape Colony. . . Under this (Representation of Natives) Bill it was proposed to take every Native off the register, which was absolutely contrary to the Act of Union. . . . and it is against the assurances given to the Imperial Government when the Act of Union was passed."—(J. W. Jagger, M.L.A., *Cape Times*, December 16, 1926.)

These facts are incontestable and cannot lightly be dismissed as political opportunism or platform chicanery. Since then a change for the worse has become manifest from the spirit that obtained in 1854 and 1910. The Northern provinces have undergone no change of heart during the last 16 years. On the contrary, there is cumulative evidence that they have steadily overpowered the Cape policy. Indeed their dominance has given birth to the Colour Bar Act of 1926, and to the Native Bills, of which we are to consider clause by clause the one entitled "The Representation of Natives in Parliament."

The Franchise Bill.

The preamble to this Bill contains three extraordinary proposals:—(a) The first is to alter sub-section (2) of Section *thirty-five* of the South Africa Act in order to remove all the names of Native voters from the registers. The original law guaranteed that "No person who at the passing of any such law (*i.e.*, to disqualify any person by reason of his race or colour only) is registered as a voter in any province shall be removed from the register by reason only of any disqualification based on race or colour." This proposal constitutes a revolutionary violation of both the letter and spirit of the Union Act.

(b) The second is "to make special and uniform provision for the representation of the Native inhabitants of the Union in the House of Assembly." This proposal postulates what we cannot accept, namely that the members of Parliament should be split into two sections according as they represent whites and blacks who live territorially mixed. It is further vitiated by its preliminary basis of depriving one section of the Natives of its franchise rights enjoyed for more than seventy years without abuse or misuse.

(c) The third is "to alter certain other provisions of the South Africa Act, 1909, and the laws governing voters' rolls and parliamentary elections, with a view to effect such representation."

There appears to be no justification for tampering with the Constitution for the purpose of introducing an injustice at the expense of the Cape Native voters.

On this preamble we would offer as a constructive suggestion that no alteration whatever be made in section 35 of the Union Act, but that special provision be introduced to initiate the Natives of the three Northern Provinces into a modified form of the franchise with a high educational and property qualification. That would be a step in the direction of honouring the assurances given in England in 1909 by the Convention deputation. Incidentally it would rectify the longstanding anomaly of the existence of voteless

educated Natives and create justice where it is clamantly wanted.

Clause I of this Bill definitely disfranchises the Cape Native voters because it repeals sub-section (2) of section 35 of the Union Act.

As we oppose the retrogressive step of the disfranchisement of the Cape Natives, we respectfully suggest that Clause 1 be deleted from the Bill.

Clause 2 establishes seven European members to represent all the Natives of the Union and divides each of the larger provinces into two electoral constituencies where voting is to be carried on only by Chiefs, Headmen, members of local Councils, or by other groups to be organised by Government machinery. This clause is both revolutionary and indefensible; revolutionary because such a system of group voting is without precedent in the British Empire; and indefensible because, (a) the number of members will be clearly inadequate for the immense population concerned; (b) the geographical size of the constituencies will be unwieldy for efficient management; (c) the character of the electoral brigades will be that of men indebted to the Government either as servants or nominees; (d) it supplies only a shadow of its intended substance because the proposed electorates, being all but suborned in advance, give but a faint reflex of real representation.

As a constructive suggestion we would eliminate this clause and substitute instead a modified individual franchise for the three Northern Provinces based on an educational and property qualification.

Clause 3 lays out the manner, date and place of elections.

Clause 4 makes the seven members additional to those in the Union Act, and perpetuates the old and contentious Colour Bar of section 43 of the Union Act.

Clauses 5 and 6 limit the privileges of the seven members in certain respects, and these respects are just those matters in which the Native voters are at least as deeply concerned as are the European voters.

Clause 7 completes the process of the disfranchisement of the old-time Cape Native voter begun under Clause 1 of the Bill.

Now, clauses 3 to 7 should be deleted

under our scheme inasmuch as they logically depend for their validity upon clause 1 and 2 which we have already expunged.

Clause 8 is a legal riddle. According to the reading of General Smuts it preserves the status quo of the Native voters in their relation to the Provincial Council. According to Sir Charles Crewe it abolishes it. The ambiguity of this clause thus permits of two diametrically opposed legal interpretations. In either case it is difficult to imagine how the Cape Native voters will continue to vote for their Provincial Council once their names are struck off the register as provided under Clauses 1 and 2 of this Bill. This confusion of aim on the part of the authors of the Bill somewhat upholds our suggestion against any tampering with the old Cape Native Vote.

Clauses 9 to 11 are negligible as they merely define terms.

Thus we are left with nothing to approve in the Bill except the constructive suggestions already outlined.

In support of this position we may at this juncture state that the Natives of the Northern provinces have, by means of their organizations, journals, meetings and all other methods of expression, unequivocally rejected the offers made under this Bill.

They do not want the Bill so long as its advantages to them involve the whittling down of the old Cape Native vote. They prefer to wait until in God's good time the European race of South Africa may be induced to start them on a franchise similar, even if modified, to that of the Cape. It will therefore be purposeless to foist upon these people a pseudo-franchise they unanimously repudiate.

On the other hand the Cape Natives have already lost so many of their old treasured privileges since Union (that is, by the disabilities under the Colour Bar clause in the Constitution, the restrictions arising out of the 1913 Lands Act, the Poll Tax, Pass Laws, the abolition of the right to appeal to the Privy Council, the dispossession of the right to land tenure under the Urban Areas Act, The Colour Bar Act of 1926), they have already lost so many of their privileges, I say, that they can hardly be blamed for being now unwilling to sacrifice their greatest asset for the sake of conferring the franchise on somebody who says he does not [sic.]

We shall now discuss eight arguments levelled against the Cape Native franchise by the Prime Minister at Smithfield (November 13th, 1925) and by others from time to time.

Firstly, the Cape Native Vote is a danger to European civilization.

Our answer to that is that a little thinking will show that this is erroneous because the ordinary Native cannot be a voter until he satisfies the standard set for all civilized men. To become civilized he begins by renouncing barbarism and develops political aspirations that are harmonious with progress and modern culture. Barbarism, as an inferior stage of ethnic development, can always be subjugated by civilization. Therefore it is a logical fallacy to assume that the Cape Native vote can by any possibility be a menace to European civilization. On the contrary the history of the last forty years contains abundant proof that the Native vote has substantially advanced the cause of European civilization, because it has been wisely exercised, producing parliamentarians of the calibre of Sir James Rose-Innes who first entered Parliament in the early eighties as a direct choice of the Victoria East Native voters. Far from being amenable to bribery by unscrupulous orators, it has exhibited judicious selection, decorating the House of Assembly with illustrious statesmen like Mr. Merriman, Mr. Sauer, Sir Richard Solomon, Sir Charles Crewe, and many more. It has never committed any mistakes. Therefore theory and experience are entirely on the side of the Cape Native vote.

Secondly, we are told it is a danger because it will in time swamp the European vote by reason of its numerical preponderance, transferring political ascendancy from white to black and making this a black man's country.

Our reply is that this is a confession of an unjustifiable fear. Past history provides no more ground for fear on this account than the Cassandra prophecies deduced from census figures by a Government official two years ago. A study of the figures reveals that in 1910 there were 6,633 Native voters to 121,346 European voters, that is one to eighteen; and now sixteen years after that there are 14,182 to 156,531, one to eleven. This comparative slowness of Native growth is in keeping with the slow process of a true education, a natural course of development. Supposing it did swamp the whites in our present day, what reason is there to fear four million uncivilized Natives on the part of a million civilized European population backed by forty-five million Englishmen plus the whole League of Nations? A lion might as well fear the future of the mouse. Just as Natal has framed laws stringent enough to limit its franchise to a few Natives, so will the Union Parliament always be in a position to circumscribe the Native vote to within whatever standard of Natives it judges to be adequate for the sentimental purpose of maintaining white dominance in Parliament. Furthermore, when the Native voters of five centuries hereafter are numerous enough to swamp the whites they will *ipso facto* be civilized enough to run the country on civilized lines and with the intelligence and dignity associated with civilized races elsewhere in the world.

Thirdly, it is argued that political equality will lead to social equality, a position repugnant to Europeans.

In answer, we say political equality is by no means synonymous with social intermixture and miscegenation any more than the present Native voters seek intermarriage with European women. We desire political equality not for social intercourse but in order to rise in our economic and political circumstances. We cannot thrive economically until we have our due share to the land rightly adjusted. And we cannot obtain our land rights until we get a direct voice in Parliament, that is, political equality. We are already inextricably bound up with Europeans in our territorial occupation of the land, but minus the means wherewith to protect our interests in the land we jointly occupy. Without political equality there is no hope of our attaining justice in our territorial problems; and it is obvious that territorial segregation will for ever be a physical impossibility in South Africa. Christianity alone has failed to secure justice for the Natives. The Natives will get justice only when they get political equality. It follows then that political equality is the only practical policy which Christianity should adopt for the Bantu

of South Africa. This has nothing to do with social intercourse.

Fourthly, it is averred that the vote is in essence contrary to the African tradition of tribal rule by chiefs.

Against this we submit that African tribal rule has undergone such disintegration that it can never be re-established among detribalised Natives. Our tribal system is being gradually dislodged by the European democratic system and will ultimately be eliminated according as education spreads. It is useless to urge tribal communism as our ultimate goal in face of the Union Act based on British individualism, which is the enemy of communism. Even a racial or differential *imperium in imperio* will be ineffectual in this country.

Fifthly, it has been said that the Cape Native vote is obnoxious because it places the Cape Native on a higher footing than the Northern Native.

Against this we would point out that the reason why the Cape Native stands politically on a higher footing than his Northern compatriot is that the Cape tradition was historically based upon impartial justice. Christian morality, so far as we understand it, requires that the happy man shall not be penalised by degradation in order to establish a uniform injustice. Rather, the unhappy Native helot of the Orange Free State should be sympathetically raised to the rightful citizenship enjoyed by his more fortunate Cape brother.

Sixthly, political advantage granted to the Native will recoil detrimentally to European interests.

This is a favourite Northern argument based on the theory that the Natives are children and should therefore be treated as political minors. Plausible as this theory sounds, it will be found on closer examination to be faulty because the Native people in the Union are not all children or barbarians. Some have achieved considerable progress and we cannot afford to despise or defy their vanguard of worthy leaders who are already fit to exercise the franchise by their unobtrusive qualification of good character, education and substance. Another mistake lies in the assumption that they will perpetually remain children and never grow out of childhood. A wise policy is that which makes due provision for such members of the population as grow out of the condition of childhood, as was done at the Cape. Under such a policy the Bantu leaders develop confidence in, and loyalty and love for their government system, leading the masses behind them to a similar appreciation of authority, thus eliminating any possible detriment to the interest of the rulers.

Seventhly, it is affirmed that the political interests of the Europeans are distinct from those of the Natives.

Our reply is that all political affairs are, in the last analysis, governed by economic interests. Now in the Union it is admitted on all sides that white and black are economically interdependent. In Native affairs the land question is supreme because the land is the indispensable asset that governs the economic status of the Native. All Native prosperity automatically increases European prosperity. Every Native wealthy enough to contribute a substantial income tax is by that much a more valuable citizen to the white government than his impecunious brother who pays only the poll tax, and accordingly deserves a voice in the counsels of the State in which he has so much property at stake. The identity of white and black political and economic interests should be accepted as an indisputable axiom in this country. The only alternative left for those who deny this identity of interest is the impossible task of effecting absolute territorial segregation, placing the blacks on some virgin land where they shall conduct their own separate administration directly under the Imperial Government.

Lastly, it has been recently stated that "As the voting power of the Native increases, so the feeling of bitterness against him will take possession of the white man. It will then doubtless come to pass that the basis of popular government, that is, honest difference of opinion on great questions, will give place to a division on colour and race lines to the neglect of everything else."

This is perhaps the strongest of all the arguments ever advanced against the Native franchise; and it is of paramount importance that the whole of the intelligent public opinion of South Africa be familiarized with the truth that will explode the fallacies that

underlie this and the other seven propositions just discussed.

This particular argument presupposes two things to which we cannot subscribe, namely, (a) that the white man holds an incorrigible hatred against the black man; and (b) that white and black in South Africa are irreconcilable enemies.

So far as the Cape Province is concerned we venture to state that the voting power of the black man has never produced bitterness against him. Division on racial lines has from the very beginning been conspicuous by its absence. The Natives have always divided along ordinary Parliamentary lines. We remember in the days of the old Afrikander Bond that Onze Jan Hofmeyr was in league with John Tengo Jabavu with a big following of Native voters; whilst the Progressives had Dr. Jameson with the Rev. Walter Benson Rubusana and an equally large share of the Native voters behind them. These were divisions on lines of honest differences of opinion persisting down to the year 1909 with the South African Party and the Unionists each claiming a substantial following of Native voters. There was not even the mention of racialism. These are the historical facts. This situation was due to the kind of spirit that ruled in the Cape. Probably it is an approximation of a Christian spirit of nonracialism. If others are incapable of rising to it, then there appears no good reason for them to blame the Cape Europeans for being good Christians. The pessimistic expectation of a division on race lines is destitute of historical foundation, and either betrays a lack of faith in Christianity, or amounts to a confession that Christianity as we know it in South Africa is bankrupt.

It is desirable that the view of the black possessor towards his franchise should be known.

He regards his vote as a treasured gift of justice inherited from Queen Victoria, the Good. This Queen attracted the Basuto, the Bechuana and the Pondo chiefs voluntarily to surrender their unconquered lands under British tutelage. This franchise is ethically moral because it places a premium on merit rather than colour. It is Christian, indicating the white man's humanitarian duty towards the black. It is economically sound, for it confers equality of opportunity on all to rise freely in the scale of civilization. It fulfills the challenge of the New Testament towards peace as against hate. It has bestowed the highest mundane privilege of man, citizenship, as opposed to serfdom. The Cape Natives being full-fledged citizens have been immune from the rigours of the Pass Laws which are the curse of their voteless comrades in the Transvaal. Likewise have they been saved by the grace of the franchise from the operation of the 1913 Lands Act with its painful evictions. They have good reason for being vigilant against any impending dispossession of this citizenship lest such a misfortune be followed by an era of mutual hatred that can only end in the dim and dismal future with a sanguinary conflict. This franchise is thus nothing less than the noblest monument of the white man's rule, emblematic of his genuineness in practising the precepts of Holy Scripture towards the subject races.

The obvious Christian policy is that which will in our day truly lay the foundations for a glorious future of co-operation and good understanding. There seems to be no likelihood of keeping the black man down or back from his march towards ultimate liberty in education, economic life and political privilege any more than it was possible for King Canute to block the ocean tide by an act of volition.

Oppression and restriction will perhaps serve as useful expedients for a time, but the unerring course of evolution and the ultimate destiny of Christianity will inevitably predominate.

All the Native people of the Union pray that the white citizens of South Africa will respond to the call of Christian duty at this momentous hour when we are at the crossroads of Native policy, exhorting public opinion to abandon the fatal path of mere expediency and injustice, guiding all to the safe haven of self-denial, peace and goodwill towards men.

. . . .

With reference to the question of the Native franchise, the first point I wish to bring to the attention of the Committee is that we, as natives, throughout the country would like to be of help to the Government in regard to the formation of a native policy. We would like to take part as far as we can do, but in such way that we shall win the confidence of our people for the decisions made by Parliament. Therefore our remarks will be made with the view of helping the Government and not destroying the efforts of the Government. In that connection we are appreciative of the efforts made by the Government to focus the attention of the country on these things in a way it has never been done before. We feel perhaps that the Committee has many views and interests to consider which are in conflict, and we shall endeavour to look at both sides and suggest what we think will be for the benefit of the country as a whole. The first point is this. We feel that these Bills represent such different interests that they may bring about unnecessary friction between black and white if taken as one indivisible block. If they can each be dealt with on their merits it will be more useful to the Committee and to the Government. We see no reason why one or two of them should not be proceeded with straight away, while the others need longer time and deliberation. Also, we feel that while we may like to approve of some things in one Bill and of others in another Bill, we are uncompromisingly against some things in another. One of the Bills we are solidly against; but we would not like it to be in the way of other Bills; therefore we feel that if the clause which binds them together be eliminated it will be of help to us and to the Committee.

With reference to the Cape Native Franchise, the feeling is that it represents a definite tradition in this country — the tradition which impressed us and our fathers as one of absolute justice in this country, namely, the Cape policy under which we were born. We regard that as the true solution which will satisfy all concerned on the native side and make for good feeling in the future. We consider not merely present convenience. It may be very convenient for present purposes to make changes but at the same time they may prove to be the undoing of goodwill in this country in the future. We feel that the Cape policy is necessary for goodwill. It gave absolute freedom to the black man to rise to his highest scale not only in education but even in political influence. Judging by results this policy has produced goodwill, and the native vote has been handled in such a way, so far as I know, that there has never been a single mistake in using it. They have used it for the benefit of the country. To take it away now will create bad blood and ill-will in the country. I and many of us have endeavoured to examine the objections which have been raised against this Cape Native franchise, and every one of them, both those mentioned in this House of Assembly, as well as others, can be answered. I will be prepared to answer questions there-anent and satisfy members that the objections can be proved to be chimerical. There need be no fear. The most potent objection is that if the franchise were extended to the rest of the country it will bring civilization down to ruins; because it will be giving strength to the backward part of the country which would do harm to those who are civilized. Far from that being the case, it will have the opposite result. Every black man who is a voter has *ipso facto* abandoned the position of barbarism. We are ranged on the side of civilization. Our interests are intertwined with civilized interests. We would not like to go back naked to the kraals and live a barbarous life. We have renounced that life once and for all. In fact if to-day there were a war between barbarism and civilization, we would be on the side of civilization. The Europeans regard us as a solid block of undifferentiated barbarism, and the Europeans as a solid block of innate capacity to govern; whereas the division is not on these lines. The division is between civilization and ignorance, which may be found in both blocks. There are many Europeans not capable of governing just as there may be a few black men who are so far removed from their conditions that they would not make a mess of civilized interests. The fact is that we are growing and developing under civilization and we shall be more and more a power on the side of civilization. The franchise is what may be familiarly called a safety valve for these natives who have developed and grown out of barbarism. It is an encouragement to feel that there is an opening at the top where they will have the opportunity to exercise their powers which they have learned to appreciate, and

the present Bill impresses one as a Bill calculated to block the progress of those who like to advance and to dam them back to the slough of ignorance. We feel so strongly in the matter that we are prepared to forego any advantage which is offered in the Bill to our northern compeers if it means touching or whittling down the Cape Native franchise as it stands to-day. The northern natives also feel that we are jointly so well protected by the Cape franchise that if there is any offer made to them but which involves the whittling down of the Cape franchise they are prepared rather to remain as they are and trust to the working of providence to change public opinion, perhaps gradually and slowly, but at any rate finally, that the Europeans may grow to realize in the future that the only sound policy for this country to adopt is to open the gates of freedom for self development rather than to make temporary measures of a repressive character or which will cause ill will amongst those debarred from advancing. That is the view of the associations I represent. I trust the Committee will understand our position, that we are giving what we really believe will be the salvation of this country. We think this policy has justified itself in the past and will continue to justify itself in the future and make for a better country and greater happiness amongst us than if we embark upon the changes proposed in this Bill.

. . . .

(*Dr. Rubusana.*) I want to emphasise what has been placed before this Committee by Professor Jabavu on the question of the franchise. I wish to say at the very outset I have never yet heard anybody in this country or in the House say that the franchise has been abused by the natives who have exercised it for the last 50 years. I think they elected very able members to the Cape Parliament. Secondly, if the policy of the Government is to equalise things and to give the natives in the north also a franchise, then I say why take away the present franchise from the Cape native. It seems to be a policy of robbing Paul to pay Peter. Apart from that I wish to say this, that if it is held by the members of the Committee that the Cape native is not benefited economically by use of the vote then it stands to reason that our white brethren who have not been benefited economically by the exercise of the franchise should also be deprived of the franchise. We know it for a fact in this country that there are Europeans as well as natives — if that is the argument used to deprive the natives of the franchise, that economically he has not been of help — to whom the same argument may be applied. But that would not need argument. I do not think that the economic conditions have anything to do with the exercise of the franchise. Apart from that, there has been in the Cape franchise the safeguard of the educational test. If I am not mistaken, in the other provinces there are no such safeguards. I believe in the Transvaal and the Free State you have manhood suffrage. Thus when a man becomes 21 years of age he becomes a voter. In the Cape it is not so. There the uneducated and unqualified man cannot exercise the vote. There is that educational test which the late Jan Hofmeyr introduced. That was a very wise provision because it prevented any idea of the native swamping the European vote in the Cape Province. All these years there has been no fear of the European vote being swamped by the native vote. There is therefore no reason for taking away the Cape vote. I have seen no cause why it should be taken away. Speaking generally, I fear on account of the passage of these Native Bills the natives in the country will be in a state of ferment in anticipation of the Bills becoming law. I happen to have had the privilege of knowing every native chief this side of the Kei as well as in the Transkei, and these native Bills are being keenly watched by these native chiefs because they are afraid that there is really something behind the Bills, and that the policy of the Government is to take away every right the native has in the country. I have no doubt in my mind, with the experience I have in the country, that the passage of these Bills into law will create hatred between the black and white people in this country. That is very undesirable. It will also shake the loyalty and confidence of the native in the justice and honesty of the white man in this country when he comes to deal with the native or man of another colour. Therefore I do sincerely hope that this Com-mittee and Parliament in their wisdom will drop these Bills so that we may have peace in the country. It has never been questioned that the natives are loyal. Drop all four bills for the time being so that things may be coolly considered later on and you will create peace in the country. We cannot afford just now to do anything which is likely to shake the confidence and loyalty of the natives in the Transkei and on this side of the Kei. I would therefore on behalf of the people I represent beg you and Parliament to drop these Bills.

(*Rev. Mtimkulu.*) I support what Mr. Jabavu has said and also wish to make a few observations with regard to the Land Bill. It is a well-known fact that the crux of the native question is the land question. In that Bill in sub-sections (1) and (2) on page 1 provision is made for released areas. It takes away the reserved areas and converts them straight away into released areas, and as such it allows competition between Europeans and natives. It ignores the fact that the native is at the present moment living under every difficulty. He has got to contend with the civilized labour policy and with the colour bar, and therefore his earning capacity is very much reduced. He cannot earn as much money as the European and cannot compete with him. Therefore it is considered very unfair that with the disabilities of the policy of the colour bar and civilized labour, the black man should be handicapped by being put on the same footing with the European in the matter of acquiring land because he cannot compete with him. I wish to make some observations also in regard to the detribalised natives. It is a well-known fact that hundreds and thousands of young men at the present time live in the towns, even men of 20, 30 or 40 years, and no provision is made for these men in the Bill. The standard of living of these men is as good as that of the coloured man or some of the poor Europeans. The Bill does not take account in this case of his nationality.

With regard to the licence for native labour tenants and squatters. These provisions create a difficulty straight away and will induce the young natives to go to the towns. As soon as a young man reaches 18 the licence has got to be found for him, and if he does not want to work on that farm he has to be sent away. He cannot live on the farm. That is going to add to the influx of natives into the towns and to the question of unemployment in the towns. It also breaks down the native custom of parental control, and is therefore regarded by the native people as one of those things that ought to receive the best consideration. We feel that to send a young man of 18 into the towns lays him open to all sorts of temptation; some are unable to think for themselves and are carried away, and by that action we will be increasing the criminal class among the natives. I may also point out in regard to these licences that it is not stated how much a man is going to be paid. It may be on the farms as is being done to-day the young men will only get 10s., 15s. or £1 per month as the case may be. Out of that the licence will have to be paid and that means that he will be bound to his baas for a number of years because the baas will get the licence for him and charge him. So he will continually be bound and this is again a policy of compelling the natives to work. If some arrangement can be made that these licences be free it will be of some advantage to the natives.

Coming to the question of land, the ratio at present is 105 morgen to every European and 3 morgen to every native. As you know, the native people generally have the hills and stony places. If the land question is going to be tackled at all it must be in such a way as to give a fairer proportion to the natives, and the native will develop himself and be a useful member of the community.

(*Professor Jabavu.*) The Cape native is very much opposed to the franchise being taken away from him. You say what the Bill provides for is merely an alteration of the franchise, but the changes which are suggested in the Bill amount to such a re-organisation of the vote that it takes away what we prize in the present state of the franchise. The individual vote is being abolished and substituted by group voting. I would not like to be responsible for supporting the suggestion that the native voters at present on the roll should remain there, and that no more be added, nor that the natives should vote separately for representation in Parliament. I stand for the *status quo*. If I were to suggest anything it

would simply be the same franchise for the other provinces, although it may be a dream that will never be realised. You ask whether it will not be for the general good of the native in South Africa if we in the Cape curtailed our rights in order to give the northern natives some share in the Parliamentary business of the country. Whatever that may be in theory we have found in practice that we lose too much when once the position is put into the melting pot. We have lost so many privileges since we came into Union through the invasion of the northern policy that to-day we feel our safety lies in the *status quo* and nothing else. I quite follow that the purpose of the Bill is to give the northern natives a vote to a certain extent, but I have the word of the northern natives themselves that they so value the privilege that we have here that they would not recognize this concession as a gift to them if it involved the whittling down of the present franchise. The Transvaal and Natal natives feel exactly as we do in regard to this question. They say if European feeling is not liberal enough to let those of the Cape keep what they have, and not to take away the rights of others, they will be better off as they are. I think the vote which I have here is helping to uplift the natives in the north. When I elect a good member for Parliament he does not say, "I am standing only for the Cape native," but he will speak for the good of all the natives and will benefit us all round. That is why we feel this offer will be no gain to us if it means the whittling down of the present system. You ask whether I have ever tried to place myself in the position of the white man and view these Bills from his standpoint. Yes, I have done that, and I feel if I were a white man I would take the view which the liberal minority of white men in the country take, and would be more generous than the average white man is to-day.

(*Mr. Pelem.*) Our Union is in favour of separate representation for natives. Where the interests of the European and the native clash, where does the native come in? He has no one to look after his interest then. If the native cannot get direct representation, which is most unlikely, then I think that the Europeans who represent him ought to be elected by the native vote solely, so that the Europeans will have no claim on that man at all. It is impossible for a man to serve two masters. A member not elected solely by the native vote cannot serve the native as well as he can his own people. That is how I look at it. I say that if I am honest and faithful and true to my people and their interests I will have to look after them, and I say the same of the European. If the native has no direct representation he must have separate representation, as he is at present he is really unrepresented in the Union Parliament. (*Dr. Rubusana.*) I may say I am a member of the Bantu Union and I do not share the view of Mr. Pelem. He is giving his personal opinion; we are not united on that question. (*Mr. Pelem.*) I have read a resolution which bears out the views I have expressed which was carried by a majority at our meeting. (*Dr. Rubusana.*) I dispute the majority unless it is tested. That resolution was taken at a congress but the men there were not all members of the Bantu Union.

(*Mr. Pelem.*) I cannot say they were all members, but a large number represented the Bantu Union.

Coming to the *Union Native Council Bill*, it is the opinion of our committee that the chairman has too much power in his hands. We do not want the members to retire by rotation but to stay on for the full three years. We want a voters' roll on which the members for the Native Council will be elected. Our view is that we like this Bill to stand in abeyance for the present and first of all let the Bunga system be extended to the provinces before we have this Council. That is my own opinion and the view of the committee. I have not considered the question whether the member for the Union Council should be elected by the Bunga or by the natives individually. (*Dr. Rubusana.*) The representation of natives through their chiefs and headmen is most unsatisfactory. They are ratepayers and hut tax payers, why not give them the vote? Why should one man who is the headman, and who may be a nominee of the Government, have to vote for the whole location? It would be more satisfactory if the people were called together by a Government official and their vote taken by him.

Africans and Whites in Dialogue

DOCUMENTS 41a-41d. Views of Africans

DOCUMENT 41a. "The Race Problem." Article in *The Guardian* by R.V. Selope Thema, September 1922

In discussing South Africa's race problem, which to my mind has been wrongly termed the "Native or Black Problem," it is extremely difficult for those who are themselves actors in the drama to avoid the attitude of partisans and advocates. And yet I take it that the examination of this (to use General Smuts' words) "the gravest of our problems" is not in the nature of debate, but rather an earnest endeavour to seek the truth beneath a mass of assertion and opinion, of passion and distress. Consequently I trust that whatever difference may exist between the views of the European and the African, it will be rather in the nature of additional information than of contradiction. It cannot be denied that Europeans have so far failed to find the solution of this burning question through lack of information from this side of the colour line. But happily right-thinking men of both races have come to the realisation of the fact that the problem cannot be solved until both races have learned to cooperate in finding its solution. In consequence societies are being organised and formed in large centres, so as to enable the advanced members of both races to exchange views in the mutual discussion of the various phases of this complex problem.

In the past the two races tried to solve the problem by means of WAR, MURDER, SLAVERY and extermination, but these proved a complete failure, simply because the Bantu could not be exterminated and enslaved, and likewise the European could not be destroyed or be driven out of the country. Since then the two races have lived side by side for nearly three hundred years. And the days of the cannon and the assegai are gone, and I hope to return no more. But the race problem is still with us, and, with the advance of the Africans and the increase of European population, it has grown in magnitude and gravity, and has become more baffling than ever. Indeed, it seems to me that the advancement of the African makes it more complex. It is well known that the European has really no objection against Africans so long as they remain a race of servants. What he dislikes is to see them becoming as free and as independent in means as himself. His spirit of domination makes it impossible for him to realise that other members of the human race are as entitled to freedom and to the enjoyment of the blessings of creation as himself. He wants to dominate and to be master of the destinies of other races. In consequence he cannot view the race problem, be it in India or Africa, from the standpoint of humanity, but from that of materialism. That is the reason why he has failed to find the solution of the problem. And as long as he continues to look at it from the point of view of POUNDS, SHILLINGS AND PENCE, there can be no hope of its solution. This is a human problem, which can only be solved by approaching it in the spirit of humanity. The right to live of every race of mankind is indisputable. This being so, each race of mankind has the right to work out its own destiny and live its own life without let or hindrance. This right can only be limited by the equal right of others. It is, therefore, necessary that before the European proceeds to solve the race problem in this country, he must first recognise that the African has the right to live and has a place in God's scheme of creation, that he was not created in the image of God to occupy a position of servitude in the affairs of mankind, but "to make his distinct contributions to the gathering achievement of the race."

But the average white man is not yet ready to take such a broad view of the race problem. Although the policy of repression has not only failed, but proved detrimental to the best interests of this country, he still believes that if "the Kaffir was kept in his proper place" everything would be all right. There are others again, and these are found among the advanced class of Europeans, who maintain that the solution of the problem would be found in segregation. They say: "Segregate the native so as to enable him to develop according to his own lines." But this policy cannot be successfully carried out today when

the interests of both races are so interwoven, when there is no land in South Africa which is not occupied by Europeans, and when the industries of the country cannot be developed without native labour. This policy was possible perhaps when the two races first met at the Great Fish River, but today it is impossible, unless it is ready to recognise THE PRINCIPLE OF SELF DETERMINATION. But this principle means the division of the country into two parts to be controlled respectively by Europeans and Africans. That is to say, each race will have its own sovereign rights to manage its affairs in its portion of the country without interference from the other. That this is the segregation scheme which the segregationists do not advocate was shown by the way in which the land was demarcated by the Land Commission of 1913. The segregation they want is one which will make South Africa "a white man's land." Under the scheme Africans will be relegated to the barren and malarial parts of the country, to be crowded there like a flock of sheep, and only be allowed to come now and again into European areas to administer to the economic needs of the whites. The white man and his Parliament will have the sovereign right to rule over them without their consent and knowledge. To my mind, between this policy and that of repression there is no difference. If there is to be a segregation of the races let it be logical and fair in its application. It must not aim at keeping one race under the permanent control of the other. For I do not see how the Africans can develop along their own lines when they are kept under European hegemony. To develop along their own lines and evolve their own civilisation, they must not only have a place in the sun, but must have freedom of thought and action.

When I denounce this policy, I do not suggest for a moment that there should be INTERMIXTURE OF THE RACES in any shape or form. I should be the last to advocate inter-marriages between the races. I love my race and its colour, and I am just as proud of it as the European is of his. And when I say the African is determined to keep the purity of his race, if only he could secure the assistance of the State to protect his womenfolk against the low-class white men, I am voicing the feeling of every sensible and intelligent African. While we do not wish to encroach upon the society of the whites, nevertheless we claim our rights of citizenship first as the aboriginals of this country, and second as British subjects; we claim equal opportunities and facilities for improvement; we claim a voice in the government of our country and in the administration of moneys which we pay to the Treasury of the State; we claim the equal protection of the law with the other citizens of the State--in short we claim equal political rights with our fellow-subjects. Under democratic institutions it is only the interests of those who have the power of the ballot that are considered and safeguarded. And in my opinion no justice can be done to the African until he has been equipped with this power. Today he is being rendered LANDLESS AND HOMELESS, taxed heavily and cruelly exploited, because he has no voice in the making of laws. Daily he is coming more and more to look upon the laws of the country not as protecting safeguards, but as sources of humiliation and oppression. The laws are made by men who as yet have little interest in him; they are executed and administered by men who have absolutely no desire to treat the black people with courtesy and consideration. Such is the position of the African under the "democratic" Government of the Union of South Africa. And I ask if the continuance of this state of affairs is in the best interests of the Country? There can be no doubt that the perpetuation of this system will only serve to aggravate the race bitterness and prejudice which now exist.

What is wanted is a policy which will promote MUTUAL UNDERSTANDING and cooperation between the races. The policy of "White South Africa" has naturally given rise on this side of the colour line to a cry of "Africa for the Africans." And as the result the two races are drifting apart. Unless a change is made now the coming generation will be separated by active hatred and hostility. Perhaps the European, relying on the superiority which his scientific knowledge has given him, and on his ability to kill eight millions of human beings in four years, feels his position secure and tenable, and therefore

does not care; but we read in history of civilisations and empires that were destroyed by the very glory of their magnificence. Where are the civilisations and greatness of Egypt, of Babylonia, Rome and Greece today? They are no more. We only read of their magnificence in history. God is not a mockery: His eternal law is not a lie.

"Lo, all the pomp of yesterday
Is one with Ninevah and Tyre."

DOCUMENT 41b. "Christianity, Basis of Native Policy?" Article in *The Workers' Herald* by James S. Thaele, December 21, 1923

Ambitious men and women of the Race, in the third instalment of this "bluff" (the Johannesburg-Pretoria Conference), I shall deal with that part of it which purports and is deliberately intended to abuse further the religion of Christ under the pretext that it is to be made the basis of native policy.

In my last article I threw down the gauntlet against our contemporary, the Bantu-Batho, for having taken a too optimistic view, as its editorial lead, *inter alia*, had gone so far as to say "the door which had been banged, bolted and barred since the days of Van Riebeek,"—a meaningless historical blunder, often committed by school boys in matriculation when given an "essay on flies," to improve upon their English, for I am sure any student of socio-political evolution knows that as late as Moshweshue's time, those were the treaty-making days—days indeed when the vivacity, vigour and man-power of the Zulu army had reached its zenith; hence any attempt on the part of one Van Riebeek and his congeners would have been all "tommy rot". It is therefore equally important, if not more, that in this issue of this widely read periodical, that I trace some discrepancies from their origin, especially as they touch upon Christianity, a doctrine good in all its essentials, yet the direct course and immediate one, when it comes down to accounting for the seemingly religious apostasy among the aboriginal races of the Dark Continent, their loss of confidence in the white man (thank God), their ready acceptance of Pan Islamic religion; and I may point out as far as it lies in me, the individuals who have condescended to stoop so low as to be used as mere tools by the other fellow in order to exploit the African Race.

Taking them in their order of magnitude, "the good boys" who subscribed to the whiteman's usual hypocrisy that "Christianity be made the basis of Native policy" are none other than men of our own race, men, indeed, above the mediocre, luminaries of the indigent African race—graduates somebody, whose knowledge, if not acquaintance, with the academic world would in the least, if you please, allow perspective. But behold the contradiction in terms!

Let me state my syllogism as the basis for our deductive reasoning so as to be within bounds. The Dutch Reformed Church and Union Government is one and the same ring. It is solidly and compactly a church and a government of, by, and for the Boers, dominated diagonally and diametrically by "boorish" principles and ideals.

It is this church which, in the Grondwet of the Republics of Transvaal and Free State not long ago, stated that there was to be no equality in church or state between the Blacks and whites. And recently, if you choose, the Dutch Reformed Church of the Cape has introduced segregation into church matters. This then, is the body that has taken the initiative in this hypocrisy. It is not a bit to be wondered at that it is supported and is working in conjunction with the then government—the capitalistic machine whose capitalistic bugaboo and inconsistencies and wanton systematic butchery of helpless women and children by machine guns have baffled the human understanding! "Thy vengeance, oh God, is too slow!" We are fed-up with the white man's camouflage, his hypocrisy, his policy of pinpricks in "the land of our forefathers." I am appealing to the racial consciousness of the radical aboriginal to use all the means to rouse the African race to wake from their long sleep of many decades. The voice of posterity is calling upon us men to play our part, and play it nobly. Law and authority must be respected, even as we did before the aliens came here; but when those in authority become so unreasonably notorious at your expense, disregard that authority, be blind and "damn the consequences."

It is a fact that our present Prime Minister, now at the head of the Union Government, made a speech devoid of all common sense and unbecoming of any Christian, at the Savoy Hotel, when he said that "the early Christians made a mistake in putting into practice the principles of brotherhood."

In the light of these foregoing statements, how in the name of God and all that is holy can "Christianity be made the basis of Native policy" by the South African white man who has countenanced it already as "impracticable for statesmanship," a "counsel of perfection?" What is the good of any hypocrite or a group of hypocrites telling us to "do as I tell you but don't do as I do." The peace-making psychology of the white man is rapidly becoming a farce, particularly here in the Union of South Africa. Is it a wonder that the League of Nations should condemn the policy of the Union Government as being one-sided and operating in the interests of the whites only?

Our white brothers have got to translate their actions into realms of practicalities and learn to practice what they preach. Hitherto, their evils have hit the thermometer of our auditory nerves many degrees beyond their normal registry that it is almost a physical impossibility to hear what they say. It is indeed amazing to see that delegates accept in good faith and with genuine integrity a quasi hypocritical policy that emanates from such a source as the Dutch Reformed Church—a source that has made itself notorious without that source, making a public confession of its notoriety.

Equally amazing and puzzling is the fact that our delegates accept in bona fide the mixing up of Christianity with politics without General Smuts retracting his infamous speech on the eve of his banquet at the Savoy Hotel in England. Can you beat it?

Poor Blacks accept this, of course, apologetically. One of the delegates is reported to have said he never "mixed up politics with religion." He has got to be told that politics rule the world, not religion, don't fool yourself. That is why the wily Union Government has it down that civil servants must not engage in politics.

The Blacks have got to be told by students

of theological thought that in the cosmogonies of Moses, or of Biblical history, we find the Prophet Isaiah breathing politics. The fundamental maxims of his statesmanship come first into the limelight in the crisis of the Syro-Epraimitic invasion; in that memorable interview with Ahaz (recorded, Isaiah, chapter 7) is nothing but politics sane and sound.

Space will not allow me to enter into Biblical exegisis of this matter as I would like to do. It is a disgraceful public confession of the worst kind I have ever heard or read of. Politics is the science and art of government, the study of the state, its life and its conduct. Whether looked on as a field of study or as a field of practical endeavour, politics is a noble sphere of manly thought, energy and enterprise.

Education in politics is not chiefly a question of knowledge; it is a question of character.

Sidney Smith has well said "the only foundation of political liberty is the spirit of the people."

President Hadley one day said: "Better the worst form of government with character and righteousness in the rulers and the ruled, than the best form of government with rulers and ruled indifferent to moral principles."

Because of the close and vital relation of politics to ethics, one would naturally see the feasibility of Mr. De Tocqueville's saying that "politics is the end and aim of American education." What America, "home of the brave and land of the free," wishes to put into the life of the nation she must first put into her schools.

The idea of some wily autocratic government prohibiting the civil servants from engaging in politics, think of it!

Do you blame student-graduates from such centres for being so narrow-minded on the present day issues that affect our life?

It is the law of economics as well as that of psychology that "the beneficiary of a system will not antagonise it," and "power over man's subsistence is power over his will."

The programme of the Industrial and Commercial Workers Union of the African race is well defined, this the radicals must realise through and through. In it we have a weapon that can paralyse "the whole industry," as the able champion, Dr. Abdurahman, has put it, "within twenty-four hours."

The calling of this Johannesburg-Pretoria Conference is prompted, not by Christian attitude on the part of the white men; it is because of the awakened attitude on our part, as the African Race, from our long sleep of decades. We, of the Industrial and Commercial Workers Union would recommend the "radicals" of the race that roads must converge at East London for the annual Conference next month.

DOCUMENT 41c. "The Native Problem." Article in *The Cape Times* by the Rev. Abner Mtimkulu, May 30, 1924

Of all the agencies that may be employed for the solution of the native problem, without doubt the greatest of these is the knowledge of the problem and the people of whom the solution is sought to benefit and intended to apply to. It is the study of the relation of the white and black races with a view to forge a connecting link for mutual understanding.

This knowledge cannot be obtained from Government Blue Books, nor from Government official interviews, compressed and bound-up as they are with official red tape; but in meetings such as this, composed of men and women who have elected to stand for right and humanity—a meeting of the old and tried friends of the natives who, behind the scenes, have for some time past been working for the interest and welfare of the native people.

The Welfare Societies of to-day cannot be other than the continuation of the great work of those noble men and women who singly held the fort for humanity and right until the formation of the Welfare Societies of to-day. The Welfare Societies and the joint council have supplied a long-felt need, and should bridge the gulf between Europeans and natives; should educate public opinion of their wants and needs, and create confidence by assisting them as they did during the discussion in Parliament of the Urban Areas Act, the

Langa Township, and the Bondelzwarts affair.

It must not be forgotten that it is only about two centuries ago since the advent of the European into this country, with a system of Government and codes of law entirely different from those of the native. The native Courts were Courts of Justice, while the European's was a Court of Law.

All New to Him.

The democratic form of Government is new to him; the continual chopping, changing, and amending of laws, and the continual change of those in authority is unknown to him. He needs guidance, he requires help. In his state of transition, awakening up from his sleep of centuries, he finds a new order of things, he finds a changed world, his pastimes are considered illegal; he must buy land, or compulsorily go to service, his wants have been increased, he must pay taxes, and his movements regulated; in his effort to make up for the lost time he becomes restless, and he is immediately diagnosed as a sure case for military operations; guns and bayonets are brought to play, and much suffering is caused, even to women and children.

We are inclined to believe that if all our leading and thoughtful Britishers were to join the Welfare Societies the tragedies of Bullhoek and that of the Bondelzwarts would never again occur, for then the public would have been educated in the psychology of the native mind. On the other hand, the native would have had the chance to ventilate his grievances, whether real or imaginary, to some one or some society, whose influence and sympathy would in some way deaden the force of impact. For that reason the Welfare Societies and joint councils have the support of the leading native opinion in the Union.

Sunshine of Progress.

The incoming of the European brought education and civilisation, with its dazzling beauty and freedom, and the native began to warm himself in the sunshine of light and progress, and to drink from the universal well of knowledge. He begins to ask questions, and to reason out things. He desires as others do,

but civilisation being "the survival of the fittest," he goes to the wall because he is unprepared. In his haste to proceed he has not observed the dangerous pitfalls that are responsible for many a death.

We look up to the Welfare Societies to set up warning lights along the danger zone of drink and its concomitant evil. We have not yet understood the logic of convicting a man for drinking poison, and the supplier to be regarded as innocent, and yet daily such conviction takes place in the Magistrates' Courts. The Welfare Societies should help to get both the supplier and the supplied under the arm of the law.

The Urban Native.

The new order of things brought with it the new problem in the native question—the urban native, one whose grandfather before him broke off all ties with the tribal system. He is as ignorant of heathen life as any of the nationalities that come from abroad. He finds that he must work, but the colour of his face is against him. His cost of living is practically as high as that of anybody, because the landlord, the grocer, and the butcher have no margin for blacks in their books, and charge the same. He finds that rings, unions, and federations have built barriers which he cannot enter. In the commercial world distribution and exchange are disheartening and perplexing. He turns to the street in disgust, and the next that we hear of him is in the Police Court charged with housebreaking, theft, or shebeening. The Welfare Society should interest themselves in these cases by striking out a way for getting employment for natives, without having to go the length of inducing them to sign a contract, which suggests to them slavery. In the democratic form of Government, such as we enjoy, the native needs all the help and protection that may be given him. In fact, the native question should be raised from the duststorms of party politics, and should be regarded as a sacred trust. When one realises how the parties are competing as to which can draw a most destructive policy for a people who are politically mute and dumb fear of the result of its operation, and austerity of the human heart asserts itself.

Policy of Despair.

The segregation policy is a policy of despair. It is a reply to the question "What shall we do with the natives?" It suggests extermination. It means giving the native the length of the rope; because in his backward state he will relapse to heathenism and will rebel. We shall then have an excuse for exterminating him. It is also a policy of regret. It would appear that the propounders of this policy regret to find the native improving himself and forging ahead. As a menace he may take away the bread intended for the European, and therefore it is suggested that the native be allowed to develop in his own line. Human nature being what it is he may then relapse to barbarism, thereby trampling down the work of the missionaries who have made him what he is.

It is likewise a policy of oppression. If the segregation policy had referred to Europeans it would not have been discussed and be made an election plank without first being brought before the electorate, and perhaps decided by a referendum. When this land was first granted for colonisation it was directed under "Letters Patent." That there shall not be in the eyes of the law any discrimination by reason of colour, races, or creed. I suppose that, to-day, is only a "scrap of paper" and beneath notice where natives are concerned. The British nation only a few years ago entered the World War to suppress the policy of oppression, the policy of Might is Right. Europeans could not be held back from coming South, although the Almighty had segregated them by some thousands of miles of water—and will a strand of water do it?

Although the segregation policy is about as old as the Union, we have not been told how it is proposed to make it operative. Where is the land to which the native may be sent? Will the farmer give up his farm? Will a native agree to go to the Sahara? Is this a suggestion for an "Imperium in imperio"? If so, who is responsible? We look up to the Welfare Society for guidance in these matters, and if all our Societies share in the social, religious, and political welfare of our people the future is assured, and there is a great hope for the native races of South Africa.

DOCUMENT 41d. "Bridging the Gap Between White and Black in South Africa." Address by Dr. A.B. Xuma at the Conference of European and Bantu Christian Student Associations at Fort Hare, June 27-July 3, 1930 [Extracts] (Printed, 20 pages)

On September 10th, 1840, at Bunkers Hill, Daniel Webster said:—

"When men pause from their ordinary occupations and assemble in great numbers, a proper respect for the judgment of the country and of the age requires that they should clearly set forth the *grave causes* which have brought them together, and the *purposes* which they seek to promote."

This evening, as I stand before you, I feel the force of this obligation. I shall in keeping with it endeavour, in my humble way, to place before you certain facts and suggestions which I believe are worthy of the study and consideration of all. I shall dictate to, and prescribe for, no man. The purpose of this paper is, not to convince or convert any one, but to stimulate in you a desire to seek the truth and facts and apply them. I shall state certain facts and interpret them according to what light I have as to their bearing upon the subject of our discussion. All are alike at liberty to reject or receive what opinions I shall express. I have neither desire nor design to offend the feelings of any, but I mean in perfect plainness to express my views.

I believe that a conference like this can be a success and justify its existence only if we can have the bare facts placed before us and bitter truths told us. We want facts, we want truth; we want a way out. Without the true facts, we have no way towards a just solution of our problem. Unless we know the truth, according to Paul the Apostle we are not free.

It must be clear to all that I have no pet prescriptions for the permanent cure of the ills of our race relations. I realise as well as any thinking person that there is no such a thing as "solving" the Native question once and for all even if it is on "Non-Party lines." It *does not stay fixed.* It is a *human problem* and like all other human problems, it is ever *changing.* We must recognise its changeability and legislate accordingly. Above all there can be no just solution of this question as long as the *chief factor* in the problem, the African with his interests and opinions, is excluded from the Councils of the State.

Throughout our country to-day, there seems to be a spirit of excitement, of fear, of unrest, and of uncertainty. Everywhere our European community seems to have a nightmare of the rising black masses encroaching upon their position of privilege, hence we have had the "Black Manifesto." The farmer presses upon the Government, to bind the Native down to the farms by restrictive legislation. The Mines are crying for more labour, more "Cheap Native labour." The Municipalities are clamouring for more powers to deal with the unemployed, "redundant" Native in the urban areas. The Government, without asking why is the African leaving the farms or where the "redundant" urban Native must be repatriated to, feverishly introduces more restrictive legislation to give effect to these cries. "Colour Bar" legislation appears on the Statute Book in one form or another at every session. The idea seems to be to legislate in haste and to think and discover the facts and mistakes at leisure.

In all this, the African, for whom the Government legislates, has no voice. His part is merely to obey the law without protest or expression of even his most legitimate grievance. If he expresses himself he is in danger of being charged for sedition either under Section 29 of the Native Administration Act 1925 or under the Riotous Assemblies Act 1930; because even his most legitimate claims may be in conflict with the interests of White voters of whom alone the lawmakers must think in connection with the next election.

The African is dissatisfied with his present lot, uncertain and anxious over his future. He is disgruntled, sullen and has largely lost confidence in the justice of the White. He is now becoming the *object* and *victim* of agitators—why? What is the reason for this? Is there any justification for this attitude on any or either side of the colour line?

As we intend to build bridges between White and Black, we can dismiss the case of the Coloured man by stating that the missionaries fought and secured some of the rights for the Hottentot until the Coloured man of to-day is, in *principle*, accepted as a White

man politically, industrially, economically, and educationally.

The Indian in South Africa does not fall within the purview of our discussion, because, according to the Rt. Hon. S. Sastri, the Indian cannot make common cause with the African without alienating the right of intervention on their behalf on the part of the Government of India.

While the missionaries were fighting for the rights of the Hottentots and later of the Coloured man, the colonists had more or less a free hand with the African—the Bantu. Our legacy is a different policy for each Province reflecting the attitude of the earlier colonists towards their Native population.

As a conference of Christian students in a Christian country, we should ask ourselves whether the practices of our country between White and Black are in keeping with our profession of the Christian faith? Would Christ, whose followers and messengers we profess to be, approve of our Native Policy in practice? Has the Black man a real grievance? Has the White man been just to the Black man? Why did Mr. Jansen, present Minister of Native Affairs, say, to a deputation that waited upon him, "I shall do all in my power to make life more bearable for the Native?" What have we come here for? In short, what is our part and share in this great task? How are we going to bridge the gap between White and Black?

The stormy voyage of Bartholomew Diaz and the fitting name of his discovery which he called "Cape of Storms," which was later changed to Cape of Good Hope, presaged the conflicts and interracial "storms" which were to be almost the rule rather than the exception in South Africa. The Good Hope, like a rainbow, recedes as we move toward it.

It was however the arrival of Jan Van Riebeck and his fleet on April 6th, 1652, which began the history of contact between Europeans and the then Natives—Hottentots and Bushmen. The introduction of slaves to supply the shortage of labour in 1658 complicated the problem of race relations. A new mentality was acquired by the free Burghers, and a new outlook and attitude toward manual labour and the Non-European developed in their minds.

It was not until 1686 that the Europeans came in contact with the Bantu when the crew of the wrecked "Stavenesse" tried to reach the Cape by land. A series of wars was to take place between the Europeans and Bantu beginning in 1779.

The British occupied the Cape Colony first in 1795 and again in 1806. The largest number of British Settlers arrived in 1820—5,000 strong.

By this time the pioneers or burghers had become accustomed to the institution of slavery. There was bound to be a conflict of attitude and outlook toward the people of colour between the pioneers, on the one hand, and the new settlers on the other.

The passing of Ordinance No. 50 in 1828 which gave legal and economic status to the people of colour was an unbearable boil on the neck of the free burghers. The boil burst when slaves were emancipated in 1833 and under the same ordinance acquired the status of free persons of colour. These two incidents combined had much to do with the initiation of the Great Dutch Trek of 1836. The Burghers marched northward giving the following reasons for their trek, according to Mrs. Anna Steenkamp, a daughter of Piet Retief.

First: "The continual depredations and robberies of the Kaffirs (with unfulfilled promises of compensation for stolen property).

Second: "The shameful and unjust proceedings with reference to the freedom of our slaves, and yet it is not so much their freedom that drove us to such lengths as their being placed on an equal footing with Christians, contrary to the laws of God and the natural distinctions of race and religion. So that, it was intolerable for any decent Christians to bow down beneath such a yoke, wherefore we rather withdrew in order thus to preserve our doctrine of purity."

This great people, determined to have their way and freedom, trekked Northward and in 1858 declared their articles of freedom in the Grondwet (Constitution of the Republics): "There shall be no equality between Black and White either in Church or in State."

Parallel to this, in the Cape Colony, the people of colour (Natives) were being granted the right of franchise with a property qualification—thus giving the non-European a political status.

Nominally the Native policy of Natal can be dismissed in a simple statement. "In the Letters Patent of 1848 by which Natal became a separate Colony, it was laid down that there shall be no interference with Native law and custom except in so far as these were repugnant to the principles of humanity, but Natal, though British in nationality, really developed the trekkers' attitude on the Native issue."

The tradition of segregation between Black and White more or less prevailed until the discovery of diamond and gold in 1867 and 1886. These discoveries were going to break down the barriers of segregation. Labour and cheap labour was necessary; and, consequently, Africans and Chinese were used.

The parallel but distinct policies on Native affairs continued to develop in each Province until after the Anglo-Boer war when one would think that the principle of the Grondwet would die a natural death. However, one finds, as the late Mr. Maurice Evans stated, that: "The Grondwet, which so clearly, concisely, and cynically laid down the relative positions of Black and White, disappeared as a defined policy at the close of the war in 1902, but the practice was not greatly changed."

As a matter of fact, a study of agreements and compromises on "Native Policy" affecting Africans, from the Treaty of Vereeniging through the Act of the Union of South Africa to the Miners' Phthisis Act Further Amendment Act passed on May 27th, 1930, by our last session of Parliament, shows that one may safely say that though the Republicans lost the war physically they won it morally, because much of our legislation on Native Affairs is a series of colour bars and an expression of the principle of the Grondwet.

The Union of the White races in South Africa through the South Africa Act, 1909, has meant disunion and loss of liberty to the Black—especially in the Cape Province where he had attained citizenship rights. From the Act of the Union on, the negative and restrictive legislation has left the African in an inferior position.

The South Africa Act yields to the Republican principle in that in the former Republics the African by provision of the constitution shall neither exercise the right of franchise nor sit as representative in the Union Parliament even for the Cape Province. A Colour Bar in the legislature! Besides, though the Cape franchise seemed entrenched under section 35 of the South Africa Act 1909, yet, any day, it may be abolished "if the bill be passed by both Houses of Parliament sitting together and at the third reading be agreed to by not less than two-thirds of the total number of members of both Houses." Thus we see that the very Act of the Constitution of our country was conceived and born in an atmosphere charged with Colour Bars and prejudice. All hope for liberty and justice for the African was dimmed. This was his first grievance which was to be followed one after another, by a series of further disabilities and colour bars, thus making the African a promising and well prepared hot-bed for the nurture of the seeds of agitation.

If we compare certain portions of the constitution of the Union of South Africa with that of the United States of America, we find that the Constitution of the latter country was based on a code of morals and ethics recognising liberties for all citizens of the country as expressed in the preamble, and the XIV and the XVth amendments.

The preamble recognises all the people in the United States, including the former slaves and their descendants, in the following words: —

"We, the people of the United States, in order to form a more perfect Union, establish justice, insure domestic tranquility, provide from the common defence, promote the general welfare, and secure the blessings of liberty to ourselves and our posterity, do ordain and establish this constitution for the United States."

Sections 1 of both 14th and 15th amendments respectively give full citizenship rights to all "persons" without regard to colour or any other distinction as follows: —

"All persons born or naturalised in the United States and subject to the jurisdiction thereof, are citizens of the United States and of the States wherein they reside. No State shall make or enforce any law which shall abridge the privileges or immunities of the citizens of the United States, nor shall any State deprive any person of life, liberty, or property without due process of law; nor deny to any person within its jurisdiction the *equal* protection of the laws."

". . . . The right of the citizens of the United States to vote shall not be denied or abridged by the United States or by any State on account of race or colour, or previous condition of servitude."

Thus we see that whatever may be the practice in certain sections of the United States, the principles of liberty and justice is the foundation stone in the law of the land. It gives hope and citizenship rights to all alike. Besides, in test cases of serious consequence the Supreme Court of the United States has, often, if not always, upheld the spirit and the letter of the Constitution.

Now coming back to South Africa, our land of colour bars and differential legislation and treatment, we find that following the South Africa Act 1909, the Land Act of 1913 is a constant, caustic irritant to the African. Through the provisions of this Act over 80 per cent of the land in the Union of South Africa went to the 1,500,000 Europeans and less than 20 per cent was left for the 5,000,000 Africans. The Beaumont Commission reported in 1917 that twice as much land was necessary for the immediate needs of the African community. It is now 13 years since this report but nothing has been done by the Government to relieve this tense situation. Through evictions of the Africans from European farms the Native reserves are crowded to overflowing. Many Natives have lost their stock; they are landless and poverty-stricken. Economic pressure is one of the many causes which drive the Natives into Urban areas.

Section 7 of the Native Administration Act of 1927 on "Land Registration and Tenure" makes land tenure for the individual African extremely insecure and yet, as Mr. A. G. Fraser has said, "Land is to the African (he might as well have said to every race of mankind) what the sea is to the fish; it is essential to his life. Without it he becomes detribalised. More harm has been done to African life and morals, except in West Africa, by European land hunger than by any drink trade."

If we look into the United States land policy, or practice, we again find no comparison but a striking contrast to South African land policy. Land in city or country can be bought by any citizen of the United States. For instance, there are today over 1,000,000 Negro farmers most of whom own their land; others rent or plough on shares. These people were, only 70 years ago, so poor as slaves that they did not even own themselves. Today, some are landlords owning millions of acres with full title deeds to the land in the same way as any other American citizen. In the cities, the Negroes buy and reside on their own property in any part of the city, notwithstanding the fact that in certain sections individual Whites had protested. In test cases on this principle of residential segregation, the Supreme Court of the United States has handed down its most considered and reasoned judgment that residential segregation cannot be upheld under the constitution of the United States. Thus we see the striking contrast between a country whose foundation is principle and the other whose structure is expediency.

Ejected from the farms, pressed by hunger or heavy taxation, the Black man enters one of the Northern cities (in the Transvaal or the Free State) and finds himself arrested for a new criminal offence; that is, failure to produce his *"pass"* or "exemption" pass on demand by any constable and by even plain clothes men, anywhere and at any time. Every African, no matter what his standing may be, is not exempt from this indiscriminate stopping of African males on the street or "night raiding of Native dwellings and locations." If a professional African man or another African in independent business produces his business cards or any other personal papers for identification instead of the prescribed pass, he is under arrest and must pay a fine or be locked up. It is the question as to whether one has the particular pass the constable happens to demand—Poll Tax receipt? Night special? Service Contract Pass? Special to seek employment? Or any other. Failure to produce any of these there and then when demanded constitutes a criminal offence with a penalty

of a fine or imprisonment. Thus many a man has been introduced into our prison system and initiated into a criminal career by such trivial and technical offences. Criminals are thus manufactured by many of our unnecessary restrictions.

The only probable but most irritating excuse for continuance of the pass system is that stated by a former member of the Native Affairs Commission on May 9th 1930, at Johannesburg. This gentleman admitted that the pass system was no longer serving the purpose for which it was intended. "But," said he, "I personally believe that where there is a highly civilised minority in the midst of a backward majority, the pass system is a necessary means of control by the civilised minority over the backward and less civilised masses." All one can say is

"He who is convinced against his will
Is of the same opinion still."

None of us would object very much if there was only a single "pass" which was demanded by a uniformed constable with a warrant for arrest, or when one was under suspicion of having committed a crime or disturbed public peace.

Let us now suppose that this Black man secures employment before he is arrested under the Pass laws, he then finds out that, under the Masters and Servants Act, "breach of contract is a criminal offence for him but not for the European employer." Under this same law, "a strike of Native workers is a criminal offence."

Because this African carries a "pass" which is required by law, he finds this a disability against him in that he cannot be legislated for under the Conciliation Act 1924. Besides, the pass system limits his freedom of movement and thereby destroys his bargaining power in a free labour market. He must therefore take such wages as are offered where he is.

Further, we find that any African over 18 years or "apparently" over 18 years of age with or without income must pay his annual Poll Tax of £1 or must suffer a term of imprisonment for failure to do so. A European, on the other hand, must not pay income-tax until he is *actually* 21 years of age with an annual income of £300, or £400 if he is married. Upon the strength of these facts, I ask you to draw your own conclusions.

The next question is a delicate case in social legislation—The Immorality Act of 1927. The object of this Act is "To prohibit illicit carnal intercourse between Europeans and Natives and other acts in relation thereto." The penalty is a term of imprisonment not to exceed five years for the offence. We do not intend to criticise the provisions of the Act; but, we are disturbed over the one-sided way in which it sometimes operates against the Native women and in favour of White men concerned. Cases have come to our notice where African women had been charged, sentenced and served terms of imprisonment under this law while the White man concerned in the case was acquitted by a jury or discharged by a Magistrate. The cases of Nogale Gwemba who was sentenced to nine months imprisonment at Grahamstown and that of Nellie Mofokeng who was sentenced to six months imprisonment in Johannesburg prove the truth of our statement. This is another colour bar and preferential treatment in favour of the White man.

I believe we all realise that no parliament can make people more moral by legislation. The sex impulse is stronger over the individual than social and racial loyalties. It knows no racial repugnance; it even challenges the law. It is a known fact that White men are strong advocates of race purity and are dead against intermarriage, but Black women and even slave Black women continue to give birth to children of mixed parentage. We protest strongly against the "double standards of morals in regard to race." We would urge that *all women* be protected and safeguarded irrespective of race or colour.

The last Bill on Native Policy was the Miners' Phthisis Act Further Amendment Act, passed on May 27th, 1930. "The amendment was designed to legalise the payment of compensation calculated on the basis of actual wages only." This is really legalising a wrong because when one complains that the Native wages in the mines are low, one is, at once, told that the Native miner receives more wages in kind, in the form of food, shelter and medical services. However, when the Native miner becomes a phthisis victim, the wages in kind are never included in the calculation of

the compensation; consequently, the Native miner never receives his full compensation.

The compensation paid the Native is indeed small. "Since 1919 the compensation paid," according to Sir Robert Kotze, "had been £25 for the anteprimary, £55 for the primary stage, and £72 for the secondary." It is well to remember that these small sums of money are often the last earnings of men, many of whom may have families of from one to ten children. These dependants get no further benefits of any kind should the breadwinner die after the full amount is received and spent. The statement made by Mr. MacMinamen showed the disparity between the compensation paid the European and that paid the African. He "pointed out that of the £10,000,000 paid in compensation the Natives had received £600,000 although they out-numbered the Whites by 20 to 1."

If we now turn to education, we find that in the Cape Colony, the earlier educational curriculum was identical for both Europeans and Bantu. Lovedale Mission Institution was opened with a class of 9 Europeans and of 11 Bantu students. From the time of the Rev. Mr. Govan through the period of Dr. Stewart, European and African students studied side by side. None seemed the worst for it. As a matter of fact, these generations of students produced some of the ablest and most prominent men in South Africa on both sides of the colour line. The Africans suffered no disabilities by this arrangement. The Europeans lost nothing in prestige by it. They were all being prepared and trained to play their part as citizens in their common country. It was in these generations that the best leaders among the Bantu were produced without any special system of education adapted to African mentality and for the African mind. (I often wonder if there is such a thing anyway.) No one would deny that men like the Rev. Tiyo Soga, pioneer missionary, Mr. John Tengo Jabavu, editor and journalist, the gifted Rev. Walter Benson Rubusana, and the versatile Rev. John Knox Bokwe, were leaders of thought of their day without regard to race or colour. They were educated to be full citizens, able to stand alone, as men, in church, in the school, in public affairs and not to be assistants to someone else. The point worthy of note is that these boys when they began their schooling were raw "Kaffir boys." They were primitive men so-called, not a day removed from savagery or from the life of barbarism, and yet side by side with White boys, they mastered the White man's education without special adaptation to Native mentality and needs and above all made the best use of their education for the good of their country.

Later on, however, the schools became separate and the change extended also into the quality and content of the curriculum as well as the qualifying certificates; so that to-day we have what are known as "N.P.L." and "N.P.H.," meaning "Native Primary Lower" and "Native Primary Higher," perhaps signifying that Africans in South Africa have a different mentality from that of other races.

It is, perhaps, from the point of view of finance that "Native Education" suffers most. In most civilised countries, the financing of education is the responsibility of the State. In South Africa, however, this is true only in so far as it affects the Europeans, Coloured, and Indians; because, under the Durban Agreement of 1923, the African in education was to be treated differently and exclusively. The Union Government spends over £8,000,000 for the education of the children of the 1,500,000 Europeans and only £500,000 for the education of the children of 5,000,000 Africans. Even this amount of £500,000 is taken from a direct tax imposed upon the Africans for the purpose, over and above what he pays indirectly, in customs duties and low wages. The consequence is that only less than one-third of Native children of school age (7-14 years) can attend the elementary schools, the other two-thirds are not and cannot be provided with any schooling under this arrangement. The funds are too small, and hence, no expansion or progress is possible in Native education.

Professional education for the African here at home is not provided for. Only in the last session the Union Parliament turned down an offer of £65,000 from the Rockefeller Foundation for the erection of a medical school for Africans. Why? We Africans, as in other things that concern us, are kept in the dark. For the present, we shall reserve our observations on the Government's decision to reject the proposed offer. We, however, venture to express the view that, until such time as the Government would deem it fit to make provision for the medical training of Africans here at home, the State would be making a friendly gesture as well as assuming its proper responsibility if a system of bursaries and loans were introduced to assist properly qualified African students to proceed overseas in order to complete their medical training.

Twenty-one years since the Union of South Africa was established, the Union Parliament created a Joint Select Committee to consider the so-called "Prime Minister's Native Bills." What are these Bills for? "To solve the Native problem once and for all," we are told. How? By taking away the Cape franchise for any substitute or nothing as the Joint Committee and joint sitting of both Houses may deem fit by two-thirds vote of all members of both Houses. Why is this necessary? Has the African ever abused the privilege? No, that is just the reason, he uses it so intelligently that he becomes a factor to be reckoned with in those constituencies where he exercises the right. Representatives of such constituencies must study his interests as well as those of the Europeans. Where he has no vote he may be treated in any way or ignored because he has no means for redress or remedy for the wrongs committed against him.

The Union Parliament would have a clear coast to establish a "White South Africa" if they could remove this last stumbling block, the "Cape Franchise," and thus consummate their unparalleled and unexcelled series of colour bars. I still believe that our Parliament will soon discover its wrong course and rectify it.

The African protests strongly against this violation of the last vestige of his Cape citizenship. He knows all too well that without a vote he cannot maintain the ground he holds. He has no hope to gain new ground or even to regain lost ground. He is at the mercy of those who alone exercise this right. To use the words of Mr. J.H. Oldham, "Deprived of political influence an unfranchised class find themselves helpless to obtain redress or defend themselves against injustice. Without the franchise Natives of South Africa have no hope of obtaining a fairer share of the land. . . . . . .A class excluded from all share in political power is condemned to permanent subordination. It becomes a servant of the interests of others, having no share or partnership in a common life."

Here and there the African begins to express himself. The pressure is getting too great. He must express his hopes and despair. Instead of finding out what his real grievance is, the Government has tried to muzzle him by Section 29 of the Native Administration Act 1927 and finally by the Riotous Assemblies Act 1930. Through this legislation freedom of speech and the airing of even the most legitimate grievances and expression are driven under ground after the ostrich philosophy. It were better that we suffered both fools and the wise to speak; because, as the Most Rev. Dr. Carter, Archbishop of Cape Town, has said, "repression can only lead to reaction later on, and this is not so very much later on."

If anybody wishes to know whether justice is being done to the Native, I say to him "Study our Union Legislation." Who is the cause of agitation and unrest among the Natives? Is it the Communists? In reply, I would say in the laconic style of Colonel Denys Reitz in answer to Mr. Jansen, Minister of Native Affairs, "Your kind of legislation."

In Chapter X of the "Union of South Africa" entitled "The Natives," the author, the Hon. R. H. Brand, says:—"One may freely admit that a great deal of our South African opinion is ignorant, unintelligent, and crude. The man in the street and the man on the veld seldom realise even the elements of the stupendous problem with which they are faced. The policy which attracts them is often one of simple repression. Take away . . . . from the Native the land which he possesses, and there will be more compulsion for him to work for the White man (hence Land Act 1913). Do not educate him, or else he will become too independent (hence no adequate budget for Native education). Keep him in his place. That is the simple creed of the average White man. He fails to see that in his own interest it is fatal. For, if the Black man sinks, he will inevitably drag the White man down . . . . . . .By raising in their breasts a sense of wrong the White man will merely be

digging his own grave." This "simple creed of the average White Man" is often the policy of "simple repression" of the man in the street and man on the veldt, and has become the approved policy and practice of our Parliament; because, under our Northern system of manhood franchise whose only qualification is that a man or woman must be 21 years of age with a White skin, it is the "man in the street" and "the man on the veldt" who elects and sends Parliamentary representatives. These representatives are responsible to them and they must carry out their policy, however crude it may seem, or else they are not again returned. In this connection the words of Schiller seem to be sound advice for my country when he said:—

"Majority—what does that mean? Sense has ever centred in the few. Votes should be *weighed* not counted. That state must soon or later go to ruin where numbers sway and ignorance decides."

When one studies and ponders over these legal disabilities of the African one is less inclined to blame him for little or no progress. His position is fixed by statutory bonds. One's feeling is expressed best in the words of John X. Merriman who said, writing from Kingwilliamstown:—

"What I regret most is the bitter feeling of race hatred which is being sown broadcast, and the terrible sacrifice of life which must take place before this wretched business is ended. Then what a task will be left for those who have to take up the reins of Government to evolve order out of chaos and by justice, honesty, and fair dealing try to remove some of the bitterness and animosity which will long survive the futile effort to establish the supremacy of the White man by might and not by right." Thus we have seen that the restrictive, repressive Union legislation has created more new problems than it has solved in our difficulties in race relations; because, this legislation has been based on the idea that the 1,500,000 Whites must for ever remain supreme over the 5,000,000 Blacks.

Although I emphasised the ascendency of Grondwetism in our Union legislation, I should not be understood to put the whole blame of race prejudice on the Dutch-speaking section. This section has no monopoly of colour prejudice. The Britons in South Africa, especially in Natal and in the former Republics share and fan the flame of these colour bars. To support this my conviction, I shall quote Mr. Maurice Evans who says in one of his books: "It is notorious that persons born and brought up in England, in the traditions of race equality are often more prejudiced when they come to live in a bi-racial country, than those brought up amongst a backward people. It is the rule and not the exception that those from Britain, who have been supporters of missions, and hold orthodox views on religious matters, who land in South Africa with these ideas undimmed, soon absorb the racial opinions current in the country of their adoption."

In spite of this conviction, I am not unmindful of the fact that there is a group, and thank God, an increasing group of fair minded, sympathetic and just people among both Boers and Britons. I, personally, have many friends in both sections. Some of these people will go any length to see that the scales of justice are held evenly between White and Black. Messrs. Fischer and Marquard, both Dutch-speaking Europeans, have, through their work as leaders of the Bloemfontein Joint Council of Europeans and Bantu (one of the best) and through their private night school for Africans, shown a devotion to the cause of the African which can hardly be excelled and is worthy of emulation by all. No more convincing evidence of this noble spirit can be found than the presence of, the interest and attitude of our delegates here. It is the hopeful sign of a better day between White and Black in South Africa.

I would not be fair, I would not be honest, I would not be just, if I did not mention two institutions which are a credit to South Africa and compare very favourably with the best of their kind anywhere in the world. I refer to our Bench of Judges and to the better class newspapers in South Africa.

By their impartiality, by their "blind justice," by their disregard for colour even in cases between White and Black, our Judges have kept faith with the African. To the African our Judges are the final hope and safety valve especially as they have more than once upset judgments of lower Courts and declared certain differential and preferential legislation ultra vires. May they always uphold the high standards and ethics of their esteemed profession for the preservation of the best in the world-civilisation namely, justice. So great is the African's faith in the justice of our Bench that I would not mind having to appeal against a judgment under the Liquor Law 1928 and appear before Mr. Justice Tielman Roos, its author, now one of our honoured Judges on the Bench. One can realise, therefore, how disturbed and agitated the African's mind is when the Riotous Assemblies Act 1930 eliminates our Bench as a Court of Appeal, in preference for one man, the Minister of Justice, with absolute power.

Besides, most of our leading newspapers have elevated journalism in South Africa. They have shunned "yellow-journalism" by refusing to play upon the African's weaknesses and foibles. They have steadied public opinion and kept it sane and civilised when political demagogues were undermining the foundation of the very civilisation they profess to build.

These two institutions are the pillars by the aid of which and upon which we hope to build our bridges.

. . . .

Our task then, is to build our bridge between White and Black by pointing out and emphasizing the danger of a restrictive, repressive policy such as the "Union Native Policy." Such a policy leads to a spirit of discontent, sullenness, and suspicion on the part of its victim, instead of contentment, good-will, and co-operation, which only justice and due consideration can bring about. While South Africa must be persuaded to realize that only through the path of justice and fair dealing can it be hoped to establish and preserve the Western civilization, whose "true signs," according to Lord Russell, "are thought for the poor and the suffering, chivalrous regard and respect for woman, the frank recognition of human brotherhood, irrespective of race, or colour, or nation or religion, the narrowing of the domain of *mere force* as a governing factor in the world, the love of ordered freedom, abhorrence of what is mean and cruel and vile, ceaseless devotion to the claims of justice." Do our European friends, who talk so proudly of protecting "European Civilization," ever realize as Mr. G. P. Gooch has well said, that, "Civilization is a co-operative achievement. The civilization which we praise so highly is the result of the co-operative efforts of men and women known and unknown through all the ages belonging to all countries and all races and creeds. It is the most wonderful thing that the world has ever seen and it is the result of the common efforts of the human family."

What we need most is a revolution of the people's thoughts, their ideas, their ideals, and their spirit to recognize the African as a human being with human desires and aspirations which must be satisfied; to concede to the African "his reasonable demand to be considered a human being with full scope for human growth and human happiness."

The educated African is our hope, our bridge. He is an asset that responsible and thinking White South Africa cannot afford either to ignore or to alienate without disastrous results in the long run. He should be brought into close contact and co-operation with the thinking European. He must be consulted in all matters affecting the African community. It is he, and he alone, who can best interpret the European to the African, and the African to the European.

In our humble efforts to accomplish this task may we always remember the words of J. H. Oldham, who says, "Christians may help infuse the right spirit—the spirit which seeks the truth, is afraid of no facts, harbours no prejudices, condones no injustice, and sets the common good above all sectional and selfish interests."

May I, in conclusion, suggest that our aim, our motto, our ideal should be, therefore, "Freedom, liberty, justice to all and privilege to none." Then, and not until then are we justified in saying, "God our Father, Christ our Redeemer, and Man our Brother."

DOCUMENTS 42a-42b. Dutch Reformed Church Conferences
DOCUMENT 42a. Proceedings and Resolutions of the Dutch Reformed Church Conference, September 1923 [Extracts] (Published in *European and Bantu*)

VI. Natives and the Land Act of 1913.

Chief F. F. Zibi.

All the authorities on the native question are agreed that the land question is the native question. The natives are a pastoral people, who lived and moved with ease when there was no land hunger. To-day the scene is changed, and they are crying out throughout the whole Union for land. Contentment among the natives, better understanding between the white and black races, and the solution of the native question itself depend mainly on a sound and satisfactory adjustment of land rights. For the purpose of this question the natives may be divided into four classes: (1) Those who live on reserves or locations under communal tenure; (2) those in surveyed locations whose ownership of their land is conditional; (3) squatters in surveyed locations and on privately-owned farms; and (4) those living in urban areas.

Natives living in reserves and locations are merely occupiers, not owners, of the land. The Government is the owner. How they can improve themselves is a difficult question. I heard from an authority on the subject "that he would not advise a man to build a decent house on Crown land"—and these reserves and locations are Crown lands set aside for the exclusive use of natives. Furthermore, according to regulations that were proclaimed to be in force last year, the white man—in spite of the segregation policy of the country—has framed rules to govern in these segregated areas, the native through a white man instead of governing him through a native. "Develop on your own lines," he says, "but I am going to tell you what those lines are to be."

The rule in the surveyed areas is "One man one lot," and no provision whatsoever is made for increase. The result is that all the sons of the lot-owners are squatters. We have been held, and are held, responsible by both Government and officials for allowing squatters into our areas. I admit we are responsible—not for allowing squatters into our locations but for breeding them. We come now to squatters on privately-owned farms commonly called "morow com" (come back to work even to-morrow). What future have these people?

The farmer wants them as long as they and their families work for him. What if a man becomes an invalid? What about his wife and children if he die? Where are they to go? These are questions the legislators should have asked themselves before they passed the law.

Origin Of The Act.

The Europeans, the governing race in this country, have through their Parliament, sought to solve the native question by first attempting to effect territorial separation of land rights between Europeans and natives, as the first instalment of the Union's native policy. This they did by passing the Natives' Land Act in 1913, a little over 10 years ago. The Act became law on June 19, 1913.

The official statement issued in November, 1913, on this matter, inter alia, stated that the Parliament had decided that an effort should be made to put a stop to the many social and other evils which result from too close contact between Europeans and natives. It is difficult to accept this statement as being the sole and only origin of the Natives' Land Act. On February 18, 1913, during the Parliamentary session of that year, the Minister for Lands was asked: (a) How many farms or portions of farms in the Transvaal Province have during the last three years been registered in the names of natives? (b) What is the extent of the land so registered? (c) How much was paid for it? The Minister replied: (a) 78 farms; (b) 144,416 morgen; and (c) £94,907. On February 28, 1913, Mr. J. G. Keyter, Free State member, moved: "That the Government be requested to submit to the House during the present session a general Pass and Squatters Bill to prohibit coloured people (1) from wandering about without a proper pass; (2) from squatting on farms; and (3) from sowing on the share system." Mr. P. G. W. Grobler, a Transvaaler, moved (as an amendment) to add at the end of the motion: "and further to take effective measures to restrict purchase and lease of land by natives." As a result of these the Natives' Land Bill was introduced and passed towards the end of the same session. The Bill complied with the motion of Mr. J. G. Keyter and the amendment of Mr. P. G. W. Grobler.

Considering all these origins as a whole, and the fact that the Bill was passed by a Parliament of white men only, we can safely say that the Europeans in this country became apprehensive, and considered that the development of the natives and the growing desire on the part of the natives would eventually seriously jeopardise the future of the white man. That, in my opinion, was the true origin of the Natives' Land Act. And it was passed with little or no regard for the welfare and interests of the natives, and no thought given to the increase of the native population and the increasing desire of the natives to acquire land property of their own.

Three points are very important to be kept in view: Firstly, immediately the Act was passed it stopped the natives from purchasing, hiring, or acquiring any land or interest in land outside the "scheduled native areas." This was in terms of Section I of the Act. Secondly, the Act contains a schedule of native areas in which natives only may buy, hire, or acquire land or interest in land. Thirdly, outside these scheduled areas no black man can buy or hire land.

The Scheduled Areas.

What are these "scheduled native areas"? The recent official statement issued by the Department of Native Affairs, to whose lot has fallen the administration of this Act, says: "The areas mentioned in the schedule of the Act comprised all the then existing native reserves or locations throughout the Union, and in addition much land privately owned by natives for tribal purposes." We have now got the answer in the clearest language possible. The scheduled native areas are the existing overcrowded and congested native reserves and/or locations plus much (?) (question mark in original text) land privately owned by natives for tribal purposes.

There is a wrong impression abroad that the Act protected native occupation of reserves and locations from being purchased or encroached upon by Europeans. A greater mistake and a more misleading statement could not be made. These reserves or locations have been granted to, and reserved for the exclusive use of certain native tribes, under certain laws. They were, and still are, protected by those laws under which they were granted to natives. The deeds of grant of these reserves are, like all other grants, filed in the offices of the Registrar of Deeds of the various provinces. The terms of some—if not all—of these grants clearly declare that these reserves are inalienable, and cannot be bought or sold, the reserves being exclusively granted to the tribes concerned. These reserves being inalienable, not even members of the tribes, for whose benefit the reserves or locations are held in trust can buy land therein. Under the terms of certain of these grants some of the locations could only be sold if the whole tribe rebelled, in which case the location could be confiscated.

Policy Of The Government.

The native areas recommended by the Beaumont Commission were rejected by the Parliamentary Select Committee, on whose recommendation the local committees were appointed. The local committee reports "were received with the same antagonism as had been exhibited in many quarters . . . towards the recommendations of the Beaumont Commission."

As already shown, the Act made it at once illegal for a native to purchase or hire land outside the scheduled native areas. These restrictions were regarded as temporary, and only to operate until the Parliament made further provision, acting on the report of the Natives' Land Commission, commonly known as the Beaumont Commission. Notwithstanding that, the Government has, according to the official statement, decided that "the time is not ripe to deal finally with the position arising out of the legislation of 1913." This is ten years after the passing of the Act, and ten years after "taking effective measures to restrict the purchase and lease of land by natives," no relief in the meantime being provided for the possible hardships and difficulties that might happen to the poor natives as the result of the administration of the Act! The restrictions that were taken to be temporary can well be taken as permanent, for the Government states "it would be premature to ask Parliament to set aside definite native and non-native areas." This can be taken to mean that from June, 1913, the Act was greatly made operative against the natives only, who were confined to buy or hire land in the scheduled native areas; this restriction was to be temporary. Investigation and the consideration of the matter in the meantime went on. Finally, it is found the "Parliament cannot be asked to set aside definite areas for black and white," while retaining the restrictions imposed on the natives.

The Government in 1922 decided that local committee areas are to be regarded as areas in which natives could buy or lease land. (Sec. 16 of the Statement.) But the statement says, "it must be clearly understood that the Government does not propose to expropriate privately-owned ground within committee areas with view to making such land available for native occupation, nor does it propose to make free grants of land for tribal locations." And, "as regards Crown land in the committee areas the Government does not purpose to authorise permanent alienation without Parliamentary authority." And "time has come when it must be recognised that any additional land which a man or community now needs must be paid for, either by way of purchase or of lease." Privately-owned ground within committee areas not to be expropriated: no free grants of land for tribal locations: Government not to authorise alienation of Crown land in committee areas. Where then can the natives buy or lease land? The answer is in Section 16 of the statement: "Local committee areas are to be regarded as areas in which natives can buy or lease land." Now what are these local committee areas? They are the existing overcrowded native reserves or locations, with additional adjoining Crown lands and two, three or four privately-owned farms, which by the demarcation of these areas fell within these areas owing to their close proximity to native reserves or locations.

No Land To Buy.

The policy followed by the Government is fully and clearly explained in the official statement, and on that statement's own showing the committee areas, as the law at present stands, are a mere theory and of no practical help to the natives. As I have shown that these committee areas consist of native reserves or locations, Crown land and privately owned farms, the Government does not purpose to authorise alienation of Crown land in those committee areas, nor does the Government propose to expropriate privately-owned farms within those areas, and, even if the natives have the money with which to buy those privately-owned farms, no farmer, under the Act, can be compelled to sell his farm against his wish. Boiled down, the whole policy comes to this, natives are practically allowed to purchase or hire land only in their own existing overcrowded locations or reserves.

The writer of the paper proceeds to consider the actual working of the Act and this policy, quoting statements to show that it is not only inequitable but also the cause of the actual hardships suffered by the natives, individually and collectively.

Evidently (he continues) a mistake was made in making and enforcing the Natives' Land Act before provision was made for the possible evictions of natives from farms as the result of the working of the Act. And now, this state of things has resulted in: (1) Other natives through circumstances beyond their control, have to enter into labour contracts with farmers under shocking, inhuman and unchristian conditions. (2) It has resulted in such natives wandering about with their families and stock looking for better places where they can get better terms. This treking about reduces the number of their stock and thus makes the natives poorer and poorer. (3) Great numbers of these wandering natives, or natives so turned out from farms, have gone to towns only to swell the great army of the native unemployed, and what is worse, some have become criminals in the town slums; some their homes broken—their wives and daughters and sons breaking away from paternal authority as the result of the undesirable influence of town slum life. Women have become illicit liquor traffickers. Young boys have joined the criminal gangs. One only has to go to native locations of big towns like Pretoria and Johannesburg, to see great numbers of men and women in their raw state, which is evidenced that they are fresh from the native kraals in their locations.

The Natives' Land Act having done its "bit" towards harassing the natives and rendering them homeless in rural and country areas, and driving large numbers of them yearly into towns, the Urban Areas Act has now been passed which will have the effect of driving hundreds of thousands of natives out of towns, as only natives in employ will remain in the native villages in towns. The question arises now: Where will these people go to?

. . . .

IX. Resolutions.

Unopposed motion by Mr. M. Pelem—

That this Conference of Representatives of various Christian Churches and races of the Union of South Africa, in meeting assembled, wishes to place on record its profound sense of gratitude, admiration and appreciation of the wise, timely and thoughtful appeal and invitation which has been addressed by the Federal Council of the Dutch Reformed Churches to the Churches and other bodies engaged in philanthropic work among the Bantu people of this country, calling upon them for co-operation and united effort and action in dealing with the solution of the Native question. This Conference would, moreover, and above all, humbly, but joyfully express its thankfulness to the Almighty God for the special gift of the Christian spirit of wisdom, grace and philanthropy which inspired and led the Rev. A. F. Louw to the conception and initiation of his grand idea and proposition.

This was seconded by Mr. W. W. Ndlovu, and passed with acclamation.

Native Education.

This Conference recommends that the Government should as soon as possible consider the advisability of introducing a Native Education Act, the objects of which will be:—

(1) To place Native Education under the direct control of the Union Government;

(2) To provide funds to place the salaries of Native Teachers on a uniform and equitable scale;

(3) To remodel our system of Native

Education so that it shall be characterised by the greater adaptation of subjects and methods to practical needs, and that a larger place shall be given to industrial and agricultural training, domestic economy and hygiene;

(4) To provide a special place in the curricula for biblical and simple doctrinal knowledge, which should form a subject of examination, as the Conference is of opinion that there is no force like religion for raising the Native, and greatly deplores the tendency towards the neglect of religious and moral training in Native schools due to its not being subject of examination;

(5) To arrange for the administration of Native education under Government control by Advisory Councils on which the Government, the Missionary Societies and the Natives will be represented.

Christian Native Policy.

This Conference of Christian leaders among the European and Native sections of the population desires to declare its utmost emphatic conviction that the only sound and safe Native policy for our country is one based on the teachings of Christianity, and would therefore impress upon the Christian Churches and other responsible bodies and persons, the urgent need of employing every means for educating public opinion with reference to this subject of supreme importance. The Conference would especially call upon the Churches to do all they can to stir up interest in missionary effort among their members, and to quicken their sense of responsibility towards the Native and his conditions and aspirations. With an eye to this end the establishment of Native Welfare Associations is heartily recommended, and the training of the young to take an interest in their fellow citizens of another colour.

The Conference further resolves to appoint a Committee to co-operate with the standing Committee of the South African General Missionary Conference and the Native Welfare Associations in order to influence public opinion, *inter alia*, through Municipal and Divisional Council Congresses, and to watch proposed legislative measures, and if necessary to bring influence to bear on the Government

in order to safeguard the rights of the Natives.

Urban Areas Act.

(1) *Regulations.* Resolved that this Conference approach the Government through its Board of Officers, with a view to ensure that no regulations, either by Government or by Urban local authorities, shall be gazetted until they have first been published and time has been allowed for the full expression of public opinion thereon, both Native and European, and that the minimum period of 7 days provided in Sec. 23, Sub. Sec. 3, is not adequate; and further that in the framing of regulations by the Governor-General, the Minister, or the local Urban Authority, the spirit of consultation should be observed.

(2) *Leases.* Resolved that this Conference urge upon the Government and local Urban Authorities that the system of leasehold tenure in Native vallages established under the Act be generally adopted and generously administered, so as to meet the legitimate aspirations of the Native for security of homestead tenure. To this end the Conference urges that the Government prepare and submit to Urban local authorities model leases.

The Conference also commends to the Native Welfare Societies, the working out of a common policy as to the terms and conditions of such leases, especially with reference to period of tenure and fairness of conditions.

(3) *Building.* Conference urges that in the construction of Native Villages facilities may be given whereby Natives may be encouraged to build their own houses (and also that Native contractors be allowed to tender for the erection of such houses as may be erected by the Urban Local Authority.)

N.B. The words in brackets were added by the Conference.

(4) *Superintendents.* That the Conference urge upon Urban local authorities the exercise of the greatest care in the selection of Location Superintendents, as the successful working of the Act will depend in a large measure upon the securing of suitable men of broad human sympathy for these posts.

(5) *Reformatories.* That in order to make possible the carrying out of Section 17, Sub. Sec. 2 of the Act which provides for the

commitment of habitually idle or disorderly Natives to reformatory institutions, the attention of the Government be called to the urgent necessity of establishing such institutions which must provide for both sexes.

All except No. 5 were adopted.

Social Betterment.

(1) In the opinion of this Conference the conditions under which the Natives live in urban areas, and the paucity of the opportunities available to them for social improvement and social expression make it urgently necessary that efforts for social betterment of Natives in urban areas be inaugurated.

(2) That such efforts should aim to providing similar facilities to those provided for Europeans by the Y.M.C.A. and Y.W.C.A. and that organizations for the carrying out of such efforts should be on Christian and interdenominational lines.

(3) That this Conference notes with gratification the inauguration of such efforts in several South African cities and commends the subject to the attention of the National Council of the Y.M.C.A. with a view to the extension and co-ordination of such efforts.

Segregation.

Resolution of Segregation proposed by Rev. Z. R. Mahabane.

That this representative Conference respectfully recommends the Government of the Union of South Africa to convene a Conference representative of the Government, the Churches, the European community and the Bantu population to consider and report upon the question of the advisability, desirability or feasibility or otherwise of segregation of the races as the best possible solution of the problem of race adjustment in this country.

This was carried 28 to 7.

Resolutions proposed by Mr. Brooke.

(1) This Conference is in favour of the principle of the differential development of the Bantu, so far as such differentiation is based on Bantu traditions and requirements, and is not used as a means of repression;

(2) So far as this general differential development can be described as "Segrega-tion," the Conference is in favour of segregation;

(3) Understanding "Segregation" in its limited geographical sense, the Conference believes that complete segregation is neither possible or desirable. It considers, however, that a partial possessory segregation (i.e., segregation based on prescriptive or other rights to the occupation of land) while not providing a panacea for the Native problem, is a useful subsidiary measure tending to facilitate administration, and it therefore especially recommends that the integrity of the existing locations be respected and preserved.

The Land Question.

The Resolution Committee's resolutions on the Land Question were then read as follows:—

That the Conference resolve

(1) That it would call the urgent attention of the Government to the very serious unsettlement and anxiety caused amongst the Natives generally by the operation of the Natives Land Act, by the confusion and uncertainty with regard to its provisions, and especially by the failure to make adequate "further provision" as recommended by the Beaumont Commission and the local Committees.

It being the intention of the Act that any prohibition to purchase land arising under Section 1 of the Act should be counterbalanced by the power to purchase other lands to be defined by the Commission appointed under Section 2. The two should be inseparable.

The increased and increasing congestion in Native areas is intensifying competition between white and black in the labour market, and therefore it is in the interest of both races to proceed immediately to relieve that pressure by the provision of land for Natives.

(2) That with regard to provision of land for Natives:—

(a) The Government should give earnest attention to the possibility of organising financial help by Land Settlement Board, Banks, or other means, to facilitate the acquisition of land to be held by Natives on individual tenure.

(b) That it will be necessary for some time to come, to provide land for Natives to be held on tribal or communal tenure.

(3) That, in order to clear up the confused position that has arisen under the Act, definite answers be requested to the following questions:—

(a) What local Councils have been recommended to the Governor-General by the Native Affairs Commission under Section 5 of the Native Affairs Act, 1920?

(b) What local Councils have been appointed by the Governor-General as the result of these recommendations?

(c) What recommendations as to land have been made by the local Councils appointed?

(d) Under Section 14 of the Native Affairs Department Statement the Governor-General can be asked to approve of Natives buying or leasing land in areas recommended by the Beaumont Commission and a local committee if the price or rent was reasonable. Are there cases of the Governor-General's approval having been asked for? If so, (a) What is the number of farms bought or leased by Natives in Committee areas? (b) What is the proportion of Committee areas still occupied and owned by Natives?

(e) What steps have been taken to inform Natives of the available land in each area? How may a Native ascertain this information?

(f) Under Section 18 the Government does not propose to "expropriate privately-owned land in areas with a view to making such land available for Native occupation." Is it not, therefore, the case that action under Section 14 can be completely blocked by any individual European holding land to-day in such areas placing upon it an unreasonable price or rent?

(g) Has the Commission discussed with the Government the position of Crown Land in the Committee Areas, and has any land whether Crown Land or privately owned in these Areas been alienated or leased to Natives?

(h) Has the Government decided not to alienate any more Crown Lands whether to Europeans or Natives? In any cases, have there been alienations of Crown lands in Committee areas to non-Natives since the Act came into operation?

(i) Will the Government bring up the whole question of Native lands for the consideration of Parliament at its next Session?

These were adopted unanimously.

Self-Government.

(1) This Conference believes the time has come for the State to devise machinery aimed at granting to all the Natives of the Union some method by which they may be enabled to have a voice in the management of their affairs.

(2) That in response to the legitimate claims made by their representatives, a beginning should be made in training the Native people on safe and wise lines in the forms of self-government by the establishment of Native local councils as contemplated under Act 23 of 1920.

These were adopted unanimously.

DOCUMENT 42b. Report on proceedings and resolutions of the Dutch Reformed Church Conference, February 3, 1927 [Extracts] (Published in *The Cape Times*)

The third day's sitting of the European–Bantu Conference was opened by a short devotional service.

The first speaker was Senator Sir Walter Stanford, who recalled the Inter-State Commission on Native Affairs, on which he served in 1903-5. That Commission recommended that South Africa should follow the example of New Zealand in dealing with representations of the aboriginal races. It could not be said, declared Sir Walter, that the natives in the Cape Province had abused their right to vote. On the other hand, they had materially assisted by sending sound representatives to the Cape Parliament. The matter should not be influenced by existing party considerations, which might change in a day.

He considered there was no justification for depriving the Cape natives of a right which they had held for so many years, and which brought them a large measure of protection which they valued greatly. The Prime Minister should let well alone in the Cape Province, and try experiments in Provinces where no provision for the native vote had been made. Repressive legislation on the part of the Europeans would not bring contentment. The feelings of the natives who had given their loyal friendship in the four Provinces were entitled to fair consideration.

Sir Walter, in conclusion, emphatically declared that he had not the slightest fear of the natives. There was no need to fear the native when the wealth and commerce of South Africa was in the hands of the Europeans. The natives realised that for the large majority of them there was nothing but manual labour.

Four Principles.

Professor Du Plessis said that any consideration of the representation of natives in Parliament should start with the Native Commission of 1905. Four principles were then laid down: (a) The native is entitled to a certain amount of representation. (b) The native should have separate representation from the European. (c) The proportion of such representation to the European representation shall be decided by legislation. (d) The qualifications of the native elector should be equal to that of the European. The Commission referred to the danger of the constantly increasing native voting, which might lead to a conflict, which would be fatal to the good understanding hitherto existing between Europeans and natives. It was considered by the Commission that it would be impracticable to take away the franchise from the natives of the Cape who already had it. These recommendations were unanimous. If therefore, 20 years ago those responsible men regarded franchise legislation to be urgent, surely it was more urgent in 1927.

Professor Du Plessis quoted from General Hertzog's Smithfield speech: "Circumstances are changing so rapidly that within a limited time the necessary conditions for the solution will not be present any more. It is my desire, therefore, that people should recognize the necessity for tackling it now and not to delay."

The recommendations of the Commission, proceeded Professor Du Plessis, were largely embodied in the Bill now under consideration. The Bill proposed to give to the natives throughout the Union representation in Parliament. This was in accordance with the first principle of the 1905 Commission. It also proposed to give the natives separate representation. Confining the number of such representatives to seven was a wide difference, however, from the fourth principle of the Commission, that the qualification of the native elector should be equivalent to that of the European. The Bill differed from that because it was not a single native vote, but certain chiefs, members of local councils or persons nominated by the Government exercised to vote. This meant the withdrawing of the franchise from 14,000 natives in the Cape.

An Anomaly.

Professor Du Plessis, continuing, thought the Conference would agree, without much discussion, to the first and second principles. It was an anomaly that the natives should be without representation in the Legislature. This anomaly should now, if possible, be removed, and he could conceive of nothing which would improve their prestige in the eyes of the world more than such an action. This Conference would also agree, said Professor Du Plessis, to separate ballot boxes for Europeans and natives, and thus do away with the unedifying spectacle of Europeans canvassing for native votes, which would thus disappear. The Northern Transvaal did not want the Cape franchise introduced there.

The Bill proposed seven representatives, and since the number was fixed at seven it was surely immaterial to the Government how they were elected, provided they were elected by the natives. There were serious objections to the representatives of the natives being selected by the Government. It would also be a mistake to disfranchise the 14,000 natives in the Cape. They had not deserved this, and would rightly object. He hoped the report that this was to be dropped was correct, as if the franchise was retained a good deal of the objections would disappear.

Professor Du Plessis suggested that instead of limiting the number of representatives to seven they might make the quota of voters for each constituency 4,000. When that quota was exceeded the number of native constituencies should be increased so as to stand in the proportion of one native to 15 European; when the Europeans in Parliament reached 150, then the native representation would advance to 10. He also wished that the representatives of the natives should have their duties in Parliament free and unrestricted. Still, if the Bill could not be passed without Section 6, then let it be passed.

Summing up Professor Du Plessis said the suggestions were that the franchise qualifications throughout the Union should be raised, with the gradual disappearance of the present voters' list; a representation of seven for the present, but to be allowed to rise until the proportion was one native representative to 15 Europeans; a simple method of nominating candidates and recording votes; the release if possible of the seven representatives of the natives from the disabilities imposed by Section 6 of the Bill.

Bantu Opinion.

Special Representatives Needed.

Mr. W. A. Russell, of Cape Town, said he fully agreed with those who held that the settlement of the native question ought not to be based on fear. The present conditions for placing Bantus on the Voters' Roll in the Cape Province and Natal should be abrogated.

The Bantu people, he contended, should be given special representatives in the Union Parliament, adequate in numbers and competent in qualifications to keep a watchful eye over Bantu interests, to draw attention to Bantu grievances, and generally to voice Bantu opinion. So far as was practicable, this representation should be disconnected from all the ordinary divisions and controversies of party politics.

Mr. Russell then advanced his reasons why such a policy was imperative at the present time.

As regards the Cape Franchise, the qualifications required were virtually a sham. They no longer fulfilled their original purpose. Many had voted in the Cape whose only literary accomplishment was the ability to write a name and occupation. He had heard of raw Kafirs having exercised franchise rights. The wage earning qualification of £50 per annum worked out at 3s. 2d. a day. Forty years ago this was a respectable wage, but not to-day. In his opinion a decent Bantu boy in the Peninsula was under-paid with less than 3s. 6d. a day.

Proceeding, Mr. Russell said it might readily happen under present circumstances that the European voters in the Cape Province would be outnumbered by the Bantu voters of a low class.

"A Serious Decline."

He believed the transference of political supremacy at the polls from the Europeans to the Bantus would initiate a serious decline in all that was best in European civilisation in South Africa, and would finally cause its extinction. If a large mass of Bantu voters were added to the European voters, the fundamental conditions of successful democratic government would certainly be violated.

Mr. Russell endeavoured to show, by referring to American investigations regarding negro mentality, that native ability was lower than that of the white man.

It had been said that the Bantus never abused their franchise privileges, and always voted for excellent representatives, and that was true.

"The reason is," said the speaker, "That they voted as their missionary leaders advised them; and the missionaries advised them wisely and well."

They used to act like docile children, he said, but there were clear signs that this docility was coming to an end. Christianised natives were beginning to show even a certain amount of antagonism to the leadership of European missionaries, and there was a very considerable movement towards separation from European churches.

Prof. Jabavu's Views.

Prof. D. D. T. Jabavu prefaced his remarks

by observing that most of what he had to say had already appeared in the Press, and he would, therefore, only speak on certain points. He wished to say that the native's feeling on this matter was strong, and its unanimity unprecedented in history. All were speaking with one voice, and he did not know of any native, outside a mental asylum, who was prepared to temporise on this. They did not want to see the native vote tampered with. In the preamble they had a proposal to remove all the names of native voters from the register. He would not argue this, as he thought all were agreed that they did not want it. But the natives did not wish the door to be barred against their sons going on the register.

Referring to special and uniform representation in the Upper House, Mr. Jabavu said he was against uniformity. When Union came in the natives did not want Union; they wanted Federation, as then the best-governed Colony might bring the others up to its level, but to-day the Cape was being attacked by the North, where they were not so generous. There appeared to him to be no justification for tampering with the Constitution for the purpose, and he would suggest that no alteration be made, but special provision be made to introduce into the other three Provinces a limited form of franchise. Clause 2 was objectionable, as the people who voted would be in some position of subordination to the Government. Clause 3 proposed the old colour bar. Clauses 5 and 6 limited the representatives with regard to certain privileges, and they should certainly ask that this be removed. Clause 8 was a legal riddle capable of two legal interpretations. Thus the natives were left with nothing to approve in the Bill, except those suggestions already outlined. The natives did not want the Bill as long as it involved the whittling down of the Cape voting qualifications. They were prepared to agree to a higher qualification for voting.

In conclusion, Mr. Jabavu referred to the fact that fear was at the back of the Bill, and said there was no fear of a black future. The natives, with the exception of some fire-eaters—who were the exceptions that proved the rule—were law-abiding.

The Colour Line.

Two Distinct Civilisations.

Mr. S. Msimang (Johannesburg) declared they should ask themselves whether it was in the interests of the country to create and maintain two distinct civilisations under one tribunal. Was it possible that the laws which discriminated according to colour, and ignored the essential bonds binding mankind together, were likely to conduce to future peace and contentment? Should the answer be in the negative, then separate representation and the grouping of parties along the colour line must constitute a danger and aggravate the problem of the clash of colour. Supporters of separate representation belonged to that school which thought only of present needs and expediencies. It appealed to them because they dreaded what General Hertzog described as "the ruin of the white population and of European civilisation in the Union." Their argument lay in a fear complex.

If, however, the Cape native vote offered a standard by which a fair estimate of the rate of increase of the number of enfranchised natives could be made, in comparison with that of Europeans, one could accept the conclusion that such fears as entertained by the Northern Provinces were without foundation. The history of the Cape native vote contained an assurance that the natives were not only amenable to civilised influences, but they were equally sensible of the responsibilities they entailed.

Native voters had never drawn a line between Briton and Boer. With them the deciding factor had been only the return of the best man. There was absolutely no evidence to support the dangerous statement that the extension of the native franchise would mean the ruin of the white population.

"A Backward Step."

Mr. H. Mazwi (Queen's Town) said it was clear that wrong existed because the present relationship required definition and amendment.

"On a close examination of the Premier's Bill it is difficult to see what he is exactly driving at," said the speaker. "The vagueness of his expressions leave safety holes through which he may escape, perhaps, later on, or may use for the purpose of attack if he may choose.

"But whatever the Premier may introduce with which to guard himself, these uncertainties leave us not only embarrassed but in a very precarious position.

"The present Bills, if carried into effect, will be so limited in their privileges, so guarded in their rights, so scant in their allowances, and will be such a distinct step backward that it will take us a decade perhaps to remake the lost ground, whereas in that decade we should have gained more ground in the recognition of our status as fellow citizens."

Referendum Suggested.

Mr. Zimi thought that if the legislation went through, the principle of referendum should be included, by which natives would have power to repeal any objectionable measure.

Mr. R. V. S. Thema (Johannesburg) said he always held that we were one nation. Two people could not live in one country and develop two nationalities. That in the end must create strife. The Conference had agreed that they formed one economic system, and they could not now say they did not form one political body.

"I now appreciate what the demand of the educated native is," said Advocate C. T. Stallard (Johannesburg). "Their demand is for complete equality with the white races, politically and economically. They demand equal rights, and it is in the light of that demand that the whole of this debate has been made.

"Personally I believe that if that demand were granted it would mean ruination to the white races, and it would harm the natives, too.

"Right from the beginning, in our resolutions, we have evaded the issue—segregation or no segregation. The public of South Africa are looking for a lead from us, and I say there is no half-way house.

"If you will not tolerate equality it is idle to talk about getting native members of Parliament. I suggest the resolutions already drafted have been very unfortunate. The whole of the resolutions have been based on a fundamental doubt as to whether you are going for segregation or amalgamation. Do let us determine now whether we are going to vote for segregation or amalgamation and equality. The lines on which we are going are leading us absolutely into the wilderness."

"Segregation Impossible."

Mr. Howard Pim (Johannesburg) said he could not accept Mr. Stallard's dilemma. There could be no such thing as segregation in South Africa.

Voice: Question!

"Quite impossible," said Mr. Pim, "except under conditions of slavery."

Loud cries of "No!"

Proceeding, Mr. Pim argued that the question of amalgamation should have been brought up before.

"The object of every scientist," he went on, "is to find a master experiment which will decide his investigations, and this Cape Franchise seems to be that master experiment. It was introduced at a time when there was no passion in this matter. It has survived minor storms, and is coming to the biggest storm. If it survives this it will mean a definite step to what our knowledge of the application of democratic government to the backward races means—a most tremendous issue. Any interference with the Cape Franchise will mean that that experiment will be lost, and I tremble at the thought of anybody taking that responsibility."

Not Necessarily Repression.

Mr. J. G. Strydom emphasised that differentiation did not imply repression, but it was a definite solution for black and white. All natives were not as calm and as intelligent as those present. If they were, he would say, "Give them a chance." But the I.C.U. and Ethiopian movement had a great majority, and he felt the few intelligent natives would never keep them down.

Mrs. Walsh said that if the rights of the Cape natives were taken away now they would be making a ghastly mistake.

"The Franchise is the precious heritage of all nations," she said. Only on national lines could any question in South Africa be faced to-day. It was imperative that they took the national outlook.

"Your only qualification for employment should be efficiency, and your qualification for the vote should be education and property," she went on.

She hoped that from the Conference would go the strongest resolution that such rights as the natives had in the Cape to-day would never be taken from them. (Applause.)

Bishop Karney considered it impossible to expect the natives to settle down on one-fifth of the land. Were they prepared to disorganise farm life by allowing all native labour to be withdrawn from them? Segregation meant all white people doing their own work, and he did not think it ever would be possible.

Advocate Stallard replied that the difficulty could be overcome by taking in the farms on the outer edge of the native reserves. A beginning should be made in the congested areas—in the towns—and redundant natives should be removed and not replaced.

Native Council Bill.

Resolutions.

After further discussion the following resolutions concerning the Union Native Council Bill were passed unanimously:

(1) That the Bill be considered independently of the other Native Bills.

(2) With regard to the method of election of the Council, the Conference consider that a register should be formed of qualified natives who shall exercise a personal vote, while unqualified natives shall be represented through chiefs and headmen.

(3) That the Council should meet at such place as shall be appointed by the Governor-General in Council.

(4) Members of the Council should retain their seats for longer periods than is suggested in the Bill.

(5) The penalty of a fine for insubordination in the Council should be deleted.

(6) Greater power should be given to the Council in initiating discussions.

(7) The Government should accelerate the establishment of local native councils.

No Agreement On Franchise.

Committee's Divergence of Opinion.

Professor du Plessis created a great surprise, particularly among the natives, when he announced that the Committee had agreed that no resolution should be taken on the Franchise Bill. He explained that the divergence of opinion in the Committee could not be overcome. Most of their resolutions had been unanimously passed, but on the Franchise they were hopelessly divergent. The European members could not meet the natives' viewpoint, and the natives said that if they let the question drop there was no knowing that they would get anything. In the circumstances it was felt unwise to advance a resolution that would not receive unanimous support.

Mrs. Walsh immediately moved as an amendment that "this Council recommends that the Government retains the Franchise as it now is in the Cape Province."

This was greeted with cheers from the native members.

Mr. Rheinallt Jones (Johannesburg University): I believe that the spirit of this Conference, despite all that has been said and done, has been one of growing goodwill and co-operation. I believe the amendment would pass, but if we passed it what would it mean? Let us agree to differ and hope to meet again before long and find a solution.

Rev. A. Mtimkulu: Does this mean that we shall achieve nothing on the franchise question?

A Year Must Elapse.

Mr. Rheinallt Jones explained that the measure would not come before Parliament until a year had elapsed after its introduction. It would not come forward this session, and he suggested that the Federal Council should call another Conference at an early date.

Mrs. Walsh: Guided by Mr. Jones, I think the wisest thing I can do is to withdraw. I am convinced I should carry this amendment, but

I am guided by those who have had a greater experience than I have. I withdraw on the clear assurance and understanding that we shall have another opportunity to discuss it before Parliament deals with it.

Prof. Jabavu said that although he would have liked to go to the extreme limit, he was glad Mrs. Walsh had withdrawn. By so doing the natives were keeping in favour with their friends in the North. The debate alone, he thought, would do good to their cause.

Original Motion Adopted.

In order to meet all wishes of the Conference the original motion was then re-drafted as follows and adopted:

"Inasmuch as the other resolutions of the conference have been reached with unanimity, or practical unanimity, and a vote on the question of the representation of Natives Bill is sure to divide the meeting, the conference decides to abide by the full and frank discussion which has been held."

The following deputation was then elected to present the Council's resolutions to the Minister of Native Affairs: The Rev. D. S. Botha, the Archbishop of Cape Town, the Rev. P. G. J. Meiring, Professor J. du Plessis, Professor D. D. T. Jabavu and Mr. Rheinallt Jones.

It was also agreed "that it be a request to the Federal Council that another conference be called on this all-important question."

In drawing the conference to a close the Chairman (the Rev. D. S. Botha) said they had reason to congratulate themselves on the good work done. They should be thankful for the good spirit which had prevailed. (Applause.) He also tendered thanks to the Archbishop and Dean for the use of the hall, and to the committees which had done excellent work. He trusted that when the resolutions were submitted to the Government the deputation would achieve the success that they had achieved in the conference.

Stating he had something in his heart which he must unfold, the reverend gentleman went on to give his views regarding segregation—views which he could not give as chairman.

"In my humble opinion what we need in South Africa is segregation of the natives as far as it is practicable," he said. Everyone knew that entire segregation was utterly impossible, but it would be in the interest of white and blacks to have segregation as far as it was practicable.

Professor Jabavu tendered the appreciation and thanks of the natives for the efforts of the Europeans on their behalf, and the conference closed with prayer, the Archbishop pronouncing the blessing.

DOCUMENTS 43a-43b. National European-Bantu Conferences

DOCUMENT 43a. Proceedings and Resolutions of the National European-Bantu Conference, February 1929 [Extracts] (Published in *Report of the National European Bantu Conference*)

The following motions drafted by the Committee on Native Agricultural Development were then considered and adopted unanimously:—

Native Agricultural Development.

The Conference records its hearty appreciation of the Government's action in appointing a senior officer of the Agricultural Department to the important work of supervising the agricultural interests and activities of the Native population of the Union.

The Conference urges all Native chiefs, leaders, and societies, to render every possible assistance to this officer, and is confident that such co-operation will lead to a vast improvement in the agricultural prosperity of the Native peoples.

This Conference is impressed by the need for the development of Native Agriculture whether in Native areas or elsewhere, both for the sake of the uplift of the Native peoples themselves and for the general advancement of the country's social and economic resources.

The Conference, having had before it the progressive measures adopted by the Transkeian Administration and the Transkeian Territories General Council which have already resulted in considerable progress in that area, supports the following agricultural policy, for the carrying out of which the establishment of Native Local Councils should be actively encouraged:—

1. The extension of individual land tenure for Natives.

2. The establishment of agricultural schools for Natives, both Government and Government-aided, using wherever possible existing Institutions.

3. The training and employment of Native farm-demonstrators in increasing numbers.

4. The extension to other areas of the Transkeian system whereby grants are made towards the cost of boundary fences on the £ for £ principle, and also the erection of camp fences partitioning the commonages.

5. The extension of the privileges of the Land Bank to Native agriculturalists.

6. (a) The encouragement of co-operative credit societies among Natives.

(b) The encouragement of co-operative buying and selling, under suitable regulations.

7. The encouragement of an improved quality of stock by the elimination of undesirable sires and the purchase of standard sires from the agricultural school farms.

8. The convenient supply of seeds of good quality, through the school farms or otherwise.

9. The limitation of the stock running on Native grazings to the ascertained stock carrying capacity of the district.

10. The encouragement of preventive measures against overstocking and soil erosion and measures for the conservation of water both by energetic propaganda and other educational means, and by practical demonstration and experiments, including boring for water and irrigation works where possible in Native areas.

11. The organisation of Native agricultural shows with the aid of Government grants, and also the extension of the practice of European Agricultural Societies providing Native sections to their shows for the advancement of Native agriculture and animal husbandry in European areas.

12. The establishment of a Native Agricultural Section in the Native Affairs Department, and the use of the specialist resources of the Union Department of Agriculture for the advancement of Native Agriculture.

That the Government be urged to introduce, through the Native Affairs Commission or otherwise, a system of leasehold tenure for Natives, both without and within the Native Areas for small-holders, to be developed and carried on by an *ad hoc* Board.

That School gardening be extended and developed, and that through the co-operation of the Departments of Education and Agriculture, acting through the District Inspector of Schools and the Supervisor of Demonstrators, the agricultural work of the school be extended to the lands of the people by means of Boys' and Girls' Clubs and similar organisations, which should be framed to include adolescents when they leave school.

The following motions drafted by the Committee on Industrial Organisation were, with slight alterations, adopted unanimously:—

Industrial Organisation.

This Conference is of opinion that the best interests of South Africa will be served by the adoption in Industry of the following principles:—

1. Recognition of the fact that the Native must be given a permanent place in Industry with the same legal and economic rights as the European, by

(a) Amending of the Industrial Conciliation Act to provide for the inclusion of pass-bearing Natives under the provisions of the Act.

(b) Removing of Natives thus brought under the Industrial Conciliation Act from the operation of the Masters and Servants Laws and such portions of the Recruiting Act as would be in conflict with the amended Industrial Conciliation Act.

(c) Repealing of the 'Colour Bar' Act.

2. Organisation of Native workers in trade unions.

3. Representation of Native interests on Industrial Councils and Conciliation Boards through such unions, or, where no such unions exist, through specially appointed representatives, with the right of appeal to the Wage Board if Native interests are not adequately represented on Industrial Councils or Conciliation Boards.

4. Use of the Wage Act in those occupations in which the Industrial Conciliation Act is inoperative, particularly where Native wages are unduly low.

5. The Industrial Conciliation Act and the Wage Act must not be used for the exclusion of Natives and other non-Europeans from Industry.

. . . .

Administration Of Justice.

Professor Brookes introduced a discussion on "The Administration of Justice." He referred to a pamphlet recently issued by the Pretoria Joint-Council dealing with this matter (copies of which were made available to members of the Conference), and replied to certain adverse criticisms that had been brought against it. That it expressed the views of persons who were outside the administration was no disparagement. Most of the great reforms of the past century had been begun by outsiders. That it exposed to the world a weakness of, or blemish on, South Africa's character was not necessarily a fault or unpatriotic. The true patriot is not he who is always praising his country, but he who always tries to make his country worthy of being praised. That it stirred up trouble and unrest among the Native people was not true. The trouble was already there. It had actually done good and helped to allay trouble by revealing to Natives suffering and fretting under a sense of injustice that they had some at least who sympathised with them and would help them. He argued further that while there was no conscious intention to do other than justice in our Courts there were preconceptions and prejudices in the minds of many of those concerned with its administration—especially in jury cases—that made it impossible for them to take an impartial view. As it was not practicable to have both Europeans and Natives serving on juries in cases where both races were concerned, the jury system should in such cases be withdrawn. He urged that death in murder cases should not be the sole penalty, but the maximum penalty. He cited the experience of American investigators as to the execution of

justice as between black and white to show that the defects in the administration of justice alleged to exist in South Africa were exactly paralleled in the United States. This greatly strengthened the claim for investigation and inquiry.

Professor Jabavu followed and dealt with the treatment meted out to Native accused in Court, and showed, with striking examples, how the faults and errors of Court interpreters were the causes of serious grievance and of miscarriage of justice. He advocated the employment of Natives as interpreters in the place of Europeans. He also stressed the fact that no Native, even in the Transkei, in spite of the advocacy of segregation, has any office in a Court of Justice in that area, not even a junior clerkship.

Sir Clarkson Tredgold, from his experience, first as Attorney General and later as a Judge in Southern Rhodesia, advocated the abolition of the Jury System. He did not think that the complaints regarding interpretation in the Courts were due to the employment of Europeans. The remedy would be found in giving interpreters a better status and higher salaries so that better men, both European and Native, could be secured for this important work. He approved of the resolution urging that there was a case for inquiry, but deprecated criticisms of sentences imposed in particular cases since the judges alone possessed the necessary data to reach right conclusions.

Sir James Rose-Innes agreed with Sir Clarkson Tredgold that the apportionment of sentence was the most difficult task that fell to any judge or magistrate. He did not claim that mistakes were never made, but he did claim that no one who had not heard the whole case through had a right to offer criticism on any sentence. He agreed that at least a case had been made out for inquiry into the Jury System and was himself inclined to favour its abolition. There should be a change made in the penalty for murder; and inducements should be given to magistrates in the Transkei to make themselves acquainted with the Native languages as this would tend to do away with much of the grievance that existed as to Court interpreters. The Native Affairs service should be a *corps d'elite*.

The Rev. Z. R. Mahabane paid a tribute to the judiciary of South Africa, but stated that recent cases had aroused grave misgivings in Native minds, referring to specific instances. The principle of the Jury System was that a man should be tried by his peers, but in cases where black and white were involved the Native was not tried by his peers. Either the Jury System should be withdrawn in such cases or the Jury should be impanelled from both races.

Mr. Selope Thema argued that a great deal of injustice complained of arose from two assumptions—that Natives were naturally and always inclined to do wrong and that the Native must be kept in his place. This created a wrong and mischievous situation as between Natives and the police and led to the policeman being regarded as a foe and not as a friend.

The Chairman called attention to the fact that was being lost sight of—that any Native had the right of claiming to be tried by a judge and not by a jury, so that the question was not so much one of Natives being overpunished, but of Europeans in mixed cases being underpunished.

Mr. R. W. Msimang believed that the police were very much what their officers made them: policemen copied the manners of their superiors. This accounted for much of the ill-treatment of Natives by the police. The defects of interpreters were largely due to the low rate at which these men were paid and the inferior quality of man that was appointed.

Archdeacon Hulme thought that for trivial offences the fines inflicted were often grossly excessive. He believed that a good deal of the wrong from which the Native suffered in regard to the dispensing of justice arose from two causes—a firm belief in the inferior grade of humanity to which he belongs and a relic of the old custom of taking the law into one's own hands.

Mr. Rheinallt Jones summarised the complaints that had reached the Johannesburg Joint Council under five headings. (1) The Jury System, (2) The Character of the Sentences, (3) The Manner of taking Evidence, (4) The Police Treatment of Witnesses and Prisoners, and (5) the Congestion of the Courts leading to hasty and consequent unsatisfactory dealing with cases. It has been ascertained that ill-treatment by the police of both prisoners and witnesses occurred frequently; and that the method of taking evidence was in many cases utterly unsuitable. He stated that immediately the present Minister of Justice had been made aware of the facts he had taken steps to remedy some of these wrongs and some improvement had already been effected, although very much remained to be done.

Mrs. Maxeke sought to have Juvenile Courts set up to deal with cases of children. She asked for Women Magistrates for these Courts. The present method of treating them as adults and sending them to gaols or reformatories was utterly ruinous.

Rev. A. E. Jennings claimed that a man accused of an offence ought always to have access to the law dealing with that offence in his own language, and that accused Natives ought to have a Public Defender.

The discussion was adjourned at 10.15 p.m.

The Conference reassembled on Friday, February 8th at 9.30 a.m.

The proceedings were opened with prayer in Zulu by Rev. J. L. Dube.

The Minutes of Thursday's sessions by the Recording Secretaries were read and confirmed.

Conference Photograph.

Conference adjourned for a brief period for the taking of a Conference photograph.

Administration of Justice *(Continued.)*

Discussion was resumed on "The Administration of Justice."

Mr. Advocate C. E. Nixon pointed out that judges of the higher courts deserved the highest praise for their efforts to secure justice in Native cases. They frequently refused to accept pleas of guilty in order that the cases might have full trial and also called the attention of Natives to their right to demand trial by judges. He also advocated that only interpreters of proved competence be used and that these go on circuit to increase their availability, and that it should be made easier for Native prisoners to appeal.

Mr. Doyle Modiakgotla related incidents of unnecessary violence on the part of the police and the action of the I. C. U. in bringing these to the attention of the Attorney-General.

Mr. A. R. H. Welsh corrected Prof. Jabavu's statement that no Natives were employed as clerks in the Transkei courts, pointing to several specific instances.

Prof. Jabavu replied that these were of very recent appointment and were not yet full clerks.

Mr. D. A. Hunter supported the suggestion of Rev. A. E. Jennings that a Public Defender of Natives be provided.

Rev. A. J. Lennard feared that long delay would be involved in the correction of the grievances as to the under-punishment of Europeans guilty of crimes against Natives, if the matter were referred to a Commission. He feared that if the condition continued the old law of retaliation might be revived. He urged continued efforts to educate public opinion.

Rev. W. Y. St. George-Stead pointed out the contrast between the practice of giving suspended sentences in the cases of Europeans convicted of serious offences, and the imposing of severe sentences on Natives.

Mr. W. G. Ballinger referred to the extortionate charges made by Attorneys for small services, and to the punishment of Natives for purely technical offences.

The discussion was then closed.

The Chairman proposed a vote of thanks to Prof. E. H. Brookes, Sir Clarkson Tredgold, Sir James Rose-Innes and Prof. D. D. T. Jabavu, for their addresses. The printed motion was referred to the Committee appointed.

. . . .

Friday afternoon.

The Conference resumed at 2.30 p.m.

Mr. Mapikela continued the discussion on the pass-laws, which was then concluded; the printed motions and several other motions being referred to the Committee on Justice.

Native Franchise.

The Cape Town Joint Council, having given notice of motion on the Native Franchise, Sir Clarkson Tredgold was called upon to speak to the motion. *Dr. Loram*, however, first obtained the leave of the Conference to address it on the question whether or not the matter should be discussed by the Conference. He urged that the introduction of the subject would vitiate the excellent results already obtained in the discussions. A vote on the Native Franchise would divide the Conference which was otherwise in agreement. The matter was not on the printed agenda and delegates had had no opportunity of securing mandates. It was urgently necessary to carry all sections together on the economic and social questions and Dr. Loram quoted the late Dr. Aggrey as saying "It is better to take all the people a little way than to take a few people a long way." The Prime Minister's revised Bills were not yet published and these the Prime Minister had said would be different from previous drafts. Shouldn't the Conference await these?

Mr. Mushet opposed this view. He referred to his own position at a previous sitting when he was alone in opposing discussion of industrial questions. He hoped Dr. Loram would find himself in a similar position. The Franchise had been enshrined in the Constitution and they could not stand by while this right was being taken away.

Dr. Loram then moved "that the Franchise question be not discussed by this Conference of Joint Councils."

Rev. A. E. Jennings seconded *pro forma.*

Professor du Plessis pleaded for a free talk on the point. He reminded the meeting of a similar situation at the Conference convened by the Federal Council of D. R. Churches in 1927, when it was felt that a vote on the Native Franchise would not be an interpretation of the mind of the Conference. He added, "We are all agreed that there shall be no infringement of existing rights, but there is room for discussion on the larger issues."

Sir James Rose-Innes suggested that the motion be put.

After a considerable discussion as to procedure during which certain amendments were submitted, but either ruled out or defeated, *Dr. Loram* amended his motion to meet a proposal by Professor Brookes, the amended motion reading:—

"That this Conference of Joint Councils do not discuss the franchise question and adjourn until 8 p.m."

Rev. E. W. Grant moved, "That the motion be now put."

Rev. J. A. Calata seconded.

This was carried by 37 votes to 6.

The motion was now put and defeated by 39 votes to 14.

Sir Clarkson Tredgold then addressed the Conference on the main question. He said that he spoke for the Cape Town Joint Council. He considered that civilised governments should encourage all persons capable of taking part in the government to share in the responsibilities and privileges. There should be no bar on grounds of colour. There were three different schools of thought on this question, (1) Those who would deny the vote to the Native, (2) those who would grant the franchise to every qualified Native, and (3) those who were in favour of a differentiated franchise.

The first was based on fear of the numerical superiority of the Natives, but it failed to note that the European voters were increasing at a greater rate than Native voters and that, as Dr. Mitchell had said, the natural rate of increase in the European population was greater than that of the non-European. There were three fallacies in this view, (1) apparent numerical superiority really proved nothing, (2) the Bantu people would not think alike on all subjects, (3) Bantu and Europeans would not necessarily be opposed to each other.

With regard to those who supported a separate franchise they overlooked the principle that representation should be based on local community of interests. Further, if it was derogatory for Europeans to represent Europeans and Natives it was surely more derogatory to represent Natives only, although he did not think so.

Sir Clarkson Tredgold then submitted a resolution in support of the retention of the present franchise in the Cape. (This motion was later referred to the Franchise Committee.)

Professor Jabavu, referring to the earlier discussion as to the desirability of debating the Native Franchise at this Conference said that it was merely chance that the issue was political. An abstract principle was involved and it could not be just ignored because it happened to rub shoulders with politicians. Franchise rights were being attacked, rights which had not only never been abused, but had been so prized that those whom the Natives had sent to Parliament had adorned it. Members of the Conference could not allow these rights to disappear without a struggle.

Attacking such current phrases as "Develop along your own lines," Professor Jabavu claimed that all civilisation was the heritage of every one. He challenged those who said "The black man is a danger to civilisation" to explain its meaning. Such phrases should be eliminated from the currency of language.

Professor Brookes held that the Conference was competent to discuss the subject before it, and it was necessary that it should do so because (1) there should be no general election on this issue, (2) the time was most inopportune for an election of that nature, and (3) consequently it was necessary to see how such an election could be prevented. He then pleaded that legislation on the Native Franchise be deferred until after the election and an effort made to secure the consent of both races concerned to any such legislation. The matter should be discussed in a Conference atmosphere. He himself was not tied down to the Cape Franchise as it stood for he was alarmed at the disproportion between the rights of Natives in the Cape and those in other Provinces. If however it was still to be an election issue he would join in resisting the attempt to take away the Cape Native Franchise without having reached an honourable agreement. He then submitted a series of resolutions which were later referred to the Franchise Committee. These deprecated the Native Franchise being made an election issue, and suggested settlement by a national convention or failing this that all who wished to secure a fair settlement should now join in resisting the present proposals.

Professor Jabavu seconded.

Mr. Musbet said that no one in 1910 even in the North had thought of taking away the Native franchise. All had regarded it as sacrosanct. The franchise rights had never been abused and its abolition would be treason.

Rev. Z. R. Mahabane supported Professor Brookes' motion.

Professor du Plessis urged the Natives to recognise that the Franchise was not a panacea for their ills. Long experience and training was necessary for a people to exercise the franchise effectively. Was the bulk of the Native population fit for it? He expressed doubt whether the Conference was the place for the adoption of Sir Clarkson Tredgold's resolution.

The Conference then adjourned.

. . . .

Administration Of Justice

The following findings of the Committee on the Administration of Justice were adopted unanimously: —

"1. The Conference is of opinion that, in view of the appreciable number of instances where the verdicts of juries have aroused deep dissatisfaction in cases where Europeans are charged with crimes of violence against Natives, the Government should be asked to appoint a Commission to investigate the operation of the jury system in such cases and to make such recommendations for the future as may be expected to remove all grounds for suspicion or discontent.

2. The Conference is further of opinion that there is room for considerable improvement in the general administration of justice in so far as it affects the Native population, especially with regard to the following matters, which it feels should be fully gone into, either by the Commission referred to in paragraph 1 or in some other adequate manner: —

(a) Interpretation in the Courts; the status and qualifications of interpreters; language qualification of Police.

(b) Special difficulties of procedure affecting Natives;

(c) Disproportionate sentences in Magistrates' Courts, especially heavy fines;

(d) Indiscriminate or unnecessary arrests;

(e) Unnecessarily rough handling of Native accused or witnesses by Police;

(f) Failure to release accused as soon as possible after acquittal;

(g) Lack of adequate and sympathetic arrangements for the handling of Native juveniles, especially first offenders;

(h) Arrangements for defence of accused persons unable to engage legal assistance.

3. The Conference requests the Prime Minister and the Minister of Justice to receive a deputation which shall present these Resolutions. The Deputation to consist of: —

Sir James Rose-Innes	Sir W. E. Stanford
Sir Clarkson Tredgold	Rev. Dr. Flint
Mrs. Spilhaus	Mr. Howard Pim
Adv. C. E. Nixon	Rev. H. Booth Coventry
Professor E. H. Brookes	Prof. Du Plessis
Professor Roseveare	Rev. A. Mtimkulu
Adv. Ramsbottom	Prof. Jabavu
Mr. J. Malangabi	Mr. R. W. Msimang
Mr. T. M. Mapikela	

with power to add to their number, Adv. Nixon to act as Secretary and Convener.

4. The Conference appoints the members of the Deputation mentioned in the preceding paragraph as a Vigilance Committee to continue in office until the next Conference, and to take such action as they may deem advisable within the terms of reference mentioned in paragraphs 1 and 2.

5. The Conference recommends that every local Joint Council or Welfare Society should closely watch the administration of justice in its own area, and communicate important facts to the Vigilance Committee through the Acting Secretary, Advocate Nixon."

Native Franchise (Continued).

The *Rev. H. Booth Coventry*, continuing the discussion on the Franchise made the points that the Franchise question is fundamental to the whole matter of Native welfare; and that it is not only a political but a moral question. The ideals laid down with regard to Health, Agriculture, Administration of Justice, etc., will be regarded as unnecessarily high unless there be the recognition of the full human status of the Native implied in the franchise.

Rev. Abner Mtimkulu urged that instead of the fear that the Native franchise will undermine civilisation there should be the recognition that every Native who qualifies for the franchise adds to the forces of civilisation. The Cape franchise, he said, is regarded by the Natives as the earnest of better things for all the Natives of the Union.

Mr. R. A. Sello felt that the threat to the Cape franchise undermined the Natives' hope for ultimate justice and suggested a National Convention of all parties including Natives.

Rev. Dr. D. Wark said that we were not so much concerned with the details of method by which the franchise should be extended as with the maintenance of the principle that every qualified man should be able to aspire to the franchise; that it is spiritual and not merely a political question.

Mr. R. V. Selope Thema urged that the granting of a differential franchise would perpetuate the idea of Africa for the Africans. The Native desired a franchise which would make Europeans and Natives one in spirit. The Natives of the Northern provinces would rather wait 50 years for the franchise than have the Cape franchise cancelled.

Sir James Rose-Innes said that the European population proposed to decide this matter in their own parliament. This was in effect being judge in their own cause which was not good for any man. It therefore behoved them to be meticulously just. It was not wise to drive all the Natives into one camp, which would be the effect of the differential franchise.

Rev. J. Calata claimed that the coloured people of the Cape were ready to support the maintenance of the Cape franchise by refusing any special rights dependent upon its abolition.

Archdeacon Hulme said that part of the definition of a gentleman was, "He that sweareth to his neighbour and disappointeth him not." We had sworn to our neighbour in this matter and must not disappoint him.

Mrs. Lyon explained the fear on the part of a section of the Europeans by the illustration that too many bass drums in the orchestra would spoil a symphony. So the pressure of a large Native vote would throw out of harmony the country's political institutions. She urged the land question as the paramount issue.

Mr. S. B. M. Ncwana deprecated the dragging of the Native franchise into party politics. European prestige would best be maintained by a liberal policy.

Mr. J. D. Rheinallt Jones closed the discussion. He said it was just over 100 years since

the 50th Ordinance made the non-Europeans in the Cape legally and economically free. In 1852 the Franchise Ordinance gave political freedom. The Land Act of 1913 would have taken away the economic freedom of the Native, but for the impartial attitude of the judiciary. The whole question of status was implied in the common franchise. Under the proposed differentiated franchise, in which Native representation was fixed and final, every increase in European representation would reduce the effectiveness of Native representation, eventually destroying Native political status altogether. Disruptive influences would be fostered by a differentiated franchise, whereas a common citizenship would save the land from such influences.

The Chairman stated that after the afternoon session it had become known that the Joint Sitting of the two Houses of Parliament would begin on Tuesday, although the Native Bills in their amended form were not yet in the hands of Members. He read a suggested appeal to the Prime Minister for the delay of action until the Bills had been submitted to the Native Conference, this appeal to be signed by all present.

A Committee consisting of Sir James Rose-Innes, Prof. Brookes, Prof. Jabavu, and Rev. H. Booth Coventry, was appointed to revise the wording of the appeal. As this Committee was not prepared to report before the adjournment of the evening session the matter was held over until the next morning's session.

Economic And Social Conditions.

The Rev. H. Booth Coventry presented the following resolution which was seconded by Rev. Z. R. Mahabane and adopted:

"That this Conference respectfully urges the Prime Minister to arrange for a thorough scientific investigation by trained experts into the economic condition of the Native people of South Africa as a necessary preliminary to all efforts to deal adequately and usefully with the many problems connected with the development of the Native people. The Conference considers that such investigation of essential facts is an urgent necessity both for the sake of the Native people themselves and for the welfare of the country as a whole."

Conference agreed that Resolutions appearing in the Agenda from the Durban Joint Council, being sufficiently covered by resolutions already adopted, be allowed to fall away.

The Conference adjourned at 9.45 p.m.

Saturday February 9th.

The Conference reassembled at 9.30 a.m.

The Rev. W. Y. St. George-Stead led the Conference in prayer.

The Recording Secretaries presented the Minutes of the previous day's proceedings, and these were accepted by the Conference, with the addition of a resolution on Hostels which had been omitted from the findings of the Committee on Social Activities submitted to the Conference on the previous day (see findings on "Social Activities").

Race Relations Sunday.

Professor W. N. Roseveare presented the following motion on behalf of the Pietermaritzburg Joint Council:—

"That a Race Relations Sunday be arranged."

Rev. J. A. Calata seconded.

After discussion it was agreed, on the suggestion of the Chairman, "that the Conference accepts the principle of a Race Relations Sunday being arranged."

Pass Laws.

The following findings of the Committee on the Pass-Laws were submitted:—

"1. That the Conference respectfully urges the Government to repeal the Pass Laws and as steps in this direction urges that:

(a) In no circumstances whatever should women or girls carry passes.

(b) The present multiplicity of passes in the three Northern Provinces should be replaced by one single life-long document for all non-exempted Natives.

(c) Instructions should be issued by the proper authorities that no Police Official other than a commissioned officer in uniform should ask for the production of the above mentioned document except for identification purposes with regard to a civil criminal case.

2. That exemption from the operation of pass laws should be granted to the following classes of persons:

(a) Adult Natives who have passed the fifth standard.

(b) Adult Natives who own or rent fixed property of the value of £75.

(c) Natives engaged in skilled occupations whether on their own behalf or otherwise.

(d) Natives who have been for a considerable time in the service of the same or consecutive employers, one or more of whom recommend them for such exemption.

3. That all Municipal regulations as to passes, should be in full harmony with the foregoing principles.

Note:—Your Committee make no suggestions as to the undebated exemptions (top of page 7 printed agenda) which go beyond the Pass Law."

Professor Roseveare expressed surprise that the findings omitted the suggestion that the Tax Receipt should take the place of the present Passes.

Discussion showed that the Conference was not unanimous on the proposal.

The findings as drafted were adopted unanimously.

Native Franchise.

The Committee on the Native Franchise submitted the following resolution, which was adopted:—

"This Conference deprecates any alteration of the law which would result in depriving the Natives of the Cape Province of the franchise in its present form."

DOCUMENT 43b. Proceedings and Resolutions of the National European-Bantu Conference, July 1933 [Extracts] (Published in *Report of the Fifth National European-Bantu Conference*)

After the tea interval, the Conference considered:—

Urban Areas Administration

Mr. W. G. A. Mears, Chairman of the Native Advisory Board, Cape Town, read his

247

paper on "Urban Conditions with special reference to the Urban Areas Act and Municipal Administration." He explained how the Urban Areas had grown up and the difficulties the growth of these areas created. The Urban Areas Act was passed to deal with these difficulties. He indicated the difficulties which still exist and he criticised the housing clauses and the financial burden placed on the Native. Other matters dealt with by Mr. Mears were: Location superintendents and their work, Advisory Boards, the brewing of beer, education, pensions for Natives, and the Native Revenue Account.

Mr. R. H. Godlo, ex-president of the Congress of Advisory Boards, read a paper on Urban Native Conditions. The speaker gave an account of the urbanisation of the Natives at East London and the reasons which lead Natives to enter such areas. The difficulties we now have to face are partly due to the fact that each municipality deals with the matter in a different way. A condition of overcrowding without proper sanitation leads to the increase of tuberculosis and other diseases. The speaker looked upon the Urban Areas Act as a boon to the Native, giving him for the first time some semblance of a status.

After showing the great value of the Act, Mr.Godlo criticised the clause dealing with the powers of Advisory Boards, which were not determined by the Act, and the fact that fines under the Act went to the Treasury. He considered it high time that permanent Bantu villages were created in place of locations as existing at present.

Referring to trading the speaker complained that in spite of the trading clauses of the Act, some municipalities bluntly refuse the necessary permission, and he considered it time that defaulting municipalities were made to conform with the provisions of the Act.

Mr. J. R. Cooper, Superintendent, Municipal Native Administration, Bloemfontein, also read a paper on Urban conditions. He referred to the undesirable state of affairs in most locations particularly with regard to housing conditions. This matter has been brought to the notice of the governments from time to time, but with little practical effect. With the passing of the Urban Areas Act, however, there has been a great improvement in the

position of Natives especially with regard to housing and administration.

At this stage (12.25 p.m.) the Conference adjourned to enable Bantu delegates to travel by bus to the location for their luncheon.

AFTERNOON

Mr. Cooper's paper was continued in the afternoon session which commenced at 2.15 p.m. *Dr. Moroka* occupied the chair.

Mr. Cooper dealt with the details of Native Administration of locations pointing out that satisfactory administration could be made possible only by personal contact with individuals. It is essential that there should be prompt settlement of minor difficulties, so that confidence might be established. Effective administration of urban Natives require sympathy and knowledge. Mr. Cooper concluded his remarks by emphasizing the fact that Native locations are governed by European Municipal Councils which are not compelled to follow the advice of the Advisory Boards. He considered it necessary that the administration of locations should be along definitely democratic lines.

Mr. Bennet Ncwana (King William's Town) opened the discussion on the papers read, by complaining that the Native Urban Administration makes no effort to give citizenship to Urban Natives.

Mr. J. R. Brent (Superintendent, Kroonstad) dealt with three points—the lodgers' permit, in respect of which he said that some form of control of lodgers is necessary; the formation of Advisory Boards—he thought the Municipal nomination of members a mistake and added that at Kroonstad the members are elected; the relations of the Boards with the Municipality—at Kroonstad there is a monthly conference between the Native Affairs Committee of the Town Council and the Location Advisory Board.

Mr. Mtwane (Ventersdorp) complained that superintendents in small towns keep the Natives in ignorance. The Native Advisory Boards are overlooked and many never meet.

Bishop D. H. Sims (A.M.E. Church) pointed out that many difficulties might be removed if the philosophy of government were right. As a first essential it should be accepted that the function of government was to educate the people to citizenship. Secondly, every man should be allowed to live up to his maximum ability, remembering that his character and brain and the contribution he makes to the body politic, are what makes a man, and not the colour of his face. Thirdly, it is necessary for the Government to inspire confidence, to give hope so that Natives may live up to something higher. The only programme to solve the whole problem was absolute economic, social and educational justice for all the people of the country.

Rev. Z. R. Mahabane (Kimberley), referring to the Kafir beer question, said that total prohibition has proved a failure because it arises out of sectional legislation. He was opposed to the municipal control of Kafir beer, and appealed to the Conference to urge the Durban Municipality to give it up. The remedy lies in licensing certain individuals of high character to brew and supply Kafir beer. The earning capacity of the bread winner must be improved so that the women who brew beer may not be compelled to eke out existence by selling liquor. Advisory Boards should be so composed as to inspire confidence. All the members should be elected. Trading Rights in locations are strongly objected to in some quarters, especially in the Orange Free State. He considered it a very unreasonable attitude on the part of the White man.

Rev. Father Martin Knight (Kroonstad), hoped the Conference would press for trading rights being granted to Natives in Urban locations. At Kroonstad they are awaiting the decision of the Minister as a result of the enquiry held by the Magistrate there in September 1932. He understood that the Native Affairs Commission have the matter before them.

Mrs. Demas (Bloemfontein) said that beer is the cause of most of the trouble in the locations and emphasized that it is not a food. The only remedy is the raising of wages.

Mr. T. Klaaste (Joint Council, Kimberley) recognised the value of what Europeans had already done for Natives in urban areas. He appealed for help with regard to the boy who lives with his parents, and who has to pay a lodger's fee. Sometimes he is put in prison for

not paying this tax and becomes a criminal or leaves home and is without parental control. He complained that Advisory Boards are useless and that the Municipalities take no notice of them, so that the people lose confidence.

Mrs. Eva Kubene (Kroonstad) pleaded that lodger's fees should be uniform and moderate; and that helpful advice on health and domestic matters should be given to Native mothers.

Mr. Keble Moti (Kroonstad Advisory Board) was of opinion that paid officials of the Municipality should not be members of Advisory Boards.

Mr. Leshodi (African National Congress) asked that the lodger's tax should be abolished with respect to bona fide members of a family, and married people hiring rooms.

Mr. Selope Thema (Johannesburg) drew attention to the fact that people did not fully realise that there are a great many of the Natives living in towns who have no other home. Many Natives are developing a new life apart from the kraal life, and want freedom to develop. The chief objection to the Urban Areas Act is that it puts too great emphasis upon control. A wise and sympathetic Superintendent can manage without excessive powers of control. Mr. Thema thought owners should pay the lodger's tax, as it is payment for extra services rendered by the Municipality.

Rev. D. W. Alexander (African Orthodox Church) urged that the Natives should be allowed to purchase their plots in the location; this disability is the cause of a great deal of discontent and of much of the trouble in the locations.

Mr. J. M. Dippa (Port Elizabeth) strongly objected to beer brewing of any kind whatsoever, as it has brought nothing but harm to the Native people.

Mr. J. D. Mogaicho (Bloemfontein) did not object to the lodger's fee provided the collection is properly administered.

The Vice Chairman, in closing the discussion expressed regret that more legislators were not present to hear the discussions and give their views. There have undoubtedly been improvements in urban areas in the past ten years. Mere criticism—the throwing of stones—

only antagonises those who are trying to improve things.

Senator the Honourable Reverend C. J. van Rooyen Smit, addressing the Conference in Sesuto, spoke of the distress among Natives owing to the prolonged drought. He had seen the Prime Minister, in the absence of the Minister of Native Affairs, and had represented the position to him. He was sure that if representations were made in deserving cases, help would be forthcoming.

The Venerable Archdeacon W. Parker gave notice of motion regarding the action of the Minister of Native Affairs in refusing to allow Pathfinders to proceed to the International Scout Jamboree in Hungary.

The Conference adjourned at 5.30.

EVENING

The evening public session commencing at 8.0 p.m. was devoted to addresses on

Public Opinion On European-Bantu Relations As Reflected in (A) Legislation And (B) The Press.

Mr. J. C. Buys, M.E.C. (Orange Free State) introduced his address with a few words in Xosa giving his reasons for speaking in Afrikaans.

Mr. Buys said it may be considered the aim of all well-meaning and thinking citizens of South Africa to deal with inter-racial questions in such a way that a clash of interests between different sections is avoided.

It is essential that each section develop in such a way that each maintains his identity as far as possible. It is not true that the White man deliberately wants to keep the Black man down. Such a policy would not only be unwise, but would be doomed to failure as it is impossible to check permanently the progress and development of any section of the people of the country. The only reasonable solution is that each section be allowed to develop according to its own nature and traditions. What we require to meet the interests of all sections is what may be termed mass-segregation and mutual co-operation. The ideal for which we must strive is a two-stream policy with coalition and co-

operation. Mass-segregation, however difficult it may seem, should not be impossible and should ultimately help to make both sections strong and progressive.

Professor D. D. T. Jabavu, B.A. (South African Native College, Fort Hare):—"There are two main schools of thought—the repressionist and the liberal, and it is important to keep in mind their historical development. While in other countries such as Egypt and India a solution of the problems is being sought on liberal lines—with extended franchise, in South Africa legislation is being increasingly influenced by the repressionist school, so that the Native franchise in the Cape is being seriously threatened.

The franchise is valued not merely because it gives potential influence, but because, as in Native government, it is a symbol of manhood. Those Natives who have the franchise feel that they have a status in the country. When he and others were approached some time ago by a member of the Select Committee on the Native Bills to agree to the disappearance of the Cape Franchise, they were told that if they gave up the vote, Parliament would vote £30,000,000 for Native Development. He himself refused to entertain the proposal. And while the granting of the vote to women has lessened the power of the franchise, yet Native leaders wish to retain it, for they hope that the coming generation, who will be separated from memories of past wars, will prove more liberal-minded. As the Native increases in culture he will be able to make himself more intelligible to the White man to explain his position, and thus prevent misunderstandings, which now occur so frequently. His vote will be more and more intelligent and more useful as an expression of Native opinion.

Many of our difficulties come from the use of catchwords and phrases. One of these is uniformity and through it the franchise is threatened. At Union each Province decided to keep its own Native Administration, now uniformity has become the fashion, and therefore the Cape franchise must be sacrificed.

'Segregation' is a mere catchword, for segregation is no longer possible. There is not the land to accommodate the Natives, and they are now too much bound up with the general economic organisation of the country for separation.

'Develop along their own lines' has perhaps many meanings, but in the minds of those who use the phrase most it means divorcing the Native from those institutions of modern civilisation for which there are no substitutes in Native life. It is not merely because these are European institutions that the Native wants them, it is because they give satisfaction for new needs which have come to stay—schools, homes with furniture and comfort, clothes and many others, part of the equipment of civilisation that is necessary for any civilised people.

'European civilisation' then is a misnomer. Civilisation involves ability to do things, to control one's environment, mastery and efficiency, and has no relation to nationality or race.

'Social equality' brings to the mind the dangers of miscegenation, and the civilisation and advancement of the Native are feared because they may involve the 'social equality' of marriage with White women. Of the thousands of educated Natives and of the large number educated in Europe, I know only one who has married a White woman. Miscegenation takes place in those ranks where there is least self-respect—among the very poor and ignorant and rarely among the educated.

Thus it is important that all classes of Europeans should be educated, and it is important that they should be made to realise the fallacies of these catchwords. While the Universities must continue their scientific study of racial questions, the children must learn to avoid race prejudices. If catchwords and phrases must be used, let them be 'The Native is not a danger,' 'Native success is not a danger to White sucess,' 'The low condition of the Black man makes for the low condition of the White man,' Repression of the Native holds down the White man.'

Rev. Z. R. Mahabane (Kimberley) said: The subject of Race Relations between White and Black in this land of many colours and variety of problems is such a complex matter and presents such difficulties that public opinion thereon must perforce be sharply divided into two or three schools of thought. On the one hand is that school that has been described as Repressionist, on the side of which is ranged the segregationist, while on the other hand is what may be regarded as the Liberal school. There is also the Native point of view.

The first school of thought is represented by a political party that nearly came into being towards the end of last year, called the Republican Party, the Draft Constitution of which was published in the Public press on the 2nd September, 1932. One of the provisions of the Constitution reads: "The Party insists on segregation of the Native, socially, politically, industrially, and as far as possible, territorially." Take also the spirit underlying Dr. W. P. Steenkamp's Manifesto published in the Press in February, 1931, and headed, "Whom I will join." Under item 7 (c) the Manifesto reads, "To maintain South Africa as a White man's country through industrial segregation, i.e., the prohibition of Native Labour where a European can be employed. Let the Native in the towns where he can be displaced by Europeans return to the farms, the Native Reserves or the Mines." See also the theory of segregation adumbrated by Senator T. C. Visser before the Bantu Studies Society of the University of the Witwatersrand published in the Press on the 29th September, 1931, when he said: "The physical facts should be sufficient to show the hopelessness of Negrophilist apostles trying to persuade a generation growing in knowledge based on scientific facts that the Native is the equal of the White man. He never can be and never will be. That," said the Doctor, "was all the more reason that he (the Native) should be safeguarded territorially, socially, economically and politically from the Whites."

This school of thought insists that the Kafir must be "kept in his place," and that is that he must continued for all time as "a hewer of wood and drawer of water." In the political sphere this body of public opinion detests the Cape Franchise which makes no differentiation between the races. It maintains that the Cape Native Vote must go or be fundamentally altered unless South Africa "wants to see either civil war or the White man's ruin or the ruin of European civilization."

The advocates of segregation of the Native

races now urge the incorporation of the Native territories of Basutoland, Swaziland and the Bechuanaland Protectorate into the Union of South Africa, holding that the solution of the Native Problem, the problem of race relations in the country as well as the problem of congestion in the Native Reserves, lies in this direction. This course has been advocated from time to time since the coming into being of Union in South Africa. It has, however, been brought more forcibly to the notice of the public during the last two or three years. The "Republican Party" declared itself in favour of this course. The following declaration appears as an article of faith in its constitution. "The Party is convinced that the Native Problem in the Union will never be solved with any degree of finality until Bechuanaland, Swaziland and Basutoland are administered by the Union Government." (Vide *The Star*, September 2nd, 1932).

Perhaps the latest pronouncement on the question from a responsible quarter is that made by Senator the Hon. F. C. Matabele Thompson, who, in supporting a request from the White settlers in Bechuanaland to the Prime Minister to receive a deputation with the object of emphasising the urgency of the matter, is reported to have said, "I want to suggest, with a full sense of responsibility attaching to my position, the advisability of incorporating the Bechuanaland Protectorate and Basutoland in the Union, not with a view to securing cheap land for Whites as has been said as a jibe, but purely as a solution of the Native land question." The Senator visualises, by this move, a solution of the problem of settlement of the African people who are crowded out of the Native Reserves and Territories of the Union as well as the urban locations.

What may be regarded as the liberal school of public thought believes in the wisdom and statesmanlikeness as well as the practicability of the late Cecil Rhodes formula of "Equal rights for all civilized men south of the Zambesi, irrespective of race or class or colour or creed." It believes also in the policy of equal opportunities for all human beings irrespective of colour; it is prepared to accept what Professor D. D. Tengo Jabavu claimed for the people he represents when he said:

"The Black man does not ask for much— only for justice, justice in land distribution, justice in economic opportunity and justice in political representation."

This school of thought has from time to time fought tooth and nail all legislative measures that appear to be of an oppressive, repressive and suppressive tendency, such as the Colour Bar provisions of the Imperial Act constituting the Union of South Africa, the Industrial Colour Bar Bill of 1926, the Native Service Contract Bill of 1932, the Native Franchise Bill now engaging the attention of Parliament, etc. This body of public opinion has characterised the Native Service Contract Act as a "repressive Bill." In a leading article the *Diamond Fields Advertiser* of Kimberley of 13th May, 1932, made the trenchant observation: "the Bill . . . . .will find a place on the statute book to the lasting disgrace of the Union Parliament."

On the question of segregation the Native point of view has been very succinctly put by Dr. P. Ka Isaka Seme, when in his closing address delivered at the Annual Convention of the African National Congress held in Bloemfontein in April last he said, "If the advocates of segregation are sincere, let them come out and give the Natives enough land for all their reasonable requirements. Let them draw up a dividing line from North to South or from East to West. Then let the Government order every White man to cross the line and go to his own corner and the Native to go to his own likewise." "I beg to ask," Dr. Seme concluded, "if there is any Government in this country which would dare to put such a policy into practice." (Vide *Umteteli* of 29th April, 1933.)

The Native view of this question of the proposed incorporation of the Native Territories into the Union was correctly given expression to by Mr. S. M. Makgatho of Pretoria in his Presidential Address to the Native Congress delivered some fifteen years ago when he quoted the pathetic words of the Rich Man in Hell when he pleaded with Father Abraham, that he would send Lazarus to his father's house, for, said he, "I have five brethren, that he may testify unto them, lest they also come into this place of torment."

The Union must first set its own house in

order, adopt and pursue a liberal policy towards the African section of its population, admit the non-European community as an integral and inseparable part and parcel of the Union populace and adopt the Cape System of statecraft, before it ventures to extend an invitation to the Protectorates to enter the fold of its political household.

Native public opinion on the whole subject of Race Relations in South Africa is fairly adequately summed up, I believe, in the declaration of rights adopted at the Annual Convention of the African National Congress held at this City of Congresses in April, 1929. I cull the following among other points, to wit:

(1) "That the aboriginal African is a member in full of, and with the human race, as well as an integral and inseparable member of the whole family of mankind;"

(2) "That as such he is entitled to all those rights, duties, privileges and responsibilities that have been conferred by a gracious Providence upon members of the human race;"

(3) "That such rights include the right of self-determination, the right to decide his own fate and determine his own destiny, as well as the right to choose his own rulers;"

(4) "That such rights involve the right of direct representation in the legislative bodies of the land of his habitation, the right to the full and unrestricted franchise on the same basis as applies to other races."

(5) "That the Black man possesses the right to lease or occupy land in any part of South Africa."

(6) "That his children are entitled to the same education facilities as those enjoyed by the children of other races of the land."

Now, one fact needs to be emphasised, and that is that as White and Black live in juxtaposition in South Africa the one group depends upon the other; the Black man is dependent upon the brain and the organising ability and the resources of the White man, while the latter depends upon the brawn and the labour of the former. This interdependence between the two races rules out segregation as an impossible and impracticable proposition.

The best solution of the problem of race relations in South Africa as in any other country which is confronted with the same problem, lies in the fearless and courageous adoption of the formula: "Co-operation between the White and Black races in this country in the development of the material, mineral, agricultural and industrial resources of this vast country; co-operation in the governance of the land and in promoting the best interests of the country." There must be co-operation in the building up of a strong and virile manhood made up of the whole heterogeneous mass of racial groups or units of all colours, creeds, classes, conditions and cultures.

And with co-operation as the settled policy of the land we can proudly feel that

> All are architects of Fate
> Working in these walls of Time
> Some with massive deeds and
> Some with ornaments of rhyme.

Professor E. H. Brookes pointed out that the conference showed that in the Joint Council movement there is room for more than one school of thought; and that however conflicting the views, they can be expressed, provided they breathe the spirit of sincerity and sympathy as evinced at the conference.

The Press serves to mould and train public opinion and it is therefore of the utmost importance. Bantu papers are as a rule much more severe in their criticism of the Europeans than the European papers are of the Bantu. The Bantu not only read their own papers, but also those of the European Press. This fact involves a tremendous responsibility, which should be fully realised by all those connected with the Press.

The speaker stated that no European paper is propagating an anti-Native policy. With regard to the Bantu Press, it is only too frequent that sincere friends of the Natives are severely criticised. In all its aspects the Press is the most important influence on public opinion. Dr. Brookes concluded by paying a tribute to the high standard maintained by the South African Press with regard to the education of the South African public.

The Chairman in conclusion stated that "if the whole public of South Africa can be educated to view these questions in the same spirit of tolerance and open-mindedness as that shown here this evening, we need have no fears for the future."

The speakers were warmly thanked and the session closed at 9.50 p.m.

. . . .

I. Urban Areas Act and Municipal Native Administration

This Conference recognises the great efforts that have been made by many Municipalities and the Native Affairs Department to effect improvements in the conditions of Native life in towns since the passing of the Natives' (Urban Areas) Act. It believes, however, that there are still a great many directions in which improvements can and must be effected to make conditions more favourable to the proper development of individual, family and communal life. The Conference recognises that the difficulties vary in kind and size from centre to centre, but it is convinced that the experience already gained of the working of the Act has yielded results which can be helpfully reviewed.

Therefore the Conference puts forward the following proposals which cover amendments to the Act, as well as administrative changes, in the expectation that the proposals will receive the favourable consideration of the Government and of Municipalities.

As a guide to the interpretation of these proposals, it should be stated, the Conference is of opinion that the time has come when the existence of a permanent urban Native population must be frankly recognised. From this conclusion it follows that the administration of the Native townships must be directed towards decent conditions of individual and family life, and towards the creation of a civic pride and interest which will enable the Natives in due time to bear their share of the communal responsibility and to qualify them for the control of their own townships. The immediate possibilities in this direction vary according to the town, but everywhere there is the possibility of modifying the harsher operation of clauses of the Act which were drafted without due recognition of the existence of a permanent urban Native population.

The Conference feels that public attention should be specially directed towards the racial problems that are developing rapidly in all urban areas. In part these are due to the transition from tribal to urban conditions; but to a much greater extent they are due to the low wages earned by Natives, so that the wife as well as the husband must daily leave home and children in search of work. The children are thus left to grow up without parental control or supervision of any kind, because the Union Government makes no adequate provision for the education of the children, and because there are few opportunities for young boys and girls to obtain regular employment. The low-earning capacity of the urban Native is affecting the whole future of all sections of the community.

Further the Conference is of opinion that the local governments in Urban areas are being unfairly forced to attempt the solution of problems which can be satisfactorily settled only by the Union Government. The fact that many Natives are not temporary dwellers and that restrictive legislation cannot alter this position does not relieve the central Government of its major responsibilities. In this connection particular mention is made of the necessity for a proper system of education for Native children, the support of indigent Natives too old to work, and the great and increasing difficulty of unemployment.

Amendments To The Act

1. *Freehold*

In order to give security of tenure, provision should be made whereby Natives may hold land in freehold in the locations.

N.B. i. The Natives Urban Areas Bill as originally submitted to Parliament provided for ownership of lots in Native villages.

ii. Paragraph 503 of the Native Economic Commission Report recommends greater security of tenure.

iii. Special consideration may in this way be given to the needs of the advanced group of Natives.

2. *Criminal Proceedings*

At as early a date as possible, there should be an abolition of criminal proceedings for the recovery of rents and that for it there should be substituted an equally expeditious way of proceeding in the matter which shall be less costly than the present civil procedure.

N.B. At the present time Municipalities must choose between criminal procedure, which is cheap, but bears harshly on the Native, and civil procedure, which is milder in its action but adds considerably to the debt of the Native.

3. *Native Advisory Boards*

Section 10 of the Act dealing with Native Advisory Boards should be re-drafted in such a way as to provide: —

(a) That all members of the Advisory Boards shall be elected in accordance with regulations laid down by the Union Government and that elections shall be supervised by an official of the Union Government.

(b) That each Advisory Board may either elect a Chairman from its own members, or, subject to the approval of the Municipal Authority, nominate a European as a Chairman.

(c) That minutes of all meetings of the Advisory Board shall be properly and regularly kept and that copies of these minutes shall be regularly submitted to the Municipal Authority.

(d) That for voters there shall be a residential qualification of six months in a location or village established under the Act, and they shall be registered occupiers.

(e) That not less than once in every six months it shall be obligatory for the committee dealing with Native Affairs in a municipality to meet the Native Advisory Board or Boards for a full discussion of such matters as either the Committee or Board may place on the agenda.

(f) That the status and powers of the Advisory Boards shall be more clearly defined, and provision made for regular meetings of the Advisory Boards.

(g) Municipal employees shall not be eligible for membership of Advisory Boards.

Administrative Improvements

1. The normal rent basis in other countries for working-class housing schemes, which is not more than 20% of the worker's average wage plus the cost of services, should be taken into account when assessing rents for houses.

2. The services of Natives should be utilised in locations as far as is possible.

3. The Conference is convinced of the great importance of training a body of men and women of character in social service and Native Administration. It is convinced that the appointment of the right persons to such posts as deal with the administration of Urban Native Affairs is of far-reaching importance, and that much harm is done by the appointment of persons with no other qualifications than an alleged "knowledge of Natives." The Conference wishes that local authorities be advised of the importance of appointing persons of real knowledge and character to administrative posts.

In this connection it also recommends: —

(a) that location superintendents should be directly responsible to the councils which they serve and should have direct access to such councils or the appropriate committee.

(b) that the Minister of Native Affairs should exercise the greatest care in the issue of licences under Section eleven of the Act, to officers administering Urban Native Affairs.

(c) that the Minister should have no hesitation in withdrawing such licences where the officer concerned is proved to be unsuitable for the post.

4. The Minister should exercise the powers conferred upon him by Section 11 of the Act for the inspection of Native locations, and for the inspection of Native Revenue Accounts to restrict undue burdening with Corporation and other charges.

5. That, to replace the so-called "lodger's fee," standholders should be required to take out a licence and pay fees to be prescribed by the local authority for the right to sublet. For this purpose any *bona fide* dependent of the standholder and *bona fide* unmarried children should not be counted as sub-tenants.

Special Recommendations

1. This Conference urges the Government where Municipalities refuse to grant trading licences to Natives, to exercise its power of granting trading rights to Natives in Native Locations.

2. This Conference strongly recommends all Municipalities to support the Annual Conference of Advisory Boards.

VII. Special Resolutions

i. The Ban on Pathfinders.
ii. Native Bills.
iii. Justice.
iv. Bantu Studies in Universities and Schools.
v. Co-operation with Farmers' Associations.
vi. Wages on Railways.
vii. Tot System.
viii. Native Arts and Crafts.
ix. Fort Hare Students.
x. The Terms "Kafir" and "Native."
xi. Medical Training Facilities for Natives.

i. *The Ban on Pathfinders*

This Conference expresses its profound dissatisfaction and regret at the action of the Government in refusing to grant passports to the Pathfinders selected to attend the International Scout Jamboree in Hungary; and authorises the Conveners in the name of the Conference to take all possible steps to secure the removal of the Ban.

ii. *Native Bills*

In view of the magnitude and complexity of the subjects dealt with by the Prime Minister's Native Bills and the desirability of securing, so far as possible, the acceptability to every section affected of any decisions to be taken, and the proved success of the Conference method as a means for the fruitful exchange of opinion between Europeans and Bantu, this Conference requests the Government to give serious consideration to the possibility and advisability of summoning a special Consultative Conference on which the Bantu themselves shall be adequately represented, for the full consideration of the Bills before their final submission to Parliament.

iii. *Justice*

That the South African Institute of Race Relations be asked to organise an enquiry (through the organisations represented at this Conference) into the many complaints regarding the relations between Native accused persons, witnesses and members of the public

and the Police and Gaol authorities, and of injustice in the Courts, and to arrange for these matters to be considered by the next National European-Bantu Conference.

iv. *Bantu Studies in Universities and Schools*

This Conference

(i) records its appreciation of the work done in the Universities in the direction of the study of Bantu Life and Languages and problems of contact;

(ii) requests the Institute of Race Relations, in consultation with the Inter-University Committee on African Studies, the N.U.S.A.S., and other appropriate bodies, to consider the possibility of the fruitful extension of these studies both in the Universities and the Schools (both European and Non-European) and also in Public Service and Police Training, referring to it in this connection the proposals of the Bantu Studies Circle of the University of Stellenbosch laid before the Conference.

v. *Co-operation with Farmers' Associations*

This Conference commends to the attention of its rural members, European and Bantu, the desirability of encouraging wherever possible consultation between Bantu leaders and representatives of local Farmers' Associations and other Europeans with a view to co-operation on matters of common interest such as agricultural shows, improvement of Native Agriculture and Education.

vi. *Wages and Railways*

This Conference urges the Government to restore the cuts made in the wages of Native railway employees.

vii. *Tot System*

This Conference records its strong objection to any further extension of the Tot System to Natives.

viii. *Native Arts and Crafts*

This Conference is of opinion that the encouragement of Native arts and crafts and music should form a part of any programme of Native development; and welcomes the efforts of the Institute of Race Relations to give effect to this aspiration.

That this Conference warmly endorses the proposal put before the National Union of Students (as presented by student members to the Conference) that students of the South African Native College at Fort Hare be admitted to full membership of the Union.

x. *Terms "Kafir" and "Native"*

(1) In view of the widespread use of the word "Kafir" as a term of contempt, this Conference is of opinion that every step should be taken to eliminate its use especially in school text-books, and in the Press.

(2) The question of the most useful, accurate and generally acceptable term to describe Bantu-speaking South Africans should be carefully considered by the next National Conference.

xi. *Medical Training Facilities for Natives*

That this Conference urges upon the Union Government the necessity for providing immediate facilities for the full medical training of Native students in this country.

Non-Europeans Meet Together

DOCUMENT 44. Proceedings and Resolutions of the Non-European Conference, June 1927 [Extracts] (Published in *Minutes of the First Non-European Conference*)

Dr. ABDURAHMAN announced that the Subjects Committee had met, and that several resolutions were ready to be placed before Conference, and that a mover and seconder had been appointed for each. In the absence of Dr. Rubusana, he called upon Mr. Plaatje to move the first one.

Mr. SOL PLAATJE moved:—

"That this Conference, representing the Non-European organisations and communities in the Four Provinces of the Union and South-West Africa, assembled in the City Hall, Kimberley, on June 23rd, 1927, resolves that the interests of South Africa as a whole can best be served by—

(a) Closer co-operation among the non-European sections of South Africa, and

(b) Closer co-operation between Europeans and non-Europeans."

The mover said that the resolutions had been thoroughly threshed out by the Committee to which these matters had been entrusted. Some of them believed that they could fight their battles better single-handed, but he for one did not think so. The non-European was regarded more as a British object than a British subject (laughter), but they claimed the enjoyment of all the rights and privileges possessed by British people of every colour in all parts of the Empire. That being so, it was only natural that they should all co-operate. But before they could hope to co-operate with the European section, co-operation among non-whites must be the first essential. Real co-operation first among the several non-European organisations and also as between white and black, would be to the advantage of all.

Mr. I. P. JOSHUA (Kimberley) seconded. It seemed to him appropriate that two Kimberley men should sponsor this resolution, because co-operation had been a matter of practical politics in Kimberley for many years. In this city, non-Europeans had co-operated in all matters—political, social and industrial—and had achieved good results. Co-operation was one of the first principles which, put into practice, brought peace, harmony and union where before there had been discord. The Conference was called primarily to discuss and evolve methods of co-operation between non-Europeans. He had no doubt the resolution would be adopted and the principle put into operation forthwith. It was essential in every part of the Union that non-Europeans should co-operate. He felt the Conference would be a great success if the resolution alone was carried and the great principle brought into practice. It was most necessary in South Africa, a country where race prejudice was more rampant than anywhere else. That was the only solution.

Prof. D. D. T. JABAVU was anxious not to be misunderstood by the world outside. Their purposes were absolutely innocent. If politics were introduced, they would fly asunder at once. They needed greater mutual knowledge, greater respect for each other, and loyalty. They must have greater co-operation so that they could combine better with Europeans. They as black men had their own prejudices between race and race. Europeans also had their racial prejudices. They must combine, blot out all prejudices, present a solid front, and help each other to rise in education and in the great struggle for existence. They should help each other by organising and getting facilities for mutual improvement, foster that good spirit throughout the country, and thus give a lead to the so-called civilised communities.

Mr. ALEXANDER M. JABAVU (I.C.U., King Williamstown), in supporting, said that as an I.C.U. man he felt that one of their greatest dreams had been realised. The I.C.U. stood for the economic development of non-Europeans. He hoped their efforts would reach a successful end.

Mr. V. LAWRENCE (Natal) wished to make clear the position of the Indians. The presence of his Chairman and himself clearly proved that they were heartily in sympathy with the movement. He always held the view that the salvation of the non-Europeans lay in unity. Unless they combined they could not get what they wanted from Europeans. The Constitution of the S.A. Indian Congress, while preventing them from committing that body in any way, did not prevent their attendance at that Conference as it was composed. He wholeheartedly endorsed the views of the previous speakers. He felt that there was no one present who could not identify himself with the resolution.

Mr. B. MAKAPELA (African Native Congress, Kimberley) also spoke in support of the resolution.

Mr. J. T. GUMEDE (Vice-President, African Native Congress) followed the lines of previous speakers. He hoped they would all strive to make the Conference a success. They had no desire to drive the white man out of South Africa. They were against injustice and oppression. They were British subjects and were promised freedom, justice, liberty and fair play. With these four principles it was heaven, and without them hopeless. Their duty was to work peaceably and constitutionally for the welfare of their people in this country. They were not, as Mr. Plaatje suggested, British objects, but British subjects. They did not want promises, nor did they ask for concessions. The present Government had no concessions to give them. They simply wanted the four principles he had enumerated.

Rt. Rev. D. W. ALEXANDER (Bishop, African Orthodox Church) expressed great pleasure in addressing such a great assembly. When the Conference was first mooted, he said, it seemed an impossibility. He was sure the eyes of South Africa were on Kimberley today. Even its European citizens should feel proud that Kimberley had been selected as the place of that Conference. He referred to his approaching visit to America and to the questions likely to be asked him there about their position in South Africa. He felt proud that now he could tell them they had come together at last to put all their prejudices in one box and bury them. They wanted no concessions from the Government but their just rights, which were theirs as free men. They claimed to be just as good as the Europeans and wanted to steer their own ship, and could steer it clear of the rocks.

Mr. W. W. WALTHEW (Natal Welfare Association) felt that the gathering was a heaven-sent blessing to the coloured races in South Africa. He hoped when it was finished they would have bound themselves in one parcel. They knew they had differences of opinion and these differences were stirred up and magnified by outsiders. They came together in no opposition to Europeans, but it was their duty to protect their rights. When they were united in one body they would be given a hearing. If they did not combine different sections might get different offers, as was already evident.

Dr. W. B. RUBUSANA (East London Native Voters' Association) congratulated the previous speakers on ther moderation under very trying circumstances. If God Almighty were not moved by that meeting to help them, he did not know what would help.

Dr. A. ABDURAHMAN, in closing the debate, said the resolution brought to a head what had passed through the minds of every thinking non-European. Many of them had thought of it for years, others had openly striven for it. He was one of the latter. He wanted to thank the Conference for not uttering one word against those non-Europeans who had done their utmost to make the Conference a failure. The Government had done all in its power to wreck it, and at one time it seemed unlikely that a Conference would be held at all. He trusted nothing would be done at the Conference to keep away from next Conference those who had stayed away, but that everything would be done to welcome them when they did join them.

The resolution was put and carried, with great enthusiasm.

. . . .

Second Day—Morning Session.

Conference resumed Friday, 24th June, at 11 a.m., Dr. Abdurahman being in the Chair.

THE CHAIRMAN said that the first resolution to be proposed was contingent on the one passed yesterday.

Prof. D. D. T. JABAVU proposed:—

"That in order to give practical effect to the foregoing resolution, the Conference urges upon all non-European organisations and recognised communities to associate as far as possible in their respective districts, and to co-operate with one another in their respective districts on all local and national questions."

Mr. DOYLE MODIAGOTLA seconded, and asked who was to recognise these bodies. Government, Town Councils, and other local bodies might refuse recognition. It was absolutely necessary to delete the word "recognised."

BISHOP ALEXANDER supported. The word "recognised" had been so pushed down their throats that even when they themselves used it they misunderstood it. So long as they knew that someone as a non-European was doing something to uplift his brother, they should work with him.

Mr. DIPPA (Alexandria) agreed. The first object was to find ways and means to bring together all non-Europeans to exchange views in connection with matters affecting them as a people. When they used the word "recognised" they began to limit their scope. They

had to devise methods to establish a stronger organisation. They must find out who was going to recognise these people. They had no organisation and no constitution yet. The word "community" also had different interpretations and different meanings. A person not a member of any particular organisation would be ineligible to be a member of the Conference. They must try to bring all non-Europeans together, whether belonging to an organisation or not, so long as such were trying to foster that feeling which animated them that day.

Mr. MOTIYANA (Thabanchu) said the question was who was to recognise such a body, the people themselves or the community? He thought they should retain the word "recognised," but did not see any difficulty in deleting it.

Mr. ISMAIL (Cape Town) saw no difficulty in retaining the words. There were so many organisations amongst their people that he did not wish to see any more. They might have a few people coming together and refusing to recognise their work with existing organisations. He urged that they had come there to organise themselves, and their duty was to recognise existing organisations and help them. They could not recognise every small group of people who disagreed with others and formed new organisations. They should be urged to join existing organisations. That Conference represented the opinion of non-Europeans in South Africa; therefore why allow a loophole for a few disgruntled persons to form rival organisations.

Dr. ABDURAHMAN pointed out the difficulties they had experienced in drafting the resolution, and explained their object in drafting it as it stood. He explained the words "recognised" and "communities." They might pass it and see how it worked. It was not like the laws of the Medes and Persians, but could be altered from time to time as experience dictated.

The resolution was put and declared carried unanimously.

Prof. JABAVU (Alice) proposed:—

"That this Conference deeply deplores the unsympathetic attitude of the Legislature towards non-Europeans as expressed in some of the contemplated legislation, which has a

259

tendency also to divide, and urges the respective organisations to take whatever steps they deem necessary to prevent the continuance of such policy."

The mover said that one of the reasons for the resolution was that they had found to their cost during many a year that they had suffered much more than they would have done had they combined as they had done that day in that Conference. Their sufferings were not only amongst themselves but had been imposed from above. He strongly urged the acceptance of the resolution, believing that it would go a long way to bring about that solidarity they were all aiming at.

Mr. JAS. NGOJO (General Secretary, Cape African Congress, Cape Town) seconded.

The resolution was carried.

Mr. J. J. JOSHUA (Kimberley) proposed:—

"That this Conference views with alarm and misgiving the tendency of the Union Parliament, as evidenced by recent legislation and the general policy of the administration, to estrange the various sections of the non-European population of the Union. That this Conference realises that while such legislation and policy are detrimental to certain sections, no material advantage is brought to any. That Conference recognises no other policy but that of justice and equal opportunity to all sections of the population, and in this connection resolves to take effective steps to combat any policy of differentiation on the grounds of colour or race."

Mr. CHAMPION, in seconding, said that he prayed night and day that one day we should see all races in South Africa on a footing of absolute equality as regards education, the vote, economic conditions, titles and honours, and the right to sit in the House of Assembly and Senate on a par with Europeans. Many men and women were working very hard to bring that to pass.

One speaker objected to the last portion of the resolution. They did not ask for any favours but only for equality of opportunity with the Europeans of this country, who claimed to be superior races yet at every opportunity demanded a special artificial advantage over the Native. If they were really superior they should give non-Europeans the advantage. In support of that he instanced the

method of handicapping in horse races. The political practice was not in conformity with the sporting spirit. In politics and economics he would ask the Europeans to carry it a little further and not seize every advantage for themselves. They (the Europeans) had been doing an injustice to themselves and their children by giving themselves those advantages inasmuch as they were not in so doing building up a virile race. They might say that was what they were doing with them (the Coloured people), but in the long run the Natives would be the better race in that country. He wanted to encourage his people to organise. The Europeans had taken a mean advantage of them by handicapping them in every walk of life.

Mr. CHAMPION (who had been interrupted on a point of order) continued his remarks, and dealt with four points on which he claimed the non-European should have equal opportunities: Church, School, Politics and Economics. He thought if the Union Government were true and honest, Dr. Abdurahman should already have been given the title of "Sir." He wished to point out that he did not know the Doctor personally. The policy of the Government was to divide and rule. He believed in equal pay for all men, irrespective of colour. He prayed every night for equality of opportunity and equality of pay for work. To-day the Government was spending large sums on work for Europeans, and had striven hard to interfere with the success of that Conference. He referred to Dr. Molema of Mafeking, and hoped that one day he might represent them in Parliament.

Mr. J. A. SISHUBA (Queenstown) spoke feelingly and temperately in support of the resolution, and urged them to be moderate in their language.

Dr. RUBUSANA proposed to add after "equal opportunity" the words "and an open door," but found no seconder.

The resolution was put to the meeting and declared carried.

. . . .

Mr. B. MAKAPELA (Kimberley) moved: "That this Conference supports the considered condemnation and rejection of the Representation of Natives in Parliament Bill, as has been expressed in resolutions passed at the Government's and other Native conferences, and affirms that the only effective means of ensuring the harmonious co-operation of Bantu and European is by direct representation in the Union Parliament."

Chief S. F. ZIBI (Rustenburg, Transvaal) seconded. He represented no organisation, but a community. Those of the Northern Provinces who were voteless and who were supposed to benefit by the Bill, felt that it was wrong to deprive their fellow-men of the Cape of rights they at present possessed in order to help those in the North.

Mr. J. A. SISHUBA referred to the Bill providing for the repeal of Section 35 of the Act of Union. If once that section was repealed anything might happen. They must stubbornly oppose it.

Mr. J. T. GUMEDE (Natal) said they were now coming to the real business of the Conference. The Black man had never abused the vote he possessed. The Voortrekkers left the Cape because they did not want to be on an equality with the Blacks; and when they established their own Republics they laid it down in their constitution that the Black man should never get the vote.

Conference adjourned for ten minutes to be photographed.

On resumption the Chairman referred to the unauthorised distribution of literature in the Hall. A delegate explained satisfactorily.

Mr. CHAMPION moved as an amendment: "Non-representative Government Conference."

Mr. R. J. MAZOMBA (Phillipstown) asked for the meaning of the amendment.

Mr. CHAMPION said it referred to the action of the Government in organising opposition to that Conference.

Several points of order having been raised, Dr. RUBUSANA protested against the discussion being monopolised by a few members.

Mr. E. S. MAKALIMA (General Secretary, Bantu Union) agreed personally with the resolution, but thought it was a universal condemnation and rejection. His society had not opposed it and he wanted to know his duty.

Mr. A. K. SOGA (Transkei) supported the motion. For once he was in agreement with the irrepressible Champion of the I.C.U. He

hoped that these delegates of non-Europeans would see that delegates to the Government Conference were properly representative in future.

Dr. RUBUSANA moved as an amendment: "Passed at the Conference of Government nominees." He had heard so many speeches, and so many speakers referred to the Colour Bar. The white man did not understand what the Colour Bar was. What was a man's colour? An accident of birth. A black colour was of more value than a white. (A voice: "Yes, for funeral purposes.") Ask the Clergy why they invest in black. It was more presentable and more costly. If a man went to an evening function in any other than black he would be the laughing stock of all the guests.

THE CHAIRMAN asked delegates to keep to the point.

Mr. C. JULIUS (Pearston) complained that members of the Subjects Committee were taking up most of the time although they had already thoroughly threshed out the whole subject. He moved the question be now put.

Mr. DIPPA (Alexandria) supported Mr. Champion's amendment.

Dr. RUBUSANA'S amendment was also seconded.

Chief S. F. ZIBI (Rustenburg) said not all the people who attended the Government Conference were Government nominees. He was appointed constitutionally by the Chiefs of the Rustenburg District, and the amendment proposed to place a stigma on all of them.

The first amendment was lost, receiving little support.

The second amendment was lost by 16 votes to 20.

The resolution was then put and carried.

The Conference adjourned to give the Subjects Committee time to prepare a further agenda.

THE CHAIRMAN said they would now resolve into Committee.

THE CHAIRMAN asked Dr. Abdurahman to explain certain matters relative to their Asiatic friends.

Dr. ABDURAHMAN said it was at some risk that their Indian friends attended the Conference. They were there because their action might be misunderstood. They were in a very difficult and delicate position. If they themselves had regard to that feeling, no very strong resolutions affecting Indians would be passed that day. It must be understood that though they remained during the day, they had not voted on any resolutions that were adopted. He was satisfied the Conference had their support, but it would be awkward if, during the negotiations which would continue, Conference resolutions were thrown up against them. It was then recorded that they took no part in the Conference. He moved: "That the Indian delegates be relieved from responsibility from any part in the passing of the resolutions."

Dr. RUBUSANA seconded. They should not in any way compromise their Indian friends. They should not, in the absence of Mr. Sastri, do anything to compromise them. Agreed to.

THE CHAIRMAN said the Subjects Committee would now meet.

Conference adjourned to 8.30 p.m.

Second Day—Evening Session.

Conference resumed at 8.30 p.m., 24th June, 1927, Prof. D. D. Tengo Jabavu in the Chair.

Mr. C. A. F. CALVERT (Kimberley) proposed:—

"(a) That in view of the great contribution being made by Natives through their labour, to the wealth of this country, and the fact of their contributing largely also through indirect taxation, in common with other sections of the population, this Conference enters its emphatic protest against Act No. 41 of 1925, which imposes on Natives in the Cape Province for the first time a direct tax, and which also reaffirms the principle of direct taxation, a form of taxation which is considered in all civilised countries as oppressive and repressive.

"(b) In the event of the Government not accepting Resolution (a) above, this Conference respectfully urges the Government to so amend Act 41 of 1925 as to exempt from its operation—

(i) Natives over the age of sixty years;
(ii) Natives who already pay urban rates and taxes; and
(iii) Those who earn less than ten shillings per month."

The mover quoted numerous instances of hardship and unfairness due to the present system of taxation. It was impossible for persons earning the small wages which many Natives did, to pay such heavy taxes. If the Government must exact those unjust taxes, then the exemptions and reductions proposed were badly needed.

Mr. J. A. SISHUBA seconded, but thought it was a bit too moderate. However, he would take half a loaf rather than nothing.

Mr. P. K. MOTIYANE (Thabanchu) supported, but felt it was a mistake to urge that they should pay no taxes at all. That would be going a bit too far, and he felt it was a privilege and a duty for those who could afford it to pay taxes.

THE CHAIRMAN thought an explanation might save much oratory. The Committee had spent an hour debating the matter, and there were many good reasons for it. It was felt that Natives already paid heavily in indirect taxation through Customs, etc. Many people were suffering through this taxation.

Mr. J. D. NGOJO (Cape Town) was of opinion that the Poll Tax was illegal and only imposed on Natives. The Native man having paid income tax and indirect taxation, should appeal to the Government to repeal the Poll Tax.

Mr. MODIAKGOTLA took exception to the exemption of those who paid urban rates and taxes. It was very unmanly to run away from their brothers in rural areas who earned less than those in town did. He moved that sub-section (ii) be deleted, and he felt that the whole gathering would agree with him.

Mr. MAKALIMA spoke on the exemption of town Natives. They must keep their eyes wide open, as that was the way to develop a white man.

Mr. DIPPA said the Native people were already overburdened with taxation. The Poll Tax was doing great harm amongst them. He spoke of the hardships of labourers on farms in his area. The town Natives paid for many municipal services, while their average pay was £3 per month. They had to use trains and trams and buy postage stamps, etc.—all indirect taxation. The country Natives earned £6 a year, and the town Natives £50 to £60, and all had to pay the same Poll Tax. The proceeds of the tax were supposed to go into a Development Fund, but that had not been done yet. The tax had already been two years in existence, but the Government had not yet made up its mind what to do with the money.

Mr. DANIELS supported, but did not think the town Natives were in a worse position. When the Minister of Finance introduced the Poll Tax he hoped to collect £1,200,000, or £1,400,000 per annum. He put aside £300,000 for development, while £900,000 was spent on the white people. He argued that from figures given by Sir Ernest Oppenheimer it would appear the Natives paid more taxes than Europeans.

Mr. SOL PLAATJE said he did not intend to say anything about taxes, but the system was complicated and unfair. He once saw thirteen lions at the Zoo ten minutes before they were fed. When they got their food he thought he could defy any man to take the chunks of beef from their jaws. It was the same with the tax. Recognising that, they simply asked the Government to gobble the tax, but relieve three sections of Natives who were hard hit. It was never suggested that a man should be exempted because he lived in a town; but ratepayers should be relieved from double taxation—a town tax and location tax. Location Natives paid no rates, only taxes, but do not let one man pay town rates and location taxes also.

Chief ZIBI informed Mr. Daniels that town Natives did not pay the 30/ - Poll Tax. He pointed out that the rates paid in towns are not taxes. What townspeople paid in taxes helped to develop the country, and what they paid in rates helped to develop the towns. Town people were asking, in effect, that those in the country should be taxed to develop the country, but that they should not be so taxed. In fact, they wanted development to happen at others' expense, not theirs.

Mr. BEN MAKAPELA (Kimberley) supported.

Mr. A. F. PENDLA (Port Elizabeth) in supporting asked if Coloured people were liable for the Poll Tax.

Mr. DALY (Bloemfontein) had asked his Magistrate in the Free State, and was told that he did come under the tax as the old tax was repealed by new laws.

THE CHAIRMAN said he would now put the motion.

The first section was unanimously accepted. The amendment was then defeated, and the motion adopted as originally proposed.

Chief ZIBI moved: "That this Conference draws the attention of the Government to the fact that all those people who have made an impartial study of the Land Bill agree with the Natives that the distribution of land according to its schedules was hopelessly unfair to the Bantu people, especially in the Cape and O.F.S. Provinces, and attest that there can be no settlement of the Land question until there is a more equitable distribution of the areas. With regard to Chapter II. of the Bill, the Conference commends to the careful consideration of the Government the constructive proposals made by the Joint Council of Johannesburg in their Memorandum."

The mover, in an eloquent and amusing speech, said the Natives of the Orange Free State were practically given nothing, and the Transvaal Natives got very little. He asked them to accept the motion as it stood, in the interests of the Natives as a whole. In the Cape they gained nothing and lost much. In fact, it was officially stated that the Cape Natives got nothing under the Bill because there was nothing to give.

(At this stage the Chairman retired and Mr. Reagon took the Chair.)

Mr. SOGA, seconding, said he was pleased they had referred to the Joint Council, Johannesburg, in the resolution. They should co-operate with those in urban areas who were doing good work for Native welfare.

Mr. P. K. MOTIYANE (Thabanchu) said they in the O.F.S. would be debarred from crossing the border to buy land elsewhere. The Bill would also prevent them from buying an island farm among white people. It would be possible for white people to arrange not to sell farms, and thus prevent access to island Native farms. He referred to the Thabanchu scheme. In the O.F.S. twenty-three Native farms were "released" by the Bill to be bought by free competition between whites and Blacks. People went so far as to ask if those farms belonged to Government or to private owners. His Chief's farm was not released, and no Native would be able to buy it. In that manner they would lose about 17,000 morgen, which to-day they could buy.

Mr. MAPAKELA also spoke.

Mr. J. A. SISHUBA said many failed to grasp the meaning of the Land Act Amendment Bill. The Transvaal might gain something, but to-day in the Cape they had a free right to buy ground anywhere, so he could not quite follow the Chief's argument. The Bill was taking away the right of Natives in the Cape. It would prevent Natives buying land when they had got the money.

Mr. GUMEDE supported. The Bill was taking those Native areas and giving them to white people again. They wanted a fairer distribution of the land.

Mr. DIPPA also supported.

It being proposed that the question be now put, the resolution was carried unanimously.

Mr. SOL PLAATJE moved: "That this Conference protests against the Native Administration Bill because (a) it abolishes the Magna Charta right, the right of appeal to the law courts, (b) suppresses free speech, (c) confers unnecessarily wide powers on the Governor-General, and (d) abrogates the Hofmeyr Act and other existing exemption laws."

The mover said the question was a very serious one. It was a fact that no one there had travelled and written so much as the speaker had done in connection with the Land Act, and his experience was that the Bill was even more serious. They were no longer to be ruled or controlled by Parliament, but by the Governor-General. That in practice meant the Head of the Native Affairs Department. He quoted cases in Transvaal where the system had for years been in operation, where men were debarred from holding meetings and expelled from their homes. In some instances they appealed to the Judge, who held it was barbarous to prevent free citizens from holding meetings. Under the Bill such people would have no right of appeal. In fact, if the Bill became law, the police could march into that Hall and arrest the whole Conference under the sedition clause, because it was called without the permission of the Governor-General. It meant that gentlemen of the I.C.U. would no longer have the right to go about asking Natives to join their Organisation which was against the interests of employers.

Mr. A. M. JABAVU seconded, and spoke strongly in favour. He referred to a reported case where it was stated that the Natal Supreme Court was not suited for Natives. If a Native had said that, what a hullaballoo there would have been. The I.C.U. had appealed and taken cases to the Supreme Court lately, and one after another of Durban's bye-laws had been declared *ultra vires*. He did not know what the Natal High Court was like, but they could rely on the fairness of the Supreme Court throughout South Africa. There was great danger in the Sedition Clause of the Bill. If they could not meet and speak publicly they were going to meet privately, and what might then be done privately!

Mr. A. J. SISHUBA was sorry that the resolution made no reference to the title deeds that had been revoked. The Government wanted to remove Natives to where it liked and when it liked. It was like Satan rebuking sin. It incited whites against non-Europeans but prevented non-Europeans from meeting and speaking.

Mr. NGOJO (Cape Town) supported, but thought other grievances should be included.

Dr. A. ABDURAHMAN, M.P.C., thought it impossible for the Conference to deal with every grievance. They must read all these laws not in the light of how they might affect them that day, but how they might affect them 15 or 20 years hence. They must not blame the unhappy white man for his attitude in his endeavour to protect his future. The Native was clamouring for more land, the Coloured demanded more education. The white man saw what was ahead, and realized that in the near future he would have to surrender some of the rights he held at present, and would have to readjust himself. The battle for rights would be a long-drawn and strenuous one, but in the end truth would prevail.

The resolution was carried unanimously.

Dr. ABDURAHMAN moved: "That this Conference urges all the associations to take steps towards mutual economic improvement by starting businesses controlled by non-Europeans to provide labour for their people and to support existing business concerns organised by non-Europeans." The moving of this resolution ought to have been entrusted to one of the members of the I.C.U., who were more familiar with industrial and commercial enterprises. If it was true that a man's character was formed by the manner in which he earned his living, then their duty was to strive for opportunities to improve their economic status. They ought therefore to create conditions to enable their own men to become employers of labour. The vast majority of them—in fact, almost all of them—were still workers, and on the lowest scale. Of course there was no indignity in that. Nevertheless they should work along the lines of the resolution and create conditions which would enable some of the younger generation not only to make money but to give employment to their own people. The rivalry between black and white capitalists would be good for the worker, as the majority of the workers in this country would be black men. He hoped the black men would prove to be better employers of labour than some of the existing employers.

Mr. CALVERT seconded, and instanced what the A.P.O. had done in its building society, which had in its possession wealth which played an important part in modern industrial life. If they could form co-operative societies, they would be able to obtain the necessities of life cheaper, and could then see the amount of good that could be done by it in many walks of life. It would be one of the finest steps they could take to uplift the non-European in South Africa.

Mr. JOSHUA thought that was one of the best methods whereby they as a people could advance. The position they occupied socially and politically resulted from their economic position. Most of them possessed nothing in a material sense, and therefore they counted for nothing. The majority of Asiatics were a commercial people, and their superior position was due to their commercial position. They, the other parties to the Conference—Native and Coloured—must try to foster the commercial spirit in their people. A clever salesman need never starve. If one could only buy and sell he was all right. They should carry out the spirit of co-operation not only in politics but in business. If each put up £1 they could start at once. He dwelt at some length on the co-operative movement in England, its millions of members, enormous capital, gigantic turnover, scholarships for children, highest wages for employees, wholesale co-operation and co-operative farming. He asked them to study that subject, practise it, and preach it as a religion.

Mr. A. JABAVU felt that everything necessary had been said, but the Natives, his own people, needed a particular homily. If they were true to their convictions and carried out their aspirations, there would be no competition between European and non-European. The non-European was the chief buyer, and white people would be too clever not to recognise the weapon that fact would give. The Asiatics and white men who had come here had business acumen. If the Natives had shops and non-Europeans bought there, the movement would be an enormous success. They could buy safely from each other as they would not be afraid that the Native seller would be out to batten on them. Not one of these Sedition Bills or Native Bills would be there threatening them if they were economically strong and sound. He particularly addressed his own people, and asked them to take home the fact that co-operation had been decided upon.

Mr. SISHUBA, in supporting, suggested that a committee be appointed to decide on something constructive, otherwise the enthusiasm might die away.

Mr. S. P. AKENA (Middelburg Vigilance Association) thought that was the most important resolution of all. But for it he would not have known what to report on his return home. He supported the idea of a small committee to go into details. If nothing was done by the Conference but passing that resolution, it would be a great success.

Mr. W. T. McLEOD (Kimberley) testified to the enormous knowledge he, as a young man, had gained at that Conference. In Kimberley and Cape Town it was a common thing for a Coloured man to earn £25 to £30 per month, but they spent it as fast as they earned it. But what was to become of their children? Must they follow on the same lines? In this country the white Labourite was supposed to be their friend, but he was up against them. Men like Schlesinger had become fabulously wealthy through the tickeys and sixpences put up weekly by their people, yet such men put up advertisements, "100 per cent. White Labour." He spoke in praise of the A.P.O. Burial Society, which employs 30 to 40 whole-time men, and urged them to help it to greater success. He made some practical suggestions for the utilisation of the capital when raised.

Mr. DIPPA (Alexandria) detailed the experiment started in his small native town, and explained it for the benefit of those not having much money. Their nominal capital was £3,000. They got a farm in their name and on it employed 50 families. The Native owners in the company employed young men to cut wood for firewood, fencing poles, etc. They had now opened an office in New Brighton (P.E.) to sell firewood there at a good price. His point was that they should not say they could do nothing merely because they only £1 per week. His people were getting from nothing up to 10s. per month.

THE CHAIRMAN said the resolution was on the lines of the thrift movement on which they heard an address that afternoon. They must first get the money, and then they could find the channel in which to use it.

The resolution was carried unanimously.

The Chairman announced the programme for the 25th:—

9.15 a.m., Visit to Kimberley Mine, Mine Compound, and Mine Hospital, tram leaving Market Square at 9.15 sharp. 11 a.m., Conference meets; 8 p.m., Public Meeting.

Third Day—One Session.

Conference resumed at 11.45 a.m. on the 25th June, 1927. Prof. Jabavu in the Chair.

THE CHAIRMAN said he hoped that would be the final session of the Conference, but it could only be the last with the co-operation of those present, who should learn to curb their loquacity and not repeat what other speakers had said.

Mr. MOTINJANA (Thabanchu) proposed: "That this Conference is convinced from practical experience gained since 1913 that a policy of segregation, territorial, political, industrial and economic, based on colour or race, is detrimental to the best interests of South Africa as a whole," and added a few brief words of explanation.

Bp. ALEXANDER seconded formally.

Mr. G. J. KUSHWAYO (Sterkstroom) supported, saying he represented districts which did not understand the attitude of the Conference. They appreciated the resolutions, but were unable to understand how they were going to carry them out.

Mr. AKENA said that the Association he represented was not against the policy of segregation, but if segregation took place, perhaps it would not be bad if accompanied by an equable distribution of land. He concluded, however, by hoping that the Conference would agree with him against the policy of segregation.

Mr. NGOJO said the policy of segregation had failed industrially, territorially, and *in toto*.

Headman H. L. PHOOKO (Herschel) hoped Conference would vote and pass on to other business to save time.

The resolution was put and carried unanimously.

Dr. ABDURAHMAN moved: "That the civilised labour policy of the Government is cruel and unjust, because it has thrown out of work and impoverished large numbers of non-Europeans; it has closed many avenues of employment hitherto open to them, besides placing a heavy burden on the whole country in the form of additional taxation to subsidise the policy." The mover very briefly pointed out that the motion expressed not only the view of the Conference but expressed the opinion of Natives and non-Europeans in South Africa and of Europeans, not only in South Africa but outside of South Africa.

Mr. D. E. WESSELS (A.P.O., Claremont) seconded, saying that they all knew the disabilities under which they laboured, and little discussion was needed.

The resolution was carried unanimously.

BISHOP ALEXANDER moved: "That this Conference desires to enter its emphatic protest against the Colour Bar Act, because it was deliberately aimed at depriving, and does in fact deprive, certain sections of the community of their inherent right of earning an honest livelihood in accordance with the capacity with which Almighty God has endowed them, and thus driving them into poverty, misery and crime." The Colour Bar, he said, was against the dictates of the Master Builder of the Universe, and if one section legislated against another section, he was afraid that section was doomed.

Mr. A. F. PENDLA seconded.

Dr. RUBUSANA said that when Asquith in England found that a good many Members of Parliament would not vote for the Union Bill because of the Colour Bar in it, he (Asquith) said he had appealed to all four Prime Ministers, who gave him positive assurances. He (Dr. Rubusana) then said to some friends that Asquith did not know the unscrupulous Britisher and the Dutchmen of South Africa. He urged that the Colour Bar should not be inserted. Members of the House of Commons felt so angry that 150 would not vote for the Bill, saying that this clause was un-British. He must express these things very strongly. There was at least a tacit understanding between their representatives who went to England that this Colour Bar would not be enforced. They (South Africa) never acted on that understanding, but those members would not vote because they would not allow themselves to be made registering machines for the Union of South Africa.

A delegate interposed to correct Dr. Rubusana, and said that all white people were unjust.

Dr. ABDURAHMAN said that in the initial stages they could do no more than protest emphatically against unjust steps. They must be constitutional. Afterwards their friends might be able to devise better steps. They would not leave that question of the Colour Bar where it was. They could not sit still under it. It deliberately robbed men of the opportunity of earning a livelihood according to the capacity God Almighty gave them, and when they deprived a man of that opportunity, they murdered his wife and children, and were nothing less than cold-blooded murderers. After they had gone to war and shed their blood, they were deliberately deprived of political rights. The very men, the Germans, whom they had fought, were already allowed to sit in the S.W.A. Parliament and make laws for the Coloured men

who fought against them. It was wrong to say that the present Colour Bar was the second. The second was in 1925 in S.W.A. The present one was the third Colour Bar, but the first economic one. It ought to be the determination of every one of them to express himself and work against it until it was removed.

The resolution was put and carried unanimously.

Rev. JAS. A. CALATA (Non-European Association, Somerset East) proposed: "That the inadequate educational facilities provided for non-European children constitute the greatest factor in hampering the economic development of South Africa. This Conference therefore impresses upon the Government that there can be no satisfactory progress unless there is a substantial increase in the grants by the Government to the Provincial Councils."

Mr. DIPPA seconded.

Dr. RUBUSANA proposed to add at end: "under the Financial Relations Act." This was agreed to, and the resolution as amended carried unanimously.

DOCUMENT 45. Report on proceedings and resolutions of the Non-European Conference, in *The Cape Times,* January 4 and 6, 1930 [Extracts].

There was a stormy scene at the Non-European Conference in Cape Town yesterday following the chairman's decision to jettison a proposal for passive resistance to Mr. Pirow's Riotous Assemblies Amendment Bill, should it become law.

Out of two motions from the I. and C. Workers' Federation and the Coloured and Bantu People's Organisation at De Aar was compounded a resolution condemning the proposed legislation on the ground that it was repressive, perpetuated racial antagonism and differentiated between races industrially, politically and socially.

To this Mr. Brown (Cape Town) moved as a rider that there should be a demonstration at the opening of Parliament, and that a day should be set aside for mass protest meetings.

Moving the resolution, Mr. Schuba (I. and C. Federation) described the proposed legislation as "shameful."

267

"Foul Play."

"What is Pirow that he tries to muzzle the mouths of non-Europeans," asked Mr. Samuels (Cape Town), seconding. "It is not fair play. It is foul play.

"It only proves they lack the supremacy they boast about. If they do not fear non-Europeans why do they bring in this Bill?"

"If this Bill becomes law my organisation will disobey it," declared Mr. Raynard (Cape Town). "It is an attempt to crush the I.C.U. and the other native unions. The African National Congress have decided not to take any orders from Mr. Pirow or any police officer or magistrate if we wish to hold meetings to express our views.

"These men who are trying to crush us are the people who played the traitor and prayed to God to crush England. The time has come to ignore the Union Cabinet and carry on our own campaign."

In a similar vein Mr. Nolobe (Cape Town) described Mr. Pirow as "nothing more or less than a Minister of machine guns."

"If any man is afraid to go to gaol for his fellows," he said, "his place is outside this Conference."

Passive Resistance.

The Rev. Mtimkulu warned delegates that the proposal meant the beginning of the end; and thereafter non-Europeans would be voiceless.

Professor Theale (Cape Town) pleaded for some practical form of action to be taken.

Mr. de Norman advocated passive resistance to the Bill if it became law, and moved accordingly.

"Too long have we played with resolutions," he said. "The time has come for action. If we resisted they could not force us to pay the poll tax, for instance."

Mr. Rahim, an Indian delegate, was also doubtful of the value of resolutions.

A campaign of passive resistance was opposed by the Rev. C. B. Lipkuko (Kimberley).

"There is not a single man in South Africa who could make a success of passive resistance," said Dr. A. Abdurahman. "You must have a leader who is prepared to make sacrifices, such as Gandhi in India. We have not such a man.

"Passive resistance is a weapon that should be properly organised and prepared so that if and when the time comes we shall be ready and could then use it. It is quite possible this Bill will never come before Parliament at all."

"We have waited too long," declared Mr. de Norman. "We have been good boys too long, tools of political parties too long and passed resolutions too long. It is time to act."

There was a chorus of indignation when the Chairman, to whom the question whether the proposal for passive resistance was in order had been referred, announced that it would be held in abeyance. With uproar going on all the time, Mr. Brown withdrew his rider, and the original motion was put and agreed to.

The Chairman later intimated that to satisfy the Conference he was prepared to put the amendments again.

The result of this course was that an amendment requesting delegates to impress on their conventions the advisability of adopting passive resistance to the Bill, if passed, was agreed to.

Mr. de Norman's motion pledging delegates to a campaign of passive resistance was then defeated. The proposals for a demonstration at the opening of Parliament and for mass meetings were also lost, and the original motion was then agreed to.

There was an attempt to move a vote of no confidence in the Chairman, but the malcontent element was shouted down.

The Conference then discussed a resolution on the Native Bills, moved by Dr. A. Abdurahman and seconded by the Rev. Mahabane, to the effect that the Prime Minister should be asked to consider arranging a convention or round-table conference of the European and non-European leaders.

"This conference," added the resolution, "is convinced that the attempt to solve questions of race relationship by means of Select Committees has proved to be wholly unsatisfactory."

Mr. Gamiet denounced the Native Bills, and moved: "This conference strongly condemns any legislation based on colour or race, and requests the Government to scrap the Bills."

A further amendment, by Mr. Calvert, provided that, failing Government action, the non-European communities should convene a round-table conference themselves.

Dr. I. Abdurahman thought the Bills might be modified to some extent.

"But the natives and coloured people will be sold once again just as they were in 1909," he added. "Do not let them invite you behind closed doors."

Dr. A. Abdurahman, replying to the debate, said the amendments merely expressed what they had already affirmed, that they were totally opposed to the four Native Bills.

"Non-Europeans, alone cannot settle these problems," he said. "We have not all the brains or integrity amongst ourselves. There are just as idealistic and honourable men among the white people.

"It is only by co-operation with these men, by showing them at a conference where they are wrong, where they have been influenced by emotional prejudice to see the facts in wrong perspective, that you can show them they have founded their opinions not on facts, but on emotion, prejudice and sentiment. It is the only way.

"The Indians said, 'We want a round-table conference, because you misunderstand the position.' You will never attain your proper place by standing away and refusing to co-operate with the white man. The very best men, from the Prime Minister down, need education in our social and political questions."

The motion, with the amendments moved as addenda, was carried.

A motion dealing with the poll tax described the tax as "cruel and indefensible" and a source of grievous hardship to natives, and appealed for its abolition.

"The only remedy is to tell the Government that we refused to pay the tax," declared Mr. Ndobe (Cape Town). "Then Pirow can send out his machine guns."

Urging the same course of action, Dr. I. Abdurahman said innumerable abortive attempts had been made for the removal of the tax.

"The only way is by passive resistance," he said. "The duty of every delegate when he returns is to impress that upon his people. If you refuse to pay the poll tax what can the Government do? Can they put 7,000,000 men in prison?"

The motion was agreed to.

The view that the present economic position of non-Europeans would within a generation produce a "poor black menace" was expressed in a resolution dealing with industrial grievances. This pointed to racial differentiation on the railways and alleged that coloured and native workers were removed from employment to create political votes by giving jobs to "poor whites."

Industrialised and landless non-Europeans, urged the motion, were largely employed at a poverty rate of wages which, allied to repressive legislation, were destroying the non-European physically, spiritually and morally.

Mr. W. G. Ballinger, speaking, he said, at the wish of the I.C.U., said that in the Transvaal and the Free State conditions were 10 times worse than in the Cape.

"The majority of native workers in Johannesburg get less than £3 10s. a month," he said. "Out of that they have to pay £1 5s. for rent. A man with a wife and, say, three children, has only 17s. 6d. with which to carry on through the month. That is the poor black menace which is developing in South Africa."

The Conference adjourned until this morning, after passing a resolution urging the need for immediate legislation to provide for free education for all non-European children in the Union and compulsory education up to Standard VI. in all urban areas; extension of educational facilities to all non-European children in rural areas; sound professional training for non-European teachers and an increased and adequate Government subsidy for non-European education.

. . . .

The non-European Conference, which meets again at the City Hall this morning, is to be asked to make a "declaration of war against the Dutch Reformed Church," the following motion having been tabled by the Western Province African National Congress:

"Seeing that the Dutch Reformed Church in South Africa is instigating and abetting and conniving at the persecution of the non-European, this conference now calls for an emphatic 'declaration of war' against this church—it declares every predicant and missionary to be the mortal enemy of our people; calls upon every non-European to leave this unchristian church within a period of three months; instruct every non-European to boycott and ostracise any of their people who still remain in this Church after the aforesaid period; and will get into communication with chiefs and headmen in the Sudan, Nyasaland and all African territories where this church is carrying on missionary work, calling upon them to expel all missionaries and emissaries of this Church who are in their midst not to enlighten and evangelise them, but to enslave them."

Another resolution from the same source reads: "Seeing that both Nationalist and South African Parties are unreliable, and not to be trusted any further, as in the past they have co-operated and declared themselves willing further to co-operate to rob non-Europeans of their inherent and just rights as British subjects. This conference declares that the time has now arrived when non-Europeans should cease to vote to place Europeans in Parliament, and to instruct non-Europeans to refrain from voting or taking part in any general or by-election for the House of Assembly till such time as the Constitution is amended, so as to allow representation in Parliament by non-Europeans."

Another resolution seeks to have "a distinct policy laid down to be adopted towards all Europeans"; and the attention of the conference is drawn to "the question of wholesale drunkenness amongst non-Europeans" with a view to checking the evil.

Other motions strenuously oppose Mr. Pirow's "slavery" Bill and demand better housing and educational facilities.

. . . .

The non-European Conference, which concluded its sittings in Cape Town on Saturday, carried a resolution re-affirming its determination to strive for equal political franchise for all people of the Union, irrespective of colour, creed or sex, and calling on affiliated organisations to oppose by all constitutional means any movement designed to rob any section of the population of rights they at present enjoy, such as the Cape Native franchise, conferred when the Cape of Good Hope became a self-governing Colony.

"There is nothing to show how the franchise is to be extended to our brothers in the northern Provinces," said Mr. Brown, during the discussion.

Proceeding, after interruption, Mr. Brown observed that the Chairman "steam-rollered" everything.

"Chairman Insulted."

Dr. A. Abdurahman, intervening on a point of order, said: "This is the second time the chairman has been insulted. I call upon the speaker to withdraw those words or leave the conference."

After vainly trying to make himself heard amid cries of "Withdraw!" and general uproar, Mr. Brown withdrew the expression used.

The Chairman having invited him to make some suggestion as to what should be done in regard to equal political franchise, Mr. Brown said: "We should adopt the principles of the Communist Party." Cries of dissent prevented him from proceeding.

Mr. Champion said that some people evidently regarded the conference as an opportunity of demonstrating their ability to talk, but its object was mutual understanding of principles of co-operation.

As representative of the people of Natal, he said that they would not be prepared to assist the Government at the expense of their brethren in the Cape.

Sympathy With India.

Stating that India was divided on the question of absolute independence and Dominion status, the Rev. Z. R. Mahabane moved:

"That this conference desires to express its sincere sympathy with the people of India in their noble struggle for the application in their country of the democratic principle of self-determination, and to express the earnest hope that an amicable settlement of the grave crisis which faces that country may be arrived at."

Professor Theale, seconding the motion, which was carried, said they admired the noble efforts which had been made in India, by virtue of which her people were on the eve of real independence and the attainment of their aspirations.

The Rev. J. S. Likhing (Kimberley) referred to the shooting incident at Potchefstroom, and said that had the Europeans abstained from attendance nothing would have happened.

A motion was carried sympathising with the widow and family of Mr. Hermanus, who died from wounds as a result of the shooting.

It was not the first time that Potchefstroom had been the scene of activities of the "white hooligan," said Mr. Ismail (Cape British Indian Council). It was there that Mr. Sastri had suffered indignities at the hands of this class of whites. White hooligans with revolvers in their pockets were always ready to shoot down the non-Europeans.

The matter must be brought to the notice of the Government and the hooliganism stopped, or dire results would follow.

Forced Labour.

Attention was drawn by Mr. Ballinger to the fact that the representatives of the League of Nations, so far as South Africa was concerned, were there to represent merely the South African point of view, not the non-European point of view "You ought to be represented at the conference on forced labour," Mr. Ballinger continued.

It has been stated that there is no forced labour in South Africa. This may be relatively true if a comparison is made with conditions in the Congo. Nevertheless, there is forced labour, for instance, the Labour service contract. The diamond industry in Kimberley is supported by forced labour, 1,200 convicts taking diamonds from the ground.

"In the Pirow Bill," continued Mr. Ballinger, "we have the suggestion that convict labour should be put on farms. No convict labour should be employed where there is an unemployed black problem, as in Kimberley."

"Even if you do not get a representative of non-Europeans," Mr. Ballinger urged, "you are entitled to a number of advisers to be sent at Government expense."

Referring to a resolution introduced by Dr. I. Abdurahman at the previous sitting of the conference, Dr. A. A. Abdurahman moved:

"That this conference condemns Mr. Pirow's proposed legislation to amend the Transvaal and Natal law relating to Masters and Servants to amplify the Native Land Act of 1913 and to impose a tax on certain natives in the Transvaal and Natal who are not under contract service.

"We have no right to assume," said Dr. Abdurahman, "that this proposed legislation is merely an electioneering dodge. When responsible Ministers give to the world a draft of what they intend to introduce in Parliament, we must take their intimation in good faith. If they do it merely for electioneering purposes, they are doing incalculable harm.

"Nothing Less Than Slavery."

"If a native, in Natal or the Transvaal enters into a contract for longer than one month, it forces him to remain on a farm for three years at least. During that three years, he must give three months service to his master, and more if necessary. It may be he will be required to give six months of the year just at the season when he wants to plough the small portion of the land set apart for his own use. Then when he is free, the ploughing season is over, and he can get nothing from his own land.

"When that native breaks the law, he can be given five lashes. When a master breaks the law, he may be fined £10, but that is the maximum fine, and it would probably be only 10s. When the farm is sold, the native is sold with the farm and the cattle. He must obey the new master. Before he leaves that farm, he must produce a clearance certificate to show that he has served three years for which he was originally indentured.

"This is nothing less than slavery," continued Dr. Abdurahman.

"If a native elects to go somewhere else, he may go to a location, but if he is found outside the location, he may be fined £5 in addition to having to pay poll tax. In the Free State, according to Mr. Ghandi, if a native did not pay the poll tax because he had not the money, then he could be fined £5. If he did not pay the £5—and presumably if he could not pay £1 he could not pay £5— he could then be indentured at the rate of 5s. a month to a farmer until he had worked off the sum of £5.

"And here we have a similar thing," said Dr. Abdurahman, "because Mr. Pirow has said that the farmers want native labour, and convicts are going to be supplied. A native who does not want voluntary slavery, and does not want to go to the location, hires himself out to somebody else, and has to pay £5. If he cannot pay £5, Mr. Pirow fines him and lets him out to the people of the Transvaal for perhaps 1s. a day.

"Since we have had democratic institutions in the Cape Province, this is the most disgraceful thing that was ever proposed to be placed on the statute book. It is a great pity that those who want to go in for passive resistance are not natives; then they could be sent to the Free State."

"Manufacture Of Criminals."

The resolution was supported by the Rev. Mtimkulu, who quoted the opinion of one of his young men that "the Government, in the Masters and Servants Act, has given to the farmer a right that God had never given to any man, the right to hand over a man's soul to the keeping of someone else." The proposed legislation could only have the effect of manufacturing criminals.

"I have heard it said," said Mr. Mtimkulu, "that Magistrates sometimes ask: 'Do you think the white man can tell a lie?' Every white man, it seems, must be an angel in the eyes of the law. If the white man says the native is a bad man, that man must be a bad man for all time."

"Even the native's cattle would belong to the farmer," said Mr. Mtimkulu; "he can milk them; he can work them; his children and his wife belong to the white man. I myself have seen women with children on their backs taking bags of mealies and putting them into the trucks.

"This Masters and Servants Act would make natives into slaves without souls of their own."

An amendment was proposed by Mr. Brown:

"That, should the Government succeed in carrying this measure, we pledge ourselves to compromise with the resolutions as passed by the Communist Party's Conference recently held."

The amendment was not carried.

Dr. A. Abdurahman said they were faced with the alternative of slavery or indentured labour, a choice between two evils.

Mr. McLeod (Kimberley) said that passive resistance was all nonsense. When the father went to gaol, the wife and children starved. "We cannot support passive resistance."

An interruption was followed by shouts of "Order!"

"When the time comes for action, we must oppose this tooth and nail."

Scenes Of Disorder.

Amid scenes of excitement and disorder, Mr. Richards moved the closure, the chairman reminding the meeting that "this place is not a Chinaman's shop." The motion was carried.

The following was put as an unopposed motion by the Rev. Mtimkulu:

"That this Conference solemnly protests against the militaristic raid by a large police force made on a defenceless community at Durban in the early hours of the morning of November 14 at the command of the Minister of Justice (for the purpose of collecting poll tax) armed with tear gas bombs, fixed bayonets and a squadron of aeroplanes, as highhanded, cowardly and reprehensible, and unworthy of a civilised Government that poses as the guardian of a people not represented in the Parliament of the country.

"Nothing has undermined the prestige of white government in the eyes of nonEuropeans more than this savage and brutal action of the Government of this country," he said.

Mr. Brown suggested the addition of a "rider": "That, should such action recur, delegates pledge themselves to call upon organised labour to support a general strike." It, however, obtained no supporters.

Mr. Reagon proposed "that the Government be requested to suspend the operation of the Wage Act to permit of non-European skilled labourers building their own houses and that on farms where housing forms part of the wages, Government action be taken to ensure that decent accommodations be provided."

Mr. Reagon said housing for non-Europeans was of a low standard and rentals were excessive. The City Council had put up wood and iron houses for the very poor, but on account of the Wage Act £1 4s. a day had to be paid to the carpenters who were building houses for people who got 4s. a day to live on. A new utility company was going to build houses but, though the company was to receive a subsidy, it would be unable to provide houses for the very people who were most in need of them. What was needed was a subsidy in favour of houses, for the very poor. The country received the benefit of labour at a low rate which these people provided. They should be allowed to build houses for themselves from their earnings. That was the only way they could achieve an economic rent with wages so low.

"Government Action Needed."

"On farms the cattle are far better housed than the natives," said Mr. Reagon. "Government action is necessary."

The following resolution was adopted: This conference deplores the differentiation made in granting old age pensions. It requests the executive to petition the Government to include within the scope of the Old Age Pensions Act all non-Europeans over 65 years of age.

It was resolved to direct the attention of the Minister of Railways to the excessive overcrowding and the inadequate and inferior accommodation provided for non-European passengers in the railway coaches and in waiting rooms on railway stations.

It also protested against the "inadequate transport facilities provided by municipalities such as Johannesburg and Pretoria," and asked that an inquiry be held into the method of administering native affairs in many towns in the Union.

Equal Rights

Another motion submitted was: That this conference instructs its executive to circularise all party headquarters and Ms.L.A., asking them for definite replies to questionnaire which shall embody an undertaking on the part of political party candidates to support legislation granting to non-Europeans the rights embodied in the old Cape Constitution of Equal Rights. In the event of unsatisfactory replies, the conference instructs its executive to collaborate with suitable representatives in constituencies where there is a non-European vote, with a view to instituting a campaign of educational propaganda to refuse to support candidates who despise the call of the non-European and the general policy of this conference.

As an amendment it was moved that, failing to get favourable replies, the conference in conjunction with other organisations, put up candidates in certain constituencies; also in Provincial and Municipal elections; further, that at the next Provincial election as many non-Europeans as possible be nominated to contest, and in the event of more than one candidate being nominated, a non-European meeting be called to elect a nominee.

The amendment was carried, and the resolution, modified, adopted.

DOCUMENT 46. Proceedings and Resolutions of the Non-European Conference, January 1931 [Extracts] (Published in *Minutes of the Third Non-European Conference*)

Minutes.

Monday, 5th January, 1931, 10.30 a.m. Delegates gathered for Registration [at Bloemfontein].

2.30 p.m. Conference was officially opened with the singing of *Nkosi Sikelel' i-Afrika* and a prayer by the Rev. Z. Mahabane. In the absence of the Mayor, the Chairman, Professor Jabavu, called upon Dr. Abdurahman to officially open the Conference.

Dr. Abdurahman began by saying that the aim of the Conference was to promote the spirit of co-operation between non-Europeans and Europeans and thus help to solve the perplexing problem of the relationship between Black and White.

He reviewed briefly the position of the non-Europeans and touched on what he called the iniquitous *Colour Bar Act; Pirow's Riotous Assemblys Act*, which was designed to stifle free speech and under which a Native could be imprisoned for presuming to do what every member of the present Government had done and was doing; *The Civilised Labour Policy*, which had driven thousands into starvation; *The Poll Tax Law* by which the Government was taxing Natives to educate White children, and the *Native Service Contract Bill*, which was designed to keep the Natives as slaves on White farms.

Small wonder, then, said the Doctor, that White and Black were drifting further and further apart, and that non-Europeans were showing hostility towards Europeans.

The non-European Conference was endeavouring to point out the errors in the White Man's Rule and thus prevent disaster to the country. That could be done by co-operation.

During the present depression, South Africa should be reminded that it was depending upon the Gold and Coal mines which could not be worked without Native Labour. It was the Native that was carrying the whole of South Africa on his back.

A vote of thanks was proposed by S. M. Bennett Ncwana and seconded by Mr. W. McLeod.

Mr. Ballinger advised Conference to concentrate on the necessity of unity among the non-Europeans. Secondly, the non-Europeans should not look overseas as the British Empire ceased to exist in 1914. Thirdly, no emancipation of the Black people would ever be obtained by going to the Law Courts. Fourthly, the Cape Vote has lost its power since the Women Enfranchisement Act. Fifthly, non-Europeans must not introduce racial issues in their organisations as these would bar progress.

Conference adjourned until 4 p.m. for tea and at 4.30 p.m. Conference resumed, with Professor Jabavu in the Chair.

Mr. Kadalie questioned the status of the Conference. Dr. Abdurahman replied that there was a Draft Constitution but in view of the amount of business before the Conference, they thought it wise to defer the discussion of the Constitution and get on with the business.

Resolutions.

"In view of the fact that General Hertzog has definitely expressed his opinion in England on the non-European problem outside South Africa, and as he has urged the Imperial Government to shape its future African Policy so as to harmonise with that of the present Union Government, and as the latter's policy is based on the principle of no equality in Church or State between Black and White, this Conference considers that the time has arrived to send a deputation to England to place before the British Government and the British people a full statement of its views on the matter of equal rights and the status of non-European citizens in the British Empire."

Dr. Abdurahman moved and was seconded by the Rev. Z. Mahabane.

Dr. Abdurahman said that he was fully aware of the fact that England would not intervene in South African domestic affairs, but in view of the fact that General Hertzog—whose South African Native Policy had not met approval but had rather received condemnation by the world outside—had asked the Imperial Government to shape their African Native Policy to harmonise with his policy, he felt that there was need on the part of the non-Europeans to educate public opinion overseas by submitting a full statement of the position of non-Europeans in South Africa, and acquaint England and Europe with what was happening in South Africa under the policy advocated by General Hertzog.

The Rev. Z. Mahabane added that there was already a proposal to incorporate Native Territories such as Basutoland and Swaziland into the Union against the wishes of the inhabitants of these Territories and that the deputation would also help those people.

The following spoke in favour:—Messrs. Bennet Ncwana (Molteno), Kadalie (Johannesburg), Sesedi (Hopetown), Sishuba (Queenstown), Calvert (Kimberley), and Professor Jabavu.

Professor Jabavu stated that there was at the present time a group of men in London who were watching with great interest the trend of legislation in this country and who would be glad to get a mandate from the non-Europeans of South Africa. He said people in England did realise that the British Principle of Equal Rights was at stake in South Africa, they were wondering what the non-Europeans were doing in refuting General Hertzog's statements. He knew Mr. MacDonald, the British Prime Minister, would receive the deputation for he was sympathetic.

Mr. Keable Mote of the I.C.U. opposed the resolution on the following grounds:—

1. South Africa had obtained sovereign independence and no deputation from Natives would receive official recognition.

2. At the present time the Natives were very poor and the money collected for the purpose of sending a deputation to England would be wasted.

3. That there were other means of informing the Public.

(a) Through the Press.

(b) By obtaining an international adviser in London.

(c) The South African Bishops had already expressed the non-European view of the situation.

Mr. Mancoe (Heilbron) and Mr. Matseke (Pretoria) supported the opposition.

Mr. Ballinger suggested that the Deputation might arrange for a platform in the Lobby of the House of Commons, of all parties of the British Parliament and afterwards approach the League of Nations at Geneva with a view to obtaining international advice on the situation.

The motion was put to the vote and carried with only two dissentients.

Mr. Champion moved and it was unanimously adopted:—

"That a Committee be appointed to devise ways and means of raising the necessary funds for the deputation." The following were then elected the committee:

Dr. A. Abdurahman, Professor Jabavu, Messrs. Kadalie, Champion, Selope Thema, Rev. Z. R. Mahabane.

Conference adjourned at 5.30 p.m.

Tuesday, 6th January, 1931. Conference resumed at 9.30 a.m.

The Convener, Dr. Abdurahman, read a telegram from the President of the Malay Association of Cape Town, in which he expressed regret at being unable to attend Conference and wished it success. He further welcomed Dr. Rubusana, who had arrived that morning.

The Chairman, Professor Jabavu, proceeded to business.

Resolution 9.

Mr. Kadalie moved, seconded by Mr. Sishuba:—

(a) That the constitutional relations between His Majesty's British Government and His Majesty's Dominion of South Africa, should be retained and further that the British judicial committee of his Majesty's Privy Council shall be retained as constituted and that it shall exercise its functions of supervising the Empire Laws.

(b) That His Majesty the King shall not abandon his right of veto under the advice of his Majesty's Privy Council or his British Ministers.

(c) That His Majesty will not accede to any petition from the Dominion of South Africa to secede from the British Empire.

(d) That His Majesty should call for a referendum of his Majesty's subjects of the Union of South Africa, irrespective of race or colour, before any decision is reached concerning Secession.

Mr. Matseke (Pretoria) objected to (a) and (c). He said the Privy Council had South African representatives in General Smuts and Dr. Malan and could not give an impartial judgment.

Mr. Mote opposed the resolution. He asked where was the King's veto when the iniquitous Land Act was passed.

Mr. Champion opposed the resolution and asked for its withdrawal.

Mr. Elias also opposed.

Rev. J. Calata gave the history of the Native Policy in the Cape and the Native Policy of the North showing thereby that the Cape Policy was British and under it the Natives enjoyed great privileges such as the

Franchise and ownership of land, but since Union the tendency of the Government has been to introduce into the Cape the policy of the North, which he called the policy of the sjambok, until to-day we are faced with such Bills as the Masters' and Servants' Contract Bill. He therefore appealed to all the non-Europeans to support the Native Policy of the Cape which would be more or less a British Policy.

Dr. Abdurahman spoke in favour of the Resolution.

Dr. Rubusana speaking in favour said that the King of England was a Constitutional Monarch. As far as he remembered the King's veto has never been asked for except only once. The British Government may have its faults but it is the most humane Government he had ever known.

Mr. Selope Thema spoke in favour saying that under the British Policy there is room for growth, even the Dutch people had grown under it to what they were to-day. We can only have peace in this country under the British Government.

Mr. Sesedi asked for the Resolution to be withdrawn in view of the Prime Minister's change of front.

Mr. McLeod spoke in favour and reminded the Conference of what Queen Victoria had done for the non-Europeans.

Mr. Kadalie withdrew as mover and Rev. J. Calata moved the resolution. A vote was taken and the resolution was carried by 33 to 13.

Conference adjourned for tea at 11 a.m. and at 11.45 a.m. Conference resumed.

Mr. Mahabane moved Resolution 2 on the Agenda:—

"That Conference re-affirms its condemnation of the Native Bills, and the Coloured Persons' Rights Bill, and earnestly requests the Government to summon a round-table conference of accredited leaders of the European race on the one hand and of non-Europeans on the other, to discuss the political relationship of White and non-White in South Africa."

Mr. J. B. Crutse (Kroonstad) seconded.

The mover said that for the last five years the subject contained in these Bills had been engaging the attention of the country but no resolution had been arrived at yet. The Government had used very strenuous efforts to get the bills through but without avail. Select Committees do not serve any useful purpose as they do not give the opportunity of exchanging views.

The non-Europeans form an integral part of the political system in the Union. Indians had claimed a Round-table Conference and had got it. Franchise rights had been extended to the European women, and we were still left outside.

As the original motion had been passed last year Mr. Mahabane asked leave to read it again. He concluded by saying that he saw no grounds for the Europeans to fear the Bantu in this country.

Dr. Abdurahman at this stage read the correspondence he had had with the Prime Minister over the resolutions of previous Conferences and the Round-table Conference. The Prime Minister was reluctant to give an opinion or would not give it. He had refused to meet a deputation and said that the Bills referred to had been already in the hands of the Select Committee.

Dr. Abdurahman in speaking to the motion stressed the importance of the principle of co-operation between Europeans and non-European. He said that he did not believe in Select Committees, as they were not only useless but dangerous; no one claimed responsibility for any Bill after the Select Committee. He would rather see General Hertzog proceed with his Bills, and accept the responsibility for them. He had instructed the A.P.O. not to give evidence before a Select Committee.

"Fancy the Parliament of a civilised country doing such a low and mean thing as actually dragging their women folk and giving them the franchise for the purpose of robbing the Native of his vote," said the Doctor in conclusion.

Mr. Kadalie moved that the Resolution be put, a vote was taken and the resolution carried unanimously.

The next motion was No. 1 on the Agenda, moved by Dr. Abdurahman.

"This Conference is of opinion that the present depression in South Africa is to some extent due to the underpayment of non-European labourers, and that its economic position will never be placed on a sound footing unless there is a fairer distribution of the wealth of this country, which would increase the spending power of non-Europeans.'

Dr. Abdurahman said that it was generally stated by economists that the distribution of wealth was amongst a few and the only way to save the world from depression lay in the workers receiving better pay. Common sense tells us that if the Native and Coloured workers were paid more the secondary industries in which Europeans were employed would be kept going.

Mr. Mancoe, in seconding said:—"We have been getting a deaf ear from the Government. If the capitalists or employers of labour will not listen to us, we should organise a revolution."

Mr. Calvert (Kimberley) said that this matter touched at the root of our economic position. All organisations should unite and decide what further steps to take. He asked Mr. Ballinger to explain the attitude of the New Independent Labour Party in the Cape, toward this problem.

Mr. Elias objected to Mr. Ballinger being allowed to participate in a non-European Conference. The Chairman stated that Mr. Ballinger had the permission of the Conference.

Mr. Ballinger observed at this stage, that in order to arrive at a system of higher wages, educational methods of approach, involving the study of co-operation, production and exchange would need to be used; it would be the duty of the more cultured Natives to teach their less cultured brothers.

Referring to the new Independent Labour Party in the Cape, he stated that if its tenets were based on those of the Independent Labour Party in Britain, it would be able to help the non-Europeans to a great extent. In aiming at their object of higher wages they would meet with much difficulty, especially from the other Labour Party in the Union, which observed a Colour Bar. That was why he (Mr. Ballinger) could have no position in the Labour Parties of South Africa.

He further observed that the production per head in South Africa was lower than in any other country.

Dr. Abdurahman supported by Rev. J.

Calata, who thought that the solution lay in following Mr. Ballinger's suggestions, and advised the substitution of the word "non-European" for the word "Unskilled," but Conference did not accept the amendment and the original motion was carried. Conference adjourned at 1 p.m. and at 2.45 p.m. Conference resumed.

The Deputation Committee presented the following report.

"The Committee, consisting of the Rev. Z.R. Mahabane, Dr. A. Abdurahman, M.P.C., Professor D. D. T. Jabavu, Messrs. R. V. Selope-Thema, Clements Kadalie and A. W. Champion has given careful consideration to the subject of the proposed Deputation and recommends that:—

1. The Delegation consist of not more than five men.

2. The Conference appoint the present committee as a Selection Committee whose duty it shall be to receive nominations from Organisations which have taken part in this non-European Conference, as also from other accredited Organisations.

3. Each Organisation should submit not more than five names from which the final selection shall be made by the Selection Committee.

4. The nominations from the Organisations should reach the Selection Committee not later than 15th March, 1931.

5. The Delegates should be under the charge of a Manager who should be responsible for the financial affairs of the delegation on business lines and should appoint its own leader.

6. The Selection Committee should also be entrusted with the duty of collecting and collating information and data for the use of the Delegates.

7. The Committee estimates that the cost of the delegation will be approximately £1000, which should cover the cost of transportation, subsistence and other expenses incidental to the project.

8. The Committee further ventures to recommend that the Deputation shall place the non-European point of view in South Africa before the people of Europe, endeavour to secure a non-party meeting of British Members of the House of Commons, place the

facts before the Minorities Commission of the League of Nations at Geneva, and further endeavour to present a verbal and written statement of the non-European point of view before the fifty Government representatives who will assemble at Geneva during September 1931. The Deputation should also address public meetings, arrange interviews and so forth in Europe.

After Mr. Keable Mote, Mr. Maqolo (Transkei) and Mr. Ngogodo had spoken the debate was adjourned in order to have typed copies of recommendations to distribute among the delegates of the Conference.

The Conference proceeded with Resolutions 3, 10, and 11 on the Agenda:—

3. "That this Conference is convinced that any legislation based on the principle of differentiation on the grounds of race, colour or creed, will in the end prove disastrous to our country."

10. "That the Civilised Labour Policy of the Government is cruel and unjust because it has thrown out of work and impoverished large numbers of non-Europeans; it has closed many avenues of employment hitherto open to them besides placing a heavy burden on the whole country in the form of additional taxation to subsidise the Policy."

11. "That this Conference desires to enter its emphatic protest against the Colour Bar Act because it was deliberately aimed at depriving, and does in fact deprive, certain sections of the community of their inherent right of earning an honest livelihood in accordance with the capacity with which Almighty God has endowed them and thus driving them into poverty, misery and crime."

Mr. Kadalie in seconding moved an addition of the words "Conference asks for immediate repeal of this Act" to 11.

Mr. Sesedi supported the original resolution as it was.

Mr. Champion wanted to know if the Colour Bar Act was in operation. The answer being in the negative, he moved the deletion of the Clause.

Rev. Mr. Calata seconded on the grounds that it was due to many protests from all sections that the Colour Bar Act regulations had not yet been drawn.

Mr. Mapikela favoured all three going through together.

The three Resolutions were carried. Conference adjourned for tea at 4.30 p.m. and at 5. p.m. Conference resumed.

Dr. Abdurahman asked leave of Conference to move a Motion that was not on the Agenda, a Motion of Unity, and got leave to move it in the evening session of the day.

Resolution 6 on the Agenda was moved by the Rev. J. A. Calata of Cradock:—

"This Conference expresses its appreciation of the attitude adopted by the South African Bishops in opposing strenuously the African Policy as outlined by General Hertzog in his speeches in London."

Before the mover could speak there were many cries of "unopposed" from various members of the Conference. The motion was therefore adopted as an unopposed motion.

Resolution 7 on the Agenda was then taken.

"This Conference records its emphatic protest against the Native Servants Contract Bill which is tantamount to the introduction of forced labour in South Africa, and is designed to keep the Natives as helots on the White farms."

Moved by the Rev. Z. R. Mahabane and seconded by Mr. Elias.

Rev. Mahabane described the infliction of corporal punishment on an elderly man as preposterous. Mr. Selope Thema quoted the Minister of Justice as saying that illegal flogging was going on in farms and he was legalising it to prevent it being done illegally. He said that we were now reverting to the old days when every farmer in the Transvaal was a law unto himself.

Mr. Matseke supported the motion.

Dr. Abdurahman asserted that Mr. Pirow was meeting with the demands of the people in the Transvaal, where an attempt had been made to introduce forced labour some time ago.

There was one provision in particular in the Bill, however, at which no decent man could but feel disgusted:— This was that which compelled the Native to sign a three years' contract when he became a farm labourer whether he liked it or not. As a result of this a farm became valuable as it possessed an assured source of labour; the Natives passed on to a new owner with the rest of the goods and chattels. In fact these human beings were sold like stock, without regard to whether they wished to serve the new owner or not.

Continuing, Dr. Abdurahman observed that he could not think of a human being conceiving anything more wicked. It looked like the work of the devil, not of a man, said Dr. Abdurahman. He would rather see a Native leave a farm in such circumstances than that he be forced into slavery. When one combined this Bill with the Tot System Bill one could rightly say that Mr. Pirow was once more introducing the "Dop and Strop Acts in the Land."

The Motion was carried unanimously.

. . . .

At this stage Mr. Kadalie moved the following resolution as additional to Resolution 1, which had been passed earlier:—

"This Conference of non-Europeans of South Africa welcomes the appointment of the Native Economic Commission and hopes that the Commission will thoroughly investigate the economic position of the non-Europeans with a view of fixing a generous minimum wage throughout the Union."

Rev. J. Calata seconded, and carried unanimously.

Then Mr. Ncwana moved:—

"That in view of the present depression in South Africa as affecting the non-European labourers, the Government should consider the immediate necessity of placing the previous economic conditions on a sound footing by increasing the spending-power of the non-European peoples commensurately with the cost of living."

Carried unanimously.

The Unity Resolution

Dr. Abdurahman moved the following resolution:—

"That as the want of unity was the greatest stumbling block to the improvement of non-European conditions in the Union of South Africa, this Congress resolves:—

(a) That the various non-European industrial and political organisations should unite and present demands for the improvement of non-European conditions in the Union on economic, social and political lines to Conferences of Employers and the Government.

(b) That there should be one Organisation with supervisory headquarters in Johannesburg, to exercise decentralised financial and administration control at central towns in the four provinces.

(c) That the details of organisation should be left to a co-ordinating Committee, with instructions to work out details of a plan whereby monthly payment of fees shall be made by members."

Rev. J. A. Calata seconded.

Dr. Abdurahman said that unity was the first and primary essential to controlling power, they must first put their house in order before they could improve conditions. The time had arrived, in fact the rank and file were demanding that they should pool their brains and resources, unite the multifarious non-European Organisations into one powerful body and direct and guide the enormous power that lay in the non-European workers.

There was too much stomping about the country and making grandiose speeches at the expense of the stupid man, who was the man who should be helped, but who was not in the least benefited.

The power that could spring from unity was a power that could not be withstood by any Government in this country. It was for them to get hold of that power and use it properly.

Mr. Clements Kadalie, leader in the independent I.C.U., suspected the resolution to be influenced by Mr. Ballinger and stated that it was interfering with the objects of the I.C.U. He said that the Conveners of the Congress had deceived the country. Instead of discussing unity they were discussing trade-unionism and the Conference was not competent for that. The voice of the Conveners was the voice of Jacob but their hand was the hand of Esau.

He was strongly in favour of unity and to confine the Conference to the purpose for which it had been convened, moved:-

"This third annual non-European Conference re-affirms the draft constitution adopted last year with reference to the constituent Associations of Bantu, Coloured and Indian Organisations of South Africa, it hereby resolves that the time is opportune to form such an Organisation to be known as "All Non-European Federal Council of South Africa," all existing Organisations shall be affiliated to such body and the affiliated bodies to pay a capitation fee to the Council."

Mr. Bennett Ncwana in seconding the amendment made a plea for unity among non-Europeans from the Cape to Cairo.

Mr. Richards asked Dr. Abdurahman to withdraw his motion.

Mr. S. Reagon, M.P.C. (Cape Town) in appealing for the withdrawal of both motions said that the time was not opportune for union as proposed in the motions.

There were many difficulties to overcome and the preamble of Mr. Kadalie's amendment was incorrect as there was no draft constitution as yet. He advocated that they should continue with the non-European Conference so as to understand and trust one another better and gradually develop to the point with mutual enthusiasm.

Dr. Abdurahman withdrew his resolution.

Mr. Champion, leader of the I.C.U. Yase Natal, vehemently denounced Mr. Ballinger as the source of suspicion at the Congress, and in support of Mr. Kadalie said that they simply could not trust him. (There were many cries of dissent from the Conference.)

Mr. Champion proceeding put the blame of the disintegration of the I.C.U. to Mr. Ballinger's interference. As long as Mr. Ballinger attended these Congresses there would always be trouble.

The Conference became disorderly, many members resented the attitude taken up by the leaders of the I.C.U. in dragging the quarrelsome issues into the Conference.

At last Dr. Rubusana appealed to Mr. Kadalie to withdraw his motion as it was a mis-statement of facts.

The resolution was ruled out of order because of its preamble and finally withdrawn.

Then Resolution 4 on the Agenda was taken:—

"That in view of the great contribution being made by the Natives through their labour, to the wealth of this country, and the fact of their contributing largely also through indirect taxation, in common with other sections of the community, this Conference enters its emphatic protest against Act No. 41 of 1925, which imposes on Natives in the Cape Province for the first time a direct tax and which also re-affirms the principle of direct taxation, a form of taxation which is considered in all civilised countries as oppressive and repressive."

"In the event of the Government not accepting Resolution above, this Conference respectfully urges the Government to amend Act 41 of 1925, as to exempt from its operation:—

1. Natives over the age of sixty years.

2. Natives who already pay urban rates and taxes.

3. Those who earn less than 10s. per month.

Moved by Mr. Richards, seconded by Mr. Reagon, the following took part in the discussion, Messrs. Sishuba, Mancoe and Mapikela.

Rev. J. A. Calata moved the following amendment:—

"That in view of the great contribution being made by Natives through their labour, to the wealth of this country, and to the fact of their contribution largely also through indirect taxation, in common with other sections of the population, this Conference enters its emphatic protest against Act No. 41 of 1925 which re-affirms the principle of direct poll tax, a form of taxation which is considered in all civilised countries as oppressive and repressive, and asks for its repeal."

The amendment was unanimously carried.

The Unity Resolution.

After a caucus between Messrs. Kadalie, Champion, Dr. Abdurahman and Rev. Z. R. Mahabane a compromise was arrived at which was moved by the Rev. Mahabane and seconded by Mr. Richards:—

"That this third non-European Conference hereby approves of the urgent necessity of establishing a central body of the constituent Associations of Bantu, Coloured and Indian Organisations of South Africa and resolves that the time is opportune to form such an Organisation to be known as the 'All Non-European Federal Council of South Africa' and that the draft constitution be circulated and adopted at the next Conference, unless amendments are received by the Convener before the end of June 1931."

Mr. Reagon moved the deletion of the Clause "to be known as the *All Non-European Federal Council of South Africa.* The following spoke in favour, Messrs. Kadalie and Rathebe, and those against Messrs. Calvert and Sesedi, and the amended resolution was carried with only three dissentients.

DOCUMENT 47. "Native Disabilities in South Africa." Pamphlet by Professor D.D.T. Jabavu, July 1932 (Printed, 18 pages)

The Non-European Conference.

The South African Non-European Conference was founded four years ago when all the existing political, semi-political, industrial, agricultural, educational and other organisations, over thirty in number, of Bantu and Coloured people, came together for the first time in South African history under the direction and influence of a single control. From the beginning the Convener has been Dr. A. Abdurahman, M.P.C., and I have been the Chairman.

Among the subjects discussed last January (1931) by this Conference at Bloemfontein was the speech made by the South African Premier, General Hertzog, in London, September 1930, when he urged the British Government to adopt in its African Colonies, especially Kenya, the policy he had himself instituted in the Union of South Africa, namely, the denial to all non-Europeans of equal treatment in Church and State.

After an exhaustive discussion the following motion was adopted:—

"In view of the fact that General Hertzog has definitely expressed his opinion in England on the Non-European problem outside South Africa, and as he has urged the Imperial Government to shape its future policy so as to harmonize with that of the present Union Government, and as the latter's policy is based on the principle of *no Equality in Church or State between Black and White,* this Conference considers that the time has arrived to send a deputation to England to place before the British people a full state-ment of its views on the matter of equal rights and the status of Non-European citizens in the British Empire."

Originally, the Conference had intended to send a deputation of at least five representatives, of which I happen to be among those nominated, in order that they may address the British public on the matter from as many platforms as possible, to educate public opinion on their view.

The financial depression that has befallen the whole civilised world has rendered it impossible for us to carry out our original programme beyond its present attenuated form in the shape of myself as the sole representative to have managed to reach England with this all-important message. Therefore small though I am in numbers I shall, however, do my best to convey to you the intention of my conference.

In the first place I wish it to be clearly understood that I have not come to ask the British Government or public to intervene directly on our behalf in local South Africa politics, nor to take up the question of our local grievances as such; because we are fully aware that South Africa is a self-governing Dominion with an independent status that enables her to manage all her domestic affairs without external interference even by Great Britain. Our Prime Minister himself openly resents outside interference in South African domestic affairs such as the Native question inasmuch as the British Parliament of 1909 endowed his country with full autonomy under the South Africa Act. But in September 1930 he himself deliberately stepped over this barrier from his own side by claiming, in London, to advise the Imperial Government and making an appeal to the British public to change the British traditional policy of equal rights and paramountcy of Native interests in African colonies, asking that this policy be altered so as to harmonise with his own domestic Native policy in South Africa whereby all non-Whites are placed under a constitutional Colour Bar and are statutorily excluded by means of minor legislation and regulations from all equality of treatment in Church or State as citizens. He clearly ruled out the principle of equality of citizenship with the paramountcy of Native interests as an impossible and undesirable formula. The conference that I represent regards this as a challenge for it to express its opinion per contra.

Sir James Rose-Innes in a letter to the London *Times* rightly pointed out at the time that General Hertzog's claim to be heard in appealing to British opinion on a matter of British policy in colonies outside the Union of South Africa involves a concession to the British people to criticise or comment on his own Union policy, because Great Britain has enormous interests in Africa, namely, three Crown Colonies, a mandated territory, three Protectorates contiguous to the Union (Basutoland, Swaziland and Bechuanaland) and an Indian problem.

Under the circumstances we welcome the new platform thus created; for the matter of a general African policy, including that of the Union, is now placed on a wider foundation than heretofore. Our concern is purely for the other non-White races who come under direct British tutelage, in that we wish them to be spared from undergoing the lot that is ours.

It is necessary first to examine the grounds on which General Hertzog justifies his appeal. These are four:—

i. That his policy is the only policy that is calculated to secure White dominance as against Black dominance.

ii. That his is the only policy that will create goodwill in the hearts of local Europeans towards the Blacks.

iii. It is the policy found by the experience of Europeans on the spot to be the best.

iv. The effect of a contrary policy elsewhere in Africa will react with unfavourable repercussion on his Native policy in the Union.

This, I think, is a fair summary of what General Hertzog and his Cabinet colleague Mr. P. Grobler, Minister of Lands, gave out to the world twelve months ago in support of their appeal to the British public.

In reply thereto I submit that:

i. The Union Native policy referred to is based on a foundation of repression and as such cannot guarantee the security wanted. The Africans are too virile a race to be governed permanently by the mere force of machine guns and police. Repression, besides,

is contrary to all considerations of moral and ethical principles. European domination will last only if founded on righteousness, for, of a truth, righteousness exalteth a nation.

Anent this my Conference resolved that:—

"Any legislation based on the principle of differentiation on the grounds of Race, Colour, or Creed, will in the end prove disastrous to our Country."

ii. Only the backward and unthinking sections of South African Whites are likely to be pleased with a policy of barefaced repression. Happily, there are many liberal-minded Whites in our country, not by any means Negrophilists, who honestly believe in giving justice and a square deal to the Blacks, and to whom the present policy of repression is repellent.

iii. During the last half-a-century the policy of repression as practised by the three Northern Provinces of Transvaal, Natal, and the Orange Free State has failed to justify itself. The policy of the Cape Province with its liberal tradition supplies a direct negation to the contention of General Hertzog.

iv. The effect of a liberal British policy in other African colonies is exactly what is needed as an education to a young Dominion to correct dangerous experimentation on mistaken lines of policy.

So much for the point of view of General Hertzog.

The non-Whites of South Africa have their reasons for urging that the policy of the present Union Government be not imitated in the other British possessions in Africa.

1. The South Africa Act of Union is based on a Colour Bar clause that precludes all Non-Europeans from being eligible to become members of Parliament.

2. This Colour Bar in the constitution is called "Segregation" and when translated into practice it means the repression of all Non-Europeans in every conceivable form, being used as a lever to curtail Native freedom of movement, to deny the Natives the rights of trading in their areas, to cripple their education grants, and generally to deny them the common human rights and privileges of equality of opportunity in economic development, undermining all fairplay. It originates from the Transvaal,

Natal and the Orange Free State where the ideals of ruling policy are under predominantly un-British and often anti-British influences. Since the consummation of Union, when it was fondly hoped that the old Cape Colony policy would tend to liberalise the Northern Provinces, it has steadily overwhelmed the Cape, giving birth to a perfect code of consistent repression and Native disabilities such as the following:—

3. The Native Land Act (1913) under which the European population of one and a half millions is allotted more than 80 per cent of the total land in the Union, while the Native population of five and a half millions gets less than 20 per cent. Under another Act of 1927 the Government has taken the revolutionary procedure of calling in all Native title-deeds, in order to introduce a number of fresh restrictions on ownership and Native rights in the disposal of their lands. The latter Act has produced an alarm among the Natives that has resulted in a series of lost appeals in all the local courts; and a desperate and final appeal has now been noted in, and accepted by, the Privy Council where it may be opened for hearing, if the necessary funds can be raised by the Natives to proceed with the case.

Under the Land and Agricultural State Bank that disburses upwards of ten million pounds to which Black and White jointly contribute by taxation, the right to get any money is restricted by a Colour Bar to White alone: "To qualify for an advance in first mortgage the applicant (and his wife, if married) must be European."

4. Pass Laws. The Transvaal relic of martial law during war and peace, in the shape of Pass Laws, has remained as an anachronism of medieval persecution down to our present day: when a Native, only because he is a Native, may be required to carry about his person as many as *twelve* different legal documents in order to avoid being imprisoned when challenged by the police. Instead of a diminution of this semi-barbarous system in a time of civilization we behold rather an aggravation of it. As a corollary of it the Government has recently enacted another law to empower its officials to remove "any Native from any place to any other place" for any reason, and at any time! Truly a law of the jungle, and one of Might is Right.

5. Masters and Servants Law. This law enables the Transvaal farmers to repudiate a contract entered into with a Native servant and then to turn round and imprison that servant if he refuses to serve, notwithstanding the farmer's dishonest repudiation of his own contract. It further institutes punishment by lashing—surely a barbaric anachronism!

6. The Colour Bar Act (Mines and Works Act 1911, Amendment Act 1926) closes all skilled occupations to Natives. This is the notorious law that shook all Christendom with dismay when it was forced through Parliament five years ago in the teeth of universal execration on the part of conscientious people; since when it has made South Africa a byword in civilisation, so that nowadays we are often greeted overseas with the stigmatic insult: "Oh! you are from South Africa, the land of colour bars, are you?"

Apropos this I attach the following resolutions from my conference:—

(a) "That this Conference desires to enter its emphatic protest against the Colour Bar Act, because it was deliberately aimed at depriving, and does in fact deprive, certain sections of the community of their inherent right of earning an honest livelihood in accordance with the capacity with which Almighty God has endowed them, and thus driving them into poverty, misery and crime." *And on the "Civilised Labour" policy—the corollary of the Colour Bar Act whereby the Government seeks to rule out all non-Whites from skilled employment:—*

(b) "That the 'Civilised Labour' policy of the Government is cruel and unjust, because it has thrown out of work and impoverished large numbers of Non-Europeans; it has closed many avenues of employment hitherto open to them, besides placing a heavy burden on the whole country in the form of additional taxation to subsidise the policy."

7. Industrial Conciliation Act 1924. No Native industrial organisation has the legal recognition accorded to European trades unions under this law. Therefore, so far as the Native worker is concerned, there can be no such thing as collective bargaining, whatever his just grievances may be.

8. Direct Taxation. Under the Poll Tax law the great majority of Natives are called upon to pay a tax altogether disproportionate to their earnings. Details of this may be seen in a small pamphlet that I produced early this year (1931) entitled *Native Taxation* being my evidence before a Government Commission on Native economic conditions; and in this it will be noticed that this tax makes unconscionable inroads into the earnings of most Bantu people. To-day this brutal tax constitutes the most heart-rending single grievance among the Union Natives as a whole.

On this, my Conference resolved:—

"That in view of the great contribution being made by Natives—through their labour—to the wealth of the Country, and to the fact of their contributing largely also—through indirect taxation, in common with other sections of the population,—this Conference registers its emphatic protest against Act No. 41 of 1925 which re-affirms the principle of direct poll-tax—a form of taxation which is considered in all civilised countries as oppressive and repressive . . and asks for its repeal."

9. Taxation of Boys. Young boys of eighteen are legally compelled to pay this Poll Tax of one pound per head per annum along with their fathers; and as magistrates are allowed to judge from appearance, this tax is being collected from many boys well under the age of eighteen—a painful experience for many Black fathers.

10. The Poll Tax Receipt has, further, been made a kind of pass, so that when a Native fails to exhibit it to a policeman on being challenged, he is prosecuted on a criminal charge and is liable to imprisonment. Draconian legislation, this.

11. The Taxation of Natives is also used as an indirect means of compulsion to labour in the service of Europeans. For example, one proposed Bill framed by the present Minister for Justice suggests an additional tax of five pounds per annum on Native males not under contract of service. This is in direct conflict with the principles laid down by the International Conference on Forced Labour at Geneva, 1929. (This bill has now become an Act.)

My Conference accordingly resolved:—

"This Conference records its emphatic protest against the Native Servants Contract Bill which is tantamount to the introduction of Forced Labour in South Africa, and is designed to keep the Natives as helots on the White farms."

12. Taxation of Native Blankets. The excessive "protective" duty of 25 per cent on imported blankets that are an indispensable article of apparel among rural Natives, is an instance of the cruel heaviness of indirect taxation of the Native.

13. Old Age Pensions Colour Bar. Old Age Pensions are paid every month to European old men but not to Bantu old men. On the contrary, the Bantu aged men are compelled to pay the universal Native Poll Tax till the day of their death if, in the judgment of the magistrate, they happen to have enough cattle.

"The Conference appeals to the Government to eliminate from the Old Age Pension Laws the racial discrimination which precludes the Bantu people from participating in the benefits conferred upon other sections of the Community."

14. Native Education Colour Bar. The funds for the education of European, Coloured and Indian children are allocated out of the ordinary government revenue to which the Natives jointly contribute; but the Natives are made to pay for their education separately out of their own pocket from a special fund raised by themselves alone. Even these allocations have now been amazingly cut down with the result that Native education has had to remain stationary since 1925. Further spasmodic "cuts" have lately reduced the salaries of many Transvaal Native teachers to the miserable figure of two pounds ten shillings per month, while in the same Province the primary education of European children costs the State thirteen pounds thirteen shillings and ninepence per head per annum, that of Coloured children, six pounds per head, but that of Native children one pound seventeen shillings. In one of my books ("*The Segregation Fallacy*") I have shown that the South African Government juggles its funds in such a way that part of European education is somehow paid for out of Native taxation.

The Conference accordingly resolved:—

"That the inadequacy of educational

facilities provided for Non-European children constitutes the greatest factor in hampering the economic development of South Africa. This Conference, therefore, impresses upon the Government that there can be no satisfactory progress unless there is a substantial increase in the grants by the Government to the Provincial Councils under the Financial Relations Act, and that the grants to Native Education be placed on a per capita basis, as those of European, Coloured and Indian children."

15. Agriculture is expressly barred from the operation of the Wage Act of 1925 under which a minimum wage for a given industry may be determined. Many farmers pay wages in kind only, and some take advantage of ignorant Natives by paying their One Pound Poll Tax and binding them for a year at a time.

16. Parliamentary Representation. The Natives of the three Northern Provinces have no representation in Parliament, and the Cape Native franchise is now threatened.

Accordingly, "The Conference reaffirms its condemnation of the Native Bills, and the Coloured Persons' Rights Bill, and earnestly requests the Government to summon a round-table conference of accredited leaders of the European race on the one hand—and of Non-Europeans on the other, to discuss the political relationship of White and non-White in South Africa."

17. Curfew Regulations make it a criminal offence for a Native male to be abroad without a night pass after 9 p.m. (in most towns). There is now a move to include Native women also under this restriction in the Transvaal. In the Cape the females are included.

"In view of the fact that the Pass System is regarded as a badge of slavery, the Conference respectfully but strongly urges the Government to take steps in the direction of the total abolition of the system from the Statute Books."

18. Security of Tenure is not obtainable by Natives who build their own houses in urban locations.

19. Excessive Rents. The houses of urban Natives are in most cases built by European labour at trade union rates of pay. Perforce the rents become excessively high for current Native wages. If Native labour were used (as at Bloemfontein) this complaint would vanish. This unwisdom, strange to say, is repeated in town after town, crushing the Native between the pincers of high costs in building and low wages in industry wherewith to pay rent.

20. Transport. Lack of adequate transport facilities to and from work and the high cost of existing transport are perennial complaints that stand for adjustment by sympathetic town councils.

21. Justice. In Law Courts much miscarriage of justice is due to the inefficiency of White interpreters. This can be obviously remedied by the substitution of Native interpreters of whom many are available.

22. Disproportionate sentences and fines against Natives in the magistrates' courts are difficult to understand outside of the common prejudice against colour, because although the money scale must have been based on incomes received by Europeans one would expect the arbiter to take into account the fact that the income of a Native is at most only a third of that of a White man in any given industry.

23. The Jury System should be altogether dispensed with in cases involving Black and White contestants because the killing of Blacks by Whites in South Africa has become alarmingly common and the offending Europeans tend to come off with unjustifiably light sentences. One might instance, the notorious Barberton case (1925) where two Whites were only fined twenty pounds each for beating a Native to death; the Standerton case of 1924 where a European was given only six weeks' imprisonment for tying a Native girl of sixteen to a waggon wheel and whipping her to death; and last month when a Nylstroom farmer was only fined twenty-five pounds for shooting a Native dead, pleading as his excuse that he intended only to frighten the Native with his loaded gun. Anent this the Johannesburg *Star* comments: "If the police were to compile and publish a complete list of fatalities of this kind, their number would stagger even the apparently callous South African countryside."

24. Medical Services for Natives are hopelessly inadequate. In South Africa hospitals

provide one bed for every 334 Europeans and one bed for every 2,231 Non-Europeans.

25. The Colour Bar may be further illustrated by the fact that the following are criminal offences only when committed by Natives:—

(a.) Breach of contract of service.

(b.) Striking for higher wages.

(c.) Failure to pay tax.

(d.) Failure to produce tax receipt on demand by the police.

(e.) All breaches of the Pass Laws.

26. Projected Legislation. Projected bills and legislation seem to indicate further hardening towards the Natives on the part of the South African government; especially with reference to the old Native franchise in the Cape Province which is now threatened with the process of "Segregation." This proposal has been characterised by the Churches of South Africa as a "denial of our common faith." "We believe that rights to full citizenship in any country are not dependent on race or colour, but on men's fitness to discharge the responsibilities which such citizenship involves. On the one hand, the principle of trusteeship forbids that the determining voice in government should be given to those who are still uncivilised and ignorant (for otherwise the stronger abdicates from his trusteeship): on the other hand, it requires a full recognition that as individuals and peoples progress, trusteeship should pass into partnership. We would emphasize the imperative need of regarding from a definitely Christian standpoint all questions which concern the relations between the different races in our land. The only policy which can succeed or survive is that which is in accord with the will of God."

A distinguished Transvaal Native leader, R. V. Selope Thema spoke four years ago to a meeting of the Cape Native voters in the following touching manner:—"I have never been a voter myself, but we in the Transvaal have always aspired to getting the franchise on the same terms as you. Our grievance against the English is that they did not straightway give us the vote after conquering the Dutch in 1901. For that reason we feel much more grieved against the English than against the Dutch, for we entertained high expectations of getting it. At Vereeniging the Boers characteristically declined to discuss the vote and asked for a postponement of the consideration of it in the full knowledge that they would meantime educate and convert the British to their own illiberal view. When responsible government was eventually granted, the British were not manly enough to renew the question. That is where we lost our opportunity. You are very fortunate for your Cape Native franchise constitutes the foundation of the Black man's upward progress in every way. You hold this right in trust for all of us Bantu of South Africa. Whether General Hertzog denies it to us in the North, please remember that you are keeping it in trust for us. Stick fast to it. If you lightly let it slip from your possession the future historian will condemn and execrate your bones long after you are dead in your graves."

Advocate W. H. Stuart speaking at Grahamstown four years ago characterised the Premier's Native vote proposals as being a "deliberate, brutal annihilation of all Native aspirations forever by the complete crushing of the effecting Cape vote under a smoke screen of 'Segregation' that had nothing whatever to do with it."

Dr. W. E. B. du Bois, the famous Negro author, rightly holds that: "In modern industrial civilisation a disfranchised working class is worse than helpless: it will be diseased; it will be criminal; it will be ignorant; it will be the plaything of mobs; and it will be insulted by caste restrictions."

It is universally admitted that the Cape Native franchise has never been misused. Even General Hertzog does not intend to abolish it or emasculate it or "segregate" it for that reason. In fact he has no reason against it except the colour prejudice and fear of Bantu civilisation that rule the backveld voters. The Native franchise with its concomitant equality of citizenship, far from imparting disrespect for Europeans in the Cape Native, has been responsible for developing an unchanging loyalty to the British, reverence for the Union Jack as the emblem of undiluted justice, and an affection for British governmental institutions that induced the African Paramount Potentates of Basutoland, Pondoland, and Bechuanaland spontaneously to offer their unconquered territories to the protection of Great Britain. The value of this Native vote, according to Leonard Barnes, has been that it compels attention to Native interests where everything else fails; it secures education, land and freedom from Pass Laws; it guarantees better treatment for the inhabitants of the rural reserves; it ensures peace and contentment; it confers a status of dignity in national affairs; it has proved to be the key experiment in the whole world, so that though it may not be the absolute ideal, yet it is the best of the present available practical possibilities.

27. Our Recommendations. With regard to your African Colonies and Protectorates outside of the Union of South Africa, we desire to urge, for the good of both the non-White inhabitants therein and of the mother-country, that Great Britain should adopt the policy of keeping her direct hold on the Protectorates contiguous to the Union; namely, Basutoland, Swaziland, and Bechuanaland. Your power of protection over these and the other British possessions in North-Eastern Africa should be firmly tightened rather than relaxed.

28. Do not be in any haste in conferring self-government in any of your Colonies. We Blacks much prefer direct rule under the Imperial Government; for we still look to Great Britain as our fountain of justice and regard her as our paramount protector. Hence we are anxious that the legal right of appeal to the Privy Council on extra-mural questions and constitutional disputes be preserved intact as it obtains under the present laws.

Hereanent my Conference resolved:—

(a) "That the constitutional relations between His Majesty's British Government and His Majesty's Dominion of South Africa should be retained; and, further, that the British Judicial Committee of His Majesty's Privy Council shall be retained as constituted, and that it shall exercise its functions of supervising the Empire Laws."

(b) "That His Majesty the King shall not abandon his right of veto under the advice of His Majesty's Privy Council or his British Ministers."

29. We wish to see your African Colonies treated and governed more liberally than we are under the Union. In this connection we call your attention to the report made in August 1930 by Mr. te Water before the Mandates Commission on behalf of the Union's trusteeship of the South-West Africa Mandated Territory, in which it was stated that

(a) The taking away of Native land without compensation was "a perfectly usual practice in South Africa;" and

(b) That the money spent on European education was ten times that spent on Native education.

Referring to these confessions, M. Rappard appositely remarked that "The mandate system represented a protest against the tendency to allow the Black to go to the wall." Evidently the local policy has yet to vindicate its claim to being liberal towards indigenous Africans.

30. High Commissioners and other representative officials we like to see selected, for your Colonies, from men in Great Britain rather than from outside. We, therefore, appreciate the creation of a special High Commissioner for the Protectorates that surround the Union, as distinct from Union officials.

31. New Markets are awaiting you in all Africa as well as in South Africa if only you undertake to help civilise the submerged scores of millions of Black people who are at present largely neglected. Once these Africans are advanced in education of every line they will furnish new markets of raw manufactures and primary products and become heavy buyers of British produced goods. Africa holds out infinite possibilities in these respects that have yet to be tapped.

32. Some South African Theories. Expressions of opinion by recent writers both Dutch and English in South Africa have gone to show that the forces of justice, notwithstanding the leadership of the present Cabinet, are slowly but surely gaining ground on the regiments of repression in discussions over the question of White and Black race-relationship.

33. Many Whites in South Africa have openly attempted to justify the policy of injustice on the ground of self-preservation. They are however steadily losing ground; and I have been sent here to help further diminish their remaining ground such as it is. One may

well ask at this juncture: What is the explanation, or probable explanation, of this South African mentality of inflexible prejudice?

Ordinarily in other parts of the world this resolves itself into a social class question with all the antagonisms associated with the clash between the aristocracy and middle classes, and as between traders and unskilled labourers, each class being jealous for its group in regard to its security of income, comfort, monopoly, privilege, social isolation and exclusive intermarriage,—constantly vigilant and fearing any loss of these. Now, the indigenous African started by being the proletariat upon whose unusually cheap labour in farms, industry, mines and domestic service the whole superstructure of White civilisation rested. White capital, brains, organizing power, administration and enterprise made the Whites inevitably both physical conquerors and spiritual guides to the Blacks. The situation was then complicated by the factor of differences in colour, social habits, living standards, primitive historical traditions, economic competition and the tacit jealousy against Blacks being seen or advertised in England in any capacity superior to that of tending a specimen set of Friesland cattle or grooming a rhinoceros.

Another complicating factor has been the so-called 2,000 years' theory: namely, if the White man has taken 2,000 years to reach his present stage of civilisation, the Black man must wait for his 2,000 years before claiming equality of treatment. Yes, if you consider only the heathen as they subsist in their primitive kraal environment; but not their sons who to-day are the "livery-attired skilful Black drivers of Chrysler Imperial eighty sedans through the thick of Johannesburg traffic, attending in full evening dress a soiree dance in one of their numerous Johannesburg night clubs, or listening to a White Communist denouncing the government, the capitalist, the missionary and labour recruiter."

Most of our "baases" who term themselves "Afrikaaners" are behind the times in their ideas on race questions. Socially, they are the most lovable and kindly Europeans if you are fortunate enough to strike an understanding with them. You can then depend more reliably on them than on any other group of Whites in the country. On the contrary they are most adamant, unforgetting, unforgiving, bitter, religious, vengeful, hard-headed and unsympathetic while they are unconverted on the racial question. They then keep you on an inexorable cat and dog life of persecution. Our experience, however, is that even dogs cease to attack the cats once they are domesticated, trained and educated.

34. The basic policy of our present masters is that the African should be precluded from civilisation, forced to develop along his primitive lines, stopped where he presently is, and pushed back to where he was a century ago. Now, the African mind once moved from its old anchorage by European money, machinery, bicycles, clothes, gramophones, cannot be moved back to where it formerly was. And it seems rather illogical to fear the African and at the same time preach that he is an inferior and a barbarian. Fear is a perilous guide in human affairs. It blinds men's eyes to truth and justice. It puts its sponsors down as beyond the reach of reason, for if the European can only maintain his civilisation by keeping his foot on the neck of the African, then he has already surrendered his mental superiority. And a mentality of this nature, if encouraged, will react in a demoralising fashion on any ruling race that puts it into practice; because it will deaden its conscience on all ideas of right and wrong where Blacks are concerned inasmuch as it will regard them as being animals of a sub-human species.

35. This is exactly why the question of the Native franchise requires a liberal spirit and a broad mind unhampered by parochial prejudice; and it is fortunate that under the Union Act the final decision on any change in the Cape Native franchise rests with the British public and the Imperial Parliament, according to the Letters of Instruction to the Governor-General of South Africa signed by the late King Edward VII. We repose our faith on this final reference to England and this is where we hope to appeal to you to help us some day in the future whensoever any change is sought which may be detrimental to the interests of the Cape Native voters. At present we would heartily welcome the enfranchisement of the Natives in Transvaal, Natal, and Orange Free State if that is done without prejudice to the

old franchise in the Cape. We want no change whatever in the Cape Native franchise and it is as well that in a question of such fundamental importance no narrow-minded solution is permitted; because no nation to-day can live in a water-tight compartment, shut off from the life of the world's ideals. For "segregation" is a narrow-minded formula which, in the words of its protagonists, "aims directly and without equivocation at a complete divorcement of the Black and White races on every plane of human activity." While segregation is a counterfoil to equal rights, the question of equal rights in economic and political development is a burning question vitally stirring the inmost passions of all non-White communities in the present-day world, especially in India and the United States of America. This world aspect of it appears great odds even against Mr. Grobler's resolve to apply segregation "with Divine guidance from above" (November 1930).

My conference is grateful for the London *Times* reply made over the signatures of H. G. Wells, Dr. Furse the Bishop of St. Albans, Lord Sanderson, Lord Olivier, and others directed to General Hertzog and Mr. Grobler, in the course of which they properly remarked that "The experience of history proves that the ideal of equal rights is the best ultimate safeguard for fair treatment. The results of the policy at present followed in South Africa are more useful as a warning than as an example."

These results are such that General Byron, a prominent South African Member of Parliament, in the course of a public speech delivered last January observed that—he had found during his recent visit to Europe that South Africa was engaging much unfavourable comment in the world because of her Native policy which, if continued, might result in the punishment of South Africa by the League of Nations in the form of an economic boycott. He was no Negrophilist but he felt it was wrong to oppress the Natives by denying them the rights to education, to justice, to the freedom of labour, to live within a natural national organisation, to habitation, and to freedom of movement.

36. We too think the attitude unfair that regards the Native as "A teeming swarming enemy," the Native first and last an "enemy" with anti-civilisation proclivities (according to the 1929 "Kaffir Manifesto" signed by three South African Cabinet Ministers), with anti-White intentions, with anti-Government ambitions, longing day in, night out, by plot to overturn good government in order to rule the Whites and wreck their pent-up vengeance of them. Such a distorted picture of my loyal people is distressing, incredible, slanderous. If it be a genuine representation of what the secessionists make of us, then we would like to revert to the direct rule of the Imperial Government when the day of South African secession arrives. To be charitable, we may take it that this is not meant to be a true picture but an intentional travesty due to electioneering run amok. Unfortunately the backveld voters who have placed the Government in power take these manifestoes seriously and not as a mere aberration of political propaganda. But in each case the life and death interests of the Natives lie between the hammer of the Cabinet Ministers and the anvil of their electorate. The Black man upon whose labour the whole edifice of primary industries,—gold, diamonds, coal, agriculture,—is built, fails to comprehend why his reward should just be this sort of vilification along with humiliating laws calculated to make him a helot in the country of his birth. How, he asks, did Great Britain abandon him so mercilessly? Can there be any Christian religion in people who set up an "Anti-Negrophilist Association" for the purpose of counteracting all movements working for the improvement of the Black man's lot in South Africa? Can Chesterton be correct when he states that "The Christian ideal has not been tried and found wanting; it has been found difficult and left untried"? Do our rulers follow the Christian ethic and morals in their governing? Are we to become Christians while our White mentors turn pagan? Then it were fruitless to preach Christian principles to men who do not accept them as capable of application to their statesmanship. These men can only be brought to submit to it by the force of a world public opinion which has grown too strong for them as it has about such things as bull-fights, duelling, cock-fights and slavery.

37. Conclusion. It is this world public opinion that we wish to see established in Great Britain and in the League of Nations; for the White race has gone to Africa to stay for good or for ill, and will not leave Africa, and the Black race cannot leave Africa even if it would. The two must learn to live together in neighbourliness and friendship. An urgent task before Christian men and women in Great Britain is the creation and enforcement of a Christian public opinion on all matters connected with White and Black in Africa. The grant of Union in 1909 did not divest Britain of all moral influence over Native Affairs by reason of the solemn mutual pledges then given as between the Crown and the South African Whites.

A test proposition will be the fate of the Cape Native franchise in case the worst should happen under the pressure of anti-Native agitation that may cause this franchise to undergo a mutilation tantamount to destruction. The treatment of the so-called subject races ceases to be the private concern of this or that colonising power and becomes in an important sense an international responsibility.

It is on record, says Leonard Barnes, that the late King Nicholas of Montenegro once boiled in oil a Prime Minister who had the temerity to oppose his wishes. That is not long ago, but in the interval a change has taken place. Civilised opinion has drawn an invisible line, and Europe at least understands that human oil-boilings lie on the wrong side of it. One may say that Europe is now a place where such things do not happen. Perhaps Africa one day may become a place where it is equally impossible even for a civilised race to conduct a policy of repression at the expense of a subject race without provoking at least a chorus of protests from other civilised races. In such an event a solemn protest addressed to the South African Union Government by the British Government conjointly with the governments of the other Dominions would be an impressive gesture and might conceivably not only improve the lot of the Bantu people but also serve to overrule and remedy the general world problem of Black and White race relationships.

Africans Acting Alone

DOCUMENTS 48a-48m. The African National Congress Strives for Unity

DOCUMENT 48a. "The Exclusion of the Bantu." Address by the Rev. Z.R. Mahabane, President, Cape Province National Congress, 1921 (Printed, 13 pages)

Chiefs, headmen, ladies and gentlemen,

It affords me great pleasure to have to stand before you once more and speak to you on what I consider to be the subject of transcendant importance to our people. Since our last and first annual meeting since the reorganisation of the Cape branch of the S. A. Native National Congress, the year under review, 1920-21, has been an eventful one, both in this country and elsewhere in the world. What is known as the League of Nations, formed under the Covenant of Peace, held its first General Assembly in Geneva towards the end of the year 1920, when forty-two of the civilised nations of the world were represented at this Congress of Congresses. But perhaps nothing has attracted the eyes of the whole world more than the grim struggle for liberty that has been going on in Ireland for the last four years or so, culminating in 1920 in an event of the greatest historic significance, the death of Mr. MacSwiney, the Lord Mayor of the City of Cork who suffered martyrdom for the great cause. In the East we note with encouragement the grant of a representative form of Government to India, whereby the Indians are to be directly represented not only on the Legislature but also on the governing councils of the country by Indian Ministers of the Crown. Steps were also taken during the year by Great Britain to give Egypt her practical Independence as a State, although this has not become an accomplished fact. In the West an event of far-reaching importance and of very great interest to the African was the Negro Congress held at New York, U. S. A., in August, and which we understand, was representative of the entire Negro world. This gathering marked the inauguration of what has been described as movement of the black people domiciled in the New World and elsewhere. We "wait and see."

In South Africa there was held at Bloemfontein, O. F. S., what was known as the "Hereniging" Conference, which was an attempt to heal the breach between two sections of the Dutch-speaking community, who have been seriously divided since 1912 on the principles preached respectively by the late General Botha on the one hand and General Hertzog on the other, or in other words on the issue of Imperialism vs Republicanism or Bothaism versus Hertzogism. The failure of this historical Conference was the occasion for the birth of a new Centre Party in South African politics, formed of the S. A. Party and the late Unionist Party, under the masterly leadership of General the Right Hon. J. C. Smuts.

This gallant soldier-statesman and political strategist seized upon the golden opportunity thus offered to call upon the entire European population of this country to make a "new start." It is significant that this happened soon after the tenth anniversary of the coming into being of the Union of South Africa.

Both the English and the loyal Dutch responded in a wonderful manner to this clarion call for national Unity. They thus agreed to let the "dead past bury its dead," to let by-gones be by-gones, sink racial differences and join hands in the formation of a new party on non-racial lines; and the truth of the saying that "Unity is Strength" was amply demonstrated at the last general election when the United Party won a glorious victory and gained a clean majority of over 40 over all possible combinations. The Bantu community may profitably learn the great lessons and sinking their petty, weakening and destructive differences purely on racial or tribal personal lines, make a new start by uniting all their labour and political forces under one great national organisation embracing all the various Bantu tribes of Southern Africa. Such an amalgamation of forces would certainly help to solve what is known as the "Native Problem."

Of the events of the year must be mentioned the manly and heroic protest of the non-European labourers of Port Elizabeth against the unlawful and unwarrantable arrest of their leader, Mr. S. M. Masabalala. This ill-advised action of the Police authorities of the Bay resulted, as have all ill-advised actions, in the unscrupulous and callous murder of twenty-three Natives and coloured men and the unnecessary death of three innocent Europeans, one of whom was a young woman who was visiting the Port from Johannesburg for health reasons. For the loss of so many precious lives the employers of Port Elizabeth, by reason of their turning a deaf ear to the claims of their employees, are primarily responsible for the "contributory causes" of the tragic happenings of the black 23rd day of October, 1920.

Time would fail me to refer to the troubles of our Israelite friends at Kamastone. I shall now pass on to deal with what I consider to be an event of more paramount importance in the history of the Bantu population of the sub-Continent, and that is the passing of the Union Parliament of

The Native Affairs Act, 1920.

This measure makes provision for the creation and appointment of a permanent Commission of Native Affairs, whose duties will be to study the Bantu questions on all its bearings, or, to be precise or follow the wording of the Act, "to consider any matter relating to the general conduct of Native Affairs or to legislation in so far as it may affect the Native population and recommendations to the Minister of Native Affairs." The Act further provides for the establishment of Native Councils in Native areas and for the convening of Native conferences of Chiefs and other delegates from any Native organisations or congresses for the purposes of ascertaining the sentiments and views of the Native people in regard to any legislative measure in so far as it affects the Bantu population or any portion thereof. The Queenstown Congress of last year took exception to the measures as marking, according to some of the speakers who spoke on the question, a "final exclusion of the black man, the original inhabitant of the land, from participation in the Government of the affairs of this the country of his birth," his Divine appointment and of his permanent abode, and the final denial to him of political rights in the country and further marking the formal inauguration of the objectionable policy of the

Segregation Or Separation

of the African or black races from the European or white races of this the country of their common domicilium, a policy which, to our mind, is fraught with dire consequences for this country. Perhaps one would have no objection to separation if due provision had been made for the partition of the land into "hemispheres" of equal size and like quality for locating the respective races, each race being given the right to manage its own internal affairs, even though the assistance or advice of the more developed race might be necessary in connection with the affairs of the less developed race. It must be admitted that the Native Affairs Act, represents a serious attempt at the solution of what has been described as the

Native Problem

or "Native question" and to allay the state of unrest alleged to exist among the black people of the land, by providing channels for the ventilation of any grievances the Natives may have and by creating a medium of communication between the Government and the people. Now, looking at the history of the movement for the solution of the problem, one is struck by the fact that the whites seem to have decided to start on three propositions, namely, assimilation, extermination, segregation. The tendency seems to be in favour of the last-named. To General Hertzog falls the honour or discredit of being the first Minister since Union who had the courage to put forward the first proposals for a scheme for the segregation of Natives. He was, however, not permitted to put this scheme before Parliament, for no sooner had he propounded his policy than fundamental differences arose between him and General Botha on the question of the connection with Great Britain, and he was consequently excluded from General Botha's reconstituted Cabinet. Then the late Mr. J. W. Sauer became Minister of Native Affairs, and he was the first to place before the House of Assembly legislative proposals in the discussion of

"Territorial Separation"

which is a milder form of segregation. He succeeded in placing on the Statute Book the famous Natives' Land Act of 1913, the operations of which inflicted untold hardships on thousands of landless Natives, many of whom became homeless. It must be said, however, that to such as possessed landed property the Sauer measure gave some security of tenure. A Commission was appointed under the provisions of the Act with Judge Beaumont as Chairman, to investigate conditions in regard to land and make recommendations. Of this Commission the late General Botha, who was then Minister of Native Affairs, introduced to Parliament what was known as the Native Affairs Administration Bill of 1917 and succeeded in carrying through the House of Assembly the second reading of the measure. This Bill aimed at carrying out the policy of the Separation of the Natives, territorial as well as political, initiated by the Act of 1913. This measure met with strenuous opposition from the English-speaking section of the House, led by the Rt. Hon. John X. Merriman and the Hon. Sir Thomas Smartt, then leader of the Opposition. The matter rested there. At the death of General Botha in 1919, General the Rt. Hon Jan C. Smuts became Prime Minister and Minister for Native Affairs. He took up the matter and made another attempt at a solution of the apparently big problem of the relations between black and white in South Africa. His scheme embodied in the Native Affairs Act No. 23 of 1920, aims first of all at political segregation, a system of class legislation on race lines. We say this, for the right honourable gentleman had said that he could not allow black men to sit in the white men's Parliament.

These statesmen, however, appear to be only carrying out what is the general view of the white inhabitants of this country as voiced by such writers as one Roderick Jones, who wrote on the "Black Peril" about 14 years ago, and Fred W. Bell, who read a paper on the subject of "The South African Native Problem: A Suggested Solution," before the Union Club of South Africa and the Native Society of the Transvaal on October 14th, 1909. As a matter of fact Gen. Smuts declared in his reply to the debate on the second reading of the Native Affairs Bill, 1920, that segregation was the law of this country. Where these theorists make a grave mistake is in that they start from a very faulty point of view—the self-preservation and self-protection of the white race and the maintenance of white supremacy in the country. Schemes founded on such foundation of sand are

Foredoomed To Failure

The only solution that is calculated to prove a success is one that would be founded on the bedrock basis of justice and right, the whole justice and nothing but justice, or in other words on Christian equity: "Do unto others as ye would it should be done unto you."

You will recall that in his great speech on moving the second reading of the Native Affairs Bill in the Union House of Assembly last year, the Prime Minister declared that the "Natives were losing faith in the white man, in the white man's education and in the white man's religion." One would have thought therefore, that the measure would have been a serious attempt to remove this state of the native mind, restore the confidence of the black man in his white neighbour and in the civilisation of the white man, remove all grounds for the black man's suspicion and scepticism. But unfortunately the enactments have come short of this glorious achievement. I make bold to say that if native opinion had been consulted in regard to this measure it would not have been accepted, in its present form at least. As it is, only half a dozen of supposed leaders of native thought were asked for their views of the Bill, but as a matter of fact the measure was forced down the throat of the Bantu people. It has been, as usual in these matters, a case of "Government without the consent of the governed."

A Further Blunder

Let it be clearly understood that no self-respecting race of people in these days of enlightenment and democracy can consent to be governed by means of local or divisional councils and commissions, possessing and discharging functions of an advisory character only. And the Government has made the further blunder of refusing to accede to the request of the native people for the appointment of at least a couple of natives on the Commission of Native Affairs. This at once makes it impossible for the Bantu to place any confidence on the Commission, even though they have confidence in men like Dr. Roberts and Dr. Loram, who have proved to be friendly and sympathetically disposed towards the united races of Africa. Further, we should not lose sight of the fact that supreme power is vested in Parliament. This august body consists of representatives of all sections and classes of the European population—the commercial, the agricultural, the industrial and the professional. All schools of political thought are represented. The Bantu population, the largest population of the land, by the way is denied this right of rights, the right of direct representation in the Legislature, the supreme legislative and administrative council of the land. The Native Affairs Commission itself will have to report to this body, through the Minister of Native Affairs. This must in itself render it imperative that the Bantu point of view be directly represented on the Commission as well as in Parliament. Our patience has been exhausted in permitting the white man to continue to legislate for us. If the white man fears the possibility of being swamped, surely South African statesmanship is not so bankrupt as to be unable to devise a plan for the due representation of Bantu interests by Bantu members that would, however, secure the supremacy of the European.

This brings us to the question of.

The Colour Bar

To be something approaching perfection

293

the Native Affairs Bill should have endeavoured to effect at least a partial removal of the Colour Bar from the Constitutional machinery of this country. This stigma of our constitution constitutes the source of all the unrest, discontent and ill-feeling that exists, among members of the non-European races in this country, and there can be no peace and contentment and happiness as long as this condition of things is allowed to continue. Why, the position may be put in a nutshell. The European came to Africa, robbed the African of his God-given land and then deprived the African of all rights of citizenship in a country originally intended by Providence to be his home. Why, did not the Almighty in His wisdom and prescience divide the earth into four continents—Europe, Africa, Asia and America? The man whom He created was planted on this earthly planet. He made them white, black, yellow. To the white man He gave Europe to be his abode, Africa He gave to the black man, and Asia He allocated to the yellow man. America God seems to have intended as the land of the surplus population of each of the three great divisions of mankind named above. The amazing thing to-day is that the white man claims Africa as the white man's country, and by his legislative action he has practically excluded the black man. This is injustice.

That Little Phrase

In supporting the motion for the second reading of the "Treaty of Peace and South-West Africa Mandate Bill" in the House of Assembly on the 10th September, 1920, the Hon. Sir Thomas Smartt, then leader of the Unionist Party, declared: "The statesmen who gathered together for the purpose of formulating the Treaty of peace would have been wanting in their duty if they had not given example to the world of what the just punishments were to be of people who had so ruthlessly trampled or tried to trample upon the rights of other people as the Central Powers had tried to do." Now, does this not hold true of the action of the white man of South Africa? Has he not ruthlessly, wantonly and brutally trampled upon the rights of the Bantu people of the sub-continent by excluding them, by the insertion in the Constitution of that little phrase "of European descent" from the rights of full citizenship in their country with all that that connotes. This is by far a worse crime than the action of the Central Powers, because these Powers made no attempt to deprive the Serbians or the Belgians of their citizenship in their respective countries. General Smuts and General Hertzog, as well as Sir Thos. Smartt, know full well that an injustice of an incomparably worse form is to deprive a man of such rights, and that in the land of his birth and adoption.

Inalienable Rights.

Let the European community of South Africa only deal out justice to the African and recognise the humanity and manhood of the latter, and so extend to them these inalienable rights of citizenship in their entirety, and then and not until then, can we all say with President Brandt, "Alles zullen recht komen." As a preliminary step in the direction of justice, let our white rulers remove the Colour Bar of the Constitution and make provision for some modicum of direct representation of native interests and the native point of view by native members in all the most important Councils of State, such as the Native Affairs Commission, the Provincial Councils in all the four Provinces of the Union and in both Houses of Parliaments. This might be done by the creation and delimitation of native electoral constituencies in each of the four Provinces, each returning one or two members to each of the legislative bodies mentioned above. This is wise statesmanship well worth trying.

Era Of Democracy.

We are living in an age of democracy, when all the peoples of the earth have become conscious of their divine right to rule themselves by men chosen by themselves, and for the benefit of themselves. They will no longer submit to rule by autocrats for their own selfish aggrandisement. The native people of India are claiming this right and the Imperial Parliament has granted them a measure of self or representative government, whereby the management of the affairs of the country will now be in their hands. The Egyptians have also demanded that the great democratic principle of the self-determination of nations be extended to them, and an Imperial commission headed by Lord Milner has recommended that this request be conceded to them. The black people of British West Africa, comprising the Gold Coast, Nigeria, Gambia, and Sierra Leone, who enjoy a measure of direct representation in the legislatures of their respective colonies, are also clamouring for a fuller measure of self-government and, in pursuance of a series of resolutions passed by their National Congress in 1920, they sent a deputation to England composed of their leading lights, members and ex-members of the legislative councils of their countries, a Chief and others, to present before His Majesty King George V. a series of resolutions embodied in a memorial.

The Devil of Disunion.

A large section of the Dutch population of South Africa also caught the fire of the new doctrine of the "self-determination" of the nationalities of the earth and they have been clamouring for the abolition of British rule in South Africa and the grant to them of the right to develop their own form of self-government, independently of any connection whatsoever with the British Commonwealth of Nations. Of course, by reason of the fact that they could not present a united front, and also that they disregarded the English, Bantu and Coloured elements of the population of the country, they have utterly and hopelessly failed to achieve their objective.

The Irish people are demanding their right of self-determination as a distinct people. Unfortunately for them, too, the devil of disunion has frustrated their efforts in this direction. They are, however, determined and have made and still are making supreme sacrifices. They have given of their best sons and sacrificed their lives on the altar for the cause of causes, the cause of freedom and liberty, notably amongst whom is one of the Lord Mayors of the City of Cork, James MacSwiney, who suffered martyrdom in the cause of the liberty of the great Irish people.

Several of the people of Ireland who were imprisoned for what they believed to be their inalienable right as a nation, but what the Powers that be regarded as high treason, decided on a hunger strike and the Lord Mayor of Cork referred to above was one of the heroic souls who succumbed to self-starvation lasting nearly ninety days.

A Precious Thing

All these things should show the Bantu people of this country what a precious thing liberty is. Individuals as well as nations have made the supreme sacrifice for this great cause. Jesus, the Christ of God, gave the lead to mankind and the liberation from the thraldom of wickedness. Over 6,000,000 of the best sons of the four Continents of the earth made the supreme sacrifice in the Great War 1914-1918 for the liberation of the people of the earth from the thraldom of autocracy, despotism and militarism. The Dutch people of South Africa fought and suffered privations and final destruction as a distinct nation for this cause in the Boer war of 1899-1902. The American colonists also fought in 1775 for liberty, and the outcome was the coming into being of one of the greatest free States of the earth.

I am not urging the Bantu races to take up arms against the Powers that be, but I want to urge them with the whole might of persuasion that I can command to launch a big Constitutional fight for this divine right of peoples, for it was God himself who gave man the right of self-determination. It was in the Garden of Eden—right in the beginning of things—that the Almighty gave man perfect freedom to choose between right and wrong, good and evil, life and death. Why should we now have to submit to a condition of things which does not give us this God-given right, the inalienable right of self-determination and self-government?

Treated As Children

For reasons of self-preservation, self-protection and self-aggrandisement, the white man has elected to treat the Bantu peoples of Africa as an "inferior race," or as Earl

Buxton, in his Presidential address at the annual meeting of the African Society in London on the 15th of March last, described our people as the "child races" of the Empire. They have carried this to a logical conclusion by denying us the right, privileges and responsibilities of manhood. And thus as children, we have no voice in the affairs of the country. Our self-constituted "fathers" or our "step-fathers" for that, the white men, must think for us, legislate for us and determine our destiny and decide our fate. I refuse to submit to the unreasonable humiliation of a great historic people. I emphatically refuse to submit or subscribe to this policy of treating men of maturer years as children or youths. According to the custom of the Bantu, only males who have not undergone the rights of circumcision are treated as youths or "Amakwenkwe," or "Maqai" and, no matter how old they may be or how bearded they may be, or what number of children they may have; as a matter of fact they were not even allowed to marry wives until they have undergone this rite of formal initiation into manhood. While in this stage they have no say in affairs, domestic or national.

The black man in South Africa is treated in exactly the same manner. He is a "political child," a political "Nkwenkwe" or "Maqai" or as the Sesuto saying is "Mosheman-mpshase-lanloa leboea ("What is boy a mere dog to be cast away, hairs and all."). The poor black man is consequently reduced to a position of utter voicelessness and votelessness, hopelessness, powerlessness, helplessness, defencelessness, homelessness, landlessness, a condition of deepest humiliation and absolute dependency. God forbid that we, as human beings, made in the image of and after the likeness of Himself, should permit other human beings, made in like manner, to abrogate to themselves a position of superiority over us.

Chiefs, councillors, ladies and gentlemen, a new thing has just happened in the political life of South Africa. A Bill is engaging the attention of the Union Parliament purporting to extend franchise and citizen rights to the women folk of the European community of this land. The omens are overwhelmingly favourable to the measure, and in all probability it will find its way to the Statute Book of the Union, and in the event of that becoming an accomplished fact (I don't begrudge the ladies the right) then all persons of "European descent," irrespective of sex, will have been included in the political economy of the land and all male persons of African or non-European descent excluded, save only to a limited extent in one of the four Provinces constituting the Dominion of S. Africa, and then the ideal of a "White South Africa" will have been fully realised. The African will then be relegated to a position of an alien or political slave in his own country. In Egypt the position under the Pharaohs was quite the reverse. Only aliens or foreigners—the Israelites—were treated as slaves, not the natives of Egypt.

Even if the position be viewed from an ethnological point the South African position is strangely anomalous as well as it is untenable. A race of people cannot be held in a sort of "political slavery" only because that race happens to be primitive, untutored or uncivilised. Yet the Bantu of South Africa can no longer be said to be in a state of barbarism or savagism.

Co-operation Of All Races

Chiefs, ladies and gentlemen, I want to declare, in conclusion, that South Africa will never attain her noble ideal of peacefulness, happiness, prosperity, greatness and national unity, of which the Prime Minister and all lovers of Africa have been rightly dreaming, without the full and free co-operation of all the white and black races of the land and of all classes and conditions of men. Industrially, agriculturally and commercially we have been working together for the development of our common country. Let this policy of full co-operation be extended to our political system; let no race or class or creed be driven to such a condition of despair as it might be compelled to adopt the Gandhian policy of "non-co-operation"—taxation without representation leads to this.

And then when our common task in this country has been completed and the end of all things has fully come, we can look back and exclaim

"All's well that ends well."

DOCUMENT 48b. Resolutions of the Annual Conference of the African National Congress, May 28-29, 1923 (Published in *The Friend*)

"That the South African National Congress in annual convention assembled at Bloemfontein on this the 24th day of May (Empire Day), 1923, records its full conviction of the determination of the Union Parliament to reduce the Bantu people to a position of perpetual serfdom, as indicated by the trend of legislation since 1913, and solemnly expresses its alarm and disappointment at the rejection by the House of Assembly of the principle, as contemplated by the Native (Urban Areas) Bill of 1923, of the right of Bantu ownership of landed property in urban areas set apart for Native occupation.

"This Congress further declares that the Bill in its amended form is utterly unacceptable to the Bantu population, whom the measure purports to benefit.

"Further, that the declaration by Parliament that the Black man, the man of African descent and origin has no right to ownership of land in this, an African, land, and that only the man of European origin has landed rights in this, a non-European country, is injustice of the grossest magnitude: is a direct challenge to the loyalty of the Bantu and an insult of a most provocative character to the sense of fairness to the Bantu.

"Also, that the incorporation of certain clauses from the Registration Bill into the measure under review, without first consultation with the Bantu population, is a contravention of the provision of the Native Affairs Act, 1920, and is calculated to shake the confidence of the Black people in the word of honour of members of the ruling races in this land.

"This Congress appoints a deputation to proceed to Capetown and place the views of the Bantu population before the authorities with a view to respectfully requesting them to recommend to his Royal Highness the Governor-General to withhold his assent to the Bill, and that the subject matter of the Bill be referred to the Government for reconsideration."

. . . .

"The South African Native National Congress in annual convention assembled at Bloemfontein on the 24th day of May, 1923, and being representative of the Bantu population of the four Provinces of the Union of South Africa, hereby solemnly resolves to place on record the following declaration, statement or Bill of Rights, viz.:—

"(1) That the Bantu inhabitants of the Union have, as human beings, the indisputable right to a place of abode in this land of their fathers.

"(2) That all Africans have, as the sons of this soil, the God-given right to unrestricted ownership of land in this, the land of their birth.

"(3) That the Bantu, as well as their coloured brethren, have, as British subjects, the inalienable right to the enjoyment of those British principles of the 'liberty of the subject, justice and equality of all classes in the eyes of the law' that have made Great Britain one of the greatest world Powers.

Cecil Rhodes' Formula.

"(4) That the Bantu have, as subjects of His Majesty King George, the legal and moral right to claim the application or extension to them of Cecil Rhodes' famous formula of 'equal rights for all civilised men south of the Zambesi,' as well as the democratic principles of equality of treatment and equality of citizenship in the land, irrespective of race, class, creed or origin.

"(5) That the peoples of African descent have, as an integral and inseparable element in the population of the great Dominion of South Africa, and as undisputed contributors to the growth and development of the country, the constitutional right of an equal share in the management and direction of the affairs of this the land of their permanent abode, and to direct representation by members of their own race in all the legislative bodies of the land, otherwise, there can be 'no taxation without representation.'

"Congress therefore, respectfully urges members of the great European races of the Union to take the whole question into their serious consideration, and calls upon Parliament to take steps in the direction of so amending the South Africa Act of 1909 as to make provision for some adequate representation of the non-European races domiciled within the borders of the Union of South Africa in the Parliament of the Union and in the Provincial Councils thereof.

Native (Urban Areas) Bill.

"That in view of the gravity of the political situation confronting the country and people of the Union, this session of the annual convention of the National Congress be adjourned, pending the return of the deputation from Capetown.

"That, whereas it is desirable and expedient that all peoples of African descent domiciled within the borders of the Union of South Africa and in other parts of the Continent of Africa,

"And whereas it is in the best interests of the African people that all existing Bantu organisations, such as inter-denominational Native Ministers' Association, Native Teachers' Association, Native Farmers' Association, Workers' Union, Bantu Women's Leagues, Vigilance Committees, and so forth, shall be affiliated with this Native National Association,

"It is resolved that the South African Native National Congress shall henceforth be known and described for all intents and purposes as 'The African National Congress.' "

DOCUMENT 48c. Resolutions of the Annual Conference of the African National Congress, May 31, 1924 (Published in *The Friend*)

Government Official Native Conferences.

The Congress appreciates the action of the Union Government in summoning periodical conferences of Chiefs and representatives of the Bantu population for the purpose of ascertaining the sentiments of the Bantu people in regard to legislative measures affecting the Native people of the Union.

Congress, however, calls the attention of the Government to the fact that the conferences as at present constituted are incapable of inspiring the respecting and commanding the confidence of the Bantu of South Africa.

Congress urges, therefore, that steps be taken to make facilities for the Bantu people, partly through their principal Chiefs and partly through their existing political, industrial and agricultural association, to elect their own representatives to these conferences.

The Colour Bar

The Congress, being convinced, after 14 years' experience, that the non-representation of the Bantu population and other non-European communities of the country in the legislative bodies is highly inimical to the economic, industrial, educational, civil and political interests of the said populations, resolves to launch forth a vigorous campaign for the removal of the colour bar in the Imperial Act constituting the Union of South Africa.

It was resolved to seek the co-operation of all other non-European associations, political, industrial, educational or agricultural, in the carrying out of the aims and objects of this resolution.

Native Education

Resolved: That, whereas it is desirable and expedient, in the interests of the existence of the Bantu race as a people, and whereas the economic interests of the Union as a whole would be better promoted if educational facilities were brought within the reach of every child in the Union, the African National Congress respectfully, yet strongly, urges the Union Government to take into serious consideration the question of introducing a legislative measure providing for the introduction of a free, compulsory and public system of Native education for the whole Union of South Africa.

Further, that, in the humble opinion of the Congress, the time has arrived when Native education shall be placed under the direct control of the Union: also, that system of native education is desirable which would be better adapted to the peculiar and practical needs of the Bantu people along the lines of the Natal system. Further, Congress urges the creation of an Advisory Council on Native Education representatives of all the authorities engaged in Bantu education as well as of the Bantu people.

Shooting Of Natives

From the reports of the Provincial Congresses it appears that the cynical shooting of the Bantu people in various parts of the country is still being practised under this, a Christian Government. Congress desires to bring to the notice of the Government the fact that the perpetration of such wanton shooting of members of a law-abiding race like the Bantu, without the authorities taking effective measures for the protection of the Bantu, can no longer be tolerated.

Another resolution urges the infliction of capital punishment on men, White or Black, found guilty of criminal assaults upon women, irrespective of race or colour.

DOCUMENT 48d. Report on proceedings and resolutions of the Annual Conference of the African National Congress, January 4-5, 1926 [Extracts] (Published in *The Friend*)

When business was resumed on Saturday morning there was some difficulty about the language that should be used by delegates. Mr. J. T. Gumede, the President of the Natal Congress, who had just arrived, chided delegates on using the language of "our conquerors," and stirringly appealed that delegates should use their own language. "We have been conquered," he said, "but I do not admit that we are slaves yet."

Voices: We are worse than slaves.

Mr. Gumede said their compatriots in America had been carried away as slaves, and to-day could speak nothing but the language of their conquerors. They here could still speak their own language, and should use it.

The Chairman said delegates could express themselves better in their own languages, and so he ruled that delegates could use any language.

Mr. Clements Kadalie declared that interpreted speeches were often misunderstood. The result was that delegates might be innocently made to deliver seditious speeches. He moved that the President of the Convention should speak in one of the official languages of the Union. This was agreed to.

The Rev. Z. R. Mahabane, the President, then introduced the discussion on General Hertzog's segregation proposals. The South Africa Act, he said, laid down a colour bar. The time had come when they should declare whether they were satisfied with that. They should now agitate more than ever before. By the White races they were regarded as children, who should be seen but not heard. Were they satisfied with that? He had never yet heard why a "child" should be taxed. No child could be taxed. The law said only adult males should be taxed. It was a basic principle of British justice that there should be no taxation without representation. It was on that ground that the American colonies broke away from England. If the Natives must be regarded as children, then they should not be taxed, but clothed, fed and educated as children.

Tribute To Prime Minister's Courage

The Rev. Mr. Pitso, of Winburg, then moved that the Congress place on record its sincere and hearty appreciation of the Prime Minister's courage in tackling the vexed question known as the Native problem in a practical and sympathetic way, showing thereby that there were still statesmen in South Africa who recognised the fact that there is no such thing as a Black or White Africa, and that the so-called Native problem cannot be solved by any one section of the people alone.

Mr. C. S. Mabaso, the vice-president was puzzled to know why such a motion had been submitted. They should discuss segregation, he said.

The Chairman (Mr. T. M. Mapikela) ruled the vice-president out of order.

The Rev. Z. R. Mahabane seconded the motion of the Rev. Mr. Pitso. It did not commit them to the Prime Minister's proposals. It merely thanked the Prime Minister for placing his policy before the people. Statesmen before him would not declare their Native policy for fear of losing votes. They followed a policy of drift. But General

Hertzog had had the courage to show what was the mind of the White man. The Prime Minister's policy was "a snake that has come out of the grass." They could thank the Prime Minister for bringing the snake into the open. By the motion they would approach the Prime Minister in a tactful manner.

Mr. Kadalie moved the rejection of the motion. The late General Botha and General Smuts, he declared, had been spoiled by compromise. They knew that General Hertzog wanted to take away the Native franchise altogether. It was no use beating about the bush.

Weakness, Greed And Robbery

"We have to tell the Prime Minister and the White people emphatically that we cannot and will not accept the proposals of the Prime Minister. You can pass such a resolution at the Government Conference at Pretoria, but you will not pass it at the African National Convention." (Thunderous applause.) His amendment, said Mr. Kadalie, did not issue from London or India, but from the seven millions of Natives in the Union, whom the Prime Minister wanted to place in a position of inferiority in the land of their birth. They spoke of a Native problem. This is no Native problem, but a European problem of weakness, greed and robbery. (Loud applause.) It did not behove them to congratulate the enemy of their womenfolk and wives and children. "This is a White problem of robbing the aboriginal races of South Africa of their inheritance, and we cannot congratulate the enemy of our race, our wives and children - " (the rest of the sentence was drowned in applause).

The Chairman pulled Mr. Kadalie up, saying he had spoken quite enough already.

Mr. L. T. Mvabaza (Johannesburg), in a strong speech, seconded the amendment to reject the Rev. Mr. Pitso's motion. General Hertzog's proposals, he stated, showed that they could trust the White man no longer. Black and White were to-day facing each other on the edge of a dangerous precipice. Either one or the other had to fall down it. General Hertzog had said the Native was a danger to the White man. The White man claimed to be

the father, the guardian of the Native as a child. He had never yet heard that a child was a danger to his parent.

At this stage feeling was running very high, and the Chairman intimated that the Rev. Mr. Pitso had asked leave to withdraw his motion. A large section protested against its withdrawal, claiming that they had rejected it. In the end the Chairman announced that the motion had been withdrawn, but Kadalie and his supporters contended that it had been rejected.

"Cannot Accept Defeat Like Men."

Mr. Pitso: I did not want to divide the house.

There was a good deal of confusion and several delegates wished to know where they were. "The whole trouble," shouted Kadalie, "is that some people cannot accept defeat like men."

After considering the position for a while, the Chairman adjourned the "house" for 10 minutes to allow delegates to "cool down."

When the Convention was resumed, the Chairman announced that segregation was now before them. The President said before the matter was referred to a committee to draft a concrete resolution, he would like to hear what the sense of the meeting was.

Mr. Mvabaza said the Smithfield pronouncement should not be dealt with piecemeal but taken in its entirety.

The President said they had seven notices of motion relating to segregation.

Mr. Kadalie said they should not rush to a Select Committee, but first discuss segregation in its broad aspects in relation to the different motions before them.

Mr. Mvabaza said General Hertzog's segregation policy had been before them since 1913. The principle of segregation was, were they going to allow Mr. Whiteman to "divide our nose." In 1923 they had already declared they did not want segregation. If now they allowed General Hertzog to segregate them, then he would later on say they had agreed to the abolition of the Cape Native vote and the alienation of their land. They were told they were children, but at the same time they were asked to sacrifice the heritage of their posterity.

Mr. Kadalie moved that segregation be discussed in open session.

The Rev. Mr. Pitso moved that the question of segregation be referred to a Select Committee.

Mr. Kadalie's motion was carried by an overwhelming majority.

The Rev. Mr. Pitso immediately moved again that, having heard the proposals of General Hertzog, the Prime Minister, for solving the so-called Native problems read out, the Convention do now go into committee to deliberate in camera on the proposals. He took this course, he said, because the Convention was without effective leadership. Before they submitted their views to the Government they should be united and speak with one voice; if that was not done, the Government might get contradictory opinions placed before them. Their enemies were taking advantage of their disunion.

"The Europeans Are Rascals."

Mr. Kadalie seconded the motion. "We Natives," he said, "have always given the game away." They were playing into the hands of their enemies. "We are dealing with rascals - the Europeans are rascals."

The Chairman asked Kadalie to withdraw this "unparliamentary expression."

Mr. Kadalie said the Europeans were very clever, and in dealing with clever people they should use high tactics. It was most desirable to exclude the Press from their deliberations, and so he supported the motion.

The motion was agreed to, and the Press was accordingly excluded from the further sessions of the Convention.

. . . .

Having considered the Prime Minister's Native policy, as declared at Smithfield on November 13, 1925, the African National Congress, in special convention, resolves to re-affirm its decisions embodied in the Bill of Rights adopted at the 1923 Convention . . . [Paragraphs (1) through (5) of Document 48b, but substituting "African" for "Bantu."]

Adequate Direct Representation

(6) "Congress, therefore, seriously urges members of the great European race of the Union to take the whole question into their consideration, and calls upon Parliament to take steps in the direction of so amending the South Africa Act of 1909 as to make provision for adequate representation of the Non-European races domiciled within the borders of the Union of South Africa in the Parliament of the Union and in the Provincial Councils thereof.

(7) "Further, in the event of the Union Government insisting upon the disenfranchisement of the Cape African voters, as indicated in the Prime Minister's speech at Smithfield, this special Convention of the African National Congress, held this day, January 2, 1926, at Bloemfontein, resolves to take steps in the direction of meeting the challenge thus thrown out.

(8) "That whereas this Convention is convinced that the grant and exercise of the Cape Native vote is a heritage of vital importance to the Africans, which has not at any time been abused or misused, but on the contrary has ameliorated Native African conditions and instilled confidence in the traditional justice and fairplay of civilised Christian Governments, Congress therefore resolves that the Cape franchise be allowed to continue as it has obtained since its grant in 1853, and urges for its further extension to the Northern Provinces of the Union.

Political And Industrial Segregation

(9) "In view of the fact that the supreme need of the country, as well as the world at large, is peace, good-will, harmony and co-operation among the racial groups composing the population of the land; and whereas any policy of discrimination, non-co-operation, as well as political and industrial segregation on racial or colour line, is, in the considered opinion of this Convention, calculated to produce undesirable results—such as race antagonism; and whereas the solution of the problem of the adjustment of the relations between White, Black and Coloured in South

Africa is as urgent as it is insistent, this Convention is convinced that a solution that is likely to be acceptable to all parties concerned would be found if a round table conference of an equal number of the representatives of the Union Government and the African National Congress, as well as other non-European organisations, could be called together at as early a date as possible.

Propaganda Work

(10) "In order to carry out the objects of the foregoing resolutions, Congress further resolves that strenuous propaganda be instituted henceforth.

(11) "In this connection, Congress resolves that it is imperative to centralise the financial resources of the African National Congress without any further delay.

(12) "The Convention desires to bring to the notice of the Government, as well as to members of the farming community, the hardships from which the Native African people, living as squatters on European-owned farms, are suffering as a result of the operation of the Native Land Act of 1913, the Convention strongly urges the Government to consider the amendment of the Act so as to restore the status quo ante the passing of the Act of 1913.

(13) "The African National Congress strongly deprecates the attitude of the Government with regard to the alienation of certain portions of Native reserves and locations in Natal and the Transvaal by the Native Lands (Natal and Transvaal) Release Act of 1925; therefore, the Congress reaffirms the resolution it passed in 1923, authorising the fighting of the land question before the Courts of the land."

A Deputation Elected.

At the afternoon session yesterday the Convention resolved that a deputation be appointed to proceed to Capetown, whose duty it shall be to watch the proceedings of the forth-coming session of Parliament when the segregation proposals of the Government are laid on the table of the House, to note down any happenings affecting our people,

get into touch with Parliamentary opinion and generally to watch over our interests and to report to the next Convention.

The following were appointed to serve on the deputation: The President-General (the Rev. Z. R. Mahabane), the general secretary (Mr. T. D. Mweli Skota), Mr. J. T. Gumede (President National Congress), Mr. C. Doyle Modiagotla (Free State), Mr. M. Mphahlele (Transvaal), Prof. J. S. Thaele (Capetown), Mr. J. Dlwata (Capetown) and Mr. J. M. Dunjwa (Johannesburg).

In regard to the council system, the following resolution was passed: "That the African National Congress, assembled in convention, strongly disapproves of the council system, as it is a bar to direct representation in Parliament."

DOCUMENT 48e. Resolutions of the Convention of Bantu Chiefs, Held under the auspices of the African National Congress, April 15, 1927 (Published in *Minutes of Evidence, Select Committee on Subject of Native Bills*)

(*Rev. Z. R. Mahabane.*) I would like to submit the resolutions of the Convention of Bantu Chiefs held at Bloemfontein on the 15th April, 1927, under the auspices of the African National Congress. The first is on the *Representation of Natives in Parliament Bill*, and reads as follows:

"The Convention, having considered the Representation of Natives in Parliament Bill, declares that after 16 years' experience of indirect representation of Bantu interests in Parliament, the Bill is not capable of acceptance by the Bantu population of the Union unless—

"(1) The Franchise Rights conferred upon the African people of the Province of the Cape of Good Hope by Her Majesty's Government and Parliament in the year 1853 are left intact;

"(2) The Bill is so amended as to provide for the direct representation in Parliament of African interests by members of the African race.

"The Convention therefore respectfully and yet strongly submits that the time has arrived when the Colour Bar clauses of the South Africa Act, 1909, shall be eliminated, and members of the non-European populations of the Union, as forming an integral and inseparable element of the population, received into full citizen rights in this the land of their common habitation.

"In case Parliament is not prepared to give favourable consideration to these representations the Chiefs in Convention respectfully urge the Government to withdraw the Bill for the present."

The second is a resolution on the *Coloured Persons Rights Bill*, as follows:

"This special Convention of Chiefs further deplores the proposal of the Government in the direction of creating a three-stream policy in the national life of the Union by an attempt to separate members of the African races of the Union into two opposing camps by the introduction of the Coloured Persons Rights Bill.

"In the opinion of this Convention this measure is calculated to create a spirit of antagonism among those concerned."

Then there are two on the *Land Bill*. First:

"The Convention expresses the conviction that no satisfactory solution of the land problem will ever be found unless a Round Table Conference between the Government and duly elected representatives of the African people, on the lines of the recent Conference on the Indian question, is held, the method of a Select Committee in which the African is not represented being absolutely unsatisfactory."

The second resolution was taken on the 1st January, 1926, and is as follows:

"The Convention desires to bring to the notice of the Government, as well as to members of the farming community, the hardships from which the native African people living as squatters on European-owned farms are suffering as a result of the operation of the Natives Land Act of 1913. The Convention strongly urges the Government to consider the amendment of the Act so as to restore the *status quo ante* the passing of the Act of 1913."

And then I have resolutions on the franchise taken on the 1st January at a special Convention of the African National Congress held at Bloemfontein. They are as follows:

"That the Africans have, as subjects of His Majesty King George V, the legal and moral right to claim the application or the extension to them of Cecil Rhodes' famous formula of 'Equal rights of all civilized men South of the Zambesi,' as well as the democratic principles of equality of treatment and equality of citizenship in the land, irrespective of race, class, creed or origin;

"That the peoples of African descent have, as an integral and inseparable element in the population of the great Dominion of South Africa, and as undisputed contributors to the growth and development of the country, the constitutional right of an equal share in the management and direction of the affairs of this the land of their permanent abode, and to direct representation by members of their own race on all the legislative bodies of the land, otherwise there can be no taxation without representation.

"Congress, therefore, seriously urges members of the great European race of the Union to take the whole question into their consideration, and calls upon Parliament to take steps in the direction of so amending the South Africa Act of 1909 as to make provision for adequate representation of the non-European races domiciled within the borders of the Union of South Africa in the Parliament of the Union and in the Provincial Councils thereof.

"That whereas this Convention is convinced that the grant and exercise of the Cape native vote is a heritage of vital importance to the Africans, which has not at any time been abused or misused, but on the contrary, has ameliorated native African conditions and instilled confidence in the traditional justice and fairplay of civilized Christian Governments, Congress therefore resolves that the Cape Franchise be allowed to continue as it has obtained since its grant in 1853, and urges for its further extension to the Northern Provinces of the Union.

"In view of the fact that the supreme need of the country, as well as the world at large, is peace, goodwill, harmony and co-operation among the racial groups composing the population of the land, and whereas any policy of discrimination, non-co-operation as well as political and industrial segregation on racial or colour lines is, in the considered opinion of this Convention, calculated to produce undesirable results—such as race antagonism—and whereas the solution of the problem of the adjustment of the relations between white, black and coloured in South Africa is as urgent as it is insistent, this Convention is convinced that a solution that is likely to be acceptable to all parties concerned would be found if a Round Table Conference of an equal number of the representatives of the Union Government and the African National Congress as well as other non-European organizations could be called together at as early a date as possible."

DOCUMENT 48f. "To All Leaders of the African People." Statement by J.T. Gumede, President, ANC, September 7, 1927 (Published in *The National Gazette*)

Sirs,

In June last I was elected National President of the African National Congress at Bloemfontein. The task before me is great, and I feel I cannot perform it successfully without the cooperation of, and active support of, all leaders of the race. I know some of you are not members of the Executive Council of this National Association, but whether or not you are members you can by using your influence with the people, make it easy for the Officers of the Congress to organise the people and bring them within the fold of this National Association.

It is my earnest desire to create mutual understanding among all the leaders of our race, and to secure their cooperative support particularly at this hour of the destiny of the race. Gentlemen, this is a critical time in our history; it is a time when we should sink our differences, when we should sacrifice our personal ambitions for the greater ambitions of the race. It is the time for cooperative action.

I know, there are two wings to Bantu movement for political and economic emancipation from the tyranny of European rule, the conservative and the radical. These wings are absolutely necessary for our progress. They are the right and left wings of a great movement. Just as a bird must have both wings for successful flight, so must any movement have the conservative and radical wings. That is to say, we may differ in our views but this should not necessarily mean divisions and bickerings. We can differ (and there is plenty of room for that within this national organisation) and yet work together harmoniously for the good of our oppressed people.

I shall esteem it a great favour if you will give us your unselfish support in carrying out the task that lies before us.

God Bless Africa,

Yours respectfully,
J. T. Gumede
National President.

DOCUMENT 48g. "What Do the People Say?" Editorial in *Abantu-Batho*, January 26, 1928*

"What do the People Say?

"They say: The department of Native Affairs has sent to the Johannesburg [Municipal] Council a Bill which seeks to amend the Natives (Urban Areas) Act of 1923. The purpose of this amendment is to give authority to town councils to make regulations to stop the movement of Africans and to move them anywhere.

"They say: The Council seeks powers to prevent Africans in various places and in the reserves from bringing their families to town, alternatively to prevent the entry of African women into urban areas and to compel those who are already in such areas to carry service contract passes.

"They say: This segregation which the Hertzog government and their white followers want to enforce between Africans and Europeans means:

"I: That Africans must agree to be removed from the places they already occupy and for which they hold title deeds; such places to be taken over by the government without giving the people alternative freehold-ing land.

*Translated from Xhosa by J. Congress Mbata

304

II: The creation of homelessness among Africans.

III: An increase in the number of roving African slaves, who, for want of a place to live, will give themselves over to European farms [to work on white farms].

IV: The escalation of poverty among Africans, because even those of them who own stock will lose much of it as they move from place to place looking for grazing ground on European farms and paying for it with their stock, as happens at present on the farms.

V: Continuing illiteracy among the young because they will grow up labourers with their parents on farms where there are no schools; and even where schools exist, the parents will not be able to pay for the education of their children because of poverty.

VI: The compulsory return of urban Africans to their Reserves which are already crowded to overflowing because of the natural population increase and the crowding that is normal in these circumstances.

VII: The prevention of contact between Black and White because the Africans tend to assimilate in a very short time the education and culture of the White people and often excel in it.

VIII: Being forced into outside areas which are disease-ridden and which have no preventive health facilities - areas where they will be herded together to die from poverty, to be the victims of disease and thus not increase, and to be decimated and ultimately become extinct.

IX: Arresting the progress of those leading Africans who are educated; turning them back into darkness and ignorance, with no understanding or knowledge of enlightened government such as would enable them to demand a share in the running of the country, or complete control over their own affairs.

X: The setting up of squatters' camps and compounds for African women and girls where they will have to pay for a place to sleep, and where they will be treated like female prisoners of war, with white women to guard and watch over them; where white housewives will be able to select servants to work for them for almost nothing, seeing that these African women will be driven to do this by their destitute condition, and by the urge to escape from being treated like prisoners. In addition to all this the African men have long been inmates of compounds, and have been separated for many years from their families which they left at home because of pressure from taxes and because of circumstances which made it difficult for them to support their families.

XI: The segregation of White and Black means that people must not have any places of their own. They will be liable to be moved from one place to another, and will not be able to multiply and prosper; they will remain scattered. Meanwhile, the immigration of Europeans into this country is being stepped up so that the places of the Africans may be taken up by immigrants.

XII: It means being treated in a humiliating manner in their own properties — i.e. for those (Africans) who still have some land of their own. It means being treated differently in the courts of law. In the administration of estates and in the contracting of marriages the treatment will be different. Administration will be placed in the hands of the police, the authority of the Chiefs will be ended and civil servants who have come from the police force will exercise authority instead. All will be forced to carry passes, and those who were formerly released from the obligation of carrying passes will have their exemption papers taken away from them and will revert to the position of being pass-bearers.

XIII: They will be expelled from the towns and from the locations. Meantime, they will have no place in the rural areas which are their reserves. They will wander about with no fixed abode and will be arrested for vagrancy and put in prison where employers will be able to hire them, paying them nothing, all payments for their work being made to the government. The situation will be very much as it is in the Kimberley diamond mines and the gold compounds of the Transvaal where use is made of convict labor.

XIV: Segregation means the separation of the Coloured people from the Black, the Coloured people being placed in the same racial groupings as the Europeans. The result will be a tendency for the Coloured people to look down on us. They will move away from us and misunderstanding between us and them will grow. They [Coloured and White] will take our women and girls to work for them as servants; they will make them bear children to increase the population classified as European so that this country will ultimately become a land of Europeans only.

XV: [It means] Taking away the vote from the Africans in the Cape and substituting a system under which they will not be able to embarrass their Parliamentary representatives with questions. Seven Europeans will represent them, and the number will remain seven no matter how big the African voters' roll is; for, at the present moment, it is clear that the African voters in the Cape control twelve to fourteen seats held by Europeans who are in Parliament as a result solely of the decisive vote of the Africans.

XVI: Segregation means that the African vote must be exercised by government servants; by policemen and headmen who are government appointed, and who will vote according to the wishes of the ruling power.

XVII: It means suppressing freedom of speech so that we may not build ourselves up through meetings. It means denial of free speech to the African by which he would be in a position to reply to the wicked propaganda that is spread about us, and to react to the rough treatment we receive from the government and its supporters. Requests for the holding of meetings have to be directed to magistrates, headmen and the police.

XVIII: Segregation means that Africans must abandon their identity and [try to] become Coloured people, while the Coloured people will be obliged to cross over to become whites.

XIX: [It means] The end of all ambition for Africans to build themselves up as a people, because such ambitions can only come to people who are free from hunger; the African cannot achieve this in his present circumstances.

XX: Segregation means the retrenching of African workers from their jobs and their replacement by European and Coloured persons. Recently there was talk of importing White mine workers to take the place of African workers in this country.

XXI: Segregation means the Poll Tax and being taxed without a say in expenditure of the money which the government uses in any way it likes.

XXII: It means giving the Africans — and even then only a few — a type of education which is different from, and inferior to, that given to the other races, with the prospect of progressively fewer children proceeding to institutes of higher education because of poverty among the parents.

XXIII: It means this: The exodus of Africans from the Churches [White-controlled] must slow down, become dry, and not flourish because the congregations will consist of poor people who will not be able to support their ministers, who in turn will not be able to teach the people anything.

XXIV: [It means] The deposing of African Chiefs and the imposition of restrictions to prevent them from speaking with one voice and coming together to fight for their rights: all this, because there is denial of free speech.

XXV: It means the break-up of tribes ruled over by Chiefs, with people being removed from the jurisdiction of a chief and being placed wherever the government wishes; where a chief dares to complain, he will be stripped of his authority and some ordinary person appointed in his place.

XXVI: Segregation means that if the Africans cannot swim they must sink in the pool of oppression and in the sea of [competition in] building and pushing oneself to the top.

XXVII: Segregation means that, if the African cannot recognize that for him the way of salvation and success lies in his own efforts and in unity, then he will be destroyed by oppression, by poverty and by persecution, all of which will result from his failure to do things for himself and failure to work together."

DOCUMENT 48h. Report of T.D. Mweli Skota, Secretary-General of the African National Congress, January, 1930 [?] (Typewritten, 2 pages)

African National Congress

Secretary General's Report.

Mr. Speaker, Leader of the House, Chiefs, Delegates, Ladies and Gentlemen, it grieves me very much that I am not in a position to attend this momentous Convention of the Organisation we are serving for the rights and interests of the Black masses. I am therefore forwarding you my report which I hope you will be good enough to read to the House. It is my sincere prayer that the Almighty's Blessings; the Blessings of the God of Africa will crown your deliberations. Mr. Speaker, last year was perhaps the worse year of the African National Congress I ever experienced. This obviously is due to the fact that all Provincial Congresses failed hopelessly not only by violating the Constitution, but also in disregarding the resolutions arrived at in the Convention. Orders and Instructions of the President-in-Council have been treated with contempt. The expulsion by the Convention of officers who failed to carry out the Constitution were disregarded and open rebellion was manifested. Resolutions were passed particularly by the Transvaal African Congress and the Western Province Congress of far reaching effects without first submitting same to the Executive for approval or sanction—this no doubt created Provincial independence that is detrimental to the best interests of the mother body. There has been a crying need for tickets, but as the Treasurer General lives in Rustenberg, we could not get in personal touch with him, and a request in writing had no effect. When I did see him later it was at the General Hospital Johannesburg where the Chief was seriously ill—it was therefore out of the question to repeat my request under such circumstances. Another matter of importance which I must report is the expulsion of Mr. Mvalo from the Executive Committee. This matter Mr. Speaker caused much unpleasantness, but Mr. Mvalo was reinstated at the request of some of the members of the Executive Committee who claimed that he was wrongfully dismissed. Mr. Mvalo, I am informed, has since got into trouble somewhere in Herschel. To the best of my knowledge and belief Chief Mandlesilo Nkosi is the only Chief who rendered financial assistance. Lack of funds prevented Officers to tour for the purpose of organising and collecting funds. The only persons who did succeed to take long trips are the President who went to Natal, and was there during the Kafir Beer

disturbances. Messrs. Letanloa and Matseke toured the North Western Transvaal. Mr. Mvabaza and Mr. Mvalo left for the Cape after the rising of the last Convention. The Abantu Batho affair is somewhat complicated, but I am sure the President and other officers will submit a clear report on the Abantu Batho. All the correspondence have been handed to the officers. Delegates were elected to represent the African National Congress at the Bantu Leaders Conference which met at Bloemfontein on the 4th of December last, and the Non-European Conference at Capetown which met on the 2nd of this month. The Transvaal African Congress sent its resolutions of their April Conference which met at Pretoria. It seems to me Mr. Speaker, Congress will have to take drastic steps to put its house in order. The Provincial Congresses refuse to send in the number of their branches and members as well as their dues to the Congress. It is therefore impossible to know if Congress has any members at all. Even the tickets that were sent out last year and the year before to the various Provinces have to the best of my knowledge never been accounted for. In other words Sir, there seems to be no Law and Order. Everybody seems to have the right, or thinks he has the right to do as he pleases. The Executive Committee is powerless. I suggest that immediate steps be taken to register the Constitution, NKOSI SIKELELA I AFRIKA and MAYIBUYE to enable Congress to take such legal steps to recover Congress funds, and interdict whenever it deems it necessary so to do. Lastly Mr. Speaker, President, Chiefs, Delegates Ladies and Gentlemen I have a suggestion to make which I hope you will accept in all seriousness. The position in which the Blackman finds himself in his own Country today from Cape to Cairo makes it imperative for him to take immediate action if he is to avoid perpetual slavery of the very worse type. I need not repeat the press reports of the letters, articles, and speeches of men like General Hertzog on the Native question, of General Smuts in Europe, of Mr. Pirow, of Mr. Abercrombe and others. I need not recount the deliberate murder of Africans by Europeans with impunity, I need not recall the gas-Machine gun scheme to recover a tax that amounts to robbery. I need not repeat the convict service scheme to force our people to work for nothing, I need not recall the £5 tax Bill and the Riotous Assembly Act amendment Bill to prove that we are in the greatest danger of our lives and the lives of our children. I therefore repeat that the time is *NOW* to formulate some way by which redress of all these oppression, suppression, can be arrived at. I now humbly submit to the Honourable House, the Speaker, the Leader of the House, the Chiefs and the Delegates that a monster Conclave be summoned to meet say—in Capetown or Delegoa Bay or such other place as the Congress shall see fit. That invitations be sent to the National Party of Egypt, to the National Party of Abyssinia, the West African Congress, the Progressive Association of Kanya, the National Association of Nyasaland, the Christian Association of North and Southern Rhodesia, the Lekgotla la Bafo of Basutoland, the Chiefs of Swaziland and Bechuanaland Protectorate and all African Organisations of the Union of South Africa. It will be seen at once that if all these bodies of various parts of Africa attend (and I submit most of them will attend) it will be the most representative meeting ever held in Africa—a meeting that will not fail to create a lasting impression on our white neighbour, while it will cement close and beneficial relations among the various tribes of Africa. There is definite proof that our more fortunate brothers in the north and west are prepared to render us material as well as financial assistance. It is their wish that we should invite them. If we fail other organisations will take the lead. General Hertzog's speeches in the Union, and those of General Smuts in Europe have been an eye opener not to us only, but to the negro throughout the whole World. Our friends in the north see in them a serious danger looming over the sky of the black or negro race. They are resolved to leave no stone unturned to destroy the danger that threatens the rights and liberty of Africans. It is therefore my humble suggestion that you seriously but favourably consider this my motion of an ALL AFRICAN CONVENTION. Lastly my humble prayer is that the ALMIGHTY direct that Honourable House with the wisdom of Heaven, and with the best wishes for the new year.

NKOSI SIKELELA I AFRIKA.
T. D. Mweli Skota,
Secretary General.

DOCUMENT 48i. Report on the proceedings of the Annual Conference of the African National Congress, in *Umteteli wa Bantu*, May 3, 1930

The 19th annual convention of the African National Congress was held at Bloemfontein during the Easter holidays. There were many delegates from all provinces of the Union, as well as representatives of the territories of Basutoland, Swaziland and Bechuanaland and the Transkei. Also present were Chiefs from the Northern Transvaal and Zululand, and among the achnowledged leaders were Messrs J. T. Gumede, S. M. Makgatho, T. M. Mapikela, Revs. John L. Dube and Z. R. Mahabane, Dr. P. ka I. Seme, and Messrs T. B. Lujisa (I.C.U. of Africa), A. Z. Mazingi (Durban), A. W. G. Champion (I.C.U. yase Natal), W. Bhulose (Durban), B. Ndobe and E. Tonjeni (Cape Town), H. Selby Msimang, C. S. Mabaso, L. T. Mvabaza and R. V. Selope-Thema (Johannesburg).

The gathering was momentous in the history of Congress, taking place as it did at a time when South Africa was called upon to determine the black man's place in the national life of the country. There can be no doubt that South Africa is at the crossroads, and the people of South Africa both white and black are asked to decide which road should be taken. The significant feature of the convention was the presence of a strong element of the Communist Party, led by a European, one S. Malkenson of Bloemfontein. The actual number of Communist delegates was only four, but their number was swelled by recruits from the ranks of the African National Congress, (Western Province branch) and the I.C.U. of Africa.

It is the belief of many members of the Congress that the Western Province of the Cape is to a large extent influenced by the Communist Party. "The South African Worker," the organ of the Communist Party, commenting recently on the convention of the Congress, said; "Following the example of Ndobe, Tonjeni and other courageous leaders of the Cape, and making hard work among the masses a sine qua non of leadership, a single fighting policy should be hammered out in place of the several incoherent or downright reactionary policies which exist at the present." This is reasonable proof that there is a connection between the Western Province Section of the Congress and the Communist Party.

The convention was opened by Dr. Walter Carey, Bishop of Bloemfontein, who in the course of his address, said he was glad to be present at that momentous gathering. He believed that God was asking three things of South Africa, and that the whole world was looking to South Africa for these three things. The circumstances were such that South Africa, and South Africa alone could settle the three questions. "God," declared the Bishop, "is asking South Africa to find a settlement and solution of the Native problem on the basis of equal justice and freedom. No other part of the world can find the solution of this burning question besides South Africa. We must get rid of prejudice and fear and base the solution of our inter-racial problems on justice and freedom. The second question is how Boer, Briton and Bantu can build up a State founded on mutual goodwill, and the third question is how we can bring the gospel of Christ to everyone in the continent of Africa. What we need for a just solution of the Native problem is statesmanship on the part of the white man. Prejudiced, hurried and panicky legislation will not solve the question. The whites must recognise that when a nation begins to move no one can stop it. A feeling of nationhood is a divine instinct and cannot be suppressed. But if it is true that the white man needs all the statesmanship he possesses, it is equally true of the Bantu people. You need principles of statesmanship clearly carried out. You want to put your case before the public in such a manner that the public will recognise the justice of it, and then you are bound to win."

After Chief S. Mini and Mr. R. V. Selope Thema had responded to the Bishop's address, Mr. J. T. Gumede delivered his presidential address, in the course of which he condemned the Government's Native legislation which, he said, was putting the Africans deeper into slavery. He challenged the legality

and justification of "this anti-African legislation." The Bills were so intolerable that speedy and drastic measures must be adopted if they were to gain their liberty and maintain their manhood and self-respect. In looking round the world one found that there were everywhere risings of oppressed peoples against their exploiters, there were, for instance, the Chinese revolution directed mainly against British Imperialism; the Javanese revolt against Dutch Imperialism; and now there was the impending Indian revolution. In fact a terrible economic crisis was threatening the capitalistic world. Millions of unemployed were being added to an already chronic number, and there was an immediate threat of international wars. All the talk about the League of Nations and Naval Disarmament were so many smoke-screens to hide the preparations for war. Referring to Soviet Russia, Mr. Gumede said that his sympathies were with the peasant workers of Russia, and he urged Congress to consider the matter of defending them against the onslaught of the enemies of the oppressed peoples of the world. Everywhere the oppressed peoples were being inspired by that ideal of emancipation which found expression in the Russian revolution. There was still an illusion that the people would obtain justice from the British Government. But the plain truth was that they had again and again failed in their petitions to the British Government, and that their supplications to the Governor-General had been futile. "We have now to rely on our own strength, on the strength of the revolutionary masses of white workers the world over with whom we must join forces. We have to demand our equal economic, social and political rights. That cannot be expressed more clearly than to demand a South African Native Republic, with equal rights for all, but free from all foreign and local domination."

The effect of this startling speech was to raise a storm of protest from the majority of the delegates who made it plain that the address did not express their views. Probably Mr. Gumede's object in making such a fiery speech was to catch votes, but if so he failed hopelessly.

The election of Dr. P. ka I. Seme as

president-general was accepted by the Communist Party as a challenge to the workers. Mr. S. Malkenson, who was given an opportunity of stating the case of the Communists, said no longer would the fight be a secret within the Congress; it would become a struggle outside Congress; and the militant masses would decide the issue.

Dr. Seme on behalf of the new Executive welcomed this declaration of war, and said that they did not want any militant organisation to hide under the name of the Congress. They were determined to get rid of Communist influences.

In addition to the resolutions published in last week's Umteteli the following were passed: —

"While the convention expresses its appreciation of the Government's action in appointing a commission to inquire into the economic conditions of Natives in urban areas, it requests the Minister of Native Affairs not to proceed with the Natives (Urban Areas) Act Amendment Bill until the commission has reported."

"Further the convention prays that the terms of reference should include the investigation of the conditions of rural Natives as the migration of Natives to urban areas is largely due to the operation of the Natives Land Act, as also the congestion in Native Reserves.

"That Union Day, May 31, be observed by the Bantu community throughout South Africa as a day of humiliation, prayer and protest against the policy of political domination and economic strangulation of the Bantu race inaugurated by Europeans with the consummation of Union in 1910."

The Executive of the Congress for the next three years is as follows: —

Dr. P. ka I. Seme, B.A., L.L.B., president-general; Rev. Z. R. Mahabane, senior chaplain and parliamentary reporter on Native legislation, T. M. Mapikela, speaker; C. P. Matseke, deputy-speaker and chairman of committees; Chief Stephen Mini, president of the Chiefs' Council; T. D. Mweli Skota, secretary-general; S. M. Makgatho, senior treasurer; R. V. Selope-Thema corresponding secretary; D. S. Letanka, secretary of the Upper House; C. S. Mabaso, financial secretary; A. Z. Mazingi, clerk of the House; Rev. J. L. Dube, education; H. Selby Msimang, labour; Dr. A. B. Xuma, health, urban areas and assistant treasurer; Rev. J. S. Likhing, representing Griqualand West; Mrs. Mahabane and Mrs. Matambo, chairwomen of Women's Auxiliary.

DOCUMENT 48j. "ANC Calls for Passive Resistance." Statement in *Umteteli wa Bantu* June 27, 1931

A mass meeting was held last Sunday in Johannesburg and was attended by representatives from all over the Reef, Pretoria, and Evaton.... The heat with which the question of passes was discussed evidenced the intense indignation of the Native people. Eventually the meeting adopted the statement which appears below.

Since 1910 the African people, particularly in the Transvaal and the Free State, have been engaged in a fierce struggle against the pass laws for the following reasons

(1) The pass laws restrict their movements and brand them as criminals, (2) they make it difficult for them to bargain with their labour to their advantage, (3) they exclude them from the benefits derived from the Industrial Conciliation Act and the Wage Act and (4) they are to a large extent responsible for the lawlessness which prevails among them.

On more than one occasion women in the Free State defied the law with the result that eventually the pass laws in the Province were relaxed so far as women were concerned.

In 1918 and 1919 Natives on the Witwatersrand, after exhausting every constitutional means, resorted to a passive resistance against these iniquitous laws. There may be recalled the disturbances which took place in Johannesburg and which eventually led to the imprisonment of hundreds of our people and a baton attack on our womenfolk by the police. In view of the present situation it is essential that the public should be reminded of these happenings. The passive resistance of 1919 was not prompted by the agitators but by the disabilities under which our people were labouring under the pass laws. It was the indignity to which they were subjected under the pass laws that made thousands of Natives prefer imprisonment to a life of perpetual humiliation. No race of men will tolerate a system of government which does not recognise the elements of human rights such as the right to move freely in one's own country and to bargain with one's labour without restriction. The result of these disturbances was the appointment of the Moffat Commission in 1918. This Commission after taking evidence found that the majority of Native grievances were legitimate and that one of the causes of Native unrest was the pass laws. After condemning the pass system, the Commission recommended their modification, adding that under no circumstances should Native women be included in the pass laws. It was in accordance with the recommendations of this commission that the Department of Native Affairs decided to issue the travelling pass free of charge.

In 1919, as the result of the passive resistance movement which culminated in the throwing away of passes and an outbreak of violence another Commission consisting of officials of the Departments of Native Affairs and Justice was appointed to inquire into the workings of the pass laws. The Commission went all over South Africa taking evidence from both Europeans and Natives. In 1920 the Commission issued its report in which it was recommended that the existing pass laws should be repealed and be substituted by one life long document for purposes of identification, and that it should be demanded, if necessary, only by an authorised police sergeant. The Commission condemned the multiplicity of passes.

Acting on the Commission's recommendations the Smuts Government framed a measure entitled the "Native Registration and Protection Bill." This Bill was placed before the official Native conference in 1923; but for reasons known only to the Government it was not submitted to Parliament while some of its clauses were transferred to the Natives (Urban Areas) Act.

It may interest the public to know that in his speech on the second reading of the Native Affairs Act in 1920 General Smuts declared that the Commission which was to be appointed under that Act would assist the Government in finding a solution of the pass law problem. He emphasised the fact that Natives were chafing under these irritating laws and that therefore a solution should be found.

The Native Affairs Department, so far as it can be ascertained, is in favour of the modification of the pass laws. The Secretary for Native Affairs, Major Herbst, told a conference of farmers at Durban in 1928 that the Department favoured the substitution of the present system by a single document, preferably the Poll Tax receipt. The Minister of Native Affairs told a joint deputation of Europeans and Natives last year that the Government would be willing to consider the simplification of the pass laws "to the extent that public opinion would allow." He reiterated this statement at the last official Native conference. It will be seen therefore that white public opinion hinders Government action in this matter.

The legal position, we understand, is that the application of the pass laws can be modified or withdrawn by the Native Affairs Department without reference to Parliament. This step, however, the Native Affairs Department is not prepared to take until such time as white public opinion shall have been so educated as to realise the futility of the pass laws for the prevention of crime among Natives.

Since 1910 we have been hoping that the Government will bring about relief in this matter of the pass laws. But by the reenforcement of the night pass laws against our womenfolk, after it had cost us over £300 in 1926 to free them from these iniquitous laws, we are convinced that the Government is not prepared to consider the relaxation of the pass laws. Rightly or wrongly we consider this action of the Government as a challenge to our manhood, and as we have for upwards of twenty years patiently pleaded in vain for relief we feel compelled to accept the challenge. We have all along trusted in the goodwill of the white race and its sense of justice; but today we find that our trust has been betrayed. As men we can submit to injustice as long as we must; but we cannot tolerate the subjection of our womenfolk to the indignities and barbarities of the pass laws.

While we are grateful to the City Council of Johannesburg and those Europeans who are championing our cause, nevertheless we feel that the time has come when we should organise passive resistance throughout the country. With this end in view, this mass meeting calls upon the Executive Council of the African National Congress to organise a campaign of passive resistance against these iniquitous and barbarous laws.

DOCUMENT 48k. Report on the proceedings of the Special Emergency Convention of the African National Congress in *Umteteli wa Bantu*, July 23, 1932

A special emergency convention of the African National Congress was held at Kimberley on July 2. The meeting was convened by members of the "Cabinet" who in a statement published in Umteteli of May 21 accused the president-general, Mr. P. ka I. Seme, of "culpable inertia." At the Kimberley meeting a telegram from the president was read in which he declared his intention to summon a general conference at Bloemfontein on August 1. The special meeting thereupon passed the following resolution: —

Whereas the President General had failed to convene the Annual General or ordinary Convention of the African National Congress for the last two years; whereas many things have happened in the meantime which are detrimental to the moral, economic, industrial and political welfare of the African people; whereas the organisation of the African National Congress is in a state of chaos and confusion, this meeting directs the chairman thereof to approach the President General by respectful address not to summon the general conference in August but to prepare for the annual convention in Easter so that any alteration or change to and in the constitution of the Congress may be considered, if need be, by the duly elected representatives of the people; and that this conference appoints two officers to assist the General Secretary to bring about a thorough reorganisation of the Congress.

The two officers appointed to assist the general secretary (Mr. D. T. Mweli Skota) were Messrs. R. V. Selope-Thema and H. Selby Msimang.

The following manifesto was adopted:

"The special emergency convention of the African National Congress held at Kimberley this 2nd day of July, 1932, convened under a resolution of a meeting of some members of the National Executive Council held at Johannesburg on the 26th April, 1932, for the purpose of devising ways and means of reorganising same, views with grave concern the state of disorganisation not only of the Congress, but also of all other kindred organisations of the African peoples, more particularly rival factions in some Provinces which tend to stultify the cause of unity among the African peoples.

"Never was there the time, the need and the necessity for the existence of a powerful organisation representing the African people of the Union more than the present, in view of the increasing burdens and disabilities inflicted upon the race by retrograde and medieval laws aggravated by the economic depression and other causes the majority of which would have been obviated had a liberal policy been the keystone of the administration of African affairs.

"This special convention deplores the fact that the voice of the African people, which has been conspicuous by its absence in the following among other matters, has lent colour to a silent acquiescence thereto:

"That the African people raised no united protest against (a) the Service Contract Bill when it passed through Parliament last session. (b) The Government took no measures to combat malaria when it swept off more than four thousand of our people in Zululand. (c) 150 African families have been evicted at a Lydenburg farm, because the land is wanted for forests. No provision has been made for their settlement. Besides, thousands living near the towns in Natal are also notified to leave, without any provision being made for their settlement.

(d) The country being under an unparalleled depression, the Africans are left destitute owing to their displacement from work by the whites in accordance with the Government policy and the non-development of reserves (e) while all the authorities pursue this policy they make no provision for relief work for Africans despite the £4,000,000 they contribute to the National Treasury. The arbitrary cuts in the teachers' salaries and inadequate Parliamentary grants have reduced the standard of education among Africans. (f) While appreciating the Government's efforts to relieve starvation in Zululand, Northern

Transvaal and other famine areas, there is a fear that with the expiration of the credit period, the people will be compelled to pay despite their hardships — and there is no organisation to plead for them.

(g) The African people have been considerably alarmed at the trend of legislation which undermines their confidence in the white man's rule besides penalising them for their loyalty to the British throne."

DOCUMENT 48l. "The African National Congress—Is it Dead?" Pamphlet by Pixley ka Isaka Seme, 1932 [Extract] (Printed, 16 pages)

It appears as if there has never been such a strong demand amongst the Native African people for the Congress in the past as there is to-day. The persistent personal attacks from my friends and enemies in the "Native Press" may be proofs or evidence of this re-awakening. This new love for the African National Congress amongst those who had hitherto been indifferent. If, therefore, my supposed inertia can cause such a wide-spread desire for unity to arise, then I am glad. But I am sure it is the dreadful vision of chattel slavery which has so easily passed unopposed in both Houses of the Union Parliament under the guise of the Service Contract Bill, which has opened the eyes of the natives in this country to-day. There is no other alternative. We shall be made slaves indeed unless we can unite and become a nation. If we desire unity then we must form the African National Congress into a solid and impregnable fortress for the defence of our Liberty, even on this Continent, which is our birthright.

By Congress I mean a duly constituted assemblage of African men and women in one Conference which may truthfully be regarded as representing all our African people. I mean all African people who have the pride in the African blood which runs through their brains. My conviction is that here in Africa, as in America, the Africans should refuse to be divided. We need a strong body of men and women to give the leading daily thought and guidance to all our people in their daily duties and struggles as a nation. Such a leading voice can only be produced by a conference, composed of the chosen leaders of the people come together for the purpose of building up the nation and not for the purpose of creating difficulties or racial stumbling blocks for those who today are earnestly working for our unity and strength. I cannot ever forget the great vision of national power which I saw at Atlanta Georgia in 1907 when the late Dr. Booker T. Washington L.L.D., presided over the Annual Conference of the Negro Business League of America with delegates representing all Negro enterprises in that New World and representing 20 million Africans in the United States of America, the most advanced of my own race.

I must come back to the subject of our own Congress, which I am now rightly or wrongly being accused of killing. Time is very precious. I shall not waste it by publishing personal incriminations against my enemies or facts which would go very far to prove that my work of organising the Congress has been seriously retarded by the want of co-operation between the leaders and myself, and more especially through the want of co-operation between the members of my own National Executive and myself. It is urgent that our Constitution should be amended so as to provide an easy way out of such difficulties in the future, if the President-General of the Congress is to be expected to lead our people during his term of office. No member of the Executive should be allowed to defy his chosen leader and then simply stand in the way and refuse to resign. The well-known rule which is observed amongst all nations is that the subordinate in the Cabinet should readily resign if so requested by the Head of his Government. In the same way, the President-General of the African National Congress, as the Chief Executive, should be obeyed and followed by his Cabinet because he is responsible for their failures. They are his subordinates, and because he alone appointed them, he should be allowed to replace any one of them who proves to be useless or unsuitable. The Constitution of the Congress should be amended so as to fall into line with this well-known rule. There can be no unity amongst us until we shall acquire the habit and the will to recognise one man as head over us. Until we shall learn to do this we shall continue to be slaves.

Ladies and gentlemen, my firm conviction is that if our Congress is to be made a real success, it should be founded more firmly upon its original Constitution, namely: that the African National Congress be made really and truly to consist of two Houses—the Upper House of Chiefs and the Lower House of representatives or delegates. The members of the Upper House to be in the nature of a permanent body whose members succeed each other by hereditary rights and not by election. The Lower House should be composed of delegates elected by the branches of the Congress for the period of two years. I carefully suggest that the delegates should be elected by the branches and not by the Provinces, because in this way only can we get the rural population to be properly represented in the Congress. My friends will agree with me that by departing from this foundation, the African National Congress has been made to lose its former influence, when I used to invite all our great Chiefs to attend the Congress. The Chiefs should be made to feel that they have a House of their own in the African National Congress, wherein they can meet alone as Chiefs and without being inconvenienced by strangers. They should feel through this Great House that it is their duty to meet with the other Chiefs of the Nation for the purpose of exchanging views in connection with the new problems which face them to-day, the problems of employment for their people, the problems of conserving national pride, customs and traditions.

It is time that our Chiefs came to realise that their office of Chiefs has very important duties attached to it. They must lead their people and their tribes unto salvation. Our Chiefs should realise that their people to-day in the country, as well as in the towns, are face to face with the grim and difficult times which the old kings and prophets of Africa have foretold. Tshaka, when he fell under the sword of his royal assassins, saw this day and uttered grave warnings just before he died, King Sobhuza I. in Swaziland caves told his people before his death that the white man was coming and that they should not kill the white man when he comes; the great Xosa prophet Ntsikane also foretold these days and gave positive warnings to his people. Africans, you must unite this day and consider the ways and means of earning a living as a nation which is destined to live amongst strongly organised and more advanced nations in your own country. No other nation or white men Councils or Joint Councils will be able to do this for you.

The Chiefs to-day should realise that their forefathers won these positions of honour and high esteem by fighting hard for the salvation of their own people and not by lying down and seeking personal comforts and pleasures. No Chief should be satisfied with his own position until he has exchanged views in an African Conference with his brother Chiefs of South Africa in the Upper House of the African National Congress. It is their duty as Chiefs to create such a Great House for their own good and for the good of their own people. As your chosen leader this year, I hereby appeal to you and to every Chief to come out and help build up the African National Congress. I must depend upon your financial assistance and patriotism. I depend upon every Chief in South Africa to help me in the difficult task of inviting the African people to come into their own inheritance and become a nation.

I am pleased to see so many of our young educated men and news writers criticising me for doing nothing for the Congress, or for killing the Congress, as some have written in their ignorance. I feel, therefore, that I can also appeal to these same men, as teachers and leaders of thought amongst our young people to-day, to come forward and join the Congress movement, for which I am pleading in this leaflet. I have no other means of reaching you—all my other efforts have failed before. I want to address myself, as I am doing in this paragraph, to our young educated men and women. The present is very bad indeed for you, but the future is bound to be worse for you and your children unless we all unite and form one strong, well organised National Congress. We really don't need much of that common agitator, who only wants to create strife and class hatred. We need the white man in this country as much as the white man really needs us. Our welfare as a nation can never be served by sowing hatred between whites and blacks in this or in any other country or by disseminating cowardly slanders against the Government, who have no means of knowing what our wishes as a nation may be. Let us unite and form the African National Congress, make it really and truthfully to represent our people. Then, and not until then, can we be able to place before the Government, or, if necessary, before the whole world, the evidence of our desire to co-operate in making Africa the greater and the happier Continent of them all.

I feel, too, that I should carry this denunciation of this spirit of non-co-operation amongst educated Africans one more point further. The time has really passed when educated men and women of any country could stand aloof and watch the uneducated folk suffer. Some time ago the missionaries came into this country to look after the heathen and to love them, but by a strange contrast, every "native" who got educated by these missionaries immediately became disinterested in the heathen and, in fact, despised his heathen brothers. The result has been that the greatest bulk of our people who are still heathen have no educated men to lead them amongst their own tribes. The Chiefs and their uneducated people are despised and forsaken by their own educated tribesmen.

This attitude of despising your own people has created antipathies between the new leaders and the old population, which are most regrettable. There is no reason why the educated Africans should throw away their tribal connections and so much desire to be regarded as being detribalised natives. I fear that in this sense the so-called "detribalised natives" have not properly considered their positions and their duty towards their own people. We need more of what the American Negro calls "Race Pride." In that country you find coloured people most highly educated and efficient in the leading professions who cannot be distinguished from the white people, nevertheless refusing to be regarded as whites. Their mothers are Negro Africans and they want to remain as Africans also. If our African people would only take a leaf from this book of Negro life in America, how much richer our people would be from trading

between ourselves. I wish to urge our educated young men and women not to lose contact with your own tribes. You should make your Chiefs and your tribal Councils feel that education is really a good thing. It does not spoil their people nor detribalise them. Most of the misery which our people suffer in the towns and the country to-day is due to this one factor, no confidence between the educated classes and their own uneducated people. The former cannot open any business relations amongst the latter and get good support because to be able to establish a business anywhere you want confidence. The Indian trader succeeds because he makes friends with all classes and ever tries to win their confidence. You must learn to do likewise.

Moreover the so-called "educated native" is the loser in the show because by cutting himself adrift from all tribal ties he becomes a prey and a victim to false standards of living. He copies the white man, his tastes and standards of living, without the least thought that all that must cost more money than what he can possibly afford or be able to earn in his position. I say that we can and should, through the African National Congress, be able to regulate our own standard of living and adjust ourselves to all the necessary changes of dress and progress as a nation. Congress can make us learn how to produce our own wants as a nation. We can learn to grow up cotton and wool and make our own clothes and blankets in our own factories; make our own leather, boots, bags and harness from the hides of our own cattle; we can cut African timber and supply good furniture to all African homes. The African National Congress will teach us "Race Pride," and this "Race Pride" will teach us how to become a nation and to be self dependent. Instead of concentrating our efforts into building up one organisation with a stable tradition, our young educated folk are developing the craze for ever creating new organisations, churches and whatnots in order to weaken the old ones. No other nation does that. The new blood is required to strengthen the old and not to break them down as you do.

. . . .

DOCUMENT 48m. "I Appeal to the African Nation." Article by Pixley ka Isaka Seme, in *Umteteli wa Bantu*, November 10, 1934

The success of my policy and administration of the African National Congress must depend upon the success of the African Congress Clubs. All that I have ever said about the necessity of building our future upon a sound economic foundation should be realised by Africans through the success of these African Congress Clubs.

Young Africans should ignore all the useless squabbles of their leaders and concentrate upon establishing these local clubs in every district or town throughout South Africa. I ask every young African to make up his mind to join a local African Congress Club and help in every way to make it as strong as possible. It is your duty and it is your great privilege to make these National Clubs as popular as possible in your own district. They are the official residence of the African National Congress in your own town. They bring to the door of every African home the messages of Hope, Co-operation and Good Will from every corner of South Africa.

Property Of The Nation

In my previous articles I have tried to show that these National Clubs will cater for all economic needs of our people, in the towns as well as in the country. Beside giving hotel facilities and providing recreation rooms the "A.C.C." will keep general stores, groceries and meat for the benefit of its members.

The clubs will be maintained from the General National Funds of the African National Congress, and all the monies which each Congress branch contributes must remain with each branch under the control of its own local officers and the trustees of the African National Congress duly appointed by the Provincial Administration by authority of the General Conference of the African National Congress.

The amended constitution of the Congress ensures general uniformity and the undoubted security of the funds and all the business of the "A.C.C." The very fact that they belong to the nation as a whole and are not the property of any private individuals, will give a powerful reason for their general support. Every African will be able to point to them with pride as the property of the African Nation—an institution which has been established and is maintained by their own efforts.

After any "A.C.C." has been duly established, under the authority of the African National Congress, the General Conference of the Congress will assume the responsibility of helping to keep them going by granting loans from the General National Fund on application.

Old Loose Methods

The advocates of the old constitution want to go back to work under the old loose methods which permitted them to go about the country collecting monies in the name of the Congress. The new constitution wants to plant the Congress tree in every district and centre of our Native population.

The "A.C.C." will encourage all Native business enterprises. It will help the Native shopkeeper, the hawker and the pedlars by giving them supplies through the wholesale departments. The chiefs will be able to get their motor cars more cheaply and the Native transport service will be much improved owing to the supervision of the motor car mechanics of the "A.C.C." It will pay our motor mechanics to join these local clubs so that they may get their supplies through the general garage of the Congress.

Management Of Clubs

In conclusion I wish to point out that the "A.C.C.," like every institution, will be capable of great growth. It is a great national insurance system against unemployment and it should ensure the steady progress of the African nation. For this reason we must take every precaution to make it a success and to avoid all chances of failure. Therefore I shall propose that we start by employing the very best and most reliable Europeans to assist us in managing the Congress's business undertakings. The Revenue Department for instance, should be placed under an ex-senior officer of the Native Affairs Department, who shall enjoy the full confidence of the African National Congress.

And we should always remember that it is the duty of the Congress to satisfy the Minister for Native Affairs of our good intentions. We must always try to win his confidence as the father appointed by the Government to watch over our interests as well as our progress. The Minister has proved in every respect that he is very worthy of all our confidence.

Meeting Place For The People

Our policy shall be to make the "A.C.C." a meeting place for a busy hardworking and anxious people who are doing their best to get into the world markets. They shall not be encouraged to become mere offices for receiving complaints and grievances. The African must be taught to build himself up and not to expect all other people to get out of his way and give him an open road to progress. He has to fight for his freedom so as to learn its great value.

The qualified young men and young women who will be drafted into the Congress National Services (C.N.S.) shall not fail to inspire the African audiences in the halls of the "A.C.C." with the new spirit of fellowship and to help to break down this cursed racialism. I ask all African leaders to remember the initial success of the old I.C.U. They fell upon this country like a mighty army. The Basuto leaders were drafted to Zululand, the Zulus to the Transvaal and the Xosas and the Coloured people all worked under one African spirit of Fellowship. I urge all you young men and women to seize your opportunity today and help me to build up the "A.C.C." under the constitutional authority of the African National Congress.

DOCUMENTS 49a—49c. The Voice of Labor

DOCUMENTS 49a—1—49a—3. Predecessors of the I.C.U.

DOCUMENT 49a-1. Address by Selby Msimang, President, Industrial and Commercial Workers' Union of South Africa, July 23, 1921 (Published in *The Cape Times*)

At Thursday evening's session of the Industrial Commercial Workers (Amalgamated) Union of South Africa, Mr. Selby Msimang (president) delivered his annual address. He began by congratulating the visiting delegates upon their labours at this the second meeting of the Assembly of the I.C.W.U. When they had first assembled together at Bloemfontein last year, few had guessed the full importance of this great and ever-growing movement. That conference had been a very important one in that it had been composed of several independent unions which had sprung up spontaneously here and there throughout the Union of South Africa. All these unions had professed practically the same ideals, with the same ideas and objects in view. The forces with which they had to contend had become so formidable that it was now essential to contrive and effect closer corporate association with each other, and so it was that the Bloemfontein conference last year had accomplished much in joining together various independent unions, with the gratifying result that a big composite union had there and then been formed.

What Had Been Achieved

They were again reassembled that day to review the work begun by that conference, and transacted during the past year. An account of their various activities during the past twelve months must be given, so that it might be seen what had been done, and what had been left undone. No doubt mistakes had been made, and some of these we might live long to forget, but such mistakes were inevitable with such a young organisation. "And yet, as an old Scotsman had put it," went on the president, "these mistakes give to youth the wit of old age. They illuminated the truth and taught us to know ourselves. Indeed, they made us realise our weaknesses, for the events of the last year should make us wiser. Now what was the naked truth that we have been compelled to see? A need for organisation. We have been often tempted, or was it mere force of circumstances and of economic difficulties, to force the issues when peaceful negotiations might have produced better and more lasting results. At such times when we might have concentrated upon organisation and mobilisation of those forces already at our disposal for the purpose of insisting upon our rights, circumstances had compelled issues which had lacked success by reason of disorganisation. There had been too many temptations to strike, and such strikes had been organised by people who were ignorant of the doctrines of Trade Unionism. These people were ignorant in regard to the great secrets of passive resistance. I will be failing in my duty if I do not warn you against the wild talk, which serves merely to rouse the passions of the people; at any rate, for the present.

Organise! Organise!!

"Our first duty should be to organise all non-European workers, wherever they may be, and to educate them and make them understand and appreciate the obligations falling upon them as workers in safeguarding the interests which are theirs and inalienable. Drive the point home that it is no fault of the employers to exploit them, but that it is their own fault and that they can only ward against exploitation by some distinct bond of comradeship.

"I am not at all blind about the pressure of the high cost of living upon our already poorly paid comrades, but the awakening that has been responsible for the formation of workers' unions should inspire courage and patience, and should prevent hasty councils. We must organise patiently and vigorously, and so make a speedier end to our present difficulties. If the workers are sufficiently awake they should demonstrate that wakefulness by endeavouring to bring about a solidarity of effort without which no strike or lock-out might succeed. If awakened we should be compelled to unite by the knowledge that every variation from unity is but a progression towards nullity."

There were other reasons, moreover, proceeded the speaker, for renewing their determination to bring all workers into closer union. There were two desperate forces to contend against. There was the European Trade Union menace, which was becoming too exasperating in certain respects. That Union looked upon them as a monster threatening to filch their patrimony. All over this country they could discover men with their hands in their pockets, playing the boss over sweated workers, and for which lazy job they were paid 20s. per diem as against 2s. a day paid to the actual workers and producers of the country's wealth. The waste in industry was, at present, larger than the power of production. It now remained to decide whether to accept the challenge or to ignore it, to extend a hand of fellowship or to reciprocate the insolence. Before they could do either they must organise.

Government Indicted.

On the other hand, they had the Union Government, evidently a club of incorrigible magnates, whose miserly hearts created a greed which Shakespeare had envisaged in Shylock.

They made such laws as would convert a Christian to Atheism. Study the laws for the distribution of land, the pass laws, the humbug of segregation. After a reference to the Native Affairs Commission, the president proceeded: "Politicians will say, 'It is all politics.' Let them say that, but I am convinced in my own mind that it is industrial propaganda organised for the deliberate purpose of reducing non-Europeans to a condition of economic slavery. Round about us we find a system for parcelling out lands for immigrants which ignores the vast population of coloured people. Go where you like, you will find non-Europeans being ousted out of land, industry, and even domestic employ. The badge of slavery, which has been christened a pass for the purpose of hood-winking the civilised world, has already been responsible for the exploitation of cheap labour. Still you hear M.P.'s agitating for the resuscitation of 'isibalo,' or forced labour, in the Union, in order, it is alleged, to meet the shortage of labour on the farms. Who can think of South Africa becoming a den of unemployment with her vast potentialities and unlimited resources? One great authority says: 'Wherever you see want and misery or degradation in this world about you, there, be sure, either industry has been wanting or industry has been in error. It is not accident, it is no Heaven-commanded calamity; it is not the original and inevitable evil of man's nature which fills your streets with lamentations and your graves with prey. It is only that when there should have been providence there has been waste.' This is exactly the position in this unhappy country of ours. There has been too much greed, too much Europeanism, too much prejudice."

Overflow Of Labour.

"We shall have," he continued, "to consider seriously the question of putting a stop to the influx of casual labour into industrial centres. There is no greater danger to the Union than the unchecked flooding of unrequired labour into industrial centres. Some towns were overflooded with labour, and as long as the supply exceeded the demand labour was bound to be cheap. Last year a resolution had been submitted to fix the standard wage for men at 10s., and for women at 7s.6d. To his mind the champions of the movement had not weighed their subject properly since they had overlooked the superfluous supply of labour. To get one-half of such a demand supplies of labour must be scarce. The sources of such a superfluity of labour were the territories and protectorates. It would be their duty to go out to these people and instruct them, and to persuade them to turn their hands to something useful and to make them realise the wealth lying dormant in the lands they occupy. They must be taught independence.

They must be taught a racial consciousness, and independence without instilling race hatred. Agriculture would seem to be a failing industry amongst the people, and this was one of the difficulties in the territories. Many men left their lands untilled to go to labour centres where they were paid one-hundredth part of what they might have made out of their lands. Some drifted to towns out of poverty, or lack of capital. It should be their endeavour to keep these men behind their ploughs. If there was one sphere of activity neglected it was bound in course of time, to prove a drag on other spheres.

Barrier Against Coloured Labour

Proceeding, the President discussed the fact that many employers felt compelled to employ whites, although they would prefer to employ coloured skilled labourers. The European Trades Unions had created a strong barrier against coloured artisans. Some European Unions at the Cape had actually admitted coloured members, but such Unions were the exceptions which only served to prove the rule, and were probably forced by circumstances to admit the coloured man. In the larger Unions, such as the leather industry, the barrier was fixed. In those other Unions the insufficiency of the European workers had compelled employers to open their doors temporarily to skilled coloured men. Promotion by racial preference kept many a good and efficient man down. There were many coloured men who were now enjoying the privilege of admission to European trades avenues who would sooner desert their fellows than assist in lifting them to achieve a similar plane. They are carrying their selfishness too far, and are ready to argue to-day that two and two did not make four if their interests were involved in that question. They were responsible for the exploitation of their less fortunate fellows.

Disparity Of Pay Of White And Coloured

"Ladies and gentlemen," continued the president, "I fail to see why the scale of pay should be regulated by the colour of the skin. It was argued that the standard of wages should correspond with the standard of living, but that seems to me to be an absurd argument. Does it mean that because the bulk of the people are extravagant one should dance to their music or that if they expend £5 a day on drink and luxuries we must follow that example!"

He urged that a via media should be found. All classes of non-Europeans must unite under common principles and aspirations, and not descend to the status of unthinking mimics of Europeans. He appealed to all other unions to throw in their lot with the I.C.W.U. for the general uplift of downtrodden races and for the facilitation of such fortifying virtues as would induce them to assist, persist, desist and resist.

Continuing, the speaker said: "We are tired of things as they exist to-day and desire a change. Whatever has or is imagined to possess a power to produce changes in other things, or in itself, is a cause; and a good cause sustains more injury from a weak defence than from frivolous accusations. When holding October 23 sacred, we should also remember Johannesburg in 1917. Comrades, I ask you to join with me in paying respect to our martyred dead by rising."

The Bulhoek Affair.

"But these," he proceeded, "do not make the total sum of our roll or honour. Persuaded as I am by a deep conviction that if the Land Laws of this country were not as they are, and believing fully, as I do, that if Enoch Mgijima had ordered his proselytes to indenture their labour to the surrounding farmers of Kamastone or to give it gratis in the name of his Church, the killing and wounding of 400 natives would not have taken place. I cannot without shame ignore these men as if they had not suffered in the same cause and under similar reasons as the rest of our worthy comrades, who now lie buried in Port Elizabeth and Johannesburg. It is not for me to pass judgment against Ngijima's teachings, but I think it is within our right to condemn any system of Government which encourages lawlessness and defiance to constituted authority. Man is not bound to confess loyalty to a tyrant. History has shown that the human soul naturally revolts against injustice."

"Russian workers had been forced to revolution in order to do away with Russian autocracy. Gladstone had declared that 'the proper function of a Government is to make it easy for people to do good and difficult for them to do evil.' Is this Government in South Africa making it easy for the coloured people to do good? All that was evident was a multiplicity of laws. With Ngijima's following they had fallen the victims to bad influences brought about by bad administration. The Acting Prime Minister had disappointed every black man in the country. The Government had adopted a policy of drifting whilst the coloured workers were smarting under irritating disabilities in every walk of life. There was no definite policy apparent. Black men were disqualified from all other rights and privileges but the right to indenture their labour for a pittance.

"Can we safely say—even supposing the 'Israelites' were wrong—that their mistakes were deliberate and without cause? The worth of a State, in the long run, is the worth of the individuals composing it. How much are we worth? Perhaps we suffer for our own sluggishness, foolishness, selfishness, and want of co-operation, self-help, and all those other virtues which go to the full sum of national progress."

DOCUMENT 49a-2. Memorandum from the Transvaal Native Mine Clerks' Association to the Mining Industry Board, 1922 (Typewritten - 7 pages)

This is the only Native labour Association in existance and is recognised by the Mining Industry, its members are all educated natives and all holding responsible positions in the Mine Compounds, Time Offices, Hospital Offices, and Shaft Offices, as Head Police Natives, Native Clerks, Checkers and ticket sorters, etc. Its Constitution allows any native to join the Association who is educated but not actually doing Police or Clerical work at the time, provided he can read and write English.

This Association was formed in 1920 and received its letter of recognition from the Chamber of Mines dated July 1920.

Objects

The main objects of this Association amongst many others are the following;

(a) To improve the position of its members socially, economically and educationally.

(b) To facilitate mutual interchange of experience between members representing different tribes and races.

(c) To discover means by which Mine Authorities may be provided with native labour in time of labour shortage.

(d) To facilitate mutual good understanding between the Compound Managers and natives working under their supervision.

(e) To educate its members and the mine natives generally to avoid unnecessary agitation and strife.

(f) To afford opportunities for discussion upon subjects of interest and of improving the conditions of native labourers working in the mining industry.

(g) To be the means of communication between the native and all Governing Authorities and Employers of Labour.

(h) To use endeavour to cause the Association to be represented on any Commission or Board of Reference or Enquiry appointed by the Government or local Authority in connection with any matter affecting mine native labourers.

(i) To agitate for the promotion of the native interests in such a way as is best calculated to bring about contentment and efficiency amongst natives.

History

This is the first time in the life of this association that we have given evidence before any Commission or Board of Enquiry.

Although this Association had not been invited to give evidence the members thought it necessary in the interests of all the parties in dispute to get an opinion of the natives working in the mines through their native representative solely as they would have a different view from even that of their white sympathizers.

This Association has also reasons to believe that this honourable Board would not have done justice to the country if it had not had the opinion of natives before making its recommendation to the Government.

In the opinion of this Association the natives are deeply concerned in this dispute and there is therefore a fear that this Board may determine the future of the natives upon misinformation.

This Association has not deemed it advisable to make a long written statement but has sent men who will stand in front of the Honourable Board for cross-examination on all the points affecting the natives from the statements given by various witnesses specially the Chamber of Mines and the Labour Unions.

This Association wishes to make it clear to the Hon. Board that its delegates come to give independent evidence, not supporting Capital or the Labour Unions, but giving the viewpoint of the native.

The revulsion of native feeling came to a head in a general Passive Resistance Movement in the Free State, the Witwatersrand and elsewhere in 1918 when natives mutually agreed to throw away their passes and undergo voluntary imprisonment. In 1920 when the mine native labourers mutually agreed to defy the Authority of their contracts and undergo loss of life and imprisonment in support of their claims for higher wages.

This record of dissatisfaction amongst the natives has no precedent in the history of South Africa.

All these events must bring home to all self-respecting Europeans that if the natives are not given proper channels through which they can voice their genuine grievances they may be stampeded by a burst from any and every kind of agitator.

The Educated Natives working in the Mining Industry in the year 1920 decided to form an Association in order that they might safeguard their fellow men from all sorts of misleading, and to take the responsibility as a body for whatever might occur as provided in the objects of the Association.

It is not so easy to mislead an educated native to commit an offence as it is an uneducated native, and it is a known fact that although the educated natives are very few in South Africa—in the mining industry in particular—they have succeeded in having their influence so felt by the bulk of their native brothers that the latter have come to recognise them as their only hope of salvation.

The fact is indisputable to those who have followed the changes of native life in South Africa.

To ignore the voice of the educated native is to labour under misapprehension and court disaster. From the two years life of this

Association we are able to state that although the times have been so bad and the atmosphere charged with electricity on many occasions we have been able to control our native brethren on the mines.

The behaviour of the natives during the recent disturbance can be put forward as a clear proof of this. So much has been said in front of this board in favour and against the Natives by Europeans that nothing has been said by the Natives themselves.

Although the terms of reference for this Board do not distinctly make it known that the native evidence is required we have decided to ask permission to be given an opportunity to give evidence which will be helpful to the Hon. Board and prevent injustice to all parties in the dispute and to the natives who are intimately concerned as to their future.

We have taken particular notice from the Press report that this Board is trying to lay a strong foundation for the future prosperity of South Africa and if possible to devise ways and means of preventing future industrial crises.

In our opinion as natives of this country we wish to submit that we are satisfied that there can be no permanent settlement nor desired good will and looked for prosperity unless the natives have been given a proper place in the management of their industrial affairs.

In order to get the desired ends we ask the real genius of the British race which is the spirit of compromise as opposed to the bullying spirit.

We ask the workers to give away something which they claim as their right namely their superiority by the virtue of their colour and we are willing to meet them with the same spirit namely our respect for their higher standard of living. We honestly believe that there can be no permanent peace between Capital and Labour if the natives are not put on a proper footing for their development as necessitated by European civilization. In the mines you will find all kinds of natives. Educated natives trained and semitrained natives. It is these natives who feel the operation of the Colour Bar. To the uneducated native it gives a dangerous impression creating in him a sullenness which is antagonistic to efficiency, considering that he has no education, no cultivated reasoning and practically speaking does not see the reasons why that while he the native can do work without the presence of a European he is prevented from doing it because of his colour.

It was the white who taught him the blessing of work, it is also the white man who prevents him from working to the best of his abilities.

Generally speaking the length of time a native has been working on a property—a long period is not considered a recommendation in many cases it has the reverse result—that of being looked upon as a spoilt native. The fact is he has become too efficient—knows too much for ill-disposed persons.

This Association has no objection as to the system of recruiting as done by the native Recruiting Corporation through its labour Agents, but is opposed to the recruiting done by the traders in the Native Areas, on the grounds that they encourage Natives to accumulate debts and persuade them to join for the Mines; making double profit in each individual head of native.

1. We therefore beg to recommend that this Association should be recognised on the same status as all White Labour Associations.

2. That this Commission recommend the Abolition of all Colour Restrictions in the Mining Industry.

The Manager to appoint any one for any job, if he is capable of doing it satisfactorily, be he White or a Native.

3. That the formation of Native trade Unions in the Mines should not be discouraged by the authorities.

4. That the status quo Agreement of 1918, better known as the "Colour Bar" should be abolished soon to enable the natives to work themselves up to efficiency.

5. That the new system which has been adopted underground viz. The cleaning Shift which starts at 7.p.m. to 2.a.m. and the breaking Shift starting at 7.a.m. to 3.p.m. should be encouraged as much as possible, as it enables the native to do more work within the required length of time.

6. That all boss boys of underground managers, Mine Captains, and shift bosses

should be educated natives who will be able to interpret for all the disputes between the gangers and their natives.

7. That in all the Mine Groups the Compound Managers should be invested with superior powers to decide all cases between the Underground Authorities and Natives, and his finding to be final as far as the disputes between the mine natives and Mine Authorities are concerned.

8. That encouragement should be given to all natives who are doing skilled work and engaged on responsible jobs, such as drill sharpening and blasting, by the way of extra pay and certificates.

9. That the Low Grade mines should be worked by the Natives with a few Europeans as supervisors.

10. That the Recruiting should be taken away from the Traders in the Locations and Territories, and be done by the Labour Agents who have nothing to do with Stores in the Native Areas.

The native may be thought a rough diamond among the many gem races that are at present in South Africa but this Association is of the opinion that with a little chiselling and polishing he will become a sculptured leaf in the Capitals of the grand columns that sustain our Empire.

We respectfully ask this honourable Board to recommend that the strangle-hold of the "Industrial Colour Bar" be gradually removed from us.

To keep us wallowing in the mud the white man must wallow along with us to keep us down there.

WHY NOT ALL GO UP HIGHER

DOCUMENT 49a-3. Petition to the Prince of Wales, from the Transvaal Native Mine Clerks' Association, June 23, 1925 (Typewritten, 1 page)

The Transvaal Native Mine Clerks' Association.

To His Royal Highness Edward Albert Christian George Andrew Patrick David, Prince of Wales and Earl of Chester, Duke of Cornwall, Duke of Rothesay, Earl of Carrick, Baron of Renfrew, Lord of the Isles and Great Steward of Scotland, High Steward of Windsor, K.C., P.C., K.T., G.C.S.I., G.M.M.G., G.C.I.E., G.C.V.O., G.M.B.E., I.S.O., M.C., F.R.S.

May it please Your Royal Highness,

We His Majesty's most respectful and loyal Native working subjects employed in the Gold Mining Industry, the President, General Secretary, Members of the Transvaal Native Mine Clerks' Association and Mine Natives generally respectfully beg to extend to Your Royal Highness a hearty welcome on the occasion of this your first visit to the gold fields of the Rand.

We wish that your visit to us as Native Labourers will impress you with our backwardness more than being impressed by us as good singers and war dancers. The deplorable events at Bloemfontein of few weeks ago and the subsequent resolutions of the African Native Congress in Johannesburg are symptomatic of a widespread discontent among the Natives which is due to many causes, political, economic, social and industrial. The Natives have many just grievances, which have become aggravated since the Union owing to Parliament's disregard of the Natives' legitimate claims. The Natives are to-day becoming more and more out of touch with the Government and feel friendless and neglected. They resent the arbitrary restrictions on their earning capacity which are embodied in the Colour Bar Laws, while Pass Laws pinpricks create a feeling of irritation especially when they are applied even to women folk.

We respectfully beg to assure Your Royal Highness of our continued loyalty and devotion to the Throne and person of His Most Gracious Majesty, the King, your Royal father and our indelible good memory to Your Royal Great Grand Mother, the late Queen Victoria.

On behalf of all the Native Labourers of the Witwatersrand gold fields, we beg to be
Your Royal Highness's
Most respectful and
loyal subjects,
Allison W. G. Champion, President.

23rd. June 1925,
Villag Deep Sports Ground.

DOCUMENTS 49b-1—49b-6. Kadalie's I.C.U.

DOCUMENT 49b-1. "African Labour Congress." Article by Clements Kadalie, National Secretary, I.C.U., in *The Workers' Herald*, December 21, 1923

We are at the threshold of a New Year, we might just as well call it, a new era. The church bells will soon chime and herald the dawn of a New Year—1924. A question worth while to be considered by all sons and daughters of the African race, is whether we are fit for the new struggles, obstacles, failures and success, also torment awaiting us as a people.

The New Year 1924 promises to be of historical importance to South Africa as a whole. Our statesmen will probably be faced to meet another General Election—a General Election that will surpass all previous General Elections in South Africa. The new event in the year will be the South African Labour Party Conference to be held in Pretoria where the Nationalist and Labour Pact will be brought up for ratification. It is also antic- ipated that the South African Mine Workers' Union will consider at their Annual Con- ference the admission of Black workers into their Union. Our Parliament will be sum- moned together to ratify the decisions of the Imperial Conference held in London recently. It cannot be denied that South Africa will face so many vital problems in the New Year that is before us. What will become of the black toilers of this sunny land of our forefathers? We shall at least be expected to stoop down to further humiliating laws such as the operation of the Pass System being intended to extend to the Cape Province. God alone knows what shall be our lot!

We live in a scientific world, a world which is good and beneficial to the industrious, adventurous and ambitious men and women. That now for five years we have carried on "industrial organisation" being the only weapon to effect our real economic emancipa- tion. We did not in the least despair at difficulties, the way was hid from us, but

thank God we at last found the way to the new Jerusalem. We are now at the brink of Jordan, receiving invigorating command. "Be strong and of a good courage, be not afraid, neither be thou dismayed...for unto this people shall thou divide for an inheritance the land which I swore unto their fathers to give them." With this grand biblical motto we shall enter that momentous Congress soon to open at East London as from January 17th, 1924. We shall not turn from it to the right or to the left, we have placed our hands to the plough, and it is high time that the white capitalistic press in this land take notice of our declara- tion. The African Native of to-day is a new man and is therefore quite different from his forefathers whom the white man found here some two hundred years ago, and whom you duped. We would like to remind the white capitalistic press, that although you profess to have studied thoroughly, through your own experts, the African Native, you have arrived most hopelessly at a very poor conclusion of this most romantic man ever created by Dieu. You keep on making noise in your press about Bolshevism as a dangerous doctrine, fright- ening the African Native, you will soon find that the so-called illiterate masses will jump in, simply for the sake of curiosity to see for himself. The African Native has been a law- abiding person from time immemorial. No African leader will join any political move- ment purporting to upset any Constitution. It is not an easy matter to sway an African audience. In no time in the history of the African people of this vast Continent it is recorded of rebellion against any constituted authority, whereas we read of Cromwellian revolution in Great Britain, the formation of Republican France and secession from Great Britain by the American Colonies in 1776. Give us what we desire, economic freedom, we must have a say in the affairs of our country and for God's sake do not make Bolshevism as an excuse.

Workers of this land, how long shall you halt between two ways? Your bosses have very nice time of your labour. It is cheap and abundant, through it it was possible to build these great cities in South Africa. You were forced to dig the earth, you brought from hell, gold, diamonds, copper and coal, some piled in the Bank of England, diamonds being demonstrated throughout the civilised Europe and America. Your wives and children, yourselves included, are continually sweating making the white man and woman's life so easy, practically living in a paradise, while you are condemned to live in hell. The reason why the white man's press is against the I.C.U. to-day is because we have directed you to eat that forbidden fruit in the centre of the garden. We believe that our race is just as good as any other race, if only given same opportunity, since we were all made in the likeness of the Creator. We have never cringed to any white politician, rather we have followed our own convictions, and it is also anticipated that this journal will face strong opposition from these exploiters of the race, since we dare to call a spade a spade.

Invitations have been issued in time to various minor unions to send their representatives to this forthcoming Congress. We have a large comprehensive agenda that needs determined men and women with a vision. A new development of far-reaching effect will be made so as to create a central organisation which must operate throughout South Africa and beyond its borders if necessary. We have reached a stage when as a race of people we must forget the past and go forward as new men and women. Our Branches in particular and also other unions should see that best men and women are delegated to this Congress. It is an opportunity that rarely occurs. Whatever the path may be, the forthcoming Congress must determine to establish a formidable Labour Organisation, through which the African workers shall more and more win a real emancipation for himself and take his rightful place in the ranks of those who do the world's useful work.

DOCUMENT 49b-2. Revised Constitution of the I.C.U., 1925 [Extracts] (Printed, 40 pages)

1. Name

The name of the Organisation shall be the Industrial and Commercial Workers Union of Africa, herein referred to as the I.C.U., which shall cater for the following sections under its aegis: Municipal Workers, Waterside Workers, Miner Workers, Building Workers, Agricultural Workers, Marine Workers, Transport Workers, Railway Workers, Factory Workers, Domestic Workers, Warehouse Workers and its Registered Head Office shall be at Cape Town, South Africa.

2. Preamble

Whereas the interest of the workers and those of the employers are opposed to each other, the former living by selling their labour, receiving for it only part of the wealth they produce; and the latter living by exploiting the labour of the workers; depriving the workers of a part of the product of their labour in the form of profit, no peace can be between the two classes, a struggle must always obtain about the division of the products of human labour, until the workers through their industrial organisations take from the capitalist class the means of production, to be owned and controlled by the workers for the benefit of all, instead of for the profit of a few. Under such a system he who does not work, neither shall he eat. The basis of remuneration shall be the principle, from every man according to his abilities, to every man according to his needs. This is the goal for which the I.C.U. strives along with all other organised workers throughout the world. Further this Organisation does not foster or encourage antagonism towards other established bodies, political or otherwise, of African peoples, or of organised European Labour.

3. Objects

The objects of the I.C.U. shall include:—

(a) To regulate the wages and conditions of labour, and to foster the best interests of its members in their different spheres of occupation, irrespective of sex.

(b) To provide legal assistance to the Organisation, and to its members in matters connected with their daily employment.

(c) To establish sick, unemployment, old age, and death benefits for its members.

(d) To take shares in any syndicate approved by the National Council, or the Board of Arbitration, and to establish such commercial enterprises as may be deemed necessary for the progress of the Organisation and its members.

(e) To establish Branches of the Organisation throughout the African Continent.

(f) To become attached to, or to federate with other Unions, and to be represented on public bodies or other Unions.

(g) To establish Clubs, Debating Societies, etc., with the object of educating the workers, especially on Labour Questions.

(h) To publish pamphlets, newspapers, or any other literature that may be deemed necessary by the National Council or the Board of Arbitration, for the material and spiritual welfare of the members of the Organisation.

(i) To impose levies upon its members to carry out the foregoing objects and for such other National purposes as the National Council may from time to time decide.

(j) All monies expended for any or all of the foregoing objects shall be deemed the capital or current expenditure of the Organisation.

4. Membership

(a) Persons desirous of enrolling in the I.C.U. shall pay an entrance fee at the time of application for enrollment, a weekly contribution as herein laid down, and such other levies as the National Council may impose when deemed necessary.

(b) Europeans are eligible for membership, but under no circumstance shall such member hold office in this Organisation.

(c) Persons wishing to become Honorary members must have their application proposed, seconded, and carried by a majority vote of the members of the Branch to which the application is made.

(d) Honorary members will be admitted to all meetings of their Branch, and may by permission of the Chairman of such Branch speak upon any question, but will not be allowed to vote.

(e) Honorary members shall pay a yearly contribution of not less than five shillings, but shall not be entitled to any benefits.

DOCUMENT 49b-3. Resolutions of demonstration against the Prime Minister's Native Bills, 1926 (Mimeographed, 2 pages)

The Industrial and Commercial Workers Union of Africa, having in mind the definite promises and frequently re-iterated by the Prime Minister that the legislation embodying his Native policy would make provisions whereby the Natives would be assisted by the Government to become possessed of the land which became their heritage under the Act of 1913; and further, that provisions would be made encouraging the development and progress of the Native people —, is compelled to regard the Prime Minister's Native Bills as failing to fulfill his solemn promises, and as constituting a breach of faith which can only result in the most serious menace to the peace and security of this land. It is obvious that the disfranchisement of the Natives in the Cape Province, the serfdom inaugurated by the license-conditions of labour tenants, the nugatory effect of the restricted functions of both the proposed Native Council and the representatives of the Natives in the House of Assembly, as well as the subtle methods by which all representations of the Natives in both the Council and the House are (directly or indirectly) Government nominees, all evidence: —

(1) to refuse the Natives any real participation and responsibility in the Government of the land of their birth;

(2) to discourage the progress or development of the more enlightened section of the people; and

(3) to inaugurate, through forced-labour conditions a fresh era of slavery.

The I.C.U. therefore resolves: —

(1) That the proposed measures, as embodied in the Prime Minister's Native Bills, be strenuously and unconditionally opposed as being a retrogade step in legislation on Native affairs, and as being inimical to the welfare of the Native people.

(2) That the Prime Minister be requested to drop the present proposals, as embodied in the Native Bills, in TOTO; and that organisations and individuals—European and non-Europeans—interested in the welfare of Natives, be asked to submit constructive proposals which shall embrace the following principles: —

(a) The allocation of territories specifically for Native occupation, on such terms and with such reasonable Government assistance as will make it possible for tribes, registered companies and aggregations of Natives to procure land on a secure tenure;

(b) The encouragement of a system of "small-holdings" which shall assist progressive agricultural development by enlightened Natives and aggregations of Natives;

(c) The gradual abolition of the squatting system in such a manner as to avoid hardship and to encourage settlement and development in specifically Native territories;

(d) The revision of the Masters and Servants Acts to render their operation equitable and just.

(e) The abolition of the Pass Laws and the institution of a more equitable and humane system of police supervision and control.

(g)* The repeal of the iniquitous Colour Bar Act, and the institution of some system encouraging the opening up of agricultural, industrial and commercial enterprise by non-Europeans in non-European areas;

(h) The revision of the constitution of the present Annual Native Conference so as to make it more truly representative of the Native people in every walk of life, through a direct vote;

(i) The granting to that Conference, when so re-constituted, of real power of legislation on matters directly affecting the welfare of Natives; and the recognition of such a Conference's opinion on matters indirectly affecting them;

(k)* The retention of the franchise by Native voters in the Cape and the extension of this franchise to Natives and other non-Europeans elsewhere: the qualifications-particularly educational of voters to be raised considerably;

(l) The direct representation of Native opinion in the Native Affairs Commission by the appointment of a Native member thereto;

(m) The revision of the constitution of the Senate so as to make it primarily elective; and the election of a longer portion of the Senate to be representative of Native opinion and interests—such election to be by the direct vote of duly qualified Native voters;

*Items "f" and "j" do not appear in the available manuscript.

(n) The exercise of the provisions of the Electoral Act of 1911 to safeguard and control all elections by Natives; and provision made—with all due safeguards—for the recording of Native voters by post where necessary;

(o) That a period of not less than two years be allowed for such recommendations and schemes to be submitted; and

(p) The provision that any enactments subsequently made shall be scrutinised and revised by the Native Affairs Commission, the Native Annual Conference and the Government, at the end of five years after the commencement of the Act.

It is further resolved:

That the I.C.U. pledges itself to devise and submit a constructive scheme for the removal of disabilities and restrictions imposed by

(a) The Pass Laws,

(b) The Masters and Servants Acts,

(c) The Colour Bar Act;

for the more just treatment of the non-European workers and for the improvement of their conditions of service, and for the encouragement and training with a view to personal advancement and the improvement of the economic and social life of the non-European workers.

DOCUMENT 49b-4. Letter to the Prime Minister, from A.W.G. Champion, Acting National Secretary, I.C.U., May 23, 1927 [Extracts] (Mimeographed, 2 pages)

I.C.U. Head Offices,
16 Market Street,
JOHANNESBURG.
23rd May, 1927.

The Hon. J. B. Hertzog,
Prime Minister, and
Minister for Native Affairs,
House of Assembly,
CAPETOWN.

Honourable Sir,

As one who has been in charge of the I.C.U. movement in Natal, for two years, and as one who is at present in charge of this Union at the Headquarters, in the absence of Mr. Clements Kadalie, I beg leave to submit this statement for your favourable consideration.

(1) Many reports have been put to you by different and respectable members of the European race about the agitation pursued by the Officials of this Union particularly in Natal.

(2) Members of Parliament have made some many unfortunate remarks about the alleged behaviour of the Natives. I have been persuaded to feel that some of the statements have been actuated by political motives.

(3) The Government has been urged to pass Legislation muzzling the legitimate movements of this Organisation. Two weeks ago you were good enough to send the Natal Chief Native Commissioner to Greytown District to ascertain the true position on the spot. On seeing the reports in the Press I offered my services to go there with him, but he refused my offer.

(4) In Orange Free State also, according to the Press reports, Europeans are very much agitated over our movement. I feel that I should ask you to consider our point of view, and, if possible, to grant us the desired opportunity to place our views personally, and, where possible, to receive your personal advice. We feel that the reports that have been taken to you are exaggerative and misleading. I admit that here and there—there has been some irresponsible statements made by some of our Officials.
. . . .

With full knowledge that your hands are full with work at your disposal, I feel, compelled to appeal to you to receive representatives of this Union, who, I have no doubt, will try to give the position as known to them.

There is a feeling in the minds of the Natives, particularly in Natal, that some evidence should be taken of their grievances.

The Government has been made to believe that it is the I.C.U. who are misleading the Natives, but the Government overlook the fact that it is the members of the European public that are doing more harm than the Native agitators, because they are busy telling natives that "We have a bad Government" and etc.

Without trying to exonerate the Union, I represent, I beg to submit that we have been told from the pulpits and the Press, and nearly everywhere, where Natives are employed, that this is a bad Government.

With these facts I again beg to appeal to you to receive a deputation from us with a view of placing our policy before the Government, . . .

I have the honour to be,
Honourable Sir,
Your Humble Servant,
A.W.Geo. Champion
ACTING NATIONAL SECRETARY.

DOCUMENT 49b-5. "Open Letter to Blackpool." Article by Clements Kadalie, in *The New Leader*, September 30, 1927

Most Europeans have some knowledge of the opening up of the "Dark Continent" by the white races, from the commencement of the Slave Trade and the invasion of the Continent by missionaries and white settlers, through the successive stages of colonisation and industrialisation, until 1909, when the separate Colonies of South Africa were grouped into a self-governing unit.

After 1909, most British people, except those directly connected with any of the vast profit-making mining or industrial concerns of the country, have ceased to be particularly interested in events in South Africa. The whole fate of the country, and of her millions of people of subject races, has been left to a small minority of white men, whose immediate interests have been diametrically opposed to the welfare of the vast mass of the population.

The Foundations Of African Civilisation

White civilisation in Africa has been built up on the assumption that the black man is inherently inferior to the white, and that this alleged inferiority gave the white man the right to exploit the black economically, and to oppress him socially and politically. It has been built up on the assumption of the natives forming to all eternity a huge labouring class, satisfied to live on the level of animals, and with little opportunities for education or advancement, and of the white men forming the aristocracy of the country, holding all legislative power in their hands, and doing none but skilled and administrative work, of which the natives, *quo* natives, were assumed to be incapable.

The South African Act of 1909 robbed the natives of political power, the Native Land Act of 1913 robbed them of whatever land still remained to them, and the Colour Bar Act of 1926 forbade them the use of machinery and robbed them of the opportunity for any economic advancement.

The Cracking Of The Foundations

No one but those blinded by self-interest and racial prejudice could have supposed the foundations on which the white men had built their civilisation to be sound. The tide of progress among the natives was inevitable. The men who were called upon to fight in the Great War for "the rights of small nations," and who were stirred by President Wilson's vision of "a world made safe for democracy"—men, moreover, who were learning how civilisation worked from the very labour which the white man forced upon them in the mines and industries of the country—could not long be satisfied to live as animals, with neither rights nor heritage in the country of their birth.

Deprived of all political means of redress for their grievances, the African workers saw in economic organisation their one hope of freedom. In 1919 the Industrial and Commercial Workers' Union of Africa was formed, with a membership of 24. Despite every imaginable persecution and oppression, and the non-cooperation and in some cases even the enmity of the white Trade Unions, the I.C.U. now has a membership of some hundred thousand aboriginal natives, coloured (mixed race) and Indian workers. It must be reckoned with as one of the biggest factors in the history of South Africa at the present time.

The White Trade Unions

The attitude of the white Trade Unions and of the Labour Party in South Africa to the growing movement among the natives for better conditions of life and labour may seem incomprehensible to the workers of other countries whose social philosophy has been built upon a belief in racial equality.

The white Trade Unionists of South Africa have never openly repudiated that philosophy; but the fact must be faced that the wages of the white workers (which are higher than anywhere else in the world) are high because the wages paid to the black workers are so far below subsistence level.

The white Trade Unions have from the first refused to accept natives as members, and in spite of the often-repeated desire of the I.C.U. to cooperate with them, they have refused to do so. The result has been that native strikes to secure better wages and conditions of labour have been broken by the white Trade Unionists, who have filled the places of the black workers, and the I.C.U. has been unable to prevent itself being used as an instrument by the employers to render action by the white Trade Unions non-effective.

In April, 1926, the South African Trades Union Congress, which was sitting simultaneously with the I.C.U. Congress in Johannesburg, refused either to send a representative to the I.C.U. Congress, or to receive a fraternal delegate from the I.C.U. to their own Congress.

The I.C.U., denied the help of the white workers of its own country, and threatened by General Hertzog's Segregation Policy—the Government was about to introduce four native Bills—decided to seek help outside South Africa. The 1926 Congress passed a resolution that affiliation should be sought with the British Trades Union Congress. By the British Trades Union Congress it was advised to seek affiliation instead with the International Federation of Trades Unions, and its application was accepted by that body. At the same time the "Imperialist" Committee of the I.L.P. and various influential individuals in England were doing good work on its behalf. All these factors affected to some extent the attitude of the white Trade Union and Labour Movement in South Africa.

A Gesture To The Whites

The 1927 Congress of the I.C.U. adopted the following resolution:

That in the opinion of this Congress the time has now arrived when both black and white workers of South Africa should join in one national Trade Union Movement, with a view to presenting a united front to one common enemy—namely, the arbitrary and unlimited power of Capitalism—and that this resolution be telegraphed to the South African Trades Union Congress now in session at Cape Town.

The I.C.U. gesture this time met with a more cordial response, and a resolution was adopted by the South African Trades Union Congress to seek ways and means of closer cooperation between the two organisations.

It seemed, therefore, that a rapid change was taking place, and that the work of the I.C.U. was to be made easier by the cooperation of the white workers.

In July, however, came the bombshell. The Union Government, with the support of all but three Labour Party members, passed the Native Administration Act—one of the most iniquitous and drastic repressive measures which any modern Government has ever enacted.

The Real Motive

The real motive of the Act is clearly the suppression of the growing movement among the natives to secure a living wage and decent conditions of existence. It is, in effect, a proclamation of martial law. The Governor General is empowered to prevent any native meetings, to deport any native from one town to another, and to define Pass areas, outside which no native is allowed to go without a special permit, which can be refused on purely arbitrary grounds, or on no grounds at all. The Government states that the Act is designed "to prevent the promotion of any feelings of hostility between natives and Europeans"!

Already the Act is being put into force. I.C.U. meetings are being prohibited. Officials are being forbidden to go from one town to another, and the farmers of Natal, Transvaal and the Orange Free State, taking advantage of the resulting situation, have announced that any black workers known to be members of the I.C.U. will be ejected. Already the farmers have put their policy into operation;

thousands of natives are being rendered homeless, and the efforts of the I.C.U. to assist them, by buying land on which they can live, are blocked by the Native Land Act of 1913, which makes it illegal for natives to purchase any but Crown Lands—which the Government now refuse to sell to them.

The Possibility Of Racial Warfare

If this Act is allowed to remain on the Statute Book the future of South Africa will be dark indeed. Denied all legitimate expression for his grievances and aspirations, who can blame the African if he takes what will seem to him the only possible path to freedom, if he comes to hate the white man as his oppressor, and if the attainment of justice and liberty comes for him to be a thing synonymous with the crushing of the civilisation the white man has built up?

None knows better than we do how fatal is the narrow spirit of nationalism; but, if the present ungenerous and shortsighted policy is continued by the Union Government, what other path will there be for us to take, and who among us will be able to show the African worker, maddened and humiliated by the white man's injustice and oppression, that white civilisation can yet be a fine and beautiful thing, that many of its constructive ideals are sane and desirable, and that its destruction in Africa will be immeasurably to the hurt of the African?

Before It Is Too Late

Before it is too late the workers of the world must come to our assistance. They must force on the South African Government, and on the Labour Party and Trade Union Movement in South Africa, the realisation that civilisation has grown beyond the stage where the happiness and prosperity of the few could be held to justify the oppression and misery of the many. The recognition must be driven home to them that slavery destroys not only the slaves but the slave-owners.

Upon the workers of Britain rests a special responsibility, and to them we appeal for immediate action to be taken. Protection must be assured to millions of defenceless souls, and the subjection of the native races of Africa must end.

DOCUMENT 49b-6. "Economic and Political Program for 1928." Statement by Clements Kadalie, 1928 (Mimeographed, 5 pages)

Industrial And Commercial Workers' Union Of Africa. A Programme For The Year, 1928.

Introductory

Opponents of the I.C.U. have frequently asserted that the Organisation is not a trade union in the sense that the term is generally understood in South Africa, but that it is a kind of pseudo-political body. The ground on which this assertion has been based is the fact that I.C.U. has concentrated its attention on matters in which the issues involved have not been 'purely economic' whilst these 'purely economic' issues have been very largely neglected.

The new constitution, which was adopted at the Special Congress at Kimberley in December last, definitely establishes the I.C.U. as a trade union, albeit one of the native workers whose rights of organisation are only now earning recognition. In these circumstances it has become necessary for the organisation to have a clearly defined economic programme, corresponding to the interests of the membership at large. At the same time it must be clearly understood that we have no intention of copying the stupid and futile "Non-political" attitude of our White contemporaries. As Karl Marx said, every economic question is, in the last analysis, a political question also, and we must recognise that in neglecting to concern ourselves with current politics, in leaving the political machines to the unchallenged control of our class enemies, we are rendering a disservice to those tens of thousands of our members who are groaning under oppressive laws and who are looking to the I.C.U. for a lead.

In the past, the officers of the I.C.U. in the field have had no definite programme to follow, and this has resulted not merely in confusion of ideas, but it has lead to the dissemination of conflicting politics. This being so, I make no apology for introducing the subject of an Economic and Political Programme for the Organisation at this stage. The I.C.U. is a homogeneous national organisation. As such it must have a national policy, consonant with the terms of its constitution, which will serve as a programme of action by which its officials will be guided in their work. The framing of such a policy or programme is essentially the work of Congress, and I propose to give here the broad outlines for a programme, which I trust will serve as a basis of discussion. In view of what I said above it will be realised that it is not necessary to divide the programme into political and economic sections, the two being closely bound up with each other.

I will further preface the proposals I have to make by remarking that our programme must be largely of an agrarian character, for the reason that the greater proportion of our membership comprises rural workers, landless peasants, whose dissatisfaction with conditions is with good reason greater than that of the workers in urban areas. These conditions are only too well known to you to require any restatement from me. The town workers must not, however, be neglected. More attention must in the future be given to their grievances, desires and aspirations if their loyalty to the I.C.U. is to be secured. At the present stage of our development it is inevitable that our activities should be almost entirely of an agitational character for we are not recognised as citizens in our own country, being almost entirely disfranchised and debarred from exercising a say in state affairs closely affecting our lives and welfare. Our programme will therefore be almost entirely agitational in character.

I now detail my proposals, as follows:—

(1) WAGES: A consistent and persistent agitation for improved wages for native workers must be conducted by all branches of the Union. The agitation must be Union-wide, and regard must always be had to local conditions and circumstances. Improvements, however small in themselves, must be welcomed and made the basis on which to agitate for further advances. Every endeavour should be made to enter into friendly negotia-

tions with farmers' associations, employers' Organisations and individual employers in the towns, with a view to securing improvements. If no results are obtained branch secretaries should, wherever practicable, invoke the aid of the Wage Board. In this connection a study of the Wage Act, 1925, is urged.

As an immediate objective, a minimum wage of £5 per month (plus food and housing in country districts) should be striven for. The reasonableness of this claim cannot be disputed by anyone. The attainment of this admittedly low rate, which it must be said few native workers are receiving, is not to be regarded as an end in itself, but as a stepping stone to the ultimate achievement of the full economic rights of the native workers.

(2) HOURS: Insistence should be made on a maximum working day of eight hours and a working week of 5½ days for town and country workers alike. This demand will have the support of all right-thinking and justice-loving people, and members who refuse to exceed this working-time should be given every possible support and encouragement.

(3) ILLEGAL PRACTICES: Illegal practices by employers, such as withholding wages, seizing stock, etc. should be reported to the local Magistrate and Native Affairs Department, with fullest particulars. Any refusal by these officials to deal with complaints, or failure to secure satisfaction for the members concerned should be reported to the Head Office of the Organisation for submission to the higher authorities.

(4) THE FRANCHISE: The proposal of the present government to withdraw the very limited franchise granted to Natives in the Cape Province should be unequivocally condemned at every public gathering of the I.C.U. Further, on the principle: "No taxation without representation" an extension of the franchise to Natives should be demanded. We would suggest that a monster petition be organised by the I.C.U. against the present reactionary proposal and presented to Parliament during the present session.

In the event of the Bill being passed and the franchise being withdrawn a protest should be made by means of a mammoth petition calling into question the necessity and legality of taxing and legislating for a section of the population and citizens without granting them the same representation as provided for the Europeans, at the same time asking for tangible and unbiased reasons why the Natives should not refuse to pay taxes without representation.

(5) PASS LAWS: The Pass Laws are a legal expression of Native enslavement, corresponding with the dark days of Tzarist Russia. They manufacture criminals and possess no moral or ethical justification. It is therefore the duty of the I.C.U. to oppose them by every possible means at its disposal. I would propose that the government be petitioned to suspend the Pass Laws for, say, a period of six months. If, during that period it is found that there has been no increase of lawlessness among the Natives, but that they are just as law-abiding without passes as with them, then the Government should be asked to repeal the Pass Laws in their entirety as there will no longer be any reason or justification, either real or imaginary, for their continuance.

In the event of the government refusing to comply with such a petition, Congress should fix a day of national protest against the Pass Laws, to be marked by mass demonstrations at which all natives should be asked to hand in their passports, the same to be burned in public, by the demonstrations. In addition, those assembled should be pledged by solemn resolution to refuse to carry any further passports or to give any further recognition to the Pass Laws.

(6) LAND: The total area of land set aside for exclusive native occupation in the Union is notoriously inadequate. Parliament should be petitioned through one or more of its members to increase the Native reserves so as to make provision for the landless native farmers. The assistance of labour organisation overseas should be invoked in this matter. In addition, an agitation should be started against the laws prohibiting native squatting.

(7) FREE SPEECH: Vigorous propaganda must be carried on against those provisions in the Native Administration Act which place restricitons on the right of free speech. Ostensibly these provisions are designed to prevent the stirring-up of hostility between the white and black races. Actually they are intended to limit the opportunities

for trade union propaganda and organisation among the native workers. These provisions must therefore be strenuously fought against and their legality challenged where wrongful arrests are carried out. In this connection, no opportunity must be lost of stressing the fact that the I.C.U. is not an anti-European organisation, and that where it has occasion to criticise Europeans it is on grounds of their actions (usually as employers of labour) towards the natives and not on account of the colour of their skins.

(8) PROPAGANDA: Members must be kept fully informed of the activities of the organisation and of all happenings affecting their interests. For this purpose regular members' meetings must be called by Branch Secretaries and the speeches made thereat must not, as heretofore, be of a vague or general agitational character but must deal with concrete and immediate problems. Every endeavour must be made to stimulate a direct personal interest in the affairs of the organisation and to this end questions and discussions by the audience must be encouraged.

The "Workers Herald", our official organ, must be further popularised among the members. If every member bought the paper its circulation could be easily quadrupled and more. The paper could be made to possess an interest for each district if Branch Secretaries would take the trouble to contribute notes concerning local happenings with their comments thereon.

(9) NEW RECRUITS: There are large numbers of native workers to whom the I.C.U. is scarcely known. I refer to the workers on the Witwatersrand gold mines, the Natal Coal Mines and the Railways. Branch Secretaries in these areas should make every endeavour to rope these men in as members of the I.C.U. as they would be an undoubted source of strength. The good work commenced some years ago among Dock Workers has unfortunately been discontinued very largely. Renewed efforts must be made during the ensuing year to bring the strayed ones back to the fold.

(10) REPRESENTATION ON PUBLIC BODIES: It was decided at a previous Congress that advantage be taken of the laws governing Provincial Council elections in the Cape to run official I.C.U. candidates. Native Parliamentary voters are qualified to enter the Cape Provincial Council, and definite steps should be taken to select candidates to stand on behalf of the I.C.U. in Cape constituencies where there is a possibility of securing a fair vote at least. An instruction should be issued to the National Council accordingly, and full preparations should be made by the branch or branches concerned for a thorough election campaign in the next Cape Provincial Council elections. Propaganda must be the main consideration, although every effort must be made to secure the return of any candidates put up.

The question of candidates in the Parliamentary General Elections forms a separate item on the agenda.

In submitting the above outline, I trust that delegates will see with me the urgent necessity for a national policy for the organisation. Once a policy is adopted, and a programme arranged, it must not be allowed to remain on paper, and every official will be expected to do his utmost to translate the same into practice. Only in this way can the organisation grow and become an effective agency for liberating the African workers from the thraldom of slavery.

DOCUMENTS 49c-1—49c-2. Successors of the I.C.U.: I.C.U. Yase Natal

DOCUMENT 49c-1. Constitution, Rules and Bye-Laws, I.C.U. Yase Natal, 1929 [Extracts] (Printed, 21 pages)

1. Name And Jurisdiction

The Organization shall be known as the Industrial and Commercial Workers Union Yase Natal (hereinafter referred to as the I.C.U. or the Union) and shall have jurisdiction over its members in Natal, Zululand and such Branches as may be formed and established in other parts of Africa. In it alone is vested authority to establish Branches and reserves to itself the right to negotiate, regulate and determine all matters affecting the well-being or interests of all its members.

2. Head Quarters And Constitution

(1) The Head Office and management of the Union shall be located at Durban, Natal, but any Branch may demand a ballot of the Union for its removal to any other centre having more than 1000 members.

(2) The I.C.U. Yase Natal shall be a registered Trade Union and shall be constituted of all persons employed in any Undertaking, Industry, Trade, Commerce or other occupation.

(3) The membership shall be divided into the following sections or Branches or such other divisions as may be deemed expedient or necessary:—

    (A) AGRICULTURAL WORKERS
    (B) BUILDING WORKERS
    (C) CLERKS AND SHOP WORKERS
    (D) DOMESTIC WORKERS
    (E) FACTORY WORKERS
    (F) MUNICIPAL WORKERS
    (G) MINE WORKERS
    (H) MARINE WORKERS
    (I) PROFESSIONAL WORKERS
    (J) RAILWAY WORKERS
    (K) TRANSPORT WORKERS
    (L) WAREHOUSE WORKERS
    (M) WATERSIDE WORKERS &
    (N) GENERAL WORKERS.

3. Others

Recognising that all human beings have a body to nourish, a brain to develop and a soul to unfold and express itself in right living, the I.C.U. *Yase* Natal stands, primarily, for the emancipation of the African Workers by the gradual introduction of industrial, political and social democracy, with equality of opportunity for all men in all spheres of life, therefore the objects of the Union shall be:—

(1) To organise wherever possible Branches of the I.C.U. Yase Natal, to protect, regulate and increase the wages of its members and to obtain and maintain just and proper hours of work and conditions of employment.

(2) To establish a Land Fund to acquire, lease, mortgage, hold, or otherwise deal with land, building farms, holdings, stock cattle, and implements, or such other methods as may be deemed expedient to find homes and employment for its members who are or may be evicted or thrown out of work.

(3) To establish and open up Branches of the African Workers Co-operative Society, to secure the greatest possible value for its members when spending their wages on the food, clothes or goods they need or when selling the products of their land or labour.

(4) To negotiate and settle differences and disputes between the members of the Union and their employers and other persons through Conferences, collective bargaining, agreements, conciliation boards, industrial boards, withdrawal of labour or other legal action.

(5) To participate, affiliate, federate, financially or otherwise, directly or indirectly, with all properly constituted Trade Unions, Federations, Congresses or other organizations having for their objects the furthering of the interests of labour and Trade-unionism, locally, nationally and/or internationally as may be deemed expedient.

(6) To assist financially or otherwise its members in distress, sickness, old age, and to make provisions for mortality allowance and funeral expenses on the death of a member.

(7) To provide legal advice and assistance to the Union and its members wherever it is necessary or expedient.

(8) To strive constitutionally for Political emancipation and the full rights of citizenship, free primary and secondary education and, ultimately, equality in Church, State and social life.

(9) To establish Schools, Leagues, Debating Societies, Churches, Clubs and such like Institutions having among their objects the training, education and upliftment of Trade Unionist and their children.

(10) To make provisions and opportunities for social intercourse and the promotion of sport and social events among its members.

(11) To establish, or carry on, or participate financially or otherwise, directly or indirectly, the business of printing or publishing of books or pamphlets, journals, newspapers or other literature that may be deemed necessary for the material, intellectual and spiritual welfare of its members.

(12) The I.C.U. *Yase* Natal shall have power to raise funds by borrowing money on

any real or personal property of the Union in such manner and on such terms as may be necessary and shall also have power to provide Funds by subscription, levy or otherwise as the Union may direct for maintaining these objects or some of the benefits from time to time authorised in pursuance of these Rules and for the establishment or maintenance of any undertaking of any kind financially or otherwise authorised by the Union calculated to further the interests of the Union or its members or the Trade Union or Co-operative movement generally.

DOCUMENT 49c-2. "Blood and Tears." Pamphlet by A.W.G. Champion, 1929 [Extracts] (Published in *History of Durban Native Riots*)

The author wishes to put on record in the second edition of this book that it is not because he wants to create ill-feeling between the natives and Europeans that he has published this book, nor because he wants to encourage the native to resist the constituted authority. Far from it. He has been persuaded to write this history by those who are familiar with the history of South Africa, which is full of misrepresentation. Right from Kings Tshaka, Dingaan and Chief Bambata, the native point of view has been misrepresented. Those who took part in Bambata's rebellion truly believe that, if the Natives who led the organisations then only did their duty and had the point of view of the Natives who had carried the armed protest the late Chief Dinizulu could not have been convicted for anything, and many of the Natives who were sentenced by the Native High Court would have been discharged. The damage that swept through the Natal and Zululand Native districts could not have taken place. At that time the leaders of the Native people in Natal were Ministers of Christian religion. They only prayed instead of getting up and doing something practical. We have the lesson in the Five Shillings rebellion, when a number of Dutchmen led by General De Wet and Manie Maritz revolted against the Union Government. Their action was defended by men like our present Minister even in the House of Assembly. It was an armed protest—not rebellion—they said. The same applied to Bambata's rebellion, and there shall always be armed protests as long as the rulers that be are not prepared to respond to the genuine grievances of those who are governed. I know I was present during the Rand Revolution, when the workers of the Rand armed themselves and protested against not only the Mining Industry, but against the action of the Smuts Government. Men died and men were imprisoned. There was blood and tears such as was seen in Durban on the 14th, 17th and 18th June, 1929, when men were killed on both sides and others were imprisoned. We have the arresting pictures of two native workers who died, and their photos were taken after death in the Hospital. We have the other two pictures, one of the men who lost his eye and another who lost his leg. I have been accused by some Europeans of justifying this by calling it an armed protest. It was an armed protest and was used for warning both the employers and the Government that unless they were prepared to respond to the genuine grievances of the black workers there would be a repetition of these armed protests on a bigger scale.

Durban has too much reliance on heads of the Departments, who claim to know the mind of the Natives because of the fact that they were born and brought up amongst the Natives and speak their language fluently.

These officials believe that the proper way of controlling the Native is through their own Native Chiefs; that each Native who has a complaint must individually appeal personally to the head of the Department concerned. They discourage any attempt at collective bargaining by Natives.

Durban has the Joint Council of Europeans and Natives, which is officially recognised by the Town Council. This Council consists of equal numbers of Europeans and Natives. The election of the members is left entirely in the hands of the members of the Council themselves. They choose those whom they like from the public, and as such their membership is limited to a circle of friends, who invite each other whenever an opportunity occurs. This is not the position in Pietermaritzburg or Johannesburg. Natives have two organizations—the Natal Native Congress and the

Industrial and Commercial Workers' Union Yase Natal. These two are not represented in the Joint Council. These two are the only ones who hold public meetings with the Natives of Durban and peri-Durban.

Durban has reached the stage of Johannesburg of 1919 and 1920, when the Native had lost every hope with white officials, and was losing confidence with many good things which were being organised by European friends.

This hopeless position was met by men like the late Mr. F. B. Bridgman, Mr. Howard Pim, Rev. Winifred Parker and others, who, after obtaining the Rev. R. E. Phillips finally organised the Joint Council of Europeans and Natives, which, I believe, was suggested by the late Dr. K. Aggrey. This Joint Council consisted of the members representing different rival organisations—Native Congress, Teachers' Union, Ministers' Association, and Clerks' Association sent in their elected representatives, while the Joint Council invited men who belonged to no other organisations.

To listen to these rival leaders talking their own minds was educative and inspiring.

The slogan was co-operation between Europeans and Natives in the true sense, never mind who has sinned the most.

The writer represented the Transvaal Native Mine Clerks' Association, and actually took part in some of the most memorable debates of 1921 up to 1925.

Ministers came forward with their case. Commercial men came forward, while the Professors of the Witwatersrand brought forward bombs, and the Natives, represented by their soap-box orators, ventilated their views without fear or favour.

The result was that from the frank discussion extremists on both sides began to appreciate each other's point of view, and loose talk on the Native platform diminished, as well as loose talk on the European side; in the Bench, pulpit, and the press it subsided, as all these had to be opposed by a group of men and women who met for one purpose only—that of co-operation between white and black and eradication of colour prejudice.

The Government began to respect the voice of this mixed Union.

The danger that we see looming in Durban was evaded by men some of whom had encouraged hatred and despair between the two races. The office of the Locations Department in Johannesburg was the centre of all the storms. This office being similar to that of the Municipal Native Affairs Department, Durban, was controlled by a Zulu linguist, who ruled with a firm hand and had the absolute support of his Council always. It was not until there was a conflict between the white and black that the authorities began to see, and as the result of the recommendation his absolute powers were diminished.

The policy of strong will, which creates the feeling of oppression in the minds of those who are controlled, never succeeds. It always leads to bloodshed and tears such as we have seen in Durban on June 14, 17 and 18, 1929. You can oppress people for some time, but you cannot oppress them for ever without creating in them that feeling whose symptoms always lead to the conflict between them and their rulers. The amendments of the Native Urban Areas Act, giving power to Local Authorities, will not help the situation. These are the means of oppression, which is bound to react. The increasing hatred between Natives in Durban and the Police Authorities will not diminish because they get more powers to arrest and convict, because the Native Affairs officials are to be crowned with absolute administrative powers. The Natives of Durban have now eyes to see and ears to hear.

Mr. Justice D. de Waal in his report says:—

"Mr. Champion, their leader, has failed in his laudable object he said he had in view, of bettering the conditions of the Native worker. Where he had much success, however, is in sowing the seeds of discontent in the minds of his fellow Natives less favoured than himself, and causing much friction between employer and Native employee and between the Borough Council and the Native."

During the inquiry, Mr. Cecil Cowley, cross-examining John Chester, Chief Clerk for Native Affairs, Borough of Durban, remarked:

"The Fact is that Natives have suffered under so many grievances that they have been forced to conclude that they cannot receive any attention from Municipal Department of

Native Affairs except harsh laws harshly administered. No sympathy or response to be obtained; a round dozen of laws and by-laws made by the Department have been declared ultra vires during the last twelve months.

The position in Durban is very peculiar. Here we have men whose qualifications to manage Native Affairs Department are that they were born amongst the Natives and they can speak their language. It matters not whether they are not educated. These men have to be the means of communication between the Europeans and Natives, and, in fact, to help the Governing Bodies to legislate for the good of the Natives of the land. On these men rests the responsibility for the welfare of the Natives of this land in their varying degrees. To them alone the country looks for the lasting peace between the white and black races in South Africa.

The fact is admitted, rightly or wrongly, that one man in the person of Mr. A. W. G. Champion has succeeded in sowing the seeds of discontent, and the question at once arises forcibly: Will harsh laws administered harshly destroy little plants of discontent which are fast growing to bear fruit? We have seen the bloodshed and tears in Durban. We see the Kaffir beer boycott which has cleaned dry the beer halls, not only in Durban, but is threatening the whole Province. We see the increase of the "Kill me quick drink" and the increasing bitterness between the general Native public and the police officers, particularly those of the Borough of Durban. Are the present officers capable of restoring confidence, which is admittedly lost, or are they not? If not, may one trust that the Government will not depend upon their advice, admittedly actuated by the spirit of defeat, but rather encourage the spirit of consultation by men whose personalities are beyond any doubt, men who are not born and bred amongst Natives nor speak their tongue—may one say, men of Dutch race, Afrikanders, whose attitude as far as Natal is concerned, has been one of square deal for everybody as against that of English rulers of keep all classes of Natives under the rule of their ignorant Chiefs.

DOCUMENTS 50a -50b. Cape Voters

DOCUMENT 50a. Petition to the South African Parliament, from the Cape Native Voters' Convention, January 3, 1928 (Published in *Imvo Zabantsundu*)

The third conference of the Cape Native Voters' Convention which met in East London on the 17th December was very largely attended by delegates from every section of the Cape Province. The following petition to Parliament was framed and unanimously passed:—

To the Hon. the Speaker and Gentlemen of the House of Assembly and the Hon. the President and Gentlemen of the Senate in Parliament assembled:

The petition of the undersigned registered native voters and acting under the authority of the Cape Native Voters' Convention assembled in congress at East London on Dec. 19, 1927, humbly sheweth—

1. That whereas the Government has found it expedient to introduce the Representation of Natives in Parliament Bill as part of its native policy which is embodied in the four native Bills published as Government Notice No. 1290 of 1926 framed by the Prime Minister of the Union of South Africa, your humble petitioners representing the Cape Native Voters' Convention have enjoyed the franchise privilege since 1854, having been granted by the late Queen Victoria through her representative Sir George Grey.

2. That your petitioners regard their franchise right as a charter of liberties on behalf of both themselves and all other natives of the Union as well as their posterity, viewing this as an inalienable privilege of all genuine British native citizens.

3. That no cause has been shown by any adverse critic to prove that this privilege has ever been misused or abused.

4. That such adverse criticism as has been levelled against our franchise has been fully collated and sufficiently refuted in a pamphlet "The Cape Native Franchise" (by Prof. D. D. T. Jabavu).

5. And that whereas the deprivation of the civic right of the franchise in all known historical precedents has always been inflicted

as an extreme penalty for treason and rebellion, there is no justification for this unwarranted procedure in the case of your petitioners.

6. That whilst your petitioners gratefully recognise the Premier's declared intention to grant some measure of Parliamentary representation to the natives of the Northern Provinces, your petitioners humbly submit that the solid and undivided opinion of all thinking natives in the Union uncompromisingly opposes any tampering with the Cape Native Franchise in its existing form.

7. Further that whilst your petitioners appreciate the offers made under the Union Council Bill, your petitioners do not regard such as an equivalent, as substitute for the Cape Native Franchise.

8. Wherefore your petitioners humbly and respectfully pray that the Union Government of South Africa may be pleased to abandon the Representation of Natives in Parliament Bill as being totally undesired and not calculated to advance the political aspirations of the Bantu races.

9. And as in duty bound your petitioners will ever pray.

DOCUMENT 50b. Report on the proceedings of the Annual Conference of the Cape Native Voters' Convention, in *Imvo Zabantsundu*, January 8, 1929

After some discussion regarding the internal affairs of the Convention, the most important matter of the session was the election policy of the Convention for the coming general election. The Chairman called upon Mr. Godlo to open the discussion. Mr. Godlo, after making a number of introductory remarks, which he concluded by saying that a thing to be eaten by the big men was to be tested by the young men, came directly to the point by saying that at present no Native knew what he was going to do. Vote they must, but then there were two parties which wanted their votes, the Pact and the S.A.P.

The Convention must not compromise itself. Its members must be united in protecting the Cape Native franchise. Unity in this was essential, for without unity they might as well cease to strive altogether and leave the whole matter in the hands of their rulers and have no voice in it. "In your hands," he said, "lies the destiny of your people."

In paying a tribute to Professor Jabavu, he said, that if the Europeans ever had a means of judging the Natives' right to the franchise Professor Jabavu had. supplied the means. Continuing, he said that all the Natives were aware of the expressions of opinion made about them by the political leaders of to-day. General Hertzog was all fire and brimstone and had always been the same. It had been said that the Europeans first duty was to study his own interests and that view still obtained widely. They all knew that General Hertzog daily reminded the country of his opinion that the Native franchise was a menace to its white civilisation, and had urged its abolition. Then there was General Smuts. There were occasions when one had Hobson's choice and had to choose one of two evils. General Smuts had repeatedly postponed the Native question in the past and said today, "Let us leave the Cape Native franchise alone for the time being."

It was now for the delegates to make a choice and their clear considered opinions were wanted as it was their custom to decide at the Convention on a course of action and to abide by what was said there.

A delegate here expressed the opinion that the Natives should vote S.A.P. as there were many reasons against voting for Hertzog's party. They all knew General Smuts' faults but he appeared to be the lesser evil.

Mr. A.M. Jabavu said he knew both Smuts and Hertzog wanted the Natives' votes but they all definitely knew that General Smuts was merely in favour of leaving the matter of the Native franchise in abeyance. He had not been definite as to whether it was to be abolished or not. At a recent S.A.P. Congress he had noted that the matter of white women's franchise was urged while the Native franchise hardly concerned the Congress. Hertzog, on the other hand, had recently in the O.F.S. said that the white women should wait for their vote until the Native question was settled. There was nothing to convince the Native, however, that the S.A.P. would fight for his franchise. The matter was left in abeyance as he considered Smuts wanted to get into power. "Is it not better to kill a cow to-day," he asked, "than to let it know it must be killed and keep it until to-morrow before taking it to slaughter?" (Laughter.)

Another reason why the Convention should not decide yet upon which party it was to vote for was the fact that the Native really had no power. The Natives working in the towns voted as their white masters did and so did those labouring on the farms. They were, in fact, led by the nose by the white people. "Whether we like it or not", he said, "it is the truth. We can't say we'll do a thing and then go and do it." If the employer told his Native employee to vote for the devil he would.

Continuing Mr. Jabavu gave a possible example in the imaginary case of a young Native in the country who owned say £30 to a Jew trader. The Jew would tell him how to vote and might threaten him with suing him for the money he owed if he didn't vote as he had been told. The young man would then vote that way, remembering only the summons and forgetting that the Jew would not know how he had voted as the ballot was secret. (Laughter.)

"So I oppose the proposal to support any certain party," he said. "My conviction is that we should protect our franchise right without consideration for the election." There were Nationalists who supported the retention of the Native Franchise as well as S.A.P. It was wrong for the Natives to choose political parties. Let them rather support those candidates who favoured and would support the retention of the Cape Native Franchise.

The Editor of the *Izwi LaBantu* said it might pay them to put their heads in the sand like the proverbial ostrich but as the Bills in connection with the Native question had not yet been discussed, the whole matter might be considered as "sub judice". They should not go to any party yet. The Native question should not be made a political party question. It appeared that certain parties had persuaded the Prime Minister to keep it out of the political arena, and they must remember this. In any case as Mr. A.M. Jabavu had pointed out the real fact of how a vote was cast was a secret in the ballot box. The Native need not differentiate much between Dutch and

English—they were both his rulers and the Convention must find a via media so as to be able to go to both races. The best policy for the Natives was a neutral one.

Mr. Mentoor remarked that if it was decided to give the Natives votes to any certain political party it meant that they might have to vote for any unwise man who was labelled by that party. They wanted as members men of high moral character, men who would make no difference between the black and white races when legislating for the country. He went on to say that the system in New Zealand would suit this country very well. If they were treated like the Maoris the Natives of South Africa would lose nothing and could support the side that had their interests at heart.

Other delegates spoke in support of Mr. A.M. Jabavu and one delegate asserted that General Smuts had definitely declared that he was in favour of the retention of the Native franchise and the Convention should therefore identify itself with General Smuts' Party. He received no support, however, and after a little further discussion, it was moved and carried "that the Cape Native Voters' Convention are not going to commit themselves to support any political party but will vote so the candidates serve, and only for candidates who favour the Cape Native franchise".

DOCUMENTS 51a-51c. Urban Africans Organize

DOCUMENT 51a. "Urban Native Legislation." Address by R.H. Godlo, President, Location Advisory Boards' Congress of South Africa, December 19, 1929 (Published in the *Report of the Location Advisory Boards' Congress of South Africa*)

Mr. Chairman, Friends and Fellow-Delegates,

It is with much fear and trembling that I venture to stand before you to address you as first president of the "Location Advisory Boards' Congress of South Africa" since its inauguration as a duly constituted body.

Never before have I been so deeply conscious of the fact that I do not possess any of the necessary qualifications for the highly responsible position I occupy. My only consolation lies in the hope that this, our first Congress, will lose no time in calling upon one of our respected and tried leaders who are present here to-day, such as the Rev. Dr. W. B. Rubusana, Messrs. T. M. Mapikela, A. M. Jabavu and others, to assume this important position; and I can assure you that when that hour comes I shall only be too glad to abdicate in favour of any of them.

My heart is filled with unfeigned joy at seeing such a large gathering assembled here from distant parts of the Union to take part in this very important conference. To every patriot and thinking man who loves his people and takes a keen interest in their affairs, it is a favourable sign, as it indicates an awakening from lethargy and bestirring ourselves to face the issues now confronting us. Therefore, in the name of this Congress, I greet you all with heartfelt gratitude for your presence here to-day, and I desire to extend to you all a cordial welcome to this our first Congress.

Now to come to the subject that has brought us together, it is necessary that I should put you in the way of understanding the basis upon which this Congress is founded. Some of you will remember that about twelve months ago, Mr. A. M. Jabavu, our Vice President, in response to numerous correspondents in the Bantu press, convened a meeting of Location Advisory Boards to meet in Queenstown. The invitation met with a good response and no fewer than fourteen Boards were represented at that Conference.

The result of that meeting was the formation of this the "Location Advisory Boards' Congress of South Africa," which has as its objects:—(a) To unite all Urban Location Advisory Boards constituted under the Natives (Urban Areas), Act No. 21 of 1923; and to secure the better adjustment of conditions socially, economically and generally of Natives resident in Municipal Locations; (b) to induce co-operation and promote understanding between Municipal Authorities and Natives residing in urban areas; and (c) to make such representations to the Union Government, Provincial Councils, Municipal Congresses, Municipal Councils and other public bodies as may be thought necessary.

It was pointed out at that meeting that the Bantu people in these Locations were suffering from many disabilities, the foremost among which were the refusal of certain municipalities to grant trading facilities to the Bantu in such Locations; the insecurity of land tenure; the unsatisfactory conditions under which some Natives are housed therein; the irksomeness of some of the Regulations framed under Section 23 (3), of the Natives (Urban Areas), Act of 1923, and the failure of municipalities generally to establish Native Villages in terms of Section 1 (1) (b) of the Act.

The meeting felt that it was the duty of the leaders of Bantu thought to endeavour to use all constitutional means in order to ameliorate these disabilities. Being mindful of the fact that their people in these areas were governed under the Natives (Urban Areas) Act which was introduced by the late Government for the social improvement of Native life in the towns, and the operation of which to a large extent depended upon the good faith of Local Authorities, the delegates emphasised the point that one of the aims of the Congress should be as far as possible to establish harmony and good understanding between Local Authorities and town Natives.

Therefore, you are called here to-day to put these aims and objects into definite shape.

My original intention was to review in this my humble Address, the provisions of the Natives (Urban Areas) Act, and if possible, to give a brief resume of legislation affecting urban Natives prior to the passing of that Act. Unfortunately, my recent illness, which was somewhat severe, interrupted my researches with the result that everything towards that end was completely put out of gear. However, I hope my successor will take the matter up.

The year just ended has been an uneventful one as no legislation of importance affecting urban Natives has been placed on the Statute Book, and furthermore, my colleagues and I have been occupied with the task of laying the foundation of this great organisation. But as you will observe when we resume the routine business of the Congress, a Bill of paramount importance as far as we are concerned has been published. I refer to the Bill to amend the Natives (Urban Areas) Act of 1923, and you will soon be called upon to make such comments and suggestions as you may deem necessary.

As you are no doubt aware, municipalities all over the Union are faced with the problem of the unprecedented migration of Natives to urban centres noticeable in recent years, with the result that some of them are unable to cope with the surplus Native population in the way of employment and housing. In consequence certain local authorities approached the Government with a view to the amendment of the principal Act in such form as to allow them not only to close their doors against Native ingress into, but to repatriate them from the towns.

The point of view of the municipalities in this respect is not altogether unreasonable as this unsatisfactory state of affairs has been created by the Government in passing the repressive provisions of the Natives Land Act, of 1913, which restricted the purchase and lease of land by Natives in certain areas. Commerce and industry come under the same category, as the inadequacy of wages paid to Natives is one of the contributory causes to the existing state of affairs, because commerce and industry are benefitting at the expense of both the municipalities and Natives. These latter together make up the deficiency in Native wages. The municipalities make it up by loan charges, which are borne either by the Native Revenue Account to which all monies expended for improvements in areas set apart for Native occupation are chargeable, or by contributions from general rates. The Natives make up their share of the difference by practising rigid economy in their mode of living with the inevitable result that in all big industrial and commercial centres with large Native populations, the death rate among infants is always appalling. As proof of this contention, all investigations in this connection point to the fact that this high infantile death rate is not wholly due to ignorance on the part of their parents, as some would have us believe.

I have endeavoured to show that the point of view of the municipalities is by no means altogether unreasonable, but the attitude they propose to take up is wrong, and will never lead the country to a satisfactory solution of this phase of the Native complex. The only way towards a solution of this problem lies in the adjustment of the conditions of rural Natives, and unless the Natives Land Act is amended as suggested, the chances for a sure remedy are as remote as the Greek Kalends. At this juncture I may remind you that it has been suggested by some foolish and inconsiderate persons that the welfare and prosperity of the black and white races in South Africa depended in a large measure on the complete segregation from the towns and the gradual repatriation of all male Natives to the country, except such as are housed under the compound system while serving periods of employment. As a preliminary to this novel suggestion the Government was urged to substitute such words as "compounds" for "locations" and "compound annexure" for "native hostel."

You will agree with me that these "suggestions" amount to nothing less than an agitation for the abolition of the existing Native townships and the substitution therefore of reservoirs of cheap labour to be styled "compounds." The repatriation theory is as absurd and as puerile as to aver that the non use of petrol in motor cars would accelerate their motion.

I shall not waste any more of your valuable time in dealing with these "excellent" expositions of superficial nonsense. Suffice it to say that the least examination knocks the bottom out of this new theory.

Your duty as trusted leaders of the great Bantu race is to sink all your petty tribal and provincial differences and take counsel together upon these matters which are embittering our inter-racial relationships.

I sincerely hope that when we arrive at the stage of considering the new Bill I have referred to, the criticism and suggestions of this Congress, in the interests of our people, will be of a constructive nature, and thereby demonstrate to the European community that with the Bantu people colour prejudice does not outweigh discretion.

My desire and prayer is that you will be happy and comfortable during the short time you will be in this beautiful town. [Bloemfontein.]

DOCUMENT 51b. "Urban Native Legislation." Memorandum to the Minister for Native Affairs from the Location Advisory Boards' Congress of South Africa, September 8, 1930 (Published in the *Report of the Location Advisory Boards' Congress of South Africa*)

The "Location Advisory Boards' Congress of South Africa" has examined the Natives (Urban Areas) Act, Amendment Act No. 25, of 1930, without prejudice or hostility, and regrets that it is compelled to view some of its provisions with disappointment.

Therefore, the president of the Congress (Mr. R. H. Godlo), availed himself of the opportunity afforded by the visit of the Honourable the Minister for Native Affairs to East London and submitted the following observations on behalf of the Urban Native community:—

1. The Act amends Act No. 21, of 1923, by giving urban local authorities additional powers to restrict the ingress of Natives into urban areas and to remove all Natives from European areas, save certain classes who may be exempted; to prosecute and to repatriate all Natives believed to be habitually unemployed; to prohibit the entry of female Natives into proclaimed areas and to tighten up the laws governing Curfew Regulations.

2. In the humble opinion of the Congress the foregoing provisions are altogether of a far-reaching character. The Congress has been, and still is, under the impression that it was not the intention of the framers of the 1923 Act to unduly restrict the movements of Natives to industrial and commercial centres, but to regulate their ingress into such centres so that they will not become a burden to the urban authorities.

3. The principal Act, according to the preamble, was intended *"to provide for improved conditions of residence for Natives in or near urban areas and the better administration of Native affairs in such areas; for the registration and better control of contracts of service with Natives in certain areas and the regulation of the ingress of Natives into and their residence in such areas; for the restriction and regulation of the possession and use of kafir-beer and other intoxicating liquor by Natives in certain areas, and for other incidental purposes."*

4. From the foregoing it would appear that the Congress is more than justified in coming to the conclusion that this Act goes farther than the Principal Act. In reality it touches the whole question of the relations between white and black in this country. For these reasons the Congress is of opinion that the wise course for the Government would have been to consult both the urban local authorities and Native opinion before bringing the Bill to Parliament.

5. In dealing with Native legislation it should always be borne in mind that the Bantu people are almost entirely unrepresented in the Councils of State. They have no means of having their views placed directly before the legislature, except in the Cape Province where they enjoy a modicum of representation. This brings us face to face with another phase of the Native complex, namely, the desirability or otherwise of consulting Natives on matters affecting their welfare.

6. Needless to say, the principle of consultation was accepted by those in authority more than ten years ago, and the matter was brought to its logical conclusion by being embodied in the Native Affairs Act, of 1920. That Act lays it down in unmistakable terms that Natives will be consulted on any legislation affecting them. But for nearly five years the annual conference between the Government and representatives of Native organisations has ceased to function. As a matter of fact the failure of the Government to summon such a conference during the last four years was regarded as a strong argument in favour of referring the Bill to a Select Committee so as to enable the Natives to come forward and give evidence.

7. Therefore, it is not to be wondered at that certain responsible leaders of the Bantu race, rightly or wrongly, have been forced to the conclusion that the Government has abandoned the principle of consultation as far as Natives are concerned. However, it was gratifying to receive the assurance of the Prime Minister that the conference has not been abandoned; and we cherish the hope that the Honourable the Minister for Native Affairs

will be pleased to summon another such conference at his earliest convenience and show the Natives that it is the desire of the present Government to take them into confidence in matters affecting their welfare.

8. Regarding the provisions of the amending Act, the clauses to which exception is taken may be summarised thus:—

1. Section 2 (b) which becomes (f) of sub-section 1, section 1 of the Principal Act, empowers urban local authorities to remove from the urban areas every Native residing in but is not employed in such areas, save certain classes exempted under paragraphs (a), (b), (c), and (d) of sub-section (2) of section five of the Principal Act.

2. Section seven (a) which becomes paragraph (d) of (1) of section twelve of the present Act, gives local authorities powers to prohibit female Natives from entering proclaimed areas, unless such females obtain certificates of approval from the local authorities concerned, which certificates should be produced on demand by an authorised officer.

3. Section eight which repeals section seventeen (1) of the Principal Act authorises the prosecution of Natives believed to be habitually unemployed, or are leading idle or dissolute lives, etc., or have been convicted for contravening certain provisions of the Native Administration Act of 1927, or have committed any offence mentioned in the Third Schedule to the Criminal Procedure and Evidence Act, No. 31 of 1917 or some other offence mentioned in paragraph (e) of this section; or is a female contravening the provisions of the preceding section.

9. Taking the three clauses seriatim, the Congress desires to make the following humble observations:—

1. As the Congress is not opposed to separate residence for Natives in these areas no exception is taken to the principle of this clause, but we fail to understand the reason why Natives employed as night-watchmen or caretakers for whom accommodation is provided in or near the business centres of the towns are not exempted from the operation of this clause in the same way as domestic servants. Therefore, Congress humbly requests the Minister to reconsider the question of

amending the same so as to exempt these classes of Natives

2. Whilst Congress is not opposed to the regulation of the movements of unattached females and minors, the application of these restrictions to married women whose husbands are employed in these areas and unmarried daughters whose fathers reside therein, is viewed with alarm and disappointment. The enforced separation of married couples for a period of not less than two years is calculated to shake the moral stability of the male Natives residing in such areas. The Natives view this restriction as an unnecessary interference with family life and the liberty of the subject. Therefore, the Congress respectfully requests the Minister to exempt married women whose husbands reside in such areas; and in the case of unmarried daughters whose fathers also reside therein, from the operation of the provisions of this clause.

3. Whilst the Congress has no desire to see the locations turned into places of refuge for all sorts of undesirables, we submit that most of the people now forming the urban Native population have been forced to migrate to the towns by forces over which they have no control. Among them may be found honest and well-meaning Natives who have become victims of the repressive provisions of the Natives Land Act of 1913 and others who have come to the industrial and commercial centres for the purpose of seeking employment to meet the present taxation which is altogether out of all proportion to their means.

10. These items again bring us face to face with other phases of the Native question, namely, scarcity of land and disproportionate taxation. It may be argued that the provisions of the Natives Land Act do not apply to the Cape Province (which has admittedly the poorest Native community). We submit that that Act affects the Cape to the same extent as the other three Provinces, because evictions of squatters and labour-tenants from European-owned farms in the other Provinces have led to the unprecedented drift to the towns. Moreover, there are certain areas in this Province where the purchase of land by Natives is allowed only by special permission of the Governor-General. As to overcrowding in the Native reserves, the fact that 1½ million

Europeans own about 80 per cent of the land while 5½ million Natives own 20 per cent speaks for itself. It is therefore hoped that when the Commission recently appointed by the Government has submitted its report on the condition of Natives, the Minister will see that the remedy is applied immediately.

11. TRADING LICENCES: Regarding the amounts charged for these licences, experience has shown that the scale laid down in the Second Schedule to the Licences Consolidation Act, No. 32, of 1925, is rather too excessive for people whose trade is confined solely to Natives. Therefore, we would humbly urge the Minister to consider the advisability of amending the Act so as to make the scale applicable to the Native Territories apply to urban locations as well, because the same consideration that prompted the framers of that Act to grant this relief to the Territories applies to the urban Native locations.

12. NATIVE ADVISORY BOARDS: The Congress is pleased to note that both the Government and the municipalities are agreed that these Boards are working well and have justified their existence. But in our humble opinion it would facilitate their work and bring about more harmony and good understanding between them and local authorities if their functions were clearly defined. At present although the phrase "functions of Advisory Boards" is made use of in both the principal and the amending Acts, these "functions" are not defined or interpreted in either of these statutes.

13. CURFEW REGULATIONS: The Congress still regrets that it fails to appreciate the reason for the determination of the Government in maintaining curfew laws in this country. The solid and undivided opinion of the Bantu people as well as unbiased Europeans is that these Pass Laws have completely outlived their usefulness. However, while this opinion has not yet convinced those in authority, we would humbly urge the Government to extend the exemptions so as to include all classes of Natives hitherto exempted from the operation of the Curfew Regulations under Sections 2 and 3 of the Local Authorities Increased Powers Act, No. 30, of 1895.

DOCUMENT 51c. "Social Conditions Among Bantu Women and Girls." Address by Charlotte Maxeke at the Conference of European and Bantu Christian Student Associations at Fort Hare, June 27-July 3, 1930 [Extract] (Published in *Christian Students and Modern South Africa*)

In speaking of Bantu women in urban areas, the first thing to be considered is the Home, around which and in which the whole activity of family life circulates. First of all, the Home is the residence of the family, and home and family life are successful only where husband and wife live happily together, bringing up their family in a sensible way, sharing the responsibilities naturally involved in a fair and wholehearted spirit. The woman, the wife, is the keystone of the household: she holds a position of supreme importance, for is she not directly and intimately concerned with the nurturing and upbringing of the *children* of the family, the future generation? She is their first counsellor, and teacher; on her rests the responsibility of implanting in the flexible minds of her young, the right principles and teachings of modern civilisation. Indeed, on her rests the failure or success of her children when they go out into life. It is therefore essential that the home atmosphere be right, that the mother be the real "queen" of the home, the inspiration of her family, if her children are to go out into the world equipped for the battles of life.

There are many problems pressing in upon us Bantu, to disturb the peaceful working of our homes. One of the chief is perhaps the stream of Native life into the towns. Men leave their homes, and go into big towns like Johannesburg, where they get a glimpse of a life such as they had never dreamed existed. At the end of their term of employment they receive the wages for which they have worked hard, and which should be used for the sustenance of their families, but the attractive luxuries of civilisation are in many instances too much for them, they waste their hard earned wages, and seem to forget completely the crying need of their family out in the veld.

The wife finds that her husband has apparently forgotten her existence, and she therefore makes her hard and weary way to the town in search of him. When she gets there, and starts looking round for a house of some sort in which to accommodate herself and her children, she meets with the first rebuff. The Location Superintendent informs her that she cannot rent accommodation unless she has a husband. Thus she is driven to the first step on the downward path, for if she would have a roof to cover her children's heads a husband must be found, and so we get these poor women forced by circumstances to consort with men in order to provide shelter for their families. Thus we see that the authorities in enforcing the restrictions in regard to accommodation are often doing Bantu society a grievous harm, for they are forcing its womanhood, its wedded womanhood, to the first step on the downward path of sin and crime.

Many Bantu women live in the cities at a great price, the price of their children; for these women, even when they live with their husbands, are forced in most cases to go out and work, to bring sufficient into the homes to keep their children alive. The children of these unfortunate people therefore run wild, and as there are not sufficient schools to house them, it is easy for them to live an aimless existence, learning crime of all sorts in their infancy almost.

If these circumstances obtain when husband and wife live together in the towns, imagine the case of the woman, whose husband has gone to town and left her, forgetting apparently all his responsibilities. Here we get young women, the flower of the youth of the Bantu, going up to towns in search of their husbands, and as I have already stated, living as the reputed wives of other men, because of the location requirements, or becoming housekeepers to men in the locations and towns, and eventually their nominal wives.

In Johannesburg, and other large towns, the male Natives are employed to do domestic work, in the majority of instances, and a female domestic servant is a rarity. We thus have a very dangerous environment existing for any woman who goes into any kind of domestic service in these towns, and naturally immorality of various kinds ensues, as the inevitable outcome of this situation. Thus we see that the European is by his treatment of the Native in these ways which I have mentioned, only pushing him further and further down in the social scale, forgetting that it was he and his kind who brought these conditions about in South Africa, forgetting his responsibilities to those who labour for him and to whom he introduced the benefits, and evils, of civilisation. These facts do not sound very pleasant I know, but this Conference is, according to my belief, intended to give us all the opportunity of expressing our views, our problems, and of discussing them in an attitude of friendliness and fairmindedness, so that we may perhaps be enabled to see some way out of them.

Then we come to the *Land Question*. This is very acute in South Africa, especially from the Bantu point of view. South Africa in terms of available land is shrinking daily owing to increased population, and to many other economic and climatic causes. Cattle diseases have crept into the country, ruining many a stock farmer, and thus Bantu wealth is gradually decaying. As a result there are more and more workers making their way to the towns and cities such as Johannesburg to earn a living. And what a living! The majority earn about £3 10s. per month, out of which they must pay 25s. for rent, and 10s. for tram fares, so I leave you to imagine what sort of existence they lead on the remainder.

Here again we come back to the same old problem that I outlined before,—that of the woman of the home being obliged to find work in order to supplement her husband's wages, with the children growing up undisciplined and uncared for, and the natural following rapid decay of morality among the people. We find that in this state of affairs, the woman in despair very often decides that she cannot leave her children thus uncared for, and she therefore throws up her employment in order to care for them, but is naturally forced into some form of home industry, which, as there is very little choice for her in this direction, more often than not takes the form of the brewing and selling of Skokiaan. Thus the woman starts on a career of crime for herself and her children, a career which often takes her and her children right down the depths of immorality and misery.

345

The woman, poor unfortunate victim of circumstances, goes to prison, and the children are left even more desolate than when their mother left them to earn her living. Again they are uncared for, undisciplined, no-one's responsibility, the prey of the undesirables with whom their mother has come into contact in her frantic endeavour to provide for them by selling skokiaan. The children thus become decadent, never having had a chance in life. About ten years ago, there was talk of Industrial schools being started for such unfortunate children, but it was only talk, and we are to-day in the same position, aggravated by the increased numbers steadily streaming in from the rural areas, all undergoing very similar experiences to those I have just outlined.

I would suggest that there might be a conference of Native and European women, where we could get to understand each others point of view, each others difficulties and problems, and where, actuated by the real spirit of love, we might find some basis on which we could work for the common good of European and Bantu womanhood.

Many of the Bantu feel and rightly too that the laws of the land are not made for Black and White alike. Take the question of permits for the right to look for work. To look for work, mark you! The poor unfortunate Native, fresh from the country does not know of these rules and regulations, naturally breaks them and is thrown into prison; or if he does happen to know the regulations and obtains a pass for six days, and is obliged to renew it several times, as is of course very often the case, he will find that when he turns up for the third or fourth time for the renewal of his permit, he is put into prison, because he has been unsuccessful in obtaining work. And not only do the Bantu feel that the law for the White and the Black is not similar, but we even find some of them convinced that there are two Gods, one for the White and one for the Black. I had an instance of this in an old Native woman who had suffered much, and could not be convinced that the same God watched over and cared for us all, but felt that the God who gave the Europeans their life of comparative comfort and ease, could not possibly be the same God who allowed his poor Bantu to suffer so. As another instance of the inequalities existing in our social scheme, we have the fact of Natives not being allowed to travel on buses and trams in many towns, except those specially designed for them.

In connection with the difficulty experienced through men being employed almost exclusively in domestic work in the cities, I would mention that this is of course one of the chief reasons for young women, who should rightly be doing that work, going rapidly down in the social life of the community; and it is here that joint service councils of Bantu and White women would be able to do so much for the good of the community. The solution to the problem seems to me to be to get women into service, and to give them proper accommodation, where they know they are safe. Provide hostels, and club-rooms, and rest rooms for these domestic servants, where they may spend their leisure hours, and I think you will find the problem of the employment of female domestic servants will solve itself, and that a better and happier condition of life will come into being for the Bantu.

If you definitely and earnestly set out to lift women and children up in the social life of the Bantu, you will find the men will benefit, and thus the whole community, both White and Black. Johannesburg is, to my knowledge, a great example of endeavour for the uplift of the Bantu woman, but we must put all our energies into this task if we would succeed. What we want is more co-operation and friendship between the two races, and more definite display of real Christianity to help us in the solving of these riddles. Let us try to make our Christianity practical.

Chronology of Chief Events, 1882-1934

Bibliographical Notes

Contents for Volumes II and III

Index

CHRONOLOGY OF CHIEF EVENTS, 1882-1934

1882

Imbumba Yama Afrika formed in Eastern Cape Colony

1884

Native Education Association formed in Eastern Cape Colony

Native Electoral Association formed in Kingwilliamstown

Start of publication of *Imvo Zabantsundu* (Native Opinion) in Kingwilliamstown (first African-edited newspaper)

Rev. Nehemiah Tile, having left Methodist Church, forms Independent Tembu National Church

1886

Gold discovered on the Witwatersrand

1887

Natal annexes Zululand

Parliamentary Voters Registration Act, Cape Colony (redefinition of voting qualifications)

1889

Jabavu promotes deputation against Vagrancy Act of 1889, Cape Colony

Dube leaves American Board Mission School for U.S.A.

1890

Cecil Rhodes becomes Prime Minister, Cape Colony (July)

1892

Rev. Mangena Mokone founds Ethiopian Church in Pretoria (November)

Franchise and Ballot Act, Cape Colony (property qualifications raised and literacy qualification added)

1893

Mohandas Gandhi arrives in Natal

Africans restive in eastern Transvaal over land issue

1894

Glen Grey Act, Cape Colony (August)

District Councils formed in four districts in Transkei, Eastern Cape Colony

Cape Colony annexes Pondoland (September)

Natal Act. No. 8 denies franchise to Indians

Natal Indian Congress formed (Mohandas Gandhi, president)

1895

Transkeian General Council formed

Jameson Raid (December 29)

1896

Ethiopian Church joins African Methodist Episcopal Church

1898

Start of publication of *Izwi Labantu* (Voice of the People) in East London

Bishop H.M. Turner of the African Methodist Episcopal Church in America visits South Africa

1899

Commencement of the Anglo-Boer War (October)

Rev. James Dwane leaves African Methodist Episcopal Church to form Order of Ethiopia (October)

John Dube founds Zulu Christian Industrial School, first school founded by professionally trained African educator

1902

Peace Treaty at Vereeniging, end of Anglo-Boer War (May 31)

South African Native Congress formed in Eastern Cape Province

African Political (later People's) organization (Coloured) founded in Cape Town by Dr. Abdullah Abdurahman.

Chamberlain meets delegation from South African Native Congress during visit to South Africa

1903

The South African Native Affairs Commission begins to collect evidence

Statement of South African Native Congress to Secretary of Colonies in London on rights in Cape Colony

1904

First Chinese laborers imported to the Witwatersrand

Start of publication of *Ilanga lase Natal* (editor, John Dube)

1905

Report of the South African Native Affairs Commission

1906

Bambata's Rebellion, Natal. Dube summoned to Government House and rebuked for his criticism of the Natal Government's handling of the Bambata affair

Indians in Transvaal required to carry passes

Gandhi leads passive resistance in Transvaal

John Tengo Jabavu and 13 other Africans petition the House of Commons to extend nonracial franchise to Transvaal and Orange River Colony. Other petitions by African organizations in Transvaal and Orange River Colony

Natal Native Affairs Commission established

1907

Repatriation of last Chinese laborers from the Witwatersrand

Transvaal and Orange River Colony granted responsible government with all-white suffrage

White miners strike on the Witwatersrand (May)

1908

South African National Convention meets in Durban to discuss union (October)

Native Administration Bill, Natal

1909

South African Native Convention (March 24-26)

Multiracial delegation travels to Great Britain to protest proposed South African Act

British Parliament passes South Africa Act (August)

Indian passive resistance in the Transvaal

1910

Union of South Africa proclaimed (May 31)

Dr. Walter Rubusana (African) and Dr. Abdullah Abdurahman (Coloured) elected to Cape Provincial Council

General Louis Botha becomes first Prime Minister of the Union of South Africa

1911

Mines and Works Act (establishes 'Color Bar' in employment)

Native Labour Regulation Act

District Councils established in West Pondoland

Pixley ka I. Seme proposes "Native Union" (October 24)

Universal Races Congress in London (John Tengo Jabavu and Walter Rubusana present)

1912

South African Native National Congress formed in Bloemfontein. John Dube elected president (January)

Squatters Bill proposed (March)

South African Races Congress formed under leadership of John Tengo Jabavu (April)

General J.B.M. Hertzog leaves Botha's cabinet (December)

Start of the publication of *Abantu-Batho* (The People), newspaper of the South African Native National Congress

1913

Natives Land Act (June)

White miners' general strike on the Witwatersrand (July)

Indian 'general strike' and passive resistance against Immigration Act (November)

African women demonstrate against pass laws in Orange Free State

Emergency meeting of the South African Native National Congress Executive Committee to discuss Natives' Land Act

1914

General Strike of white workers called on the Witwatersrand. Martial law declared and strike leaders deported by General Smuts (January)

Nationalist Party formed under leadership of General Hertzog (January)

Riotous Assemblies and Criminal Law Amendment Act (directed against militant white trade unions)

Delegation of South African Native National Congress travels to Great Britain to protest Natives Land Act

Solomon Plaatje remains in England when other Congress delegates return

World War I begins (August)

Revolt by anti-war Afrikaner nationalists

John Tengo Jabavu opposes Walter Rubusana in Cape Provincial elections

1915

National elections. Botha government retains parliamentary majority (October)

1916

Dedication of the South African Native College at Fort Hare

Report of the Native Lands (Beaumont) Commission

Solomon Plaatje's *Native Life in South Africa* published

1917

Industrial Workers of Africa founded

Native Administration Bill proposed

South African Native National Congress Executive Committee splits, with John Dube accepting theory of territorial segregation. Samuel Makgatho assumes office as president

1918

Strike of African sanitation workers in Johannesburg (June)

Reports of Provincial Natives Land Committees (Natal, Orange Free State, Eastern Transvaal, Western Transvaal)

Natives Urban Areas Bill proposed

Formal *Status Quo* Agreement between Chamber of Mines and white trade unions

1919

Industrial and Commercial Union formed in Cape Town under leadership of Clements Kadalie (January)

Demonstrations in Bloemfontein location. Selby Msimang arrested (March)

Anti-pass demonstrations on the Witwatersrand led by the South African Native National Congress (March-April)

Constitution of the South African Native National Congress approved

Bantu Union formed in Queenstown under leadership of Meshach Pelem

Delegation of South African Native National Congress travels to Great Britain and Europe to present African case at Versailles Peace Conference

Native Education Commission reports

General Botha dies. General Smuts becomes Prime Minister (August)

Union Parliament ratifies Treaty of Versailles and accepts League of Nations mandate for South-West Africa (August)

Dock strike by African and Coloured dock-workers in Cape Town led by the Industrial and Commercial Union under Clements Kadalie (October)

1920

African mineworkers strike on the Witwatersrand (February)

National elections. Smuts forms government with narrow parliamentary majority (March)

Report of Low Grade Mines Commission

Native Affairs Act

Industrial and Commercial Workers' Union of South Africa (ICU) established as national non-white trade union, Bloemfontein (July)

African demonstrators shot in Port Elizabeth (October 23)

Transvaal Mine Clerks' Association formed under the leadership of A.W.G. Champion

1921

Death of John Tengo Jabavu

National elections. Smuts government remains in power with increased parliamentary majority (February)

Israelites shot at Bulhoek resisting police efforts to move them (May)

Communist Party of South Africa formed in Cape Town (July)

John Dube attends the Second Pan-African Congress in London

J. E. G. Aggrey of Gold Coast visits South Africa

First European-African Joint Council formed in Johannesburg

Start of publication of *Umteteli wa Bantu*, African newspaper linked to the Chamber of Mines

1922

Bondelswarts rebellion in South West Africa

White miners' general strike becomes armed clash between strikers and government (March)

Clements Kadalie assumes dominant position in national ICU

First Native Conference held under provisions of Native Affairs Act of 1920

1923

Nationalist Party and South African Labor Party conclude electoral pact to challenge Smuts government (April)

Start of publication of *Workers' Herald*, newspaper of the ICU

South African Native National Congress renamed African National Congress (May)

African National Congress adopts 'Bill of Rights' (May)

First European-African Conference sponsored by the Dutch Reformed Church (September)

Natives (Urban Areas) Act

Natives Registration and Protection Bill proposed (consolidation of pass laws)

Z.K. Matthews graduates from Fort Hare — first African graduate from South African institution

1924

Industrial Conciliation Act

Rev. Z.R. Mahabane elected president of the African National Congress (May)

National elections. Nationalist Party-South African Labor Party win parliamentary majority. General Hertzog becomes prime minister (June)

Native Tax Bill proposed

1925

Wage Act

Economic and Wages Commission

Attempt to extend pass laws to African women blocked by court decision in suit instigated by African National Congress

ICU headquarters shifted from Cape Town to Johannesburg

Visit of the Prince of Wales

General Hertzog outlines his "solution" for the 'Native Question' at Smithfield (November 13)

Afrikaans recognized as an official language

1926

South African Trade Union Congress formed (April)

Mines and Works Amendment Act ('Colour Bar' Act) (May)

Communists expelled from ICU (December)

Kadalie defies order forbidding him entry into Natal

Balfour Declaration defines relations of Great Britain and the Dominions

Hertzog "Native Bills" published

1927

Nationality and Flag Act

Immorality Act

Native Administration Act

District Councils established in East Pondoland. Pondoland General Council formed

First Communist-sponsored African trade union formed

Clements Kadalie visits Europe (June-November)

First Non-European Conference meets in Bloemfontein under the leadership of Dr. Abdullah Abdurahman (June)

James Gumede elected president of the African National Congress (June)

James Gumede travels to Europe and the Soviet Union under Communist sponsorship

Second (and last) European–African Conference sponsored by the Dutch Reformed Church (February)

1928

South African Trade Union Congress rejects application of ICU for affiliation (January)

Natal branch of ICU secedes. ICU *yase Natal* formed under leadership of A.W.G. Champion

William G. Ballinger arrives as adviser to ICU (July)

Walter Madeley, Labor Minister of Posts and

Telegraphs, receives ICU deputation. General Hertzog drops Madeley from Cabinet and forms new government (November)

1929

First National European–Bantu Conference (February)

Clements Kadalie resigns from ICU after disputes with W.G. Ballinger (January)

Independent ICU formed under the leadership of Clements Kadalie (April)

National elections. Nationalists gain parliamentary majority. General Hertzog forms government without aid of South African Labor Party (June)

Africans of Natal boycott municipal beer halls. Demonstrations in Durban around office of ICU *yase Natal* result in loss of African and European lives (June)

Oswald Pirow, Minister of Justice, leads police expedition to Durban to force Africans to pay poll tax (November)

Location Advisory Boards' Congress formed

South African Institute of Race Relations formed

1930

Second Non-European Conference, Cape Town (January)

Riotous Assemblies (Amendment) Act

Natives (Urban Areas) Amendment Act

Enfranchisement of European women

Pixley ka I. Seme elected president of the African National Congress (April)

Conference of European and Bantu Christian Student Associations at Fort Hare (July)

A.W.G. Champion barred from Natal under provisions of Riotous Assemblies (Amendment) Act (September)

General Hertzog at Imperial Conference in London asks South African voice in British Imperial policy in Africa (September)

1931

Third Non-European Conference, in Bloemfontein, votes to send deputation to Europe (January)

Communist-sponsored pass-burning campaigns culminating in disturbances in Durban (December)

Abantu-Batho (The People) ceases publication as an African National Congress organ (July)

United Transkeian Territories General Council formed (amalgamation of Transkeian General Council and Pondoland General Council)

Franchise Laws Amendment Act (removes all property and literacy tests for white voters)

1932

Start of publication of *Bantu World*, European-sponsored African newspaper (March)

Native Service Contract Act

Report of the Carnegie Commission on the Poor White Problem

Report of the Native Economic Commission

South Africa goes off the gold standard (December)

Attempt to apply curfew regulations to African women in the Transvaal sparks discussions of passive resistance against passes (June)

1933

General Hertzog invites General Smuts to form coalition government (March)

National elections. Coalition parties win overwhelming parliamentary majority. Fusion government formed with General Hertzog as prime minister and General Smuts as deputy prime minister (May)

1934

'Purified' Nationalist Party formed under leadership of Daniel Malan (July)

United Party formed by majority of supporters of Nationalist Party and South African Party. General Hertzog is leader; General Smuts deputy (December)

BIBLIOGRAPHICAL NOTES

In the preparation of the introduction for this volume, the documents themselves, of which this collection includes only a relatively small proportion of those available, have been by far the most valuable. Useful insights have also been secured from contemporary and later works by Africans. T. D. Mweli Skota, prominent in the ANC in the 1920s and 1930s, edited a unique compendium of facts about early African personalities and organizations, *The African Yearly Register, Being an Illustrated National Biographical Dictionary (Who's Who) of Black Folks in Africa* (Johannesburg: R. L. Esson and Co., Ltd., 1930). A second edition was published in 1932. A further edition came out in 1965 as *The African Who's Who: An Illustrated Classified Register and National Biographical Dictionary of the Africans in the Transvaal* (3d ed.: Central News Agency, Limited). Solomon T. Plaatje, the first Secretary-General of the ANC, wrote a widely read book called *Native Life in South Africa, Before and Since the European War and the Boer Rebellion* (2d ed.: London: P. S. King & Son, 1916), which is excerpted in this volume. D. D. T. Jabavu wrote of his father in *The Life of John Tengo Jabavu, Editor of Imvo Zabantsundu, 1884-1921* (Lovedale, Cape Province: Lovedale Institution Press, 1922). Among later works by Africans who knew participants in early nationalist activities are Chief Albert Lutuli's *Let My People Go* (New York: McGraw—Hill Book Company, Inc., 1962) and Jordan Ngubane's provocative *An African Explains Apartheid* (London: Pall Mall Press, 1963 and New York: Praeger, 1963).

A few studies have been made of topics particularly relevant to the period of the documents in this volume. Stanley Trapido has provided detailed evidence of African participation in the Cape Colony's nonracial political system in "African Divisional Politics in the Cape Colony, 1884 to 1910," *Journal of African History* (January 1968), 79-98, and "John Tengo Jabavu and Cape Party Politics, 1893 to 1898," which was delivered before the Institute of Commonwealth Studies, London. So also does J. L. McCracken, *The Cape Parliament, 1854-1910* (Oxford: Clarendon Press, 1967). Along a different line, Lionel Forman's pioneering pamphlet, *Chapters in the History of the March to Freedom* (Cape Town: Real Printing and Publishing Co., 1959) is a politically oriented effort to analyze the development of early African political groupings. See also A. P. Walshe, "The Origins of African Political Consciousness in South Africa," *Journal of Modern African Studies* (December 1969), 583-610.

The Swedish scholar B. G. M. Sundkler, in *Bantu Prophets in South Africa* (2d ed.: London: Oxford University Press, 1961), provides authoritative information on the Ethiopian movement, while two articles by George Shepperson, "Ethiopianism and African Nationalism," *Phylon*, XIV, 1 (1953), 9-18, and "Notes on Negro American Influences on the Emergence of African Nationalism," *Journal of African History*, I, 2 (1960), 299-312, elaborate the important international ramifications of this phenomenon.

For the history of the ICU, Clements Kadalie's autobiography, "My Life and the I.C.U.," is useful. It has been edited for publication by Stanley Trapido (London: Frank Cass & Co. Ltd., 1970). See also the analytical treatment of the movement by Sheridan W. Johns, III, "The Industrial and Commercial Workers' Union of Africa, ICU: Trade Union, Political Pressure Group, or Mass Movement?" which has appeared in *Protest and Power in Black Africa* (New York: Oxford University Press, 1970), a symposium edited by Ali Mazrui and Robert Rotberg.

For the background against which to place this material, a classic and sometimes first-hand source is Edward Roux, *Time Longer Than Rope: A History of the Black Man's Struggle for Freedom in South Africa* (2d ed.: Madison: University of Wisconsin Press, 1964), although in certain instances the documents challenge Roux's emphases. The additions in the second edition are based on newspaper accounts of events. An invaluable analysis of class and colour as determinants in South African history has recently been published: H. J. and R. E. Simons, *Class and Colour in South Africa, 1850-1950* (Harmondsworth, Middlesex, England: Penguin Books, 1969).

The African Patriots; The Story of the African National Congress of South Africa (London: Faber & Faber, 1963) by Mary Benson, a South African journalist, is a vivid and somewhat partisan history of the ANC and its leading personalities, based on a large number of personal interviews as well as other material. Some of its detail may be questioned. Revised editions were published in 1966 and 1969 under the title *South Africa: The Struggle for a Birthright* (Harmondsworth, Middlesex, England: Penguin Books, 1966, and New York: Funk and Wagnalls, 1969). Leo Kuper's "African Nationalism in South Africa, 1910-1964" in Monica Wilson and Leonard Thompson, eds., *The Oxford History of South Africa*, Volume II (London: Oxford University Press), forthcoming, provides insight and interpretation within a more scholarly framework.

For those beginning their study of South Africa, a good introduction is Leo Marquard, *The Peoples and Policies of South Africa* (4th ed.: London: Oxford University Press, 1969). Eric A. Walker, *A History of Southern Africa* (3d ed.: London: Longmans, Green and Co., 1957) is the standard history but is weak in its coverage of African politics. A profound and more readable analysis is C. W. de Kiewiet, *A History of South Africa: Social and Economic* (London: Oxford University Press, 1964). Two more specialized historical studies are valuable for their treatment of specific periods and problems affecting Africans. L. M. Thompson, *The Unification of South Africa, 1902-1910* (Oxford: Clarendon Press, 1960) is a definitive analysis of the political developments leading to Union. C. M. Tatz, *Shadow and Substance in South Africa: A Study in Land and Franchise Policies Affecting Africans, 1910-1960* (Pietermaritzburg: University of Natal Press, 1962) provides a thorough discussion of the evolution of governmental policy with regard to African land ownership and political representation.

On white politics in South Africa, the most extensive analysis is Gwendolen M. Carter, *The Politics of Inequality: South Africa since 1948* (New York: Praeger, 1958, 1959). Several articles of special relevance to this survey are in Ellen Hellmann, ed., *Handbook on Race Relations in South Africa* (New York: Oxford University Press, 1949). For the economic perspective, the introduction of D. Hobart Houghton, *The South African Economy* (2d ed.: Cape Town: Oxford University Press, 1967), is helpful; complementary to it is the more specialized study of G. V. Doxey, *The Industrial Colour Bar in South Africa* (Cape Town: Oxford University Press, 1961), which deals with the origin and entrenchment of the segregated labor market.

CONTENTS FOR

VOLUME II: HOPE AND CHALLENGE, 1935-1952

Part One

AFRICANS UNITE UNDER
THE THREAT OF
DISENFRANCHISEMENT: 1935-1937

Introduction

Documents—Part One

Part Two

MODERATION AND MILITANCY, 1937 - 1949

Introduction

Documents—Part Two

The Rise of the African National Congress Youth League and Adoption of the Programme of Action: 1943-1949

The All African Convention and Efforts at Wider Unity

61. Resolution on the War. Adopted by the National Executive Committees of the AAC and the ANC, July 7, 1940
62. Address by I.B. Tabata, AAC Conference, December 16, 1941
63. Statement on the Atlantic Charter, by Professor D.D.T. Jabavu, June 26, 1943
64. "A Call to Unity." Manifesto adopted by the National Executive Committee of the AAC, August 26, 1943
65. "Draft Declaration of Unity" [including 10-point Programme] . Statement approved by the Continuation Committee of the Preliminary Unity Conference of Delegates from the AAC and the National Anti-C.A.D., December 17, 1943
66. "A Declaration to the Nations of the World." Statement of the Non-European Unity Movement, signed by Rev. Z.R. Mahabane, Dr. G.H. Gool, and E.C. Roberts, July 1945
67. Letter ["On the Organisations of the African People"], from I.B. Tabata to Nelson Mandela, June 16, 1948
68. "A Call for African Unity." Statement signed by Xuma, Jabavu, Moroka, Matthews, Bokwe, Godlo, Mosaka, Baloyi, Champion, Selope Thema, Ntlabati, and Mahabane, October 3, 1948
69. Minutes of the Joint Conference of the ANC and the AAC, December 16-17, 1948
70a-
70c. Joint Meeting of the National Executive Committees of the ANC and the AAC, April 17-18, 1949
    70a. Minutes, signed by C.M. Kobus [of the AAC] , Recording Secretary
    70b. Letter reporting on this meeting, from Moses Kotane to Professor Z.K. Matthews, May 8, 1949
    70c. Review of this meeting, in Minutes of the Annual Conference of the AAC, December 1949

Other Non-European or Left-Wing Activity

71. "Arms for Non-Europeans." Flyer issued by the Non-European United Front of South Africa, March 18, 1942
72. "Non-European Peoples' Manifesto." Adopted at Non-European Conference Convened by the Non-European United Front, June 28, 1942
73. Manifesto of the African Democratic Party, September 26, 1943
74. Resolution of the National Anti-Pass Conference, May 20-21, 1944
75a-
75b. First Transvaal-Orange Free State People's Assembly for Votes for All, May 22-24, 1948
    75a. "Manifesto." Call to Attend the People's Assembly, [n.d.]
    75b. "The People's Charter." Manifesto Adopted at the People's Assembly

Part Three

JOINT ACTION AND THE
DEFIANCE CAMPAIGN, 1950-1952

Introduction

Documents — Part Three

CONTENTS FOR

VOLUME III: CHALLENGE AND VIOLENCE, 1953-1964

Part One

THE CONGRESS MOVEMENT, 1953-1956

Introduction

Documents — Part One

Part Two

THE LAST STAGE OF NON-VIOLENCE, 1957 - May 1961

Introduction

Documents—Part Two

Multi-Racial Conference, December 1957

The African National Congress while its Leaders are on Trial, 1957-1959

45. "The Pan Africanist Congress Has a Message for the Down Trodden Black Masses of Afrika." Flyer issued by the PAC, [n.d.]
46. "One Central Government in Africa." Article, by R.M. Sobukwe, March 1960
47. "Calling the Nation! No Bail! No Defense!! No Fine!!!" Flyer announcing the launching of the anti-pass campaign on March 21, issued by R.M. Sobukwe, [n.d.]
48. Letter announcing the launching of the anti-pass campaign, from R.M. Sobukwe, to Major-General Rademeyer, Commissioner of Police, March 16, 1960
49. "Press Release: Call for Positive Action," announcing the launching of the anti-pass campaign, [n.d.]
50. "Launching Address" [quoting text of R.M. Sobukwe's final instructions] by Philip Kgosana, March 20, 1960
51. "A Statement by the Emergency Committee of the African National Congress." Statement, April 1, 1960
52. "Congress Fights On . . . Release the Detainees!!!" Statement in *African National Congress Voice: An Occasional Bulletin*, No. 1, April 1960

Does the ANC Advocate Violence? Treason Trial Testimony, March-October 1960

53. Testimony by Dr. Wilson Z. Conco, Chief A.J. Lutuli, Nelson R. Mandela, Robert Resha, Gert Sibande, M.B. Yengwa, Professor Z.K. Matthews

Renewed and Abortive "All-in" Efforts, December 1960-May 1961

54. Resolutions, Adopted by the Consultative Conference of African Leaders, and Cable, Sent by the Conference to the United Nations and to Oliver Tambo, December 16-17, 1960
55. "The African Leaders Call to the African People of South Africa." Leaflet announcing the All-in African Conference of March 25-26, 1961, issued by the Continuation Committee of African Leaders, [n.d.]
56. Resolutions of the All-in African Conference in Pietermaritzburg, March 25-26, 1961
57. "An Appeal to Students and Scholars." Flyer issued by the All-in African National Action Council, signed by Nelson R. Mandela, Secretary, [n.d.]
58. Letter calling on the United Party to support a national convention, from Nelson R. Mandela to Sir de Villiers Graaff, May 23, 1961
59. "Police Agents at Work . . . STAY AT HOME May 29 30 31." Flyer issued by the ANC, [n.d.]
60. "Stay at Home" [on May 29-31]. Flyer issued by National Action Council, [n.d.]
61. "Poqo, Poqo, Poqo." [opposing the stay-at-home on May 29-31]. Issued by the PAC, [n.d.]
62. "Clarion Call to African Nationalists." Article in *Mafube (The Dawn of Freedom)*, No. 1, issued by "African Nationalists", [written by A.P. Mda], May 1961

Part Three

THE TURN TO VIOLENCE, SINCE MAY 31, 1961

Introduction

Documents—Part Three

63. *The Voice of the All-African Convention Vigilance Committee.* Newsletter, July 1961
64. *"Umkonto We Sizwe"* (Spear of the Nation), Flyer "issued by command of *Umkonto We Sizwe"* and appearing on December 16, 1961

INDEX OF SELECTED ORGANIZATIONS

(All African political bodies and pressure groups mentioned in the text are included. In addition, Coloured, Indian, and multi-racial organizations in which Africans participated are listed.)

Universal Races Congress, 62

Vigilance Committees, 298

Welfare Societies (Native Welfare Societies), 216-218, 231, 245
   Cape Native Welfare Society, 150
West African Congress (*See* National Congress of British West Africa)
Western Province African National Congress (*See* African National Congress)
Western Province Congress (*See* African National Congress)
Women's Section of the African National Congress (*See* African National Congress)
Workers' Union (*See* Industrial and Commercial Workers' Union of South Africa)

INDEX OF SELECTED NAMES

(All Africans mentioned in the text are included. Coloureds, Indians, and whites who participated with Africans in political organizations and pressure groups are also listed. White politicans and government officials are not included.)